Urban planning and
real estate development

The Natural and Built Environment series

Editors: Professor Michael J. Bruton, University of Wales, Cardiff
Professor John Glasson, Oxford Brookes University

Urban planning and real estate development

John Ratcliffe & Michael Stubbs

First published in 1996 by UCL Press

UCL Press Limited
University College London
Gower Street
London WC1E 6BT

and

1900 Frost Road, Suite 101
Bristol
Pennsylvania 19007-1598

The name of University College London (UCL) is a registered
trade mark used by UCL Press with the consent of the owner.

British Library Cataloguing in Publication Data
A catalogue record for this book is available from the British Library.

Library of Congress Cataloging-in-Publication Data are available

ISBNs: 1-85728-563-8HB
     1-85728-564-6PB

Typeset in Times Roman and Optima.
Printed and bound in Great Britain by Bookcraft (Bath) Ltd.

This book is dedicated to
Vivien, Samantha, Luke and Adam Ratcliffe
and to Katherine Stubbs

Contents

Preface

There is an oft-used sequence in *Through the looking glass*, where Alice and the Red Queen are running as fast as they can, but the trees and other things appear to move with them. Alice says, "In our country, you'd generally get to somewhere else – if you ran very fast for a long time, as we've been doing." "A slow sort of country, "said the Queen. "Now, here, you see, it takes all the running you can do to keep in the same place". The world of planning and development is not "A slow sort of country". Fluctuating economic conditions, new legislative frameworks, political and social swings, advances in information technology and communications, and innovations in management theory and practice, all conspire to create a climate of constant change. Indeed, the very impetus for writing this book was to provide as up-to-date as possible a text on the twin processes of planning and development for practitioners and students alike, recognizing that pace of change and the need, so far as possible, to keep up.

This book is addressed primarily to students of real estate studies, in all its guises (estate management, land management, land economy, general practice surveying and real estate), and town and country planning in all its various forms (urban planning, urban and regional planning, environmental planning and town planning). It is also intended to provide an explanatory guide for other allied courses concerned with the stewardship of the built environment, such as architecture, urban design, engineering, building, surveying, economics and law. Those engaged in professional practice across the disciplines of the built environment should also find the text to be a useful source of reference.

The book is divided fundamentally into two portions, the first, Parts Two and Three, being devoted primarily to what might be considered "planning" matters, and the second, Parts Four and Five, dealing with essentially "development" issues. This major body of text is then topped and tailed by introductory and concluding chapters that respectively set the context for urban planning and real estate development and address some of the most pressing questions that presently face the planning profession and the development industry. It will be appreciated by readers that planning and development are two sides of the same built environment coin, the currency of which is devalued by an over-emphasis upon one at the cost to the other, and equally diminished by a neglect of the special qualities and characteristics of both. An appropriate balance has, it is hoped, been struck by the organization and treatment of material.

Separately, the related processes of urban planning and real estate development are inherently multi-and interdisciplinary. Collectively, the twin processes combine to create an environmental milieu that affects the lives of everyone. Sharp distinctions, however, can be drawn between the respective activities of planning on the one hand and development on the other. The former displaying a more formal, correct, communal, deliberate and publicly accountable character. The latter bearing a more individualistic, entrepreneurial, dynamic, opportunistic and profit motivated stamp. In similar vein, the backgrounds, attitudes and experience of those selecting urban planning or real estate courses of study and professional careers tend to differ markedly. By a mixture of design and circumstance, the same is true of the authors. The one with an estate management education, formerly an academic and now a planning and development consultant in private practice. The other with a town planning education, formerly a planner in the public sector and presently an academic in the real estate field. It is hoped that readers consider the chemistry works, despite the inevitable slight divergences in approach, style and sometimes opinion. In any event, to the best of the authors' knowledge, this is the first book of its kind, which brings together both urban planning and real estate development matters in a single text.

It would not be possible properly to recognize and thank all those individuals who have contributed to the development and preparation of this book. Our indebtedness extends to family, friends and colleagues in business and education who have provided help and support, and in particular Roger Jones, UCL Press, Professor Anthony Lavers and Professor Martin Avis, School of Real Estate Management, Oxford Brookes University and Bunty Chapman, MImiC Secretarial Services, Chesterton.

John Ratcliffe   Michael Stubbs
December 1995

PART ONE

Introduction

CHAPTER ONE

Urban planning and real estate development: the context

The need to plan

What is urban planning?

The persisting process of urbanization, the worst excesses of a post-industrial society, and the explosion in population growth and car ownership, have all contributed towards a heightened awareness, and ultimate acceptance, of the need for the introduction of some form of regulation regarding the distribution of land between competing uses (Ashworth 1954). The expression, profession and practice of urban planning, with its multidisciplinary nature, comprehensive perspective, changing character and continuing self-questioning, is extremely difficult to define. It has been variously described as "the art and science of ordering the use of land and siting of buildings and communication routes so as to secure the maximum practicable degree of economy, convenience, and beauty" (Keeble 1969) and as "an attempt to formulate the principles that should guide us in creating a civilized physical background for human life" (Sharp 1942) whose main impetus is thus ". . . foreseeing and guiding change" (McLoughlin 1969). Put another way, however, it is concerned with providing the right site, at the right time, in the right place, for the right people.

Control over the layout and design of urban settlement has been exercised since time immemorial. The early civilizations that congregated in the valleys of the Tigris and Euphrates demonstrated an ability to impose order upon comparatively high-density community living, and established an elementary system for the provision of services and facilities, as did the Inca and Maya cultures of South and Central America. Hippodamus of Miletus is generally given the accolade of being the first town planner, with his "chequerboard" or grid-iron layout of Piraeus nearly 2500 years ago in Greece. The distinctive hallmark of Roman colonial expansion was the dispersal throughout the empire of standardized uniform town plans. Not only has urban planning a long history, however, it can also be said that to some extent all development is planned. The individual dwelling is constructed so as to maximize efficiency in terms of function, daylight, outlook and convenience. Similarly, a block of offices is designed to facilitate internal movement, management and servicing. There is little difference between the planning of separate dwellings and that of whole towns; it is only the scale and the interests involved that vary.

Perhaps the most important single justification of a formal system of urban planning concerns these very interests, for planning is a reconciliation of social and economic aims, of private and public objectives (Harvey 1973). It is the allocation of resources, particularly land, in such a manner as to derive maximum efficiency, while paying heed to the nature of the built environment and the welfare of the community. In this way, planning is, therefore, the art of anticipating change, and arbitrating between the economic, social, political and physical forces that determine the location, form and effect of urban development. In a democracy, it should be the practical and technical implementation of the people's wishes operating within a legal framework, permitting the manipulation of the various urban components such as transport, power, housing and employment, in such a way as to ensure the greatest benefit to all.

Urban planning aims at securing a sensible and acceptable blend of conservation and exploitation of land, as the background or stage for human activity. This involves the process of establishing the desires of the community, formulating them in a manner that facilitates comprehension and discussion, preparing a policy for their adoption, regulating the degree and proportion of public and private investment, guiding the provision of public services, initiating action where necessary, and continually examining the effect of the adopted policy, making adjustments if required.

The very expression "planning" is now applied to almost all kinds of human activity, and consequently tends to mean all things to all men, being comprehensively defined as "the making of an orderly sequence of action that will lead to the achievement of a stated goal or goals" (Hall 1975). The practice of urban planning in particular, however, implies the introduction of a strictly spatial component in addition to other social, political or economic considerations. This sequential and goal-oriented character overtakes the more traditional stages of "survey—analysis—plan" put forward by Patrick Geddes in the 1920s, and largely adhered to until the 1960s, whereby information relating to a chosen area was collected and examined for prevailing problems and indications of change, and a plan was subsequently produced for a given future period based upon decisions at that point in time (Faludi 1973). Now, planning is seen as a cyclical process subject to continuing scrutiny and change. Although criticized for demonstrating a somewhat partial physical land-use attitude, a useful threefold ideology of planning, illuminating the spatial aspect of the discipline, has been suggested as being "to reconcile competing claims for the use of limited land so as to provide a consistent, balanced and orderly management of land uses . . . to provide a good (or better) physical environment for the promotion of a healthy and civilized life . . . And providing the physical basis for a better urban community life" (Foley 1960). In the light of recurring crises facing many inner

3

urban areas, and because of what has been contended to be a lack of understanding of urban processes and a promotion of predominantly middle-class values by planners, a more radically political school of thought evolved in the 1970s, believing that planning should seek to attain more redistributive goals in order to redress the alleged social injustices that have taken place in the city, arguing that invariably it has been the already poor and disadvantaged who have borne the costs of planning policy and suffered successive setbacks.

Planning is also said to be the application of scientific method of policy-making, but again this definition can be applied to most activities, and in many ways it only serves to camouflage the essentially political nature of urban planning, for although attempts are sometimes made to divorce planning from politics, the two are inextricably interwoven. Almost any planning decision is to some extent concerned with the allocation of resources, so that some people gain while others lose, and for this reason it is misleading if not downright dangerous to conceal the overtly political complexion of planning policy.

In this context, mention has to be made, however briefly, of the way in which the three successive Conservative governments, led by Prime Minister Thatcher, sought in the years following 1979 to alter and restructure the urban planning system in line with their ideology. The main policy themes were embodied in the work of the Adam Smith Institute and have been described succinctly by Atkinson & Moon (1994) as:

- town and country planning employed what they felt to be a spurious "sociological notion of community; not only was sociology frowned upon, so was anything that suggested any social units other than the individual, the family and the firm
- planning was elitist; it imposed planners' values and offended the populist Thatcher project
- it gave undue discretion to local government, which Conservatives wished to curb
- its subjective nature and its checks and balances caused delay and cost to the entrepreneurial wealth creators of the private sector
- although it went against the grain of New Right analysis, there was an implicit suspicion that urban riots and the state of British cities in the early 1980s were in some way a consequence of failures of town planning.

An authoritative examination of town and country planning under the various Thatcher governments is provided elsewhere (Thornley 1991), and the legislation enacted is described in Parts Two and Three of this text. Suffice it to say that, from a Conservative viewpoint, much was achieved during the 1980s in terms of reorientating the planning system to market needs. In particular, structure planning was dismantled and development control deregulated to facilitate private sector investment. From a different stance, the cost of these changes has been stated to be greater centralization, decreased participation, the removal of the social item from the planning agenda, and overt favouritism to the needs of capital (Atkinson & Moon 1994). A reaction to this reorientation now seems to characterize the 1990s, with much greater emphasis being placed upon environmental awareness and participation.

Planning and the market

In the absence of town planning, land would be apportioned between competing uses by the price mechanism and the interaction of demand and supply. In this free-market situation, land would be used for the purpose that could extract the largest net return over a foreseeable period of time, but experience has shown that, unfettered, the market can consume resources in an ill conceived and short-sighted way, creating almost insurmountable problems for generations to come. Moreover, the competition engendered in the private sector, where laissez-faire conditions prevail, can all too often breed waste. The private sector developer seeking to maximize his personal profit often neglects the provision of both social services and public utilities. The very need for planning arose out of the inequality, deprivation and squalor caused by the interplay of free-market forces and lack of social concern prevalent during the nineteenth century. Furthermore, unplanned, these forces combine to produce the fluctuating booms and slumps that epitomize private sector instability.

Planning, therefore, has properly been identified as "a concern of government and a field of public administration" (Solesbury 1974) because inherently it is involved with political choice rather than market transactions, so that public agencies have been established to control the operation of markets in the interests of the community and supplant markets in the provision of certain kinds of goods and services. Several reasons justifying the exercise of political choice through planning intervention can be advanced for this, including the provision of "public goods", such as roads and defence, which are supplied to all; the existence of other goods and services that produce side-effects upon those not involved in their consumption; the need to supply certain high-cost high-risk goods and services unattractive to private enterprises, such as electricity and aerospace, which are best placed in the care of national monopolies; the necessity to control certain complex operations such as land assembly for comprehensive redevelopment, where public regulation secures a better overall outcome than would private-market transactions; and the desire to protect or preserve particular activities or resources that are considered beneficial to society at large, such as conservation areas, historic buildings, open space and leisure facilities.

The market, operating alone, does not provide the most appropriate location for what are generally described as the non-profit-making uses of land, such as transport termini, gasworks, roads, fire stations and sewage plants. Nevertheless, the correct siting of these non-profit-making uses can render the profit-making uses of land more profitable. Proximity and accessibility to these various services and activities are often essential to commercial viability. Thus, planning assists the market in becoming more efficient.

5

At a time of ever-accelerating social, technological and political change, planning seeks to direct and control the nature of the built environment in the interests of society as a whole. In doing so, it is unlikely to please all of the people all of the time. There can be little doubt, however, about the need for some degree of intervention in private-sector decision-making, despite occasional frustration, fault and delay. Although violent political and philosophical schisms regarding the ownership, management and return from land exist, the needs of traffic management, for example, demand far wider comprehensive layout and design than can be provided by the private sector. Central area reconstruction is another instance where large-scale corporate acquisition is more effective than fragmentary private purchase. Despite the obvious merits implicit in some form of control and guidance over the nature and function of the built environment, ensuring economic efficiency, social justice and physical quality, the application of comprehensive land-use planning does not always meet with universal acclaim. Strong undercurrents, favouring a great deal less formal planning and a greater freedom of interplay of market forces, exist in some quarters. Planning and planners are often accused of setting themselves up as arbiters of public taste, often in blissful ignorance of consumer demand. The model or plan they produce, which aims to achieve balance, symmetry and order among the various elements and systems of urban organization, does not always cater for changes in taste, habit or preference.

Despite the above deficiencies, it can be said that the twin forces of the free market and the planning process tend to act as a beneficial corrective, one of the other. The planner has to operate alongside the market, directly influencing, and frequently assisting, its functioning, but in a manner that takes account of both public and private interests. Increasingly, public policy depends upon private sector development for the implementation of a large proportion of planning proposals, not only city centre redevelopment, where high costs virtually prohibit public investment alone, but also residential, industrial and commercial undertakings of all kinds. Moreover, there is a tendency towards the use of free-market methods by planning agencies, and compromise solutions and joint developments are becoming the order of the day. Above all, however, planners must be directed towards the study of uncertainty and the consequences of change, the very essence of urban planning.

The role of real estate

The role of real estate in any developed or developing economy can hardly be understated. In one way or another, it impinges upon virtually every domestic and commercial activity at all levels of society.

The real estate market is formed by the interaction of buyers and sellers in exchanging real property rights for other assets, usually money. This type of interaction occurs in different areas, for different reasons, and in relation to different types of property. Thus, the real estate market is divided into categories, based upon the differences among property types and their appeal to corresponding markets. The markets for these categories of real estate are further divided into submarkets that are based upon the preferences of buyers and sellers. These divisions facilitate the study of real estate markets.

All real estate markets are influenced by the perceptions, motivations and interactions of the buyers and sellers of real property, which in turn are subject to many social, economic, government and environmental influences. Real estate markets may be studied in terms of locational, competitive and supply and demand characteristics as they relate to overall real estate market conditions.

Real estate, as a unique form of asset, should be viewed in the context of the overall economic life of a nation. In terms of wealth in open economies, for example, it is clear that, although national and international trends influence the level and pattern of real estate values, the property industry in its turn affects many, if not most, economic activities by virtue of its collective size. Also, in the majority of countries, a significant proportion of total wealth is related to real property.

The place of real estate in a market economy

The term "real estate" embraces a wide range of concepts, uses and concerns. A sense of land and property recognizes the diverse physical, legal, economic and cultural characteristics that can exist in different geographical locations and within alternative political systems. Real estate includes the interests, benefits and rights inherent in the ownership of land and buildings. It is thus a "bundle of rights" whereby each stick in the bundle represents a distinct and separate right to use real estate, to sell it, to lease it, to enter it, or to give it away. These rights may be held separately or collectively. To varying degrees they are also subject to such powers of government as taxation, eminent domain, escheat, building ordinance, administrative regulation and planning control.

Likewise, the notion of a "market economy" is a variable concept. From a near "laissez faire" philosophy, with little or no government intervention, at one extreme, to a policy predicating a high degree of regulation at the other, with sundry systems in between. No two markets can be said to be the same. In the context of a real estate market, however, property is popularly held to demonstrate certain common features: heterogeneity, tangibility, durability, immobility, adaptability and indivisibility. It is also said to require large amounts of capital to acquire, pose difficult legal problems in respect of ownership, incur high costs of transfer and be costly to manage. Like most trite generalizations of this kind, there is some fact and some fiction. Nevertheless, what can be affirmed is that the real estate market in an open economy is a complex imbroglio of theories, practices and procedures, which alter according to situation and circumstance.

Several other major features of the real estate market in an open economy can be distinguished. First, many large private development schemes can act as a catalyst, generating interest and confidence for further investment in other development opportunities. Secondly, in like vein, public and private sector contributions to physical infrastructure projects, such as tunnels, toll roads, public utilities and transportation facilities, can produce similar results. Thirdly, a healthy, efficient and professionally managed real estate market can greatly assist in attracting foreign investment across all sectors of the economy.

The characteristics of the real estate market

Setting aside the conventional characteristics of markets described in traditional textbooks on the subject, there are practical features that distinguish the role of private sector property agencies in real estate markets from the management and control of land and buildings in largely centrally planned and publicly regulated economies. These can usefully be summarized as below.

Attitudes

Unashamedly, the driving force behind real estate markets is the profit motive. Whether the aims and objectives of those involved are short-term trading turnover, secure income flow or long-term capital growth, the maximization of return invariably remains the overriding factor in property investment and development decision-making. Without some form of comprehensive planning framework, however, individual decisions made in isolation can cause external costs that lead to a less than optimum overall return from the allocation of land between competing uses. With the advent of environmental impact analysis, the introduction of more realistic planning policies, and a growing awareness of an improved corporate image on the part of private sector property agencies, this problem is beginning to diminish. Moreover, profit is increasingly being equated with quality.

Arguably, it is also apparent that a more business-like approach towards real estate is to be expected in the private sector of the market. Even here there has been something of a revolution over recent years as leading property firms and major construction companies have adopted more modern organization and management theories and methods from other business communities.

With regard to attitude and behaviour, another feature differentiating private from public land and property dealings is the degree of confidentiality involved. In general, government is both inclined and obliged to be more open in disclosing information relating to such matters as ownership, costs, values and intentions. In terms of "knowledge", the real estate market is highly imperfect, although even this is changing as markets become more sophisticated, and those participating more aware of the need to display their insight and prowess.

Additionally, by its very nature the real estate market fosters close client relationships. There is always a pecuniary pressure to pay assiduous attention to the special needs of potential occupiers or purchasers of property.

Underlying all these attitudinal aspects is the act of negotiation. A much neglected skill in the training of real estate practitioners, the degree of success resulting from a property transaction – be it concerned with investment, development, management or marketing – is normally dependent upon effective negotiation.

Efficiency

One of the essential characteristics of a market economy is stated to be that of efficiency. In this respect, real estate, with a high degree of competition in most markets, is no exception. The days of certain markets, easy sales and soft lettings have gone, and seem unlikely to return in the immediate future. However, competition in an open economy can be a two-edged sword. On the one hand, it can stimulate the provision of a higher level of professional services. On the other, it can lead to excessive fee-cutting and result in lower standards of performance.

An obvious advantage often enjoyed by private sector agencies in the property industry over their counterparts in the public sector is that of staffing flexibility. Not only is there a greater facility to "hire and fire" according to changing economic circumstances, but it is easier to engage and deploy specialist professional expertise for individual projects, often on a "one-off" basis.

The growing accent upon greater efficiency in professional practice organization and management has already been mentioned. But it is probably true to say that the structure and operation of the larger national and international agencies in the real estate market has changed dramatically since the late 1980s, and continues to evolve in line with contemporary management thought and practice.

Accountability of decision-making is a matter of sharp distinction between public and private sector agencies in the area of land and property. Whereas government is usually compelled to follow set procedures and respect certain protocols, which can be time-consuming and costly, private participants in the real estate market in an open economy operate under far less constraint. This notwithstanding, it should be recognized that clients have become more demanding, better informed and less loyal. Moreover, the world generally has become more litigious, with clients more ready to sue for poor performance. This may result in greater efficiency in respect of professional standards – but, as always, at a cost in terms of additional expenditure upon such items as indemnity insurance, collateral warranties and legal fees.

In the context of efficiency, the watchwords of the real estate industry in a market economy are time, cost and quality, the problem being, of course, that these objectives are all too often mutually exclusive. Clients want the quickest, cheapest and best; but the best is rarely the cheapest or quickest, the quickest is rarely the cheapest or best, and the cheapest is rarely the best. This is where professional judgement, based upon experience gained from across a range of real estate markets, can enable more "efficient" decisions to be made.

Responsiveness

Given the competitiveness of real estate markets described above, there is considerable pressure placed upon professional participants in all sectors of the property industry to respond quickly to changing conditions and circumstances.

First, there are changing techniques. In the field of real estate appraisal, for example, the discipline of property valuation has advanced significantly over the past decade or so. Not merely with regard to the techniques employed and the processing of information involved, but also in respect of the situations in which valuations are required and the manner whereby they are performed. In virtually all parts of the property industry, new techniques of planning, evaluating, scheduling and controlling have had to be introduced and mastered.

Secondly, there is the question of changing locations. Throughout most market economies the shape of cities and patterns of land use are constantly in a state of flux. Improved communications, increased mobility and the desire for a better environment have, for instance, altered the traditional concepts of central place theory and complementarity. Centrifugal forces for certain functions are replacing centripetal ones. And, by and large, it is the real estate industry in a market economy, being close to client and consumer demand, that responds most promptly to such changes.

Thirdly, across most sectors of the property market there have been changing designs. Residential development has become less uniform. Retailing is always in a state of transformation. Office specifications have been heightened and the market diversified. Industrial estate development standards have been materially upgraded, and varying forms of layout and design devised according to function. And composite buildings have found favour. In all this, the keynotes of design are now flexibility and adaptability.

Fourthly, in the area of property development and investment there have been changing contractual procedures. With building procurement, for example, the traditional form of contract, although still commonly employed, has been supplemented by other systems such as design and build, package deal, management fee contracting, separate contracts and the like. With the management of investment property, changes have been witnessed in such respects as lease length, terms, conditions and the provision of services. The very contractual relationships among staff within firms has also undergone change.

Fifthly, there has been a gradual change in work practices. Largely in response again to client demand, competition in the market and the drive for greater efficiency, many work practices have been altered and other new ones introduced. Statutory reform has also played a part. In the real estate profession, this has affected such matters as fee scales, equity sharing arrangements, licensing, incorporation and inter-practice collaboration.

Sixthly, there is above all a need to be able to respond rapidly to changing economic conditions. This is relatively easy in rising markets. The real test comes in falling or highly volatile markets. Too often the "herd instinct" prevails, and market trends are exaggerated, threatening certainty, stability and predictability.

Although the foregoing comments highlight the attribute of responsiveness of real estate markets to changing needs, it should be noted that the most successful property practitioners are those who possess that rare quality of anticipation.

Enterprise and experimentation

As a direct corollary of the above, "anticipation" can be seen as almost synonymous with "enterprise". One of the hallmarks of a market economy is enterprise – the willingness to engage in novel, bold or difficult ventures. Entrepreneurs are inevitable, indeed essential, participants in the real estate market and, over recent years, several general entrepreneurial and experimental initiatives can be discerned.

To begin with, the provision of financial services has become a major function of leading real estate consultants. Either by establishing their own specialist department with a network of financial contacts, or by close association with a particular finance house, clients are able to obtain investment or development funding specially tailored to their needs, rather than engage in lengthy negotiations to secure awkward alterations to the previously available bespoke variety. A whole new range of property investment vehicles have been introduced or extended, including such devices as consortia funding, securitization with multi-option facilities, non-recourse loans, unitization by way of investment trusts, venture capital arrangements for higher-risk projects, mezzanine funding, more sophisticated forms of sale-and-leaseback, and a wider choice of mortgage facilities.

In the realms of property tenure, new opportunities for real estate ownership have been created. In addition to the familiar forms of freehold and leasehold tenure, markets internationally have witnessed the introduction of more tractable types of tenure. These include the wider application of flying freeholds or strata title, common-hold, equity participation through partnership or joint venture, land pooling and syndication.

In the face of stiffening competition, the relaxation of certain institutional regulations and market demand, there has been a marked movement towards the formation of multidisciplinary practices. This is not a trend peculiar to the real estate market. Nevertheless, within the property industry there are a growing number of clients who prefer "one-stop shopping" in obtaining real estate advice and services. There can be little doubt that this trend will continue, both among the various central disciplines within the built environment, and between allied professions such as those providing legal, banking, accounting, management and public relations services, either by way of formal amalgamation or through close and continuing association.

Since the mid-1980s there has been substantial innovation and change in the property development sector of the real estate market. Apart from improvements in the design and performance of traditional forms of building, new types of development have emerged or expanded. These include business parks, composite buildings, sheltered housing, science and high-technology parks, leisure complexes, theme parks, specialist shopping centres, discount retail estates, large shopping centres, gracious shopping malls, factory outlets, business centres and the refurbishment of old buildings for fresh uses. Another feature in market economies worldwide has been the resurrection of deteriorating or derelict inner-city waterfront land and property for a variety of residential, commercial and recreational purposes.

A marked trait in the real estate market during the late 1980s and early 1990s was the increased emphasis placed upon property research. Some would argue that such research as was conducted prior to that period was mainly for the purposes of "window-dressing" or corporate promotion on the part of those firms concerned. Also that it was of a fairly amateur and superficial nature. In the UK that situation has changed radically. Leading real estate consultants now view the research function of their practice as an essential support to the other investment, development, management, marketing and appraisal services they provide. Furthermore, research has become a recognized fee-earning activity in its own right, and independent firms specializing in property-related research have sprung up and are prospering. Nevertheless, many real estate markets remain where information and analysis is either sparse or virtually non-existent.

A recent and far-reaching characteristic of the property industry has been the internationalization of real estate markets. In property terms the world is now truly a global village. Money for investment and development moves readily between countries; concepts of design, layout and use of buildings spread quickly; and the foremost real estate firms have either expanded their own practices on a more international basis, or formed close associations or networks of reciprocal relations with local firms in other countries. This process of internationalization of real estate is bound to gain pace as more and more markets open up to opportunity.

Professionalism in real estate markets

Given the vagaries of real estate markets, the competitive cut-and-thrust of day-to-day practice and the higher levels of accountability demanded, standards of professionalism have come under closer and closer scrutiny. There are several issues and areas of professional operation that are worthy of mention.

Independence

An essential ingredient in many property situations is the need for genuine objectivity. This is not always as easy to achieve as perhaps it sounds. Client pressure is often brought to bear to produce evidence or results that justify desired outcomes. Furthermore, negative advice, properly proffered, often precludes additional fee-earning work on that, or even other, projects by the consultant concerned. In the long-run, however, the reputation for strict adherence to an objective approach eventually gains credibility and, hopefully, clients.

In some countries the role played by professional bodies is of considerable importance in achieving independence. Such societies or institutions set and maintain standards, provide consistency and continuity of practice, enhance public confidence, monitor the activity and performance of members, and act as a lobby to government in respect of legislation relating to real estate. In many other countries a system of licensing is employed to ensure certain basic levels of professional competence in their local context. Often the two exist side by side, supplying respectively the complementary functions of professional development and the upholding of minimum standards.

Evaluation and appraisal

With regard to professionalism in the field of real estate, a principal area of concern relates to evaluation and appraisal, some form of which is fundamental to all aspects of property investment, development, management and marketing.

Essential to all evaluation and appraisal situations is market information. Relevant data concerning such elements as rents, values, yields and costs, let alone ownership, planning policy and physical condition, are not always easy to obtain. In some countries land and property transactions are a matter of public record; in others a veil of secrecy is drawn across such information. Even where information is readily available, great care must be taken in always accepting it at face value. All too often, declared figures conceal more clandestine agreements between the parties involved.

Possessing market information is one thing, but conducting market analysis is often another. It can be staggering how much results can vary between different professional real estate consultants based upon exactly the same data. The core analysis of most appraisals is that of comparability. Comparable evidence is drawn from similar projects or property transactions previously completed. The figures are then adjusted for such factors as age, size, location, layout, ownership, services, facilities, physical condition, occupation, terms of tenure, time of transaction, current market climate, statutory requirements and possible future trends, and then applied to the proposal in question. It is hardly surprising that appraisal can be a hazardous affair.

To assist in reducing uncertainty and error in appraisal, various skills and techniques are adopted. There has long been a debate whether the task of valuation is an art or a science. It is, of course, a combination of both. Although there have been significant advances made in the development of techniques, especially in the areas of risk analysis and portfolio management, even the most refined techniques cannot replace the necessary professional judgement required to select suitable initial data and make informed decisions upon the results produced following analysis. Despite these advances, however, it is startling to discover how restricted their use is, even with such a simple method as discounted cashflow analysis, especially given the easy access nowadays to a choice of appropriate computer software. Hunch and intuition still play too large a part in valuation practice.

In respect of professionalism, the past decade or so has seen the formulation and adoption of some standards and guidelines. Sometimes statutory (produced by government) and sometimes advisory (promulgated by professional bodies), they aim at securing consistency and certainty in professional practice. Notably, in the field of valuation, there have been standards and guidelines introduced relating to asset valuation, mortgage valuation, the measurement of buildings and the preparation of appraisal or valuation reports. Again, some of these are gaining international recognition, amended, where appropriate, to suit local circumstances.

Property investment

Property is not only a major national asset in a market economy, it also forms a strategic role in a mixed asset portfolio, for the long-term (20 years) performance of property is competitive with other asset classes. In the short term, however, the performance of property does not coincide with that of other markets. In the short to medium term, therefore, it's role is more of a tactical nature. Nevertheless, this difference in the performance cycle to that of equities and fixed-interest investments means property is a very effective diversifier of risk in a mixed asset portfolio. It is also true that, in many open economies, property investment exhibits a high quality of income growth, especially where long-term leasing structures, with frequent upwards-only rent reviews, provide high security and predictability of income. However, the property investment market is perceived to have structural problems related to marketability and pricing. But these problems should not be seen as insoluble; they require different management solutions and warrant continuing investment decisions.

In the real estate market the property investment consultant provides services that can best be briefly listed as follows:
- supplying general property investment advice
- buying and selling interests in land and property on behalf of clients
- developing and applying analytical techniques for evaluating the performance of the property market
- disseminating relevant information to clients in a form that facilitates their decision-making
- predicting possible future changes in market performance among the various property sectors and between alternative investment opportunities
- increasingly, adopting an international approach to real estate investment.

Property development

Real estate development today determines in many respects how we will live in the future. In providing shelter, workplace, shopping and leisure, it fulfils many fundamental needs of modern society, as well as constituting a very large portion of the gross private domestic investment in most countries having a market economy. Real estate development is also unusually dynamic, with rapid changes occurring in the links between construction, regulation, marketing, finance, management, and so on.

It should be recognized that both public and private sectors in real estate development share compelling reasons for understanding the development process. The public sector aims to maximize good development, ensuring that buildings constructed are attractive and safe as well as properly located to foster the efficient functioning of a town and city as a whole. The aim of the private sector, as already stated, is to maximize profit while minimizing risk. Few businesses, however, are as heavily leveraged as real estate development where risks are high but potential returns to equity are also high. In a market economy, the real estate professions perform important functions at every stage of the development process. The principal ones can usefully be summarized as follows:

- the identification of land suitable for development or redevelopment for particular uses unhampered by preconceived and sometimes dated land-use plans
- the evaluation and appraisal of development proposals based upon current market knowledge of such factors as rent, yield, building cost, land value, interest rates and time taken
- the assembly of various sites and interests in land so as to form a comprehensive scheme unfettered by statutory requirements regarding resumption or compulsory purchase
- securing sufficient funds from suitable sources on favourable terms to finance development projects
- assisting in the selection of an effective professional team and advising on the basis of their appointment
- assessing and monitoring the layout and design of development projects in order to ensure their marketability
- advising on a preferred procedure for selecting a contractor, depending upon such factors as the technical complexity, aesthetic quality, economics, timing and scale of the scheme in question
- setting up an appraisal system to monitor the viability of projects throughout the construction period in the light of possible changing market conditions
- determining the point at which a marketing campaign is best started, how it should be conducted and by whom
- establishing an appropriate management and maintenance programme
- deciding upon the form of lease or sale contract, so as to preserve an optimum return on the investment.

Traditionally, the functions described above have normally been allocated to different individuals drawn from different backgrounds within the real estate industry. However, the changeable climate of the property market, the growing complexity of the development process, an increasing sophistication in funding arrangements, the need to reduce design and construction periods, added pressure for more positive marketing strategies, tighter fiscal and administrative regulation and ever-accelerating advances in technology have all conspired to focus attention

15

upon the need for a single professional to accept responsibility for managing a building project from start to finish. Hence, in a significant number of major schemes of property development, in both public and private sectors of the industry, the benefits have been recognized of appointing an individual charged with the task of helping to establish the overall objectives of the project and assuming the direction, control and co-ordination of the work of those contributing to the achievement of those objectives.

The discharge of these responsibilities demands a comprehension of the physical, functional and financial objectives of the scheme, an awareness of the legal issues bearing upon them, and an appreciation of and sensitivity towards the contributions made by the other members of the professional team in initiating, designing, funding, constructing, managing and marketing the development. In brief, this is the role of the project manager, whose span of control thus stretches from the inception of a proposal, often with an involvement in the decision to develop, through to the eventual disposal of the completed building, covering every aspect the development process in between, albeit to different degrees of detail.

Property management

With a growing scarcity of land for urban development and narrower margins of profit on new projects, greater accent is being placed upon property management. Better portfolio management aimed at optimizing returns, together with more discerning tenant demand, has reinforced this emphasis. Generally, there is an increasing awareness in many sectors of the real estate market of the need to look after the existing stock of buildings in a far more positive and professional manner than hitherto.

For many years shopping centre management has led the way. Management of large planned retail centres has virtually become a profession in its own right. At best, it is highly sophisticated and it requires a combination of professional skills embracing promotion, marketing, personnel relations, building services, security, environment and finance. Many lessons can be drawn from shopping centre management that could effectively be applied to other sectors of the market.

Modern office property management has improved greatly over the past few years, but positive as opposed to responsive management is largely confined to prestige blocks in prime positions. Obsolescence and depreciation is all too obvious in older office buildings located in less central or accessible positions. In terms of offices, the most recent and interesting development over recent years has been the emergence of a discipline known as "facilities management", which takes a comprehensive approach to commercial property management.

With the arrival of "high-technology" estates and science and business parks, industrial property management has been transformed. Developed to low densities, of high-quality design, well landscaped and well provided with a wide range of services and facilities, they bear little or no comparison to the industrial estates of yesteryear. Recognized now as important property assets, they attract a high level of professional management in order to sustain their investment value.

Setting aside public housing, residential property management is mainly concerned with relatively high-class or luxury accommodation. Again, however, the overall standard of management services provided has tended to improve over recent years. Major firms have established specialist departments dedicated to residential property management and carrying responsibility for several estate developments, thereby gaining a broad range of experience and enjoying the benefits of scale in respect of expert services. Even at the lower end of the market, the formation of management committees, either on a mandatory or voluntary basis, has raised the standards of property management.

The ultimate form of property management is probably refurbishment. In market economies worldwide there has been growing pressure since the early 1980s to protect and manage existing property rather than always demolish and redevelop anew. In some countries, refurbishment is seen to be the fastest expanding sector of the real estate industry. Moreover, in an open economy, almost nothing is sacred. Refurbishment potential is not just realized in the main sectors of existing office, shop, hotel and industrial buildings, but such properties as cinemas, churches, markets, power and railway stations, breweries, theatres, locomotive sheds, watermills, dock and harbour buildings and hospitals have all been targets in different cities throughout the world. The spread of refurbishment schemes is also likely to continue across all residential and commercial fields of development.

Property marketing

In most real estate markets, property as a product has become more difficult to sell, and those responsible for selling it have been forced to bring a higher degree of professionalism to the task of agency and disposal. Users' needs have to be more closely identified and more carefully related to product design. Put simply, marketing is the skill of matching the needs of a buyer with the product of a seller, for a profit. However, because those marketing property investments or developments are faced with a highly competitive and discerning market, and one that demands better information, more active and rigorous attention is being paid to the selling process. Buying and selling real estate in an open economy calls for an ever-increasing understanding of the procedures and functions of marketing. There are certain marketing tools relating to information collection, advertising, promotion and public relations that are available and becoming more and more sophisticated. But the starting point of any marketing campaign is market research, and it is really only in recent years that leading firms in real estate consultancy have committed themselves to the serious analysis of the markets in which they operate. Similarly, over the past few years there has been a significant shift towards the division of a more formally structured and deeply considered marketing strategy for investment and development projects. The advantages of

17

a more rigorous planning process are that diverse marketing activities can be better co-ordinated, crisis management reduced to a minimum, measurements of performance easier to conduct against known standards, corrective measures applied in sufficient time when required, and participation by all those involved encouraged with improvement and motivation. The prime aim of marketing remains that of selling or letting property for the highest price or rent available in the market. To achieve this, the property must be freely exposed to the market in an orderly manner, and the most appropriate method of selling a particular property will depend largely upon the nature of the premises concerned and the prevailing market conditions. Four basic methods of property disposal can be distinguished – private treaty, public auction, formal tender and informal tender – each of which has its own advantages and disadvantages.

Innovation in the process of promotion and marketing is bound to happen, especially with the spread of advanced systems of information technology available on a wider and cheaper basis. Nevertheless, there is no magic formula to marketing. It is simply a logical stage-by-stage approach that employs a range of techniques and disciplines, and it is the firm that uses all the relevant techniques and skills that creates the synergy that sells.

Urban planning and the real estate market

As the world order changes – economically, politically and socially – so urban planning systems and real estate markets are in a constant state of flux. A major consequence of the pace at which change has taken place is economic uncertainty, which has, in turn, led to wide fluctuations in real estate markets and proved a severe test of planning systems. This has happened globally, regionally, nationally, within countries and even between competing locations within a city. Boom has invariably been followed by bust.

At the risk of stating the obvious, there are several basic features that determine the nature and performance of real estate markets worldwide. Such markets are:

- subject to the fundamental laws of demand and supply
- derivatives of general economic activity
- inherently cyclical in character
- increasingly international in activity.

More specifically, in respect of the UK, there are broad international and national issues that impact upon attitudes and policies towards urban planning and real estate development. These are explored more fully in relevant chapters in the text, but can usefully be summarized as follows.

Globalization

In the fields of both urban planning and real estate, Britain has about the most sophisticated planning system and property market in the world, with a long history of land and property management, and development serviced by a wealth of experienced and dedicated professionals. At a time of growing international awareness regarding the built environment, the opportunities for overseas consultancy abound. Indeed, a global perspective is fast becoming an imperative.

Sustainable development

Having roots in the doomsday scenario painted by the Club of Rome in the early 1970s, the Global 2000 report produced in 1980, and the 1987 Brundtland Report, the term "sustainable development" has become the worldwide buzzword for environmental policy issues of all kinds. Defined as "development, which meets the needs of the present without compromising the ability of future generations to meet their own needs" (World Commission 1987), in practice the philosophy, however laudable, is fraught with contradictions and political problems. Nevertheless, the UK is determined to make sustainable development the touchstone of its environmental policies (DoE 1994c), with major ramifications for urban planning policy and property development practice.

Environmental assessment

In a similar vein, environmental assessment (EA) is a phase that has been increasingly heard in the planning and development fields since the mid-1980s. Prompted by a 1985 European Community Directive (85/337), the UK government somewhat reluctantly enacted legislation in 1988 specifying certain kinds of development for which an EA should be submitted (DoE 1988). Criticisms abound regarding the number of EA's having to be produced, their variable quality, the burdensome cost, the ability of prospective developers properly to prepare them and planners competently to assess them, and the uneasy way in which they relate to the UK planning system. Only time and experience will tell the true value of such documents.

Europe

The emergence of Europe as a powerful trading block inevitably will strengthen the case for a greater integration of both urban planning policies and practices, and property investment and development markets. For those professions involved with the built environment, Europe is at the beginning of an exciting period

19

of change and opportunity. Many of the issues pressing down upon the UK regarding such matters as shopping patterns, town centres, transportation, urban regeneration, evolving industrial and business organization, and the impact of technology upon work, will probably become agenda issues for the wider Community in the next few short years. As one of the most crowded countries in the Community, moreover, the UK has had to face and resolve some of the more difficult trade-offs between mutual responsibility and personal freedoms (Jonas 1994).

Property cycles

Since the mid-1960s, a familiar phenomenon in the UK and, for that matter, elsewhere throughout free market economies all over the world, has been the manifestation of recurrent yet irregular property cycles. These property cycles have major, often damaging, repercussions on the wellbeing of the economy as a whole. They are linked directly to the general economic cycle, but there are also additional sources of potential instability from within the property industry itself. Although a better understanding of the nature of such cycles, together with continued refinement of data sources and more widespread use of fundamental analysis, should limit the wilder results, property cycles are distinguished from economic cycles, for development is volatile not just because it is tossed about by building manias or waves of purely speculative finance, but because it is deemed to be unstable by its very nature. Building booms and slumps can be explained simply by developers' responses to current market signals and the development lag. With the benefit of hindsight, moreover, public policy changes can be seen to have served to de-stabilize the property market further. It is argued that policy- and decision-makers in both public planning and private development sectors now have at their disposal the research tools and findings to help improve on previous performance (Key et al. 1994).

Planning and commercial viability

Although the issue of commercial viability arises across the planning system as a whole in the making of both planning policy and development control decisions, its influence becomes visible only at the stage of implementation. It has been stated that, although the relevance of commercial viability in the planning system has evolved through the support of judicial authority, it has not been regarded by planners as an integral element of the system. Nevertheless, the planning system exists in the public interest and, if it is to function successfully, commercial viability must be central to it in so far as, in practice, viability determines the consequence of planning decisions (Bullock 1993). In the words of PPG12 (DOE 1992b: para. 1.1): "No development takes place unless the market and other considerations persuade owners and developers to come forward with proposals".

20

Assessments of commercial viability, however, have been treated with scepticism by both public and private sector agencies alike, but a closer dialogue and greater understanding between all concerned is clearly called for in order to ensure that those framing policy and making planning decisions are as informed as possible as to the consequences of the actions.

Public markets and privatization

In pursuit of its declared aims, the Conservative government has introduced a range of reforms in the workings of the public sector, many of which impinge upon urban planning and development. These include privatization, compulsory competitive tendering, contracting out, the private finance initiative, new funding mechanisms, market testing, and encouraging private sector firms to provide services in parallel and in competition with public providers, the pressure being upon local authorities to act as enabler rather than provider of services. Such changes have been viewed as both threats and opportunities by those involved. In certain authorities the very function of planning has been externalized. An extreme view envisages a possible local government structure solely comprising elected members, chief officers and contract managers supervising the externalized or privatized contractors (Eames 1993).

Urban regeneration

Urban regeneration can be defined as the process of reversing economic and social decay in towns and cities where it has reached the stage where market forces alone will not suffice. Further, the significance in terms of government policy is enshrined in PPG23 as follows:

> The principle of sustainable development means that, where practicable, brownfield sites, including those affected by contamination should be recycled into new uses and the pressures thereby reduced for greenfield sites to be converted into urban, industrial or commercial uses. (DOE 1994d)

The complexities of developing on brown land can include multi-ownership, contamination, outdated infrastructure, demolition of existing structures, inadequate site history, and so on. To be successful, it has been argued that the project must change the total environment (Early 1994). This means that the scale of the project can be enormous and it often involves addressing social and economic issues as well as the physical development. Several government initiatives have been aimed at promoting urban regeneration by harnessing together public planning and private development agencies. City Challenge provides government funding to act as a catalyst to attract other finance, especially private sector investment, into areas of acute deprivation. English Partnership was established in 1993 to bring derelict land and buildings back into productive use, working with both public and private sector bodies. In 1992 the government announced a new scheme, the Private Finance Initiative, to find ways of mobilizing the private sector to meet needs traditionally being met by the public sector. November 1993 saw the government promulgating a series of measures collectively called the Single Regeneration Budget, "designed to shift power from Whitehall to local authorities". And the European Union (EU) makes funding available for urban regeneration under the European Social Fund and the European Regional Development Fund. Government, generally, has moved away from its previous reactive approach to urban regeneration, money being much more targeted and not given out haphazardly to any developer with a bright idea for an inner-city scheme (Smith 1994).

Town centre and out-of-town development

A major debate rages around the future of town centres and the impact upon them of out-of-town developments. Many town centres have experienced a decline in fortune over recent years, principally as a result of growing competition from out-of-town shopping facilities, but also because of such factors as an increase in car ownership, a lack of suitable sites in town centres, higher town centre rents, the movement of multiple retail chains out of town, the loss of town centre individuality and shopping appeal, the erosion of town centre leisure and entertainment appeal, and the diversion of institutional funds towards out-of-town property (Moss & Fellows 1995). The government response to the above is primarily included in the revised PPG6 (DOE 1993a) and elements of PPG13 (DOE 1994a), which, although recognizing the need for both town centre and out-of-town retail provision, clearly favour town centres, and then edge-of-town locations, for future development. However, potential conflicts of interest are bound to arise.

Planning obligations

As the recession eases and the momentum of property development resurges, the thorny and emotive issue of "planning gain" (or using the governments preferred term, "planning obligations") inevitably will re-emerge. There have also been moves to institute a system of "developers contributions" towards the provision of transport infrastructure. With the introduction of planning obligations in the Planning and Compensation Act 1991, and Departmental guidance in Circular 16/91 (DOE 1991), the ambivalent attitude of government towards such imposts is demonstrated. While encouraging councils through advisory circulars to take an entrepreneurial approach towards raising income from the development proc-
, it also recognizes that they may be venturing into an area of law that has yet

to be tested fully. Considered on the one hand to be "the only form of lawful corruption left in the United Kingdom" and "a right and proper means by which society recoups community created values" on the other, the scene is surely set for future controversy and litigation. Revised circular guidance on planning obligations is anticipated during 1996, and will provide some clarification on the determination of acceptable behaviour in this already vexed area of development control.[1]

Property as a strategic resource

There is an increasing awareness that there is a need to place property issues higher on the strategic agenda of senior management in the field of corporate business. In the USA a project entitled Corporate Real Estate 2000 aims to promote effective corporate real estate management by developing a framework and a methodology for helping senior business managers and real estate professionals integrate property into broader corporate thinking as what is described as the fifth strategic resource. Similar research in the UK identified that the most important issues facing business organizations were identifying new market opportunities, focusing on core business, quality improvement, investment technology, and re-engineering business processes. In all of these an organization's property requirements can be seen to affect and facilitate change. Moreover, although the requirements for occupational property will always be a function of the overall nature and level of activity of the organization, in the particular light of changes in communications technology senior managers are always looking for more flexible solutions to property needs (Gibson 1995).

In addition to the issues highlighted above, there are major questions regarding such matters as local government reorganization, transportation, employment, housing, green belts, contaminated land, strategic planning for London, conservation, lifestyles, technology and demographics, which all influence the way in which planning and development processes will act and interact in future. The issues will not fade away. The challenge for all those involved in urban planning and real estate development will be in determining how these issues are to be addressed in practice.

---

1. Refer to Chapter 5.

PART TWO

Urban planning organization

CHAPTER TWO

Policy and implementation of urban planning

Since 1948 a highly regulated system of land-use control has been gradually introduced by successive legislative reforms. Today, the implementation of urban planning controls is exercised under two distinct but interconnected subject areas, dealing first with the production of planning policies and then how those policies feed into the development control system, whereby decisions are made on individual planning applications. Both of these subjects form the bedrock of the planning system. Attention will be focused upon the context of planning policy, together with a detailed study of the processing of a planning application, including the formulation of the decision whether to grant or refuse such an application. Reference is also made to illustrative (but not exhaustive) case law on matters that constitute issues relevant to the determination of a planning application. The chapter is organized as follows:

- the development plan process
- the development control process.

The post-war planning system involving both the production and implementation of locally produced planning policy was first introduced by the Town and Country Planning Act 1947. All previous town planning statutes were repealed and the new legislation heralded the introduction of a major shift in public policy, from which we may trace the evolution of the current system. The new Act came into force on 1 July 1948 (the appointed day).[1] This legislation introduced the modern system as it exists today. The very need to apply for planning permission became nationalized. Private landownership would remain, but thenceforth permission would be required to change the use of buildings or to erect new structures. Planning policy would be prepared by local councils (city, district or borough) and county councils. Such locally produced policy would shape the patterns of development across the country. However, the overall organization of town planning would be the subject of a highly centralized system of control, whereby central government would determine the function of local government. As local government is responsible for the implementation of planning functions,

---

1. This date is important in determining what is "original", so that, when calculating permitted development tolerances, anything built before the appointed day is original and therefore not considered to be an extension.

this meant that the national government dictated the nature of town planning powers and their institutional structures. Today, central government departments, in particular the Department of the Environment (or Scottish Office or Welsh Office), have responsibility for the policy outcomes of the planning system. The DOE, Scottish Office/Welsh Office issue PPGs and Circulars containing the views of the Secretary of State on a wide variety of policy areas. These documents constitute important material considerations and must be taken into account in decisions on planning applications and appeals. Other government departments, notably the Department of National Heritage and Department of Transport also influence the system.

The Town and Country Planning Act 1968 introduced a significant reform to the system of plan preparation with the introduction of structure plans and local plans. The structure plan was to be prepared by a county council or the Greater London Council and was to comprise a statement of strategic and longer-term planning objectives such as major housing allocations or green belt identification. The local plan was to be prepared by the city, district or borough, providing a more detailed and short-term list of policies to be applied specifically to individual sites. The local plan would need to be in conformity with the structure plan, and with central government advice. At first, county councils were encouraged to incorporate economic and social, as well as land use, policies in structure plans. However, in recent years central government has sought to exclude wider social policy objectives in an attempt to emphasize land-use strategies. This stance has been followed by councils, although they have not excluded considerations of issues such as transport[2] and sustainable development.

The reforms of 1968 were subsequently consolidated into the Town and Country Planning Act 1971. This statute remained the principal planning statute until the introduction of new planning legislation in the Town and Country Planning Act 1990 and Planning and Compensation Act 1991. The only other significant statutory reforms introduced between 1971 and 1990 dealt with the delivery of the planning function in the reform of the local government structure. The Local Government Act 1972 created a new system in England and Wales (which came into force in 1974), except for Greater London, which had been reorganized in the early 1960s under the London Government Act 1963 (which came into force in 1965). In Scotland similar reforms to local government structure were introduced by the Local Government (Scotland) Act 1973 (which came into force in 1975).

The reforms to local government structure are shown in Table 2.1. The reforms of 1973 and 1974 increased the number of local government bodies (counties and districts) from 177 to 454 in England and Wales (Redcliffe-Maud Report 1969), whereas in Scotland it reduced them from 430 to 65. Across Britain the new structure involved a two-tier basis whereby the county/region (metropolitan or non-metropolitan) would be responsible for strategic planning matters and the district

2. Policies set out in the yearly Transport Policies and Programmes Statement (TPP) produced by a county will draw upon strategic issues laid out in the structure plan.

Table 2.1   Local government, 1974–94.

England	39	county councils
	296	district and city councils
(except Greater London)	6	metropolitan councils
	36	metropolitan districts and borough councils
Greater London	Greater London Council	
	32	London boroughs
	+	City of London (special status being excluded from local government reforms)
Wales	8	county councils
	37	district and city councils
Scotland	9	regional councils and three island authorities
	53	district or city councils

or city council, and London boroughs would be responsible for day-to-day matters, especially dealing with planning applications.[3] In the metropolitan areas of and surrounding Manchester, Liverpool, Newcastle, Sheffield, Leeds and Birmingham, a two-tier system of metropolitan counties and districts was established. The objectives of the Local Government Act 1972 and Local Government (Scotland) Act 1973 were to introduce reforms to simplify and streamline the structure of local government and implementation of local services, including town planning controls.

Today that two-tier system has been replaced by a confusing mix of two-tier and single-tier structures, a consequence of reforms introduced in 1986 and 1995. In 1986 the Greater London Council and six metropolitan counties were abolished, with their powers being passed on to the London boroughs and the metropolitan district councils. Therefore, in each of these urban areas only one body would be responsible for the implementation of local government including the town planning function, so the London borough or metropolitan district would be responsible for both structure and local plan policy. Policy would reflect an amalgamation of both objectives and would be called a unitary development plan. In 1995 and following a widespread review of local government structure undertaken by the Local Government Commission for England, the Scottish Office and the Welsh Office, the government announced further reforms, whereby some county and regional councils would be abolished, with their powers passing to the districts. Again, these councils would be responsible for producing a unitary development plan.

No formal regional planning function is established in Britain. Areas such as the South East region of England do not have their own formal regional body of government. Informal groupings of the many local government bodies have assembled to create regional forums such as the Standing Conference of South

---

3. In Scottish regional councils (Borders, Dumfries, Highlands), all planning functions are implemented at regional level. No district authorities exist in the Island Regional Authorities, so all planning is undertaken by the island councils.

East Planning (SERPLAN) or the Standing Conference of East Anglia Local Authorities (SCEALA). However, they enjoy little real power. Since 1989 the government has issued Regional Planning Guidance Notes (RPGs) for England, which provide for a series of broad regional planning strategies. When preparing structure plan policy, the county council must take account of such regional guidance, yet this is not the same as having a regional tier of government as exists in Germany, France and Spain. Although the structure of local government has been changed several times since the mid-1980s, the district or borough has retained the power of control over planning applications (development control). These bodies are commonly called the local planning authority (LPA). The vast majority of planning applications are submitted to and determined by the LPA. The parish council is outside this system. It does not enjoy any formal local government powers, although it may be consulted on planning applications. Around 10000 parish councils exist in England (called community councils in Scotland and Wales). Today the system is as shown in Table 2.2.

Table 2.2   Local government post-1995.

Non-metropolitan England (shires)	(i)*	19	Two-tier country and district councils
	(ii)*	20	Mixed single-tier and two-tier, in which principal towns are unitary and remaining area in the county retains two-tier county and districts structure.
Metropolitan England (London and conurbations)	(i)		London: 32 single-tier unitary London boroughs and City of London
	(ii)		Newcastle, South Yorkshire, West Yorkshire, West Midlands, Merseyside and Manchester: 36 single-tier Unitary Metropolitan district Councils.
Scotland		28	Single-tier unitary councils
		3	Island councils
Wales		22	Single-tier unitary councils

Key notes
In a two-tier system both county council and district council enjoy responsibility for local government.
In a single-tier "unitary" system these functions are amalgamated into one unitary council.
* Subject to Parliamentary approval, as at December 1995.

The development plan process

The development plan is an "umbrella" expression that covers all statutory planning policies produced by local planning authorities (Healey 1983). These policies are found in four principal documents:
- the structure plan produced by regions or non-metropolitan counties
- the local plan produced by district or city councils
- the unitary development plan produced by the London boroughs, metro-

29

politan districts or metropolitan districts with no county tier
- old-style development[4] plans produced by district/city prior to 1968 reforms.

Sometimes the LPA will introduce Supplementary Planning Guidance, policy that is used in decision-making on applications, but has not been included in the local plan or UDP. Such policy should supplement the plan and not seek to replace it. This practice is best used on technical guidance such as carparking standards or visibility splays from road junctions. It does not carry the same status as the plan and should be clearly cross-referenced to the local plan. If it is not related to such policy and has not been the subject of any public consultation, it will be considered as a "bottom drawer" policy that carries little weight as a planning consideration. Refusals based solely on such "bottom drawer" policy guidance will stand little chance of being supported by an Inspector when considering any subsequent planning appeal.

These policies "guide" development proposals by establishing a series of rules that may shape future development proposals and influence the chances of gaining planning permission (Bruton & Nicholson 1987, Healey et al. 1988). They also provide a "starting point" for the consideration of various development proposals. Satisfying development plan policy does not guarantee that planning permission will be granted, however, the various development plan policies form an important and significant material consideration. These policies should always be examined in the first instance before submitting planning applications as they constitute an important material consideration in the decision whether to grant or refuse planning permission. The "weight" attached to such policy increases as it proceeds through the various stages of its production. When policy has completed these stages, it will be "adopted" (if a local plan or unitary development plan), or "approved" (if a structure plan). This will mean that:

> Where in making any determination under the planning Acts, regard is to be had to the development plan, the determination shall be made in accordance with the plan unless material considerations indicate otherwise.[5]

The local plan produced by the district council (or city council) deals with more detailed and local issues identifying specific land uses suitable for individual sites and detailed policies for particular development proposals. Some local plans are also called action area plans (specific sites, usually town centre development) or subject plans (dealing with specific policies that cross district boundaries, usually green belts), although they carry the same status as local plans. The unitary development plan is a combination of both structure plan strategic issues (Part I) and local plan site-specific issues (Part II) in areas with only a single tier "unitary" authority, e.g. London boroughs.

---

4. A few of these are still in place, but are being replaced by local plans.
5. Section 54A of the Town and Country Planning Act 1990. Refer to the section entitled "The decision-makers duty".

In 1991, the introduction of reforms resulted in greater weight to the legal status of development plan policy within the decision-making process.[6] It is therefore important that landowners and developers monitor the production of planning policy and become involved in that process to influence the final outcome (Table 2.3). Once policies have completed this process, they become "adopted" or approved; resulting in considerable influence over the outcome of future planning applications. These reforms also made the production and adoption of district-/borough-wide local plans (or unitary development plans) a mandatory requirement across England and Wales (this had been a requirement in Scotland since 1973). In spite of DOE targets that these should be in place for England by 1996, delay in the production of policy and scheduling of all the necessary Local Plan Inquiries mean that in reality total coverage for the country should be reached at some time between 1998 and 2000.[7]

Table 2.3   The production of development plans policy.

Structure plan/local plan/unitary development plan process	
Stages	What happens
A – Survey	Council gathers data on land use and other relevant information (e.g. transport patterns and population trends).
B – Prepare draft	Council formulates policies and supporting information.
C – Deposit	Plan is "deposited" for a formal period of publicity and for the submission of objections against individual policies in the plan.
D – Review	Review by panel at Examination in Public (Structure Plan) or Inspector at Public Local Inquiry (local plan or UDP). Each will publish a report with recommended amendments.
E – Modification	Council may modify in line with the report. This may require another review to be opened.
F – Notice to adopt	Council submits notice to adopt to Secretary of State, who has a 28-day period to "call-in" the plan and approve plan in whole or part.
G – Adoption	If no "call-in" plan becomes adopted and now carries full statutory weight.

* Full details of all procedures can be found in Sections 10 to 54A of the Town and Country Planning Act, 1990.

Groups interested in the planning process such as landowners, developers and local or national interest groups, are advised to monitor the production of plan policy, especially in the early stages (Stages A, B and C). Structure plan revision

6. This legislation has been enacted across England, Wales and Scotland.
7. The DOE produces updates on the production of local planning policy, published several times a year. Copies are available from their headquarters at Marsham Street, London SW1.

and alteration should take place every 10–15 years and local plan/UDP every 10 years. Any person or group who disagrees with a particular policy should submit objections following the deposit stage (Stages B and C). If they do not object, and the policy becomes adopted, it will carry the full weight of Section 54A, making it unlikely that it could be ignored when dealing with a planning application or appeal. Objection to local plan or unitary development plan policies can be made in writing or in person before the Inspector. In the local plan/UDP Inquiry, any objector has the right to appear before the Inspector to explain their case. Anyone doing so is open to cross-examination by the LPA. Legal representation is allowed in similar format to a planning appeal submitted by way of public inquiry. Similarly, it is common for many objectors to instruct planning consultants to prepare proofs in support of their objection and to appear at the local plan Inquiry. The structure plan Examination in Public allows the "panel"[8] to select issues and invite certain participants to make a contribution. No one who objects to a policy has the automatic right to appear before the panel. The examination takes the form of a discussion led by the chairman between panel members, representatives of the county council and the invited participants. Planning consultants and legal representatives are allowed to appear. Both the local plan Inspector and structure plan Panel will consider the views of objectors and invited participants. A report is sent, in either case, to the relevant district/city/borough council or county council. The Inspector/Panel may recommend modifications that the respective council must consider. There is no obligation to implement such modifications, but they should provide good reasons for not so doing. In both types of plan the Secretary of State enjoys powers to object to policies in the plan, to direct the structure plan authority to modify a policy or to "call-in" a local plan/UDP and direct that a policy be modified or altered. In extreme cases he may reject in whole or part a structure plan or local plan/UDP.

The development control process: a definition?

Development control is a process by which society represented by locally elected councils regulates changes in the use and appearance of the environment. (Audit Commission 1992).

The development control function is of itself difficult to define. It has been referred to as the Cinderella of the planning system in that it deals with the day-to-day administration of planning control. In many ways this function operates at the "sharp end" of the system, as it deals with decision-making on planning applications, representations at appeal, and the enforcement of planning control.

8. The panel is appointed by the Secretary of State and consists usually of three independent experts, usually one each from the Planning Inspectorate, the DOE and an experienced planning solicitor or barrister.

Case study 2.1: Local plan objection

Prefabricated Engineering Ltd owns a hectare of land occupied by a series of single storey light engineering buildings.

The local council proposes in its local plan that the site be identified for industrial use for the plan period (ten years). The owners wish to vacate in the next two years and consider that the site is better suited to residential redevelopment. They lodge an objection to the local plan policy and instruct a town planning consultant to appear at the Local Plan Inquiry. The Inspector considers the objection and reports that the land is suitable for residential redevelopment and should be so designated. The local council modifies the plan to delete this site from industrial allocation and include it in residential allocation.

However, the local council is not compelled always to follow the Inspector's recommendations, although if it opposes such modifications it must provide good reasons, otherwise the Secretary of State may intervene during the final stage prior to adoption (Stage F in Table 2.3).

This all takes place within a political system whereby locally elected politicians make decisions within a planning committee or delegate such decision-making powers to officials, principally the chief planning officer of a local authority. To understand how this system operates, it is necessary first to examine the historical background of development control, as well as the debate surrounding the quality and service delivery of this function. The basis of today's planning system can be found in the reforms introduced by the Town and Country Planning Act of 1947. This legislation introduced a system of comprehensive control over development. What constituted development was defined by statute and would require planning permission by means of an application to a local authority. The system would be overseen by a government department (initially the Ministry of Housing and Local Government and today the Department of the Environment in England and Welsh and Scottish Offices), although the emphasis was on local control.

The Dobry Report, 1975

The first comprehensive review of the development control system took place in 1973, led by George Dobry QC (Dobry 1975). The review was established to consider the current arrangements for planning appeals as well as appraising whether the development control system adequately met current needs, with a view to advising on areas for improvement. The report was commissioned against a background of dramatic increases in the numbers of planning applications and appeals submitted between 1968 and 1972. By 1972 the number of planning applications submitted had increased by more than 67 per cent over 1968 levels. Dobry concluded that, although the system was very good, its procedures did not adequately meet current needs, and he criticized them for being slow and cumbersome. A series of detailed recommendations were designed to speed the administrative and procedural side of the development control function, rather than the quality of the decisions made (a recurrent theme in subsequent reviews of development control).

The most significant recommendation, which the government considered to be too radical to enact, proposed that all planning applications be split into two categories with differing procedural requirements. Category (A) would be "simple" applications of a small-scale nature or non-contentious (i.e. those in accordance with the development plan). Category (B) would be large-scale proposals or contentious proposals (i.e. not in accordance with the development plan). The planning authority would be required to issue a decision on (A) applications within 42 days of submission and on (B) applications within three months of submission. Failure to issue a decision on Category (A) within 42 days would result in a deemed grant of planning permission. No such deemed consent would apply to Category (B).

Although Dobry's major recommendation of Category (A) and (B) was rejected by the government, several of its minor recommendations were to be incorporated into various administrative reforms, notably the use of a standard application form when applying for permission, greater delegation of decisions to officers, publicity and public consultation for planning applications, and the introduction of a charge for submitting a planning application. The Dobry Report dealt with areas for improvement of efficiency within the system and it is important to distinguish between the desire to improve the efficiency of the development control process and the quality of the decisions made. Dobry dealt almost exclusively with seeking to improve the speed of decisions without affecting their quality.

This philosophy has been followed through more recently with the publication of three reports into the operation of development control, as follow.

The Royal Town Planning Institute Report 1991

In identifying the strengths and weaknesses of the current system, this report dealt with the problems surrounding an examination of "effectiveness" within that system. The report stated: "Attempts at defining an effective planning service can easily open up a debate on the ideology and philosophy of planning itself" (Royal Town Planning Institute 1991).

It was acknowledged that statistics could be employed to measure procedural issues (for example the percentage of planning applications determined within a particular time period). However, such methods could not be used to measure the quality of decisions made, as this was a largely subjective matter. It is a paradox of the system that the more carefully a planning officer negotiates to improve an application, the less likely it is that a decision will be made within the eight-week statutory period that constitutes the only measure of quality control. The study therefore found that "effectiveness" in the planning service does not necessarily equate with speed. With regard to development control, the study identified the following as the key attributes that contribute towards an effective planning service: clarity, speed, user involvement, openness and certainty. Recommendations were made, including several designed to improve service delivery, such as the need for concise reports to planning committee, encouragement to hold pre-application meetings, and greater delegation of decisions by planning committee to the Chief Planning Officer.

In conclusion, the report emphasized that, for a planning service to operate effectively, a "service culture" must be built upon the concept of customer care. In development control, such a concept of care requires the process to be both "accessible" to developers and the public, in that decisions are clearly and easily explained, as well as procedurally efficient in that administrative targets are set for the speedy despatch of decisions or responses to enquiries.

The Audit Commission: building in quality 1992

Like the Dobry Report, the Audit Commission's report (Audit Commission 1992) was concerned with the speed and efficiency of the development control function, but, unlike Dobry, its principal terms of reference were defined as improving the quality and effectiveness of the system. The report focused upon the attainment of quality outcomes. The Audit Commission had considered the views of both developers and consultants, as well as existing statistical performance indicators, such as the net expenditure per application by the local authority, or the percentage of applications considered under delegated authority. These quality outcomes were similar to the RTPI (1991) study in that they identified a series of administrative areas of concern as follows:

- Service objectives need to be established – encompassing all the publications or policy documents of the LPA.
- Pre-application discussions and advice – should be encouraged and guidance published on applications, as well as the existence of an accessible planning department reception.
- Efficient administrative backup – To register applications upon receipt and pass promptly to a planner.
- Consultation and notification – encouraging the notification objectives to be clearly set out in correspondence, together with guidance on the relevance of particular responses to avoid replies with no planning relevance.
- Assessment and negotiation – following any negotiation it must be necessary to demonstrate the achievements gained from this process. LPAs should utilize the services of specialist in-house staff to ensure consistency and quality in specific areas (e.g. economic development, design, traffic or ecological matters).
- Documentation – written reports to committee upon a case, dealing with the merits or otherwise of the case; jargon is to be avoided.
- Decision-taking and committees – potential for greater delegation to Chief Planning Officer and a frequent committee cycle.
- Decision notification – to ensure speedy delivery of decision reached.

35

Confederation of British Industry (CBI)/Royal Institution of Chartered Surveyors (RICS) (1992)

This report was the result of a CBI appointed task force of 21 business leaders and planning professionals, charged with examining the planning system and identifying areas where improvement would help the successful operation of businesses (CBI & RICS 1992).

The most far-reaching recommendation was for the creation of a National Framework of Strategic Guidance, with relevant central government departments producing a policy framework covering land use and infrastructure, over a projected five-year period and with the most immediate priorities identified for the next year, together with a funding commitment from the Treasury. This represented a call for greater direction by central government over strategic planning issues, together with associated financial commitment. The business community identified the need for a greater degree of direction regarding major land-use and transport proposals to ensure greater certainty for the property investment industry. Such a call was seemingly at odds with government philosophy, which in 1983 had proclaimed that strategic planning was an outdated concept of the 1960s and 1970s, followed in 1985, by the abolition of the Greater London Council and six metropolitan county councils (HMSO 1983).

Perhaps not surprisingly, the then Secretary of State for the Environment, Michael Howard, soon dismissed any possibility of the government adopting such a strategic framework.[9] The report considered that pre-application discussion should be made a statutory requirement and that the business community should seek to make a more cohesive and systematic input into plan preparation to ensure that planning policy adequately dealt with the needs of the business community.

Appraising quality within development control

These reports have all sought to appraise the development control function. It is far easier to identify quality within the system by examining administrative and procedural matters such as the frequency of committee meetings or the time taken to issue a decision notice. It is harder to examine the concept of quality when dealing with the actual quality of the decision. To appraise whether or not a particular local planning authority has issued a "good" or "bad" decision would be fraught with problems, as many planning decisions rely on professional judgement, based on policy and other material considerations. Appraisal of the quality of decisions made is further complicated by the fact that planning officers, committee, developers or the public may all hold differing views on the desirable outcome of the whole process and, therefore, what is a good decision to one group may not be a good decision to another group. The Audit Commission did attempt

---

9. "Shaping the nation", editorial opinion in *Estates Gazette*, 14 November 1992.

to link service delivery with the assessment of, and negotiation on, a planning application. This would be achieved by utilizing specialist contributions to the appraisal of a planning application (e.g. for conservation, landscape, economic development issues) and ensuring that the development control service is guided by the local authority's overall objectives. However, in the vast majority of recommendations in all of these reports, the overriding concern is service delivery and how it can be made more open and apparent to the public, quicker in dealing with administration and able to establish targets and guidelines. This is not to say that the current system is wholly inefficient, but that, in the past, little real attention has been paid towards a review of targets and performance. Some authorities have subsequently published Service Charters[10] setting out mission statements and targets for performance, and in some cases attention has been paid to improving public perception by allowing greater access for the public, on particular cases, to speak in committee meetings.[11]

When appraising development control, it is easy merely to associate quality with speed of decision-making. The eight-week statutory period encourages this,[12] as the Department of the Environment will release annual statistics on the percentages of planning applications decided within eight weeks or in excess of eight weeks. This measure does allow for a crude indication of quality in that the more minor applications should be decided within such a period. However, for anything more complex, involving the consideration of many technical issues, the eight-week period is unreasonably short. In effect, to stay within it encourages LPAs to avoid negotiations seeking amendment, as the submission of amended plans (and associated requirement to go back to public consultation), will take the application outside the statutory period. It may be of benefit to their statistical returns for the LPA to refuse an application and pursue discussions prior to resubmission of a revised, fresh planning application. This would delay the developer, but would reflect a more efficient approach by the LPA. The Dobry recommendation of a two-tier system based upon Category A and B applications would reflect the workings of the system more accurately. Both the recent RTPI and Audit Commission reports have criticized the statutory period as not providing a measure of quality. As long as it remains, it provides a benchmark to assess the speed of decision-making, but it is necessary to acknowledge that caution should be exercised when using it to assess the effective delivery of the development control service.

---

10. For example, Woking Borough Council in 1992 published a series of targets dealing with such matters as responding to letters and dealing with pre-application advice.
11. See the report on the practice adopted by Newbury planners in *Planning*, 12 February 1993.
12. Under provision of the General Development Procedure Order, Article 20, the LPA must give notice of a decision on a planning application within eight weeks of receipt. This period may be extended by written agreement between both parties. DOE target figures aim for 80 per cent of all applications to be decided within this period. Adherence to this target is subject to wide fluctuations across the country, with some LPAs as low as 35 per cent within eight weeks.

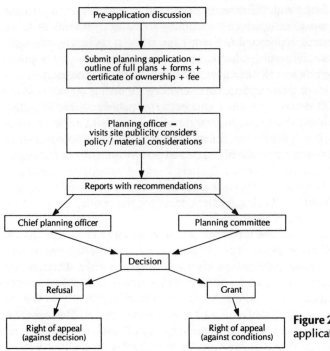

Figure 2.1 The planning application process.

The planning application process

Once it has been established that: the proposal constitutes development, in that it represents either a material change of use or operational development,[13] and that it would not otherwise be exempt from control by provisions within the General Permitted Development Order or Use Classes Order, then it is necessary to apply for planning permission by submission of a planning application to the local planning authority.

Two specific topics must be considered: the processing of the application, and how one arrives at the decision to grant or refuse planning permission.

Processing the application (Fig. 2.1)

Pre-application discussions
Before the application is submitted, the developer may wish to approach the LPA to seek either the informal views of the planning officer on the likelihood of permission being granted, or to clarify whether permission is required for the

---

13. See section beginning on p. 55.

proposal in the first place.[14] The developer would be well advised at this stage to check the planning history of the site or its surroundings (previous application approvals or refusals and appeal decisions, i.e. whether these were allowed or dismissed, and any Inspector's comments).

The planning history constitutes an important material consideration.[15] The developer may leave the meeting in the knowledge that the proposal would be acceptable subject to certain issues or details being amended or that the proposal is unacceptable in principle (i.e. contrary to policy) and that the likelihood of a recommendation for approval by officers is unlikely. These meetings may also help the developer to decide whether to submit an application at all.

Which application?

The application can be made in either full or outline. In both cases it is necessary to submit the following documents:

- *Plans* The exact detail or type of plan will depend largely on the proposal and whether the application is made in full or outline. Common to both will be an Ordnance Survey extract showing the site outlined in red and any other adjoining land also owned by the applicant outlined in blue. Full applications will require detailed elevational drawings and floorplans together with a siting drawing (showing proposed access, parking, relationship of proposal to adjoining land and, possibly, landscaping). Outline applications may only require the Ordnance Survey extract, although a siting plan may also be submitted, depending upon which matters are to be reserved for subsequent approval.
- *Forms* The application must be made on standard forms issued by the LPA.
- *Certificate of ownership* A certificate that only the applicant owns the land or has given notice of his application to all relevant landowners, and whether or not the land is on an agricultural holding, must be signed by the applicant or agent. It is therefore possible to make a planning application on land that is not within the ownership of the potential developer.
- *Fee* Charges for planning applications were first introduced in 1980, the government's view being that some part of the cost of development control should be recovered from the applicant and not solely borne by the LPA. The fee structure changes approximately every two or three years. Reference should be made to the current Town and Country Planning (Fees for Applications and Deemed Applications) Regulations to ascertain the current charges.

---

14. To avoid any uncertainty regarding whether permission is required, an application can be made for a Certificate of Lawfulness of Existing or Proposed Use or Development; see section beginning on p. 65.
15. See section beginning on p. 46.

Outline applications

An outline planning application seeks to establish the principle of operational development on a particular site (applications for changes of use cannot be made in outline). The outline planning permission is one that is made subject to a condition requiring the subsequent approval by the LPA of reserved matters. These reserved matters cover five key areas of development control, namely siting, design, external appearance, means of access, and landscaping. The application form requests that the applicant nominates which matters are to be considered at the outline stage and which "reserved" for subsequent approval. It is possible for all of the five matters to be reserved, although it is common practice for the applicant to request (and supply necessary information) that siting and means of access are considered at the outline stage.

The LPA has powers to request that further details are required and that the application will not be considered until such details are received. However, it is rare for this request to go beyond the details required for access and siting.

Once outline planning permission has been granted, any application for the approval of reserved matters must be made within three years of the outline approval, and the development must be started within five years of that date, otherwise the permission will lapse.

The distinct advantage of outline planning permission is that it establishes certainty within the development process, namely that a particular scheme is acceptable, subject to reserved matters. This allows the developer the guarantee of a scheme without recourse to an appeal. Thus, outline approvals may enhance the value of land by establishing the principle of redevelopment without needing to draw up full plans.

Full applications

An application for full planning permission is for detailed approval. Full planning applications will therefore require submission of elevational drawings and floorplans, together with site plans showing access, landscaping and other treatment, such as carparking or servicing areas. It is usually the case that, although a good deal of detail will be submitted, the full planning permission may be granted subject to some conditions. These conditions may, similar to reserved matters on outline approvals, permit the proposal, while reserving for future consideration certain technical matters (e.g. details of internal matters such as soundproofing between converted flats). Conditions may also limit specific land-use matters, for example hours of operation, or maintenance of an approved landscaping scheme.[16] The full planning permission must be begun within a period of five years from the date of the approval or it will lapse.

---

16. Guidance on planning conditions can be found in DOE Circular 11/95: *The use of conditions in planning permissions*, or in Scottish Office Circular 18/86 or Welsh Office 35/95.

Formal submission of a planning application

When the application is made to the LPA it will be checked to ensure that all the documentation is correct and the necessary fee has been submitted. The application will then be acknowledged by the LPA and the date of the applications receipt will constitute the starting date for the two-month statutory period within which the LPA is required to issue a decision.

Following acknowledgement, it will be normal practice for most LPAs to undertake consultations with and publicity to various bodies or individuals.

Call-in powers

The Secretary of State for the Environment enjoys wide ranging powers to call-in any planning or listed building consent application for his own determination. These powers are rarely employed. Around 1000 planning applications are called in every year by the Secretary of State in England and of these some 151 will be formally determined, with the remainder referred back to the LPA. Most of these applications involve large-scale or controversial applications or applications that involve a departure from development plan policy, such as residential development within a green belt. If the LPA proposes to grant planning permission to such a "departure application" it must consult with the Secretary of State to allow for "call-in" to be enacted if the DOE considers the matter worthy of greater scrutiny or refusal. The Secretary of State also enjoys the power to give directions to the LPA that he must also be consulted on specific types of application, whereby he may then consider the use of "call-in" powers, an example being the Town and Country Planning (Shopping Development) (England and Wales) Direction 1993, requiring consultation on shopping development of in excess of 20000 m² gross floorspace.

Publicity for planning applications

Publicity surrounding planning applications can be taken to mean advertisements in local newspapers, on site or by neighbour notification.[17] Examples are shown in Table 2.4.

Third parties

Until 1991, LPAs were only encouraged to notify local residents who were neighbours considered to be affected by a proposal. However, it became increasingly apparent that different LPAs adopted different internal practices towards such consultation. An RTPI report (RTPI 1991) discovered that over three-quarters of all authorities undertook discretionary publicity and notification of planning applications. Yet, considerable differences existed between councils, with some only contacting immediately neighbouring occupiers, and others would contact widely within a set radius around the proposal site. Third parties did not enjoy any direct redress against the Council for failure to consult them, as no statutory duty existed

---

17. See DOE Circular 15/92, *Publicity for planning applications.*

Table 2.4 Specified publicity for planning applications.

Application	Publicity
1. Major development – 10+ dwellings, 1000+m² floorspace, waste processing or working of minerals.	Advertisement by applicant in local newspaper and on site.
2. Developments affecting a conservation area and/or a Listed Building.	Advertisement by LPA in local newspaper and site notice.
3. Applications that depart from the development plan.	Advertisement by LPA in local newspaper and site notice.
4. Applications involving submission of an environmental statement.	Advertisement by applicant in local newspaper and site notice.
5. Minor development such as changes of use or extensions.	Site notice or neighbour notification.

for notification to take place at all. Out of anger, or frustration, or both, many people lodged complaints with the Commissioner for Local Government Administration ("Ombudsman") on the grounds that the councils had been procedurally unfair in not consulting them.

In May 1991 the government accepted that all planning applications in England and Wales should receive some publicity, and regulations came into force in 1992.[18] Despite this, a problem still exists over the exact purpose of neighbour notification and publicity for planning applications. The Audit Commission (1992) identified a desire in many authorities to use neighbour notification as a public relations exercise, without informing the public about the exact purpose of such consultations. This devalues the process.

Third parties may draw the conclusion that the entire process is a waste of time if their comments are deemed irrelevant by the Chief Planning Officer in the report to planning committee. The Audit Commission recommended that authorities focus greater attention on providing the public with realistic expectations on both the process by which views will be taken into account, as well as the relevance of a particular type of response.

Consideration by planning officer
The application passes to a case officer who will also deal with the results of the publicity and consultation exercise. The case officer will visit the site and consider planning policy and other relevant planning matters not covered by policy. The consideration of these issues is not the consequence of a haphazard interaction of factors but the discharge of a particular statutory duty imposed upon the decision-maker by planning legislation. This duty affects all decision-makers within the planning process, namely the local planning authority (i.e. planning committee or Chief Planning Officer), the Secretary of State (as regards called-

---

18. Introduced by the Planning and Compensation Act 1991, in which responsibility for publishing all planning applications was imposed on LPAs.

in applications or appeal decisions) and Inspectors appointed by the Secretary of State to decide planning appeals. This duty will be considered below. As a consequence of such considerations, the planning officer may seek amendments to the proposal. The desire for amendment usually results in some element of discussion and negotiation between the officer and applicant (or agent appointed to deal with the application).

What emerges from this consideration is a recommendation from the case officer to the Chief Planning Officer either to grant planning permission subject to conditions[19] or to refuse permission, stating a reason or reasons. The consideration of the application may be deferred to allow for further information to be brought to a subsequent meeting (e.g. for amendments, details of proposed use or additional consultations). The planning committee may accept or reject (overturn) the recommendation of the Chief Planning Officer. If it rejects a recommendation to grant permission, and refuses the application, this must be a decision based upon sound planning judgement. The introduction of the award of costs in planning appeals means that any unreasonable refusal of planning permission may result in the "punishment" of the LPA by an award of costs. However, overturning the recommendation of the Chief Planning Officer does not automatically constitute unreasonable behaviour from which costs will follow. Circular 8/93 on costs states "While planning authorities are not bound to follow advice from their officers. . . they will be expected to show that they had reasonable planning grounds for a decision taken against such advice".[20]

Delegated applications (i.e. decision-making delegated by committee to officers) will usually be considered by the Chief Planning Officer; the criteria that determines suitability for delegation will vary from authority to authority. In most cases such delegated powers apply to small-scale proposals (e.g. household extensions), usually with little or no third-party objection.

The use of such delegated authority benefits the development control function in that, by avoiding the need to report the matter to committee, the decision time can be reduced. The officer simply reports, verbally or by a short written summary, to the Chief Planning Officer. If this is accepted, then a decision notice can be prepared and despatched. When dealing with committees it must be remembered that such bodies function on a cycle of meetings throughout the year. To report, an application requires considerable administration, as draft reports must be prepared and circulated to senior officers and then placed upon the agenda for the forthcoming meeting. With most committees on a cycle of one

---

19. The LPA may impose conditions on a planning permission "as they think fit". Such planning conditions will need to be related to land-use planning as well as the development being permitted. In all cases they must be reasonable. Government guidance on the use of such conditions is contained in DOE Circular advice, which states that all conditions must be necessary, relevant to planning, relevant to "the development" enforceable, precise and reasonable. Further Guidance on Planning conditions can be found in Circular 11/95, *The use of conditions in planning permissions.*

20. DOE Circular 8/93, *Award of costs incurred in planning and other proceedings* (para. 9 of Annex 3). In Scotland similar advice is contained in Scottish Office Circular 6/90.

meeting every three to four weeks, to miss one committee would take the decision period to between six and eight weeks, greatly increasing the chances of it falling outside the statutory period. The further complication of awaiting consultation and publicity responses before reporting to a committee provides additional procedural problems in determining applications within the eight-week statutory period. LPAs can improve their performance by increased use of delegated powers and shorter committee cycles.

The decision-maker's duty - how the decision to grant or refuse is made: Section 54A

The decision-maker in arriving at a decision on a planning application must discharge a legislative duty. Under the provisions of Section 29 of the Town and Country Planning Act 1971, which became incorporated into Section 70(2) of the Town and Country Planning Act 1990, this duty was that the decision-maker "shall have regard to the provisions of the development plan so far as material to the application and to any other material considerations".

In 1991 this was significantly changed by the introduction of Section 26 of the Planning and Compensation Act 1991, which introduced a new Section 54A into the 1990 Act as follows: "Where in making any determination under the planning Acts regard is to be had to the development plan, the determination shall be in accordance with the plan unless material considerations indicate otherwise".

This legislative change resulted in a considerable flurry of debate among planning professionals regarding its implications for decision-making. The previous system was based on a clear "presumption in favour of allowing applications for development".[21] The courts had held that the words "shall have regard to" did not mean slavish adherence to the contents of development plan policy.[22] The development plan was but one of possibly many material considerations. Certainly, on first impression, Section 54A gave greater weight to planning policy than was previously the case. In introducing the new section, the then Planning Minister, Sir George Young, said in the House of Commons:

> . . . if the development plan has something to say on a particular application the starting point would be that the plan should be followed unless the weight of the other considerations tell against it. In other words, there would be a presumption in favour of the development plan.

Section 54A has meant that:
- Greater attention needs to be paid to development plan policy. Although

---

21. Contained in DOE Circular 14/85, *Development and employment*, which was cancelled in 1990.
22. See *Enfield London Borough Council* vs *Secretary of State for the Environment* (1975), JPL 155, and *Chelmsford Borough Council* vs *Secretary of State for the Environment and Halifax Building Society* (1985), JPL 555.

Section 70(2) was not repealed, the new Section 54A gives more weight to the contents of the development plan.

- Greater importance is given to adopted policy rather than emerging policy in the course of preparation. Both Section 70 (2) and Section 54A apply to adopted policy. Emerging policy passing through the adoption process does not benefit from these provisions, although policy is said to "gather weight" as a material consideration as it moves through the various stages towards adoption (refer to PPG1).
- A greater degree of certainty in the development process as developers/LPAs realize that, if a proposal is in conflict with policy, a presumption exists that permission will be refused and, if the proposal is in accord with policy, a presumption exists that permission will be granted.
- Greater attention will be focused towards the procedures by which policy is formulated, as developers and other interested parties realize that the weight attached to policy warrants greater attention to its content. Policy formulation will need to be monitored so that objections may be considered at the appropriate stage.
- Material considerations will still be of importance in the development process and capable of outweighing policy, yet where policy is adopted and up to date it will carry considerable weight in influencing the decision-making progress.

Section 54A has undoubtedly introduced changes to the perception of the role of planning policy by developers, planners and consultants.[23] Fundamentally, it seeks to steer the decision-makers towards examination of policy, unless for some reason a material consideration outweighs such policy. Consider the example in Case Study 2.2 from the employment policies in the Oxford City Council local plan, regarding the former North and South Rover car facilities at Cowley.

Case study 2.2: Applying local plan policy

Policy EM5 Any land released for development on the Cowley Works site will be retained primarily for B1 and B2 uses and some limited B8 uses, together with ancillary uses such as an hotel. Any other uses will only be considered if it can be demonstrated that they will assist in achieving the rapid development of the site in an acceptable manner . . .

The emphasis of this policy is to secure B1 (Business), B2 (General Industry) and B8 (Storage) redevelopment on the former Cowley Works site. The consequence of Section 54A is that any proposal outside the terms of EM5 will be required to demonstrate that it will bring benefits that will outweigh these employment-related objectives.

---

23. For some case law on this refer to *St Albans District Council* vs *Secretary of State for the Environment* [1993] 1 PLR88.

What are material considerations?

Any consideration which relates to the use and development of land is capable of being a planning consideration.[24]

The courts have provided detailed interpretation as to exactly what can be considered to be a material consideration. A useful starting point in this area is *Westminster City Council* vs *Great Portland Estates* (1985), in which Lord Scarman stated that a material consideration was a consideration that served a planning purpose and that a planning purpose was one that related to the development and the use of the land.

So although the term "material considerations" may throw a wide net with a vast array of issues potentially of material importance, it is important to remember that the key test is whether it serves a planning purpose. For example, the developer's desire for profit would not be material.

Several key material considerations that have emerged from the Courts can be summarized as follows:[25]

Precedent: the granting of permission and its influence on adjoining land.

Case law	Issues
Collis Radio vs Secretary of State for the Environment [1975] 29 P&C R 390.	**Held** that there is no error of law if an application is judged according to its consequences of the development of other sites.
Poundstretcher Ltd, Harris Queensway plc vs Secretary of State for the Environment and Liverpool City Council [1989] JPL 90.	**Held** that where precedent was relied upon some form of evidence must be required. Mere fear of precedent was not sufficient.

Comment: Every planning application and appeal site must be considered on its own individual merits; however, this does not exclude concern regarding the cumulative impact, whereby in granting permission on site A it will probably follow that permission will be granted on sites B, C and D. This logic is influenced by the fact that the decision-making must be consistent and that the grant of development on site A would influence similar decisions on sites B, C and D, unless distinguishing reasons can be shown. So, precedent can be material, yet caution

---

24. See *Stringer and Minister of Housing and Local Government* (1970) I WLR 1281 and comments of Justice Cooke.
25. Legal references are cited as follows:
    P&CR: Property, Planning and Compensation Reports
    JPL: Journal of Planning and Environment Law
    All ER: All England Law Reports
    WLR: Weekly Law Reports
    PLR: Planning Law Reports
    AC: Appeal Cases
    EGCS: *Estates Gazette* Case Summary.

is required here, as it refers to consistency of decision-making or the cumulative impact of decisions. It is not some kind of binding legal principle where the LPA must grant permissions on comparable sites.

Planning history: previous granting of permission on proposal site.

Case law	Issues
Spackman vs Secretary of State for the Environment [1977] 1 All ER 257. South Oxfordshire District Council vs Secretary of State for the Environment [1981] 1 WLR 1092.	**Held** in both cases that a previous planning permission is capable of being material even if it has expired (i.e. over five years old and not implemented).

Comment: The history of previous decisions on the site in question is a matter of some importance. Unimplemented and expired (i.e. more than five years old) permissions will be material yet, as with precedent, the LPA or Inspector on appeal is not automatically obliged to renew such permissions and must consider the merits of the case, which will include whether any change in circumstances has occurred.

Financial considerations: economic viability of a proposal.

Case law	Issues
Sosmo Trust vs Secretary of State for the Environment, London Borough of Camden [1983] JPL 806. R vs Westminster City Council, ex parte Monahan [1989] 3 WLR 408 and 2 All ER 74 sometimes referred to as "Covent Garden Royal Opera House case". See below.	**Held** that it was material to consider the financial viability of a proposed scheme where it would have planning consequences.

Comment: The desire of the developer to make a profit from development is not a material consideration and never will be. However, the financial and economic viability of a proposal may have planning consequences and this, perhaps, may be the key determining factor. So, the developer's plea during negotiation, that not permitting a certain amount of additional floorspace will result in a proposal being economically unviable, can be a material consideration. LPAs may be sceptical about such arguments, although they will need to give them some attention. In such instances as the Covent Garden Royal Opera House case, issues of financial viability were material and considered sufficient to outweigh local plan policy, which would have otherwise resisted any commercial proposal on that site. The Opera House had argued that some commercial redevelopment (offices/shops) were required on their site in Covent Garden to fund and maintain the future existence of the theatrical use. This was accepted by Westminster City Council, the LPA and, following a legal challenge of the decision by a local Community Association, was held to be the correct approach.

Objections by third parties: residents or other people affected by a proposal

| Multi Media Productions vs Secretary of State for the Environment and Islington London Borough Council [1989] JPL 96. | **Held** that it was perfectly correct for an Inspector to dismiss an appeal on issues raised by third parties and not by LPA. |

Comment: Objections by third parties are all capable of being material, provided that these objections are based upon sound planning considerations. In many ways it is not so much the sheer quantity of objection letters submitted in relation to an application or appeal but instead their quality in the extent towards which they deal with planning matters.

The development plan: combination of local plan and structure plan or UDP.

Case law	Issues
St Albans District Council vs Secretary of State for the Environment [1993] 1 PLR 88.	**Held** that Section 54A of the T&CP Act 1990 meant that the policies in the plan shall prevail unless material considerations indicate that it should not.

Comment: It must be remembered that the development plan itself is a material consideration, as it is a matter concerned with the use and development of land. It is convenient to consider the development plan policies separately from material considerations, as town planning statutes tend to distinguish between the two when stating "unless material considerations indicate otherwise". All planning decisions will involve a balancing of issues. Section 54A attaches greater importance to the development plan as a matter of law. It follows that, after the introduction of this revision, the existence of a relevant and up-to-date development plan policy will be the strongest indicator of whether planning permission is likely to be granted or refused.

Government planning policy: combination of PPGs, Mineral Policy Guidance Notes (MPGs), Regional Policy Guidance Notes (RPGs) and government Circulars.

Comment: central government departments issue guidance to local government in the form of various policy guidance notes and Circulars. Such documents provide important, if broadly based, advice upon a range of development control issues and areas. Such information constitutes an important material consideration in determining applications and it establishes the broad direction in which the government wishes the development plan and development control system to progress. Although local planning authorities are not duty-bound always to follow this advice, they will need to show good reasons for any decisions that run counter to the government's view. It must also be remembered that if a matter proceeds to an appeal, the Inspector will take such guidance into consideration. Each of these documents carries the same weight; the principal difference between PPGs and Circulars is that the latter tend to deal with technical guidance, whereas the former provide more general advice on the operation of the system. The government has indicated, however, that in time all Circulars will be replaced by PPGs. The most widely used statements of government planning policy can be found in the following documents:

Document	Year issued	Topic
Circular 13/87	1987	Use Classes Order
PPG1	1992	General principles of planning (revision 1996/7)
PPG2	1995	Green belts
PPG3	1992	Housing
PPG6	1993	Retailing (revision expected 1996)
PPG13	1994	Transport and planning
Circular 11/95	1995	Conditions on planning permissions

Source: Grant (1995a).

Advertisement control

Control over outdoor advertisements is made under town planning statute and regulations.[26] Such control is self-contained from the rest of the planning system, with the creation of a separate category of advertisement control instead of planning permission. In addition to this, a series of exclusions and deemed consents are established, which reduce the need to seek consent for certain types of advertisements.

What is an advertisement?

An advertisement is defined by statute as meaning:

> any word, letter, model sign, placard, board, notice, device or representation whether illuminated or not in the nature of, and employed wholly or partly for the purposes of advertisements, announcement or direction . . . and includes any hoarding or similar structure.[27]

In addition, an awning or blind (usually a "canopy" outside a shop front) has been added to this definition. Examples of advertisements include a painted shop fascia or illuminated shop sign, projecting box sign, "For Sale" or "To Let" sign, and a canopy or blind to a shop.

26. Section 220 of the Town and Country Planning Act 1990 and Town and Country Planning (Control of Advertisements) Regulations 1995. Also see PPG19 (1992), *Outdoor advertising control*, and DOE Circular 5/95 *Town and country planning* (Control of Advertisement) Regulations 1995.
27. Section 336 of the Town and Country Planning Act 1990.

The need for advertisement consent

The 1995 Regulations divide advertisements into three broad groupings:

Grouping	Examples
Exclusions, i.e. no control is exercised	Traffic signs, national flags, those on a moving vehicle or displayed within a building
Deemed consent, i.e. would require consent, but this is granted by the regulations, so no application is required	14 specific categories including: * Sale/letting of a building * on business premises (relating to size, number and siting) * Flag adverts, on housebuilding sites during construction and temporary hoardings (1–3 months)
Express consent, i.e. Advertisement Consent is required from LPA and an application is made on standard forms together with a fee to LPA	Most illuminated signs or non-illuminated, which are above first-floor window level

If the LPA wishes to refuse permission for an application for express advertisement consent, it should only do so if it is considered that the advertisement will harm the visual amenity of the area (for example, because of its proximity to a listed building or its location within a Conservation Area) or the location will be detrimental to public safety (for example, it may obscure visibility of a highway or traffic signal). A right of appeal exists against such refusals. If the LPA wishes to grant permission for an application for express consent, it may impose a set of standard conditions as set out in the 1995 Regulations (for example, requiring the advertisement to be maintained in a clean and tidy condition).

Powers over contraventions

Display of an advertisement in contravention of the regulations is a criminal offence and if found guilty may be punished by a fine. The LPA has three distinct powers in respect of such matters. First, it may serve discontinuance proceedings that require discontinuance of an advertisement or use of a site for the display of an advertisement, whether or not it enjoys deemed consent. A right of appeal exists against such a notice. Secondly, it may seek an order to create an area of special control in which various restrictions of classes of deemed consent may apply, subject to the exact area to be protected. Such orders are commonly used to protect the appearance of conservation areas. Approval and consent must be given by the Secretary of State. Finally, it may seek special directions to be issued by the Secretary of State to limit specific areas of deemed consent. An example in recent years had been where such a direction excludes Class 3 ("for sale" and "to let" temporary advertisements) in conservation areas and locations of predominantly flatted accommodation. Some LPAs had approached the Secretary of

State following concern over the visual impact of many such boards in streets where former townhouses were subdivided into flats.

Maladministration and town planning

Maladministration refers to faulty administration resulting in some form of injustice to a person or group of people.

In 1974 the government created an Office of Commissioner for Local Authority Administration, commonly, referred to as the Local Government Ombudsman,[28] with powers to investigate maladministration in all areas of local government. A Parliamentary Ombudsman had been created in 1967 to investigate complaints about central government departments.

Maladministration is not defined by statute. Examples include bias, delays, neglect, carelessness, or failure to observe procedure, which have all resulted in injustice. Separate Ombudsman offices have been established for England, Scotland and Wales. Once a complaint is received, it will be investigated to see if the matter falls within their jurisdiction and that some maladministration is evident before a final investigation will be undertaken. The services of the Ombudsman are free and their staff are independent and impartial. If they find that maladministration has occurred, they may recommend a remedy to the matter, usually compensation paid to the complainants by the local authority. If the local authority decides to ignore the recommendation to pay compensation, no legal power exists whereby the Ombudsman may enforce payment.

Town planning matters often constitute the second most common area of complaints to the Ombudsman.[29] The lodging of a complaint does not mean that maladministration has occurred or been proven. It may be of little surprise that town planning does encourage complaints, because not all local people, some of whom may have been consulted on the application, will agree with a decision to grant permission. Although the system encourages public participation, such comment on applications is but one of the many material considerations. Frequently, public comment avoids planning matters and raises non-planning issues. Yet although some people will feel aggrieved by planning decisions they consider "unpalatable", this does not of itself constitute maladministration. Around 96 per cent of all complaints received do not proceed to a formal investigation. Matters found to constitute town planning maladministration have included a council's failure to enforce compliance with a landscaping scheme on a site; a delay of ten years to deal with unauthorized tipping of soil in an Area of Outstanding Natural Beauty; delay and conflicting advice by a council in deciding whether to save a tree protected by a Tree Preservation Order; and failure to take account of town

28. Ombudsman powers are found in the Local Government Act (1974: part III).
29. Annual statistics published by the ombudsman reveal that housing issues constitute the largest number of complaints at 35–40 per cent, with planning second at 20–25 per cent of all complaints.

planning history on a site and incorrectly informing the owner that a matter was permitted development when it was not.

A finding of maladministration in town planning is rare. Around 500000 planning applications are dealt with every year in England, around 4000 planning related complaints are submitted to the Ombudsman. The Local Government Ombudsman Annual Report for 1994 revealed that 76 complaints were investigated and in only 34 cases the Ombudsman concluded that maladministration had occurred.[30] The Ombudsman plays a limited role in town planning, albeit an important one, in providing a mechanism for the investigation of bad practice and the ability to expose procedural problems. This may result in not just financial compensation to the complainant, but it also allows the local authority the opportunity to introduce reforms to its working practices to prevent a repeat in the future.

Conclusions

The creation of a policy for future land-use control and the implementation of that policy by development control represents the central component of the entire planning system. This system is highly regulated, yet has evolved from the premise that the implementation of planning decisions should be subject to a degree of flexibility. This flexibility means that a local planning authority does not have to follow slavishly all that is written down in planning policy (see Case Study 2.3 for an extreme example of this). It is possible to weigh the policy implications against other planning (or "material") considerations. Policies provide valuable guidance and not a rigid code. This distinguishes the British system from other planning systems (notably continental western Europe) based upon a zoning principle in which the zone stipulates what type of development must be implemented in a particular location. However, the inbuilt flexibility in the British model exacts a particular price, in that the outcome of the decision-making process will be less certain than under a zoning system. In spite of legislative reforms in the early 1990s, which place greater weight on the status of planning policy, the local planning authority still is afforded the opportunity to examine a broad range of material considerations in reaching a decision on a planning application. Examination of policy must always be the key starting point in any assessment of a development proposal. Any relevant guidance will be important but not always decisive in the outcome of a planning application. The UK system of planning policy and development control has been the subject of varied criticisms, based on the apparently negative stance of council planners towards development proposals, or delay in the determination of applications. The vast majority of planning applications are granted. However, performance measured against speed of decision-making is the subject of wide fluctuations across different local

---

30. In the remaining cases the Ombudsman found no maladministration had occurred, or that there was maladministration with no injustice, or that the investigation had been discontinued.

Case study 2.3: Planning and property development in the City of London

The ancient heart of London, "The City of London", comprises one square mile in area (2.6 km^2) and incorporates the capital's financial sector. The Great Fire of London in 1666 destroyed approximately 75 per cent of the medieval City and bombing during the second world war destroyed approximately 30 per cent (Marriott 1989).

The City Corporation is the local planning authority for this area. In the immediate post-war years the City Corporation was subject to the newly introduced planning regulations of the Town and Country Planning Act 1947. A statutory development plan was approved in 1951 under the guidance of Charles Holden and William Holford, who were themselves previously responsible for development of the London transport system (Holden) and for the redevelopment of the Paternoster district within the City (Holford).†

Since the early 1950s the City has been the subject of two property booms, those of the 1960s and the 1980s. The nature of each boom and its influence upon commercial development was shaped by the town planning system, and the buildings resulting from each boom may be distinguished by their contrasting architectural styles.

In the 1960s the demands for new office accommodation in the financial heart of London fuelled a building boom that was able to use newly acquired building methods involving concrete and steel construction to build high-rise office blocks. Architects such as Mies Van der Rohe (1886–1969) considered that concrete used in construction should be "seen and not screened" (Ross-Goobey 1992). Redevelopment around London Wall and Paternoster Square provides good examples of the style of the age, notably external concrete facings and curtain walling, whereby the external walls are hung like curtains from the concrete floors.

Town planning policies were an influence, mostly by the imposition of plot ratio controls. These controls restricted the amount of lettable floorspace as a portion of every square metre of land within the plot. This would restrict the resulting height and bulk of a building, so that a common ratio of say 5:1 or 3:1 would allow 5 or 3 m of lettable floorspace for every 1 m of site area. Conservation area controls were not introduced until the late 1960s and the City Corporation made few design-related decisions during this period. The architect and developer was allowed a free reign to design the fashionable brutalistic-looking tower blocks of the age, so long as they satisfied the plot ratio criterion.

During the 1980s the City of London was to experience a second boom, yet one whose impact upon development was to be far more dramatic than that experienced during the 1960s. The growth in information technology, increased levels of economic activity, financial deregulation, a reaction by many people against the architectural style of the previous boom, and a relaxation of town planning controls, were all to contribute towards a second boom in commercial development. The rate of property development is largely controlled by the town planning system, because the amount of floorspace permitted will influence the level of market activity. During the 1980s the City Corporation relaxed the application of its own planning policies and increased plot ratios to permit more floorspace on a site in an attempt to encourage developers to come forward with redevelopment schemes. It was hoped that a relaxed town planning regime would be perceived by many developers as a positive move. In 1986 the City Corporation made provision for an increase in office floorspace. At that time the City accommodated around 2 694 000 m^2 (29 million ft^2) office floorspace Taking the development cycle between 1986 and 1994 2 276 050 m^2 (24.5 million ft^2) office floor space was completed. At June 1994 a further 1 263 440 m^2 (13.6 million ft^2) was the subject of unimplemented planning permission.

(continued overleaf)

This almost relentless drive by the City Corporation planners and Planning Committee to permit new offices was not motivated by some desire to accommodate the needs of property developers but instead was a reaction to the threat posed by massive office development in the London Docklands, only a few kilometres to the east. Canary Wharf, the 244m high tower on the Isle of Dogs created 929000m^2 (10 million ft^2) of new offices alone, and the London Docklands Development Corporation created a total of 13 million ft^2 (1 208000m^2) of new office floorspace between 1981 and 1994. The London Docklands Development Corporation (LDDC) and the Enterprise zone within it, were established by the Conservative Government in 1981 to redevelop the designated 2226ha (5500 acres) of derelict former docks to the east of the City of London. The LDDC saw office redevelopment as a key part of its strategy. The new office floorspace could offer cheaper rents than the City, and new floorspace incorporating all the necessary information technology and modern services. The City, fearing an exodus of office occupiers, fought back by granting as many office planning permissions as it could. The LDDC itself was a deregulated planning body whose planning powers overrode the existing London boroughs. The City Corporation, although not a deregulated planning body, merely served to throw away many of its own development plan policies to achieve the same effect. With the following economic slump in 1989, the permissions of the 1980s created a massive oversupply in the 1990s, resulting in both much empty floorspace and a considerable drop in rents. Some of this new office floorspace may never be let. In 1994 (Williams & Wood 1994), it was estimated that in Docklands some office floorspace has a vacancy rate of 50 per cent with rents as low as £0.92m^2 achieved in the late 1980s. LDDC's[‡] own statistics put this figure at 418050m^2 (4.5 million ft^2) or 35 per cent of all floorspace being vacant. No comparable figure is available for the City.

In the City itself some of the new office floorspace may also never be let. Before market demand can be found, new technology may render obsolete some of the schemes of the 1980s. Their glittering architectural styling incorporating post-modern hi-tech and classical revival styles[¶] may serve as a monument to the inability of the planners to predict an oversupply and to apply a braking mechanism to the ferocious activity of the property developers combined with the planning policies pursued by the London Docklands Development Corporation to permit large-scale office redevelopments such as Canary Wharf.

[†] Refer to Study on Paternoster.
[‡] London Docklands Development Corporation Property Facts Sheet, updated periodically and available from LDDC Information Centre.
[¶] **High-tech** buildings are characterized by exposed steel structures, use of glass and external siting of piping and ducting, a good example being the Lloyds Building in London, by Richard Rogers.
   Classical revival employs plentiful use of Greek and Roman decoration, sometimes called "fake Georgian", a good example being Richmond Riverside, London, by Quinlan Terry.
   Postmodern employs a mix of historic detailing with "symbolism", where the building incorporates unusual shapes and forms. A good example being Alban Gate on London Wall by Terry Farrell.

planning authorities, and, so far, this crude measurement is the only widely utilized quality standard within the system. Indeed, it is unlikely that the concept of quality will ever be the subject of universal agreement, as appraisal of what is "good" or "bad" in development control is so subjective. However, local planning authorities are looking increasingly at ways to improve administrative efficiency and they involve the public more fully in the policy-making process so that their views on environmental issues can be incorporated at an early stage in the development control process.

CHAPTER THREE
Town planning law and regulation

A system of comprehensive control over all development was introduced by the TCPA 1947, which required that all building development and any material changes in the use of a building and of land would, henceforth, require planning permission, to be issued by the local planning authority. The legislation established just what would or would not require planning permission. Since 1947 all town planning legislation has provided a definition of "development". To understand the workings of the system it is necessary to understand just what falls within the provisions of the definition of development to establish what does and does not require planning permission.

This chapter will examine the principal legislation that defines what does and what does not require the submission of an application for planning permission. Detailed reference will be made to the TCPA 1990, Town and Country (Use Classes Order) 1987 and Town and Country Planning (General Permitted Development) Order 1995. The latter section of the chapter will deal with the enforcement of town planning control, a specialist area of planning legislation that deals with remedial action against the development of land undertaken without the benefit of planning permission. The chapter will be subdivided as follows:

- the definition of development
- Use Classes Order and General Permitted Development Order
- enforcing town planning control

The definition of development

Section 55 (1) of the 1990 TCPA defines "development" as:

> "the carrying out of building, engineering, mining or other operations in, on, over or under land or the making of any material change in the use of any buildings or other land.

This definition of development provides the very basis for the development control system and introduces a distinction between operations (building, engineering, mining or other) and material change of use (activity). The definition is itself broad in content and must be considered alongside the General Permitted Development Order (GPDO) and Use Classes Order (UCO). Read in isolation it would result in a vast number of operations and uses falling within the definition. The GPDO and UCO create a whole series of exceptions to the need for planning permission, effectively releasing many types of development from the need for planning permission (Grant 1992).

The TCPA 1990 does help clarify some issues that either do or do not fall within the definition. For the avoidance of doubt, the matters that do not amount to development are:

- Any internal works or external works that do not result in a material impact on the appearance of a building. Such external works would depend upon the circumstances of an individual case but include the addition of guttering and downpipes and repointing of mortar between bricks.
- Maintenance/improvement works within the boundary of a road undertaken by a highway authority or the laying out of an access to a highway.
- Inspection/repair/renewal of sewers.
- The use of any building or other land within the curtilage of a dwellinghouse for an incidental use for example the use of a garden shed for hobby activities.
- The use of land for agriculture[1] or forestry (agricultural or forestry related buildings may require permission).

However, an operation that is specifically does amount to development is the conversion of one dwelling into two (e.g. subdivision of a house into flats).

The Act does not list all matters that may or may not require planning permission beyond these specific groupings. The decision whether or not any other proposal falls within or outside the definition of development will be the subject of interpretation. The following section will now set out some guidelines that will aid such judgements.

Operational development

The principal characteristic of operational development is that it results in some permanent physical change to the appearance of the land concerned. The works may be building, engineering, mining or other operations, and these will be considered in turn.

Building operations

Building operations include the demolition of buildings, rebuilding, structural

---

1. Agriculture is defined by Section 336(1) of the TCPA 1990 as including horticulture, fruit and seed growing, dairy farming, market gardening, grazing land, meadow land and nursery land.

alterations and extensions, and are works usually undertaken by a builder. Case law dealing with what is and is not a building operation has established three tests of a building operation, namely:
- Does it have size?
- Does it have permanence?
- Is it physically attached?

In practice, if two of the three tests are satisfied, the matter in question will constitute a building operation. For example, we may conclude that the erection of a new warehouse, industrial unit, a block of flats or a dwelling house each constitutes a building operation as they incorporate size, permanence and physical attachment. They all fit the common everyday use of the word "building" and we should experience little difficulty in establishing that they are operational development. However, it is important to recall that a structure need not look like a normal building to constitute a building operation, so that erection of a radio mast aerial, satellite antenna, and metal security shutters to a shop front all constitute building operations. In 1986 a fibreglass shark sculpture was erected on the roof of a terraced house in Headington, Oxford. In similar vein, a marlin was attached by a homeowner to his roof in Croydon. The works constituted a building operation and required planning permission.

Table 3.1   Summary of building operations.

Definition	Key points to remember	NB
§336 (1) and §55 (1A) of the TCPA 1990 to **include** demolition, rebuilding, alteration, extension or addition; to **exclude** any plant or machinery comprised within a building, structure or erection.	3 Tests – size – permanence – physical attachment. If any two are decisive then it will usually follow that the proposal constitutes a building operation.	Does not have to look like a building to be a building operation, e.g. Oxford shark or Croydon marlin.

Engineering operations

Engineering operations are taken to include operations normally undertaken by a person carrying on business as an engineer. This has been interpreted in case law as not meaning that an engineer need always be employed but instead that the works in themselves call for the skills of an engineer.

It is sometimes difficult to distinguish between engineering and building operations. For example, in the construction of a new office development an engineer may be called in to survey the subsoil and deal with the foundation details (clearly an engineering operation) and then the office is constructed (clearly a building operation). In such cases it would be acceptable to regard this as both an engineering and building operation, thus amounting to development, although only one grant of planning permission (to cover both aspects) will be required. Other examples of engineering operations include the creation of a hard-standing, excavation of soil to form an artificial lake, or the deposit of soil to form a golf course or embankments.

Table 3.2   Summary of engineering operations.

Definition	Key points to remember	NB
§336 (1) of the TCPA 1990 states it **includes** the formation or laying out of a means of access to a highway.	The limited definition in the Act has been **interpreted** as including any works requiring the skills of an Engineer.	Many engineering operations may be tied in with building operations. It is acceptable to consider them together.

Mining operations

Mining operations, although specifically mentioned within the definition of development, are not defined within the Act. "Mining" can be taken to include the winning and working of minerals in, on or under land, whether by surface or underground working.[2] "Minerals" are defined within the Act as including "all minerals and substances in or under land or a kind ordinarily worked for removal by underground or surface working, except that it does not include peat cut for purposes other than sale".

Table 3.3   Summary of mining operations.

Definition	Key points to remember	NB
Not defined in the Act but taken to include surface or underground extraction of minerals.	Coal, iron ore, china clay extraction.	Any extraction of minerals.

Other operations

The inclusion of "other" within the definition of development is rather unhelpful to both student and practitioner, because of its vague "catch all" quality. The concept of "other" defies adequate definition. It may be useful to consider it where works involve some form of physical alteration to land, which appears to constitute an operation yet does not sit easily within the previous definitions of building, engineering or mining operations. For example, it was held in one appeal decision that the tipping of soil onto land for the purpose of raising the level of the land did not, in that case, constitute an engineering operation, but did constitute "other" operations. The decision as to whether raising of ground level constitutes and "engineering" or "other" operation will depend upon the merits of the individual case. However, as a general rule, it would appear that the creation of embankments or larger-scale projects such as golf courses would constitute engineering operations, whereas smaller-scale tipping and raising of ground level would fall within "other" operations.

---

2. Definition provided in Section 290, Town and Country Planning (Minerals) Regulations 1971. Also see Minerals Planning Guidance Notes (MPGs), Town and Country Planning (Minerals) Act 1981 and Schedule 14 of the Environment Act 1995.

Table 3.4   Summary of other operations.

Definition	Key points to remember	NB
Works that result in some permanent physical change to land yet do not easily fit within engineering, building or mining operations.	Consider only in exceptional cases, or as a last resort.	Rare. Not a helpful concept for students or practitioners.

Demolition and operational development

Considerable legal debate has prevailed[3] over the question as to whether demolition of buildings falls within the definition of development. Certainly, if we go back to the definition of an operation as something resulting in a change to the physical characteristics of the land, then demolition works would be covered. Demolition may involve the work of a builder or engineer and may be considered to constitute either a building or engineering operation, yet, on examination of the tests of a building operation, demolition would not easily fit within the criteria of size, physical attachment and permanence. Case law has in the past resulted in conflicting findings on this issue. The definitive statement on the subject was made in 1991 by Mr David Widdicombe QC sitting as a High Court Judge in *Cambridge City Council* vs *Secretary of State for the Environment and Another*. It was held that demolition would constitute development where it was an operation that a builder normally carried out. Thus, demolition was found to be a building operation. To avoid a vast additional burden of planning applications on local planning authorities, the Government issued a specific direction to clarify the matter. Demolition of the following would not constitute development and therefore would not require submission of a planning application:

- Any listed building or unlisted building in a Conservation area (remember that Listed Building Consent and Conservation Area Consent respectively would be required) so that some measure of control is exercised, but is not achieved by a planning application.[4]
- Any building except a dwellinghouse (includes a flat) or building adjoining a dwellinghouse.
- Any building smaller than $50\,m^3$ volume.
- Any gate, wall, fence or other means of enclosure.[5]

---

3. *Cambridge City Council* vs *Secretary of State for the Environment and Another* [1991] *JPL* **428**. Demolition control is described by Sir Desmond Heap (1991) as "a ghost which haunted planning law. The time has now come for the ghost to be laid to rest" (p. 114).
4. Please refer to sections on Listed Buildings and Conservation Area.
5. For more guidance, see the *Town and country planning (demolition – description of buildings) Direction* 1995 and DOE Circular *Guidance on planning controls over demolition*.

Material change of use

Taking the second limb of the definition of development, it is necessary to consider material changes of use. These have been defined as activities done in, alongside or on land, but do not interfere with the actual physical characteristics of the land. It is therefore important to remember that it is important to understand the concept of a material change in the use of land and that this deals only with activity (uses) and does not deal with physical works on the land, such as building operations. In dealing with material change of use it is important to establish primary uses, ancillary uses and mixed uses and to define the exact area of land affected by the change of use (the "planning unit").

What is material?

Determining whether or not a material change has occurred will depend upon the merits of the individual case. For a change or shift in use/activity to result in a material change it will be necessary to establish that the change has been substantial or significant, rather than some minor shift in activity.

To determine a material change in use it is necessary to examine the character of the use. For example, is the character retail (sale of goods to the public) or non-retail (services such as banking or food and drink users such as pubs, restaurants). Following this, it is necessary to examine the consequences of the use in terms of planning issues (e.g. noise, smells, hours of operation, traffic or pedestrian generation).

If either the consequences or character has changed to a significant degree, then it can be established that a material change of use has occurred.

In determining a material change, two problems are usually encountered. The first problem relates to the choice of the unit of land to be considered (referred to as the planning unit), which will influence the decision on materiality. For example, if we consider an industrial estate which comprises 10 factory buildings and a small office building and the office is then converted to a warehouse/storage use, the decision as to whether this is material will very much depend on the planning unit considered.

The main principle derived from case law[6] is that the planning unit should be taken to mean the unit of occupation or ownership. However, a separate unit is created if within one unit of occupation two or more physically separate and distinct areas are occupied for unrelated purposes.

Taking the previous example it would follow that, if each industrial unit and the office building are within separate ownership, then the office building forms its own planning unit and a material change of use has occurred, within that unit. If the whole industrial estate was within one ownership, it could be argued that

6. *Burdle* vs *Secretary of State for the Environment* [1972] 1WLR 1207.

the whole estate is one planning unit and no material change of use has occurred to that unit as a whole, by alteration in the use of such a small component. The second problem relates to the fact that, within any one site, several uses may take place. To help establish a material change of use it will be necessary to establish the primary (main or principal) use of the land. It will often be the case that ancillary (secondary or incidental) uses may function alongside such a primary use.

Consider the examples in Table 3.5.

Table 3.5   The relationship between primary and ancillary uses.

Primary	Ancillary
(i) Hotel with . . .	Bar, restaurant, laundry, swimming pool, sauna, open to hotel residents.
(ii) Shop unit with . . .	Office at rear dealing with associated administration.
(iii) Retail warehouse or departmental store . . .	Associated café/restaurant.
(iv) Office building with . . .	Staff gym.

Provided that the ancillary activities remain functionally related to the primary activity, then no material change will have occurred. If the ancillary activities increase to such an extent that they could no longer be said to be ancillary, then a mixed use has occurred.

Intensification is a widely misunderstood concept within consideration of change of use. The intensification of a use may occur (e.g. increased levels of production output in a factory), which in itself does not result in a change of use. Intensification can be said to result in a change of use only where the intensification itself results in a change in the character and town planning consequences of the land. For example, if a clothes shop sells more clothes, it has intensified its activity, but no material change of use has occurred. It is better practice to look for a material change in use rather than intensification.

Summary of material change of use

- To establish a material change of use consider the character of use and consequences of that use.
- Define the area to be considered by establishing the planning unit (unit of occupation in which uses are functionally linked).
- Remember that in dealing with character/consequence of a use the primary use will need to be identified, together with ancillary uses that are secondary to it. If no primary/secondary relationship can be established, then a mixed use is created. If a secondary use grows to such an extent as to create a mixed use, then a material change of use has occurred from primary to mixed.

- Intensification of use is a misleading concept; consider instead the characteristics of a material change of use.

Use Classes Order 1987 (SI 764) (UCO) and General Permitted Development Order 1995 (SI 418)[7]

The GPDO and UCO establish a series of freedoms from the need to apply for planning permission, taking each in turn:

The General Permitted Development Order (GPDO)

The GPDO has two principal benefits for the planning system:
- it covers classes of development considered to be of relatively trivial planning importance and, in most cases, are environmentally acceptable
- it relieves local planning authorities of a vast administrative workload for (generally) acceptable operations.

How does the GPDO function?

Article 3 of the current order (the current order being Statutory Instrument 418, dated 1995) grants planning permission for a variety of the operations and some changes of use identified. In other words, any operations or uses that adhere to the criteria laid down in the 33 separate classes of Schedule 2 constitute development, but permission for that development is automatically granted; that is, it is permitted by the Order without the need to submit a planning application and is therefore known as "permitted development".

The most important classes are:
- Part 1: Development within the Curtilage of a Dwellinghouse, e.g. extensions to a dwellinghouse or a certain size and siting are permitted development.
- Part 3: Changes of Use, e.g. to change from A3 (Food and Drink) to A2 (Financial and Professional Services), from A3 or A2 to A1 (Retail), from B2 (General Industry) to B1 (Business) and from B1 or B2 to B8 (storage and distribution).
- Part 8: Industrial and Warehouse Development, e.g. small extensions to such buildings.

---

7. This is not to be confused with the Town and Country Planning (General Development Procedure) Order 1995 (SI 419), which deals with procedural matters relating to the submission of a planning application, e.g. it establishes the eight-week period for the determination of an application.

Table 3.6   Some examples of permitted development within the GPDO.[a]

GPDO	Example
Part 1	Dwellinghouse, e.g. • Side or rear extensions to a cubic limit of 50–70m³ or 10–15% value of original dwelling (varies between terraced and semi- or detached). • Porch • Garage • Sheds/greenhouses/swimming pool enclosure • Hard-standing • Satellite antenna or dish (within size limits)
Part 2	Minor operations, e.g. • Gate, fence, wall or other means of enclosure • A means of access other than to a trunk or classified road • Painting exterior of building
Part 3	Changes of use, e.g. • A3/A2 to A1 • B2 to B1 • A3 to A2
Part 4	Temporary buildings and uses, e.g. • Structures/plant required in construction • 28 day temporary use in any one year (reduced to 14 if a market, motor rally or clay pigeon shooting)
Part 5	Caravan sites
Part 6	Agricultural buildings and operations
Part 7	Forestry buildings and operations
Part 8	Industrial and warehouse development

a. Examples to illustrate some freedoms from planning permission established by the GPDO. Refer to the Order for an exact list of the criteria that must be satisfied to constitute permitted development.

Where permitted development may not apply

- Residential permitted development does not apply to flats, only to dwelling-houses.
- Residential permitted development rights are reduced on Article 1 (5) land, i.e. in National Parks, Areas of Outstanding Natural Beauty, or Conservation Areas.
- Where the local planning authority has served an Article 4 Direction.[8] Such Directions require the direct approval of the Secretary of State. Normally Article 4 Directions withdraw permitted development rights for a particular class of development within a specified area. This is mostly employed in Conservation Areas; it protects the amenity and gives the planners greater control over development, for example, requiring planning permission for such activities as exterior painting or the installation of double glazing.

8. Served under Article 4(1) of the Town and Country Planning (General Permitted Development) Order 1995.

The local planning authority in granting planning permission for new development may seek to remove future permitted development rights by imposing a condition. However, they must have good reason to do this; for example, in high-density residential developments this will protect the amenities of the neighbouring occupiers.

As we have seen, we must refer to the General Permitted Development Order with operational development, whereas with the vast majority of material changes of use, we refer to the Use Classes Order.

The Use Classes Order

The UCO places certain planning uses into classes, with a total of 16 classes and a variety of subdivisions within each class. To move from one use to another within a class is not development (Grant 1989, Home 1989). Conversely, to move between any of the 16 classes is development and therefore requires planning permission. (The current order is the 1987 Order, Statutory Instrument number 764.)

The twofold purpose of the Order is stated in Circular 13/87,[9] first to reduce the number of use classes while retaining effective control over change of use, which, because of environmental consequences or relationships with other uses, need to be subject to specific planning applications; and, secondly, to ensure that the scope of each class is wide enough to take in change of use that generally do not need to be subject to specific control.

Table 3.7 Summary of examples within the UCO.

Use class		Principal examples (not exhaustive)
A1	Retail	Any shop selling retail goods to public ⇒ post office ⇒travel agent ⇒ off licence ⇒ sale of cold food for consumption off the premises
A2	Financial and professional services	Bank ⇒ building society ⇒ estate agent
A3	Food and drink	Pub ⇒ restaurant ⇒ sale of hot food ⇒ wine bar
B1	Business	(light) Industry ⇒ office ⇒ research and development

⇒ Denotes a movement "within" the use class, which is not development and therefore would not require planning permission.

The Use Classes Order is not comprehensive. Any use not covered by the Order (and therefore outside the provision of the Order) is considered to be the *sui generis* (in a class of its own). Any movement to or from a *sui generis* use is outside the provision of the UCO and would require planning permission.

---

9. DOE Circular 13/87 *Change of use of buildings and other land: town and country planning (Use Classes) Order* 1987. In Scotland see Circular 6/89.

The relationship between the GPDO and the UCO

Consider, for example, Class A1 (shops) of the UCO. The Order states that Class A1 use is for all or any of the following purposes:

- the retail sale of goods
- as a post office
- the sale of tickets or as a travel agency
- the sale of sandwiches or other cold food for consumption off the premises
- hairdressing
- the direction of funerals
- the display of goods for sale
- the hiring out of domestic or personal goods or articles
- the reception of goods to be washed, cleaned or repaired, where the sale, display or service is to visiting members of the public

Therefore, to change from a hairdressing salon to a travel agency is within the A1 class and would not require planning permission. To change from a hairdresser to a use outside A1 would require planning permission. It follows that, in the vast majority of cases, to move between individual classes is a material change of use for which planning permission will be required. In a few cases (see Table 3.6, part 3: p. 63), such movements, although accepted as constituting a change of use and therefore development, are themselves automatically granted planning permission by Part 3 of the GPDO, so that to move from A3 (Food and Drink) use to A1 (Retail) use is development, but it falls within the provision of Part 3 of the GDPO and therefore constitutes permitted development for which no planning applications is required. Although it is somewhat confusing to include provisions relating to use in the GPDO, the simplest way to remember these issues is that after establishing that a proposed use results in movement between use classes, cross-reference to Part 3 of the GPDO to ascertain whether this is permitted development. Figure 3.1 illustrates a summary of this.

The overall relationship can be summarized in a flowchart (Fig. 3.2).

Enforcing town planning control

When the development of land is undertaken without the benefit of planning permission, the local planning authority has enforcement powers to seek a remedy to those breaches of control that they consider to be unacceptable.

A breach of town planning control is defined as the carrying out of development without the required planning permission or failure to comply with the terms of any condition attached to a grant of planning permission.[10] Such an unauthorized development does not constitute a criminal offence. It will only become a criminal offence in the event of enforcement action being taken by the LPA that is subse-

---

10. Such breaches of planning control are established by Section 72(3) of the TCPA 1990.

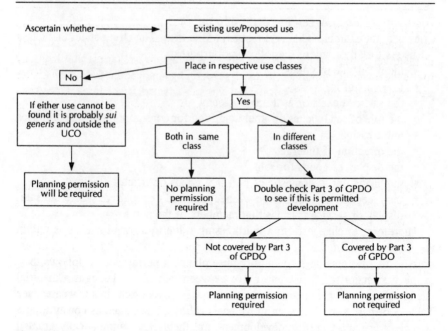

Figure 3.1 A summary of the General Permitted Development Order and the Use Classes Order.

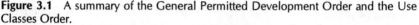

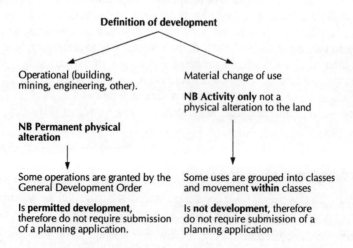

Figure 3.2 A summary of the definition of development.

quently ignored or not complied with by the landowner, or if works have been carried out to a listed building. It should also be remembered that carrying out development without planning permission is not automatically followed by enforcement action. The LPA has discretion in deciding whether or not to enforce.

Enforcement normally follows in cases where the breach of control results, in the opinion of the LPA, in some form of harm to amenity (which may be contrary to planning policy). If the LPA considers the breach to be acceptable, they may invite the owner to submit a retrospective planning application, so that the matter can be decided through the normal development control procedures. Once such a retrospective application is granted, then the matter becomes regularized.

The Carnwath Report

In 1988 the Secretary of State for the Environment appointed an eminent planning lawyer, Robert Carnwath QC, to undertake a review of enforcement procedures (Carnwath Report 1989).

The findings were published in 1989 with a series of recommendations designed to make enforcement more effective when dealing with unacceptable breaches of control. These recommendations were introduced into the system by the Planning and Compensation Act 1991, (Sections 1 to 11) that added new powers and amended those existing under the TCPA 1990.

The various enforcement powers available to the LPA in the post-1991 system can be summarized as follows:

Planning Contravention Notice (PCN)

Prior to taking formal enforcement action, the LPA needs to determine whether a breach has in fact occurred. This may not always be an easy matter to ascertain. To assist, the LPA may serve a Planning Contravention Notice requiring information from the owner or other people with an interest regarding operations, uses or matters in respect of planning conditions relating to the land.[11] For example, a landowner or operator may start digging a trench on a site or may begin to service/maintain motor vehicles. A PCN can help to ascertain whether the trench is for the construction of a building or that the motor repairs undertaken in a domestic garage are for a commercial purpose and not merely a hobby. From this response, the LPA may initiate formal enforcement action, but the service of the notice will alert the owner to the council's concern, from which further dialogue between both sides may overcome the problem without recourse to any further action. The decision to serve a PCN is an option available to the LPA. They do not have to serve one as a precondition of future action. However, once served, failure to comply with its requirements within 21 days or to give misleading information constitutes a criminal offence.

---

11. Interest in Land means a legal or equitable interest such as ownership or the grant of a tenancy or lease. A PCN may also be served on an occupier who is carrying out operations or uses such as a builder. Refer to subsections 171C and D of the TCPA 1990.

Enforcement Notice

The enforcement notice constitutes the principal enforcement mechanism at the disposal of the LPA when seeking to remedy a breach of planning control. Prior to the service of an enforcement notice the LPA should normally, as a matter of good practice, undertake a land registry search to ascertain ownership or other interest in the land. They may have previously served a Planning Contravention Notice to gather information, or they may serve a Section 330 Notice, that requires the occupier of the land to provide information of interest in the land or the interest of other persons. The enforcement notice is issued by the LPA and served upon the landowner or any other person with an interest in the land who will be affected by the enforcement action. It will stipulate a course of action (steps to be taken) to remedy the breach and will indicate a time period within which such action must be taken. Reasoning must be provided to support the decision to issue the Notice, which will in most cases allege that the continued implementation of the breach results in some form of planning harm or loss of amenity that may be contrary to policy or other material considerations. A right of appeal exists against the service of an enforcement notice.[12] Any appeal must be submitted within a 28-day period following "service" of the notice. If an appeal is lodged, then the Notice does not take effect but is held in abeyance and the matter must be determined by the Secretary of State or an appointed Inspector who may quash, uphold or vary the notice in some way. The enforcement notice appeal may be pursued by written representation, informal hearing or public inquiry method. The informal method is unsuitable if there are complex legal considerations. An award of costs is available in all three methods.[13]

Summary: characteristics of an Enforcement Notice

- Deals with remedying unacceptable breaches of planning control.
- Provides for a timescale within which the matter should be rectified.
- Allows for an appeal, in which case the effect of the notice is suspended and the matter is dealt with by the Secretary of State or Inspector. An appeal must be lodged within 28 days of service of the notice, otherwise the notice becomes ineffective.

Stop Notice

The stop notice provides the LPA with its most Draconian enforcement powers. Unlike the enforcement notice, which allows for a reasonable period for compliance, the stop notice requires a halt to activities (uses or operations) within three

---

12. This appeal must be made against one or more of seven specific grounds. Reference should be made to Section 174(2) of the TCPA 1990.
13. See p. 87.

days of its service upon the landowner or other person with an interest in the land who will be affected by the stop notice. It is therefore served only in cases of serious breaches of planning control.[14] A stop notice can be served only if an enforcement notice of similar content has also been served and before the enforcement notice takes effect. An appeal can only be lodged against the enforcement notice as no right of appeal is available against a stop notice. If on appeal the Secretary of State or Inspector either quashes the enforcement notice or varies it to the extent that the matter "stopped" no longer constitutes a breach of control, then the LPA is liable to pay financial compensation to the owner for the loss incurred by the imposed cessation of activity.

Summary: characteristics of a Stop Notice

- Deals with remedying unacceptable breaches of control that require immediate cessation.
- No appeal, however, as a stop notice can only be served alongside or after an enforcement notice (of similar content) then an appeal may be made against the enforcement notice.
- Compensation payable if enforcement notice appeal is successful in authorizing the breach stopped by the notice.

Breach of Condition Notice (BCN)

This procedure permits specific action against failure to comply with a planning condition imposed on a previous grant of permission by service of a Breach of Condition Notice.[15] As with the enforcement notice, the LPA must specify steps to be taken to remedy the matter, together with a period of compliance. Failure to comply with such a notice is a criminal offence. No right of appeal is available against such a notice; therefore, if an onerous condition is imposed on a planning permission, the landowner is well advised to pursue an appeal against the condition rather than await any future breach of condition notice.

Certificates of lawful existing use or development and proposed use or development

Such certificates are considered by LPAs in the same way as applications for planning permission. They allow an owner to have a ruling as to whether an existing operation or use of land, without the previous benefit of planning permission, is

---

14. Served under Section 183 of the TCPA 1990. Certain activities cannot be prohibited by a stop notice, namely use of a building as a dwelling, or to stop operational development that has been carried out for a period exceeding four years.
15. Served under Section 187A of the TCPA 1990.

69

lawful or to ascertain that a proposed operation or use would also be lawful and therefore not require the need for a grant of planning permission.[16] This would remove any uncertainty that a matter was outside the realm of planning control, for example it was either permitted development (e.g. a small residential extension), or not development at all (e.g. movement within a use class), or was immune from enforcement action whereby an operational development was substantially completed for at least four years,[17] or, if a change of use, for a minimum period of at least ten years.

Both certificates help to remove any uncertainty an owner may have about the planning status of a site. The LPA can refuse to grant either certificate, which carries a right of appeal to the Secretary of State.

Injunctions

The local planning authority also enjoys powers strengthened by the Planning and Compensation Act 1991[18] to seek an injunction in either the High Court or County Court to halt an actual or anticipated breach of planning control. Such injunctions are generally, but not necessarily, employed by LPAs as a second line of attack, although such a legal mechanism is a very effective way of controlling any contravention of the planning system, because, if an injunction is granted by the courts and if its terms are subsequently ignored by the owner, then the person involved risks possible imprisonment for contempt of court.

Discovering breaches of planning control

The majority of breaches of planning control are discovered by the LPA following the receipt of a complaint from a member of the public, usually a neighbouring occupier. Local planning authorities usually establish a specialist in-house team of enforcement officers who investigate such complaints and advise both owner and complainant on the possibility of action being taken. Decisions to pursue enforcement matters involve legal judgement (establishing facts to determine that a breach has occurred) and planning judgement (to remedy the situation to overcome any loss of amenity that results from the unauthorized use or operation).

For this reason, enforcement activity involves both town planning and legal personnel, and government guidance encourages a strong level of co-operation

---

16. Refer to subsection 191 and 192 of the TCPA 1990.
17. i.e. The four-year immunity does not start to run until the operational development has been largely finished.
18. Similar powers were previously available under the Local Government Act 1972 but were introduced specifically to town planning by this section. Section 3 of the Planning and Compensation Act 1991 introduced a new section, 187B, into the TCPA 1990.

between such staff to ensure effective implementation of this important planning function.

Table 3.8   Summary of enforcement powers.

Procedure	Objective	Example	Right of appeal
Planning Contravention Notice	To require information regarding the use of or operations within land	To seek information on a use of land to determine if it is a change of use, so LPA can enforce	No
Enforcement Notice	To remedy a breach of control resulting in harm	To remove a scrap metal dealer from a site	Yes
Stop Notice	To almost immediately cease an activity (use or operation) resulting in (serious) harm	To remove a scrap metal dealer and immediately stop any further activity	No
Breach of Condition Notice	To remedy the failure to comply with details of a planning condition.	Enforce hours of use imposed on a change of use permission from shop to restaurant	No
Injunction	To halt a breach or anticipated breach of planning permission	Prevent use of land for motorbike scrambling once permitted development has been used up	No Civil legal proceedings
Certificate of Lawful Use/Development	Establish existing use or development is lawful	Establish immunity under 10 (use) or 4 (operation) year rule	Yes
Certificate of Proposed Lawful Use/ Development	Establish that proposed use or development is lawful	Establish permitted development	Yes

Conclusions

Town planning legislation creates the procedures by which control may be exercised over the use of land and operations that take place on, over or under that land. Such legislation is applied consistently across England and Wales and it sets out to create a regulatory system, yet it must also establish freedoms or exemptions from the system where "development" would not result in any harmful environmental impact. Thus, a balance must be struck between necessary environmental protection and unnecessary bureaucratic burden. Such decisions are not easy and are particularly contentious in the realm of residential permitted development, where some homeowners will resent any form of planning control that will restrict their desire to extend, or otherwise alter, a dwelling. The introduction in 1988 of town planning control over external stone cladding to dwellinghouses illustrates the problem, with the government finally being convinced, after many years of debate, that the residents' right to alter their property in this way was eroding the quality of the environment.

Town planning legislation creates the all important "ground rules" that provide a structure for the planning system. All participants in the planning process must comply with these "ground rules", although it is important to remember that legislation is the subject of continual revision by case law in which the courts provide rulings on the interpretation of statutes.

CHAPTER FOUR
Planning appeals

A planning appeal is a challenge to the merits of or lack of a planning decision made by a local planning authority and should be viewed as a decision of last resort.

Most decisions made by local planning authorities carry with them the right of appeal to the Secretary of State for the Environment. Such appeals provide a form of arbitration on the town planning merits of a decision and represent the final stage of the development control process. Any further appeal is a matter of legal submission in which the decision is challenged in the courts on grounds of procedural unreasonableness, namely that matters were taken into account by the decision-maker that should not reasonably have been taken into account or were not taken into account when they should have been, or the decision was so manifestly unreasonable that no reasonable decision-maker could have come to it. Such legal appeals to the High Court, Court of Appeal or House of Lords should not be confused with a planning appeal. A planning appeal deals solely with the technical town planning merits of the case and only involves legal argument where it has some influence upon decision-making regarding technical town planning matters. It is important to draw this distinction from the start.

This chapter will set out the procedures that govern the system of town planning appeals. It will explain the advantages and disadvantages of each method, and some reference will be made to case studies to illustrate the suitability of each method to different types of development proposal. Reference also will be made to the award of costs, whereby one party is required to pay the costs of another party to the appeal. The chapter is organized as follows:

- the planning appeal system
- procedures involved in each method
- the award of costs.

The planning appeal system

Historical background

The TCPA 1932 introduced the right of planning appeal, whereby someone could challenge the decision of a local authority to refuse planning permission. The Public Inquiry had been introduced 23 years before in the Housing, Town Planning etc. Act 1909. However, at that time it did not represent a method of planning appeal as it does today, but instead was a means by which the public could voice objection to town planning schemes. The TCPA 1947 introduced a limited system of planning appeal that was tightly controlled by the Minister of Housing and Local Government. All appeals were considered by Public Inquiry. The rules governing the conduct of such inquiries were not publicly available as the relevant government department was unwilling to publish them. Although the ultimate decision either to allow or to dismiss the appeal was published, the reasoning upon which the decision had been based was kept secret. Such a system was not only secretive in its procedures but also largely excluded the public from the area of appeal decision-making.

Such a situation was to change in 1958 (Franks 1957) following the implementation of recommendations made by the Committee on Administrative Tribunals and Inquiries (the Franks Committee) (Layfield 1993) of the previous year. These reforms introduced statutory rules for procedure in Public Inquiries, publication of the Inspector's report, and established the key attributes of openness, fairness and impartiality in all appeal proceedings. These three "Franks' principles" still apply today and have governed all procedural reforms since 1958. Further changes in the early 1960s and 1980s introduced new appeal methods in the form of the Written Representation and Informal Hearing.

The Planning Appeal is a critical stage within the development process. Unnecessary delay will frustrate both developer and local planning authority. However, it is important that every decision is made in full knowledge of the proposal to enable the appeal system to produce the correct decision and therefore enhance the development control process.

Key characteristics of the Planning Appeal system can be identified: there are many different rights of appeal against LPA decisions, and these rights are exercised by the applicant (person making the planning application) and in enforcement matters the person who occupies or has an interest in the land. The decision to appeal is free of charge and the appeal is considered by the Secretary of State for the Environment or an Inspector. Administration of the appeal is co-ordinated by the Planning Inspectorate (England) or the Welsh Office or Scottish Office. The Secretary of State will issue a decision either to allow (grant) or to dismiss (refuse) the appeal, with the system being paid for by the government at a cost of around £25 million a year.[1]

Four principal purposes may be advanced. First, Planning Appeals provide a form of *arbitration* whereby an aggrieved applicant or owner may seek an independent assessment on a wide variety of decisions made by the local planning authority. Secondly, they ensure that there is a degree of *consistency* in decision-making across the country. Inspectors will consider each case on its own merit but will take some account of national planning policy in the form of Circulars and PPGs. Thirdly, they provide an opportunity for *public participation* by which third parties can view the decision-making process and make their own representations. Third parties have been defined as "those other than councils or appellants who, in relation to a particular appeal, think they will be affected by its outcome". Third parties are therefore members of the public who consider that they may be affected by a development proposal (Keeble 1985: 80). Third parties enjoy no right of appeal. They are consulted about the appeal and may participate. At Informal Hearing and Public Inquiry they appear at the discretion of the Inspector and are usually allowed to ask questions of the appellant. Fourthly, they provide a *safeguard* against unreasonable decisions by the local planning authority. Appellants are expected to pay their own costs in all appeal proceedings. An award of costs can be made against either party if unreasonable behaviour is evident. This unreasonable behaviour would cover failure to follow relevant appeal procedures or to provide evidence to support the case.

Who considers the appeal?

All planning appeals are submitted to the Secretary of State for the Environment. In practice, the jurisdiction for considering such appeals is split into either transferred or recovered decisions. Decisions are "transferred" to a Planning Inspector appointed on behalf of the Secretary of State. This applies to all Written Representations, most Informal Hearings and about 95 per cent of Public Inquiries. The Planning Inspector is an "arbitrator", with a property-related professional specialism, who is employed by government but is entirely independent in determining appeals. Decisions "recovered" (i.e. not transferred) are determined by the Secretary of State. Such appeals are usually heard by Inquiry and involve major proposals and ones that raise significant legal difficulties or public controversy. Although some of these may be personally referred to the Secretary of State for a final decision (as in the case of sensitive appeals like New Settlements), it is usual practice for a senior official within the Department of the Environment to make the decision upon receiving a recommendation from an Inspector who has been appointed to hold an Inquiry on behalf of the Secretary of State.

The necessary administration and processing of appeals are undertaken by the Planning Inspectorate, an executive agency of the Department of the Environment, or by the Welsh Office and Scottish Office. Proposals decided by the Secretary of State tend to be co-ordinated by the relevant regional office of the DOE.

---

1. See the Planning Inspectorate *Annual report and accounts* for a yearly update. This document is published towards the end of each year in question.

The decision will be conveyed in a letter format addressed to the appellant or agent and will set out in summary the case as presented by either side and any third parties, followed by the reasoning of the Secretary of State or Inspector, dealing with policy matters and other material considerations, and concluding with the decision to allow the appeal (with conditions) or to dismiss the appeal. Any appeal beyond this point is based on a point of law and is made to the High Court.

In dismissing an appeal it is possible for the decision letter to be written in a "positive" tone, stating what would be acceptable and therefore inviting a fresh planning application. It is important to remember that, although consistency is required in planning decision-making, the appeal decision does not constitute a precedent to bind the local planning authority in its consideration of other sites, no matter how similar those sites may be, but may constitute a material consideration with regard to such cases.

Types of appeal

The most common type of planning appeal is against a refusal of planning permission. It is a common misconception that this is the only type of appeal. In fact, many different types of appeal are available under the provisions of town and country planning, listed building and advertisement legislation (Table 4.1).

Submission of appeal

All planning appeals are submitted on standard forms issued by the Secretary of State and co-ordinated by the Planning Inspectorate or DOE regional office. Any appeal against refusal of permission, planning conditions or reserved matters must be submitted within six months of the LPA decision. Appeals against enforcement notices must be submitted within a prescribed period (usually 28 days), that is indicated on the notice. The appeal forms require submission of supporting documentation including plans, notices of refusal, correspondence and certificate of ownership. The right of appeal is free of charge, although in some enforcement matters the appellant may be required to pay a fee.

The choice of appeal method is an important decision. It will affect the procedure for deciding the case, the overall time over which a decision will be reached and the costs involved, not in lodging the appeal, as this is free, but in the professional time required to pursue each method. The choice of method is unfettered by the type of case or nature of evidence to be produced, although the agreement of both parties will usually be required. It is conceivable, if rare, that the most minor appeal may go to Public Inquiry. Although the Inspectorate will always seek the agreement of an LPA, the appellant has the right to choose a Public Inquiry if he wishes to have the case heard before an Inspector, no matter how small the case.

Table 4.1 Types of planning appeal.

Type of appeal	Example
Refusal of planning permission	Refusal to build on or change the use of land
Against a condition on a grant of permission	Hours of opening condition imposed on a grant of hot food take-away
Against refusal of reserved matters application following grant of outline planning permission	Reserved matters — siting, means of access, external appearance, design and landscape, e.g. refuse submitted landscape details
Against refusal of any details required by a planning condition	A condition may require details of proposed materials to be submitted, which may subsequently be refused
Against failure to determine a planning application (non-determination)	LPA do not issue decision within eight weeks or an extended period as agreed by each party
Against the issuing of an Enforcement Notice requiring some remedy against unauthorized development	Notice to remove a building or structure or cease a use – all undertaken without permission
Against failure to grant a certificate of lawfulness of existing or proposed use or development	LPA refuse applications to establish that a building without planning permission has existed for 4 years minimum or a use has existed for 10 years minimum; any appeal would need to produce evidence to prove otherwise
Against refusal of Listed Building Consent	Refusal of application to extend or alter a Listed Building
Against conditions on a grant of Listed Building Consent	A Listed Building condition may require specific materials or methods of construction to be used to match existing
Against the issuing of a Listed Building Enforcement Notice	Specific grounds similar to a planning notice, e.g. requires removal of extension built without Listed Building Consent
Against failure to grant Conservation Area Consent	LPA refuse consent to demolish an unlisted building in a Conservation Area
Against refusal of permission to display an advertisement	Consent refused as advertisement may be too large or result in highway problems
Against an application to top, lop or fell a tree preserved under a Tree Preservation Order	Permission is refused to alter a preserved tree usually due to the loss of amenity involved and/or good health of existing tree

The appeal methods

Following the initial decision to pursue an appeal, the most important decision on the appeal forms is the choice of appeal method (Lavers & Webster 1990). The choices available are Public Inquiry, Written Representation or Informal Hearing. Only one method may be chosen. The Planning Inspectorate has always sought to encourage use of the written method, which is quicker and cheaper to implement. Since September 1994 the appeal forms have displayed a clear choice of the three methods.[2]

All three methods are designed to embody the rules of Natural Justice. Such rules state that the decision-maker (Inspector or Secretary of State) is impartial and that, before a decision is taken, individuals should be given a chance to put their points of view. Inquiries and Written Representations are governed by statutory rules of procedure.[3] The Informal Hearing procedure is set out in a non-statutory Code of Practice.

These three appeal methods each represent a balance between the need for administrative expediency and for a proper examination of the planning issues of the case. It is widely accepted that the Public Inquiry results in a greater rigour of detailed examination than the written method (McCoubry 1990, Purdue 1991).[4] However, it also takes longer to process and it costs more to both the DOE (in Inspector time) and the appellant (in professional fees). Not all planning appeals involve complex policy or other issues. Therefore, it may be expedient to sacrifice the detailed examination of issues in preference to a quick and less expensive method of appeal. An appraisal of the three Planning Appeal methods is shown in Table 4.2.

Table 4.2 An appraisal of Planning Appeal methods.

	Advantages	Disadvantages
Written Representation	Cheapest method.	Evidence is not rigorously tested.
	Shortest period to get decision.	Written evidence only – little opportunity to clarify issues or allow Inspector to ask questions.
Informal Hearing	Informal atmosphere.	Role of Inspector is central to proceedings. If an Inspector does not control the discussion then this method loses its advantages.
	Some oral discussion – testing of evidence and clarification of issues.	
	Hearing avoids time-wasting – usually half-day duration.	Discussion basis, is not adversarial and may help to readily identify key issues.
	Opportunity for costs to be incurred.	Costs may also go against.
Public inquiry	Cross-examination allows for a rigorous testing of evidence and clarification of issues.	Formal and sometimes excessively adversarial.
		Most expensive.
	Opportunity for costs.	Longest period of time to get a decision. Costs may also go against.

2. Following recommendations of W. S. Atkins (planning consultants), December 1993, to the Planning Inspectorate (1993b).
3. Usually contained in Statutory Instruments, e.g. Town and Country Planning (Inquiries Procedure Rules 1992) (SI 2038).
4. See *Ricketts & Fletcher* vs *Secretary of State for the Environment and Salisbury District Council* [1988] *JPL* **768**, on how the Inquiry method may be considered as a direct, effective and efficient means by which evidence can be tested.

Which method to choose?

Determining factors can be identified that will influence the choice of appeal method (Table 4.3). The decision to appeal is a decision of last resort. Around 30–35 per cent of all appeals are allowed, so, crudely speaking, the appellant has a one in three chance of success, although the Inquiry on its own gives slightly better odds at around 40 per cent allowed.[5] If the LPA would give favourable consideration to some form of amended proposal, then this would be a more secure way of realizing development potential. Although some appeal proposals will stand a better chance than others, the appeal pathway will always remain a lottery to the developer, as the Inspector is making an entirely fresh (*de novo*) development control decision.

Table 4.3 Factors to consider when choosing a method of appeal.

Determining factor	Method
(a) Magnitude of case: the size and scale of development proposed	Public Inquiry suitable for major proposals,* Written Representation for minor ones
(b) Complexity of case: the number or depth of policy and material considerations involved	Public Inquiry for complex and Written Representations for straightforward cases
(c) Financial considerations (professional fees) imposed by (a) and (b) above	Public Inquiry will involve greater professional input to prepare evidence and appear at Inquiry
(d) Time available to appellant	Written – 18 weeks† average from submission of appeal to decision notice being received Informal – 26 weeks† Inquiry – 44 weeks†
(e) Possibility of seeking costs for unreasonable behaviour	Costs applications only available at Inquiry and Hearing, not at written method
(f) Level of third-party involvement (number of objections at application stage prior to appeal)	All appeal methods permit the appellant to deal with third party comments; however, if many are expected the Hearing is an unsuitable method within which to deal with many objections; consider either Inquiry or written

* "Major" is 10+ houses or 10000 ft² floorspace for industrial, commercial or retail.
† Expressed as overall handling time in 80% of cases, see Planning Inspectorate *Annual report* for year-to-year fluctuations.

Procedures involved in each appeal method

Written representation

These are rough justice, greater speed of determination being purchased at the cost of less thorough exploration. (Keeble 1985)

5. Every year the Planning Inspectorate publishes its *Annual report*, which includes statistical analysis of appeals allowed for each appeal method.

> ## Case study 4.1
>
> *Proposal:* The LPA refuses planning permission for a two-storey side extension to a dwell-inghouse for the reason:
>
> > The proposal by reason of its excessive bulk would result in a loss of light and over-shadowing of the neighbouring property, detrimental to the amenities enjoyed by the occupiers of that property.
>
> *Appraisal:* The planning issue is clearly defined. The case is of little magnitude or complexity. On this basis it would not warrant a great deal of professional input and the owner is keen to have a decision as soon and inexpensively as possible. In this case a Written Representation would be the best method.

Such criticism has been levelled at the written method on the basis that, in pursuing a relatively quick decision, the procedures inhibit a rigorous exploration of the planning merits of the case (McNamara et al. 1985). Such a view must be qualified by the fact that the written method is best employed in minor cases with straightforward planning issues (Case Study 4.1). The Department of the Environment encourages use of this method, as the appeal forms state "Do you agree to the written procedure?" Since this method was first introduced in 1965 as an alternative to the Public Inquiry, it has increased its percentage share of all methods from 30–35 per cent to 80–85 per cent of all appeals. The written appeal has many benefits for the Planning Inspectorate in that the cost of each appeal is cheaper, involving generally less administration or Inspector's time to reach a decision and therefore the combined advantage of offering a cheaper unit cost per appeal[6] to the Treasury and speedier decisions to appellants and local planning authorities. During the 1990s the Secretary of State for the Environment set targets for the handling of written appeals from the submission of forms to the issue of the decision notice.[7] It is therefore in the interests of the Planning Inspectorate to continue to promote the Written Representation appeal with the benefit of a decision period of around 18 weeks to be reflected in the statistical returns issued every year.

Since 1987, Written Representation procedures have been governed by statutory rules,[8] which established a timetable to govern the operation of the appeal (Table 4.4).

It is intended that this timetable should establish a set of deadlines to be followed by parties to the appeal. Such time periods are rarely observed, although failure to meet them is usually by a matter of days or weeks, and not months.

The written procedure allows for a single exchange of written statement and the opportunity to comment on that evidence. However, additional written exchanges beyond this point are discouraged. Nothing is gained from having the last word. One frequently expressed criticism of this procedure is the inability

---

6. In early 1990s this was around £700 per written appeal.
7. That 80 per cent of all Written Representations will be handled within 22 weeks.
8. Town and Country Planning (Appeals) (Written Representations Procedure) Regulations 1987 (SI 701). Also see DOE Circular 11/87 on *Written representation procedure.*

Table 4.4 Timetable for the Written Representation appeal process.

Time	Procedure
Decision to appeal is made	Appellant submits appeal forms.
Start date	Planning Inspectorate (PI) notify both sides of start date whereby process has begun.
14 days	LPA to return a questionnaire issued by the Inspectorate.
28 days	LPA to send a statement of case (their evidence) to LPA and PI. The LPA do not have to submit a statement. They may choose to attach relevant documents (officer's report, local plan, extract) to the questionnaire.
17 days after LPA questionnaire or statement	Appellant must submit a response to the LPA.
7 days after receipt of appellant statement	LPA can respond but should only deal with new material that has not been previously dealt with.
Close of representations	Date set for site inspection if site cannot be seen from public land. The site inspection permits both sides to show the Inspector various features and not to deal with arguments over the merits or otherwise of the appeal.
Site visit plus 14 days	Decision letter issued, either granting (allow) or refusing (dismiss) the appeal.

of local authorities to adhere to the procedural timetable and the unwillingness of the Planning Inspectorate to enforce it.[9]

Summary: Written Representations – key characteristics

- suitable for minor cases
- written exchange of evidence
- quickest appeal method
- cheapest appeal (in professional fees)
- preferred by Planning Inspectorate
- procedure (timetable of events) governed by statutory rules
- most used method: 80–85 per cent of appeals.

Informal Hearings

Informal Hearings were first introduced in 1981 as an alternative to the Public Inquiry. During the 1980s they grew in popularity, so that by 1993 in England and Wales more appeals were decided by the Informal Hearing method (1862 appeals) than the inquiry method (1609 appeals).[10]

The Informal Hearing has been described as a "half-way house" (Morgan & Nott 1988: 310) between the other methods, although it does have its own distinct advantage in that discussion is allowed on the site visit. The procedure involves

---

9. See Planning Inspectorate (1993a).
10. Planning Inspectorate, *Annual reports and accounts*, 1993.

Case study 4.2

Proposal: The LPA refuses planning permission for a change of use of a retail shop (A1 use class) into a restaurant/food and drink use (A3 use class). The proposal satisfies local plan policy and was recommended for a grant of planning permission by the case officer. The Committee overturned this recommendation and refused permission.

Appraisal: A straightforward case involving one policy issue. Although A3 uses involve the potential for several material considerations (especially odour emissions, late night activity, traffic generation and non-retail frontages), they are not considered to represent complex cases of great magnitude. Such a proposal could be adequately dealt with by Written Representation. However, there is some evidence of unreasonable behaviour and the possibility of an award of costs being made against the LPA.* In such a case, only Hearings/Inquiry allow either party to pursue such an award. A Hearing provides the better forum for dealing with costs in relatively straightforward or minor cases, whereas the Inquiry is the most suitable method for dealing with costs in the more complex or major cases.

* The award of costs is considered at the end of this chapter. The overturning of the recommendation of the Chief Planning Officer does not of itself constitute unreasonable behaviour, resulting in costs. However, if evidence is not forthcoming at the appeal to support the Committee's action, there is a strong chance costs may be awarded.

---

an exchange of written evidence between the parties prior to the Hearing, and at the Hearing the Inspector leads a discussion between both parties and any third parties who attend.

Legal representation and formal cross-examination is discouraged. The Inspector plays a pivotal role in proceedings, leading the discussion, structuring the debate and intervening when the procedure departs from the code of practice. The Informal Hearing has been described as a "round table discussion led by the Inspector" (Purdue 1991) or as a "significant business meeting free from archaic ritual but not by any means an unconstrained social gathering" (McCoubrey 1990). The Inspector does have considerable discretion to structure the discussion, which may result in differing approaches by different Inspectors (Stubbs 1994). Most certainly, the Informal Hearing gives the Inspector greater control over the exact workings of the process compared to either the written method or the Inquiry. The procedure is shown in Table 4.5.

In 1993 the Planning Inspectorate commissioned research into customer

Table 4.5 Timetable for the Informal Hearing appeal process.

Time	Procedure
	Appellant submits appeal forms
Start date	Start date is issued by Inspectorate; Appeal begins
Start date plus 6 weeks or 3 weeks prior to Hearing	Both sides exchange statements of evidence
Hearing (3–4 hours duration)	Discussion based format led by Inspector
Followed by site visit	Discussion may continue on site
After Hearing Decision, letter is issued (no target set)	

perceptions of the Hearing method.[11] The report findings demonstrated a high level of satisfaction with this procedure, with appellants and LPAs citing the benefits of cost (professional fees), efficiency and suitability of a discussion-based forum. One of the key recommendations was that the automatic choice of a Hearing should be available. This was accepted by the Inspectorate. From September 1994 the planning appeal forms contain a clear choice between Written Representation, Informal Hearing and Public Inquiry. The LPA would still be required to agree to a Hearing; however, this amendment clearly established the role of Hearings as a clear alternative to not just inquiries but also Written Representations.

Public Inquiry

The Public Inquiry is the most formal, as well as formidable, method of planning appeal. Procedure is governed by a set of statutory rules, which establish that written statements of evidence shall be exchanged by both sides prior to the Inquiry. At the Inquiry, each side will appear with an expert witness or witnesses who will be open to cross-examination by, in most cases, trained advocates (see Case Study 4.4 and Table 4.6).

The exact procedure varies between cases decided by Inspectors (transferred cases) and those decided by the Secretary of State (recovered cases).

Cases determined by the Secretary of State (recovered cases)

In such cases an Inspector will be appointed to hold an Inquiry and to produce a decision letter with a recommendation. The Secretary of State or a senior official will consider this recommendation and either agree or disagree with the Inspector's findings.[12] Such cases usually involve large-scale proposals, with an Inquiry lasting many weeks. A pre-inquiry meeting may be held during which practical and procedural issues will be considered, such as establishing a timetable of witness appearances for the duration of the Inquiry.

Summary: Informal Hearings – key characteristics

- written exchange of evidence followed by "round the table" discussion
- Inspector plays important role in controlling the discussion
- increasing popularity from mid-1980s onwards; since 1992/3 more popular than Inquiry
- procedure governed by a code of practice and not statutory rules
- half-way house between Written Representations and Public Inquiry in speed of decision, and professional fees involved
- since 1992, application for an award of costs can be made at Informal Hearing
- accounts for 5–10 per cent of all appeals.

---

11. Planning Inspectorate 1993b.
12. The Secretary of State may disagree, because new evidence or matters of fact have been taken into account or because he differs from the Inspector on a matter of opinion on which a conclusion or recommendation has been based.

Table 4.6   Timetable for the Public Inquiry (transferred cases).

Time	Procedure
	Appellant submits appeal forms.
Date for Inquiry is set (RD plus 20 weeks)	Secretary of State (Inspectorate) issue an acknowledgement letter the date of which is the relevant date (RD), which starts the process towards Inquiry.
Relevant date plus 6 weeks	LPA must serve a Statement of Case (also called Pre-Inquiry Statement) on Inspectorate and appellant. This is a statement of the particulars of the case and a list of documents to be referred to.
Relevant date plus 9 weeks	Appellant must serve a statement of case on Inspectorate and LPA.
Documents referred to by each side may be requested by each party.	
3 weeks before Inquiry	Both sides "exchange" proofs of evidence (detailed statements, usually one for each witness) and send copies to the Inspectorate. Each proof exceeding 1500 words must be accompanied by a summary.
Inquiry and site visit	Each witness presents evidence by reading from proof or summary, which is then open to cross-examination.
	The Inquiry site visit is governed by the same rules as the Written Representation site visit.
Decision letter issued	

Cross-examination

The Inquiry procedure rules are designed to ensure that the Inquiry time is used most effectively in helping the Inspector in arriving at an informed development control decision. The most tangible advantage of the Inquiry is the ability to cross-examine witnesses who appear on behalf of the LPA, appellant or third parties (see Case Study 4.3). In this respect the inquiry may take on the appearance of a court, with the adversarial stance taken by either side and the frequent use of barristers or solicitors to present the case for either side. It is not, then, uncommon for the Inquiry to be viewed as a judicial hearing, but this is misleading. A court hearing involves strict rules of evidence that may rule some evidence inadmissible, for example hearsay evidence. A planning Public Inquiry, although governed by statutory rules, deals with a good deal of opinion-based argument, for example the professional judgement of a witness in how to interpret a particular policy, or the relative balance between policy and other material considerations in arriving at a decision, constitute such judgement.

In an Inquiry, cross-examination should not be used to discredit any witnesses but instead to test the validity of facts or assumptions, explore how policy relates to the merits of the case and to identify and narrow the issues in dispute. Government policy advice states that Inspectors "will protect witnesses, particularly those who are unrepresented, from intimidating questioning. Inspectors are interested in the considered views of witnesses not in forced concurrence with questioning."[13]

Case study 4.3

Proposal: The LPA refuses planning permission to build two new houses within a backland site in a Conservation Area. At the application stage, considerable local opposition is voiced against the proposal. The application is refused permission for several reasons:
- The proposal is contrary to the nature and form of development within this Conservation Area.
- The proposal would result in an unacceptable loss of existing trees within the site, which make an important contribution to the appearance of the Conservation Area.
- The proposal is contrary to conservation policies within the local plan.

Appraisal: The magnitude and complexity of the case are greater than in Case Study 4.1, yet they are still relatively straightforward, principally the impact on the character and appearance of the Conservation Area. However, the possibility of considerable third-party representation rules out the Informal Hearing, leaving either a Written Representation or Public Inquiry. If the developer is happy to bear the additional cost and time involved, an Inquiry allows the opportunity to deal effectively with any third parties who wish to appear by means of cross-examination.

Case study 4.4

Proposal: The LPA refuses planning permission for an office redevelopment within a town centre location for the following reasons:
- The proposal is considered to be contrary to local plan policy that identifies the site as being suitable for retail development.
- Insufficient parking is provided within the site, resulting in congestion on the neighbouring highway.
- Excessive height, and mass, of proposal resulting in a form of development out of scale with surrounding development.
- In the absence of any contribution towards highway improvements on surrounding roads, the LPA considers that the additional traffic generated will result in an unacceptable increase in congestion, detrimental to the free flow of traffic and highway safety.

Appraisal: This appeal raises several complex technical issues (policy, material considerations and possible need for planning obligations) and a proposal of some magnitude. The financial cost of professional representation would be high, involving possibly several different professionals (planning, highway engineering and architectural) to deal with the different reasons. The Public Inquiry presents the best method with which to deal with these issues, with the significant benefit of being able to cross-examine the other side.

Inquiry format

The Inquiry format and various tactical considerations can be considered as in Table 4.7.

The nature of evidence

In all methods of planning appeal "evidence" may be produced in several ways. In all appeals this evidence may comprise both fact and opinion/judgement. For example, note the distinctions between facts and opinion in Table 4.8.

---

13. DOE Circular 24/92. The Town and Country Planning (Inquiries Procedure) Rules 1992, Annex on *Good practice at Planning Inquiries.*

Summary: Public Inquiries – key characteristics

- suitable for more complex cases
- written exchange of statements and proofs of evidence followed by Inquiry with formal rules of procedure involving evidence in chief, cross-examination, re-examination and submissions
- appeal method of longest duration
- most expensive (in professional fees) for appellant and Inspectorate (in administration and Inspector's time)
- procedures (exchange of evidence and Inquiry conduct) governed by statutory rules
- least used method but tends to deal with the most important cases
- smallest proportion of all appeals: 5–10 per cent

Table 4.7   Planning Inquiry format "on the day".

Format	Details	Tactics
Inspector opens Inquiry	Statement that Inquiry is to be held and short explanation of procedure; Inspector notes names of advocates, witnesses and any third parties	
Appellant's case		
Appellant's advocate makes an opening statement	Outline of case	Brevity required with a summary of the issues and key policy and material considerations
Appellant's Evidence in Chief	Each witness reads proof or summary plus any additional oral explanation	Deal with reasons for refusal point by point
LPA may cross-examine each witness	Opportunity to test evidence by oral examination	Agree common ground + Focus on differences + Test validity of differences
Appellant may re-examine	Advocate may deal with issues raised in cross-examination	Must avoid leading witness or introducing fresh evidence
Inspector may ask the witness questions		
Local planning authority's case		
LPA evidence in chief	As above	As above
Appellant may cross-examine		
LPA may re-examine		
Inspector may ask questions to witness		
*Third party evidence**		
Closing submissions by LPA and then appellant	Summary of case as emerged from evidence/cross/re-examination	An extremely important opportunity to target what has been conceded in cross-examination
Inspector will close Inquiry, then . . . Site visit		No discussion of the merits of the case, while on site

* Taken at a convenient break in proceedings, if third parties wish to speak or are professionally represented. Third parties may also cross-examine the appellant's witnesses.

Table 4.8 Examples of evidence produced in Planning Appeals.

Facts	Opinion
Planning policy issues, i.e. the site is or is not covered by policies A, B or C. This is a matter of fact.	Some policies are vague in detail or broad in their application and require opinion to decide on how they should be interpreted.
It is a matter of fact that the site is within a Conservation Area.	Conservation policy states that development must preserve or enhance the character/ appearance. It may be a matter of opinion that a proposal satisfies such criteria.
Carparking or amenity space standards, i.e. does the proposal satisfy such standards. This is a matter of fact; e.g. proposal provides five spaces and standards require seven spaces = fails standard by two.	Whether rigid adherence to carparking standards is required is a matter of opinion; e.g. surrounding roads contain plenty of parking on the kerbside, so two additional cars would not result in any harm to the free flow of parking.

The award of costs

In all planning appeal proceedings, each party is expected to pay their own costs. The power to award costs in planning Appeals was first introduced in 1933. Since 1972 the Local Government Act has enabled the Secretary of State or Inspector to require that one party pays the costs of another in planning appeals.[14] Key features of this provision are that:

- it is available in all Public Inquiry and Informal Hearing appeals[15]
- it is also available in all enforcement appeals or listed-building enforcement notice appeals submitted by Written Representation
- applications for an award must usually be made within the appeal procedure; at Public Inquiry or Informal Hearing this is usually before the close
- the award covers the costs of attending and preparing for the appeal. It does not deal with the financial costs relating to the purchase of a site, the development of which has been delayed by the fighting of a planning appeal, loss of profit, and so on
- the award is made because of unreasonable conduct by a party, which has caused another party unnecessary expense
- the award does not automatically follow the appeal decision, e.g. if the decision of the Inspector is to allow the appeal it does not infer costs will follow. If an LPA fails to support a reason for refusal with evidence, this can constitute unreasonable behaviour, and costs may be awarded to the developer. However, the merits of the appeal and merits of costs are dealt with entirely separately.

14. Section 250(5) of the Local Government Act 1972, and Circular 8/93, *Award of costs incurred in planning and other proceedings*.
15. Section 320 (2) and Schedule 6 of the TCPA 1990. Similar provisions are to be found in Section 89 of the Planning (Listed Buildings and Conservation Areas) Act 1990 and Section 37 of the Planning (Hazardous Substances) Act 1990.

The award of costs represents a penalty against either party for unreasonable conduct in appeal proceedings. During the 1980s the majority of awards were made against local planning authorities. Research undertaken between 1987 and 1990 indicated that costs had been awarded against an LPA 6.5 times more frequently than against appellants (Blackhall 1990, Association of Metropolitan Authorities 1989). During this period the government was seeking to "deregulate" the planning system by establishing, in policy guidance, a presumption in favour of granting planning permission. A development boom resulted in the submission of many more planning applications, and planning committees found themselves overturning officer recommendations and refusing planning permission in order to pacify local opposition to this "tide" of new development. Research (ibid.) indicated that costs were more likely to be awarded in cases where the planning committee had rejected a recommendation by the Chief Planning Officer.

This position changed dramatically in the 1990s with the property boom turning into a recession and the government's increasing emphasis on a presumption in favour of planning policy, and deletion of the presumption in favour of development per se. In the 1990s a refusal based upon the correct application of a relevant up-to-date policy would be virtually immune from the threat of a costs award at any subsequent appeal. In 1992/3 there were 263 awards of costs in favour of the appellant and 120 in favour of the LPA, a significant narrowing of the margin compared to the late 1980s. It seems likely that during the remainder of the 1990s such awards will be employed by the Secretary of State and Inspectors to ensure that both sides follow procedural rules and produce evidence at appeal to support their case.

In 1991 the government reinforced the need to comply with Inquiry procedures by enabling an award of costs to be made against any party whose unreasonable behaviour directly resulted in the late cancellation of an Inquiry or Hearing resulting in wasted expense in preparing for an appeal that was abandoned.[16]

Examples of costs

To gain an award of costs, it is necessary to establish that one party has acted unreasonably, vexatiously or frivolously and that this behaviour has resulted in unnecessary expense for the other side (LPA, appellant or, in rare cases, third party).

In the majority of cases, applications for costs can be divided into those based on procedural issues and those based on evidential issues. Table 4.9 shows a series of examples to illustrate some common features of costs applications; however, they are by no means exhaustive. It is important to remember that criteria as stated under (A) and (B) must be satisfied for an award of costs to be granted in favour of one party.

---

16. DOE Circular 8/93, *Award of costs incurred in planning and other proceedings.*

Table 4.9 Examples of the award of costs.

Procedural		Evidential	
(A) Unreasonable behaviour	(B) Resulting in unnecessary expense	(A) Unreasonable behaviour	(B) Resulting in unnecessary expense
Failure to provide adequate pre-inquiry statement i.e. not setting out case or documents to be used. **Both sides.** †	Waste of inquiry time to establish the case produced by one side **or** results in need for adjournment.	Failure to provide evidence to support refusal. **Award against LPA.** †	P/app should not have been refused in the first case or LPA have not justified their case so appeal unnecessary.
Failure to provide supporting information or late submission of proof of evidence	Waste of inquiry time to establish the case produced by one side **or** results in need for adjournment.	Planning policy establishes that proposal was in accord with policy and therefore p/app should have been granted. **Against LPA.** †	Matter should not have proceeded to appeal in the first place.
Introduce at late stage a new ground of appeal or legal ground in an enforcement appeal. **(Appellant)** † or reason for refusal **(LPA).** †	Waste of inquiry time to establish the case produced by one side or results in need for adjournment.	It was apparent from PPG or Circulars that the appeal had no reasonable chance of success (e.g. green belt policy).	Matter should not have proceeded to appeal in the first place.
Unreasonable/late withdrawal once Inquiry/Hearing has been arranged.	One side has wasted time in preparing for inquiry unnecessarily.	It was apparent from a previous appeal on the site that a resubmission with amendments would be acceptable. **Against LPA.** †	LPA should have granted resubmitted proposal, following the material consideration of the previous Inspector's decision.

† Party against whom costs would be awarded if an application for costs was made at the Inquiry/Hearing and the Inspector agreed.
* Some caution is required when considering this case. Most planning policy requires a good deal of interpretation and of course material considerations may "indicate otherwise", making it difficult to establish unreasonable behaviour against either an appellant who proceeds to appeal on a matter that appears contrary to policy or an LPA that refuses an application that appears in accord with policy.

Conclusions

The planning appeal process plays a vital role in the town planning system granting power to challenge the decisions of the LPA. The procedures upon which the system is based are themselves shaped by the needs of natural justice and administrative efficiency. Most appellants seek speedy decision on appeal, but they also seek a system that allows for a full explanation of their case and requires the LPA to account for its decision. All three methods of appeal contain a balance between administrative efficiency and the rules of natural justice. The written method is quickest, with the least rigour in its examination of evidence, and the Inquiry is the longest, with the most rigour in its examination of evidence; the Hearing falls somewhere between the two. Changes to procedures have increasingly sought to improve efficiency by introducing timetables, rules and the award of costs.

In past years this drive towards procedural efficiency has resulted in some reforming proposals that have subsequently been dropped by government, following criticism that they would compromise the ability of appeals to deliver natural justice. Such ideas have included dropping the automatic entitlement to a Public Inquiry, issuing policy guidance to the effect that pursuing an Inquiry instead of an alternative method could be grounds for the award of costs, curtailing the opportunity to cross-examine at Inquiry, and widening the power to award costs to Written Representation. None of these ideas have been acted upon[17] and both the Planning Inspectorate and the Secretary of State have supported the appellant's automatic right to insist on a Public Inquiry. However, critics of the system are concerned that the increasing support of alternatives such as Informal Hearings is only the tip of the iceberg to reduce both the costs of appeal and length of time to reach a decision by ultimately either restricting access to the Public Inquiry method or the ability to cross-examine within that method.[18] This remains to be seen; however, the final push towards such dramatic reforms may ironically be the result of the activities of the property industry.

In the property boom years of the late 1980s, the number of planning appeals received by the Inspector rose to a peak of 32000 in 1989/90, falling to 18000 by 1993 and projected to stabilize at around 20000 until 1996.[19] This demonstrates that the number of appeals submitted is subject to dramatic fluctuations depending upon the property development cycle. If this cycle were to undergo another dramatic hike in activity towards the end of the decade and the government were not prepared to fund the appointment of more appeal Inspectors, then the best way of maintaining a quick turn-round of appeal decisions would be to discourage Public Inquiries in favour of the alternative methods of appeal.

17. Although the government has stated that it will make the award of costs available in Written Representations as soon as resources allow. By the mid-1990s this had not been introduced.
18. *Estates Gazette*, editorial, 2 July 1994, p. 43.
19. The Planning Inspectorate, *Corporate plan 1993/94–1995/96*.

CHAPTER FIVE

Planning gain and planning obligations

Planning gain is a term familiar to many professionals working in property development. However, it is also a misleading and ill defined term. Since 1991 the Government discouraged its use and preferred the term "planning obligations". This chapter will seek to define the planning gain and obligations system and will consider the subject in two sections dealing with the legal and philosophical context of the subject.

The study of planning gain/planning obligations exposes the tension that exists between the town planning system and the property development industry. At its most fundamental it involves examination of who should pay for the wider environmental impact of a development proposal, the developer or the local authority. This chapter will examine the workings of the system, dealing separately with the legal or procedural rules that guide the practical implementation of planning obligations, and the broader, more philosophical, debate as to whether such obligations represent a form of development tax or a legitimate development cost. A series of case studies will focus on what is considered to constitute good and bad practice. The chapter will be subdivided as follows:

- the legal issues
- the philosophical issues.

Background

The many misconceptions surrounding this subject are in part explained by the lack of a single and widely used definition and the use of a variety of titles relating to the practice of planning gain. Research (Healey et al. 1993) discovered the use of twelve terms to describe the same function.[1] The term "planning gain"

---

1. Planning gain, community gain, community benefit, planning advantage, planning requirements, planning obligations, planning agreements, developer's contribution, legal arrangements, improvements and additional facilities, community impacts, environmental impacts.

Case study 5.1

Proposal
Residualbuild Developments submits a planning application seeking permission to build 20 detached houses. The chief executive of Residualbuild calculates the profit margins of the development and writes to the LPA, offering them £1 million to spend on community projects within the area or indeed on **"anything they so wish"**.

Tests (see Table 5.1)
Similar to Case Study 5.4, in that the cash payment will not satisfy any facilities necessary for this development to proceed. If some form of community use had previously existed on this site, or the new development would itself require community facilities, then a case could be made for a payment or offer of land to compensate for the loss. However, merely offering a "blanket" sum unrelated to the requirements of the case is not the correct approach.

Conclusions
Again, an unreasonable pursuit of a planning obligation by a developer. Such an example is used to demonstrate that the generation of unreasonable obligation is not the exclusive privilege of the public sector.

---

provides a convenient umbrella under which benefits in either cash or kind are offered to a local planning authority (LPA) by a developer, following the grant of planning permission and controlled by an agreement between the local planning authority and landowner or by planning condition. This implies a situation in which the local planning authority benefits from something for nothing, that is, by simply granting planning permission the developer will provide "sweeteners" or "goodies" (Case Study 5.1). Such a view would be an unsatisfactory start to the topic. At this stage we must acknowledge the important procedural role played by the system, which allows both local authority and developer to overcome and control the environmental impact arising from development proposals enabling planning permission to be granted in cases where, without these controls, it may have been refused (Case Study 5.2).

Provision for agreements relating to the development of land have existed in planning legislation since 1909.[2] The current system can effectively be traced back to 1968 when the need for ministerial consent was removed and such agreements were left for straightforward negotiation between the local planning authority and landowner/developer, as exists today.

In 1980 the Government commissioned the Property Advisory Group (PAG) [3]to examine the practice of planning gain. Their report (Property Advisory Group 1980) concluded: "We are unable to accept that, as a matter of general practice, planning gain has any place in our system of planning control."

However, the DOE did not accept such a finding and in 1983 they issued Circular

---

2. Housing. Town Planning Etc. Act 1909 followed by Section 34 of the TCPA 1932.
3. Advisory group composed of property professionals, independent of government.

Case study 5.2

Proposal
Ecoville Developers acquire a former land fill site within green belt land and propose to build a business park on approximately 30 per cent of the site, a golf course on 20 per cent and parkland on the remaining area. Various highway improvements are required on land adjacent to the site. A planning obligation would allow the use of the park and golf course for access by the public, together with a (single) cash payment towards the cost of adjoining highway improvements to serve the site.

Tests (see Table 5.1)
A business park within the green belt would in normal circumstances be contrary to policy. In this case the use of an obligation allows an area of previously spoiled green belt land to be brought into recreational use. The obligation is needed to allow the development to proceed and satisfies test 1. Together with the associated highway works, it is clearly both functionally and geographically related to the development.

Conclusion
An acceptable planning obligation, clearly allowing planning benefits to both sides by restoring green belt land and allowing a business park. Green belt policy is strictly applied by LPAs and this example should not be viewed as a means by which planning gain may be employed to permit exceptions to planning policy. However, it does illustrate the role of negotiation, illustrating how an obligation is used to facilitate improvements to spoilt green belt by permitting some development. A planning agreement is required as both sides are involved.

Guidance on Planning Gain. Paragraph 2 of the Circular provided a definition:

"Planning gain" is a term which has come to be applied whenever in connection with a grant of planning permission, a local planning authority seeks to impose on a developer an obligation to carry out works not included in the development for which permission has been sought or to make payment or confer some extraneous right or benefit in return for permitting development to take place.

The Circular set out a series of broad rules or "tests of reasonableness", to establish what could be considered to be acceptable practice. These tests established that any gains should be reasonable in content, and both geographically and functionally related to the development to be permitted (Case Studies 5.3, 5.4).

Planning gain practice during the 1970s and 1980s was not viewed by many local planning authorities as a quasi-legal function, based upon the application of these Circular tests, essentially to overcome objections to a scheme and allow permission to be granted. Instead, some local planning authorities were employing the system to extract community benefits from developers. This benefit in social or physical infrastructure (building a community centre or a new road) was sometimes either unrelated or shared a tenuous relationship with the development to be permitted.

Towards the end of the property boom in the 1980s, a growing suspicion emerged that both local planning authorities and developers had violated the "tests" in the pursuit of planning consent or wider benefits by the local authority. In 1989 the Royal Town Planning Institute raised doubts over some activities that were being reported as planning gain:

> Planning gain is a somewhat misleading term. A key element of our statutory land-use planning system in this country is action by local planning authorities to influence developers to come forward with proposals which are in

---

Case study 5.3

Proposal
Blackacre Developments acquire a church, now redundant, within a high street location. Behind the church is a carpark. Blackacre acquire the car park to assemble a site large enough to accommodate a new shopping mall.

The demolition of the church would provide a direct link with the existing high street and the pedestrian flow necessary for the economic viability of the new centre.

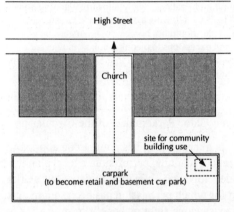

Following the sale of the carpark to the developer, a planning obligation would permit the developer to offer to build another community use elsewhere within the site to replace the church displaced by the development. The council may seek to maintain some element of public access to the car parking within the new scheme, which is likely to be in a basement underneath the new shopping mall.

Tests (see Table 5.1)
Replacement of "lost" uses (car parking, church) within these new provisions would satisfy the fifth test, namely offset the loss of amenity. The maintenance of public parking in the area would overcome any objection to the loss of car parking and would satisfy the third test. The obligation would appear to be fairly and reasonably related to the proposal.

Conclusions
An acceptable planning obligation serving a land-use purpose. A planning agreement would be the most appropriate method, with both sides benefiting in some way.

Case study 5.4

Proposal
Flexible BI Developments proposes an office building within a town centre location. The LPA seek a financial payment towards a local civic/community festival.

Tests (see Table 5.1)
A cash payment which will not contribute towards satisfying facilities necessary to allow the development to proceed (tests 1 and 2). This example is not fairly and reasonably related to the proposal.

Conclusions
Unreasonable pursuit of a planning obligation by the LPA.

---

accord with the Authorities development plans and other policies. This may include essential infrastructure provision of various kinds. This should quite properly be termed planning gain. However, the term has more recently been applied to agreements entered into by local planning authorities and applicants, to ensure that a development when permitted includes wider benefits (Byrne 1989).

The Planning and Compensation Act 1991 introduced a series of reforms and a new term: "planning obligation" (Redman 1991).

Alongside these reforms to the operation of the planning gain system, Circular 22/83 became superseded by Circular 16/91, entitled *Planning obligations* (issued on 8 October 1991). This Circular stated in paragraph B2:

The term planning gain has no statutory significance and is not found in the Planning Acts. . . . In granting planning permission, or in negotiations with developers and other interests that lead to the grant of planning permission, the local planning authority may seek to secure modifications or improvements to the proposals submitted for their approval. They may grant permission subject to conditions, and where appropriate they may seek to enter into planning obligations with a developer regarding the use or development of the land concerned or other land or buildings. Rightly used, planning obligations may enhance development proposals.

So the introduction of this new planning language was accompanied by the government's own emphasis upon the role of obligations in enabling modification or improvements to planning applications, which may in turn enhance development proposals. One objective was to provide greater focus on this planning mechanism in preference to the mere extraction of community or other benefits. This chapter will refer to "planning obligations" when dealing with the post-1991 system. Any reference to "gain" will be historical, referring to the system before 1991.

In attempting to unravel the many issues that surround planning obligations, the subject will be split into two principal areas, legal and philosophical. It is

95

important to understand how the system works (the legal side) before dealing with the wider issue of whether this system is the best way of controlling the environmental impacts of development proposals (the philosophical side).

The legal issues

Planning obligations

Planning obligations are created under Section 106 of the TCPA 1990. A new Section 106 was introduced into the 1990 Act by the Planning and Compensation Act 1991,[4] together with a new Section 106A (powers to modify or discharge an obligation) and Section 106B (appeal against refusal to modify or discharge an obligation). The Section 106 obligation forms the legal contract by which the objectives of the planning obligation are legally honoured and enforced.[5]

In addition, local planning authorities may enter into legal agreements with developers under Section 111 of the Local Government Act 1972.[6] It is common practice for such legal agreements to recite that they are made in compliance with both statutes. It is possible for a planning condition to be used to control various land-use matters instead of a planning obligation. However, a condition may be of limited use because in the majority of cases it may deal only with land-use planning related issues within the application site[7] and, this notwithstanding, many local authorities simply prefer the legal enforceability associated with Section 106 and Section 111. If a proposal involves a financial payment or an off-site matter such as a highway improvement, then a legal agreement will normally be required. With the very limited use of conditions, it follows that Section 106 planning obligations provide the most popular and effective method of control.

The 1991 Reforms to the system were:
- Planning obligations were introduced and came into force on 25th October 1991.[8] The new concept of the planning obligation comprised either a Planning Agreement, whereby the developer/landowner enters into an agreement with the local planning authority, or a unilateral undertaking, whereby the developer/landowner gives an undertaking to the LPA. Such obligations may restrict the development or use of land, require specific operations (works) or activities (uses) to be carried out on land owned by the applicant, which may be within the application site or may be on neighbouring land, require land to be used in a particular way, and require payments to the

---

4. Although a little confusing, the 1991 Act amended the 1990 Act. Therefore, the reforms came into force in 1991 on the basis of a statute of 1990.
5. By injunction against failure to comply.
6. Provides power to do anything that will facilitate the discharge of their functions.
7. See DOE Circular 11/95, *The use of conditions in planning permission.*
8. Introduced by Section 12 of the Planning and Compensation Act 1991.

local authority periodically or at one time. (This was the first statutory recognition that an obligation may include an undertaking to make a financial payment, although the practice had existed since the 1970s). There is no specific requirement within the Act that payments relate to the land itself or to the development that is the subject of the planning obligation.

- The introduction of powers to modify or discharge a planning obligation. Following a period of five years from the date the obligation is entered into, an application can be made to the local planning authority on the grounds that the planning obligation no longer serves a useful planning purpose or should be modified in some way. The right of appeal to the Secretary of State is available in the event of the local authority either failing to determine the application or deciding that the planning obligation should not be modified or discharged.[9]

- The introduction of new government policy guidance in Circular 16/91, which cancelled the previous Circular 22/83. This guidance incorporated the 1991 reforms providing policy advice on what constituted an acceptable obligation. The previously established "tests" in 22/83 of what are reasonable were incorporated into the new guidance, principally that the extent of what is required is fairly and reasonably related in scale and kind to the proposed development (which would cover the functional geographical and financial elements of the proposed benefit). The new Circular stated for the first time that a planning obligation could be used to "secure the implementation of local plan policies for a particular area or type of development" (e.g. the inclusion of an element of affordable housing in a larger residential development).[10] This additional guidance, coupled with the plan-led system also introduced by the Planning and Compensation Act 1991,[11] provided a strong incentive for local planning authorities to seek obligations in local plan policies. Research undertaken by Oxford Brookes University indicated that the reaction of consultants to this new guidance demonstrated concern over the possible inclusion of "shopping lists" of obligations; however, they did expect that Inspectors at local plan Inquiry would give greater scrutiny to such policy (Stubbs & Cripps 1993). In spite of the greater attention given to the inclusion of planning policies dealing with obligations, the new guidance was similar to the old and did little to create a radical shake-up of the system.

The reforms were designed to overcome certain procedural inadequacies of the previous system. The unilateral undertaking allowed the developer to act independently of the local authority in offering to enter into an obligation at appeal (see Case Study 5.5). This would be binding upon that developer and any successors in title. Under the old system, an Inspector could

---

9. Section 106A and 106B of 1990 Act.
10. Paragraph B8 (4) of DOE Circular 16/91, *Planning and compensation act: planning obligations*.
11. Section 54A of the 1990 Act: see the section on "The decision-maker's duty".

Case study 5.5

Proposal
Megabuild Limited proposes a new retail warehouse development on a site identified in the local plan for residential use. The eastern boundary of the site adjoins existing residential development and Megabuild offers additional tree planting on this side and will also pay for double glazing for these properties.

Tests (see Table 5.1)
It is considered that the proposed obligation would be needed to overcome a potential loss of amenity caused by delivery vehicles manoeuvring alongside this boundary. This would satisfy test 1 and would be functionally related. However, the principle of development is unacceptable to the local authority because the retail warehouse use is contrary to local plan policy. The offer of an obligation is rejected and the application is refused because:
    (a) it results in a loss of amenity to residents
    (b) is contrary to policy.

Conclusions
If Megabuild goes to appeal, it can offer a unilateral undertaking to "target" reason (a) and thereby concentrate its case on fighting reason (b).

---

consider the matter at Inquiry only if both parties had agreed to its provisions. The unilateral undertaking represents an important tactical benefit to the developer. If an application goes to appeal, then such a unilateral offer can be used to target specific objections to the scheme, such as the improvement to the neighbouring highway to overcome the impact on traffic generation from a proposed development. The introduction of unilateral undertakings will not render the planning agreement redundant, as in some instances the developer will require the local authority to do certain things, for instance, to use the money they provide to undertake certain works. A planning agreement provides a legally enforceable contract in circumstances in which both sides are required to perform certain duties as a consequence of the planning obligation.

Modification or discharge allows the lifting of obsolete obligations. Under the old system, such a result could be obtained only by application to the Lands Tribunal,[12] who could only consider if the matter was obsolete in legal terms and not on planning grounds. For example, a planning obligation may be agreed that provides for the construction of a community centre within a new residential development, as well as an access road across the site. In future, a new highway could be constructed along the eastern boundary of the site providing a road frontage to the centre. The original access road will no longer be required and its future maintenance will not serve the original planning purpose provided for in the agreement, and the planning obligation should therefore be discharged.

---

12. Under provision of Section 84 of the Law of Property Act 1925.

Examples of planning obligations

To establish what is a reasonable planning obligation, reference should be made to Circular guidance in the first instance. Satisfying one of the tests numbered 1–5 and number 6 would result in an acceptable proposal (Table 5.1).

In practice these tests are open to considerable interpretation. How far away does a highway improvement such as a new roundabout have to be before it

Table 5.1   The tests of a planning obligation.

16/91	Test	Example
1	Needed to allow development to proceed [i.e. planning permission would otherwise be refused]. AND	Provision of access road or sewerage.
2	If a financial payment, will it contribute to such facilities. OR	Cash payment towards access road or new sewer is used to implement those works.
3	So directly related that the application ought not to be permitted without it. [*Overcomes some form of planning objection*]. OR	Providing carparking, open space or double glazing to neighbouring occupiers affected by new use.
4	In mixed development will the proposal secure an acceptable balance of uses.	In a new settlement this provision could be used to provide a mix of homes for rent alongside owner occupation.
5	OR Offsets the loss of or impact on any amenity present on the site prior to development.	A proposal result in the loss of an existing community use (social club or sports field) and the obligation provides for a similar use/building on neighbouring land owned by the developer.
6	AND IN ALL CASES Is the extent of what is required fairly and reasonably related in scale and kind to proposed development.	

becomes either geographically or functionally unrelated to the development in question (see Case Study 5.6)?

Planning obligations have been classified as land-use/amenity related gains and social/economic related gains (Debenham Tewson Research 1988). Certainly, in the latter category it is harder to satisfy all the tests of reasonableness, and such provision of social and economic infrastructure within planning obligations tends to produce greater controversy and provides critics of the system with an easy target. However, it must be remembered that the ground rules established by the Circular are rigid. The starting point should be that an obligation is required only to overcome some legitimate planning objection to a proposal. Yet, the British system in general and the planning obligations system in particular, are based upon negotiation and bargaining. If a developer wishes to offer land or financial payment towards social and economic infrastructure beyond the strict requirement of the consent, then that is the prerogative of the developer. This may be viewed as "buying planning permission" on one hand or as an acceptance of the need towards betterment in society. Either way, it does not make the obligation illegal within the rules of the system.

The lack of detailed guidance by government will result in difficulty in interpreting the tests. The system has been described as "fuzzy" (Lichfield 1989). It will continue to be fuzzy for so long as the government maintains such policy guidance, which is based upon the application of "tests" to the vast array of suggested planning obligations that arise from consideration of planning applications.

These examples are used to illustrate important interpretations of Circular advice. A planning obligation is often the result of negotiation between both parties and not an offer made by one side. The application of the tests of reasonableness is an important material consideration in the assessment of any planning obligation. Several judicial pronouncements on this issue provide an important interpretation of planning legislation. In *Newbury District Council* vs *Secretary*

Case study 5.6

Proposal
Barcode Developers proposed to build a new food superstore. The local planning authority required several highway improvements around the application site, including new roundabouts, new traffic signals and upgrading of several roads. These works had been required for many years. Since traffic generation has been steadily rising from an adjoining business park, opened three years before, highway improvements had become a matter of urgency. The local planning authority argued that the new works were necessary because their scheme represented the "last straw to break the camel's back". The developers considered this unacceptable, arguing that they were being required to solve problems of traffic generation produced by other sites.

Tests (see Table 5.1)
An unreasonable pursuit of an obligation by the LPA as they are seeking to penalize one developer for traffic generation resulting from other sites. This is not fairly and reasonably related to the development to be permitted. In *Safeway Properties Limited* vs *Secretary of State* (1990),† the Court of Appeal considered such highway improvements in the general locality to be unrelated to the building of a new superstore proposed.

Conclusions
Although some highway improvements may be required to cope with the new superstore, it is unreasonable to request that this scheme shoulders the burden of previous developments. Although this obligation may pass test 1, it certainly fails tests 3 and 6. This is an example of land-use gain that is substantially unrelated in functional terms with the development and, as such, unreasonable. If the gain was more directly linked – perhaps one new roundabout opposite the application site - then it could be seen as being both reasonable and related. Traffic generation resulting from this scheme constitutes a material planning consideration and the local planning authority could refuse planning permission on this basis. However, it is unreasonable for gain to be sought (dealing with highway matter or otherwise) on the grounds that this would remedy problems (land use or social) not related to the application site.

† For a detailed report see *Journal of Planning and Environment Law*, October 1991, pp. 966–73.

---

of State for the Environment (1981),[13] the Court of Appeal said that any planning obligation should serve a planning purpose, related to the development and not be unreasonable (to the extent that no reasonable planning authority could have imposed it). In *Regina* vs *Plymouth City Council and others ex parte Plymouth and South Devon Co-operative Society Limited* (1993),[14] the Court of Appeal, in supporting a previous decision by the High Court, cast doubt on the role of the "tests" as a legal guideline. The legal test was the one stated in Newbury, the tests themselves only represented government policy and not statute. They must always be viewed in this context. The contention that planning obligations amount to the "sale of a planning permission" was considered in *Regina* vs *South Northamptonshire District Council* ex parte *Crest Homes* (1994). The LPA was seeking to finance infrastructure provision in the absence of sufficient public funding to achieve this. The Court of Appeal held that, in this case, such a policy was lawful. Particular emphasis was laid on the fact that the LPA had identified specific infrastructure projects and sought to distribute the infrastructure cost equitably among a consortium of developers and landowners in the area.

In *Tesco Stores Limited* vs *Secretary of State for the Environment*[15] (11 May 1995), the House of Lords upheld the Secretary of State's decision to grant planning permission to Sainsbury for a site in Witney, Oxfordshire (where Tesco were also promoting a superstore site). In so doing, the Secretary of State had overturned the decision of the Inspector hearing the original appeals, who had recommended in favour of the Tesco proposal, which included the offer of a £6.6 million contribution to highway works for their store. It was held, following an appeal by Tesco, that their proposed planning obligation had been taken into account, quite properly, by the Secretary of State and that it was within his discretion, and not a matter for the Courts, to accord it whatever weight he considered appropriate (apparently whether or not it was disproportionate to the development proposed).

This decision may cast further doubt on the value of Circular guidance in interpreting what is, and what is not, a reasonable offer of planning gain. The Court seems to seek to rely on a simpler, yet broader and more vague, test: that the proposed planning obligation constitutes a material consideration, that it is entirely within the decision-making body's discretion to weigh in the overall evaluation of an application. This would throw a very wide net indeed. It is clear that, with such large sums of money involved, litigation in this area of planning law will continue and the outcome of such litigation may be a need to review government guidance and to update or repeal and replace Circular 16/91.

We may go on to consider the wider philosophical issues surrounding this system in the knowledge that interpretation of the Circular's rules is a matter left to local planning authorities and developers, and the rules themselves are by no

---

13. [1988] AC578.
14. [1993] EGCS 113.
15. [1995] 1 WLR 759, [1995] AUER 636.

> ## Summary: planning obligations – key characteristics
> - Section 106 of the TCPA 1990 provides legal powers to enter into planning obligations.
> - The 1991 reforms to the system introduced the new term "planning obligation" to cover both agreements between the LPA and the developer/applicant, and unilateral undertakings offered only by the developer/applicant, as well as the power to discharge or modify an obligation.
> - Cash payments are detailed as permissible in the 1991 Statute.
> - New Circular guidance issued at this time reflected the stance of previous guidance.
> - These reforms did not result in a radical restructuring of the system but more an attempt to amend certain procedural tools or mechanisms.

means clear cut.

The philosophical issues

For some "planning gain" was a legitimate contribution from developers to community development but it has been viewed by others as both an unconstitutional tax and a form of negotiated bribery corrupting the planning system. (Healey et al. 1993)

The practice of developers offering a variety of benefits to local authorities has resulted in many emotive, if easy to remember, phrases, such as "planning blackmail", or "cheque book planning". Such a response to the system tends to ignore the more significant issue of whether or not a developer should pay something back to the community after taking profits from a development that will inevitably have some impact on the locality. The question for debate should be whether a developer should pay anything towards alleviating the impact of a development and then in what form should this charge be levied? Although these points are being considered, it should also be remembered that the planning obligation gives the developer a legal mechanism within which planning objections may be overcome, therefore improving the chances of gaining permission.

Historical background

In considering such issues, it is important to recall the historical development of the British planning system. The TCPA of 1947 nationalized the right to develop land. The ability to build or change the use of a building became a decision for society to exercise by means of the decisions of local planning authorities. However, land with planning permission would, in a country with limited land resources, carry a premium. The planning system introduced a new control mechanism, which meant that obtaining planning permission would both enhance the value of land and increase the value of adjoining land that benefits from the "amenity" created by development. These benefits introduced by the planning system or indeed any other activities of government are referred to as betterment.

The 1947 Act was based upon the key philosophical position that, alongside the nationalization of the right to develop land, any future increases in the value of land following the granting of planning permission should be the property of the state (Ward 1994: 108). The new legislation introduced by the Labour administration resulted in a 100 per cent tax on betterment (i.e. all of the increased value of land resulting from gaining planning permission would be taxed). This has been described as a contradiction at the heart of the Act (ibid.), because private ownership of land would be maintained, yet any increases resulting from the speculative grant of planning permission would be taxed, thereby killing off a good deal of private sector activity by attacking the profit motive. Not surprisingly, this proposal was unpopular and the incoming Conservative administration of 1951 soon announced their intention to end it. The Planning Act of 1953 abolished the development charge without introducing any alternative tax measure to collect betterment.

A betterment tax was not to return until the late 1960s with the Land Commission Act 1967. This time a levy of betterment at 40 per cent was introduced. A new agency, the Land Commission, would oversee the system. The new 1970 Conservative government abolished the Land Commission after one year in office. The final betterment tax came with the Development Land Tax Act 1976, which introduced a new tax on land value increases, initially set at 80 per cent of betterment, with the intention that it would eventually rise to 100 per cent. However, this Development Land Tax suffered from a poor level of implementation hampered by a serious property recession in the mid-1970s. This, then, represented the third post-war attempt at betterment and it was itself abolished in 1986.

To assess the role of the planning gain/obligations system properly, we must view developer contributions as either a modern form of betterment, or instead as a legitimate development cost.

Betterment tax?

Planning gain/obligation represents indirect betterment tax in that it imposes a charge on development proposals. The actual cost of developer contributions will vary dramatically across the country and across development proposals. The measure of tax will crudely depend upon the size of a development proposal – the larger the proposal the greater the impact and the greater proportion of gain required. It is unlikely that planning authorities undertake detailed economic appraisals of development proposals and then "top slice" a percentage towards community "goodies" in the form of obligations. Most planners lack any professional training in such matters, and little liaison is made with valuation officers employed within the local authority. It is largely a myth that planning authorities operate in this way, although it would be foolish to state that in large development proposals there is no expectation among planners and planning committees that some cash or contribution in kind will be forthcoming from the developer.

A betterment tax imposes a set of uniform criteria to be applied nationally and consistently. An obligation does not work in this way and the ultimate outcome reflected in cash terms will depend upon the merits of the case and the negotiation and bargaining between the two parties, influenced by government Circular advice. Planning gain/obligation may be viewed as at best a crude form of land taxation. It is not a continuation of betterment as introduced in 1947, 1967 and 1976, but in the absence of any other form of levy or development land tax it becomes associated with this subject.

Development cost?

The idea that developer contribution is based on the view that the planning obligation system represents a legitimate cost to a developer, who must accept that all development has some impact on the environment and that some level of contribution should be made towards either controlling or alleviating this impact. Such an impact may be physical (roads, landscaping, drainage, sewerage measures) or social (provision of social housing, community uses, access to open space or recreation facility). Government Circular advice is more aligned with this view than the betterment concept, in that it establishes guidelines for acceptable practice based upon functionally and geographically related criteria applied to each case.

It seems reasonable that the developer should make some form of contribution to the impact of a development proposal. In some ways the current system, when correctly applied, permits a developer to overcome matters that would otherwise result in refusal of permission. The problem that we return to is that the lack of clear definition and the application of vague government Circular advice means that, although obligations lean towards a development cost, they are a legitimate cost only if they are correctly applied.

To determine fully the extent to which legitimate obligations have been pursued by local authorities or indeed developers, reference should be made to research on this topic. Before the 1968 reforms, little real use was made of such legal agreements. It has been estimated that between 1932 and 1967 only some 500 such agreements were made. A dramatic increase followed over the next few years. A survey of 106 English planning authorities revealed that more than 50 per cent admitted seeking some form of planning gain (Jowell 1977). Research into the use of planning agreements by district councils (MacDonald 1991) revealed that around 70 per cent of all respondents were intending to include planning obligation policies in emerging local plans to strengthen their stance in negotiation with developers. The most comprehensive survey in recent years was published in 1992 (DoE 1992a). The survey findings of a sample of local authorities taken between 1987 and 1990 discovered that on average only 0.5 per cent of all planning applications were accompanied by a planning agreement. This could be projected to an annual total in England and Wales of between 6500 and 8000 agreements and in Scotland of between 300 and 350. Significantly, the research concluded that local authorities generally adhered to policy guidance set out in government Circular advice and that only 12 per cent of all agreements in the survey contained provisions dealing with financial payments, most notably related to infrastructure provision. Only a small proportion of obligations related to matters that involved the provision of wider benefits not considered to be necessary to the grant of planning permission. One other significant issue raised by the research was the time taken to grant planning permission when an agreement was involved. In 80 per cent of such applications it took around one year to seal the legal agreement.

In 1993, research commissioned by the Joseph Rowntree Foundation (Healey et al. 1993) examined a total of 206 legal agreements signed between 1984 and 1991.

The final recommendations stated that "The challenge for policy-makers concerned with planning agreements is to identify roles which enable market opportunities and transactions to develop efficiently while safeguarding legitimate environmental and community concerns."

In its general support for the system, it recommended, inter alia, that social economic and environmental impacts should be considered as legitimate obligations.

Conclusions

The system whereby developers contribute towards social and physical infrastructures in return for obtaining planning permission has remained largely unaltered since 1968. In spite of some important procedural changes introduced in 1991, the system is based on negotiation between developers and LPAs with, since 1983, some broad policy guidance issued by the government. Nothing is specifically prescribed as either acceptable or unacceptable, and the application of government guidelines or tests may result in considerable uncertainty as to what is acceptable. Developers may feel that they have little choice but to comply with LPA demands for benefits, as to pursue the matter at appeal has no guarantee of success. Yet, within this somewhat imperfect system and in the absence of any formal betterment taxation, it would appear that both sides in the development process have made the system work in practice. Research in the early 1990s has indicated that the tests are generally followed by the LPA and in the majority of cases the obligations were required to facilitate the grant of planning permission. As long as the system operates on this level, then it is clearly a legal mechanism by which a developer can rectify the physical and sometimes social impact of the proposal. In this respect it is clearly a development cost. The problem occurs when the system is used as a means by which LPAs can extract *wider* social benefits. Although research in the early 1990s has demonstrated that this is not the case in the vast majority of proposals, when it does occur it creates frustration and fuels the misconceptions of "planning blackmail". Further, as the system is

105

currently constructed, there is no effective braking mechanism that could prevent this occurring in future years. By taking the matter to appeal (usually against non-determination) to expose the unreasonable pursuit of an obligation, the developer risks a great deal.

Several alternatives have been proposed: for instance, the American model of impact fees (Grant 1993, 1995b) or the concept of a community benefit (Lichfield 1989). In America a standard fee is payable according to the type and size of a development proposal, which contributes towards a public schedule of a proposed infrastructure. Such a system has an element of openness and certainty within which the developer can clearly calculate the expected contribution before an application is submitted. However, it is difficult to standardize all development types into a shopping list of contributions, as development projects and their impacts are variable and prove difficult to measure uniformly. Such a system inevitably involves greater bureaucracy than currently exists.

A community benefits system would represent a reformulation of the current system, whereby each development application would be subject to a valuation appraisal, agreed by both sides, and a community benefit either on site or off site, but related to the use and development of the land, would be calculated to determine what would be affordable. This would give greater formality to the role of economic appraisal within the system and it attempts to create a refined version of a betterment tax. Its association with betterment makes such a proposal unpalatable to any Conservative government.

It appears to be unlikely that the post-1991 system of planning obligation will be the subject of a major overhaul during the 1990s. The system has been made to work. Indeed, the number of obligations is likely to increase during the decade as local government's own funding becomes increasingly squeezed by fiscal restrictions on public sector expenditure. Such trends are not exclusive to Britain. In Australia, for example, both state and local government bodies have, since the late 1980s, increasingly sought contributions from developers towards both physical and social infrastructures. It may be perceived as representing planning blackmail, but this view is not based on evidence of its operation in practice but instead, in a minority of cases, the perception of perhaps being on the receiving end of bad practice. In the current system, planning obligations represent a means of extracting development contributions to lessen the impact of planning applications. It is not a formalized form of betterment and as such represents a hidden form of taxation. The post-1991 system provides a framework within which the impacts of planning permission can be controlled. The cost is therefore concealed within a planning framework. It may be convenient for governments to keep it concealed, instead of adopting a system such as impact fees, which applies additional and formal taxation to potential developments, instead of the British system, which leaves the matter to local negotiation subject to the merits of the case.

In December 1995 the DoE issued a consultation paper on planning obligations together with a draft revision of circular 16/91.[16] The draft circular in attempting to clarify guidelines on the general policy dealing with this subject, stated that

Summary: planning obligations	
Benefits/advantages	Problems/disadvantages
Legal mechanism to lessen the impact of a development proposal or overcome a reason for refusal of planning permission. AND A means of making the developer pay towards impact.	This legal mechanism (Section 106) is subject to policy guidance (tests) requiring an obligation to be related to the proposal, resulting in interpretation over what is acceptable or unacceptable behaviour.
DoE research (1992) indicates "tests" are being correctly applied	Some of the "tests" are so broad that compliance with them would not always infer good practice.
A legitimate development cost.	A crude form of betterment tax.

planning obligations should only be sought where they are necessary to make a proposal acceptable in land-use planning terms. Such planning obligations while relating to land, roads or buildings must share a direct relationship with the planning permission to which they are attached. In helping to determine what constitutes a reasonable planning obligation the DoE proposed that account is taken of the following:

- what is required or offered is needed to enable the development to go ahead.
- Any financial payment will meet or contribute towards the cost of any necessary facility
- That the development ought not to be permitted because the planning obligation is so directly related to the proposed development.

This new guidance is expected to replace 16/91 sometime during 1996. While it would appear that the DoE are seeking to move away from the formal creation of "tests of reasonableness" (see Table 5.1), the first three tests survive in the new guidance as broad principles of what may constitute reasonable benefits arising from planning obligations.

---

16. Department of the Environment, Development Control Policy Division, issued 15 December 1995. Also see Planning, 19 January 1996 pages 8–9 for a commentary on the revised circular guidance.

PART THREE

Urban planning issues

CHAPTER SIX
Specialist town planning controls

"Specialist planning controls" provides an umbrella term under which we can examine topics dealing with the preservation of the built and natural environment. In urban areas in particular, listed building and conservation area controls seek to protect historic and architecturally significant buildings and areas, whereas urban design seeks to improve the quality of urban fabric when those areas are developed. In rural locations those considerations also apply, but many additional controls seek to ensure the protection of the natural environment for its beauty (i.e. National Parks, Areas of Outstanding Natural Beauty or National Scenic Areas) for its flora and fauna (i.e. Sites of Special Scientific Interest, Environmentally Sensitive Areas and Nature Reserves) and for its recreational value to Britain's mostly urban-based population (i.e. Country Parks and an objective of National Parks designation). Other environmental controls applicable to both urban and rural locations are Ancient Monuments, Archaeological Areas and Tree Preservation Orders. Green belt designation applies a multi-faceted approach, seeking to influence land-use issues applicable to both urban areas and rural areas located on the urban fringe (see Table 6.8 for a summary of these policies). This chapter will deal with each of these topics and will be organized as follows:
- Listed Buildings
- Conservation Areas
- design control
- green belts
- countryside planning

Listed Buildings

A building or group of buildings considered of special architectural and historic interest, which are included in a list compiled by the Secretary of State for National Heritage and protected from demolition, alteration or extension without obtaining Listed Building Consent from the local planning authority.[1]

Procedure for listing

The list is compiled by the Secretary of State for National Heritage (or respective Secretaries of State for Scotland or Wales) on the recommendation of:

- His own Inspectors, who will undertake a survey of buildings. They may act upon the recommendations of local authorities or members of the public (a procedure referred to as "spot listing").[2]
- English Heritage (The Historic Buildings and Monuments Commission), whose recommendation may be accepted with or without modification. English Heritage was created in 1983 to secure the preservation of all listed buildings in England. As a part of their role, they also provide specialist advice, acquire and manage a limited number of buildings and co-ordinate grant aid to secure the preservation of listed buildings, conservation areas and the public's enjoyment of such heritage. English Heritage undertakes periodic surveys to update the lists. A second survey was undertaken in the late 1980s to increase the proportion of Victorian and Edwardian buildings on the list and in the early 1990s to consider the listing of post-war buildings. Since 1970 the work of these re-surveys has increased the number of listed buildings fourfold to an estimated total of 500000. The equivalent bodies in Scotland (Historic Scotland) and Wales (CADW) make recommendations to the Scottish and Welsh Secretaries, respectively.

The survey of a building, and consideration of its merits for listing, may be undertaken without notice to the occupier or owner, to avoid any demolition prior to listing. In 1980 the Firestone Building, an Art Deco 1930s factory, was demolished during the weekend prior to its listing coming into effect. To avoid further recurrence of this, powers were introduced to allow the service of a Building Preservation Notice to prevent demolition, alteration or a extension of a building without consent for a period of six months while the building is considered for listing. The owner or developer may seek a certificate that a building is not intended to be listed (a Certificate of Immunity) to avoid any uncertainty regarding its future potential for development. This immunity certificate, if granted, lasts for five years, after which the building may be considered afresh for listing. Such a certificate was issued against the former Bankside Power Station on the South Bank of the River Thames in London in 1994. This allowed the owners of the site, Nuclear Electric, to market the building for sale and redevelopment without the possibility of listing until 1999. A building preservation notice cannot be served if a certificate of immunity is in existence.

---

1. Legislative provision can be found in Section 1 (1) of the Planning (Listed Buildings and Conservation Areas) Act 1990. In Scotland refer to the Town & Country Planning (Scotland) Act 1972.
2. In recent years the number of buildings listed annually has been falling, while those listed following a recommendation to spot list has increased dramatically reaching a peak of 37 per cent in 1990. See *Estates Gazette* (22 February 1992). Around 3000 requests to spot list are received every year by English Heritage.

What kinds of buildings are listed?

Specific groups may be identified in terms of listing:
- All buildings prior to 1700 that survive in anything like their original condition.
- Most buildings erected between 1700 and 1840.
- Buildings erected between 1840 and 1914 of definite quality and character, for example, the principal works of important architects, or those exhibiting particular design quality or workmanship employed in the building's construction and ultimate external or internal appearance.
- Buildings of high quality, erected between 1914 and 1939, for example, Hoover Building, Perivale, London, which has an Art Deco Facade on a 1930s factory, and Battersea Power Station (a unique power station in the middle of London). These buildings represent examples of high-quality design during the inter-war period.
- Post-war to present day: only outstanding buildings. This criterion applies to buildings more than 30 years old and if under threat of alteration/demolition, and, in exceptional cases, buildings as recent as 10 years old may be considered for listing. The first building to be listed under the 30-year rule was Bracken House in the City of London (former home of the Financial Times newspaper and designed by Sir Albert Richardson), built 1956–9 and listed in 1991.

Table 6.1 gives further examples.

What is listed?

Once a building is listed, then Listed Building Consent (LBC) is required for any works that would result in its demolition, alteration or extension in any manner likely to affect its character as a building of special architectural or historic interest. The need for planning permission is entirely separate from Listed Building Consent and, in practice, LBC extends far beyond what would require planning permission, because it deals with "any matter" affecting the character of the listed building. The building itself is protected and this includes both internal and external fabric; for example, a period plaster ceiling or a particular type of mortar used between brickwork may be considered to be of historic or architectural importance, and works to them will affect the character of the building and therefore require LBC. General cleaning works would not require LBC, whereas painting (in a different colour) probably would require consent. Any object or structure fixed to the building that is either external (e.g. guttering downpipes) or internal (e.g. wall panelling) is also protected, as is any object or structure within the curtilage and forming a part of the land since before 1 July 1948; that is, any outbuilding (garden house, statutes, gazebos) will be listed only if it was constructed before 1948.

Table 6.1 Examples of listed buildings.

	Building	Reasons
Prior to 1700	Hampton Court	1515 begun by Cardinal Wolsey and later enlarged by Henry VIII in 1531 using Renaissance architects.
1700–1840	Radcliffe Camera, Oxford. Part of the Bodleian Library, University of Oxford	1739–49 by James Gibbs. A unique building in England with a circular form and strong Italian influence in its design.
1840–1914	Midland Hotel, St Pancras railway station, London	1868–74, Victorian neo-Gothic architecture, by Sir George Gilbert Scott.
1914–1939	Penguin Pool at London Zoo	1934–38 by Berthold Lubetkin with a novel use of moulded reinforced concrete to create curved shapes.
	Red telephone box (Kiosk No 2 or K2)	1925. Design by Sir Giles Gilbert Scott. The wooden prototype is outside Burlington House, Piccadilly, London.
1945 + 30-year rule	Bracken House, City of London	Highly decorative facade. Built 1956–9.
10-year rule	Wills Faber office building	Excellent example of a modern office building with external appearance strongly influenced by lighting technology. Built 1975 and listed in April 1991 following proposals to alter the interior to construct a swimming pool within the interior.

Grading of buildings

A grading system applies, which does not affect the level of statutory protection but does indicate the importance of the building. Three grades exist, as shown in Table 6.2:[3]

Once it has been determined that a building is listed and that the proposed works affect the character of that building, then it is necessary to apply to the LPA for Listed Building Consent. Although many churches are themselves included as listed, listed building controls do not apply to works for the demolition, alteration

Table 6.2 Listed Building grades.

Grade I	of exceptional interest (around 6000 buildings or, in England, 1.4 per cent).
Grade II* (referred to as "two star")	of particular importance more than special interest (around 18000 buildings or 4.1 per cent in England).
Grade II	of special interest (around 417000 buildings or 94.5 per cent in England). In Scotland 37000 buildings are listed within a different classification of A, B and C. In Wales around 14500 buildings are listed and classified in the same manner as in England.

3. A fourth grade of "local interest" identified by the LPA but not the Secretary of State is now obsolete and carries no statutory significance.

or extension of an ecclesiastical building that is currently used for ecclesiastical purposes. This would cover the place of worship and not any building used by a minister of religion for residence.

The LPA may grant Listed Building Consent, subject to conditions, or refuse it. The LPA must notify English Heritage (or CADW, Historic Scotland) of all applications dealing with Grade I and Grade II* Buildings and whose consent must be obtained before Listed Building Consent can be granted for these buildings. Every year English Heritage processes around 6500 such consultations. If an application involves the partial or complete demolition of a listed building, then the LPA must notify six national amenity societies who each have a specific concern regarding various periods of architecture or historic interest.[4] Refusal or failure to reach a decision within eight weeks carries with it the right of appeal to the Secretary of State.[5] All these listed building matters are considered separately from applications for planning permission. It is a common occurrence that many development proposals involve both listed building and planning proposals, this will require separate applications and decisions.

Consider the following example. A brewery owns adjoining listed buildings: one is a public house, the other a retail shop. It proposes using the shop as a part of the public house and removing a party wall to connect the two buildings. The change of use requires planning permission and the removal of an internal wall requires Listed Building Consent. Each application would be considered separately with a separate decision issued. It is possible for either one to be granted and the other refused.

Other Listed Building powers

Unauthorized works
It is a criminal offence to carry out unauthorized works to a Listed Building. Therefore, the LPA may prosecute under criminal law, or it can issue an enforcement notice[6] seeking restoration of the building to its former state or other works as deemed necessary. A Listed Building Enforcement Notice carries a right of appeal.

Buildings falling into disrepair
If a building has been neglected, the LPA may undertake the necessary repair works and recover their costs from the owner, or serve a Repair's Notice, which

---

4. The six are The Ancient Monuments Society, The Council for British Archaeology, The Georgian Group, The Victorian Society, The Society for the Protection of Ancient Buildings, and The Twentieth Century Society.
5. Such an appeal may be lodged on the grounds that the building is not of special interest and should be removed from the list. In deciding upon such an appeal, the Secretary of State or Inspector may find that it should remain on or be removed from the list.
6. Served under Section 38 of the Planning (Listed Buildings and Conservation Areas) Act 1990.

requires the owner to undertake such remedial works. If this request is ignored, then, after two months, the LPA may acquire the building by compulsory purchase.[7] No right of appeal is available against a repair's notice. These powers are used only rarely. It has been estimated that, between 1984 and 1990, only 300 such notices were served in England, resulting in 40 compulsory acquisitions. Such powers of repairs notice and compulsory purchase are also available to the Secretary of State and were used in 1992 to acquire the Grade I St Ann's Hotel in The Crescent, Buxton, Derbyshire.

Case study 6.1: Repairs notice and compulsory purchase – St Ann's Hotel, Buxton, Derbyshire

The hotel was built at the end of the eighteenth century as a principal attraction in the Duke of Devonshire's attempt to make Buxton a spa town to rival Bath. The Hotel's fabric was neglected during the 1970s and 1980s, ending with its forced closure on environmental grounds in 1989.

In 1992 the Secretary of State, in consultation with High Peak District Council and English Heritage, served a repairs notice, followed by the compulsory acquisition of the property and works of repair and restoration. At the time there was some speculation among property professionals that this case heralded a new interventionist stance by the Department of National Heritage, and willingness to serve notices/acquire listed properties that had fallen into neglect and involved repairs that the LPA on its own could not afford to pay. Such speculation was unfounded and, since 1992, the Secretary of State has used these powers in only a handful of other extreme cases. If they were to be more widely used, then the Department for National Heritage or English Heritage budget would need to be greatly increased.

Listed Buildings and the development process

When a building is listed, it has consequences for the owner or developer. Listed Building Consent is required for the alteration, extension or demolition, covering both internal and external fabric. This control is in addition to planning permission and may be perceived as either an additional bureaucratic burden or important control over the nation's built heritage. Decisions on Listed Building Control involve detailed architectural and historic appraisals and decision-making on applications takes longer than for most planning applications. Government policy establishes a presumption that listed buildings should be preserved. It is highly unlikely that Listed Building Consent will be granted for demolition (see Case Study 6.2 on the Mappin & Webb site). Development potential can be restricted with greater attention required to design and materials used, resulting in higher costs. Grants are available from English Heritage for restoration and repair. Around £30 million is available in grant aid every financial year. However, no legal duty exists whereby the owner must keep the building in good repair.

---

7. Requires the consent of the Secretary of State for National Heritage.

115

Case study 6.2: Demolition of listed buildings: the Mappin & Webb Site, No. 1 Poultry in the City of London

The site comprised a group of eight Grade II listed buildings located within the Bank of England Conservation Area in the ancient heart of the City. The buildings were listed between 1970 and 1975, but towards the end of that decade the upper storeys, previously used for small offices, became vacant. Such small office suites were no longer required in the City of London, and the site's owner, Lord Palumbo, sought to redevelop it for modern office floorspace. Lord Palumbo's first proposal, in 1985, involved demolition of all the buildings and their replacement by a 90m high tower designed by the modern architect Mies Van der Rohe. The Planning Authority, the Corporation of London, refused Listed Building Consent, and planning permission and subsequent appeals were dismissed.

In 1986 a second proposal was submitted, by the architect Sir James Stirling. This also incorporated demolition of the existing buildings, but replacement with a modern building of similar bulk. Again, Listed Building Consent and planning permission were refused, but the Secretary of State granted a subsequent appeal. Save Britain's Heritage (SAVE) a heritage pressure group and third party at the appeal challenged the decision in the Courts. The matter was finally considered by the House of Lords† in 1991, five years after the submission of the original planning application. The key legal issue was whether the Secretary of State was entitled to permit demolition, contrary to his own policy in Circular guidance, in which a presumption was established in favour of the preservation of a listed building. The Inspector's decision letter, accepted and supported by the Secretary of State, concluded that the Stirling scheme was an "architectural masterpiece" and that this was considered sufficient to override that presumption. Their Lordships accepted that the Secretary of State was entitled to take this view on the merits of the case, although this did not establish that in future the demolition of all listed buildings would be permitted in the event of the replacement being considered to be of greater architectural merit.

The presumption remained intact if perhaps a little "dented" by this outcome. The appeal decision, supported by legal judgment, illustrates the wide discretion in decision-making within the British system to permit the demolition of a listed building in certain cases.

†Save Britain's Heritage vs No. 1 Poultry Ltd and the Secretary of State [1991] 1 WLR 153, The Times (1 March), Estates Gazette (Case Summary 24), Chartered Surveyor Weekly (28 March).

Repairs notices and compulsory purchase are available to Secretary of State or LPA, as well as enforcement powers and criminal proceedings against owners who have undertaken unauthorized works. The fact that a building is listed may enhance its value because of the *caché* of period features or reduce the value as many institutional investors perceive such buildings as resulting in higher costs and poorer returns compared to unlisted ones. Maintenance work to residential listed buildings is exempt from value added tax (VAT). However, research by the Investment Property Databank has shown that listed commercial buildings have resulted in an investment return comparable to unlisted ones (Scanlon et al. 1994). Some institutional investors seek a series of building standards such as special floor loading capacities, which most historic properties cannot satisfy. Research has suggested that the fall in value associated with listing is a one-time cost, normally imposed at the time of listing, and such a fall is highest in small buildings (presumably suitable for conversion to other uses) in areas of high development pressure but outside conservation areas (RICS & English Heritage 1993).

Case study 6.3: the Hoover Factory, Perivale, West London

The Hoover Building was built in 1932 and formed part of a complex of several buildings comprising factory, offices, staff club and canteen, commissioned by Hoover for its British headquarters and designed by the architectural practice of Wallace Gilbert and Partners. The frontage building incorporated into the Art Deco style of the 1930s Gilbert's love for Egyptian decoration, to create a spectacular façade. The factory buildings were hidden behind this elaborate façade.

Hoover vacated the building in 1980, and in 1985 the frontage buildings were listed as Grade II* which resulted in the automatic listing of all the factory buildings (either attached to the frontage or within the curtilage and built before 1948). The buildings remained vacant until 1990, when the entire site was acquired by Tesco Stores Limited, with a view to some form of superstore development.

The London Borough of Ealing, in consultation with English Heritage, granted a series of listed building consents and planning permissions, following a change in their own policies that had previously resisted a loss of industrial employment uses on this site. The Tesco scheme involved demolition of rearward factory buildings and construction of a new 41500ft^2 superstore, together with extensive refurbishment and restoration to the frontage buildings. Work was completed during late 1992.

By permitting the new superstore, this outstanding landmark listed building could be returned to the glory of its original 1930s architectural splendour.

Listed Building control and future directions

In 1970 120000 buildings were listed. By the mid-1990s the figure had increased to 440000 listed structures in England (about 1 in every 40 of the country's total stock of buildings). It was estimated by English Heritage in January 1992 that 83 per cent (36700) of all the listed buildings in England are "at risk" (i.e. in very bad or poor condition and unoccupied) and that a further 16.5 per cent (72850) are "vulnerable to neglect" (i.e. in a poor condition but occupied); 2400 Grade I or II* buildings were considered to be at risk (including at the time the Grade I Midland Hotel at St Pancras Station in London, which was subsequently externally repaired and refurbished by British Rail). This lamentable situation meant that around 25 per cent of all listed buildings were in an unsatisfactory state of repair at the beginning of the 1990s (English Heritage 1992a).

Three key factors that will influence whether the situation improves or deteriorates by the year 2000 may be identified:

Dialogue between public and private sectors
Greater understanding between these two groups will help to break down misplaced perceptions about listed buildings. In 1991 and 1992 a series of joint seminars were held between representatives of RICS and English Heritage.[8] From such meetings it was evident that:

---

8. See discussion in "Taking action to stop Britain's heritage going to rack and ruin", *Chartered Surveyor Weekly* (1 October 1992, p. 26).

- English Heritage staff should learn about property values, and property professionals should learn about architectural history.
- Work was required to change the negative perceptions of funding institutions towards listed buildings.
- The importance of keeping a building in an appropriate use was viewed as essential to achieve its long-term survival. Some degree of flexibility in listed building control must be exercised to maintain viable economic uses. This can be achieved without compromising the important historic or architectural fabric of a listed building.

Availability of grants

Grant aid towards listed-building preservation has traditionally been reactive in that a building has needed to fall into disrepair before it becomes eligible for assistance. The grant aid system operated by English Heritage was criticized by the National Audit Office in 1992. English Heritage had not adopted a consistent procedure for assessing the need for grant aid, nor did they collect information on the total value of private investment, which was "levered in" by each £1 of grant spent. This grant regime was not rigorous enough and, in one example cited in the report, three Grade I properties grant aided by English Heritage with a total of £53 000 in 1989, were recorded as "at risk" in the 1991 survey.

Prior to, and following, these findings, English Heritage introduced a series of reforms to its allocation procedures to ensure greater monitoring, value for money and consistency. Nevertheless, the funding of such works still amounts to a small sum in proportion to the problem of buildings in disrepair. Between 1984 and 1991, English Heritage and the National Heritage Memorial Fund have spent £220 million on a range of grants for heritage properties, of which £91 million was spent on historic buildings. Although this allocation was increased in 1992/3, it is unlikely to exceed £35 million per year during the remainder of the 1990s. Further grant aid is only given to buildings judged to be "outstanding" and therefore covers only by definition Grade I or Grade II* Buildings. The 34 300 Grade II buildings designated "at risk" in 1991 would not be eligible for any grant aid. The grant aid "cake" is too small to solve the problems of listed building neglect, no matter how well it is allocated, because it is already directed away from the majority of buildings that require some financial help. Unless this position changes, with more resources directed towards more buildings, then grant aid will not contribute towards a reduction in the numbers of buildings at risk or vulnerable to neglect. English Heritage is also responsible for managing its own properties. In its annual report for 1993/4, it anticipates that the backlog of repairs on these properties will not be cleared until the year 2000, provided that funding can be maintained.

Post-war buildings

Since the late 1980s, English Heritage's survey of post-war buildings has sought suitable examples of architecturally or historically important buildings drawn from all major building types built up until 1980. In 1993, 95 school, college and university buildings were recommended to and accepted for listing by the Secretary of State.[9] In March 1995, further recommendations were submitted by English Heritage, dealing with many other uses, including commercial, out-of-town offices, industrial and railway buildings. In addition, some post-war buildings have been listed under the 30-year or 10-year rule. The merits of post-war listing generated fierce debate between developers, heritage groups and members of the public. Most post-war buildings were built for a particular purpose and a limited life-span. Such buildings do not always easily lend themselves to conversion into alternative uses, which results in dereliction when the original use becomes redundant and conversion to another use may destroy the fabric of the original building and with it the very reason for listing.

Critics argue that such listings create an obsolete building, unsuitable for re-use, which remains empty for many years until the LPA, English Heritage or Secretary of State accept that demolition is inevitable to release land for redevelopment. Thus, the listing only serves to delay the agony; but this argument should not be used to resist all post-war listing, otherwise an important period of history would not be recorded in its built form. Instead, it should be used to justify a careful selection in which the viability of economic and acceptable re-use is taken into account in the decision to list. Failure to take into account economic re-use means that post-war additions to the list will serve to increase the number of buildings "at risk" or "vulnerable to neglect". In 1995 the Secretary of State for National Heritage announced that, for the first time, further additions to the list would be the subject of a wide-ranging public consultation of proposals to include professionals, amenity societies, private citizens and owners of the buildings.

Summary of issues concerning Listed Buildings and future directions

- Grant availability is limited. Repairs notice and CPO will be used only to limited effect because of financial restrictions.
- Improved dialogue between English Heritage and the property industry will result in better understanding of problems and should reduce the number of listed buildings in a poor state of repair. However, without increased grant aid, the private sector will be required to fund the majority of the maintenance costs.
- Post-war listing requires a balance between the preservation of the nation's heritage and the economic reality that certain post-war buildings are not capable of re-use without extensive alteration, which would dramatically change their character.

---

9. For a discussion of the merits of such post-war listing, see English Heritage (1992b).

Table 6.3 Examples of post-war buildings.

Category	Building date	Built	Listed	Reasons
Educational	Templewood School, Welwyn Garden City, Hertfordshire; Herts County Architect. Still in educational classroom use.	1949–1955	1993	Use of prefabricated building systems – architectural innovation in post-war construction methods.
Commercial, industrial	Centre Point, Charing Cross Road, London WC2	1961–5	1995	1960s office block illustrative of London speculative office development of the period
30 year rule (Grade II)	Brynwawr Rubber Factory, Gwent. Architects Co-Partnership Grade II*. *Derelict since 1980. LPA seek demolition to allow employment redevelopment use.*	1952	1986	Roof involves nine spectacular roof domes the largest of their kind in the world. Example of architectural form.
	Keeling House, New Lane, East London – Sir Denys Lasdun Grade II. Vacant and derelict, subject to a dangerous structure notice in 1994. Repairs estimated at £8 million.	1955	1993	Post-war council housing tower block. Example of social housing policies in post-war years and early example of high rise tower block architecture.
10 year rule (usually Grade I – exceptional and under threat of alteration).	Alexandra Road Estate, Camden Borough Architects Grade II*. Listed during Council renovation works. Further works require Listed Building consent. Still in residential use.	1978	1993	Medium rise council housing block if 1970s. Unique low–medium rise design.
	Wills Faber Domas Building, Ipswich. Norman Foster. Listed Grade I following threat to interior. Still in office use.	1975	1992	Novel use of a curving glass skin on the exterior to create an entirely glazed facade. The glass is not divided by mullions, but by translucent silicone to enhance the effect.

Conservation Areas

A Conservation Area is an area of special architectural or historic interest the character or appearance of which it is desirable preserve or enhance.

"Special" infers being set apart from or excelling others of its kind.[10]

Evolution of conservation policy

Conservation Areas were introduced by the Civic Amenities Act 1967. Local planning authorities were provided with statutory powers to designate such areas, resulting in a stricter regime of planning control over development proposals. The first Conservation Area was Stamford in Lincolnshire, designated by Kesteven District Council in 1967. Since that date LPAs have been enthusiastic about the additional powers that flow from Conservation Area designation, and every year has seen an additional number of designations. 1975 witnessed the highest number of individual designations, with 602, resulting in a total of 3000 Conservation Areas. By the mid-1990s this figure had risen to 7500 in England (English Heritage 1990) covering an estimated total of 1.3 million buildings (4 per cent of the nation's buildings; Rydin 1993: 108), 550 in Scotland and 350 in Wales.

Types of Conservation Area

No standard specification exists beyond the statutory definition of special architectural or historic interest. It is not always easy to separate the two limbs, and many conservation areas contain a mixture of both components. For example, Shipley Saltaire in Yorkshire is a conservation area designated by Bradford City Council in 1971. The area represents an important piece of both social and town-planning history, created by Titus Salt as a "Model" Community in the mid-nineteenth century. The architectural layout combines good quality Victorian workers' houses and a park, church, shops and library. The design and location of its buildings reflect (and are a result of) the social ideas of Titus Salt in seeking to create a better environment for his workers. Therefore, both architectural and historic issues are closely linked.

Conservation Areas are designated for a whole range of varied reasons. The one factor common to all designations is that they are based on areas, not individual buildings, whether listed or not. The spaces within Conservation Areas are just as important as the buildings. These spaces may include parks or open land, streetscapes, public squares and village greens, or simply relate to the separation between buildings.

10. This is the dictionary definition. The relevant Act provides no definition of "special" in the context of Conservation Areas.

The following examples illustrate the diversity of such areas.

- Oxford City and the University of Oxford, including many ancient and historic buildings of the University and historic streetscapes; designated 1971 and extended 1985.
- Durham: ancient cathedral and university; designated 1968, extended 1980.
- Undercliffe Cemetery, Bradford; Highgate Cemetery, London; Necropolis Glasgow: examples of Victorian cemeteries; designated 1984.
- Leeds–Liverpool Canal; designated 1988: example of Victorian engineering, not based around buildings.
- Hampstead Garden Suburb, London; designated 1968 and extended 1988: uniformity of architectural design and use of open space. Important post-Howard example of the Garden City planned layout.
- Bloomsbury (Fitzrovia), London: groups of Georgian town houses with square and open spaces; designated 1969 and extended 1985.
- Thame, Oxfordshire: medieval street pattern; designated 1969 and extended 1978.
- Royal Crescent, Bath; designated 1969 and extended 1985: Regency terraced houses with open spaces as an integral part of the layout.
- Finchingfield, Essex or Church Green, Witney, Oxfordshire; designated respectively 1969 and 1968: traditional English village green with buildings around.
- Leicester Square, London; designated 1984 (within Soho conservation area): highly varied architectural, economic and social character.

Implications of Conservation Area designation on development control

Conservation Area designation enables many additional development control powers to be exercised and will therefore influence the decision to grant or refuse planning applications.

Schemes of enhancement

The LPA is required to formulate and publish proposals, from time to time, for the preservation and enhancement of Conservation Areas. Such schemes must be submitted to a public meeting for consideration, and regard shall be paid to any views expressed. Proposals may include traffic calming measures to reduce and restrict car access, tree planting schemes, provision of street furniture (litter bins, street lights and seating, bus stops, etc.) or works to improve pavements and road surfacing (e.g. paviours or cobbles) to enhance the appearance of the area. Although many planning powers are viewed as "negative", in that LPAs refuse permission to develop, these enhancement schemes allow for a "positive" role in improving environmental quality in the Conservation Area. Unfortunately, financial squeezes on local government funding have restricted such works in recent years and many LPAs have ignored their duty under the Act to bring forward such schemes of enhancement.

Duty when considering planning applications

Conservation Area legislation imposes a duty on the decision-maker (LPA or Secretary of State/Inspector on appeal) when considering development control in Conservation Areas as follows: "Special attention shall be paid to the desirability of preserving or enhancing the character or appearance of that area."[11] This section of the legislation enables the LPA to exercise far greater control than would otherwise be possible over matters such as design or materials. "Appearance" refers to the visual impact of a proposal and "character" refers to the use or activity within a proposal. The terms "preserve" or "enhance" have proved more problematic in their definition, and the period 1988–92 witnessed considerable legal argument regarding the exact meaning of these terms in the exercise of development control and a degree of uncertainty within planning practice as to their exact interpretation (Stubbs & Lavers 1991). The matter was finally clarified in a decision of the House of Lords in *South Lakeland District Council* vs *Secretary of State for the Environment and the Carlisle Diocesan Parsonages Board* [1992].[12] Their Lordships relied upon the meaning of "preserve" in the Oxford English Dictionary – i.e. "to keep safe from harm or injury" – and therefore, where character and appearance were not harmed, they were preserved. Thus, preservation would imply a neutral impact; positive improvement goes beyond what is necessary to meet that requirement.

The meaning of the term "enhance" was not considered in the *South Lakeland* judgment. However, following from part of an earlier decision in *Steinberg vs Secretary of State for the Environment* [1988],[13] enhancement is taken to produce a positive outcome, so to "enhance" would imply a positive effect. See Table 6.4 for examples of how such legislative wording is applied to practical examples.

Summary of Conservation Area powers

Statutory duty

If a proposal results in either neutral or positive impact on the character or appearance of the conservation area, it will pass the duty and should be granted planning permission. If a proposal results in neither a neutral nor positive impact, it will invariably result in *harm* and planning permission should be refused. These decisions are not always easy ones. They require both a thorough examination of the merits of the case and the application of professional judgement.

Conservation Area consent

Demolition of all unlisted buildings within a Conservation Area requires Con-

11. Section 72 of Planning (Listed Building and Conservation Areas) Act 1990. In Scotland reference should be made to the Town & Country Planning (Scotland) Act 1972.
12. [1992] 1 All ER573 and [1992] 2 WLR204.
13. [1989] *JPL* 259.

Table 6.4 Examples of how to apply Conservation Area legislation.

Planning proposal	Harm (negative)	Preserve (neutral)	Enhance (positive)	Character (use)	Appearance (visual)
Externally refurbish existing hotel in Conservation Area by rebuilding part of structure and repaint, repair elevations.	–	–	Benefit as previously in a poor state of repair	No impact	Benefit to visual and external impact of building.
Conclusion:		Enhancement of appearance of Conservation Area (Positive).			
Remove ugly metal shopfront and replace with wooden painted version in Conservation Area.	–	–	Benefit as previously an eye-sore.	No impact	Benefit to external impact.
Conclusion:		Enhancement of appearance of Conservation Area (positive).			
Change of use shop to bank in Conservation Area.	–	No difference in impact with similar hours and activity	–	No impact	No impact as shopfront the same.
Conclusion:		Preserves existing character of Conservation Area (neutral).			
Change of use shop to pub in Conservation Area.	Late night noise and activity.	–	–	Change in character with more activity.	No impact
Conclusion:		Harms existing character of Conservation Area (negative or harmful result).			

Overall conclusions: A finding of either no impact or a positive impact to either character or appearance would satisfy the statutory duty imposed by Section 72 of the Planning (Listed Building and Conservation Areas) Act 1990. Any finding of harm (negative impact) fails the duty and planning permission would be refused on grounds of unacceptable harm to the Conservation Area in question.

servation Area Consent. A few exceptions to this have been established by the government, notably any building smaller than $115\,m^3$, any agricultural building erected since 1914, any industrial building up to $500\,m^2$ in area, or gates/walls erected before July 1948. Listed buildings are already protected by Listed Building Consent, so this provision applies only to unlisted buildings. This Conservation Area Consent was introduced in 1974[14] and it allows LPAs to protect buildings that, although not worthy of listed status, do contribute to the character of an area. Government policy advice states that . . . "consent for demolition should not be given unless there are acceptable and detailed plans for any redevelopment".[15]

14. By Town and Country Amenities Act 1974.

The decision to grant Conservation Area Consent is like any other development control decision in a conservation area and is subject to the statutory preserve/enhance duty. The decision-maker will need to consider whether the loss of existing building and the proposed replacement would preserve or enhance the character or appearance of the Conservation Area.

Restrictions on permitted development rights

Freedom from the requirement for planning permission in respect of certain development in a conservation area under the General Permitted Development Order (GPDO) is much more restrictive, especially in terms of the volume tolerances for the enlargement of a dwelling house (reduced to 50 m^3 for a side or rear extension to all types of property) and the exclusion of any external cladding (stone, timber, plastic or tiles) as permitted development.

Many LPAs seek to restrict permitted development still further by means of an Article 4 Direction. These Directions under the GPDO take away selected permitted development rights and must be approved by the Secretary of State. Without an Article 4 Direction, permitted development rights, albeit restricted, can dramatically alter the appearance of residential property. Works of maintenance are still permitted in a Conservation Area and can include extensions, re-roofing, double glazing and painting of brickwork.[16] By bringing such work within control and introducing a Direction, many house-owners are angered by the need to obtain planning permission to alter their own property and by the fact that the planners may insist on expensive materials being used in construction, such as handmade bricks or slate roof tiles to match existing period details.

Advertisement control

Advertisement powers may also be severely restricted,[17] to reduce categories of "deemed consent" (advertisements that would normally be exempt from control). So that most advertisements will require permission. Most LPAs encourage painted shop signs, without internal illumination, within conservation areas.

Control over trees

All trees within a Conservation Area, whether or not they are already protected by a Tree Preservation Order, are given limited protection. Six weeks' notice must be given to the LPA prior to removal or any lopping or topping of such a tree.[18] If the LPA considers that the tree is of amenity value and should remain, they can then serve a Tree Preservation Order to protect it.

---

15. PPG15, *Planning and the historic environment* (1994: para. 4.27).
16. From 30 March 1994, LPAs were given additional powers to withdraw selective permitted development rights without the need for an Article 4 Direction. No authority would be required from the Secretary of State. These "selective" works would include insertion of new doors, windows and roofing materials.
17. Order served under Town and Country Planning (Control of Advertisements) Regulations 1992 SI No 666.
18. Section 211 of the TCPA 1990. Also refer to DOE Circular 36/78.

Publicity

Any applications that in the opinion of the LPA would affect the character or appearance of a Conservation Area must be advertised in the local press. This will be in addition to any neighbour notification that may also be required

Conservation Area Advisory Committees

LPAs are encouraged to set up committees of local residents to advise on conservation policy and individual applications. These committees are usually composed of people drawn from local historic amenity or civic societies, as well as resident professional architects, planners or surveyors.

Exploding some myths about Conservation Areas

Do Conservation Areas prevent development?

No: Conservation Area designation only prevents unacceptable development. Although the planning regime is made tougher in a Conservation Area, government advice clearly states that "Although conservation of their character or appearance must be a major consideration, this cannot realistically take the form of preventing all new development: the emphasis will generally need to be on controlled and positive management of change. (PPG15, *Planning and the historic environment*, para. 4.16).

Conservation Areas are based around Listed Buildings?

No: they may often be centred around listed buildings but not always. The reasons for designation do not stipulate that the inclusion of a listed building is required.

Conservation Areas help preserve buildings

Yes: but they also preserve areas; therefore, open spaces and the separation of development are just as important as the buildings within.

Conservation Areas remove all permitted development rights

No: some permitted development rights remain. The only way to remove such rights is for the local planning authority to apply to the Secretary of State for the Environment to issue an Article 4 Direction (see section above).

Character and appearance represent the same thing

No: character tends to relate to use, and appearance tends to be visual (e.g. the buildings' elevations).

Conservation Areas and the abuse of designation

Conservation Areas introduce a restrictive planning regime. An LPA may designate as many conservation areas as it deems necessary. There is no statutory duty to consult anyone prior to designation although the government considers consultations with local groups to be "highly desirable". The agreement of the Secretary of State, following notification by the LPA, is only required for an Article 4 Direction, not a Conservation Area. However, the restrictive planning regime that follows designation may make planning permission harder to obtain and, subject to many factors, that will influence development cost by imposing the need for a high quality of design and materials. Conversely, this designation gives effect to valuable protection of the built environment. As conservation area designations have continued to grow over the years, critics have expressed concern that the procedure is now being abused. The early designations gained the support of the public and the development industry, but, more recently, designations have allegedly been made for political reasons, with greater control in areas that do not warrant Conservation Area Status.[19] Research commissioned by the Royal Town Planning Institute (RTPI) stated that:

> In a very small number of cases, new conservation areas appear to be designated for political reasons rather than for the benefit of the historic townscape.

This report recommended that Conservation Areas should be the subject of regular reviews by the local planning authority, which should ensure that policies and designations remain valid and up to date. There is still no legislative duty imposed upon an LPA to undertake such a review, and this recommendation is only an attempt at good practice and not a requirement of town planning legislation.

Summary: key characteristics of Conservation Areas

- strict planning regime
- development proposals must preserve or enhance the character or appearance
- debate that further designation beyond 7500 is resulting in a potential for abuse of the system.

Design control

Design control within the planning system operates at two levels covering, first, aesthetic control and, secondly, urban design or townscape. These will be considered in turn.

---

19. Views expressed by the British Property Federation in the early 1990s

Aesthetic control

The dictionary definition of "aesthetic" is an appreciation of beauty. In town planning, the term "aesthetic" refers to the external design of a building. Many architects would argue that planning authorities should not be permitted to exercise any aesthetic control over development proposals and that such matters should be left to the architect and his client, because of the subjective nature of design. Since 1980[20] government planning policy has sought to limit the exercise of such control where it does not affect and/or is located within, either a Conservation Area, an Area of Outstanding Natural Beauty, a National Park or a Listed Building (either the building or its setting).

> Good design should be the aim of all involved in the development process but it is primarily the responsibility of designers and their clients. . . . Planning authorities should reject obviously poor designs that are out of scale and character with their surroundings. But aesthetic judgements are to some extent subjective and authorities should not impose their taste on applicants for planning permission simply because they believe it to be superior.[21]

A refusal of planning permission based solely on an aesthetic judgement, such as the design of a window or door, could constitute unreasonable behaviour sufficient to warrant an award of costs on appeal in favour of the appellant.

Such restrictions on design control may frustrate many planners or members of planning committees, who inevitably associate the appearance of a building with protection of environmental quality and therefore consider the matter to be a legitimate concern of the planning system. This weakening of design control has coincided with a reduction in the number of architect–planners employed in planning departments and in the design-based content in undergraduate town planning courses (Punter 1993). However, some aesthetic control does survive, mostly in the form of design guides issued by LPAs, which contain a range of broadly based policies dealing with issues of scale, height, mass, density, layout and landscaping. Many give guidance on such matters as the need for a pitched roof on a two-storey domestic extension, or the nature of shop advertisements (printed fascia signs, with external spotlights). In past years various design guides made some bold attempts to intervene in aesthetic matters. The most famous of these was the Essex Design Guide of 1973, produced by Essex County Council, which incorporated guidance on details, materials and use of local architectural styles (Essex County Council 1973). Such an approach is no longer in vogue and current design guides tend towards broadly based policies that avoid aesthetics and focus on such considerations as landscaping, height, mass and scale of new residential planning applications.

---

20. Introduced by DOE Circular 22/80, *Development control – policy and practice*.
21. PPG1, issued 1988 and revised in 1992, *General policy and principles*, Annex on design considerations. For a critique of this approach see N. Taylor, "Aesthetic judgement and environmental design: is it entirely subjective?", *Town Planning Review* 65(1), 21–58, 1994.

Reasons for refusal based upon aesthetic grounds will be rare, but planners will occasionally negotiate on aesthetic matters, and applicants will make design alterations to please planning committees in an attempt to gain permission without the delay and uncertainty of going to appeal (see Case Study 6.4).

Urban design or townscape

Urban design represents the subject area where town planning and architecture meet, that is, the design and layout of the urban spaces. In the 1960s a distinct urban design subject area emerged as a reaction to the many failures of comprehensive redevelopment during this period and the realization that both the architectural and the planning professionals were ignoring the design of public space (Tugnett 1987) ". . . the void between buildings, the streets and spaces which constitute our everyday experience of urban places" (Hayward & McGlynn 1993).

Works by Nairn (1955), Cullen (1961) and Jacobs (1961) warned against mediocre town planning and architecture, and sought to establish a series of urban design principles. During the past 30 years, various people have added to and refined such principles, including HRH The Prince of Wales (1989). A summary of urban design principles is shown in Table 6.5.

Table 6.5   Good and bad urban design.

Urban design principles	A reaction to 1960s and 1970s architecture and town planning
Build on a human **scale**, low- or medium-rise development with regard to the nature of the surroundings.	High-rise commercial and residential buildings, with a brutal and intimidating appearance.
Use of traditional and local **materials**, e.g. stone, local brick.	Use of concrete in facing and roofing materials, with a harsh external appearance.
Ensure pedestrian **access** and **priority** within urban areas, e.g. traffic restrictions, and pedestrian only areas.	Dominance of motor car, with only secondary consideration to pedestrians (Ministry of Transport 1963).
Create a **community** with a mix of land uses (shops, residential and employment) and housing ownership (rent or buy), together with community participation in planning decisions.	Subdivision between council rental estates and private housing estates and different uses in different zones in planning policy; local people feel isolated from planning decision-making.
Reflect the importance of the **function** of a building, so a civic building is identifiable by its grand design and decoration.	Similarity of buildings, making it difficult to distinguish the function of each.
Make the urban form **diverse** and **stimulating**, with use of squares/piazzas, narrow and winding streets, landscaping and traffic calming.	Urban form dictated by rigid and detailed road layout, creating uniformity of width and building plots, resulting in a boring and monotonous urban form.

Case study 6.4: Aesthetic control and urban design – Paternoster Square redevelopment, the City of London

The Paternoster area is located to the north of St Paul's Cathedral. The area developed around the original St Paul's which was founded in 604 and rebuilt by the Saxons in the late seventh Century. The Paternoster area has been destroyed and rebuilt on two occasions. First, following the Great Fire of London in 1666, which also destroyed the Cathedral, replaced by Wren's masterpiece design, completed in 1710; and, secondly, by incendiary bomb attack in 1940. In spite of the extensive rebuilding following the Great Fire, Paternoster retained its original medieval street patterns, including principal thoroughfares and a series of tightly packed lanes and squares/courtyards incorporating three- and four-storey buildings used for residential and commercial purposes. The post-war reconstruction ignored this form and layout, with a series of 1960s high-rise buildings constructed on a grid layout. The brutal architectural style, use of concrete and separation of vehicles from pedestrians reflected the prevailing architectural and town planning thinking of the time, but it soon became unpopular among the people who worked in or visited Paternoster.

In 1992, outline planning permission was granted for the redevelopment of 1.7 ha (4.2 acres) of the total 2.8 ha (7 acre) site, which, with its location alongside St Paul's, is perhaps the most sensitive planning site in Britain this decade. The scheme submitted by Paternoster Associates proposed to re-establish the traditional street pattern, employing many urban design techniques to create a diverse and interesting street layout and provide $70000 m^2$ ($750,000 ft^2$) of offices and 80 shops. The architectural form employed neoclassical aesthetic treatment of keystones, round windows, brickwork, limestone detailing and metal railings, drawing inspiration from the work of many classical architects. This ultimate choice of design has not been without a degree of controversy, illustrating how aesthetic judgement is a matter of personal opinion. The approved scheme has been described as "... the most outrageously theatrical classical-style architectural development London has ever seen since the construction of the titanic Ministry of Defence headquarters in Whitehall"[†], and the Royal Fine Art Commission has compared a part of the scheme to Disneyland. A previous proposal by Arup Associates, incorporating a modern architectural solution, was dropped following strong criticism by HRH Prince Charles in 1987.[‡] Detailed planning permission was granted in early 1995.

The debate surrounding the redevelopment of Paternoster illustrates that the exact choice of a building's external treatment can, especially in sensitive locations, raise heated debate about what are matters of personal taste. Most property professionals and members of the public would agree on what may constitute good urban design, but it would be impossible to gain a consensus of opinion on what constitutes good architecture. Aesthetic decisions are important in conservation areas and when dealing with listed buildings. However, the many views expressed over Paternoster show that aesthetic control is a subjective matter and that local planning authorities should avoid becoming arbiters of taste concerning the external appearance of a building.

[†]The *Independent*, 3 February 1993.
[‡]His Mansion House speech, 1 December 1987.

Green belts

A green belt is a special policy defining an area within which only a highly restrictive schedule of changes constituting development under the planning acts will normally be permitted. (Elson 1986)

Evolution of green belt policy

Green belts were first introduced by Ebenezer Howard in his theory of the Garden City, published in 1898. Howard imposed his own green belt around Letchworth and Welwyn Garden City, by limiting the outward expansion of his developments into the surrounding agricultural land, which was also owned by the Garden City Corporation. It was a self-imposed restriction on future expansion. Such early examples represented isolated cases in which undeveloped land provided a "buffer" around the Garden Cities, no national or statutory system of green belts was in existence. Movement towards a national statutory system began with Raymond Unwin, who took this green belt concept and applied it to the problems of London's rapid growth during the inter-war years (Oliver et al. 1981). Unwin advised the Greater London Regional Plan Committee in 1933 and recommended that an estimated 250 km^2 of open space were required to restrict urban expansion within the belt of land surrounding London's urban fringe. Patrick Abercrombie echoed these ideas in his Greater London Plan of 1944. In 1947 the modern town planning system was created and, for the first time, a system existed whereby, through the exercise of planning policy, green belt restrictions could be imposed by local authorities.

In 1955 the government introduced planning guidance that established the purposes of green belt policy. In heralding this guidance, the then Minister for Housing and Local Government made a statement in the House of Commons:

> I am convinced that for the well-being of our people and for the preservation of our countryside, we have a clear duty to do all we can to prevent the further unrestricted sprawl of the great cities.

This was the beginning of the current system.

The original objective of preventing unrestricted urban sprawl remains valid today. Fourteen separate green belts are now in force in England, covering a total area of 1.8 million ha (4.5 million acres) of land, and five in Scotland covering a total area of 15000 ha (37000 acres) of land. No green belts have been designated in Wales. The majority of this land is in agricultural use, although this is not an essential prerequisite of green belt designation. The important issue is that the land enjoys an essentially open character, so that land may be woodland or farmland, or may incorporate some buildings as long as it maintains its open character (Thorne 1994).

Indeed, derelict or waste land without a use, and even unattractive in appear-

131

ance, may still serve a green belt purpose, although the existence of such land in the green belt serves to weaken the effectiveness of such policy.

In 1989 a study by the London Planning Advisory Committee reported that in nine outer London boroughs some 980ha of green belt land were derelict. London's green belt has a total area of 485600ha,[22] stretching out some 40km (25 miles) from the urban fringe into the surrounding counties.

Following an extensive review of green belt policy commissioned by the DOE and reported in 1993 (Elson et al. 1993, Elson & Ford 1994), the government published new policy guidance in 1995,[23] superseding the earlier guidance issued between 1955 and 1988. The 1995 guidance repeated the principal purpose of green belt policy, but for the first time set out objectives for the use of land within green belt designation (Table 6.6).

Green belts: post-1995

By the end of the 1990s a new green belt policy agenda will have emerged. The 1995 guidance heralded this new approach with a greater emphasis towards

Table 6.6   Green belt policy since 1955.

Purpose of green belts (1955, 1988 and 1995 policy)	Policy objectives for land use (1995 and onwards)
• Check unrestricted urban growth.	Provide access to open countryside.
• Prevent neighbouring towns from merging.	Promote use of land near urban areas for sport and leisure use.
• Safeguard countryside from encroachment.	Retain attractive landscapes near urban populations.
• Preserve the special character of a town.	Improve derelict land around towns.
• Assist in urban regeneration.	Secure nature conservation and retain agricultural, forestry and related land use.

enhancing the quality of green belt land and making greater use of its recreational potential for use by neighbouring urban dwellers. Since the mid-1950s green belt policy has been very successful in restricting urban sprawl. It has been less successful in protecting the quality of land on the urban fringe, and the proportion of derelict land has increased. The link between green belts and inner-city regeneration is tenuous. Little evidence has been produced to show that if developers cannot build on green belt land, then they consider inner-city sites. It has been estimated that about 61000ha (157000 acres)[24] of derelict land still exist in the

22. 1993 figure, published in PPG2 (1995) 14/84.
23. PPG2, *Green belts* (issued 1995). In Scotland similar guidance can be found in Scottish Office Circular 24/85, *Development in the countryside and green belts*.
24. Surveys of derelict land in England, Wales and Scotland, the most recent data being 1988.

urban areas of Britain, and in England the estimated annual loss of rural land to urban uses stands at about 11000ha (27170 acres) (Sinclair 1992).

It therefore appears that developers refused permission on green belt land are more likely to leapfrog the belt and look for sites beyond, instead of redirecting their attention towards the inner city. A report by the Regional Studies Association (1990) argued in favour of "green areas", that is, green belts covering a far wider area to prevent this leapfrogging and to create a more sustainable regional planning policy. Such ideas have not found favour with the government, which in past years has expressed a desire to maintain green belt policy but not to widen its geographical scope beyond current limits around the major cities. The 1995 Guidance links green belt policy with the promotion of sustainable patterns of development so that LPAs should ". . . consider the consequences for sustainable development (for example in terms of the effects on car travel) of channelling development towards urban areas inside the inner green belt boundary, towards towns and villages inset within the green belt, or towards locations beyond the outer green belt boundary".[25] The government's desire to prevent "leapfrogging" and building upon open country beyond the green belt may focus greater attention towards the regeneration of the urban area within the green belt. Yet the availability of grant aid has always been a more effective "carrot" to facilitate urban regeneration than the "big stick" of the green belts' restrictive planning regime. Green belt policy may contribute to such sustainable objectives, although in isolation from other strategies it will have little real impact on development patterns beyond its own boundaries.

Green belts or concrete collars?

Green belt policy will continue to operate into the next century. The 1994 review represents a shift in policy, not a fundamental change in direction. Yet such policy will continue to exact a price on the property market. By limiting land supply, green belts will increase land values and house prices. A 1988 survey by Business Strategies Limited estimated that green belt policy increased house prices to the extent that 4 million households in the area covered by the London green belt had to pay an additional £36 a month on their mortgage repayments. Critics argue that green belt policy strangles urban areas, preventing even limited growth necessary to provide for housing and employment needs and that many local planning authorities draw an excessively tight inner boundary that restricts the release of some land for development on the urban fringe (Evans 1988). At the other extreme, groups such as the Council for the Protection of Rural England argue that green belts are not strong enough and should be more rigorously applied to enforce the redevelopment of redundant land in inner cities.

Decisions regarding the identification and release of the "white land" (non

25. Extract from PPG2, *Green belts* (1995: para. 2.10).

Case study 6.5: the Oxford Green Belt

A green belt around Oxford was first proposed in 1958, although the outer boundary was not confirmed until 1975 and the sensitive inner boundary was not finally agreed upon until the mid-1990s, when the four local planning authorities responsible for its implementation gained approval in their local plans, resulting in a total area of 100000 acres of land "washed over" by green belt designation. The consequences of the Oxford Green Belt have been fourfold:

- virtually no outward extension of Oxford during this period
- the limited release of housing land on the city fringe on a sporadic basis to meet certain housing needs
- substantial growth of a number of smaller settlements within the Green Belt or beyond its outer boundary
- promotion by the County Council of a "county towns" strategy where a series of five market towns beyond the limits of the Oxford Green Belt would accommodate new dwellings to take pressure away from Oxford with its restrictive green belt regime: the market towns of Bicester, Didcot, Witney, Abingdon and Banbury).

---

green belt land on the urban fringe) for future development raise many problems for local authorities, who must draw a clear and defendable line between the green belt and the urban area and yet allow for some release of land for future needs without eroding the future maintenance of the inner green belt boundary.

If green belt policy is to retain its role within the planning system, it will need to address the problems of derelict green belt land and availability of suitable "white" land, so that the important policy objectives of green belts can be achieved without unacceptably increasing land values and development densities within existing urban areas (see Case Study 6.5).

Countryside planning powers

The statutory purposes of National Parks are conservation and enhancement of the natural beauty, wildlife, cultural heritage, and the promotion of the quiet enjoyment of the special qualities of such areas.[26]

National Parks are designated by the Countryside Commission in England, and Countryside Council for Wales, under powers contained in the National Parks and Access to the Countryside Act 1949. No national parks have been designated in Scotland.

The first park to be designated was the Peak District in April 1951, followed in the same year by the Lake District, Snowdonia and Dartmoor. The most recent designation was the Norfolk and Suffolk Broads, designated in 1988[27] and resulting in a total of seven National Parks in England and three in Wales, which cover

---

26. See PPG7, *The countryside and the rural economy* (1992: para. 3.2) and §61 of Part III, Environment Act 1995.

an area of $13600 km^2$ (9% of the land mass of England and Wales). The largest National Park is the Lake District ($2229 km^2$) and the smallest the Norfolk and Suffolk Broads ($288 km^2$) (MacEwen & MacEwen 1987).

National Park authorities

Each park is administered by a National Park Authority (NPA). Reforms in 1972, 1991 and the Environment Act 1995 have resulted in enhanced powers for these bodies, so that they are now responsible for development control, preparation of a National Park management plan and countryside management activities. Each NPA must produce its own local plan and will determine all planning applications submitted within the Park. Such local plan policies will need to consider the conservation of the high standard of the natural environment and the economic and social needs of the local population. Government planning advice states that major development should not take place in National Parks except in exceptional circumstances.

It is not always easy to strike a balance between the needs of the local economy and environmental protection. Some parks contain traditional mining and mineral extraction industries, which provide valuable local employment yet whose activities can scar or blight the local environment. The restoration of such workings, once they are no longer active, should usually be completed to a high standard so that the landscape is returned to its former beauty.

The most recent review of National Parks was the Edwards Report (Edwards 1991), which advocated stricter planning policies against some categories of development, including certain agricultural and forestry buildings and roads, noisy outdoor recreational pursuits (clay pigeon shooting, war games and motorcycle scrambling), farm diversification into non-agricultural uses, and installation of satellite dishes. The General Permitted Development Order of 1995 has withdrawn permitted development rights for clay pigeon shooting and war games within Sites of Special Scientific Interest. A recommendation was made that firm planning policies should be continually required to protect the special character of these areas, including the landscape and traditional buildings and structures (such as stone walling). The total annual funding of all National Parks is about £22 million every year, paid directly by government.

---

27. Unlike the others, this park was designated by Act of Parliament, although it has a similar function to the others.

Areas of Outstanding Natural Beauty (AONBs) or National Scenic Areas (Scotland)

An AONB is a countryside conservation area of high landscape beauty considered worthy of protection.

AONBs are also designated by the Countryside Commission, subject to the confirmation of the Secretary of State for the Environment. The grounds for designation are similar to National Parks in seeking to protect areas of high landscape importance. The key differences from a National Park are that:
- AONB designation does not include a duty to promote recreational use and public access may be restricted.
- AONBs tend to cover a much smaller area.
- AONBs are not governed by a special AONB Authority. All planning controls remain with the local authority. Policies to protect the landscape quality are usually incorporated into development plan policies. A strong presumption exists against any development in these areas, with the promotion of the preservation and enhancement of natural beauty.

Thirty-nine such AONBs have been designated in England and Wales, covering a total of $20400 km^2$ of land (13% of total land area). Examples include the Chiltern Hills in Buckinghamshire and Bodmin Moor in Devon. A total of 55 have been established in England, 4 in Wales and 1 shared.

In recent years, increasing importance has been attached to the co-ordinated management of such areas, and government has encouraged the creation of "joint advisory committees" to bring together local authorities, amenity groups, farming and other interested parties to agree a common strategy for protection of the landscape while facilitating activity such as agriculture, forestry and public access.

In Scotland, similar powers are vested in 40 National Scenic Areas, covering much of Scotland's beautiful landscapes, such as extensive parts of the Highlands. Planning controls, as with AONBs, are held by LPAs, although extensive consultation is required with Scottish Natural Heritage before any planning applications may be granted. Some 13 per cent of Scotland's land mass is protected by such designation. Scottish National Heritage may also designate National Heritage Areas to manage recreational and conservation needs in other parts of the country. This new power was introduced in 1991.

Sites of Special Scientific Interest (SSSIs)

SSSIs are areas of special nature conservation interest that are designated to protect habitats and wildlife/plantlife.

SSSIs are designated[28] by English Nature (the nature conservancy body for England), the Countryside Council for Wales or Scottish Natural Heritage, on the basis of detailed scientific criteria. By 1995 3794 such sites had been designated in England, 892 in Wales and 1377 in Scotland, covering a total of 9750km², (6.5% of the land area). Examples include Oxleas Wood, Greenwich, London, and Loch Sheil in Scotland. This land is not excluded from development pressures.

Environmentally Sensitive Areas (ESAs)

ESAs are areas of high, wildlife importance maintained by non-intensive agriculture.

ESAs are designated by government and administered by the Ministry of Agriculture, Fisheries and Food, following recommendations of the Countryside Commission. Such a designation will need to be considered by local councils in the exercise of development control. Farmers benefit from specific grants to continue to exercise traditional land management techniques to preserve wildlife habitats.

By 1994, 22 such areas were designated in England, 6 in Wales and 10 in Scotland. Examples include the Somerset Levels, Cambrian Mountains and Central Scottish Borders.

Nature Reserves

Nature Reserves are habitats considered to be of national importance.

Nature Reserves are designated by English Nature, Scottish Natural Heritage and the Countryside Council for Wales[29] and may deal with protection of habitats of rare and migratory birds or waterfowl, by the introduction of specialist habitat management policies. Protected wetlands are referred to as "Ramsar" sites following Britain's signature to the Convention of Wetlands of International Importance, signed in Ramsar, Iran, in 1971. Such nature reserves may be terrestrial (National Nature Reserves) or marine (Marine Nature Reserves); 273 terrestrial and 2 marine reserves have been designated. In Britain 75 Ramsar sites have been established. Examples include Lundy Island (marine), the Island of Uist, Shetland (terrestrial) and Bridgwater Bay, Somerset (Ramsar). Additional controls over wildlife are found in Special Protection Areas to protect the habitats of vulnerable or endangered species, in particular bird habitats. In England 45 exist, with 8 in Wales and 37 in Scotland.

---

28. Under powers in section 28 of the Wildlife and Countryside Act 1981.
29. Designation under provision within the Wildlife Countryside Act 1981.

Country Parks

Country Parks are areas for countryside recreational use in proximity to urban areas

Country Parks are designated[30] and managed by the local authority for the recreational benefit of the local population. An example is Aldenham on the borders between northwest London and Hertfordshire.

Special Landscape Value

An area of great landscape value not covered by AONB status.

Areas of Special Landscape Value are designated by means of the planning policy of local planning authorities. As a planning policy, it counts as a material consideration in planning decision-making but does not benefit from the status of AONBs, National Parks or other protected areas, and is something of a poor relation compared to these controls.

Tree Preservation Orders (TPOs)

A TPO constitutes an order imposed under town planning legislation to protect trees or woodland considered to be of amenity value.

- Neither "amenity" or "tree" is defined within town planning legislation. In most cases a TPO will seek to protect a fine or rare specimen, usually mature in growth and exceeding 20 cm in diameter. The decision as to what constitutes "amenity value" is left entirely to the local planning authority. The LPA must serve a notice on owners/occupiers of the relevant site, stating that they intend to make a TPO. A period of 28 days is then given for any representations or objections to be submitted, after which the LPA may confirm the Order. No right of appeal is available against the service of a TPO.
- Once a TPO is in force, consent is required from the Planning Authority before the tree can be cut down, topped, lopped or uprooted. A right of appeal exists against a refusal of such consent or failure to issue a decision. Unauthorized removal, topping, lopping or uprooting is a criminal offence, usually punishable by a fine. The LPA may also require the planting of replacement trees of the same maturity.
- In a conservation area, six weeks' notice is required to cut, lop, top or uproot *any* tree.

---

30. Countryside Act 1968 in England and Wales, or Countryside (Scotland) Act 1967.

Ancient monuments and archaeological areas

An ancient monument may constitute any building structure or work, including a cave, excavation, or remains, considered to be of public importance.

The Secretary of State for National Heritage is responsible for compiling a list[31] of ancient monuments, usually following the recommendation of English Heritage in England or specialist boards established for Scotland and Wales.

The vast majority of the 2000 scheduled ancient monuments in Britain comprise archaeological sites incorporating ancient structures and buried deposits. However, other examples include various bridges, barns, castles and other fortifications. Scheduled monument consent is required to undertake any works, including repairs to such monuments, and this is permitted only by application to the Secretary of State. No right of appeal exists if consent is refused, although compensation is payable. Unauthorized works are liable to criminal prosecution. Government policy establishes a presumption that such monuments shall be preserved.[32]

In areas of known archaeological remains, developers may be required by the LPA to permit an investigation of the ground before redevelopment and this can be controlled by planning conditions. The designation of an area of archaeological importance by a local authority or Secretary of State delays any construction work, to allow a full site investigation to extract sufficient archaeological information from the site.

Agricultural land

The Ministry of Agriculture, Fisheries and Food (MAFF) have classified all agricultural land. This does not represent a protective designation or form of special control; however, it may be a material consideration if a local authority wishes to refuse planning permission for a proposal, such as for residential development, that will result in the loss of agricultural land.

The grading of agricultural land is shown in Table 6.7.

The grading assessment is based upon the physical and chemical characteristics of the land, which determines its suitability for long-term food production.

Around 45 per cent of all land in England and Wales is covered by some form of special planning status, 15 per cent is urban and the remainder is in rural use (agriculture, forestry or horticultural). Such special powers give the planners additional controls in pursuing a variety of (sometimes overlapping) planning objectives. The maintenance of these special planning controls will involve a complex balance between the need for environmental safeguards and the need for

---

31. Under Section 1 of the Ancient Monuments and Archaeological Areas Act 1979.
32. See PPG16, *Archaeology and planning* (1990: paras 8 and 27).

139

Table 6.7 The grading of agricultural land.

Grade		Description
1	Excellent quality	All suitable for current and future agricultural needs.
2	Very good	
3a	Good quality	
3b	Moderate quality	Changes of use to non-farming use will not be restricted on agricultural grounds.
4	Poor quality	
5	Very poor	

development to satisfy the economic requirements of a modern industrialized society. Maintenance of these special policies is not sacrosanct and sometimes decisions are made to build on green belt land (such as the Bluewater Park Regional Shopping Centre in Kent) or on SSSIs (e.g. the new road building at Twyford Down near Southampton, Hampshire).

The existence of such special powers has become familiar to many members of the public, and land-use decisions that result in the erosion of these areas are usually met with strong opposition. However, the longer-term retention (into the next century) of these planning policies appears to be assured.

Conclusions

Britain, like many of its continental European neighbours, is a densely populated country in which considerable pressures are placed upon the development of land to accommodate the needs of a modern industrial society. However, the supply of land is finite and, as a consequence of being a relatively small nation in geographical terms, areas of considerable natural beauty and landscape value are often located in close proximity to major sources of population in large urban areas. The creation of the post-war system of planning control has provided the necessary mechanism by which specialist policy areas can be introduced to protect important environments, both rural and urban; it sought to reconcile these objectives with the need to permit urban expansion to facilitate economic growth. Since the mid-1940s a whole host of controls have been introduced to deal with urban and rural protection, to maintain and guarantee the future survival of significant natural and built environment, while providing for the agricultural, recreational, cultural and biological needs of a modern industrial society. In this way, the town and country planning system, in protecting many diverse facets of environment and society, seeks to ensure the future enjoyment of features such as buildings of heritage value, or countryside of high landscape value, thereby contributing simultaneously to environmental standards and quality of life.

Table 6.8 Summary of special first planning control areas.

Title	Year control was introduced	Statute today	Town and country planning objectives	Numbers in force and percentage of land or building stock
Green Belt	1955 (limited introduction in 1940s)	No green belt statute – control exercised under Town & Country Planning Act 1990.	Maintain open character around urban areas and prevent sprawl.	15 14% England
Listed Buildings	1947	Planning (Listed Building & Conservation Areas) Act 1990	Preserve buildings of historic and architectural importance.	440000 buildings in England, 37000 in Scotland, 14500 in Wales
Conservation Areas	1967	As above	Preserve/enhance areas of historic and architectural importance.	7500 Conservation Areas in England. 550 – Scotland, 350 – Wales
National Parks	1949	Environment Act 1995	Conserve natural beauty and allow public access/enjoyment.	10 9% England & Wales
Area of Outstanding Natural Beauty or National Scenic Areas (Scotland)	1949	As above	Conserve natural beauty.	35 England, 4 Wales 13% – Scotland and 40 established.
Sites of Special Scientific Interest	1981	Wildlife & Countryside Act 1981	Nature, conservation of plants, habitats, wildlife.	3794 – England, 1377 – Scotland, 892 – Wales
Environmentally Sensitive Areas	1986	Agriculture Act 1986	Protect landscape, wildlife & agricultural features.	22 – England, 6 – Wales, 10 – Scotland
Nature Reserves – National (Land) and Marine	1971 & 1981	Wildlife & Countryside Act 1981	Nature conservation of habitats.	National: 150 England, 52 Wales, 71 Scotland Marine: 1 England, 1 Wales
Country Parks	1986	Countryside Act 1968 (Scotland 1967)	Public recreation.	*
Special Landscape Value	1971	Town & Country Planning Act 1990	Development plan policy to keep landscape quality.	*
Tree Preservation Orders	1947	Town & Country Planning Act 1990	Protect trees of amenity value.	*
Ancient Monuments & Archaeological areas	1913	Ancient Monuments & Archaeological Areas Act 1979	Preserve ancient monuments in the public interest.	20000 monuments

* Figures/data not available. All figures for Britain unless otherwise stated.

CHAPTER SEVEN
Sustainable development

Sustainable development, sustainability or environmental stewardship are all terms that refer to the relationship between environmental protection and the economic development associated with industrial society. Just as the early public health legislation of the nineteenth century was a reaction against disease associated with slum housing, so in the 1990s the introduction of sustainable development is a reaction to the environmental degradation of the latter half of the twentieth century, which is associated with pollution, depletion of non-renewable resources (fossil fuels, minerals, aggregates), erosion of the ozone layer, pollution and the warming of the Earth's atmosphere because of the production of carbon dioxide (global warming).

Sustainable development is difficult to define and can mean different things to different people. As a subject area it deals with the relationship between economic growth and environmental protection. In some ways it represents a marriage between these two issues, seeking to ensure that future economic growth and development is achieved without longer-term environmental degradation. As Blowers (1993: 5) suggests:

> Sustainable development requires that we have regard to the Earth's regenerative capacity, the ability of its systems to recuperate and maintain productivity. Thus, the conservation of resources is a strong component of sustainable development.

The following definition, provided by the United Nations World Commission, commonly referred to as the Brundtland Commission after its Chairperson, Mrs Gro Harlem Brundtland, is the most quoted, and has been adopted by many national governments in their own policies on the matter:

> Sustainable development is development that meets the needs of the present without compromising the ability of future generations to meet their own needs. (World Commission 1987)

A strategy of sustainable development will therefore deliver economic growth and development without resulting in long-term damage to environmental resources. How does town planning and property development fit into this equation?

In Britain the town planning system has, since 1947, been concerned with decisions relating to land use. Sustainable development has the following implications for British town planning. It will influence the existing nature of land-use decisions so that new developments will be assessed against environmental planning criteria, such as the need to halt processes that lead to global warming or ozone depletion. It will broaden the realm of material town planning considerations so that environmental issues become important in decision-making. Planning policy will be widened to take such matters into account. The chapter is organized as follows:

- background
- current environmental problems
- conclusions.

Background

In 1972 a report entitled *The limits to growth* (Meadows 1972) was published by the Club of Rome, a group of industrialists who had commissioned research into the relationship between industrial growth and environmental protection. It argued that economic development associated with a modern industrialized society was resulting in environmental damage. The choice had to be made to continue with economic growth and create further environmental degradation or halt further economic activity and preserve the environment. It was argued that it would not be possible to "balance" economic needs with environmental protection.

In 1980, a report on World Conservation Strategy identified an increasingly alarming trend towards damage to ecological systems by economic development. However, unlike *The limits to growth*, the report concluded that, instead of a "no growth" strategy, a balance was required so that economic development could be continued as long as ecological interests were unharmed. A strategy of sustainable development would deliver this "equilibrium" between the economy and the environment, so that future industrial growth with its associated urban growth could be achieved without a continued erosion of natural resources and environmental quality. In 1987, the United Nations' World Commission on Environment and Development published a report of proceedings entitled *Our common future* (the Brundtland Report: World Commission 1987). Sustainable development was defined in a way that implied that future generations would still be able to use and benefit from environmental resources. Action would be required to arrest environmental problems of global warming, acid rain, pollution, consumption of non-renewable resources and reduction of the ozone layer. As with the 1980 report, further economic growth and development were not viewed as incompatible with such objectives.

In 1992 the UN held a Conference on Environment and Development in Rio de Janeiro.[1] The tangible outcome of the conference was published as *Agenda 21*, in which national governments committed themselves to an "action plan" of

143

strategies for sustainable development. The document[2] set out policy areas dealing with social and economic issues (combating poverty, protecting and promoting human health and promoting sustainable human settlements), and conservation of resources to allow for future development (meeting agricultural needs without destroying the land, protecting ecosystems, safeguarding the oceans and halting the spread of deserts). A United Nations Commission on Sustainable Development was established to monitor the progress made by countries in implementing *Agenda 21* within their own political systems.

In Britain and in the European Community, *Agenda 21* has found its way into several policy initiatives. The European Community published the fifth Environmental Action Programme (1993–2000) *Towards sustainability* and the fifth Environmental Action Plan. Both documents set out a broad range of policy areas in which sustainability must be considered by member nations, including control of industrial pollution, spatial land-use planning policy, education and training. The British government published discussion documents, notably the government White Paper, *This common inheritance* (DOE 1990a), that set out the broad policy agenda for sustainability in Britain, including tackling global warming and the role of land-use planning decisions. In addition, the government commissioned a series of environmental studies, notably the 1993 joint DOE and Department of Transport study *Reducing emissions through planning* (DOE 1993c) and introduction of new legislation, notably the Environmental Protection Act 1990, which imposes a duty on Her Majesty's Inspectorate of Pollution and Local Authorities to establish registers of data, on potentially polluting processes, which are open to public inspection. A requirement, under Section 143 of the Act, that all local authorities maintain a register of contaminated land (e.g., sewage sites, former industrial sites and completed landfill sites) was never introduced by the government, following opposition from the development industry, especially housebuilders. The Environment Act 1995 imposes a duty whereby a local authority must designate sites of serious contamination. The issue of government policy guidance to influence the planning system has been recognized, with several PPGs being revised to accommodate sustainable policy objectives. Finally, the government has published a series of strategy documents to set out the its aims for the implementation of sustainable development, following on from its commitment to *Agenda 21* at the Rio Earth Summit. Four documents were published in January 1994, dealing with sustainable development,[3] climate change,[4] biodiversity,[5] and sustainable forestry.[6] Each document takes a long-term view of the various environmental problems to the year 2012 (20 years from the Earth Summit). As with

1. Referred to as the "Earth Summit".
2. *The Earth Summit: Press Summary on Agenda 21*. United Nations Conference on Environment and Development, Rio de Janeiro, 3–14 June 1992.
3. *Sustainable Development – The UK Strategy 1994* (Cmnd 2426) London: HMSO
4. *Climate Change: The UK Programme 1994* (Cmnd 2424) London: HMSO
5. *Biodiversity: The UK Action Plan 1994* (Cmnd 2428) London: HMSO
6. *Sustainable Forestry: The UK Programme 1994* (Cmnd 2429) London: HMSO

Brundtland, the UK policies have always taken the view that economic development and environmental protection can be achieved together. In many ways the British government went further than Brundtland, when they stated in the *UK strategy*:

> Sustainable development does not mean having less economic development: on the contrary, a healthy economy is better able to generate the resources to meet people's needs and new investment and environmental improvement often go hand in hand. . . what it requires is that decisions throughout society are taken with proper regard to their environmental impact.

This is not a universally accepted view. Although the views of the Club of Rome are not given wide support today, many commentators on the subject still argue that sustainability brings with it a *conflict* between economic activity and environmental quality. To improve and protect the environment requires a curb on some economic activities.

A growing awareness of sustainability in the post-Rio Summit world has been translated into local *Agenda 21* strategies, whereby local government has sought to adopt policies on sustainability in many topic areas. In town planning, local government is well placed to develop and codify these local ideas into planning policy. During the 1990s, with increasing momentum in this subject area, it is envisaged that growing numbers of local Councils will publish such strategies, either incorporated within an all-embracing local *Agenda 21* document or within planning policy. By the mid-1990s it had become apparent that some county councils have taken a lead on this in reviewing the environmental content of policies in structure plans. However, this is not to preclude the emergence of such strategies at district/City or unitary development plan level, it merely reflects the more strategic function of Counties, seeking to establish a broader and longer-term view of policy within their areas. Bedfordshire and Hertfordshire county councils, in particular, have sought to recast the content of their structure plans to accommodate local sustainability issues. Economic development, conservation of natural resources, and transport strategies, are important topics covered by county councils in their capacity as strategic planning authorities. These issues readily lend themselves to the implementation of environmental policy, as envisaged by *Agenda 21*.

The problem for Britain, as it seeks to meet the challenge posed by such documents as *Agenda 21*, is not whether it has the necessary procedures within which to deliver sustainability at local or national level, because it undoubtedly does have this in the current mechanics of the planning system, but instead the more thorny problem of whether local and national government, which steer that system, have the political motivations to guarantee effective implementation.

Sustainability and town planning

Town planning can play an important role in delivering sustainable development, however, the planning system cannot on its own deliver sustainability. Planning must work alongside existing, as well as new, areas of environmental policy and the traditional land-use emphasis of post-war British planning will need to be widened to pay greater regard to environmental preservation. The remainder of this chapter will examine seven principal environmental problems of the late 1990s and then turn to consider how land-use town planning can accommodate sustainability in an attempt to address these problems.

Current environmental problems

Uses of urban land

In Britain, post-war development patterns have increasingly been influenced by the rapid growth in private ownership of the motor car. This has resulted in increasing levels of out-of-town development such as retail warehousing or business parks, not easily served by public transport. As a consequence, people and businesses have relocated away from existing urban locations. It has been estimated that by the late 1980s between 60000 and 110000ha of wasteland existed in urban areas of Britain.[7] Groups such as the Friends of the Earth and the Council for the Protection of Rural England have argued for many years that "Cities have great capacity to be more resourceful" (Houghton & Hunter 1994: 45). Clearly, sustainable planning policies can contain urban growth (e.g. by green belt policies) and ensure that derelict urban land is developed while existing land is recycled through redevelopment. However, this strategy alone will not accommodate all future land-use needs. It has been estimated by the DOE that between 1981 and 2001 the urban area of England will increase by 105000ha.[8] When one considers that 40 per cent of all urban expansion in Britain during the 1980s was on previously agricultural land, it becomes apparent that the planning system must balance competing demands for finite land resources and make difficult decisions regarding urban containment or expansion.

Global warming

The production of carbon dioxide, methane, nitrous oxide and chlorofluorocarbons creates a heat blanket around the Earth, trapping some of the sun's energy and producing a rise in global temperature. Such increases in temperature have been predicted to be around 0.3°C every decade, resulting in changes in weather

---

7. In 1988 Department of Environment statistics estimated that some 60000ha of vacant or derelict land existed in England, Scotland and Wales. Other estimates by environmental campaigners have been far higher. Stephen Joseph puts the figure at 110000 for England and Wales (Joseph 1987).
8. For more details on this debate refer to DOE (1994c: ch. 11).

patterns (affecting agricultural production) and rising sea levels, in the range of around 6 cm every ten years (Houghton et al. 1992). During the 1970s, UK emissions of greenhouse gases declined as a result of restrictions on industrial production and domestic heating. However, the dramatic rise in the number of motor vehicles meant that by 1984 any further decline was arrested and that, by the year 2000, projections anticipate an increase in such greenhouse emissions.[9]

Depletion of the ozone layer

The ozone layer protects the Earth from excessive levels of ultraviolet radiation. This layer is being reduced by chlorofluorocarbons (CFCs), which are found in chemicals such as halon, used in the manufacture and operation of air-conditioning solvents, refrigeration and aerosols.[10] An international commitment was made in 1987 to reduce such substances.[11]

Deforestation

Trees, woods and forests absorb carbon dioxide, which helps to reduce the effects of global warming. Tropical forests have been destroyed annually for a variety of reasons, including the harvesting of timber. In Britain around 10 per cent of land area (2.4 million ha) has tree cover, compared to an average of 25 per cent in the European Community. Nevertheless, this figure represents a dramatic increase on the situation prevailing at the beginning of the century and is largely the result of planting undertaken by the Forestry Commission, which was established by government in 1919.

Biological diversity

Activities such as the burning of forests, draining of wetlands and growth of urban areas and road networks have led to the loss or near extinction of many species of plant or animal life, resulting in the loss of sources of food, medicine and industrial materials. It has been estimated that about 2 per cent of agricultural land is eroded by city growth around western European cities every ten years (Houghton & Hunter 1994: 7). In Britain the amount of land occupied by urban areas continues to grow. Urban growth is usually accompanied by an increased demand for infrastructure, especially roads, and development pressure on urban fringes becomes intense. Between 1985 and 1990 around 14000 ha of land were used to build new roads in Britain (DoE 1994c).

Industrial pollution

Industrial pollution is discharged into the air, sea and ground, and includes the dumping of industrial waste at sea. Many industries in the former Soviet Union

---

9. In 1990 carbon dioxide emissions in Britain were calculated at 158 million tonnes expressed as carbon. By the year 2000, projections range between 157 and 179 million tonnes.
10. Other ozone depleting chemicals include carbon tetrachloride 1.1.1, hydrobromoflurocarbons (HBFCS) and hydrochloroflurocarbons (HCFCS).
11. Montreal Protocol on substances that deplete the ozone layer, held in 1987.

are responsible for a heavy discharge of pollutants. "Acid rain" refers to rain, snow, fog or mist that has become contaminated by contact with sulphur and nitrogen dioxide, which are produced by industrial processes. The increasing number of motor vehicles has produced a rise in the level of nitrogen dioxide in the atmosphere (an increase of 70% between 1980 and 1993) although pollution from homes and industry has steadily fallen since 1970 (sulphur dioxide has fallen by 45% and black smoke emissions fell by 70 per cent between 1970 and 1993; DoE 1994c: ch. 7).

Depletion of non-renewable resources

All of the Earth's natural resources of fossil fuel, minerals and aggregates (sand, gravel and crushed rock) are in limited supply. The long-term supply of such resources can be maintained by policies that ensure a greater degree of efficiency in the use of such finite materials and substitution of their use by renewable resources, especially in the supply of energy, by using wind power and solar power.

The role of town planning

Following an examination of these various environmental problems, it is necessary to pose the question "How can the British land-use planning system affect these environmental issues?". Several key areas may be examined (Table 7.1). Each environmental issue will be considered and reference will be made to the influence of town planning.

Table 7.1 Town planning and sustainable development.

	Environmental issue	Land-use planning influence
(1)	Greenhouse effect/ global warming	• Planning policies to restrict use of the motorcar
(2)	Use of urban land	• Green belt policy to contain urban areas. • Urban density policies to ensure urban land is used efficiently. • Strategies such as urban villages and new settlements to reduce car use by ensuring a mixture of employment and housing or shopping land use within close proximity.
(3)	Pollution Ozone depletion Resource depletion Deforestation	• Control over industrial emissions when deciding new planning applications. • Use of procedures such as Environmental Impact Assessment to assess the exact potential for pollution and other environmental harm.

Greenhouse effect

In 1990 the British government committed itself to a programme of action to curb the rise in all carbon dioxide emissions, so that by the year 2000 these emissions would be returned to their 1990 levels. This "target" requires a complete reversal of the upward trend in emissions of recent years. Emissions from vehicles are a growing source of carbon dioxide and, associated with more motor cars, an increased number of car journeys are undertaken by each owner.

In pursuit of the *Agenda 21* strategy agreed at the Rio conference, the UK government pinned great hopes on the implementation of sustainable patterns of future land-use planning, to control and restrict motor vehicle usage and therefore carbon emissions. Reducing global warming has been identified as the environmental imperative to sustainability.

> We can also employ the land-use planning system to influence the siting of new shops and offices, where we work, where we go to enjoy ourselves and where we go to shop – these choices are all significant for the use of the car . . . we need to deliver development patterns over the next 20 years that will enable people to continue to choose to walk or cycle or use public transport. We should stand firm against the urban sprawl that would deny those choices.[12]

Between 1992 and 1994, the DoE revised particular areas of its own policy guidance to local planning authorities. Three revised PPGs were issued, with important pronouncements on sustainability and town planning. First, PPG12 (issued February 1992) focused on the content of planning policy. This encourages LPAs to ensure that the principles of sustainability are enacted by introduction into local planning policy in development plans. This policy guidance identifies a wide range of land-use policy areas, which may deal with sustainable development as follows in Table 7.2. Secondly, PPG6 (issued July 1993 and a revised version is expected in 1996) deals with retailing. This introduced a new town planning material consideration, in paragraphs 12 and 38, which stated that, in future, concern about fuel efficiency could be a legitimate objection to building

Table 7.2 Sustainable planning policy outcomes.

Environmental issue	Sustainable planning policy
Global warming	Reduce the need for the private car by: • Controlling land-use patterns, e.g. ensure urban land is used "efficiently" by building at medium to high density • locate new development near to public transport networks. • Limit town centre parking.
Pollution	Produce detailed policy to control/limit specific emissions from industrial or manufacturing industry (including noise, smells and dirt).
Conservation of natural and man-made environments	Policies to protect landscapes and open, undeveloped areas and to protect buildings and urban spaces. (Listed Buildings and Conservation Areas).

12. Extract of a speech by the Secretary of State for the Environment, John Gummer, to the Town and Country Planning Association, January 1994.

schemes and that town centres are well served by public transport networks. By promoting the development or redevelopment of existing town centres, as well as complementary measures to reduce traffic flow, the government are seeking to promote the use of town centres, while discouraging the use of the private motor car. An LPA would, in theory, therefore, be entitled to refuse planning permission for out-of-town development on the grounds that vehicular journeys to and from the centre would result in an unnecessary waste of fuel (petrol) resources. Thirdly, PPG13 (issued March 1994) concentrated on transport and incorporated the strongest language of the three documents on how the planning system can restrict car use. Paragraphs 1.7 and 4.4 encouraged LPAs to incorporate policies in their development plans, which locate all forms of development in areas well served by a choice of transport modes and, through the operation of restrictive parking standards, reduce parking provision within that development to an operational minimum.

The combined impact of PPGs 6 and 13 is to steer developments away from out-of-town locations and towards the centre or edge of existing towns. Further car usage will be discouraged as towns/cities have traditionally been the focal points for interchanges between railway, tram, bus, private car and pedestrian modes of transport.

The thrust of government policy is that, by discouraging out-of-town and encouraging in-town and edge-of-town development and yet limiting use of the private car, by restricting parking provision in new schemes, people will use public transport in preference to the private car. A 1993 report, commissioned by the Departments of Environment and Transport argued:

> The evidence of the study indicates that in overall terms, the planning policies most pertinent to the objective of reducing travel demand and encouraging use of emissions-efficient modes are:
> - the focusing of development in urban areas
> - the maintenance and revitalization of existing neighbourhood, town and city centre
> - constraints on the development of small settlements and the extension of villages within the commuter belt. (DoE 1993c)

This objective to use the planning system to reduce car use was subject to several criticisms. First, the government Departments of Environment and Transport were pursuing contradictory policies with respect to this common objective. Environment was encouraging LPAs to resist car usage in dealing with planning applications, while Transport was pressing ahead with a major road-building programme, requiring an additional 9000 km of new roads in the 1990s (DoE 1994b).

> The contradictions were everywhere apparent, for example in the massive road-building programme to cater for a projected 83–142 per cent growth in traffic by 2025, or the deregulation of buses or cut backs on investment in railways. (Blowers 1993: 778).

Secondly, by seeking in-town and edge-of-town redevelopment in preference to out-of-town, it does not always follow that vehicular emissions will be reduced. A vehicle idle in a traffic queue, waiting to gain access to a busy town centre, is likely to produce more carbon dioxide than one that gains immediate access to an out-of-town shopping development with ample parking provision. PPGs 6 and 13 encourage local councils to introduce complementary highway measures to reduce traffic flows in town centres, such as re-routing through-traffic, park & ride schemes on the city boundary, traffic-calming measures and pedestrianization. Such measures will ultimately work if they "push" people away from using a car in favour of public transport.

Thirdly, the only reliable way to reduce carbon dioxide emission is to make the use of the private car a financially expensive option when compared to public transport. The town planning strategies in PPGs 6 and 13 represent a "big stick" being wielded against car ownership. A more effective strategy would be a "transport stick & carrot", whereby a financial penalty is imposed on car use by means of road pricing (to charge the motorist on the basis of mileage travelled) and there is investment in public transport, so that it would be far cheaper than using roads and run at a sufficient frequency to be accessible to many people. Furthermore, although existing roads should be maintained, the budget for new road building should be severely cut back. All these issues are beyond the realms of town planning policy *per se*, and are matters of public investment and wider public policy (CPRE 1992, Pharoah 1992)).

It must be acknowledged that, even in the mid-1990s, "sustainability" was in its infancy as a piece of public policy. The government identified the role that planning should play as part of a wider strategy. It is therefore only the start of a long process to change public, (including developers') perceptions of the whole sustainability subject area. It is important that the real impact of government policy is properly assessed at the end of the century and not before. However, all people involved in this subject area realize that land-use planning in isolation of a wider policy of supporting public transport and limiting private car usage will not be able to tackle effectively the problem of carbon emissions produced by motor vehicles.

Urban growth

The Earth Summit considered how sustainable development could be applied to patterns of human settlement to create the "sustainable city". This urban sustainability deals with the achievement of urban development subject to the condition that natural resources are not depleted so as to threaten their their long-term future.

The sustainable city must enjoy a harmonious relationship with its region or subregion, so that its existence and potential for growth are balanced against the long-term maintenance of water supply, air quality, land in agricultural production, and drainage/sanitation. Thus, urban sustainability is directly influenced by land-use controls, which ensure efficient use is made of urban land and which protect non-urban land from urban encroachment.

In Britain, some land-use policies have emerged that address such issues. Although they largely pre-date the sustainable development policies of the late 1980s and 1990s, they can be adapted to reinforce the implementation of a sustainable strategy.

Green belt policy   Until 1994, green belt policy had been principally concerned with checking urban sprawl, so that only a restricted schedule of development activity had been permitted around the major conurbations of Britain. In 1995 the government issued amended policy guidance with a new emphasis on how such policy, by operating at a regional and subregional level, can deliver sustainable patterns of development. Green belt policy, while continuing to resist outward urban expansion, can play a positive role in retaining attractive landscapes, promoting outdoor recreation, improving the quality of spoilt land (subject to tipping or extraction) and encouraging development within the existing urban envelope, whether by development of derelict land or redevelopment of existing sites within towns and cities. One problem is that such areas of restraint are "leapfrogged" by developers.

Conservation of built environment   Both listed building and conservation area controls deal with the preservation of the built environment. Such special policy regimes would satisfy the Brundtland definition in that they seek to maintain the nation's built heritage for the benefit of future generations. Such policies also focus attention on matters such as the sympathetic re-use of listed buildings or the enhancement of conservation areas.

The UK strategy on sustainable development supports the need to maintain and protect the built environment, stating that "Failure to do so would result in irreversible loss of the nation's heritage". (DOE 1994c: 88).

Conservation of natural environments   Several policies deal with the relationship between development activity and conservation of natural resources to protect biological diversity:
- Sites of Special Scientific Interest and landscape quality, introduced by the Wildlife and Countryside Act 1981.
- Controls introduced by the European Community Habitats Directive[13] or Birds Directive,[14] which establishes a European system of Special Areas of Conservation to protect wildlife and where development will only be permitted if there is no alternative solution and there are "imperative reasons of overriding public interest" (which includes economic and social considerations)[15]

---

13. *Conservation of Natural Habitats and of Wild Fauna and Flora*, EC Council Habitats Directive 92/43.
14. EC Council *Birds Directive* 79/409.
15. Article 6 of the Habitats Directive, 92/43.

- Control over trees, either by Tree Preservation Orders or by conservation area legislation (temporary protection for six weeks)
- National Nature Reserves
- National Parks
- Areas of Outstanding Natural Beauty
- Biosphere reserves
- Environmentally sensitive areas.

Efficient land use   Some planning policy initiatives dealing with new housing provision have championed the cause of sustainability and sought to be associated with this new policy agenda, including both urban villages and new settlements, providing for a mixture of residential, commercial, industrial and leisure-related activities. Urban villages promote the idea of medium- to high-density (not high-rise) mixed-use redevelopment. Such proposals offer redevelopment within existing urban areas and seem to minimize commuting by providing for both employment and housing within an area of approximately 40ha (100 acres), with most parts of the urban village within a walking time of around ten minutes. The consequence is that urban land can be "recycled", providing for industrial and residential needs without eroding land outside the city. The new settlement can create a more self-sustained community, less reliant on the motor car, as homes and workplaces can be provided side by side (DoE 1993b).

Protection of the ozone layer conserving resources and forests and reducing pollution   Conservation of resources such as minerals, aggregates and reduction of industrial emissions, with consequences for the ozone layer, fall within the realms of planning consideration.[16] Since the introduction of the modern system of planning controls in 1947, LPAs have enjoyed considerable planning powers to control industrial pollution. However, until recent years, with the introduction of a new "sustainable" agenda, these powers were largely unused, because of inadequate training for planners in this subject, lack of effective government guidance, attempts by council environmental health departments to deal with such issues, and the fear that such planning restrictions would result in job losses. Sustainability has provided the much-needed incentive to "kick start" many planners into a reconsideration of their role in the area. Such a new awareness of pollution issues within town planning has been accompanied by a wider range of controls over the regulation of industrial pollution. The Environment Act 1995 introduced new procedural systems for the regulation of industrial and water pollution, establishing a new Environment Agency to co-ordinate implementation of such powers. New Planning Policy Guidance as well as case law[17] accepts that potential pollution from a proposed development is a material consideration to be taken into account when deciding to grant or refuse planning permission. In particular, the planning

16. See *Gateshead District Council* vs *Secretary of State for the Environment and Northumbrian Water* (1994) *JPL* B8.

system should consider matters such as location, impact upon amenity, impact upon other land, nuisance, impact on road or other transport networks, and feasibility of land restoration in the longer term, when considering potential pollution issues.

The increased employment of environmental impact assessment in large-scale development proposals allows for an examination of potential pollution emissions from industrial development. However, an LPA enjoys power to refuse planning permission for any type of development proposal, with or without an environmental impact assessment, which may result in unacceptable pollution (DOE 1994d). The Earth Summit identified the contribution of industrial activity to causing airborne pollution, which is harmful to human health as well as damaging to forests and trees, creating acid rain and resulting in depletion of the ozone layer. However, the British planning system had not previously taken an active role in pursuing such policy objectives as "seeking to protect the ozone layer". Up until the mid-1990s it was unheard of for a planning permission to be refused on the grounds of "producing chemicals known to result in ozone depletion" or the "depletion of finite fossil fuel reserves". Following the guidance in PPG12 the government encouraged local planning authorities to deal with such wider environmental issues. By the mid-1990s some English county councils began to adopt structure planning policies that included language dealing with such issues as ozone layer depletion, fuel emissions, longer-term maintenance of non-renewable resources and industrial pollution (Barnard 1993). It is perfectly reasonable to anticipate that between 1995 and 2000 this initial trickle of "sustainable" policy will become, if not a flood, then most certainly a continuous flow of new policies. It is also inevitable that planning permissions will be refused for such environmental reasons and, when these decisions are the subject of a challenge at appeal, then the Secretary of State or an Inspector will be required to arbitrate on the outcome. At such a time, the government's resolve will be tested in the degree towards which it supports local councils who seek to use planning policy to protect the ozone layer or the finite supply of fossil fuels and the means by which they deal with attempts to calculate the environmental impact of schemes, for example, due to carbon emissions (Pearce 1994). Such an issue was dealt with in a decision of the High Court in 1994 regarding the construction of a new regional shopping centre at Trafford Park (also called Dumplington), in Manchester. Mr Justice Schiemann stated:

> The evidential problem of establishing the amount of CO_2 to be generated by the Trafford Centre and establishing how much of this would have been generated by shopping trips that would no longer take place if shoppers went to the Trafford Centre instead of their habitual shops is manifestly enormous. The results would inevitably have to include a vast range of error. Such a

17. Refer to PPG23, 1994, *Planning and pollution control and the comments of Lord Justice Glidewell in Gateshead MBC* vs *Secretary of State for the Environment and Northumbrian Water Group PLC*, (1994) EGCS 92, where it was accepted that pollution was a material planning consideration.

result if it turned out to show that there would be a net increase in such gases, would then need to be balanced against the undeniable benefits of the proposal.[18]

Conclusions

In 1991, legislative reforms[19] introduced a presumption in favour of the development plan, which superseded the "presumption in favour of development" that had reigned throughout the 1980s property boom. LPAs have, since 1992, been encouraged to adopt sustainable strategies within new planning policy, and the DoE has produced its own guidance, with a strong emphasis on sustainability, especially in using planning policy to discourage use of the motor car. The 1994 *UK strategy* (DoE 1994c), as a response to the Earth Summit's *Agenda 21*, represents a further move in the direction of this "greening" of the planning system, whereby environmental considerations are given considerably more weight in the decision-making process than would have been the case in the 1980s. Yet the *UK strategy* contains few detailed targets or timetables to establish guidelines by which government policy can be assessed. The climate change document (HMSO 1994a) sets out a programme for curbing carbon emissions up to the year 2000 and the *UK strategy* identifies the important role town planning can play in helping to change land-use patterns and reduce car dependency. However, no government document establishes targets to limit car ownership figures, and the rise in ownership to the year 2025 is accepted as inevitable. The government published details of its future road-building programme (DoE 1994b) which identified the need for up to 9000 additional hectares of land in England to accommodate traffic growth over the 1990s. The *UK strategy* appears to accept that new roads will be constructed and that "This will impact directly on landscapes and wildlife habitats and indirectly lead to more land being used for aggregate provision. " (DoE 1994c). The document is silent on how bus deregulation and railway privatization will help curb traffic growth.

Critics argue that government pronouncements merely serve to "shoehorn" previous planning policies into a sustainable setting, that the strategy delivers nothing new and instead just "repackages" existing commitments to the environment so that they *appear* to be pro-sustainability. However, the government's approach to sustainability *is* a step in the right direction. Although some gaps do exist, notably on public transport strategy, the new policy guidance of PPGs 6, 12 and 13 have affected, and will continue to affect, planning decisions at application and on appeal. Out-of-town retailing permissions have been harder to

---

18. *Bolton MDC* vs *Secretary of State for the Environment* (1994) JPL B37. While this decision was later overturned, these comments remain valid.

19. Section 54A of the TCPA 1990, introduced by the Planning and Compensation Act 1991. See p. 44.

obtain since PPG6, and the regional shopping centres of the 1980s are unlikely to be permitted in the 1990s.

The implementation of sustainable land-use town planning is not an unattainable vision. Town planning has an important role to play by ensuring that urban or greenfield development incorporates a mix of uses integrated with a range of public transport systems. The wider issue is whether planning can make any real impact on such issues as global warming and vehicular emissions. Any planning strategy must be linked to other areas of public policy if such objectives are to be realized. Reducing the use of the private car will require a combination of planning policy with financial policy (subsidy to public transport) and a coherent transport strategy (reduce new road building) before the real growth in car ownership can be arrested, as people will opt for other modes of transport that provide greater accessibility at lower cost. The planning system operating in isolation of these other areas will not make any significant impact on such environmental issues as global warming. The Royal Commission on Environmental Pollution (1994: 159) concluded that "In isolation, land-use planning is a relatively blunt instrument for changing travel behaviour, critical though it may be in the long term . . . The problems of traffic growth and congestion must, in the first instance, be tackled by more direct means." In considering the role of the land-use planning system, the report acknowledged the interaction between land use and transport issues, but emphasized the role of a coherent transport policy framework alongside purely planning-based strategies contained in documents such as PPGs 6 and 13.

Planning authorities are being encouraged to adopt sustainable policies in their local structure or unitary development plans. By 2000 it is evident that such policies will be widely applied throughout the system. Sustainable development has been, and will continue to be, a "buzzword" in town planning throughout the 1990s. Land-use decision-making is an important arena within which a balance may be struck between economic development and environmental protection; therefore, town planning plays a vital role. Although it alone cannot deliver sustainable development, it enjoys considerable potential to direct key areas towards these goals. The test of the 1990s and beyond will be the political will of national government to support such a role for the town planning system.

The term "sustainable development" is not subject to one universally agreed definition. This may be of little surprise when one considers the broad subject area encompassed by the term "sustainability", namely that of the relationship between economic development and global environmental conservation. This chapter has focused upon the role of land-use planning in delivering sustainable development. That in itself is a broad subject area. Nevertheless, the British government have sought to initiate some debate, as well as action, on the role of the planning system. It is too early to judge whether the UK strategy, following from the Earth Summit, will be a success or a failure.

Table 7.3 Summary of key statistics.

Issue	Statistics	Source
Derelict urban land	60000–11000 ha within existing cities (Britain)	Civic Trust *UK strategy*
Urban growth	1981–2001 urban increase of 105000 ha (Britain) By 2001, urban area will account for 11% land area (England)	*UK strategy* Houghton & Hunter (1994)
Agricultural land	77% land area (Britain) 1985–90 of all urban increase, around 40% was previously in agricultural use.	DoE land-use change statistics
Forestry	2.4 million ha (Britain)	*UK strategy*
Road building	1985–90, 9000km of new roads built (Britain) covering 14000 ha. 1989 DoT predict further 9000km required.	Department of Transport statistics
	Global warming	
All greenhouse gases (methane, nitrous oxide & carbon dioxide)	Government target: all emissions to be at 1990 levels by 2000.	Climate change document
Carbon dioxide emissions	1990 calculated at 160 million tonnes carbon. By 2000 between 157–179 million tonnes carbon.	*UK strategy*
Car/vehicle ownership	20 million 1990 30 million by 2025	*UK strategy*
Pollution	Sulphur dioxide/black smoke fallen by 70% 1970–93. Nitrogen dioxide risen by 70% 1980–93.	Climate change document
Climate change	Estimate 0.3°C increase in temperature and 6 cm rise in sea level every ten years at 1990 rates.	Climate change document and Houghton et al. (1992)
Changes in land-use patterns 1982–92	Out-of-town retail = 4.1 million m^2 and 3.4 million in town (Compare: 1960–81 = 1 million out-of-town and 6 million in town.)	*UK strategy*

CHAPTER EIGHT
Urban policy and regeneration

This chapter examines the combined impact of property-based and financially based initiatives that have attempted to generate the renewal of Britain's urban areas since the 1960s. Attention will focus upon the pronounced changes to property-based strategies that were brought about in the early to mid-1980s and the more recent financially based strategies of the 1990s. One key theme will be the extent to which traditional town planning regimes constitute a bureaucracy that acts as a disincentive to potential developers considering projects in inner-city areas and whether, by removing that layer of local control, greater levels of economic activity will be released in those areas. Evidence drawn from research into these reforms will be analyzed, so that lessons may be drawn and conclusions reached.

The chapter will be divided as follows:
- property-based regeneration
- financially based regeneration

No precise or universally agreed definition exists to cover exactly what is meant by the terms urban regeneration or indeed urban area. The following definitions are designed to provide a starting point to the study of this subject:

> Urban areas . . . extensively built up concentrations of population and employment which have usually developed over a considerable period of time. (Atkinson & Moon 1994: 1)

> Urban regeneration policy . . . a conglomeration of largely area-based policies designed to tackle social (housing and health) economic (industrial base) and environmental (quality of urban form) deprivation with a strong emphasis upon improving the physical environment by achieving redevelopment of derelict land and provision of new infrastructures. (Stubbs)

Historical background

The introduction of the Urban Programme in 1968 represented the first real move by a post-war government to tackle inner-city deprivation. The Urban Programme and its associated Community Development Projects were designed to target limited resources, estimated at around £5 million between 1968 and 1978, on particular groups. Funding was directed towards a combination of environmental improvements and community projects. Yet the whole strategy tended to ignore the causes of urban poverty (poor housing, healthcare provision, lack of employment and educational facilities). From such early initiatives we may identify the roots of many subsequent policies, notably their focus on particular areas (area-based policy) in preference to dealing with particular groups in society (socially based policy). The Inner Urban Areas Act 1978 broadened the scope of urban policy. It established seven Partnership Areas, fifteen Programme Areas and nineteen Designated Areas.

The choice of organization was influenced by the level of deprivation, with Partnership designation in the most deprived urban areas, although this classification was not an exact science and was largely influenced by political decision-making by the national government. Each partnership programme and designated area involved the bringing together of local authorities and government departments into a common management structure, with funding to improve the area's physical infrastructure (roads, recreational facilities and housing), social infrastructure (health and educational provision) and economy (financial assistance to maintain and attract employment) (Lawless 1989).

In 1979 the General Election returned a new Conservative administration under the premiership of Margaret Thatcher. This administration was returned to office in 1983, 1987 and in 1992, although Mrs Thatcher resigned as Premier in 1990. During the eleven years of the Thatcher government several new urban policy initiatives were introduced. The new government of 1979 brought with it a fresh ideological zeal towards property-based urban regeneration.

> In general terms the post-1979 Conservatives believed that the problems of British Cities derived from the flight of the private sector. This, they felt, was largely caused by rigid local government bureaucracies and inflexible labour markets squeezing the private sector out. The central need was to encourage private investors to return. (Atkinson & Moon 1994: 115)

From 1979 new policies were being designed to increase the role of investment led by the private sector in deprived areas. This regeneration was directed towards a property-led strategy in which the role of local government town planning control was to be either reduced or bypassed completely. One central premise to what would follow was that a greatly reduced level of town planning control would encourage greater levels of private sector activity, notably property development, which would introduce new housing and jobs. Three principal policy areas were based on this philosophy, those of Urban Development Corporations, Enterprise Zones and Simplified Planning Zones.[1] These policies formed the key elements of the 1980s urban policies and challenged the almost established

---

1. Other forms of planning deregulation comprised revision to the General Development Order (1988) and Use Classes Order (1987) to provide more freedom. The General Development Order (1988) has now been replaced by the General (Permitted Development) Order 1995. See Chapter 3.

norm of the post-war years that local government was the only suitable administrative body by which development activity and urban regenerative strategies could be controlled. Alongside this revolution in property-based regeneration, the government introduced a series of grant-aided financially based strategies, which were founded on co-operation, as opposed to confrontation, with local government. This chapter will examine the property- and financially based urban regeneration strategies introduced since 1979 and which continue to be in practice in the 1990s.

Property-based regeneration

The incoming Thatcher government of 1979 believed that local government was a brake on urban renewal instead of a facilitator. Although the initiatives following from the Inner Urban Areas Act of 1978 were allowed to continue, the 1980s witnessed the introduction of reforms to encourage private sector development at the expense of local government control. The principal reforms creating the "flagship" of urban policy were the introduction of Urban Development Corporations (UDCs) and Enterprise Zones (EZs) with, to a lesser extent, Simplified Planning Zones (SPZs) (see Table 8.4) (Brindley et al. 1989).

It is important to remember that such urban policy was part of a wider strategy of introducing greater deregulation of town planning control (Thornley 1993). Other reforms introduced circular guidance "to establish that planning permission should always be granted unless there are sound and clear-cut reasons for refusal" (Circular 22/80), and a presumption in favour of granting planning permission (Circular 14/85), together with additional provision for freedoms from the need for planning permission in the Town and Country Planning (Use Classes) Order 1987, as well as the abolition of six Metropolitan county councils and Greater London Council in 1985, which had exercised significant strategic town planning powers in the major English conurbations. Local government was mistrusted by central government and with that mistrust came a suspicion that by reducing the burden of local government control, private enterprise would flourish and property development activity would increase.

Urban development corporations

An Urban Development Area could be designated under Part XI of the Local Government Planning and Land Act 1980. Each "area" would be controlled by an Urban Development Corporation and the Act set out the objectives for these bodies "to secure the regeneration of the area which would include housing, social infrastructure, environmental improvements, commercial and industrial redevelopment."

Table 8.1 Urban development corporations.

Numbers	UDC area	Designation
1	London Docklands	1981
2	Merseyside	1981
3	Black Country (West Midlands)	1987
4	Cardiff Bay	1987
5	Teesside (Sunderland)	1987
6	Trafford Park (Manchester)	1987
7	Tyne and Wear (Newcastle)	1987
8	Bristol	1988
9	Central Manchester	1988
10	Leeds	1988
11	Sheffield	1988
12	Birmingham Heartlands	1992
13	Plymouth	1992
Total number — 13 between 1981 and 1992		

Four "generations" of UDCs were designated between 1981 and 1993 (see Table 8.1). They are all funded by the Treasury and were not established with a specific lifespan. However, it is anticipated that the Secretary of State will dissolve some of them during the period 1996–8. When this occurs, all planning responsibility will revert back to the LPAs within the respective UDC area. Although all UDCs have enjoyed the same powers, the relationship between UDCs and their host local authorities have changed over the years. Whereas London Docklands (designated 1981[2]), Cardiff Bay (1987) and Bristol (1989) have met with considerable local government opposition, by the time of the creation of Birmingham Heartlands (1992) and Plymouth (1993) the UDC shared a harmonious relationship with their respective local authority. However, it is important to note that, once created, the UDC is responsible for all development control powers in its area previously exercised by the host local planning authority.[3] In addition, the 1980 legislation introduced wide powers of compulsory purchase of land, whether in private or public ownership, together with the power to grant planning permission on that land. Such powers were not available to the traditional local authority and had previously been used by the New Town Development Corporations, who were vested with responsibility for building the British post-war new towns of the 1950s and 1960s. The host local authority retained its plan-making role, although there was little regard towards such policy by many UDCs especially in London Docklands as the LDDC pursued a bullish attitude to property-led regeneration in which they encouraged commercial redevelopment and privately owned housing. Such policies could be pursued contrary to local opinion because the UDC was a non-elected body, composed of professional planning and

2. Second UDC designation shortly after Merseyside, which was first.
3. Some differences occur between individual UDCs in that some may "re-employ" the local authority to carry out development control on an agency basis.

related staff under the control of a board of directors appointed by the Secretary of State for the Environment, instead of an elected planning committee composed of Councillors. The UDC considered "that its principal task was to encourage private sector interest and that the very absence of a master plan" would foster interest by housebuilders and industrialists, encouraged by a pragmatic rather than rigid plan-led strategy.

It would be unfair to portray the UDC as an unelected planning "hybrid", riding roughshod over the wishes of local people. However, the development strategies pursued by these organizations would look to a different constituency from those of the traditional planning committee, namely property development companies or commercial occupiers, rather than to pander to the desires of the local resident population. Whereas the London Docklands Development Corporation represents a unique example of an urban development corporation by dint of its proximity to the City of London, with the resulting pressures for residential and commercial redevelopment and its resources (in 1990–1 an expenditure of £332 million, compared to £24 million in Merseyside) in its early years, it was the subject of considerable criticism for pursuing a development strategy frequently at odds with community groups, as it granted permissions for high-quality office schemes (such as Canary Wharf) that provided a few jobs for local people during construction and after completion (Brownhill 1990, Coupland 1992). Although since 1988, with the collapse of the 1980s property boom, the LDDC has pursued a much more conciliatory role towards local community groups. A good deal of antagonism had been the hallmark of the years between 1981 and 1988 (Case Study 8.1).

Outside London Docklands the relationship between UDC and local authority has not been so antagonistic, yet a consistent criticism has been voiced against the undemocratic powers of these corporations and the way in which they cut across local democracy and accountability, together with increased financial resources that had not been available to local government in previous years. This was the view taken in areas such as Liverpool, where the establishment of a Merseyside UDC was greeted with mistrust by the various local government bodies who opposed its resources and organizational structures but welcomed any new funding to create much needed employment.

Enterprise zones (EZs)

Also created by the Local Government Planning and Land Act 1980, the Enterprise Zone represented a combination of taxation incentives with a greatly reduced level of planning control in an attempt to foster fast-track development and expedite redevelopment of run-down urban areas. Each EZ was designated for a ten year period. The incentives to developers in EZs are:
- *Town planning issues* A simplified planning scheme is drawn up, which grants automatic permission for anything within the uses, type or size of development listed.

Case study 8.1: Urban Development Corporations

The **London Docklands Development Corporation** is by far the most well publicized UDC. Since 1981 it has overseen the construction of 2.2 million m² (24 million ft²) of commercial/industrial floorspace, a new airport, 18 700 new homes, a new road link to the City of London (Limehouse Link) and a light rail system (Docklands Light Railway). This development has taken place on 2070 ha of land astride the River Thames and 3 km of the east of the City of London. Some £2300 million of public sector investment in the first 13 years has resulted in an estimated £6 000 000 million of private investment. By 1996 one major area remained undeveloped, that of the Royal Docks, with LDDC plans for a conference hotel facility and a major international exhibition centre. The vast majority of housing is privately owned and at the end of 1994 the vacancy rates for the 1.2 million m² (13 million ft²) of offices was 34.8 per cent.

The **Black Country Development Corporation** on the northwestern outskirts of Birmingham, established in 1987, has co-ordinated the construction of new roads, 557 400 m² (6 million ft²) of commercial/industrial floorspace, 2000 new homes and reclamation of 303 ha of land.

Merseyside Development Corporation has been responsible for the redevelopment of the former docks area of Liverpool on both eastern and western sides of the River Mersey. Between 1981 and 1994, 380 ha of land were reclaimed, together with new developments at the Albert Dock (leisure, retail uses), the Brunswick Business Park and housing schemes of New Brighton and Vauxhall.

- *Taxation issues* Exemption from rates charged on commercial and industrial property; 100 per cent allowances for corporation and income tax for capital expenditure on industrial and commercial buildings.

Between 1981 and 1990, 39 such zones were designated, 11 in the first year alone. EZs were always considered to be something of an experiment and the government announced in 1987 that further designations would only be made in exceptional circumstances. Between 1988 and 1992, only four EZs were designated. However, in early 1994 the government announced that 16 new EZs would be created in the areas of County Durham, Yorkshire and Nottinghamshire, affected by closure of coalmines during the mid-1990s (Table 8.2).

The majority of designations have been made in areas blighted by industrial decline in traditional manufacturing or heavy industry, such as shipbuilding in Sunderland or northwest Kent, and manufacturing industry in Dudley (West Midlands) or the steelworks in Corby (Northamptonshire). The EZ is designated by the Secretary of State for the Environment, and the relevant local authority or UDC responsible for the zone in question is invited to prepare an individual scheme detailing the exact schedule of planning freedoms they consider most appropriate.

The activities of the various enterprise zone authorities have been the subject of considerable research and analysis. Two questions often arise when seeking to evaluate their work. First, to what extent does the Enterprise Zone represent an experiment in free-market economics? Secondly, what has influenced development activity within the zone: freedoms from planning permission, taxation

Table 8.2   Enterprise zones.

Numbers	Enterprise Zone	Designation
1	Belfast	1981
2	Clydebank (Glasgow)	1981
3	Clydebank District	1981
4	Corby (Northamptonshire)	1981
5	Dudley (West Midlands)	1981
6	Hartlepool	1981
7	Langthwaite Grange (Wakefield)	1981
8	Lower Swansea Valley	1981
9	Salford Docks/Trafford Park	1981
10	Speke (Liverpool)	1981
11	Tyneside	1981
12	Isle of Dogs	1982
13	Dale Lane & Kinsley (Wakefield)	1983
14	Delwyn (Clwyd)	1983
15	Invergordon (Highlands)	1983
16	Londonderry	1983
17	Britannia (Middlesborough)	1983
18	North East Lancashire	1983
19–23	North West Kent (5 Zones)	1983
24	Rotherham	1983
25	Scunthorpe	1983
26	Wellingborough	1983
27	Workington (Cumbria)	1983
28	Milford Haven	1984
29	Round Oak (Dudley)	1984
30	Glanford (Flixborough)	1984
31	Tayside	1984
32	Telford	1984
33	Lower Swansea Valley No. 2	1985
34–5	North West Kent 6 & 7 (2 Zones)	1986
36	Inverclyde	1989
37–9	Sunderland (3 Zones)	1990
40–43	Easington Coalfields (Durham) (4	1994
44–7	Zones)	1994
48–51	East Midlands Coalfields (Notts) (4	1994
	Zones)	
	Yorkshire Coalfields (S Yorkshire)	
	(4 Zones)	

Total number = 51 designations 1981–94

benefits, or both in equal measure?

In response to the first question, it is difficult to conclude that EZs represent a pure free-market experiment when they are so reliant upon a whole variety of "taxation holidays" or other financial exemptions. The activities of the free market have been distorted to provide incentives to locate within the zone. Indeed, it may be that their designation may have a detrimental rather than beneficial effect upon the free market. Research published in 1987 (PA Cambridge Economic Consultants 1987) concluded that the EZ experiment has encouraged the development of new premises in previously derelict or neglected sites, creating both physical regeneration and economic activity. An estimated 35000 jobs were created as a direct result of EZ policy in 23 zones studied (at a cost of around £23000–30000 cost per job to the public sector). Zones in the more prosperous regions of the South East and Midlands achieved the fastest rate of development, with some 88 per cent of firms in the zones studied perceiving exemption from Rates to be the principal benefit. Only 3 per cent of firms considered the relaxed planning regime achieved this. Most of the additional jobs created within the zones were transferred from elsewhere in the local communities.

It would be impossible for such studies to conclude for example that such development would not have located within the Isle of Dogs if the Isle of Dogs EZ had not been created. The EZ in effect acted as a magnet drawing certain economic activity to a particular area instead of acting as a pure catalyst, in which its existence helped to create that activity. Furthermore, research published in 1988 into the Tyneside Enterprise Zone concluded that the financial benefits of the zones may provide a disincentive for firms to pursue efficient business practice:

> . . . the main effect of the incentives appears to have been a "cushioning" effect denied to their competitors outside the zone who appear to have been forced to become efficient, notably by developing new products. (Talbot 1988).

Regarding the second question, some studies have found that the planning freedoms offered by the EZs have had little influence on the decisions of firms relocating to the new zone. The significant incentives had been taxation benefits and rates holidays. Such fiscal benefits would appear to have almost totally eclipsed any reduced town planning (sometimes called "non-plan") regime in the eyes of the newly located businesses ". . . While developers developing in the EZ clearly do not regard the relaxed planning regime as a major contributing factor, attracting them to EZs, it is nevertheless regarded as of value by many of them mainly because of the time saving involved" (Roger Tym 1984: 138). The vast majority of EZs were designated in inner-city areas. It is poor quality and poorly funded infrastructure that has traditionally discouraged new businesses locating within the inner city. The many financial benefits enjoyed within the EZ would appear to have provided a very significant "carrot" to attract investors and businesses. With many EZs, the infrastructure outside the zone has remained unaltered, with continued existence of poor transport linkages and environmental quality. However, the tangible financial benefits of the EZ have outweighed even this traditional disincentive to relocating in the inner city. Enterprise zones have a limited lifespan of ten years, after which the financial benefits end and traditional planning powers are regained by the local planning authority. It is entirely possible that, with the removal of the key reason for the original relocation, the EZ occupiers of the 1980s may drift out of these areas during the 1990s in preference to areas with a better infrastructure or environmental quality within the

165

Case study 8.2: Enterprise Zones

The **Isle of Dogs** EZ within London Docklands UDC covered an area of 170ha. Manufacturing industry was not encouraged, with a preference for office redevelopment.

The 929000m² (10 million ft²) office development at Canary Wharf was located within the Enterprise Zone. This EZ was dissolved in 1992, following completion of its ten-year lifespan. The **Dudley** EZ ran between 1981 and 1991 and incorporated the regional shopping centre at Merry Hill and a major office/leisure development, The Waterfront. Both were constructed on former industrial land.

---

surrounding region (Case Study 8.2).

Simplified Planning Zone (SPZ)

The SPZ was introduced by the Housing and Planning Act 1986, with designation possible from 2 November 1987. Whereas the town planning principles contained within the Enterprise Zone were applied in isolation from all the other financial benefits, the SPZ represented a pure form of deregulation by reducing or avoiding altogether the need for developers to apply for planning permission whose proposals fall within the schedule of acceptable development within the zone. As with an EZ an SPZ is designated for a ten year period.

Any LPA or landowner could promote the adoption of such a zone, provided that the land involved was not in a National Park, Conservation Area, Area of Outstanding Natural Beauty, green belt or Site of Special Scientific Interest. The SPZ represented an extension of the government's philosophy that to reduce town planning bureaucracy would encourage development activity to take place.

This philosophical stance was stated in the policy guidance on SPZs, which was issued shortly after their designation became an option for councils and developers to consider:

> SPZs are a new planning instrument for facilitating development in designated areas. The SPZ provides for an alternative approach to the control of development which allows the planning system to operate more efficiently and effectively in designated areas and thereby encouraging development to take place where it is needed.[4]

As with the Enterprise Zone, the SPZ involved a schedule of zones, uses and building activity that would not require planning permission. Any proposal that fell outside the provisions of this schedule would require planning permission in the traditional way, which in the case of an SPZ area would require submission of an application to the local planning authority. The government promoted the idea as being suitable for the following:

- large, former industrial areas or estates

---

4. PPG5 (1988), *Simplified planning zones*. The document includes guidance, as originally issued, on the designation of SPZs.

- large single ownership sites
- employment areas, providing a mix of industry, warehousing, commercial and retail development
- large-scale residential.

Although the SPZ sought urban regeneration, it was effectively a deregulation of planning control, and the government's optimism in 1987 was that this initiative would be widely welcomed by developers who had been frustrated by delay within the planning system. However, by 1990, just over two years from the introduction of the SPZ, only three had been adopted: at Derby, Corby and Dingwall. The government commissioned research into the poor perception of SPZ schemes by developers.[5] One of its key recommendations dealt with the need to speed up the adoption procedure. The government heeded this advice and introduced certain reforms in 1991. The key reform was the waiving of the previous need for a Local Inquiry into the SPZ if any objections were received, which had created an inbuilt delay of between 12 and 22 months. Revised policy guidance was also issued in a new PPG.[6]

Between 1990 and 1992, three additional SPZs were adopted at Monklands (Scotland), Gedling (Nottingham) and Falkirk. In 1994 the proposal for the Slough Trading Estate was adopted, This SPZ is the second largest (164 ha compared to 178 ha at Corby). Its adoption represents a good example of the SPZ concept being promoted by a local landowner, Slough Estates, who sought the benefits of not requiring planning permission for a ten year period within which they will implement a comprehensive redevelopment of the many industrial and storage premises within the estate. The Slough SPZ divides the estate into a series of subzones, within which a broad range of industry, commercial and warehouse uses will be permitted. Sensitive boundary subzones separate any development from nearby residential occupiers.

The enthusiasm for the SPZ as shown by Slough Estates is still a rare phenomenon. Indeed, the Slough example is unique in being within single ownership and being located within a buoyant economic area, astride the M4 and Thames Valley corridor between London and Reading. In other parts of the country, the adoption of an SPZ has not, in itself, been a catalyst to economic activity. Again, we return to the relationship between town planning freedoms and economic or development activity. Although many developers would welcome a lifting of excessive town planning bureaucracy, this in itself would not create a flurry of economic activity.

The fact that only ten SPZs were adopted in the years between 1988 and 1994 (Table 8.3) is evidence of a lukewarm reception by the private sector. Furthermore, not all of these are examples of a "pure" form of SPZ. The Derby SPZ was promoted on the back of a £3.28 million City Grant to pay for infrastructure improvements within the site (Derby City Council 1991). Such financial benefits

---

5. Refer to the research recommendations in *Simplified Planning Zones: progress and procedures* [DOE Planning Research Programme] (London: HMSO, 1991).
6. PPG5 (1992), *Simplified planning zones*. This replaced the original issued in 1988.

Table 8.3   Simplified planning zones.

Numbers	SPZ	Adopted
1	Sir Francis Ley (Derby)	1988
2	Corby (Steelworks)	1988
3	Dingwall (Highlands)	1989
4	Monklands (Coatbridge)	1991
5–6	Gedling (Nottingham)	1991
7	Grangemouth Docks (Falkirk)	1992
8	Slough Trading Estate	1994
9–10	Broxtowe (Nottinghamshire)	1994

Total adopted = 10 between 1988 and 1994*

* By 1995 a further 3 proposals were being processed (2 in Birmingham and 1 in Newcastle) and 5 had been proposed but then dropped (Enfield, Cleethorpes, Rotherham, Scunthorpe and South Holland (Lincolnshire).

and associated infrastructure payments carry greater influence than a mere deregulation of planning procedures. The evidence so far is that SPZ designation on its own is a weak tool in achieving urban regeneration, and the government's hopes for the initiatives have not been seized upon by developers (Blackhall 1993). (For a summary of property-based regeneration, see Table 8.4.)

Financially based regeneration

Since the mid-1980s, the government has sponsored a series of new urban policy initiatives in progressing the work of the urban programme (see Table 8.5).

City Action Teams (CATs) and Task Forces

CATs were created in 1985 and Task Forces the following year, following policy initiatives by the DOE and Department of Employment respectively. Both CATs and task forces shared a common objective in seeking to co-ordinate the work of their respective departments with the activities of local authorities, voluntary organizations, private sector groups and community groups. Funding to each organization was limited, but the policy was born of a desire to co-ordinate the work of national government departments at a local level. Yet these bodies were the subject of criticism in 1990 by the National Audit Office, which identified the need to improve both their procedures and effectiveness (National Audit Office: 1990). By the early 1990s, 16 task forces and 8 CATs had been established.

Action for Cities

Action for Cities represented a loose amalgamation of ideas for the inner city, published by the government following the 1987 general election in an attempt to generate greater private sector interest in inner-city renewal and redevelopment.

> What is perhaps most important about Action for Cities is that it placed the emphasis unambiguously upon the leading role of the private sector and the need to do whatever was necessary to encourage its participation and the prioritization of economic development over social regeneration. (Atkinson & Moon 1994)

The most tangible piece of urban policy to emerge from this document was that of the City Grant. City Grant was a financial award directed by the private sector, designed to convert commercially unprofitable schemes within the inner city into financially viable ones by means of a "top-up" grant available to projects costing more than £200000. The scheme, although introduced in 1988, was by no means a new concept and was more a repackaging of previous policy, in that the City Grant merely replaced some existing grants, including the Urban Development Grant (introduced in 1982) and Urban Regeneration Grant (introduced in 1986), which had been designed to support infrastructure projects in the inner city with joint financial support from the private sector. Since 1994, all City Grant funding has been absorbed into the work of English Partnerships.

City Challenge and a review of the urban programme

City Challenge emerged out of a general review of the urban programme, itself undertaken in 1990 (DoE: 1990b). It was launched in 1991 by the then Secretary of State for the Environment, Michael Heseltine. The idea was to create a new partnership between public sector and private sectors and on a wider level to co-ordinate and integrate the work of all agencies striving towards urban renewal. The emphasis of City Challenge was to help enable the physical development of land within the urban area, yet with regard to issues of social deprivation. The emphasis on "partnership" with local government and the encouragement given to local creativity were objectives in stark contrast to the role of Urban Development Corporations during this period. UDCs had been imposed upon local areas and had pursued a largely property-led strategy of renewal, whereas City Challenge pursued a policy of working alongside local authorities in pursuit of property renewal, with a strong emphasis on social policy. The government would pursue both policies in tandem.

City Challenge funding (which did not provide additional resources but was based on monies diverted from other budgets in the urban programme) was allocated following competitive bidding or tendering, determined by the Secretary of State for the Environment. In 1991, 21 bids for funding were submitted for

169

an equal share of £82.5 million every year. Eleven bids were successful, each local authority receiving £7.5 million per year for a five-year period. In 1992 a second round of bidding was undertaken in which 20 winners shared £750 million over a five-year period. Each "winner" was responsible for agreeing a programme of operation with the DOE. These programmes have concentrated on physical works such as infrastructure improvements and site preparation (removal of contamination, demolition) but have also included training and employment initiatives and housing improvements (Case Study 8.3).

Case study 8.3: City Challenge

Bethnal Green City Challenge won a competitive bid in the first round in 1992. The £7.5 million annual sum was directed towards retraining and educational initiatives for the local population, as well as physical improvements (building a new sports centre) and an urban design strategy to improve the quality of the local environment. Grants have also been made to local housing associations and the local authority to improve the quality of existing stock and aid conversions, as well as assisting the construction of new units.

Urban regeneration agencies

Also emerging from the Action for Cities document was a desire to seek greater levels of co-ordination within the broad arena of urban regeneration, designed both to attract investment and to improve the physical environment of the inner city. In England, policy for the inner cities was fragmented across several central government departments and they had pursued their own initiatives in isolation, for example the Task Forces (Department of Employment, later handed over to Environment) and CATs (Environment, together with Trade and Industry). Michael Heseltine, when Secretary of State for the Environment, had floated the possibility of other bodies being set up to co-ordinate all urban policies during the 1992 general election campaign. In Scotland and Wales, urban regeneration policies have been based upon local participation co-ordinated by one body in each country: the Scottish Development Agency (SDA) appointed by the Scottish Office, and the Welsh Development Office (WDO) appointed by the Welsh Office. The SDA was established in 1975 to bring about industrial and urban renewal and play a central role in co-ordinating government funding with local partnership. It was dissolved in 1990 and replaced by Scottish Enterprise. The WDO has remained intact and it co-ordinates a grant regime designed to encourage investment into identified areas.

In November 1993 the government[7] established English Partnerships as the body responsible for urban regeneration projects in England, incorporating City Grant and the English Estates Assisted Area Programme. Although the work of English Partnerships deals with the regeneration of derelict land, its wider re-

---

7. Established by the Leasehold Reform Housing and Urban Development Act 1993.

sponsibility is to attract inward investment and enhance the environmental quality of identified areas. Although the annual budget of some £250 million is in part allocated to grant aid (urban investment funding), the emphasis is on establishing joint ventures in which public funding is used to attract private sector investment. Such a "pump-priming" is combined with powers of compulsory purchase, whereby English Partnerships may assemble suitable sites for redevelopment alongside reclamation works to unsightly, derelict or contaminated land (Case Study 8.4).

Case study 8.4: English Partnerships

In its first year, 1994–5, English Partnerships was allocated a budget of £250 million, with an estimated £300 million raised by joint projects with the private sector, of which £102 million was allocated to reclamation of around 7282ha of derelict land. English Partnership funding has been used to attract investment into inner-city areas such as Newcastle and Liverpool. In Liverpool, English Partnerships established a joint venture company with Liverpool City Council, to regenerate key sites in the Speke–Garston area, to attract industrial and business redevelopment.

Finally, urban regeneration projects may receive funding from the Single Regeneration Budget (SRB) and European Community Union (EC) Funding. SRB funding is designed to tackle social and economic issues, as well as environmental degradation within the inner city, and is administered either directly by regional offices of central government departments or is allocated directly to bodies operating existing projects such as English Partnerships, Urban Development Corporations or local authorities. EC funding is channelled towards the economic development of the least favoured regions of the community,[8] as well as areas that have experienced a decline in the manufacturing, industrial or agricultural employment base (Case Study 8.5). The principal source of this assistance are the European Social Fund and European Regional Development Fund (collectively referred to as the "structural funds"). (For a summary of financially based regenartion, see Table 8.5.)

---

8. Defined where gross domestic product per capita is below 75 per cent of the average for the whole European Community and including in Britain, Merseyside and Scottish Highlands and Islands.

Case study 8.5: European Community Assistance

European Community Assistance is divided into a series of classes or "objectives", together with a collection of funds targeted at specific industrial–economic restructuring.

Objective 1 applies to the identified "least favoured regions". An allocation of 2 400 000 million ECU (£1 900 000 million) has been identified for regional assistance to Merseyside and the Scottish Highlands and Islands for the period 1994–9. **Objective 2** deals with areas of industrial decline, with each round of awards resulting in some 2 000 000 million ECU (£1 600 000 million) for the industrial regions of northern England, South Wales and the central region of Scotland. **Objective 5B** deals with economic restructuring in rural areas affected by changes brought about by the Common Agricultural Policy. For the period 1994–9 an allocation of around 5 000 000 million ECU (£3 900 000 million) will be targeted towards economic restructuring parts of Somerset, Devon, Suffolk, Norfolk, Lincolnshire, North Yorkshire, Cumbria, Shropshire, the Scottish Lowlands and Clwyd in Wales. Other specific funding regimes include restructuring the fishing industry (PESCA) areas affected by defence changes following the end of the Cold War (KONVER) and closure of coal mining industries (RECHAR II), steel industry (RESIDER III) and urban areas suffering from severe social and economic depression (URBAN).

Table 8.4   Property-based regeneration.

Location	Property-based regeneration	Established	Key factors
England, Wales Scotland	Urban Development Corporation	Local Government Planning and Land Act 1980	• 13 (by 1995) • Unlimited period (probably 15/18 hours duration • Adopt development control powers from LPA • Strong compulsory purchase powers
England, Wales, Scotland	Enterprise Zone	Local Government Planning and Land Act 1980	• Ten year period • Planning freedoms and financial incentives • Funded by Treasury • 51 (by 1995)
England, Wales, Scotland	Simplified Planning Zone	1986 Housing and Planning Act	• Ten year period • Planning freedom, no financial incentive • 10 by 1995

Table 8.5 Financially based regeneration.

Location	Financially based regeneration	Established	Key features
England	City action teams/ task force	1985/86	• Co-ordinate work of government departments with local groups
England	City Grant	1988 to 1994	• Top-up grants to encourage investment • Absorbed into English Partnerships
England	Urban Programme City Challenge	1968– 1991–	• Partnership • programme and designated areas • Urban programme funding projects based on bidding by local government
England Scotland Wales	English Partnerships Scottish Enterprise Welsh Development Agency	1993– 1990– 1976–	• Urban regeneration • Attract inward investment • Improve physical environment • Co-ordinate local economic initiations
England	Single Regeneration Budget	1993–	• Tackle social and environmental decay
Britain and European Community	E. C. Social Fund and Regional Development Fund (structural funds)	1992–	• ·Economic development to include environmental measures and training/employment projects

Conclusions

. . . the anti-bureaucratic sentiments dominate the government's attitude to planners. (Thornley 1993: 212)

This chapter has examined two distinct areas of urban policy – town planning strategy and financial assistance – with both strategies sharing the common goal of seeking the regeneration of derelict and economically depressed urban areas.

Town planning strategies sought to by-pass many existing local government town planning functions, whereas the urban policy strategies sought partnerships with local government. Although emphasis on "partnerships" emerged from a good deal of policy introduced in the 1990s, such as City Challenge and English Partnerships, several 1980s policies were also based on this premise, notably City Action Teams and Task Forces. Meanwhile, during the 1980s, the Thatcher administration led an attack against local government planners by introducing UDCs, EZs and SPZs.

UDCs and EZs have attracted redevelopment. SPZs have been less successful.

Research, as cited in this chapter, has indicated that planning deregulation in itself does not attract investment. The key issue is the availability of financial induce- ments. Taking this issue further, we may examine not just the fact that develop- ment has taken place in some of these areas but how that development has been approved and what type of development has been approved. In London Dock- lands these issues have been at their most polarised. During the 1980s, the LDDC largely ignored local opinion in a bid to "tap" development demand produced by the City of London. The government argued that the need for development meant that such important decisions could not be left in the hands of existing local gov- ernment.

The debate surrounding this topic boils down to a fundamental question as to whether urban regenerative town planning strategies should be vested in local government or in some agency established by central government. As for the role of town planning, the issue seems to have been clearly established following research into UDCs, EZs and SPZs: that a deregulation of town planning controls does not in itself create development activity. The most bald attempt at following such a philosophical position, that of the SPZ, has been a policy failure when judged against the government's optimism for them when launched in 1986. Nev- ertheless, in parallel with such innovations in town planning control, a variety of financial packages have been designed to achieve physical regeneration by reclaiming hazardous, unsightly or vacant land and by attracting investment. Grants have been offered to industry and they have sought to bring together local and central government in an attempt to establish effective procedures for the allocation of limited funding to tackle the many social and economic problems. A whole myriad of bodies have been created since the introduction of the Urban Programme in 1968. What has emerged is that central government has viewed local government in sharply conflicting ways at different times. On one hand it was suspicious of entrusting town planning to local government; on the other it sought to harness and co-ordinate activities with local government when allocat- ing grant aid towards urban regeneration projects. By the end of the 1990s, many of these organizations will have been dissolved and the "experiment" can be assessed fully with respect to the physical, economic and social regeneration of these areas. However, even when such assessment is undertaken, it is important to remember that town-planning controls on their own only play a limited role and that developers and investors are attracted by financial incentives and grant aid in preference to the automatic granting of commercial planning permissions.

CHAPTER NINE
European planning

An examination of the domestic town planning system in any European nation will reveal a variety of different practices and procedures reflecting the distinct historical, geographical, political and economic factors that have shaped those countries. However, it is possible to identify specific features that help to distinguish or group the planning systems of European nations. This chapter examines the town planning systems of Germany, France, Spain, and the Netherlands (Table 9.1). Key characteristics will be identified and comparisons made with the British system. This is followed by an examination of the impact of the European Community on town planning within its member-states and the emerging planning systems in the former communist nations of central and eastern Europe.

It is important to recall that the principal characteristics of the British system are a lack of regional government and a system based upon a strong element of national (central) government, with control at the top of the hierarchy. National government is responsible for creating the planning system by the introduction of both town planning and local government legislation, and through the function of government departments that have responsibility for planning matters: the Departments of the Environment and National Heritage.

The local government system is responsible for local decision-making on planning applications at the lowest and most local level of government. Decisions are based upon a flexible combination of policy and other relevant planning matters (material considerations). Policy is adopted following a process that allows public/developers to object. A right of appeal against the refusal of permission and determination of the appeal by an independent government Inspector, with discretion to allow or dismiss the appeal based on the town planning merits of the proposal.

The chapter is organized as follows:
- examination of German, French, Dutch and Spanish systems
- role of the European Community
- European regional policy
- central and eastern Europe.

The German system

After the Second World War, the old Germany was divided into the Federal Republic (West) and German Democratic Republic (East). These two countries were reconstructed under separate political systems, with West Germany following a market economy and the GDR a communist state. In 1990 the communist system collapsed, and east and west became unified on 3 October 1990. The West German democratic model, established by "The Basic Law" (Constitution of 1949) would now prevail in the east, and reforms would introduce procedures and practices that had originated from the former west.

Power is exercised at three distinct levels, with each level enjoying a strong element of autonomy. The three levels may be summarized as follows.

Federal government (national government)

The Federal government enjoys few powers to control town planning. A government department, the Federal Ministry of Regional Planning, Building and Urban Development, produces a report every four years, which establishes broad goals, targets and objectives regarding land-use policy.

Länder (regional government)

The former West Germany comprised 11 *Länder* or regions. Following unification, the former five *Länder* of East Germany were restored to create 16 regions in the new Germany. Each region is responsible for the implementation of Federal Law and such laws include the Federal Building Act and Federal Building Law, which establish what constitutes development and therefore requires permission. The *Länder* governments produce a regional plan dealing with strategic long-term planning issues and will issue advice on how the municipalities should interpret such regional policy or relevant legislation.

Municipalities (local government)

Each *Länd* will incorporate many municipalities. Each municipality (*Gemeinden*) will produce a binding land-use plan *(Bebauungsplan)*. This document will be the subject of a formal adoption procedure that includes consultation with local people and with the *Länder* to ensure conformity with regional policy. Once formally implemented, the plan constitutes a binding document that must be followed in all local development-control decision-making.

The plan identifies specific areas of land, possibly the ones subject to or expecting development activity, and details specific planning criteria regarding use, size and siting, carparking, methods of construction and materials. If a proposal is in accordance with these details, it must be granted consent and cannot be refused. Consequentially, development control is viewed as a technical rather than political process. In the event that no land-use plan exists, the official will need to rely upon any relevant advice as issued from the *Länder*.

Two further points need to be remembered. Under the German system, applications are made for a building permit that deals with both town planning and building regulation matters. A right of appeal does exist against refusal of a building permit (i.e. planning). However, such an appeal must be based upon some irregularity in the legality of a decision, resulting in a violation of the legal rights of a citizen; for example, the administrative error of refusing consent for an application that in all respects satisfies the land-use plan. The appeal therefore is not made on the planning merits of the case but on procedural and administrative issues. The appeal, which can be made by any German citizen, is made to the *Länder* and then the courts.

Summary: key characteristics of the German system

- plan-led system with a binding land-use plan at a local level
- some areas for discretion if no local plan exists
- planning and building control considered within one permit
- appeal based on administrative/procedural grievance and not judgmental planning-based issues
- legal certainty for developers when proposals are in accordance with the local plan.

The French system

In France planning control is exercised by each of four levels of government. Since 1983 some reforms have devolved significantly more planning responsibility to the local levels, although the national government has retained important powers to oversee and co-ordinate the activity of the other tiers. These four levels may be summarized as follows.

National government

The national government produces the French National Plan, providing, in theory, the national direction for land-use planning over the next period of five years. However, such documents are by their very nature very broad in content and are poorly related to issues of detailed implementation. During recent years the importance of such a document has been superseded by planning documents produced by the communes. A definition of "development" produced by the government and a series of national regulations establish a code of town planning principles governing all development types.

Regional government

France is divided into 22 regions. Each region may produce its own planning policy (*contrat de plan*), setting out a variety of regional planning issues, mostly financial projects dealing with infrastructure issues such as road funding or economic development.

Départements (subregional level)

The French Département represents an arm of national government operating at a subregional level. Each Département will include various divisions providing technical advice to the local levels (Communes) and oversee the operation of their planning function. Each Département produces a structure plan (*schéma directeur*) providing guidance on strategic and long-term planning objectives.

The commune (local authority)

Increasingly within the French system, planning responsibilities have been devolved to the local level or *communes*. Each *commune* is responsible for preparing a local plan (*plan d'occupation des sols – POS*). The POS local plan preparation is the subject of public consultation, which may result in a formal public inquiry with an independent Commissioner hearing public comment before producing a report. The Commissioner's report must then be taken into account by the commune, which may introduce amendments before the plan can be formally implemented. This is in contrast to the top-down system adopted by the British and German systems, whereby conformity is required with the documents and policy produced by the higher tier. When the plan has completed this progress, the commune becomes responsible for planning powers at the local level. In the absence of a POS, development activity is controlled by relevant national regulations applied by government officials working at departmental level. In the absence of a local plan, the département becomes the development control authority for the local area. The plan forms a zoning map, detailing both detailed restrictions and planning criteria to encourage development. It is not a binding plan and the technical officer dealing with the application is permitted some flexibility in its implementation.

Three further areas need to be considered, as follows.

Appeal system

The French Appeal Mechanism provides a way for applicants to challenge a refusal of permission to develop, but also a mechanism whereby third parties may seek to challenge decisions. This right is a consequence of French civil law, which allows a challenge to all administrative decisions, on the grounds of maladministration as well as on the merits of the case, on the basis that the decision has prejudiced the rights of the individual. This is not comparable to the British planning appeal system, which is not concerned directly with the impact on the rights of the individual but instead with the land-use consequences, which may or may not affect the amenities enjoyed by neighbouring occupiers.

Urban renewal

In dealing with the problems of urban renewal, the French have introduced development initiatives that have echoes in urban policy within other European states, where large urban areas require public and private sector investment, most notably the British employment of Urban Development Corporations, Enterprise Zones and Simplified Planning Zones. The French *Zone d'Aménagement Concerté* or ZAC was introduced in 1967, 14 years before the first UDC was designated in Britain. The ZAC represents a public–private urban renewal initiative whereby the local commune identifies a zone for specific infrastructure investment within which planning permissions are automatically granted for a variety of mixed planning uses. The local authority/commune may own the land already or may acquire it, and can then sell it to developers with specific planning permission attached. A special company may be established by the commune to perform and co-ordinate the sale of such land. The ZAC does not incorporate tax advantages. It has enjoyed success as a tool of public–private sector co-ordination in regenerating economically depressed areas and is an example of the introduction of an ad hoc planning mechanism outside traditional forms of control and with a narrowly defined purpose, namely the rapid regeneration of economically depressed areas.

Building regulations

Building regulation matters require a separate permit to planning matters. This is similar to the British system, whereby controls over town planning and building control matters are exercised by distinct groups of council officers, whose powers are determined by separate legislation.

Summary: key characteristics of the French system

- Devolution of development control to the local commune on the adoption of a local plan. In the absence of such a plan, decision-making powers on planning matters are held by the département.
- The local plan is not a binding land-use plan and the planning officer is allowed some flexibility over the application of policy and zoning when dealing with applications.
- The right of appeal exists, although this is based on administrative law and is not directly concerned with the individual planning merits of the case.
- Planning and building regulations are the subject of separate control.

179

The Netherlands

In the Netherlands, planning responsibility is exercised at the local authority level. Government is divided into the three tiers: national government, provincial government and municipality (local government). The responsibilities of these tiers can be identified as follows.

National government

The national government is responsible for enacting town planning and administrative legislation. This legislation has effectively devolved the important development control and development planning powers to the local level. There is no single definition of what constitutes development; instead, this is left to the individual municipality to define. A department of the national government oversees the system but does not intervene in local decision-making by the municipality. It does issue government policy statements, which may affect land-use planning but such policy represents guidance and is not binding upon the lower tiers.

Provincial government (regional)

The Netherlands is split into 12 provinces or regions. Each region produces a regional plan. Such policy provides for the strategic direction of land-use and transport policy across the province.

Municipalities (local authorities)

The Dutch local authority enjoys the greatest proportion of planning powers within the system. The local municipality prepares a local plan (the *bestemmingsplan*), which is a binding land-use plan. All applications for a building and construction permits must be judged against the use and built form prescribed for any plot of land contained within the plan. Permission is granted if a matter is in accord with the plan and is refused if it is not.

The municipality is given considerable freedom in deciding its own strategy, provided that the policies do not conflict with the regional plan or policy statements made by the national government, although such conflict would be difficult, as these documents tend to be broadly based and rather non-specific. The adoption of a plan, or review of an existing plan, involves the opportunity for public comment including a public inquiry to deal with objections under the co-ordination of the provincial government. This process may take between one and two years, but has been known to take as long as five or six years. A right of appeal exists against the refusal of permission. This appeal is made to a judicial department of the Council of State and is based purely on the legality of the decision, namely whether or not it was made within the correct interpretation of national legislation.

> Summary: key characteristics of the Dutch system
> - Most important planning powers are given to the local municipality
> - The local plan is binding upon decision-makers, although it may allow for flexibility in specific areas, notably seeking redevelopment of inner-city land
> - Building and planning regulations are considered in one permit
> - The appeal system is based on administrative law and not on the planning merits of the application.

Spain

The Spanish system is divided into three distinct levels of national, regional and local government. Planning responsibilities are divided across all three levels, as follows.

National government

The national government was responsible for enacting the principal town planning statute, the Ground Law 1975, which established the system of planning regulation and control. A government department prepares a national plan that identifies those areas of a land-use policy and transportation infrastructure across the regions considered to be of national importance, for example extensions of the motorway infrastructure or areas for industrial expansion.

Regional government

Spain is divided into 17 autonomous regions, each with its own regional government and regional sovereignty. This strong tradition of regionalism is reflected in the various regional policies, although national government must approve the content of regional policy. Such policy is issued through two documents, the Regional Economic Programme and the Guidelines on Development of Territory. The region enjoys considerable powers to introduce both regional and local policies, dealing with both the strategic regional directions of planning policy and the more detailed planning criteria for individual towns.

Local government

Towns larger than 50000 in population must prepare a master plan, which applies both national and regional planning criteria at the local level. These plans incorporate zoning into various uses or sub-uses (industrial, low/medium or high-rise residential or general, heavy and light industry).

Provisions of the master plan are binding, and planning applications will be approved only if they satisfy the criteria in the plan relating to use and built form. However, some flexibility is possible on undeveloped land within the urban area. The local authority may identify such land as non-programmed land (in effect stating that no programme or strategy has been adopted in respect of it). It is then possible for any developer to submit a proposal to the municipality to redevelop the land. The municipality will consider the application against their own broad policy objectives. The concept is similar to the ZAC (in France) and UDC/ SPZ/EZ (in Britain).

Summary: key characteristics of the Spanish system

- Strong regional identity with a significant regional role in local planning.
- Local plans constitute binding land-use plans with some flexibility permitted with the non-programmed land.
- Planning and building regulations are considered together.
- There is no right of appeal against refusal of a permit.

Comparison of some western European planning systems

It is easy for any comparison of many planning systems to become saturated with a vast array of procedures and practices.

In a summary of key characteristics and distinctions it is important to distinguish between: the plan-making function dealing with the various national, regional and local plans; and the development control function dealing with the basis of decision-making on applications for planning permission (Table 9.1).

Plan-making function

In Britain there has been little tradition of regional government. Plan-making is the responsibility of the local government tier. However, continental western Europe exhibits a strong regional tier as a common feature, with plan-making powers vested in these tiers varying between nations. In France, the regional planning policy has become largely irrelevant, whereas in Spain it retains its significance. In Germany and the Netherlands, the regional tier retains important powers of co-ordination over the lower tiers.

Table 9.1 Summary of comparative systems

	Tiers of government	Development control body	Status of planning policy	Planning & building permits	Appeal system
Britain	National Local	Local Authority	Policy is not binding	Separate permits	Yes, deals with merits of planning decision
Germany	National Regional Local	Municipality	Policy is binding	Considered in one permit	Yes, but deals with administrative errors
France	National Regional Subregional Local	Département if no local plan *Commune* if local plan	Policy is not binding	Separate permits	Yes but deals with administrative errors
Netherlands	National Regional Local	Municipality	Policy is binding	Considered in one permit	Yes, but deals with administrative errors
Spain	National Regional Local	Town councils	Policy is binding for urban areas only	Considered in one permit	No right of appeal

A significant feature across these five continental systems and Britain[1] is the importance of plan-making at the local tier. The importance of a visible and publicly accessible planning system has increased the desire in many countries to provide a greater focus on locally based policy production. This process may be a "bottom-up" system (France) where the local initiatives are given authority as policy documents, or it may involve local policy co-ordinated with documents from the regional or national tier for conformity as in the Netherlands and Germany.

Development control function

The legal status of planning documents is another important comparative distinction affecting the decision-making process. In Germany and the Netherlands, the local plan becomes a statement of binding land-use commitment, and planning

---

1. See section beginning on p. 29.

permission can be granted only for applications that satisfy criteria established within the local plan. In Spain and France, the local plan is also binding, although there is some flexibility in decision-making for particular areas (e.g. in inner cities and urban regeneration). In Britain, the plan is advisory and not binding and, although of importance, it may be overridden by other material considerations.

The "binding" plan provides for certainty within the development process and the "advisory" plan permits a degree of flexibility. During the 1980s some European planning systems demonstrated a tendency towards greater flexibility when confronted with development pressures towards new forms of development in specific locations, notably out-of-town retailing and business parks (Healey & Williams 1993).

Finally, it is important to remember that in the British model the appeal system exists as a form of arbitration over the planning merits of an individual scheme. The predominant characteristic of the other European systems is of an appeal based upon legal irregularity in decision-making. A binding system is established to decide exactly what will be built over a specific time period, so the appeal is used only to challenge maladministration or administrative error and not to challenge the merits of a decision that has already been made. An advisory plan system involves considerably more judgement in interpreting policy and other relevant planning matters. Therefore, it is a logical extension of the decision-making process that any challenge to it must be based on the merits of the planning issues and not the administration involved. In Britain, if an appeal is made on administrative matters surrounding a planning decision, it must be made to the courts. A planning appeal deals only with the planning merits of a scheme.

The role of the European Community

Turning to consider the impact of the European Community on town planning, we may ask the question to, "To what extent will the EC produce a convergence between the planning systems of member states?"

Four topic areas will be considered:
- European regional policy
- the Maastricht Treaty and subsidiarity
- environmental assessment
- sustainability.

Background

On 25 March 1957, six European nations signed the Treaty of Rome, which established the European Economic Community. The six nations undertook the gradual policy of economic integration by means of reducing tariffs and trade restrictions within their region. The predominant view at the time was that closer political and social integration represented the ultimate goal, but that such an objective would be most effectively achieved by building upon economic union. With greater emphasis towards this political role, the EEC is today referred to as the European Community (EC) and in January 1995 its membership expanded to 16 nations with the addition of Norway, Sweden, Finland and Austria. Britain was not one of the original signatories to the Treaty of Rome, having joined in 1973.

The Community consists of four institutions:

- *The European Commission* The Commission represents the government or executive of the Community. The Commission is composed of civil servants and is lead by 17 Commissioners. It formally initiates legislation (regulations, directions, decision or recommendation).
- *The Council of Ministers* Composed of ministers from the national governments of member-states, who must adopt all legislation before it can be formally implemented.
- *European Parliament* The Parliament comprises 567 members who sit in a whole session 12 times a year as well as in committee. The Parliament examines legislation introduced by the Commission but enjoys only limited powers to amend or reject such legislation.
- *European Court of Justice* The Court is made up of 13 independent judges appointed by member-nations who decide upon disputes between EC institutions and member nations, challenges by individuals to the action of EC institutions, and matters referred by courts within European nations for a judgement.

European regional policy

European regional policy has been in operation under differing policy initiatives since the 1960s. Today we can divide this topic into two areas: first, "cores versus peripheries", where regional policy seeks to employ financial assistance to eliminate economic disparity between regions; and, secondly, "cities versus regions", where urban growth can be controlled so that it benefits the surrounding region. Each will be considered in turn.

EC financial assistance: the Structural Funds

Regional financial aid is administered through the Structural Funds of the EC. The Single European Act 1987 laid out five specific objectives for these funds:

- development of poorer regions
- converting regions in industrial decline
- combating long-term unemployment
- increasing youth employment
- adjustment of agricultural structures and development of rural areas.

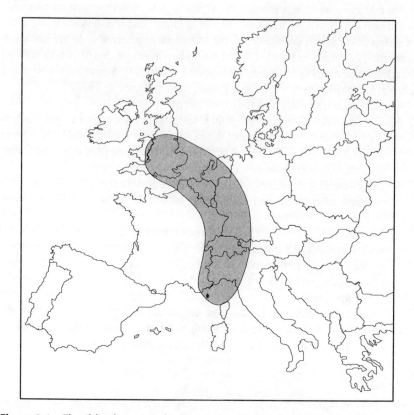

Figure 9.1 The "blue banana": the linear megalopolis that forms the urban core of western Europe (after Hall 1992: fig. 7.2).

During the period 1987–93 such funding was steadily increased to an annual sum of 14 billion ECUs (£11 billion on the basis of 1995 conversion: £1 = 1.2688 ECU). The EC has been viewed as a core prosperous region and a periphery of economically weak areas (usually below 75% of the average per capita GDP of all the EC; Hall 1992); the core has sometimes been referred to as the "blue banana", forming such a shape and including the central and southern England, northeastern France, Belgium, the Netherlands, southwest Germany and northern Italy (Fig. 9.1). The periphery includes the principally rural Ireland, northern Scotland, and areas around the Mediterranean. Financial assistance is directed towards creating economic growth in the peripheral areas, so that eventually the European Community will form an economic trading bloc of unitary strength. A 1991 report by the European Commission reinforced the view that economic and employment issues within the Community tend to cut across national boundaries, supporting the role of such a wider regional policy (CEC 1991).

EC policy and urban growth

Another way of examining regional policy is to focus on differing patterns of urban development. Cities within the northern half of the EC have undergone a complete cycle of urbanization from growth to decline and they commonly share problems relating to redevelopment of inner-city areas and planning policies such as green belts. In the southern half, some urban areas are still in the early stages of industrial growth, with its consequent outward expansion and reliance on migration of workers from rural areas. The EC has undertaken a series of studies dealing with problems surrounding urban environments, and in 1990 the Commission published a Green Paper on the urban environment (CEC 1990), which identified common problems such as the physical decay of historic urban areas, pollution, social problems. The report recommended a review of planning practice to encourage mixed-use urban development or redevelopment, with a consequent move away from a "monoculture" of land use, whereby planning serves to designate specific areas for specific functions, creating a reliance on the private car and preventing a sense of community developing.

In 1991 a new Committee for Spatial Development was established to examine issues relating to regional development, and the Commission published the Europe 2000 discussion document, which identified Europe-wide planning problems and policy agendas (CEC 1991).

The Treaty on European Union (the Maastricht Treaty)

The Treaty on European Union, signed in Maastricht in February 1992, established specific time periods for economic and monetary convergence across member-states. The Treaty required ratification by member-states, and introduced the concept of "subsidiarity" and promoted "sustainable" growth. For the first time in any Community treaty a direct reference was made to the practice of town planning (in Article 130s(8)), whereby the Council of Ministers, acting on proposals from the Commission, shall adopt "measures concerning town and country planning". Any measures would need to be agreed by all ministers, drawn from member-nations, who attend the Council of Ministers and must accord with the concept of subsidiarity, which seeks to limit community actions to measures that cannot already be adequately achieved by member-states. As regards town planning, subsidiarity would limit EC intervention to matters that cross national boundaries (such as regional policy) or involve a scale or magnitude over which the EC would be better able to act than the individual state. Subsidiarity limits the nature of EC legislation to that which focuses on Europe-wide planning issues. The Treaty also includes further initiatives on regional development issues to deal with regional policy, notably the suggested formation of a Committee of the Regions.

Environmental assessment

The EC measure that has so far resulted in the most pronounced impact on British town planning is the Directive on the Environmental Assessment of Projects.[2] This has been referred to as a piece of "supra-national" development control legislation (Healey & Williams 1993: 707) in that it affects the submission and consideration of planning applications across member-nations. The ultimate objective of the Directive is to bind the member-states, although the exact mechanism by which it is implemented is left to the individual country. In Britain, the Directive was implemented by a statutory instrument, the Town and Country Planning (Assessment of Environmental Effects) Regulations 1988 and the Environmental Assessment (Scotland) Regulations 1988. Guidance on its implementation is found in PPG12, *Development plans and regional planning guidance* (1992). Environmental impact assessment has been described as ". . . a systematic process that examines the environmental consequences of development actions, in advance" (Glasson et al. 1994: 3).

The Directive seeks one common approach to the evaluation of major development projects throughout the EC. The philosophy behind it is that the most effective environmental decision-making will prevent the creation of pollution or other nuisances at source. In Britain the 1988 Regulations categorized development types into two groups, Schedule 1 and Schedule 2 (Table 9.2), commonly referred to as an "environment impact assessment" (EIA).

Table 9.2   The British model of environmental assessment.

Schedule 1	Examples
All projects within Schedule 1 require environmental assessment.	Nuclear/thermal power station. Major airport. Railway for long-distance traffic. Steel/iron melting works.

Schedule 2	Examples
Projects that require environmental assessment only if they would be likely to have a *significant* effect on the environment by virtue of their nature, size or location.	Agriculture, e.g. salmon hatchery. Extracting peat, petroleum, natural gas and various ores. Processing of metals and manufacture of glass. A yacht marina. Holiday village or hotel complex.

Therefore, planning applications falling within Schedule 1 or Schedule 2 (with a significant impact) will require the submission of an Environmental Statement.[3] This must include information on the likely environmental impact of the proposal with specific reference to several subject areas.[4] If any significant effects are

---

2. Directive EEC/85/337 in force from July 1988.
3. Local planning authorities have powers to request a statement if one is not provided and they consider the proposal to fall within the Schedules.
4. . . . human beings, flora, fauna, soil, water, air, climate, landscape, cultural heritage.

identified, a description of measures to avoid or reduce those effects must be included. All this information must be summarized in a report written in non-technical language. The content of the statement will constitute an important material consideration in development control matters when dealing with large proposals that may involve potential widespread impact on the environment. The EIA represents a procedural mechanism by which information on such major projects is gathered, assessed and taken into account within the town planning system (Wood & McDonic 1989). Permitted development rights do apply to some Schedule 2 projects, whereby planning permission is automatically granted by the Town and Country Planning (General Permitted Development) Order 1995, for example the reclamation of land from the sea, or storage on land, of fossil fuels, natural gas or petroleum spirit. If the LPA considers that any such projects will result in a significant effect on the environment, then such permitted development rights are withdrawn and the matter will be the subject of both a planning application and an environmental assessment.[5]

The government is also encouraging county councils to incorporate policies relating to environmental impact within emerging structure plans. PPG12 (para. 6.25) states: "Environmental concerns need to be integrated into policy appraisal in all development plan preparation".

Sustainability

An increasing awareness of "green" issues within British planning has been evident since the late 1980s. Although this may be a consequence of many factors, such a trend has been identified as of greater importance because of the problems resulting from the property boom of the 1980s, including the erosion or rural areas by development activity. The concept of "sustainability" has now become a buzzword between planners and politicians. The influential Bruntland Report (World Commission 1987) provided a useful definition of sustainability "development that meets the needs of the present without compromising the ability of future generations to meet their own needs". This refers to the adverse environmental impact of development, seeking to restrict or prevent development that results in any adverse impact and to permit schemes that maintain long-term environmental quality. Such a concept is evident in the environmental assessment directive.

Between 1990 and 1992 the European Commission published a series of papers dealing with sustainability (CEC 1990, 1992a,b). The terms of reference set out in these papers signalled a move towards the inclusion of much wider aims and implications than had previously been considered by the Commission, with a focus on the agents and activities that deplete natural resources or otherwise risk dam-

---

5. For specific guidance, refer to the Town and Country Planning (Environmental Assessment and Permitted Development) Regulations 1995 (SI 1995/417).

aging the environment (Davies et al. 1993: 25). The British government introduced an environmental strategy in similar tone in a White Paper entitled *This common inheritance* (DOE 1990a).

The increasing emphasis given to this agenda of environmental protection will result in a greater impact on the planning process throughout the 1990s and beyond. This impact will affect EC legislation by building upon existing law, such as environment assessment, as well as increasing guidance issued by the Commission and encouraging environmental initiatives by individual member-states. It is not always easy to identify the specific results of such Europe-wide initiatives on the development control process within individual countries. Unlike European legislation, which has a direct bearing on decision-making procedures, EC initiatives on sustainability tend to focus on identifying problem areas and fostering debate on environment policy issues. During the 1990s the EC will play an increasingly important role by facilitating an awareness of sustainability, which in Britain will filter downwards to government policy (in PPGs) and in local planning policy (in structure plans, local plans and unitary development plans).

Conclusions for EC policy

The future role of the EC will influence planning systems through the creation of legislation to establish common criteria for development control decision-making within member nations, such as the approach taken in the Environmental Assessment Directive. Commentators have concluded that "The situation has been reached in which European environmental law has started to have an impact on the town and country planning systems in this country" (Redman 1993). During the second half of the 1990s it is possible for the approach taken in the Environmental Assessment Directive to be widened to include historic buildings and heritage areas, as well as dealing with access to information. Looking beyond legislation, the EC is having an equally significant, if indirect, bearing through the promotion of environmental awareness (substainability) and through the allocation of regional financial aid. Both areas will affect land-use policy.

The individual systems of planning regulation within individual member countries have evolved out of legal, historical and geographical circumstances (Davies & Edwards 1989). It appears highly unlikely that EC land-use policy will result in a complete integration of these planning systems. The systems will remain, but it does appear that EC policy will result in some convergence of ideas as certain topics are made the subject of EC legislation. However, this convergence of ideas should not be thought of as simply a top-down process, whereby EC legislation seeks a common approach on certain development issues. An increasing volume of EC legislation is anticipated throughout the 1990s, but the principle of subsidiarity will restrict the nature of legislation to matters that cross national boundaries. Nevertheless, a good deal of EC work will be involved in issuing guidance and fostering ideas to encourage action by individual governments. This has found favour in the increasing statutory importance of planning policy, which has emerged in several countries. In this respect, the work of the EC is to encourage a "bottom-up" approach to planning policy and procedures. EC policy has imposed common criteria upon diverse systems rather than requiring common planning systems.

By the year 2000, although it is unlikely that member-states of the EC will share a common system, they will probably share a common understanding of the problems facing Europe.

Professional bodies including, in the UK, the Royal Town Planning Institute and RICS, have developed an increasing awareness of European issues and are placing greater emphasis on EC issues in professional training and education. A 1993 report set out priorities for future action when professional bodies such as the Royal Town Planning Institute are faced with the impact of EC town planning policy.

The principal thrust of these priorities was a recommendation towards a greater Europe-wide mutual exchange of ideas on practice and planning policy, together with a review of education and membership policy to focus on European issues (Davies et al. 1993). In addition, the EC Directive on mutual recognition of professions results in professional qualifications being recognized across the Community, and pan-European professional organizations have been created to represent those professions, such as the European Council of Town Planners (Fryer 1994).

Central and eastern Europe

During the late 1980s and early 1990s, dramatic political reforms in eight[6] central and eastern European nations, together with the break up of the former Soviet Union, resulted in the fall of the European post-war communist bloc. Since these political changes, these nations have, to varying degrees, sought to embrace the democratic structures of western European nations and market-based economic systems. Such reforms will have implications for future town planning controls within these nations. As the former communist systems, with their strongly centralized concentration of power, have been cast off, new structures will be required to regulate the development pressures of a market-based economy.

The exact nature of these new structures will reflect the cultural, economic, social and geographical factors that prevail in these countries. Many differing systems will emerge and it would be foolish to speculate on their exact nature;

---

6. Albania, Bulgaria, Czechoslovakia (now the Czech and Slovak Republics) German Democratic Republic (now joined to the former Federal Republic and within the EC), Hungary, Poland, Romania and former Yugoslavia.

however, it is possible to draw some conclusions on the future directions of town planning within these states and to identify some of the development pressures to be anticipated during the late 1990s and into the next century.

Former communist systems

The principal features that distinguish land-use development in former communist countries from that of Western capitalist states can be summarized as:

- the role of the state
- ownership of land.

These will be considered in turn.

The role of the state

Under the communist system all political power was controlled by the state. The concept of "planning" was well developed in that the future economic regional and urban development was usually enshrined in a document issued by government ministries. In the Soviet Union, planned development of the nation was controlled by a national committee whose responsibility was to direct regional land-use policy, combining economic, political and sociocultural aims (French & Hamilton 1979). In Czechoslovakia, the government produced national and regional planning documents to direct development to the best location. Such policy statements provided a gloss to the reality of the situation in which the real decision-making regarding land use was vested in powerful government ministries whose prime objective was to maximize industrial output in a (vain) attempt to catch up with Western economies. These "super monopolies" made the decisions regarding the location of factories, transport infrastructure, extraction of raw materials and residential development to house the industrial workers. Land-use decisions were sometimes haphazard as the government ministries competed with each other to maximize output. This resulted in both environmental degradation and poor-quality development, especially so in housing developments.

Government ministries also controlled shops, hotels, warehouses and construction organizations. Local government was frequently powerless to influence the land-use decisions of these bodies. Although a town planning profession did exist within these communist nations, its role was to influence the decisions of the powerful ministries with only limited success. Local government did not enjoy a statutory control over new development proposals, as found in western European nations; although, planning policies and regulations were produced by local planners, the real power of implementation remained with the government ministries and it was not uncommon for such policies to be ignored by the ministries in their building programmes. The communist systems viewed town planning as an ideological beacon, a means of delivering the goals of a balanced and fair society. The reality was that town planning control was never vested in local government but in the "technocrats" who controlled state industries. Town planning became another tool by which these ministries could achieve their goals of industrial output at the expense of a balanced and co-ordinated land-use strategy.

Landownership

All land was owned by the state. In the absence of a land market, the pattern of land use was radically different from that of Western economies. The "super-monopolies" had no incentive to invest in existing city centres (Bater 1980). Their locational decisions were driven by industrial output and not, as in the West, by investment returns on commercial property. As a result, city centres were not sought after as a location for commercial and retail activity.

Following post-war reconstruction, many city centres simply failed to "evolve". Historic areas were untouched by commercial development and they avoided some of the radical redevelopment pressures resulting from property booms in Western economies, which so dramatically altered the character of the British cities such as Birmingham or the City of London. By the late 1980s, the centre of Prague looked much the same as it had in the 1930s.

The post-communist era

The break-up of communism resulted in the disintegration of the large state ministries or super-monopolies. The process of reform in the early 1990s was as rapid in its implementation as it is uncertain in its outcome. However, it is possible to identify a series of trends that have emerged in the first half of this decade, from which we may gather an understanding of the future direction for town planning practice.

Introduction of a market economy

The introduction of a free-market economy in general and a property market in particular has resulted in a change in the very motivation for property development. The transformation from state domination to a privately owned market economy has required the privatization of government property assets, to create a free-market environment in which private ownership of land encourages property development activities (Dyker 1992).

During the early 1990s most eastern European, former communist, countries adopted a "fast-track" approach, seeking the most rapid privatization possible as a "shock therapy" to increase the irreversibility of the earlier political reforms. One key issue arising from this programme is whether governments should automatically return property to the successors of its former owners (those who controlled the same prior to communism (re-privatization or restitution)) or whether property rights should be auctioned by the state to whomever can afford to buy (Grime & Duke 1993). As land becomes transferred into private ownership, both individuals and organizations will seek to enhance property values by developing land. The more land transferred, the greater the level of development activity.

Devolution of power

The break-up of large government ministries has been followed by a decentralization or devolution of power to local government. These reforms provide the mechanism for stronger town planning controls to be given to local councils.

In the Czech Republic, planning powers were transferred to such local councils. National legislation has defined the content of local plans and a government agency was appointed to oversee the system. In the former Soviet Union the reforms have been more haphazard. Increasingly, powers were transferred from national government to regional and local government bodies, yet no national legislation or other policy guidance sought to establish the nature and content of planning policy and development control activity.

As privatization of property increases and market forces take effect, then increasing amounts of development will occur. This is unlikely to happen until the late 1990s. At that stage it will be possible to assess properly the capacity of these emerging town planning systems to cope with such new development pressures.

What is important is that some mechanisms for planning control are adopted. Fear has been expressed among town planners in eastern Europe that planning controls will be swept away in the rush towards the implementation of new development or in seeking to make potential projects appear more attractive to foreign investors.

The nature of new development

Since the political changes of the 1990s, some significant development trends have emerged. Five popular areas of land uses in particular may be identified:

- *Retail* Increasing amounts of retail development have been occurring in city centre locations, especially for the sale of speciality and/or luxury goods. Such redevelopment activities have focused on residential buildings within, or close, to historical core areas. As a result, existing residents have been displaced as suitable buildings have been purchased by developers with a view to retail conversion.
- *Hotels* Central areas are also experiencing pressure for hotel redevelopment to facilitate, as well as encourage, the rising levels of tourism being experienced by these countries.
- *Commercial* Most former communist countries suffered from a lack of commercial office space. The service sector was largely ignored, as economic activity was geared towards industrial development. Increasing amounts of office floorspace will be required to satisfy both internal demand as well as the needs of foreign business seeking to trade with these countries. Centrally located office floorspace will be much sought after. With a low base of good-quality office accommodation and growing demand, it will take many years for an adequate supply to be provided. During the late 1990s the demand for such space will result in well located office floorspace commanding high rental levels (Case Study 9.1).

- *Residential* A lack of adequate family accommodation in many former communist countries, combined with displacement of people living in city centres, caused by commercial activity, creates a demand for new housing. The introduction of housing finance in the form of mortgages or other financial loans on property will combine with this existing demand to fuel a wave of new private housebuilding.

This new housing will result in suburban expansion of existing cities as development pressures push them outwards beyond existing boundaries. These changes will result in a new profile of urban form, whereby the city centre will contain almost exclusively commercial and retail activity, with residential and industrial activity spreading from the centre, and with land value dictating the type and nature of housing and industry.

Prague, Budapest, Berlin and Warsaw are poised to take advantage of new trading relations between east and west Europe because of their central location within continental Europe and their enthusiasm to embrace political, economic and social reforms (Hall 1993). The later half of the 1990s will witness rapid urban growth in these cities, provided that economic recovery is sustained until the year 2000.

Environmental degradation

Many former communist countries have to deal with severe environmental problems as a result of inadequate environmental controls exercised by the former system. The use of low-grade coal as an energy source, inefficient industrial and transportation technology, and under-investment in processing facilities, has resulted in serious air and water pollution, together with pollution-related diseases.

Conclusions

The new systems of these former communist countries of Europe will be required to deal with a legacy of environmental problems, as well as to accommodate and deal with the growing pressures associated with increasing levels of development activity as the private property market takes root. These pressures may be considerable and it is possible that they may overwhelm the system's ability to cope. Such a bleak prediction would result in an increase in environmental degradation, as polluting industries continue unchecked by regulations and planning mistakes encountered by Western countries in the 1960s and 1970s are replicated (notably the destruction of historic environments at the expense of commercial redevelopment). The need for increased town planning controls would provide the best means by which the effects of economic growth could be accommodated acceptably within the urban and rural environment. Liaison between the governments of these new nations and western European organizations representing property professionals, such as the Royal Town Planning Institute and the Royal Institution

Case study 9.1: Development in Vladimir, Russia

Vladimir is located approximately 100 km to the east of Moscow. A modern industrial town was developed around the ancient historical centre during the communist era. Following the introduction of liberal democratic reforms in the early 1990s, the City Council set about implementing a combination of town planning and marketing strategies to attract both foreign investment and tourism. The existing town of 375 000 population contains a strong manufacturing base and a magnificent historic centre built around a series of twelfth century cathedrals. Land alongside the railway station to its immediate southern boundary was identified for a hotel entertainment and conference centre to "tap" into the anticipated increase in business and holiday visitors during the remainder of the decade. The complex would include office, hotel, motel, banking and conference facilities, and would be linked to the central area by a new pedestrian walkway. By 1995 no work had started on the development, largely as a result of problems experienced in attracting Western investment, troubled by negative images of the new Russia as a result of political instability following the introduction of democratic and free-market economic reforms. However, once the political and economic situation stabilizes, then dramatic levels of foreign investment will follow. At that juncture the policies pursued by Vladimir will be followed by the many other industrial and/or historic cities in the Russian Federation.

SITUATIONAL
PLAN

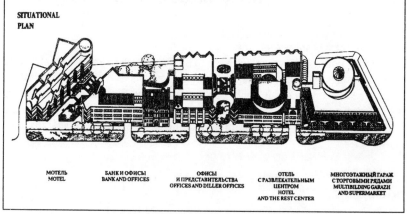

МОТЕЛЬ	БАНК И ОФИСЫ	ОФИСЫ	ОТЕЛЬ	МНОГОЭТАЖНЫЙ ГАРАЖ
MOTEL	BANK AND OFFICES	И ПРЕДСТАВИТЕЛЬСТВА	С РАЗВЛЕКАТЕЛЬНЫМ	С ТОРГОВЫМИ РЯДАМИ
		OFFICES AND DILLER OFFICES	ЦЕНТРОМ	MULTIBILDING GARAZH
			HOTEL	AND SUPERMARKET
			AND THE REST CENTER	

of Chartered Surveyors, will help to promote a greater understanding of the advantages, as well as disadvantages, of other planning systems. The role of the European Community is also vital in establishing a dialogue on such issues as environmental assessment and regional policy.

PART FOUR

The real estate
development process

CHAPTER TEN
The property development process

The property development industry is both complex and diverse: complex, in that there are many agencies, public and private, large and small, undertaking development in a variety of organizational forms and legal entities; diverse, in that it involves a vast number of businesses across a wide range of sectors, having different aims, objectives and modes of operation.

The property development industry is also risky, cyclical, highly regulated and lengthy in production. In addition, it comprises three major groups: consumers, producers, and providers of public infrastructure. This seeming imbroglio thus requires close consideration and understanding, so that the process of property development can be managed in a way that optimizes the benefit to all concerned. The point has been made more eruditely by one of the leading thinkers in the field of real estate development, as follows:

> Unlike many mass production industries, each real estate project is unique and the development process is so much a creature of the political process that society has a new opportunity with each major project to negotiate, debate and reconsider the basic issues of an enterprise economy, i.e., who pays, who benefits, who risks, and who has standing to participate in the decision process. Thus, the development process remains a high silhouette topic for an articulate and sophisticated society. The best risk management device for the producer group, which is usually the lead group in the initiation of a project, is thorough research so that the development product fits as closely as possible the needs of the tenant or purchaser, the values of the politically active collective consumers, and the land use ethic of the society. (Graaskamp 1981)

The growing intricacy and sophistication of the property development industry has led to the need for a deeper understanding of the public policy, physical planning, municipal regulation, market research, the legal framework, site appraisal, economic evaluation, financial arrangements, contractual procedures, building design, construction techniques and marketing strategy dimensions of a development scheme, together with a much more professional approach towards the management of projects in terms of time, quality, cost and asset value.

To facilitate the study and understanding of property development, several models of the development process have been devised since the mid-1950s. These have been grouped as follows (Healey 1991):

(i) **Equilibrium Models,** which assume that development activity is structured by economic signals about effective demand, as reflected in rents, yields etc. These derive directly from the neo-classical tradition in economics.

(ii) **Event Sequence Models**, which focus on the management of stages in the development process. These derive primarily from an estate management preoccupation with managing the development process.

(iii) **Agency Models**, which focus on actors in the development process and their relationships. These have been developed primarily by academics seeking to describe the development process from a behavioural or institutional point of view.

(iv) **Structure Models**, that focus on the forces which organize the relationships of the development process and which drive its dynamics. These are grounded in urban political economy.

For the sake of clarity, and in order to respect the principal aims of the text, this chapter essentially adopts an "event sequence" approach. Nevertheless, mention is made of the various agencies involved in the property development process, the respective members of the professional team responsible for development projects and those other parties concerned with or affected by development decisions. Furthermore, the point is made that the development of real estate may be seen as a set of interrelated processes and not merely a single sequential process. Indeed, it is important to recognize that, although it is helpful to distinguish a series of steps or stages in the property development process, such as in an apparently consecutive flow-chart approach, it by no means reflects the concurrent nature of most, if not all of those stages. A successful developer must maintain a perspective overview of the whole process all the time and be prepared to undertake almost constant repositioning of the constituent elements of the development scheme, as well as continually renegotiating agreements with the other participants in the process.

It should also be appreciated that there are any number of ways in which the development process can be described as a sequence of events or series of stages from the start to the finish of the project. There might be slight variations, but by and large the stages identified are similar and they embrace the same range of activities. By way of example, one relatively simple approach divides the development process into four phases (Cadman & Austin Crowe 1983):

1. evaluation
2. preparation
3. implementation
4. disposal

199

Another more detailed model of real estate development distinguishes eight stages (Miles et al. 1991):

1. inception of an idea
2. refinement of the idea
3. feasibility
4. contract negotiation
5. formal commitment
6. construction
7. completion and formal opening
8. asset and property management

To explore the process of development and those professional disciplines participating in it, this chapter is divided into two main parts:

- property development: a five-phase process
- participants in the development process.

Property development: a five-phase process

For the purpose of this text the following five phases in the property development process have been identified:

1. concept and initial consideration
2. site appraisal and feasibility study
3. detailed design and evaluation
4. contract and construction
5. marketing, management and disposal

Concept and initial consideration

Establishing objectives for the development organization and generating ideas to meet them

In the private sector of the property industry the overriding objective is unashamedly one of profit maximization. However, potential return must be weighed against potential risk and the degree of uncertainty. Operational objectives are paramount in the public sector, although strict budgetary constraints might be imposed. Image may also be an important factor in decision-making. In terms of the generation of ideas to meet established objectives, however, property development is at root about imagination, opportunity and venture. Successful developers are invariably those who arrive at different conclusions from others against similar sets of information. So too, it should be said, are unsuccessful developers.

Determine a basic strategy for the development organization

Strategy determination will normally entail a consideration of several related factors:

- the very purpose of development activity, whether it is for owner occupation or for speculation
- the size of a potential project in respect of financial commitment
- acceptable locations in terms of function and project management
- specialist knowledge related to selective sectors of the property market
- portfolio "fit", taking into account existing investments and other development proposals so as to maintain an appropriate balance
- a surfeit of capital resources leading to pressures to invest
- the need to sustain an active and credible development programme
- the capacity of the development organization to undertake the scheme
- and, perhaps above all, how auspicious is the timing.

Time, for example, might outweigh all other considerations, and the planning approval position may be of paramount importance, or acquisition itself could be a problem. Conversely, quality of design, construction and finish might be the overriding consideration, or cost the critical factor. Where the client is an industrial or business concern intending to occupy the completed property, great attention must obviously be paid to operational needs and balanced against the continued marketability of the building. In satisfying the requirement of the development organization, once established, different forms of management structure will be most suited to particular projects according to such variable factors as size, complexity, time, sophistication, economy, degree of innovation and extent of external forces. It will also be necessary to identify the key decision points in the process of development, such as when planning permission is granted, acquisition completed, building contract completed, or sale or letting agreements entered into, and to determine the consequences that flow from such events, dependencies that arise, involvements that occur and costs that are incurred. A critical path through the development will also usually be constructed at this stage to assist planning control in the decision-making process.

Undertake market research and find a suitable site

The significance of sound market research cannot be stressed too strongly. Indeed, market research and marketing underpin every stage of the property development process. Market research is fundamentally concerned with demand and supply. Demand, be it proven, perceived or latent, being the most difficult element to investigate with confidence. Although market research is commonly considered to be formal, focused and systematic, it has been pointed out that market research for generating ideas for development has a very large informal component made up of experience, observation, reading, conversation, networking and analysis. Both formal and informal approaches are necessary, as recognized elsewhere:

The generation of ideas, marketing and market research have both intuitive and rational elements. Successful developers are able to maximize both the intuitive and the rational. Formal knowledge of marketing principles and market research enhances the use of both facilities. (Miles et al. 1991)

Finding a suitable site involves establishing a set of criteria by which alternative locations can be identified and assessed. These would broadly relate to market, physical, legal and administrative conditions and constraints. Once a shortlist of say three or four options has been drawn up, a preliminary appraisal will be conducted in order to determine the most suitable choice. This is the proverbial "back of the envelope" analysis, which combines an objective assessment of likely cost against value with a more subjective judgement based upon experience and feel for the market. Ideally, of course, the right site looking for the right use meets the right use looking for the right site. But there is no magic formula.

Site appraisal and feasibility study

Undertake a more refined appraisal of the viability of the proposed project, taking into account market trends and physical constraints
Decide to what extent will further enquiries, searches, surveys and tests have to be conducted, by whom and at what cost, so that there is sufficient information available in order to analyze the financial feasibility of a development proposal. This will normally entail a more detailed assessment of market demand and supply; a close examination of the changing character of the sector; projections of rents, values and yields; and estimations of costs and time. An initial consideration of the structural engineering design foundations and subsoil will also be undertaken. Having assembled all the data, a check should be conducted to ensure that the basic concept achieves the optimum use of the site or buildings and maximizes the amount of letting or operation space.

Consult with the planning authority and other statutory agencies with regard to the proposed development

Apart from making sure that all the usual inquiries are made in respect of preparing and submitting applications for planning approval and building regulation consent, it is also essential for the developer to create a positive climate within which the development can progress. This means that the right people in all the various authorities and agencies concerned with accrediting the proposal must be carefully identified, and approaches to them properly planned and presented. It is vital for the developer to galvanize the professional team in such a way that everyone involved generates an enthusiasm for the scheme and conveys that interest to those responsible for assessing it. First impressions are always important, and simple precautions can be taken, such as consulting with all the contributors to the project to compile all the preliminary inquiries together, to avoid duplications and despatching them to the authorities and agencies in sufficient time to allow proper consideration and formulation of response. Among the principal factors the developer will seek to establish are the prospects of being expected to provide elements of planning gain by way of legal agreements and the likelihood of obtaining a consent, the possibility of having to go to appeal, the chances of success, and the consequent probable timescales and costs resulting.

Identify the likely response from other interested parties to the proposed development

The developer needs to have heightened understanding of how a particular scheme of development will be received by those likely to be affected by it, or have a voice in how, and if, it proceeds. This implies a knowledge of the distribution consequences of development and a comprehension of, say, urban renewal policy. They must, therefore, be able to predict who will oppose, why, how they might organize their opposition, what influence they exert, and how best to negotiate with them and reduce potential conflict.

Establish the availability of finance and the terms on which it might be provided

Because the parameters set by a fund can influence and even determine the design and construction of a building, great care must be taken in selecting a suitable source of finance and in tailoring the terms to meet the aims of both parties to the agreement. This will involve an evaluation of alternative arrangements for financing the project in question, including an assessment of the financial, legal and managerial consequences of different ways of structuring the deal. In doing so, it will be necessary to determine very closely the absolute limits of financial manoeuvrability within the framework of the development plan and programme, for, during the heat of negotiation, points may be conceded or matters overlooked, which could ultimately prejudice the success of the scheme. Different sources of finance will dictate different forms of control by the fund. The major financial institutions, for example, increasingly insist that some kind of development monitoring be undertaken by project management professionals on their behalf, whereas a construction firm might provide finance for development but demand more influence in the management of the building operation. The developer must be wary. Presentation of a case for funding is also a task deserving special attention, and any message should be designed to provoke a positive response. Subsequent to a loan being agreed in principle, it will be necessary for the developer, in conjunction with their lawyer and other relevant members of the professional team, to agree the various drawings and specification documents to be included in the finance agreement. These will normally comprise drawings showing floor layouts and cross sections of the entire project, together with drainage, site and floor-related levels, and outline heating and air conditioning proposals, as well as a performance specification clearly setting out the design, constructional and services standards to be met. The financial dimension to project management is critical, for a comparatively small change in the agreed take-out yield can completely outweigh a relatively large change in the building cost.

Detailed design and evaluation

Decide the appointment of the professional team and determine the basis of appointment

It is essential that the developer, or an appointed overall project manager, has a good grasp of building technology and construction methods, together with an appreciation of their effect upon the development process. To this must be added a perception of the decisions that have to be taken and an ability to devise appropriate management structures necessary to carry them out. In deciding such questions as whether to appoint a small or large firm, appoint on the basis of an individual or a firm, select professionals for the various disciplines from the same or from different firms, choose professionals who have worked together previously or who are new to each other, or opt for existing project teams or assemble one especially for the job in hand – the respective advantages and disadvantages must be explored and weighed most carefully. The chemistry is all important, but the opportunity to take such a deliberate approach towards the assembly and integration of the professional team is one of the great advantages of property project management. In this context, however, it is essential that the contractor is seen to be a central member of the team, playing a full part in the design process and not somehow placed in a competitive position. Increasingly, moreover, a choice has to be made between different methods of producing building services, such as package deal, design and build, selective competitive tender, two-stage tender, serial tender, negotiated tender, management fee contract or separate trades contract. However, a true project management approach might be said to be superior to all other methods. The members of the team, once appointed, will usually be required to enter into collateral warranties as to their professional obligations and be prepared to produce reasonable evidence of the adequacy of their professional indemnity insurance. It may also be that the fund as well as the developer will expect similar undertakings and will insist that the conditions of engagement reflect this part of the financial agreement.

Prepare a brief that outlines the basic proposals for design, budgeting, taxation, planning, marketing and disposal and sets out all the management and technical functions, together with the various boundaries of responsibility

The preparation and agreement of an initial client's brief is an indispensable stage in the project management process. Misunderstandings are common without a clearly identified set of client's objectives being established. In this, the traditional responsibility of the architect as client's representative or leader of the professional team has been found seriously wanting. Therefore, it is very important to define the separate functions and management activities of individual members of the professional team, as well as those of any project manager, and how they all relate to one another. Equally, it is necessary to ensure that everyone understands the brief. Sometimes a very formal agreement at the outset allows for greater flexibility thereafter. Furthermore, time expended at this stage can often save much wasted energy and ire later. Likewise, fee negotiations must be conducted and terms agreed at this stage, including a clear understanding and record of any departures from standard professional terms of appointment. Frequently, it is beneficial to seek outside advice on certain matters such as town planning, taxation and space planning, so that the organization of the project and functional use of the building can be optimized, even if it is expensive and provided by specialists who will not be involved in the development itself.

Arrange for the design team to prepare and submit preliminary detailed drawings for the planning approvals and budget forecasting
The most important aspect at this stage is to make sure that strong and effective liaison takes place between the architect, the quantity surveyor, the agent and the fund.

Submit the planning application and negotiate with the local authority, statutory undertakers and other interested parties
An enormous amount of time and effort can be spent on fruitless discussions unless the right relationships are established with the right people. The presentation of the submission can have a considerable effect, especially for significant schemes of a sensitive nature. In such negotiations, steps should be taken to preserve as much flexibility for future action as possible.

Make any necessary changes to the scheme, adjusting the various programmes and obtaining final approvals from all concerned
It should be appreciated that changes may have to be made and incorporated within the plans for the project at almost any time, which emphasizes the need to maintain flexibility. For example, changes may have to be made in respect of occupancy, division of space, time of completion, technology used, design, layout, materials, finishes, contractor, costs, services, and even use.

Contact and construction

Establish the preferred procedure for selecting a contractor, arrange the appointment and approve the various contract documents
There is now much wider acceptance of the benefits to be derived from selecting and involving the contractor at the earliest possible point in the design process. Alternative methods of building procurement will demand different procedures for appointing a contractor, and it is ultimately for the developer to recommend or decide how best to proceed, reconciling the two often countervailing factors

205

of competitive cost and quality of work. A combination of tender and negotiation is, therefore, frequently the preferred approach. Performance bonds of around 10–15 per cent of contract value will also have to be negotiated with the selected contractor and any nominated subcontractors, and any specialists or suppliers offering a design service will normally be required to provide a design warranty.

Establish a management structure to take account of the communication between the parties and the responsibilities borne by all those involved, paying particular attention to administration, accounting, purchasing, approvals reports and meetings

Traditional relationships established during the construction process are not always the most suitable means of communication and collaboration between the various parties engaged in a particular project. However, although it has been suggested that the quality of work is best, and the efficiency in production greatest, where discretion over detailed design is highest, it is often the case that the setting up of a very formal structure with a strict routine of meetings and reports to begin with, but allowing for subsequent and deliberate relaxation or amendment as matters progress, works best.

Set up an appraisal system to monitor the viability of the project throughout the building period

It is the fundamental responsibility of the project manager on behalf of the developer to ensure that the project brief is being satisfied. Because of the task of constantly relating the requirements of the brief to the programme of development and the constraints of the budget, it is necessary for the project manager to prepare some kind of master programme. The monitoring of this programme will mean that they must make certain that the members of the professional team are producing all the required information at the right time and in the proper form. It will also be necessary to liaise with other parties, such as the fund and the various statutory bodies, to reassure them that the building and its construction is in accordance with the requirements of the various consents and agreements. Careful control will also have to be exercised over interim and stage payments to those claiming them.

Ensure that on completion of the development, arrangements are made to check all plant, equipment and buildings before they are commissioned

It will normally be the duty of the project manager to accept the building on behalf of the client, sometimes their duty to prepare it for acceptance by the client or their advisers or the funding agency, and sometimes a mixture of both. In certain circumstances, it may be appropriate to make provision for a phased completion and handover. Generally, a minimum maintenance period of 12 months will be required of those responsible for supplying and installing building services and equipment.

Generally supervise all contractual affairs in order to anticipate and solve problems as quickly as possible
At the beginning of the construction process the development project manager should consider the desirability of appointing a nominated expert to settle any building disputes that may arise between the parties. Occasionally the project manager will assume a greater responsibility than normal for arbitrating between contributors to the building operation. In any event, part of the project management function will always be the sensitive oversight and control of the building and associated contracts on behalf of the developer. Very simply, the risks of the development vary in proportion to the degree of detail and commitment to the project produced by the members of the professional team, and to the level of successful orchestration achieved by the project manager.

Marketing, management and disposal

Determine the point at which a marketing campaign is best started, how it should be conducted and by whom
All too often, concern for marketing is too little and too late. However, the prime aim of any private sector development scheme is to produce a marketable building, even if that market is a client who is already identified. Right from the start, therefore, it is the job of the developer to focus the attention of all the contributors to the professional team upon the marketing dimension of the project. This is especially true of those concerned with the design and construction of the building, who tend to neglect the demands of the market. It is imperative for the developer or his project manager to forge a close link between the selected architect and the instructed agent. Where the project is speculative, the keynote must be flexibility – in both physical and tenurial terms. In selecting an agent, the developer will be faced with almost the same set of questions as when choosing any other member of the team, such as, national or local, small or large, firm or individual, regularly retained or new, generalist or specialist, and sole or joint instruction. Decisions must also be made between the developer and those engaged in the actual marketing of the development about the size of the marketing and promotions budget and the pattern of expenditure during the selling or letting period. As part of the process of planning the marketing campaign, it will be necessary to determine what specialist services such as market research, public relations and advertising might usefully be retained and on what basis they will work.

Decide on the form of lease or sale contract, so as to preserve an optimum return on the investment
Given the changing conditions of the market, this decision will involve the developer considering very carefully such matters as how many tenancies can be accommodated, what lengths of leases might be accepted, on what terms in respect of rent review and repairing and insuring obligations might leases be agreed, what

incentives might effectively be offered, and whether there are any tax advantages to be gained from conducting sale or letting arrangements in a particular way. In respect of a forward sale agreement transacted with a financial institution, it is important to ensure that the conditions are reasonable so far as the client is concerned. Too sanguine a view of the programme for development, and the prospects for letting can often lead to the acceptance of a contractual straitjacket. It should also be appreciated by those acting in a project management capacity on behalf of clients undertaking speculative commercial development that, with most funds, the issuing of an architect's certificate no longer automatically triggers the machinery to release development profit and the start of a lease. Normally it takes a separate document issued collectively by the architect and project manager, together with the fund's professional representative, to release payment.

Establish a management and maintenance programme and, where the development is to be retained or a prospective occupier agrees, recruiting and training the necessary personnel to provide a smooth handover
Besides making sure that the necessary operating manuals have been prepared, and the drawings, plans and approvals are collected together for transmission to the client's or purchaser's management organization, the project manager might often now have to set in train and supervise recruitment and training programmes for continuing management staff. This has been the case for some while in the development of planned shopping centres and certain forms of leisure development. It is now spreading to other commercial sectors, such as multi-occupied office schemes, and industrial and business estate developments. Even in the residential sector, large-scale housing projects will require the establishment of selling, management and maintenance operations. Certain apparently minor, but in practice very important, tasks must be commissioned and checked. These include such matters as the provision of a fire insurance valuation, the effectuation of a defects rectification programme with appropriate liabilities and the verification of other insurance and maintenance policies.

Maintain the security and safety of the building at all times
Over and above the responsibility for ensuring that the site is both secure and safe during the construction period, it is also increasingly important to produce a building that throughout its economic life complies easily and inexpensively with ever more stringent regulations regarding health and safety at work. Moreover, with the advent of more advanced systems of information technology and the movement towards multiple occupancy of commercial premises, there is a growing need to create accommodation capable of installing and operating business security systems. The project manager must take this into account at all stages of development.

Monitor the performance of the retained agents

Given that marketing is a critical ingredient in the project management process, close contact must be maintained with the agent. Regular meetings must be held, detailed reports prepared, and explanations provided for disappointing or unexpected results. The developer or project manager should also be consulted about advertising material and its placement. The image of the project and the way it is presented can be significant. Commitment and care on the part of the agent must be watched, and the developer or project manager must not be reluctant to take alternative or novel advice regarding the sales potential and marketing of a building. It is also important that, once identified, the prospective tenant or purchaser is fully involved in decisions taken during the completion of the development.

Reorganize the financial arrangements where necessary

Depending upon the progress of the development programme, the state of the market and the success of the marketing campaign, there may or may not be a need to renegotiate the terms of the funding agreement, seek additional financial support or restructure the cashflow projections and budget allocations. Aspiring tenants or purchasers might have occupational requirements that dictate a reordering of the financial arrangements. Alternatively, the original funding agreement might have certain stipulations in the way of rental guarantees or priority yield, for instance, which are either incompatible with, or detract from, potential disposal terms. Furthermore, for a variety of reasons it may be beneficial to rejig the financial agreement because of the taxation position of the parties.

Participants in the development process

The property development process involves the constant interaction of various agencies, groups and individuals. Given the all-pervasive nature of property in the lives of everyone, few, if any, are exempt from participating in the development process in one way or another.

A celebrated model of the real estate process collects the participants into three major groups:

- **The Space Consumer Group** – which includes "individual space users" attempting to rent or buy real estate space to house their specific needs; collective users generally pursuing their interests in real estate activity through the political systems that purchase open space, provide for public infrastructures, or regulate space production with pooled funds from taxation; and "future users" who are typically represented by proxy, either by developers who anticipate the need to change the use of a building in the future, or by the judiciary or special interest groups, who perceive some trusteeship of the land for future generations. Provision for future users being a hidden charge to present consumers . . .

- **The Space Production Group** – which includes all forms of expertise necessary to convert from space–time requirements to money–time. The systems includes, those who assemble the capital and those who prepare materials as well as those who contribute to the assembly of these on-site . . .

- **The Public Infrastructure Group** – which comprises all those enterprises that provide a network of tangible and intangible off-site systems for the individual space user, including physical networks of roads, sewers and other utilities, services such as education, police and fire and operational systems for land registration, government regulation, adjudication and all forms of economic activity with efficiencies of scale that suggest off-site action . . . (Graaskamp 1981)

In a more prosaic manner this text divides the participants in the property development process into "development agencies" and the "members of the development team".

Development agencies

The generic term "developer" embraces a wide heterogeneous breed of agencies, from central government at the one extreme to the small local housebuilder at the other. The aims and objectives of different property-developing organizations also varies enormously, as does their relative efficiency. Many indulge in property development as an ancillary function of a larger prime operation, such as the major retail chains and the principal banking houses, whereas others concentrate their efforts solely on the activity of land dealing and property development. Even within the mainstream of the property development industry, considerable specialization in respect of region, sector and size is experienced and a general description is difficult to manufacture. Nevertheless, the following classification serves to identify the principal agencies involved in property development.

Property development companies
As already stated, a great range in the type and size of property development companies can be discerned. There are large companies with extensive development programmes capable of undertaking complex major projects and small companies content to operate on a more modest and selective basis. Many large companies are publicly quoted on the Stock Exchange and portray a higher profile, as well as arguably bearing greater accountability for their actions than the bulk of others not so placed or exposed. Some specialize in particular sectors of the market such

as office, shop, industrial or residential, whereas others spread their attentions and apply their skills across the market. There are also those who have established a niche market in such areas as church conversions, waterside developments, sheltered housing and historic buildings refurbishment. Some development companies concentrate upon projects in or around a particular town or city; others operate regionally, nationally or even internationally. There are also companies that trade predominantly in completed developments, whereas others are more concerned with building up a sound and balanced investment portfolio. In terms of organization and structure, it is hard to characterize the typical company, for some, even the very largest, run extremely lean operations, preferring to employ outside professional expertise for virtually the whole range of development activities, whereas others maintain substantial in-house teams. It is true to say, however, that most property development companies were originally founded as the result of one man's initiative, and the importance of the individual remains paramount in the private sector property development industry. They all, moreover, share a common goal: that of profit maximization.

Financial institutions

Since the mid-1950s many insurance companies and pension funds have involved themselves to varying degrees in direct development on their own behalf. The role of developer has often willingly been sought by the more venturesome funds, seeking to secure the full measure of equity return from development projects, but has also frequently been the result of having to take over the affairs of defaulting property companies to whom they advanced loans or purchased a significant interest. The extent to which such financial institutions become active developers in their own right is largely a function of the prevailing general investment climate and the particular performance of the property market. By the mid-1990s, it is a far more attractive proposition to acquire ready-made developments at a discount than indulge in the lengthy and speculative process of building from scratch. Conversely in a buoyant or rising market, or in anticipation of one, there is much to be gained by financial institutions participating directly in development schemes.

The predominant characteristics of the financial institutions as developers are that they take a longer view of, and adopt a more cautious attitude towards, development proposals than would most private property companies, being concerned with future income and capital growth over a prolonged period of time. An inherent advantage enjoyed by institutions acting in a development capacity is, of course, the financial confidence with which, of course, they can proceed, given the underlying capital strength they command. They also seem to attract a higher degree of respectability than their property company counterparts, because, no doubt, of their policyholder, rather than personalized, ownership. Partnership schemes with local authorities and prospective owner-occupiers, as well as with property companies and construction firms, have also proved popular development vehicles for financial institutions where risks can be shared, attractive covenants gained and expertise acquired. Perhaps the major drawback that can be

211

levelled at the insurance company or pension fund as a direct developer is that, although they possess all the attributes of a large corporate organization, they also suffer from some of the associated disadvantages in lacking a certain amount of flexibility, flair and enterprise. They tend to be extremely conventional in their approach towards location, design, covenant, tenure and management.

Construction firms

Traditionally, building contractors have always been closely connected with the positive promotion of speculative development. Of recent years, most major construction firms have all been active in the development field. Construction is a high-risk undercapitalized operation with very sensitive margins, and many contracting firms have built up property portfolios of respectable size in order to ensure greater continuity of income and a more substantial and secure asset base. The most obvious advantages derived from the horizontal integration of building and development is that it can internalize the risk of obtaining contracts, facilitate the borrowing of funds, and sustain the employment of a skilled workforce. Joint ventures have often been established between contracting firms and other property development companies on an equity-sharing basis. Likewise, with financial institutions, one of the benefits gained by the builder as developer is that profitability can be viewed across both development and construction activities, providing a competitive edge in the bidding process for land.

Public sector agencies

The direct development activity undertaken by public sector agencies varies enormously according to their nature and function. Local authorities provide by far the most diverse range of development experience, with some councils pursuing an extremely adventurous approach towards commercial schemes, particularly in the light industrial sector, in locations where small nursery factories have not been provided by the private sector. Others have attempted to engage in central area shop and office schemes, but with very mixed results. Residential development has quite naturally played a traditional role in municipal development programmes, but of somewhat less significance over recent years under a Conservative government. In general terms, the degree of involvement in different forms of development naturally varies between authorities according to their geographical location, persisting problems, potential opportunities, landownership, financial resources and political complexion. Probably the main differences between public and private sector development are the degree of accountability that attaches to the former and the extent to which community consultation and participation takes place. Local authorities must demonstrate the highest levels of probity and disclosure in all that they do. They also have differing objectives in that such aims as the provision of shelter, the generation of employment, environmental protection and the supply of services outweigh the overriding profit-maximizing goal of the private sector.

The positive part performed by central government in direct development is strictly limited, as opposed to the determination of a strategic framework and the promotion and control of the property industry by way of fiscal incentives and statutory regulation. Most state development, in fact, is confined to the provision of accommodation for their own purposes and, to this end, the DOE's Property Holdings acts in the capacity of agent on the government's behalf. Regional development boards and agencies such as the Scottish and Welsh Development Agencies have also been established, but with the main task of an attracting business investment and stimulating employment, rather than pursuing the active construction of commercial premises. The various public services and utilities that require land and buildings for their respective operations, such as health, education, gas, water and electricity, also perform the role of developer, but again in a very restricted sense. Slightly different in kind are those public or quasi-public bodies who have a surplus of land for their own operational requirements, or who are able to combine their functions with other commercial endeavours on the same site and become energetic development agencies in their own right. A classic example is British Rail, which has implemented an ambitious development programme since the mid-1970s. Deserving of special mention in the context of public sector development agencies, albeit in a somewhat historic perspective, are the New and Expanded Towns, for, since their inception as part of post-war construction and interregional planning policy, they have played an ambitious and successful entrepreneurial role in providing civic, residential and commercial accommodation. In a similar vein, there have been the Urban Development Corporations and a host of other public and quasi-public agencies set up to tackle the task of regeneration in declining inner-city areas.

Large landowners

By dint of circumstance, many large landowners almost inevitably become property developers. Some of the most notable, such as the Grosvenor, Portland and Duchy of Cornwall estates, are long established and have set high standards in terms of building design and management. The Crown itself is, of course, a leading landlord and a major participant in the property market. Despite the recession of the past few years the Crown Commissioners have restructured their portfolio to great effect, although this has entailed a concentration upon investment in completed developments rather than active development on their own account. Conversely, the Church of England, another major landowner and property manager, has indulged in the development market with dire results. Oxford and Cambridge colleges have also been involved in property development over many years on land endowed to them.

Business concerns

Where there is a need for a highly specialized building, or a non-traditional location is proposed, and there is likely to be little or no general market value attached to the completed development, then it falls to the prospective occupiers to provide their own premises. This can prove a hazardous affair, and professional expertise

213

of the highest order is required. However, it should be stated that many businesses have opted to develop their own property; often in conjunction with a property development company, and using some form of sale and leaseback arrangement. In fact, there has been an appreciable growth in the involvement of various business concerns in direct property development since the mid-1970s. Many major retail shopping chains have initiated, funded and managed the development of their own schemes. Other business organizations, such as breweries, have undertaken commercial projects on their own otherwise redundant property, an activity normally seen as outside their province. It can be argued that the trend towards aspiring occupiers developing their own property is likely to grow.

The development team

It almost goes without saying that the quality of a development, and the level of efficiency by which it is produced, is dependent upon the ability and application of those involved in the process from inception to completion. Even where the individual contributions from the various disciplines are capable of producing work of the highest standard, it is imperative that their separate skills be co-ordinated in a manner that eliminates delay and harmonizes effort. Although the scale and complexity of particular projects will vary, and thus the professional demands will differ, the following catalogue of disciplines describes both the principal participants who would normally be involved in a major scheme of development and their respective terms of reference.

The developer

Developers vary enormously in the degree of expertise they bring to the development team. Their backgrounds may be in building, estate agency, engineering, finance, law, architecture or business management. They also differ in the extent to which they are involved in the actual process of development. Some assume total responsibility for the management of every stage of a project from start to finish, whereas others are content to delegate a substantial amount of responsibility to a project manager, retaining a more strategic policy role.

Above all, however, a developer is an entrepreneur: someone who can identify the need for a particular property product and is willing to take the risk to produce it for a profit. In stating this, a sharp distinction should be drawn between the private developer to whom this entrepreneurial tag truly belongs and the salary-earning corporate professional in either the public or private sector who really acts as more of a project manager. Thus, the developer is seen to play many roles.

- promoter and negotiator with regulatory and approved authorities as well as other parties with an interest in the proposed development
- market analyst and marketing agent regarding potential tenants or purchasers
- securer of financial resources from the capital markets; employer and overall manager of the professional team engaged on the project.

The job description of the developer has been said to include:

. . . shifting roles as creator, promoter, negotiator, manager, leader, risk manager and investor, adding up to a much more complex vision of an entrepreneur than a person who merely buys low to sell high. They are more innovators – people who realize an idea in the marketplace – than traders skilled at arbitrage. (Miles et al. 1991)

With regard to general matters of concern in relation to the development function, one leading developer has identified the following requirements (Jennings 1984):

- *Motivation and leadership*   Probably the most important attribute of all, without which roles and objectives become confused and confidence eroded.
- *Selection of development team*   Another most important function as a considerable amount of collaborative work is required at all stages and mutual confidence is essential if misunderstandings and wasted effort are to be avoided.
- *Funding policy*   This will inevitably be a mix of market conditions and the developer's aspirations, but it must be kept constantly in mind and the relevant members of the professional team involved as appropriate.
- *Pre-letting objectives*   Since these can often have a material effect on various aspects of design and funding, they are bound to be at the front of items for close consideration.
- *Quality requirements*   These are not always easy to lay down in detail at an early stage and can tend to be rather subjective. Nevertheless, they are important to the team and can often best be defined by comparison with other existing buildings.
- *Who does what*   Although this should not be difficult, it is important to recognize that at the creative stage of a project the crossing of traditional disciplinary lines may often be beneficial.
- *Programme*   Although form and content will change frequently, it is imperative that at all times any activity should know where it stands both as to time and as to sequence.

From all this, it can be seen that developers spend a large part of their time on a project managing the input of others. However, an alternative is the appointment of a project manager to whom the developer, as client, devolves significant managerial responsibility.

Project manager
Project management has been defined as:

The overall planning, control and co-ordination of the project from inception to completion aimed at meeting a client's requirements in order that the project will be completed on time within authorized cost and to the required quality standards. (CIOB 1992)

Likewise, the duty of the project manager acting on behalf of the client has been stated to be:

> Providing a cost effective and independent service correlating, integrating and managing different disciplines and expertise to satisfy the objectives and provisions of the project brief from inception to completion. The service provided must be to the Client's satisfaction, safeguard his interests at all times and, where possible, give consideration to the needs of the eventual user of the facility. (CIOB 1992)

The function of project management and the role of the project manager have become increasingly important in the property development process since the mid-1980s. In practice, the project manager could be an in-house executive of the client development company or an external consultant specifically appointed to the project. It is also the case that each project is unique and the means by which the task of project management is fulfilled are subject to variation.

Construction manager

A distinction is drawn in this text between project management – where the span of control normally stretches from involvement in the initial development decision, right through to the eventual disposition of the completed building, covering every aspect of development in between – and construction management, where responsibility is restricted to the building-related stages of the development process. The appointment of a construction manager is most common where the developer acts in the capacity of total project manager and, for reasons of either managerial efficiency or lack of technical expertise, or both, prefers to delegate responsibility for overseeing all the construction activity to another.

The construction manager might be an architect, a builder, an engineer, a building surveyor or a quantity surveyor, and extensive practical experience in the type of project being built is essential. The prime task is similar to that of the project manager, seeing that the building comes in to time, to cost and to specification. In doing so, the construction manager is often called upon to reconcile conflicts between other professional members of the team involved in the building process.

The architect

The role played by the architect is critical to the development process. Invariably the design team leader, except where a project is essentially an engineering problem, the architect translates the developer's concept into a workable and attractive solution. Probably the best way of describing the various functions performed by the architect during the development process is to list the "architect's services", as laid down by the Royal Institute of British Architects, which are divided into the work stages summarized in Table 10.1 (Parnell 1991)

It can, therefore, be seen that the architect is fully concerned with several major elements in the development process: the acquisition of planning approval, the design of the building and the control of the building contract.

216

Table 10.1 Architects' services: the work stages.

Inception This stage is primarily concerned with an initial analysis of the client's brief and the provision of advice regarding the appointment of other consultants and specialist contractors.

Feasibility Based on site surveys and consultations with the various regulatory authorities a set of broad alternative options are prepared and a review of the design and construction implications undertaken in the light of the client's aims.

Outline proposals From the agreed concept, option outline proposals and approximate construction costs are prepared for the clients approval.

Scheme design The design is developed according to agreed spatial arrangements, materials and appearance, coupled with a cost estimate. An indication of possible building contract start and completion dates. Application for planning permission is also made at this stage.

Detailed design In conjunction with other relevant consultants and specialist contractors, a detailed design scheme is developed. Quotations are also obtained, cost checks conducted and building regulation approval sought. At this stage the architect is also required to obtain the client's approval regarding the type of construction, quality of materials and standard of workmanship.

Production information This involves the preparation of such information as drawings, schedules and specifications of materials and workmanship. It also includes preliminary tendering procedures and the engagement of nominated subcontractors and suppliers.

Bills of quantities These are prepared with sufficiently detailed information so as to enable the contractor to prepare a realistic tender. Site inspectors are also appointed and any necessary corrections made to the drawings.

Tender The architect provides advice on the list of tenders and obtains the client's approval for those selected. Tenders are then invited, meetings held, contractors questions handled, tenders received and advice again proffered prior to a decision being made. Alternatively, a negotiated contract might be arranged.

Project planning A final decision as to the successful contractors is made, and respective responsibilities of the client, architect and contractor apportioned under the terms of the building contract. Product information as required by the building contract is also prepared. Site supervisory staff are appointed and briefed.

Operations on site The architect is responsible for administering the building contract; making general site inspections; commissioning and testing; providing, with other consultants, periodic financial reports to the client; and preparing a maintenance manual.

Completion This stage involves administering the building contract in relation to completion of the works, as well as giving general guidance on maintenance, including the production of a Building Maintenance Manual with all the necessary drawings. The architect is then responsible for pre-handover inspection, outstanding works and defects, and finally handover.

Engineers

Several engineering disciplines are involved in the construction process of a development project. Working closely with the architect, they combine to ensure that the plans are structurally sound and that the mechanical systems will service the building adequately.

Structural engineer The role of the structural engineer is to provide the skills necessary to create structures that will resist all imposed forces over the life-span of the structure with an adequate margin of safety. The relationship between the structural engineer and the architect is inevitably a close one. A decision as to the choice of structural frame – reinforced concrete, precast concrete or steel – has to be made early in the design process, as does the form of foundation adopted and the measure of resulting loads and stresses. Such decisions have consequential effects upon the basic design, construction and use of the building. It is also important to provide sufficient flexibility in the initial design to permit changes during construction and even after completion. With the growing sophistication of modern commercial buildings, flexibility in routing services through floors, ceilings and vertical ducts is another prime consideration at the structural design stage. Throughout the process, of course, attention must also be paid to building cost, and the structural engineer, together with the architect and other engineering consultants, needs to liaise with the quantity surveyor.

Geotechnical engineer Usually responsible to the structural engineer, the geotechnical engineer is retained to perform initial tests of the bearing capacity of the soil, evaluate drainage conditions and generally assist in planning to fit the proposed project onto the site in an optimum manner, balancing physical effectiveness with building costs.

Mechanical and electrical engineer or building services engineer Together, these engineering disciplines supply the life-blood of a building. It is estimated that around 60 per cent of total building cost these days can be attributed to the provision of building services in commercial development projects. Such facilities as heating, water supply, lighting, air conditioning, communications, fire precautions and lift services must be carefully planned and co-ordinated. Alternative systems must be assessed in respect of capital and running costs, energy conservation, main plant location and size, duct sizes and routes, partitioning flexibility, special computing requirements, control mechanisms and the facility to add on services or increase capacity. It should be noted that, given the singular service they provide and problems they can cause, the specialist lift engineer is an important member of the professional team.

Environmental engineer The environmental engineer is playing an increasingly important role on the design team. At one time, environmental engineering was relatively straightforward, usually dealing with water and soil run-off onto surrounding property. Following the discovery that asbestos in existing buildings posed a serious health hazard, and with the advent of "sick building syndrome", there are now a new set of environmental problems related to toxic waste and a much wider range of concerns requiring environmental impact analysis and control.

The quantity surveyor

The quantity surveyor is basically charged with the task of cost analysis and cost control. It is advisable for the quantity surveyor (or building economist) to be included in the initial design deliberations and financial appraisal, particularly as the question of construction cost has become so critical over recent years. The original function of the quantity surveyor was mainly restricted to the preparation of bills of quantities and the variations of accounts. However, they have progressively become more involved in providing cost advice throughout the development process, but they remain principally concerned with supplying cost information through the feasibility, outline and detailed design stages, culminating in an agreed cost plan linked to an acceptable preparatory design. This is followed by a process of cost checking; assistance on tendering procedures and contractual arrangements; the production of specifications for the main contract and nominated subcontractors; examination and report on submitted tenders and negotiations; approval of variation orders, interim certificates and final accounts. However, it is worth emphasizing that the concept of cost-effectiveness is of greater consequence than ever before, and the application of associated techniques such as cost-in-use, life-cycle costing and value engineering have been in the ascendant.

The builder
The builder is not normally included as a full member of the professional team at the outset of the development process, but rather is viewed as a contracted agent at the procurement stage. However, some more enlightened property developers have found that early, prompt and sympathetic advice on the building aspects of construction and design, particularly such aspects as labour, site management and materials, can be extremely useful in respect of savings in both time and cost. The builder's function in the development process can best be described as follows (Somers 1984):

- *Feasibility* Understanding the developers' overall timescale; preparing an outline network so that discussions relating to key dates can be meaningful at all principals' meetings; and providing general assistance to the whole team on matters relating to site conditions and construction.
- *Outline proposal* Participate in site investigations and any surveys and schedules of dilapidations; produce initial method statements; liaise with the quantity surveyor on a range of cost information; supply examples of contracts and subcontracts; provide material samples; draw up alternative construction programmes; and develop the project network and report progress.
- *Scheme design* Advise on design matters relating to trade sequencing and degree of difficulty; help in advising on the design details relating to weather proofing, which must be guaranteed; consider long-term delivery aspects; continue with cost information advice; interview specialist subcontractors; and update the project network to include the detailed design stage and report progress.
- *Detailed design* Prepare temporary support work designs; establish all special conditions to be included in subcontract documentation; prepare and agree the total budget for construction; detail all quality control and instruction procedures; update the project network to include construction activity

and report progress; order long-term delivery items; advise local authorities, neighbours, local residents and unions of intentions; define the extent of all remaining details to be provided by the consultant teams and complete project network accordingly; and agree all work packages.

- *Construction period* Follow the basic tenets of building safety, within budget, on time and to specification; update the project network to include show areas, letting procedures and key dates together with handover arrangements and maintenance period work; and be in a position to report time and financial progress accurately at all times.
- *Post-contract* Monitor the users' acceptance and allocate a senior member of staff to be responsible for final certification and to act as a long-term contact for the client, consultants and users.

The agent

It should be appreciated that the agent might be but one contributor to the overall process of marketing, albeit an important one. Nevertheless, the agent is an integral member of the development team, whose principal functions are fully described and discussed in Chapter 14.

The valuer

Many development agencies supply valuation expertise from within their own organization. Where this is not the case, it is common for the estate agency firm retained also to provide valuation advice. Sometimes a separate consultant is employed. In essence, the valuer might be asked to estimate the likely value of land identified for a development project, the possible level of profit that might be derived from undertaking the scheme, or the capital value of the completed project. Again, the various components of the residual valuation, and the methods of conducting development valuation, are fully explored in Chapter 12.

There may be separate valuations that have to be conducted for such purposes as land assembly, compensation, taxation, funding, letting, sale and asset valuation. The initial valuation will almost certainly have to be revised and updated during the development process, as the picture of probable income and actual expenditure becomes clearer.

The solicitor

The services of a solicitor are unavoidable in the property development process, right from acquisition through the various stages of planning approval, contracts for construction, to eventual sale or leasing. How much legal work is involved in any particular project will naturally depend upon the complexity of the scheme and the number of parties concerned. It is also possible that specialist advice might have to be sought on certain matters. In simple terms, it has been said that the solicitor is well suited to undertake several roles: of advisor, especially in the complex area of planning law and construction contract law; negotiator, to explain, to persuade, to reach agreement and to discover for and between the various parties;

advocate at meetings, representations of all kinds and inquiries; co-ordinator, between all parties to the project and all those who can regulate or otherwise have an influence upon it; and draftsman, of all the relevant formal documentation (Hawkins 1990).

Other specialist team members

According to the nature of the proposed development project and the problems encountered, a need to bring in specialist consultants will often arise. The most common of these can be listed as follows:

- *Accountant*   Who might be called in to advise on certain tax issues, funding agreements, and disposal arrangements, as well as how the development relates to the overall position of the company.
- *Town planning consultant*   Employed in circumstances where the planning position is more complicated than a matter of pure design and layout, especially if the approval is likely to be difficult to obtain and there is a possibility of the proposal going to appeal. Sometimes an actual environmental impact statement or its equivalent is required.
- *Landscape architect*   High-quality landscaping is increasing in popularity and importance, and a good landscape architect can promote the marketability of a project and enhance the value. When necessary, it can also cover up defects in design!
- *Interior design*   The internal appearance of offices, houses and especially shopping centres is of utmost importance, and an interior designer might be called in to assist the architect in beautifying the building, especially the common parts, display units, reception areas and shopping malls.
- *Facilities manager*   The management of an organization's facilities, its built environment and its infrastructure must take into account the nature of the activities that take place within the building and which the facilities are serving. For an office building where the eventual occupant is known, the introduction of a facilities manager into the team is becoming increasingly common. Even where the occupant is not known, such advice is beneficial. The equivalent in the retail sector is the early inclusion of shopping centre management expertise into the development team.
- *Others*   Might include health and safety, insurance, archaeology, party walls, traffic engineering and public relations consultants.

Conclusion

Although a description of the property development process and those professions participating within it can be relatively simple, the activity itself grows more and more complex. Increasingly, development requires more knowledge than ever before about prospective markets and marketing, patterns of urban growth, property legislation, local planning regulation, building procurement and disposal, elements of building design, site development and construction techniques, financing, controlling risk and managing time, the project and the people concerned. Greater complexity in property development has also resulted in more specialization, and as more affiliated professionals have become involved, the size of the development team has grown and the roles of some of the professional disciplines changed.

Development in real estate in the 1990s is different from that of the 1980s and is likely to be different from that of the 2000s. Although developers may not continually address societal trends and changes in the short-term, over the longer-term trends and changes have a tremendous effect on what developers build, where they build it, for whom and on what basis.

CHAPTER ELEVEN
Development site appraisal

Once a potential site has been identified, or a number of sites put up for selection, it is necessary to analyze the respective merits or otherwise of each before a formal development valuation can be conducted. In many ways, this stage of appraisal is one of the most important in the development process and, given the ever tighter margins within which development takes place, deserves more attention than it has sometimes received. Several well reported cases of professional negligence highlight the need to undertake critical surveys and investigations with care and consideration. The project size, capital resource commitment and degree of community concern evoked determines the level of analytical detail required. This chapter does not cover in depth the extensive detailed analysis that would normally underlie summary calculations and recommendations undertaken for major development projects. Rather, the intent is to indicate the basic nature of the comprehensive methodology that should be employed in the appraisal of development sites.

The first step is to consider the developers' goals and objectives regarding the project. These must be clearly established and agreed before specific uses for the site are studied. This will require consideration of the developers' motivations, business capacities and financial situation. Increasingly complex objectives underlie the goals of development agencies. It is a fair assumption, however, that the private developer is motivated by financial considerations as opposed to the social or community characteristics of the project, although the latter should be of supreme concern to government agencies because of the public responsibility they bear. Even though developers are motivated primarily by financial considerations, their objectives may still vary substantially. Developers may have nothing more than an idea that a certain type of project may profitably be developed. They may or may not have a particular site in mind. Alternatively, they may have a site and be searching for the most profitable use. Some development agencies, such as local housing authorities or municipal development departments, may be socially motivated and concerned primarily with weighing social costs against social benefits within à given budget (Barrett & Blair 1982). In any event, once the developer's goals and objectives have been established, site appraisal may commence. For convenience, the principal factors that have to be studied at appraisal have been grouped as follows:

- planning policy and practice
- economic climate for development
- site survey and analysis.

Planning policy and practice

It may seem an all too obvious starting point to state that a clear understanding of prevailing planning policies as they relate to the site or sites in question should be gained, but in one of the leading cases of professional negligence, involving a very substantial greenfield development site, it was not possible to prove that the surveyor responsible had spoken to the local planning authority, even over the telephone. It is vital to recognize, therefore, that planning policy provides the frame within which development takes place.

The formal procedures and practice of planning and development are examined elsewhere in this text (see Part Two). What the following section seeks to do is to explore some of the less formal aspects of planning policy as they affect the appraisal of sites for development.

Non-statutory documents

In addition to the statutory planning process, land planning policy is also expressed by way of a variety of non-statutory plans, briefs and guides. Planning documents treating individual subjects such as housing, transport and employment have been produced regularly by local planning authorities (LPAs). Furthermore, site-specific planning and development briefs, as well as more generalized design guides, have been produced.

A planning brief is compiled by an authority when it does not own the site in question and has no intention of doing so. It is a non-statutory written statement and site plan, sometimes accompanied by supporting maps and illustrations indicating a local authority's policy and aspirations towards a specific site or group of related sites, which possess development or redevelopment potential. The brief is intended to bring together the requirements for a particular development, hoping to form a basis of agreement between interested parties before planning permission is granted.

A development brief, on the other hand, is prepared by an authority, or other landowner, where it owns a site or intends to acquire interests in the land. It usually contains similar "core" information regarding the site and relevant planning guidance, as does the planning brief, but it also includes details concerning how interests in the land are to be disposed. It should be appreciated that development briefs can be prepared by landowners other than local authorities. Nevertheless, where they are produced by a local authority, several enquiries regarding their production are worth pursuing. Where, for example, they have been approved by resolution of council they are much more authoritative and reliable than otherwise. Those briefs that have been the subject of consultation with all the relevant departments within the authority, with other statutory authorities and undertakers outside and with the public and their representatives, tend to be a great deal more dependable than those where they have not.

Despite the degree of detail and level of commitment given by the authority producing a planning or development brief, it is important to stress that they only represent the author's standpoint. According to the relative needs and bargaining strengths of the parties concerned, they should be seen as negotiable instruments, but at least they simplify appraisal by bringing together many different policy objectives in a single document.

Another type of non-statutory planning document occasionally encountered is the design guide. This is prepared by some planning authorities for development control purposes as an advisory document, backed, where applicable, by standards and statutory requirements. It describes preferred forms of development, giving advice on design techniques and materials to be used across an entire planning area. Less important at appraisal stage than other documents, it might influence market research and the choice of architect. One good example of such a design guide is held to be that produced by North Norfolk District Council, which seeks to conserve the local vernacular and to inspire good new architecture using sensitive materials. An attempt has been made to extend the concept to an entire district area in East Anglia where areas are identified and different sets of design policies applied to them relating to design density, form, style, materials and landscape requirements. Another approach aimed at providing "development briefing" has been looked at by the Housing Research Foundation, Here, the intention is to supply supplementary guidance to ensure that developers of residential areas know what is expected of them by using a system of "housing plus" elements. These would define and cover social housing, additional open space and extra facilities, and quality of design, and they would be applied to specific sites prior to schemes being submitted, using agreed checklists in an "open process" – a trifle too interventionist and deterministic for most developers, especially as the idea is to fund such elements out of the development land value. Nevertheless, a more structured approach towards design issues might be welcome and might also reflect the requirements of Policy Planning Guidance consideration. Some authorities produce a regularly updated statement of planning policy, whereas many others prepare proposals maps showing all known proposals on a district-wide basis. Land availability schedules and maps are also frequently published, especially for industrial and residential development.

The weight that should be attached to informal plans and other non-statutory documents will depend upon their purpose, the date when prepared, and whether or not they have been approved by full council or by the planning committee exercising a delegated power.

The planning application

An examination of the past performance of a given planning authority can usually give a pretty reliable indication of the likely reception a particular development proposal will receive and the approximate length of time it might take to obtain a decision. The starting point for this examination is the Planning Register, which records applications and decisions for all current and past applications, refusals and permissions. From this can be gained an overall impression of the authority's attitude towards development: the type of conditions they are inclined to attach to planning permissions, especially where they are unusual or generous; the refusals to approve applications and the general tenor of the reasons given; and the number of applications that have been called in by the Secretary of State and appeals made to him, together with the decision letters and inspectors' reports resulting from them.

Relevant ministerial Circulars and planning policy guidance should be consulted and the manner in which these are interpreted by the local authority considered. It may transpire that the local planning authority pursues a particular policy towards certain forms of development that is not in accord with central or strategic planning policy, and are not perturbed by their failure rate at appeal. In these cases it may be apparent that an appeal is inevitable, and protracted negotiation futile except to judge the strength of the authority's argument, so that the procedural wheels are best set in motion early.

Less pejoratively perhaps, the planning history for the site in question should be studied, with note taken of past applications, previous decisions, outstanding consents and current proposals. The same exercise should be conducted for neighbouring properties in order to identify any intended development schemes that could affect the site concerned. A more comprehensive approach might benefit all parties on the one hand, whereas possible overdevelopment might detract from the viability of the proposed project on the other. Anyway, it could make a difference to the timing and presentation of an application.

One of the most difficult aspects of appraisal to describe in comparatively objective terms is the effect that personalities and politics have upon planning decisions. They can, however, be crucial. Many an application has foundered, or progressed less easily than it should, on the lack of awareness on the part of the developer or his advisers of certain individual or political sensitivities existing within the authority, its officers and its representatives. Where a developer is faced with an unfamiliar locality, it is often worthwhile compiling a scrapbook of cuttings from the local newspaper stretching back a year or so that deal with planning and development matters. The front page and the letters column are most productive. These extracts can help paint a most revealing picture, spotlighting issues and individuals in the forefront of local planning affairs. Slightly harder is the task of identifying those within the council who are most influential with regard to planning decisions. Time taken with informal contracts finding out is rarely wasted. In politically sensitive situations it pays to check the date of local elections and the likelihood of political change – either way.

These days the authority and influence of various interest groups can play an important part in the planning process, and some consideration of their presence and power at appraisal stage is expedient. Apart from those local amenity groups formed to promote and protest about particular causes, there are established national bodies concerned with specific facets of our urban heritage. These include the Georgian Society, the Victorian Society, the Society for the Protection of Ancient Buildings, the Royal Fine Arts Commission and the Town and Country Planning Association. A sympathetic attitude towards the views of such interests at an early point in the development process can often prevent unnecessary conflict and smooth the path to approval.

An absolute must in all appraisals of any significance is the holding of informal discussions with officers, and occasionally members, of the local planning authority. The main purpose of these enquiries is to elicit information and details that may not have been forthcoming from published documents, and to clarify the background to previous decisions and published statements so as to avoid confusion. Apart from those matters already mentioned, these discussions might usefully cover any relevant policy work in progress, the timetable for the production of any new plans or policies, suitable land-use survey information that could be made available, the relationship and need to consult the county council and other bodies, the dates of the appropriate committee meetings and agenda deadlines, the immediate reaction of the authority to the particular development proposal, and any special information that should be provided by the applicant. It is suggested that, at the conclusion of the meeting, the local authority be asked if there are any other matters to which the authority would like to make reference, and recommended that following the meeting the subjects discussed are confirmed in writing. It is a well known axiom in planning and development circles that the quality or usefulness of an answer obtained from planning officers in only as good as that of the question posed; it is also only as good as the person answering, and their standing. Commonly, it has been found that developers are often concerned about the quality of advice they have received at pre-application inquiry. They frequently find that junior staff are used to deal with enquiries and that their views are overridden by more senior staff at later meetings, or when a planning application is submitted. As a result, they feel misled when committees do not support officers' recommendations. In particular, frustration is felt when proposals are amended before planning applications are submitted, in response to advice received from planning officers, and officers later recommend refusal of something that they appeared to support earlier (Taussik 1992). It has further been stated that officers are often unprepared, overly cautious and preoccupied with detail. Conversely, developers have been accused of being too vague in their proposals, over-expectant of the off-the-cuff on-the-spot responses, and tending to hear what they want to hear. Nevertheless, proper preparation prior to a meeting, an appointment with the appropriate officer, a careful agenda drawn up, sufficient information provided (preferably in advance), objectives identified, notes taken and written confirmation of the discussion made after the meeting – should help make pre-application inquiries fruitful.

These days, communication is of the essence, and it has been stated that information or development proposals should be concise and frank, with a clear style of presentation that makes them easy to understand (Boys 1983). An increasingly common practice among developers and their consultants, once they are serious about a proposal, is to produce a single package of information for the authority and other involved parties. Typically, this would provide an introduction to the company's affairs, give a history and summation of the development proposal, discuss the commercial background to the company's plans, explain the development proposals in relation to various topics, and provide annexes in support of earlier parts of the statement together with any supplementary information. Later in the process this might be followed with a public exhibition, using additional aids such as enlarged plans, models and audiovisual programmes.

Consultations with other bodies

Most development projects of any size will involve consultations with at least two or three bodies in addition to any consultations with the LPA. If the proposal is thought to have strategic implications, it may be necessary to discuss it with the relevant county council planning department or, in the case of London, for strategic matters, the London Planning Advisory Committee. Similarly, where development has traffic consequences, then having discussed the matter at first instance with the district or borough council, it may be advisable to check certain points with the county council in their capacity as highway authority. This may relate to possible changes in public transport routing, any required improvements or alterations to the road system, adoption and maintenance of new roads and appropriate parking and servicing standards.

In respect of large development schemes generating a substantial amount of public transport travel, it will be necessary to consult the local passenger transport services if any rescheduling, re-routing or stopping provisions are required. Further, it is always worth checking with those services, or where appropriate with the relevant rail network operator, that local services are likely to be maintained at their present level of provision, especially where those travelling to the development for business, shopping, work, leisure or housing are dependent upon public transport.

In addition to detailed investigations regarding the supply of services to the site, it is incumbent upon the developer to approach statutory undertakers, such as the water authority and the gas and electricity companies, to ascertain if there are any capital programmes or proposals that they may have formulated and which could have a bearing on the project. Sometimes certain other bodies such as the Environmental Health Officer, the Health and Safety at Work Executive, the National Coal Board or the British Airports Authority might have to be consulted if the circumstances of the scheme dictate.

228

With regard to infrastructure requirements, most statutory undertakers are governed by statutes that enable them to assist developers either by re-routing existing services or linking-in with existing services up to the site boundary. However, the provision of major off-site infrastructure can bring major problems, financial and legal, so it needs to be assessed very carefully. For example, it is not unknown for an authority opposed to a development proposal on planning, or even political, grounds to find the most surprising highways, drainage or other service reasons for refusal. Conversely, a co-operative authority can be very helpful, even to the extent of being prepared to use their powers to assist a developer in acquiring any necessary land. The likely reaction of a local authority must, therefore, be carefully assessed.

Planning obligations and planning gain

Probably the most controversial issue surrounding planning and development since the mid-1970s has been that of "planning gain". Sometimes known as planning agreements, and now described as planning obligations, the extraction of community benefits from a development project through the exercise of the planning approval mechanism has been the subject of continuing legislation, litigation and debate. (This section should be read in conjunction with Ch. 5).

Several competing rationales justifying the imposition of planning agreements upon developers in return for the grant of planning permission have cogently been set out in a 1993 report (Healey et al. 1993). The first rationale is concerned with the implementation of planned development. In this rationale the plan provides a clear framework justifying a development. Within such a framework, agreements may be used to address management problems with respect to development, or developers may be encouraged to contribute to the provision of planned infrastructure to enable their development schemes to proceed. The second rationale focuses on the adverse impacts of the development and the subsequent need to alleviate or compensate for the social costs of that impact. Unlike the first rationale, it is not so much concerned with making the development work on its own terms as with accommodating the development over a wider area. It is suggested that this rationale can be used to justify a wide range of community benefits. Under a third rationale, the developer is seen as having a duty to return some of the profit from the development to the community – a form of local development charge. In both the first and second rationales, reasons can be established for refusing the proposal on the grounds that, without the planning gain or obligation agreement, the development would be unacceptable in planning terms, in the former by making the proposal development project fit with an already envisaged scheme, and in the latter by amelioration of the impact of the project. The third rationale, however, is founded solely on the perceived need to impose some form of local tax on the developer (Edwards & Martin 1993).

The DoE has for long been concerned over the extent to which local planning

229

authorities seek to extract planning gain from developers and the means by which they go about it. The position is now largely governed by the provisions of the TCPA 1990 as significantly amended by the Planning and Compensation Act 1991, together with Department of Environment Circulars 16/91 and 28/92, as well as the Town and Country Planning (Modification and Discharge of Planning Obligations) Regulations 1992. There has also been a DoE research report, *The use of planning agreements* (1992). One of the main changes introduced by the 1991 Act, amending the TCPA 1990 Act, was a section allowing for the possibility of unilateral undertakings. It also provides a statutory regime for modifying and discharging such unilateral undertakings and other planning obligations. A system of appeal to the Secretary of State was introduced and Crown land was brought into the ambit of unilateral undertakings and planning obligations. Furthermore, certain new formal requirements were introduced. For a planning obligation to have statutory force, it must be made by deed; it must state that it is a planning obligation for the purposes of the 1990 Act; it must identify the land to which it relates; it must identify the person entering into the obligation and their interest in the land; and it must identify the local planning authority by whom it is to be enforceable (Martin 1993).

It is now provided expressly that a planning obligation may be conditional or unconditional, and be either indefinite or limited in time. A planning obligation requires registration as a local land charge, but, controversially, it is not capable of being recorded in the public planning register. As long as the formal requirements are met, then a planning obligation is enforceable against the person entering into it and those subsequently deriving title, unless otherwise specified.

Planning obligations can be positive or negative: positive, in that they might relate to the provision of services or facilities such as highways, sewerage, low-cost housing, open space, landscaping or other physical community benefits; negative, in respect of controls over the use and occupancy of the land or building. They can also require sums of money to be paid to the local planning authority, both one-off and periodic payments. DoE Circular 16/91 provides the current policy guidance to local planning authorities on the use to be made of planning obligations. It sets out the circumstances in which certain types of benefit can reasonably be sought in connection with the grant of planning permission. Those circumstances generally are where the benefit sought is related to the development and is necessary for the grant of that permission. It stresses that planning applications should be considered on their merits and determined in accordance with the provisions of the development plan, unless material considerations indicate otherwise. It may be reasonable, however, either to impose conditions on the grant of planning permission or, where the planning objection to a development proposal cannot be overcome by means of a condition, to seek to enter into a planning obligation by agreement with the applicant, which would be associated with any planning permission granted. The point can be made that, if there is a choice between imposing conditions and entering into a planning obligation, the imposition of a condition is preferable because it enables a developer to appeal.

As with conditions, planning obligations should be sought only where they are necessary to the grant of planning permission, relevant to planning and relevant to the development to be permitted. Unacceptable development should never be permitted because of unrelated benefits offered by the applicant. The Circular then sets out a test of the reasonableness of seeking a planning obligation. It also provides guidance on the use of unilateral undertakings stressing that such undertakings are not intended to replace the use of mutual agreements but rather are to be employed only where a developer considers that negotiations with the local planning authority are being unnecessarily protracted or that unreasonable demands are being made. It follows, therefore, that the principal use of unilateral undertakings may well be at appeal, where there are planning objections that only planning obligations can resolve but the parties cannot reach agreement. Where a unilateral undertaking is then offered, provided it is in accordance with the general policy set out in the Circular, it should amount to a material consideration and will have to be taken into account (Martin 1993). The likelihood is that there will be a continued growth in the use of planning obligations, and possible refinement of their application by government. It is imperative, therefore, from the viewpoint of the developer at appraisal, that they identify the general policy and practice of a particular local authority towards planning obligations, and their success in implementing them.

Economic climate for development

A study of the market to estimate the range of specific land uses, and the rate of physical development that can be supported within the constraints imposed by demand and supply conditions, is perhaps the most important stage in the development process. However, it is one of the most difficult to undertake.

Market appraisal is used not only to inform prospective developers and to assist them in reaching a decision, but also to gain support from local planning authorities, leading financial institutions and potential tenants and purchasers. It must be conducted in a manner that is systematic, rigorous, logical, defensible and reasonably detailed. However, the degree of objectivity required is not always a trait most immediately associated with the natural optimism or bullish behaviour of the developer. Thus, the services of a more dispassionate consultant analyst are often felt advisable. Nevertheless, problems persist, most notably the basic lack of relevant data; the dated and non-comparable nature of such data as does exist; a frequent reluctance on the part public authorities and their officials readily to co-operate; a similar, though natural, recalcitrance by competing developers, estate agents, property managers and occupiers or owners to share market knowledge; and the fact that there is often no direct precedence to act as a guidepost. In similar vein, the developer invariably wishes to act at this stage with a high degree of confidentiality, if not downright secrecy. An independent consultant acting as analyst also often faces the problems of an inadequate budget for undertaking a thoroughgoing market appraisal, and sometimes a developer with a preconceived notion as to the preferred outcome of any analysis. Moreover, there is the somewhat invidious pressure placed upon the consultants themselves to produce positive results that may lead to further work on the project.

It should be appreciated that a market appraisal may be undertaken for one of two basic reasons: where the use is known, but the site has to be determined, or where the site is known but the use has to be determined. Many of the factors to be studied remain the same, but the processes of analysis are somewhat different.

General market condition

Overall economic climate

All development decisions are inevitably affected by the overall economic climate prevailing in the city, region and country concerned. Increasingly, moreover, international markets are exercising a considerable influence over national and local ones. A market appraisal should, therefore, start with an examination of global as well as national conditions and projected long-term trends, then narrow the focus upon the characteristics of the region, locality, neighbourhood and ultimately the site.

Business cycles

Within national economies, and even within regional and local economies, there are distinct business cycles that affect investment and development decisions in the property market. The reverse is also the case, because it should be borne in mind that there is also a situation of "simultaneous causation", whereby events in the property market can impact upon other sectors of the economy as well as vice versa. In this context, four types of economic fluctuation bearing upon property investment and development decision-making have been identified (Barrett & Blair 1982). These are random fluctuations, which are short-term irregular changes in business activity; seasonal fluctuations, which are regular and reasonably predictable; business cycles, which are fluctuations affecting the total economy having expansion, recession, contraction and revival phases; and secular trends, which represent the underlying economic conditions that might influence generations. Construction and property cycles do not normally match the average cycle for the economy as a whole, tending to peak before the total economy peaks, and bottoming out before the rest of the economy. This is mainly attributable to investor and consumer confidence, the fact that property is usually one of the first sectors to be adversely affected by rising interest rates and that a slowdown in construction and development activity itself depresses other parts of the economy. The important issue so far as analyzing the economic climate for development is to make sure that the timing of the development is related to the turns of the business cycles.

Urban structure theories

In searching for a site, or deciding the highest and best form of economic assessment, developers are advised to reflect upon certain basic economic theories of urban structure and change. Some regard should be paid to the traditional concepts of concentric zone theory, axial theory, sector theory and multiple nuclei theory. Concentric zone theory states that, assuming no variations in topography, transport or land supply, land uses are sorted out according to their ability to benefit from, and therefore pay for, the position of greatest accessibility. Axial theory accounts for development along transport corridors, with accessibility considered in time-cost terms so that changes in transportation lead to changes in land use and land value. Sector theory also recognizes the importance of limited transportation in urban areas, but suggests that specialization of land use takes place according to direction rather than just distance from the position of greatest accessibility. And multiple nuclei theory observes that urban areas may have more than one focal point, each of which influences the location of certain land uses.

Economic models

There are also a set of urban economic models or concepts that provide a less descriptive and more analytical approach towards the examination of growth and change. These include economic base analysis, shift and share analysis, input–output analysis, econometric models, simulation, time-series and other hybrid models. Between them, these macroeconomic tools allow a perspective of general economic forces to be gained and translated into the demand and supply of urban land and property resources. The range of forecasting techniques is large, and the choice lies with the user, and with a sound understanding of the strengths and weaknesses of each approach, as well as an equally sound understanding of the particular forecasting or analytical problem facing the developer's consultant. Only through the exercise of informed judgement based on a knowledge of local conditions, the problem to be studied, and the techniques available for studying the problem and the area concerned, is it possible to construct and present usable studies of urban economic systems.

Local markets

Most property development markets, however, are essentially local markets. Local developers will have a good understanding of their own area – the policy of the local planning authority towards property development; prevailing rents, values and costs; other projects in process or contemplated; and the potential for future expansion from contact with tenants, purchasers, financiers and the construction industry. Newcomers will obviously have to find out. Nevertheless, a broad understanding of the property market and an intuitive grasp of the particular situations should enable a prospective developer in unfamiliar surroundings to feel at the outset if they like the town, like the location and like the site. This personal judgement is not to be despised, for as in most lines of business, confidence in the final product is essential. Even without sophisticated analyses of the local market it should be possible to tell if, for example, a town is under-shopped, lacks sufficient housing, has a buoyant industrial base, is well placed for distribution services, or lends itself to office relocation.

Market delineation
It is important to define exactly what is the relevant local and non-local market area for the proposed project at a specific site. The local market might be contiguous, such as that for retailing, or diffuse, such as that for housing. Office and industrial development can be both. Apart from recognizing a geographical identity, it is also necessary to study market-area dynamics taking account of the compatibility of the proposed use with surrounding land uses and in the light of neighbourhood growth trends, the location of competitive sites and the degree of spatial monopoly (Miles et al. 1991).

Demand and supply
Any market study must focus on the determinants of demand and supply. It should be appreciated, however, that in doing so there is an inherent difficulty in differentiating the many economic factors influencing the property development industry between demand and supply. There are large areas of overlapping influence where certain factors can be said to affect both demand and supply. Nevertheless, there are certain basic forces that clearly affect one side of the demand and supply equation more than the other. These have been stated as follows (Barrett & Blair 1982):

- Demand = (population, income, employment, relative prices, taxes, interest rate, down-payment requirements and future expectations).
- Supply = (expectations of demand, planned supply, competitive environment, availability, and cost of land, labour and capital).

Demand for development

The demand for property is both derived from and driven by the market: market-derived in that many occupiers locate in a given market area in order to provide goods or services for that area, or be accessible to resources and customers, and others, to secure employment within a reasonable commuting distance; market-driven in that the local economy must remain competitive to support sustained demand for accommodation, so that spatial arrangements within an area become important in influencing firms' profitability and local residents' wellbeing. A typical market study of demand for property development would analyze a number of basic factors, of which the following may be considered to be of notable performance.

Catchment area

For most forms of commercial property development the demand for space is a function of the catchment area or hinterland commanded by the site or the activity proposed on it. The exact nature of the centripetal forces at play will vary according to the size, use, location and accessibility of the planning developments. The prime concern at appraisal is to establish whether or not those forces external to the scheme that affect the extent of the hinterland are likely to change. Rail and road closures, diversions and by-passes, motorway extensions and ringways, parking provision or restriction and traffic management schemes of all kinds can have a major impact upon development viability.

Population

The population factor would include an examination of past trends and current estimates regarding population size, birth and death rates, age structure, migration, family size, and spatial distribution. In terms of forecasting, natural births and deaths are relatively easy to gauge, but migration is more difficult. It is also hard but necessary to categorize the population properly into consuming units, especially for retail and housing studies.

Income

Again, income data are mainly required for retail and housing studies, and include a study of past trends and current estimates of personal income, socio-economic distribution, household formation and change over time. In the housing market it is important to distinguish between "need" and "effective demand" in respect of affordability. In the retail market it is necessary to estimate actual consumer expenditure between sectors, and forecast likely future disposable income on consumer durable and convenience goods.

Employment

This would include an examination of past trends and current estimates of employment among different sectors and occupations, so as to give an overall picture for a given community. This study is especially important in smaller communities, where dependence upon certain major employers can be high, and also in larger urban areas where there is an agglomeration of businesses in the same field of service or production activity. Comparatively small or selective changes can have a significant and multiplier effect upon total employment. Predictions of location and relocation of actual or potential employers, inwards and outwards, can have a dramatic impact upon forecasts of effective demand.

Labour supply

In the context of employment, several different surveys have shown the importance of labour supply to those intending to occupy completed developments, mainly in the industrial sector. In one the calibre of staff required was placed second, just after transport considerations, as the reason for selecting a particular location, while in another it was put top, so some recognition of the effect of labour supply upon property demand at appraisal is required.

Rents and values

The most reliable indicators of demand for space are rental values for commercial schemes and capital values for development land and housing. In analyzing values for property it is the general direction of rents and prices for the area over a period of time that is important, and the broad pattern of their incidence across the market, not individually quoted deals struck in isolation from the rest, which might result from pressures to purchase unconnected with the prevailing conditions of the property market. Moreover, care must be taken to ensure that only achieved rentals are used in appraisal, and not asking-rents, which may differ considerably. Any incentives to either party should also be taken into account. In the same way, where seemingly comparable transactions are being analyzed, adjustments must be made to take account of variations in location, size, use and date. As with most preliminary appraisal it is sometimes sufficient to employ a break-even rental figure as a rule of thumb to find out if it is worth pursuing investigations further.

Vacancy rate

Another useful guide to effective demand is the vacancy rate persisting in a chosen locality. Some degree of care must be exercised, however, in reacting too immediately to a forest of estate agents' signs on high street frontages. It may just be that old leases have fallen in at the same time. Nevertheless, where a surplus of existing property development has been overhanging the market for some time, it is obviously a warning sign not to be ignored.

Informal enquiries

Discussions with those actively involved in local property markets can give a good picture of the current scene. Existing tenants in competing projects, estate agents acting on behalf of buyers and sellers, property managers concerned with occupiers' requirements, investors involved with financial performance, and contractors providing building services can all provide informed and informative views of present conditions and prospects. However, it should be remembered that the picture they paint can be highly coloured.

Other factors

There are many other factors affecting the demand for development, including taxation, special incentives, interest rates, local amenities, leisure facilities and environment. All must carefully be considered.

Supply of development

An appraisal of actual and likely future supply of property is generally agreed to be easier than an appraisal of demand. It is conducted so as to compare resultant supply figures with those of demand so as to gauge the amount, if any, of excess demand and the prospects for development. Many factors need to be considered in any assessment of the demand for development, as follows.

Anticipated supply

Put simply, anticipated supply (AS) is:

> AS = existing stock + (space under construction, expected starts, planned new projects and conversions of space) – (demolitions, removals of stock and abandoned projects).

Existing and planned supply

This involves an examination of past trends, current estimates and future forecasts of stock for the particular types of property under scrutiny. Data on existing stock are relatively easy to gather, but prediction of future supply beyond a three- to five-year time horizon are difficult to make reliably. Some important assumptions regarding market behaviour, and central and local government responses to any significant market changes, need to be made. It is also important to recognize that longer-term supply is sensitive to fluctuations in the business and construction cycles.

Competition

It is essential in appraising supply to study most assiduously actual and possible competition. In general terms, this necessitates an assessment of projects under construction, their size, number of units, quality, location, special features, management and stage of development. Competitors themselves must be studied, their number, activities, aspirations, capacity, confidence, contacts, image and performance.

Land availability

It is imperative to ascertain the amount of land allocated in the development plans for the area under study, and the total amount of development that might result if taken up. Possible changes to land release, zoning policy and density control must be considered. Furthermore, the potential for conversion of existing buildings to a new use, and the refurbishment of older premises to provide competition to fresh development schemes, must be assessed.

A survey of cleared sites and other evident development opportunities should be undertaken, for latent supply can be just as telling on market conditions over time as that possessing formal recognition. Floorspace targets, land allocation and infrastructure programmes established by the local authority must be studied, so that a full picture of the potential supply of development land can be presented. In linking land release with permitted levels of commercial floorspace, a certain amount of circumspection is often advised about land owned by local authorities and the final resolution regarding the preferred location of commercial development.

The Planning Register

As already mentioned, one of the main sources of information is the Planning Register, which will show the number of outstanding planning permissions for various forms of development within the planning area. From this, a rough calculation of the probable proportionate increase in the existing stock of buildings and supply of floorspace can be performed. If possible, an attempt should be made to ascertain who is the likely developer and, even more pertinently, whether or not the scheme is designed with a prospective occupier in mind. Where the development is intended for a known owner-occupier, or has already been pre-let, it can be argued that there will be less impact upon the overall supply base. Conversely, the search of the Register might reveal one or more directly competing schemes, which, upon further inquiry, might prompt a complete reconsideration of the planned development. In any case, the prospect of the take-up of these competing schemes and their likely timing should be considered, for it might be possible to pre-empt them by swift action in progressing the planning approval and making an early start on site. However, care should be taken in scrutinizing the Register because several applications and approvals might relate to the same piece of land. Some official surveys have been distorted by adopting crude aggregates of potential floorspace with planning permission and neglecting to sift-out duplicate consents. A check should be run on permissions previously granted to ensure that they are still valid. Outline consents expire after three years and full approvals last for five, unless extensions are sought and approved.

Neighbouring markets

It is now always sufficient to restrict the appraisal of the supply of development to a particular authority area or presumed hinterland. Extensive land release and a profusion of planning consents in adjoining towns and areas can exert a very considerable influence upon property markets. This can apply across the board, but is especially significant in the retail development sector, where shopping patterns are notoriously vulnerable to changes in supply.

Local construction industry

One aspect of market conditions that is sometimes overlooked when it comes to appraising the supply of development properties is the capacity of the local building industry, and its ability to cater for the level of construction required by the proposed development programme. This check should extend to the availability of materials as well as labour. The effect of swings in the business cycle can be profound on the construction industry, but major problems emerge for the developer, of course, during boom periods where skilled labour and experienced supervisory staff are short and delays in delivery materials long.

Absorption and capture rates

The rates at which supply soaks up demand and the proposed project penetrates the market are of great consequence to the developer. There are three levels to such absorption or capture rates: the overall market for the type of property concerned, the relevant market segments, and the subject property – the intention being to ascertain what surplus or unfulfilled demand exists and the extent to which the project in question can attract that demand. Thorough market research should provide a good basis for appraisal, but it has been stressed that the capture rate of the project and its eventual profitability will actually depend on how well the developers understand demand and what the competition is doing, beyond cursory market studies (Miles et al. 1991).

Informal enquiries

As with the appraisal of demand, it pays an aspiring developer to talk to a range of parties who might be able to give insights into the supply side of the market. In the public domain, elected representatives, community associations and interest groups will give an indication of what might be favoured and what opposed. In the private sector, property owners, occupiers and managers can give an idea of what is preferred, where, when, why and how.

Other factors

Other factors also tend to affect the supply side of the development equation, including infrastructure costs, land assembly problems, landholding issues and capital investment programmes.

With the appraisal of both demand and supply for property development, it is important to recognize the inherent risks that exist. Sources of information can be suspect, long-term forecasts are notoriously unreliable, policies towards land release and planning consent can change quickly, market studies do not necessarily determine the highest and best use for a site or the best site for a given use, and the attitudes and behaviour of owners and occupiers can be volatile. Some form of risk analysis or simulation to test the sensitivity of project proposals to change is well advised.

Site survey and analysis

Having considered the planning position, and explored the likely level of potential demand and the overall prospects for supply persisting within a particular town or given locality, a developer must assure himself about the capabilities of a selected site to meet his development objectives. For convenience the various

239

surveys and analyses that are necessary to achieve this can be grouped into those of a legal, physical and functional character.

Legal considerations

Ownership

To begin with, it is clearly essential to establish the ownership of all the various interests that may subsist in the land and property. If the site is offered as a free-hold, it is necessary to ensure that full vacant possession can be obtained. It is possible that, in disposing of the freehold interest, the vendor might seek to impose legal requirements placing the developer under some form of obligation to fulfil certain conditions relating to the nature and performance of the development scheme. If the vendor is a public authority, for example, it might seek to retain certain rights to approve the layout or design of the development or to compel the developer to complete the project within a stipulated period of time. The developer will wish to be satisfied that such conditions are acceptable, that they are expressed in reasonable terms and that they allow enough flexibility for the proper execution of the scheme. If there are leasehold interests to be taken into account, then the developer will need to ascertain the period of any lease, the amount of rent payable, the review pattern, the main provisions of the lease, the position with regard to security of tenure, and the respective responsibilities on reversion. A check should also be made about any licences that might have been issued, and the terms on which they were granted. Unauthorized entry and occupation by squatters might have been effected, and both time and money could be expended in obtaining possession. Appearances of vacancy or dereliction can sometimes be deceptive.

Land assembly

The process of land assembly in the private sector can be a somewhat secretive affair. The skill and guile of the developer, or more usually his agent, is employed to piece together a site in such a way as to acquire the various interests at the lowest possible price. Sometimes a developer who has identified a site containing many different interests will instruct more than one agent to act independently on separate plots in order to maintain anonymity and suppress expectations. One of the major problems faced by the private sector in the piecing together of a mosaic of plots is the creation of what have been called "ransom" sites. These occur where a developer has been unable to secure all the land necessary for a scheme, and one or two key sites remain, such as those required for access or essential services, with the owner holding out for an extravagant price, only too aware of the "blackmail" or "marriage" value of his interest. Colourful stories can be related about commercial schemes developed above and around recalcitrant owners, but the lesson in terms of expeditious and economic assembly is that such key sites should be pinpointed and purchased at the earliest possible opportunity.

240

Option to purchase

Many private purchases can be highly speculative in nature and be undertaken well in advance of likely planning permission. A common device in such transactions is the taking of an "option to purchase", normally enforceable upon the grant of planning consent. The purchase of an option postpones the need to incur heavy capital investment in successful circumstances and it safeguards the developer where the scheme proves abortive. Care must be taken, however, to ensure that the figures determined in the option agreement are realistic, and do not unduly reflect the uncertainties of inflationary growth.

Boundaries and obligations

One of the earliest tasks to be performed in the survey of a site is the precise identification of the boundaries and the way in which they are defined. Although this may seem a somewhat obvious precaution, it is surprising how often in practice discrepancies are found with boundary alignments, and how relatively small, but frequently critical, parcels of land have been either omitted or wrongly included in the disposition.

Some very costly renegotiations have been witnessed. At the same time as identifying the boundaries of the site, the responsibilities for repair and maintenance should be determined. Furthermore, in some development situations, particularly those in congested highly developed parts of major towns and cities, it is necessary to consider rights of support that might have to be afforded to adjoining properties both during and after development. Highway agreements might also exist. In more rural locations, wayleaves, such as those to accommodate overhead cables or underground public trunk mains can cause problems. Party walls should be considered with an awareness that an award might have to be negotiated. It is essential, therefore, to obtain from the existing owners a copy of a plan showing their legal title, and to compare this with an updated Ordnance Survey sheet by walking the boundaries with the plans in hand. This may well show up anomalies between the title plan and the physical boundaries of the site. These anomalies must be checked out very carefully, for even Land Registry plans can be in error.

Covenants

Covenants running with the land that restrict its free use must be investigated and, where necessary, early steps should be taken to refer such matters to the Lands Tribunal to have them removed or modified. Rights of light, rights of way and rights of entry are the most common forms of easements encountered in a legal search for development land, and it may sometimes be possible to reach a satisfactory accommodation with those entitled to the enjoyment of the rights without recourse to the uncertainties and expense of the legal system. Again, it is important to carry out a careful inspection of the site for evidence of easements that might have been acquired by prescription and will not necessarily be disclosed on title, such as gates, doors in boundaries, or drains crossing the site. With restrictive covenants, however, they are always expressed and never implied (save only those rights of indemnity implied by the Law of Property Acts). Nevertheless, there are some very complex rules governing whether or not restrictive covenants are still binding on the land. As a rule of thumb, the best approach at initial appraisal is to assume they are still effective and to try to gauge either the likelihood of getting them amended or discharged, or the cost of taking out an indemnity policy with an insurance company.

Planning permission

It may be that the site being appraised has the benefit of an existing planning permission. Even if an alternative planning permission is to be sought, it is necessary to scrutinize the current consent and any conditions that are attached. Obviously, if the site is to be bought on the strength of a particular planning approval, a thorough perusal is essential – of the permission, the planning application and accompanying drawings, and all the subsequent correspondence leading up to the decision. Special considerations might have to be given to any planning conditions, and an assessment made of the need to have certain conditions struck out or modified, together with the chances of being able to do this. There may also be the question of an outstanding planning agreement or obligation that could constrain development, and that might outlast the expiry of any existing planning permission.

Planning and preservation

Since the introduction of "conservation areas' in the Civic Amenities Act 1967, more than 7500 "areas of special architectural or historic interest, the character of appearance of which it is desirable to preserve or enhance" have been designated. Individual buildings can also be listed for protection. The current legislation being the Planning (Listed Buildings and Conservation Areas) Act 1990. Although it is clear that conservation areas can embrace acceptable change, and should not be regarded as "preservation" areas, close attention must be paid by a prospective developer when considering a site within a conservation area, or where a conservation area impinges upon a site. Even more care must be taken where any buildings on the site are listed as being of special architectural interest, for they may well constrain development. A developer must obtain Listed Building Consent before carrying out any demolition or renovation work that could affect the character of a building. The development of land within a Conservation Area entailing any demolition work will also usually require the express consent of the local planning authority. Further, any tree on the site that is protected by a Tree Preservation Order, or any trees within a Conservation Area, must not be cut or damaged without special permission from the authority. Even if consents are eventually forthcoming for protected trees or buildings, there is often an effect on the development programme or a compromise with the proposed scheme.

Nevertheless, planning new development in a conservation area, or on a site containing protected buildings or trees, can be a particularly challenging and rewarding experience. Outstanding and profitable results can often be achieved, but this requires a sensitive and constructive attitude from both the planning authority and the private developer.

Environmental protection

Awareness of environmental issues has increased dramatically since the mid-1970s. For some major development proposals the European Community Directive 85/337, as reflected in the subsequent Town and Country Planning (Assessment of Environment Effects) Regulations 1988 for the UK demands the preparation of an environmental assessment (EA). This mandatory requirement relates to very special types of development having obvious environmental consequences such as crude oil refineries, thermal power stations, chemical installations, radioactive waste stores, major roads and the like. There is, however, a discretionary power under the Regulations where an EA may be required that includes such proposed uses as energy production, processing of metals, manufacture of glass, chemicals, rubber textiles, the food industry, infrastructure schemes and miscellaneous "other projects'. This is more significant for the conventional developer since it can include industrial estate development projects, certain urban developments, yacht marinas, holiday villages and hotel complexes. Evidence to date suggests that the majority of EAs have ben concerned with waste disposal sites and the extractive industries. Nevertheless, there is a distinct possibility that the application of the regulations could be extended and, further, that many development proposals already have to submit a form of EA or environmental impact statement in support of a planning application. There is also more and more attention being paid to such ecological issues as water quality and resource management, air quality management, wildlife management, solid waste disposal control and noise control. Developers must increasingly be able to anticipate these problems and proffer acceptable solutions.

Physical considerations

Site measurement

The first physical survey to be carried out should be an actual measurement of the site and its boundaries in order to determine the exact area. Too much reliance should not be placed on third-hand reports, estate agents' details, or figures arrived at from measurements taken off Ordnance Survey maps. An accurate assessment of the area of the site is essential in arriving at the permissible density of the development in accordance with development control standards and any agreements made with the local planning authority. It is also vital where a financial offer based upon a design scheme is to be prepared, as will usually be the case.

Ground conditions

It is necessary to discover the character and stability of the land and subsoil. There are three basic deposits beneath a site: artificial ground created by man;

243

drift deposits such as sand, clay, gravel, silt and peat; and rock such as mudstone, sandstone, siltstone and granite. If there is a shallow water table, this should be identified, especially when the site in question is located on the floodplain of a river. Particular attention should also be paid to the presence of any underground rivers, ponds or springs. The existence of any of these features will have implications for the kind of foundations that would need to be laid to support the development. For the same reason, the type of soil or soils covering the site should be classified and the degree of permeability investigated to check how easily water will drain from the site. Any contamination of the soil by a previous use (e.g. gasworks or chemical works) should be recorded and investigated, especially if the proposed development is to be residential. The load-bearing nature of the subsoil should be ascertained, particularly where the site is composed of made-up ground, or has recently had trees removed.

It is sometimes also necessary to find out if any part of the site could be liable to subsidence because of the underlying geological formation or as a result of previous mining operations. Air shafts and walls of underground activities must also be located. The appraisal of one major development site revealed the existence of a forgotten railway tunnel, another was found to mark the scene of a notorious mining disaster, and yet a further site, unbeknown to the prospective developer, concealed a vast lake not that far beneath the surface. In most circumstances, therefore, it pays to sink a few trial boreholes, or at the very least to do a little hand-auguring or probing at first instance to see what subsoil conditions are like, although more sophisticated techniques might have to be employed by geotechnical engineers at a later stage in exceptionally difficult or uncertain conditions. Ground investigations are often given too low a priority, especially in highly competitive situations where time is of the essence. Even a simple desk study, plus site visit by a specialist firm, is rarely undertaken, although the costs of a full site investigation should not exceed 2 per cent of building costs.

Topography
The topography of a site can occasionally be a significant factor in appraisal. Certainly, extreme gradients can cause problems and, although some interesting design solutions might be produced by the architects, cost penalties can be high. Where widely varying and irregular levels exist on a site, it is essential to commission a proper land survey from which the constraints on building layout and design can be gauged and implications for both development cost and value assessed. In this context, physical site appraisal might also include a consideration of the aspect and climate relating to the land in question. Views to and from the site can again affect building design and development value, especially in housing schemes, and south-facing developments benefit very generally in terms of sunlight and rainfall evaporation. There may even be odd instances when local climatic conditions are worthy of appraisal, since, in the event of severe weather the development programme might be affected, and in singularly exposed posi-

tions marketing might be difficult and viability subject to modification. On the other hand, certain existing landscape features might enhance the site, and their careful retention and exploitation be reflected in the value of the development, either directly by an uplift in rents or prices or indirectly by easier letting or sale.

Archaeological remains

Since the mid-1970s it has become increasingly important to make sure if a selected development site contains archaeological or historic remains. Almost by definition, the interests of the developer and the archaeologist are diametrically opposed, but responsible developers have normally allowed reasonable access for excavation and provided funding for it. Ever since the introduction of the Ancient Monuments and Archaeological Areas Act 1979 there have been statutory powers enabling access and postponing the start of development to allow excavation. There are also designated Areas of Archaeological Importance such as the old town cores of Canterbury, Chester, Exeter, Hereford and York. In addition, the British Property Federation and the Standing Committee of Archaeological Unit Managers have drawn up a code of practice that appears to be effective, and there is a British Archaeologists and Developers Liaison Group to further co-operation between the respective parties. Even the best codes of conduct and collaborative agreements can go awry and give cause for conflict. Because of this, a few basic rules have been suggested for developers who might face the problem of archaeological remains (Thame 1992). First, make sure a full site evaluation is undertaken. This includes trial excavations, remote radar sensing, bore holes and documentary research, so that, even if there are remains, any final archaeological agreement regarding access, an agreed timetable and financing is based on adequate knowledge of what is likely to exist below the surface. Secondly, organize an exploratory dig (Gregory 1989). There is not always a need to demolish a building for this, and the excavation of exploratory trenches in basements is standard practice in cities such as York. In any event, new government planning rules in the form of PPG16 mean that local authorities are very likely to insist on some modest evaluation work in propitious situations, and archaeological remains are now a material consideration in the planning process. Advice taken early usually pays off. Thirdly, retain experienced consultant architects and engineers who can produce sensitive and economic design solutions. And fourthly, be prepared to contribute, sometimes significantly, to the costs of excavation.

Building surveys

Most of the above searches and investigations are equally relevant where some form of refurbishment or rehabilitation of existing buildings is contemplated. In addition, of course, it will be necessary to conduct a physical survey ("referencing", as it is known) of the existing buildings. In brief, this will cover the following matters. An appraisal report on the buildings themselves will describe their design and construction, probable age, existing use, current occupation, present access, available services, provision of amenities and any special installations. Measurements of gross external, gross internal and net internal areas, as well as cubic capacity, will be calculated for different purposes, and particular attention paid to existing eaves heights, clear heights and column spacing. Performance standards will be assessed in respect of the general repair and condition of the building, together with specialist requirements relating to health and safety, fire, heating and ventilation, insulation and floor loading. A special eye will be kept open for defects such as the presence of high alumina cement, blue asbestos, woodwool roof slabs and other deleterious materials, as well as evidence of subsidence or flooding. The extent to which these investigations are pursued will depend upon the degree of redevelopment envisaged. The mere retention of a facade or external walls will call for a more restricted but highly specific survey, and the simple renovation of the existing structure will demand a comprehensive and thorough survey of the entire building. A record of existing and established uses for planning purposes might also be required. Even where existing buildings are to be demolished, there is a need to carry out a careful survey of the structure of the premises, along with any plant and machinery contained therein, to find out how much demolition will cost, how long it will take, what safety and security problems arise and whether or not much can be salvaged.

Functional conditions

Transportation

Transportation linkages to a project must be reviewed carefully at the preliminary stages of site appraisal. Proximity and access to motorways, connecting streets and the availability of public transport are all important to the competitive posture of the project. Time and distance to major sources of employment, commercial activities, schools, and health and recreational facilities should be plotted and compared to existing and planned competitive projects. In some cases, consideration will have to be given to the alteration of existing road configurations to accommodate the additional burdens imposed on the road network by the new development. As part of this appraisal process, a traffic survey studying the traffic records of the local authority, traffic counts and patterns, delay analysis and noise levels.

Mains services

Availability of mains services is crucial to development, and from the developer's point of view is likely to become more so, as utility companies are ever more alert to the possibility of extracting the costs of off-site infrastructure directly associated with the scheme from the developer. With gas supplies it should be established whether the local mains are high or low pressure and if governors will be required. With electricity, the probable loading capacity must be estimated and, when the scale or nature of the scheme dictate, the construction of a substation may be needed and a decision reached as to where and how it can be located. The only normal problem experienced with water supply, unless the scheme is particularly large or there are special industrial requirements, is with existing pressure. However, sewerage capacity can often be difficult, but at appraisal it should be ascertained whether the existing system is a joint drainage system, or a split foul and surface water system; if the size of sewer is sufficient to cope with the additional flow; and if the present configuration of the sewers is suitable for the proposed development. Alterations and improvements can be extremely expensive. It is, therefore, important to determine the need to stop up, divert or replace any such services and whether the utility companies will insist upon undertaking the work themselves. Where large distribution mains are involved, it is also common for the utility companies to insist on the work being carried out at a certain time of year; hence the need to co-ordinate this into the development programme. Where new mains services are being installed, utility companies sometimes demand that new mains are sized in excess of those required solely by the development in question, and financial contributions can be negotiated accordingly.

Other facilities

The proper and prompt provision of some facilities and services is often over-looked in development appraisal. Among these are telephone communications, refuse disposal and treatment, and postal deliveries and development nomencla-ture, and the availability of certain social amenities such as schools, shops, res-taurants and banks. Leisure and medical services should also be taken into account. It may also be necessary to identify and measure the major sources of noise within the vicinity of the development.

Problems and pitfalls

Although the preparation of site appraisals and analyses has become more pro-fessional and reliable since the mid-1980s, there are still problems, shortcomings and pitfalls that have been identified (Eldred & Zerbst 1985). These can be sum-marized as follows:

- an over-optimistic developer unduly influencing the consultant's analysis
- an unclear set of objectives established by the developer, leading to result-ant studies being incomplete, inconsistent and misleading
- consultants too concerned with producing a positive recommendation, which might lead to further fees from the project
- fragmented development planning where the full survey and analysis proc-ess has not properly been followed
- inadequate analysis of indirect forces affecting the feasibility of the project, such as changing planning policies, consumer behaviour or community reaction

247

- misrepresentation of data, either deliberately to enhance the prospects of the project, or inadvertently where key data may not be sufficiently substantiated by market fact
- mis-specification of supply and demand by the indiscriminate use of aggregate data, such as population, employment, income, values and vacancy rates, coupled with a failure to correlate supply and demand factors
- inattention to economic indicators regarding likely future conditions through the business cycle
- underestimation of infrastructure costs
- inadequate techniques of analysis
- too much statistical data and not enough analysis or judgement.
- lack of primary data and overreliance on secondary sources
- lack of consumer surveys exploring preferences and attitudes
- lack of sensitivity analysis testing the effect of potential changes to the constituent factors determining the feasibility of a project
- overvaluation of land caused by too sanguine an approach towards income flows
- faulty financial analysis and inadequate methods of computation
- avoidance of responsibility on the part of consultants.

As a cautionary note to conclude the subject of development appraisal, it is recommended that anyone concerned with the valuation of development land should read, or re-read, the decision in Singer & Friedlander, which is reported in full elsewhere (Singer & Friedlander 1977). The procedures and pitfalls are well described. Finally, it should be recognized that, although there is no unvarying approach towards appraisal, there is a necessary attitude of mind, which has been succinctly summarized by the American Institute of Real Estate Appraisers as follows:

> Making an appraisal is solving a problem. The solution requires interpretation, in terms of money, of the influences of economic, sociological and political forces on a specific real property. Characteristics of real property differ widely. This does not mean, however, that there is wide variation in the orderly procedure for solving appraisal problems. The best experience in the appraisal field has crystallized into the appraisal process.
>
> This process is an orderly programme by which the problem is defined, the work necessary to solve the problem is planned, and the data involved are acquired, classified, analyzed, and interpreted into an estimate of value. It is a dependable method of making a thorough, accurate appraisal in an efficient manner. It can also serve as an outline of the appraisal report. (AIREA 1977)

CHAPTER TWELVE
Development valuation[1]

It has been said that property possesses development potential whenever an element of latent value can be released by the expenditure of capital upon it (Baum & Mackmin 1989). Generally, this may arise through the development of a bare site where planning permission has been, or is likely to be, obtained; by redevelopment through the demolition and replacement of existing buildings following the grant of planning consent; by renovation through the upgrading of existing buildings, with or without planning approval for a change of use; or by a combination of new development, redevelopment or renovation.

There is nothing especially complex about the basic theory of development valuation, or indeed the traditional techniques employed. In fact, its very simplicity often attracts the disfavour of those seeking the mystical qualities of more advanced techniques of financial appraisal. In essence, development valuation merely involves the calculation of what can be achieved for a development once completed and let, less what it costs to create. It is, therefore, the most explicit and straightforward of valuation tasks, but can, at the same time, be the most prone to error and most responsive to individual supposition. Consequently, it depends above all upon sound professional judgement and a thorough investigation of all the circumstances prevailing in individual cases.

One fundamental factor, however, is that the reliability of any development valuation depends entirely upon the quality of the appraisal information described in the previous chapter.

The purposes

A development valuation or viability study can basically be undertaken for various different purposes, which include:

- calculating the likely value of land for development or redevelopment where

---

1. The examples used in this chapter, and some of the associated text, are taken from the chapter on development valuation by John Ratcliffe & Nigel Rapley in *Valuation: principles into practice*, W. A. Rees (ed.) (London: Estates Gazette, 4th edn, 1993).

acceptable profit margins and development costs can be estimated
- assessing the probable level of profit that may result from development where the costs of land and construction are known
- estimating the required level of rental income needed to justify the development decision
- establishing a cost ceiling for construction where minimum acceptable profit and land value are known.

A combination of the calculations can be conducted to explore alternative levels of acceptable costs and returns, but all valuations for development purposes require an agreed or anticipated level of income or capital value with which to work.

Several methods of assessing viability can be employed, with the appropriate choice of technique largely resting upon the individual circumstances and objectives of the developer concerned. The principal method used is that of capital profit, by which total development costs are deducted from gross development value and a residual profit is established. An alternative approach is the estimation of the yield or return produced by a development scheme. This can be a simple comparison of the anticipated initial income expressed as a percentage of the likely development costs; or it can be a more refined relationship between estimated income allowing for rental growth and the attainment of a specified *yield* by a selected target date. A further method, more commonly employed abroad, is that of *loan repayment* whereby the period it takes to repay a fixed interest loan is used as a comparative test of viability between alternative projects.

Component variables

To conduct a development valuation, there are variable components about which quantitative data is normally required. These are explored in more detail later in the chapter, but typically can be listed as follows:
- rental income or sale price
- investment yield for capitalization
- gross building size
- net lettable area
- construction costs
- fees
- cost of finance
- land cost (if known)
- required profit (if not the purpose)
- development period
- construction period
- acquisition and disposal costs
- contingency sum.

In examining the valuation of development properties, this chapter is organized into three subsequent sections:

- the residual method
- discounted cashflow analysis
- risk and uncertainty.

The residual method

The technique most frequently employed in the financial analysis of development projects is generally known as the residual valuation method. In essence, the residual method of valuation simply calculates what you can get for a development scheme once completed and let, less what it costs to create. Put another way, the conventional approach to a residual valuation is based upon the simple equation:

gross development value – (costs + profit) = residual value

The following two examples describe in bare outline ('back-of-the-envelope') residual valuations to find land value and development profit figures respectively. All figures are for illustrative purposes only.

Example 1: to find land value

A prospective developer finds it necessary to ascertain how much he can afford to offer for a small prime provincial site, which has planning permission for $2000\,m^2$ of offices producing $1600\,m^2$ of lettable floorspace. The projected development period is expected to be 24 months and the building contract period 12 months. Six months have been allowed before building works start to take account of detailed design, estimation and tendering. Six months following practical completion have been allowed for any possible letting voids that may occur. Finance can be arranged at 1.2 per cent per month, comparable schemes have recently yielded 6 per cent, rents of around £185 per m^2 net of all outgoings have currently been achieved on similar properties, and a developer's profit of 15 per cent on capital value is required. Construction costs have been estimated at £800 per m^2. A development valuation to assess the residual value of land can be conducted as in Table 12.1.

Example 2: to find development profit

A vacant and partially derelict deconsecrated church building in the centre of a large provincial town is being offered for sale at £2.5 million. A local property development company is interested in converting the building into a small speciality shopping centre on two floors. The reconstructed building will be approx-

251

Table 12.1   Valuation to assess land value.

Valuation	£	£
A. Capital value after development		
Anticipated net rental income	296000	
YP in perpetuity at 6%	16.67	
Estimated gross development value		4934320
B. Development costs		
(i) Building costs		
2000m² gross floor area at £800 per m²	1600000	
(ii) Building finance		
Interest on building costs 1.2% pm for 18		
months × 1/2	191606	
(iii) Professional fees		
12.5% on building costs	200000	
(iv) Interest on fees		
1.2% pm for 18 months × 2/3	31934	
(v) Promotion and marketing		
Estimated budget (including interest)	50000	
(vi) Contingency		
5% on costs (including interest)	103677	
(vii) Agents' fees		
Letting at 10% on initial rent	29600	
Sale at 3% on capital value	148030	
(viii) Developer's profit		
15% on capital value	740148	
(ix) Total development costs		3094995
C. Residual land value		
(i) Sum available for land, acquisition and interest		1839325
(ii) Let x – land value – 1.00 x		
(iii) Finance on land		
(iv) 1.2% pm for 24 months = 0.33/x		
(v) Acquisition costs		
(vi) 0.04 at 1.2% for 24 months = 0.053 x		
1.384x – £1839325 ∴ x =		
Residual land value now		1328992
	Say	£1330000

imately $3000\,m^2$ gross in size providing about $2000\,m^2$ of net lettable floorspace divided into 18 units of between $50\,m^2$ and $250\,m^2$. Rental income is predicted to average out at around £300 per m^2. An investment return of 7.5 per cent is sought. Building costs are estimated at £550 per m^2. Bridging finance is available at 1.4 per cent per month and the development will probably take 21 months to complete and let. The development company is anxious to know what will be the likely level of profit. (Table 12.2)

Table 12.2 Valuation to assess likely level of profit.

Valuation	£	£
A. *Gross development value*		
(i) Estimated rental income at £300		
(ii) per m² on 2000 m	600000	
(iii) YP in perpetuity at 7.5%	13.33	
Gross development value		7998000
B. *Development costs*		
(i) Building costs at £550 per m² on		
(ii) 3000 m	1650000	
(iii) Professional fees at 15%	247500	
(iv) Contingencies at 5% on (i) and (ii)	94875	
(v) Promotion, say	50000	
Finance on (i) to (iv) at 1.4% pm		
for 18 months x 0.65	377486	
(vi) Letting fees at 10% of rent	60000	
(vii) Sale fee at 3% of GDV	239940	
(viii) Land cost	2500000	
(ix) Acquisition at 4%	100000	
(x) Finance on land and acquisition at 1.4%		
for 21 months	881532	
(xi) Total development costs		6201333
C. *Development profit*		
(i) Residual value in 21 months		1796667
(ii) PV of £1 in 21 months at 1.4% pm		0.747
Value now		£1342110

(iii) Profit on cost in 21 months

$$\frac{1796667 \times 100}{6201333} = 28.97\%$$

Profit on cost now

(iv) $$\frac{1342110 \times 100}{6201333} = 21.64\%$$

Profit on value in 21 months

$$\frac{1796667 \times 100}{7998000} = 22.46\%$$

Profit on value now

$$\frac{1342110 \times 100}{6201333} = 16.78\%$$

Investment return on cost

$$\frac{600000 \times 100}{6201333} = 9.68\%$$

253

Component variables

Probably the most important part of the development valuation process is the analysis of all the determining factors that underlie and condition the various component variables.

Density of development

Having investigated the general climate for development and the broad planning policies in an area, it is a necessary first step in any residual valuation to establish the optimum amount of achievable gross floorspace or units of development. Assuming that no improvements can be made by further land assembly, a consideration of the relevant density controls must take place. For residential development this will usually be expressed in habitable rooms, dwellings or bed spaces per hectare. Habitable rooms are more popularly applied as a measure in concentrated urban areas; dwellings persist as the most familiar form of density control in private residential estate development; and bed spaces are normally found as a governing factor in public housing schemes. With regard to the commercial development of offices, and to some extent shops, the two major instruments of density control are floor space index and plot ratio. The former is based upon the total area of gross floorspace measured externally and expressed as a proportion of the site, plus half the width of surrounding roads up to a usual maximum of 6.1 m (20 ft), whichever is the less. The latter is similar but excludes the half width of surrounding roads. Variations occur between authorities in respect of whether or not certain elements such as basements, vaults, carparking, plant rooms, fuel stores and other kinds of special storage are included or excluded from the calculation. It is also fair to say that many local authorities now place greater emphasis upon design and other environmental considerations than they do on arithmetical formulae. With industrial development, the conventional way of assessing density is by site cover. Most modern industrial estates are developed to meet an eventual coverage of 45–55 per cent. Some inner urban projects, particularly those creating small nursery units, can produce as high as 65 per cent site cover, and at the other end of the spectrum the new business and science park concept with high-technology operations is often designed to provide around 15–25 per cent cover.

Again, it should be stressed that there are many other planning, and design considerations that determine the permissible volume, bulk and massing of new buildings. Among these are such matters as carparking, access, height, landscaping and light. There might also be the question of conservation, and the existence of listed buildings or protected trees and views, either on or around the site, can exercise a stringent control over the density of development. On the other hand, it is sometimes the case that local planning authorities will be prepared to approve schemes of development that are in excess of normal density levels as a result of a planning obligation, an exceptional design or the peculiar nature of the site.

Where the development project involves the refurbishment of existing premises, either in whole or in part, a detailed survey should be undertaken to establish gross and net areas so that existing use rights can be appraised. By rearranging the internal layout of the building, making more efficient use of common space, redesigning stair and light wells and exploiting basement and roof-space, considerable gains in lettable floorspace can be made from these existing use rights.

Economic design

In the context of property development it has been written that "The economic design is not necessarily the cheapest; it is the one that gives the best value for money". Costs in the development equation used to be taken at too crude an average and with little recognition of real design and construction implications. All parties involved in the process of property development are becoming increasingly aware of the need to create an economic design. The developer is concerned with the costs that must be borne to obtain the best return on capital seeking to maximize lettable floor area from a given gross area. The investor is more interested in the relationship between annual expenditure and the capital tied up in the project, looking for a building that is lettable and saleable and an asset that promises good rental growth with a sound economic and physical life. The occupier is concerned with the total costs of operating the building and the value it affords in terms of comfort, convenience and appearance, and the consequent effects upon business.

In attempting to minimize non-lettable floorspace it is possible to make a few generalizations about the "efficiency ratio" of different kinds of commercial development, that is, the relationship between gross external and net internal floorspace. With new offices the target is to achieve around 80 per cent, but in refurbishment schemes this figure can drop to between 60 per cent and 70 per cent. Shopping development varies considerably, but somewhere between 65 per cent and 75 per cent is normally sought. In industrial and warehouse development it is possible to achieve 90 per cent and more. Naturally, there are various factors that influence the efficiency ratio and design economics of a building, and without going into too many details it is worth recording some of them.

To begin with, the plan shape of a building has a significant effect on cost. It is, therefore, necessary to have regard to the "enclosing ratio" in order to compare the economics of various plan shapes, for the lower the ratio between the perimeter of the building and the floor area, the lower the unit cost. Heat losses can also vary according to layout, and change in shape may have an effect on the provision and cost of external works such as paved areas and drainage systems. Although the shape of a building is determined by a combination of factors, it has been ascertained that overall costs increase as the perimeter wall length increases in relation to floor area, and, further, that this becomes more marked when the building is increased in height by adding extra floors without altering the total floor area.

Because certain fixed costs connected with demolition, transportation and erection do not appreciate proportionately with increases in the size of a building, unit costs are usually reduced as a building becomes larger. Moreover, wall-to-floor ratios are again reduced with larger projects, and in some high-rise buildings there may be a cost advantage where certain services, such as a lift installation, serve a larger floor area and reduce overall costs. In certain forms of construction the grouping of buildings can affect cost. If, for example, buildings are arranged together rather than erected separately, there can be some cost saving by the combined use of separating walls between the two structures. This is particularly important when the facing walls are expensively clad.

A good economic design for a building will seek to reduce circulation and core space to a minimum. Entrance halls, corridors, stairs, plant rooms, lift wells and passages are all examples of dead space that cannot be used for any profitable purpose, yet all these areas have to be enclosed, heated, decorated or maintained in some way. Of course, cost is not the only criterion, because the value of the completed development will depend upon the appeal of the property to prospective tenants. Nevertheless, it is desirable to avoid unnecessary core provision and limit circulation space to an effective minimum.

Another factor is the height of buildings and, in very general terms, as storey height increases over about three or four storeys, upper floors become more expensive to provide. This is largely because of increased costs of scaffolding, the hoisting of materials and equipment, the extended provision of services and the need for formwork and additional reinforcements. Moreover, the demand for circulation space tends to increase slightly with height, and structural components are inclined to occupy a larger area. Wind is an important factor in high-rise buildings, which is not always considered as fully as it might be. Prevailing winds against the structure can cause eddies and whirlwinds affecting pedestrian flow at ground level, require the installation of plate glass windows at extra cost and dictate the incorporation of an air conditioning system. In addition, maintenance costs will usually be greater on high-rise buildings, but, on the other hand, heating costs can fall with the reduction in roof area, and economies can be experienced by repetition in the construction of successive floors through standardization and familiarity of work.

Therefore, it can be seen that the most economic design solution for a building is that which gives the best value for money, having regard to the need to contain initial, periodic and user costs, but taking into account the rental and capital values created. Depending upon the stage in the development process at which the residual valuation is being made, all the above design factors must be considered to varying degrees of detail in order to explore the cost–value implications.

Estimation of rental value
Possibly the most critical factor in the development equation is that of rental income, and yet all too frequently the chosen figure must rest upon hunch and intuition. Estimates of rent are usually based upon comparison with transactions conducted on similar properties in the locality, but, as already stated in the previous chapter, true comparables are sometimes difficult to discover. Adjustments

will often have to be made to allow for differences in size, location, age, condition, occupancy and lease terms. It may seem obvious, but care should be taken to ensure that quoted figures used for comparison are achieved-rents and not asking-rents, and that any premiums, discounts, rent-free periods or special lease terms are allowed for in analysis. Another problem is that, although some valuers are tempted to employ subtle zoning or apportionment techniques when comparing rental values for development proposals, this is not how the majority of commercial occupiers look at rent. In fact, it is increasingly common to find that prospective tenants tend to have greater regard to the full annual cost of occupying space, which on top of rent will include rates, maintenance and repair, insurance, cleaning, security, lighting and heating. For the purpose of valuation it is assumed that the tenant is normally responsible for all outgoings such as repairs, maintenance and insurance, or that a separate service charge would be levied to cover management costs.

Conventionally, rents are assessed on current rental values, but in practice the majority of developers also conduct valuations to take account of any likely rental growth up to completion. The argument for this is that, if rental values, which are a significant and sensitive component in valuation, were not projected in some way, then a developer would invariably be outbid at auction or when a sealed tender offer was made. The percentage to be taken for growth would depend on the local market where the scheme was situated, and a demand assessment study would be required (Marshall & Kennedy 1993).

In the absence of comparables, or in certain other special circumstances, rent may be calculated as a proportion of profit. The most notable situation where this occurs is in the use of turnover rents in planned shopping developments. These fix the rent at a percentage of current rental value plus a proportion of takings according to use. Nevertheless, in the valuation of a development scheme where such rents are proposed, many valuers will ignore the turnover element but adjust the year's purchase to reflect additional security and potential growth, others will adopt two different rates in capitalizing the rental income, one rate for the relatively secure base income and a higher rate for the riskier turnover income.

A further method of assessing rental value is by taking a percentage on cost, following the logic that rent is a return for investment risk. Very much a method of last resort, it is used occasionally in checking the viability of development projects.

The most certain conditions for establishing rental value are, of course, where a pre-letting of the development has been agreed. In this instance, it is likely that the tenant would have negotiated a preferential rent up to first review at a level something below full rental value at the date of occupation. Equally, however, it would be reasonable in any valuation to adjust the yield downwards so as to reflect the increased security conferred by a pre-let. Thus, there is a compensating effect.

Selection of capitalization rate

Most residual valuations rely upon the conventional "all-risks" yield to determine the rate at which estimated rental income should be capitalized. Also known as the initial or investment yield, it is market-derived and, one can argue, price-dominated. As already intimated, the main complication arising from the use of yields produced by analyzing allegedly similar market transactions is that prices often reflect special circumstances. Initial yields deduced from the analysis of existing investments in a current market should not be employed indiscriminately in the selection of capitalization rates for assessing the viability of development schemes. However, they do have to reflect factors including probable future rental growth, security of income, flexibility of use, ease of letting, likely economic life of the building, acceptability of design and layout and responsibility for management.

Although most projects are highly sensitive to small changes in yield, especially at times when prime commercial yields are running at very low levels, it is the component of the residual valuation over which the developer has least control. With all other factors such as costs, rents, fees, time, and even finance, much more scope exists for improving project performance by skilful negotiation or management. Invariably the yield, and thus the capitalization rate, are determined within very narrow margins by the funding institutions. Even so, it is always worth presenting a scheme to a variety of funds in the hope that the special nature of it, in terms of situation, size, tenure, covenant and use will exactly meet certain outstanding requirements of their portfolio, in which case they may be prepared to accept a slightly lower yield. As it is usually the asset value upon completion, and through time, that is the overriding objective to an investing institution, they will often take a longer-term view than the developing agency. It is not uncommon for funds to put together a package deal with a chosen developer that includes a forward sale commitment and demands a slightly higher return. In such circumstances it is vital to agree a specified yield rate at the take-out date.

For whichever party to a development proposal the valuation is being prepared, it is important to explore the possible range of yields that might be adopted by all other interested parties and to study the effects on value and profit levels. A vendor will wish to examine the likely spread of bids and a potential purchaser will want to identify the manoeuvrability of any competition.

In order to achieve a desired yield, a purchaser of the development as an investment would need to meet the costs of legal fees, agents' fees, stamp duty and other disbursements. These normally amount to around 2.5–2.75 per cent of gross development value (GDV) and would need to be deducted from the GDV to arrive at the required net yield. However, it is sometimes assumed, as in the examples described in this chapter, that the yield is analyzed net of purchasers' costs and so it would be double counting to deduct the costs again. In practice, especially where a developer has entered into a commitment to sell the project on completion to a fund, these costs would almost always be deducted.

Building costs

The precision with which building costs are gauged will differ according to circumstances, becoming more refined and exact as the valuation is worked up. At the outset it is likely that very indicative figures will be employed, drawn from roughly similar schemes on an overall basis. If the result is encouraging, then an outline scheme will normally be prepared by the architect, and slightly more detailed figures calculated against a general specification will be used. Several more stages of sophistication will follow if the auguries are propitious.

Again, a few very general factors merit attention. To begin with, demolition can be a very expensive item, particularly where heavy fixed plant has been installed, special foundations or superstructure provided, or the site is tightly positioned in a busy urban area. Likewise, in older central locations where existing and redundant underground services are present, or in fresh situations where the ground lacks stability or access to infrastructure, site preparation costs can be high.

Probably the largest single element in terms of the costs of development and the potential economic life of a building is the provision of mechanical and electrical services, and in the past too little consideration has been given to the environmental engineering aspects of a development too late in the design process. It has been suggested that over 60 per cent of building costs can be attributed to these services, and it has been argued that more problems arise around matters of power, lighting, lifts, air conditioning, heating, water supply, drainage and communications, than with any other aspect of development. The heating and ventilation system of a building, for example, should be designed in sympathy with the structure for which it is intended, and considered in respect of both initial capital costs of installation and future annual running costs.

One of the greatest irritants to occupancy is the lift system and, as a broad guideline, buildings exceeding three storeys usually have a passenger lift and those taller than six storeys require a second. In addition, where a substantial flow of goods takes place within a building, a separate goods lift will have to be provided, even at two storeys. The two most commonly used types of lift installation are electrical traction drive and oildraulic drive. From a development valuation point of view, the cost of installing an oildraulic lift can be approximately twice that of a conventional electrically driven lift. Running costs are about the same for both, but, because the oildraulic system has no large driving motor, maintenance costs during its working life are negligible, and it is a very much more flexible system to install in refurbishment schemes, tending to optimize lettable floorspace. Lifts can be of varying speeds, but faster lifts require the use of either two-speed or voltage motors to provide smother acceleration and deceleration, thereby increasing capital, maintenance and running costs. On the other hand, the extra cost of high-speed lifts is usually justified by the saving of valuable floor area.

With regard to other services, the amount of artificial lighting will depend upon the use of the property and vary according to the depth of the building, its ori-

259

entation and the type of windows incorporated. The onset of advanced technology has meant that the accommodation of communications equipment has assumed more importance, and presently the ability to bring power, telephone, audiovisual, computer and other cabling to desk, check-counter or operating position is a basic design consideration with both cost and value implications. Another fundamental factor is the supply of plumbing and waste disposal facilities, and any hot and cold water system, together with their related utilities, will be more economic the more compactly they are planned and the shorter the pipe runs that result.

To aid the accurate spread of building costs throughout the construction period, most experienced developers have drawn up cost profiles for the various sectors of the property development industry, but these are only used in an indicative way in the residual method of valuation, as opposed to DCF analyses where they can be employed more positively. Techniques for appraising total building costs, which have gained in popularity within the quantity surveying profession, are costs-in-use analysis, life-cycle costing and valve engineering, whereby the initial construction costs and annual user costs of a building can be reduced to a common measure. Initial and future expenditures for selected alternative designs are discounted to their present worth and compared in the knowledge that small changes in design can often have significant effects upon running costs as well as capital costs.

Striking a note of caution in respect of building costs, it can be argued that they have been held down over the past few years by competing contractors absorbing a substantial proportion of increasing costs in order to win contracts, but significant escalation is likely to take place within the next year or so. In practice, a majority of developers allow for an inflation in building costs in the same way as rental projections are made until practical completion.

Professional fees

Many developers prefer all fees to be expressed as a percentage of the total costs of construction. The traditional allowance is around 12.5–14.5 per cent, but may fall to 10 per cent or even lower for straightforward and repetitive work such as that in certain industrial and residential estate development, and rise as high as 15–17 per cent on unusually complex schemes or projects of refurbishment.

In very broad terms these fees may be broken down among the various contributing professionals as follows. The architect usually receives about 6 per cent on construction cost, excluding disbursements, but this figure can easily rise to 10 per cent on refurbishment schemes, and there is an entitlement to stage payments. Quantity surveyors' fees vary but are normally in the range of 2 per cent to 3 per cent inclusive on cost, depending upon the value of the work, being a lower percentage the higher the value. It is traditional for consulting engineers to relate their fees to the cost of the relevant engineering works with which they are concerned, not to total construction costs, at a rate of around 6.5 per cent exclusive of disbursements, but pressure is applied by some developers to have engineering fees expressed as a proportion of the whole. Where this is done, structural engineering fees work out at approximately 2.25 per cent of total construction cost and other engineering fees at a further 2.25 per cent to 2.75 per cent. Project management fees are around 2 per cent.

The majority of commercial agents would seek a letting fee of around 10 per cent of the initial rent, unless a specially reduced rent has been agreed with the incoming tenant. Joint agents formerly often looked to share 1.5 per cent RICS scale. All fees are to some extent negotiable, and where developers use regularly retained agents they will sometimes look to secure a discount. It should be noted in most circumstances that, on sale, the tenant will pay the legal costs of the landlord. In some development projects it will be necessary to call upon specialist advice relating to such matters as planning, tax and party walls, in which case the fees are normally charged at an appropriate hourly or daily rate by the consultant concerned.

Apart from the agent's letting fee, the finance on fees tends to be somewhat front-heavy. Architects, for example, are entitled, in theory at least, to three-quarters of their fees before building work begins.

Finance for development

Chapter 13 is devoted to this topic in some detail. For the purposes of conducting a basic residual valuation it is pertinent to make a few comments regarding how the cost of finance is accounted for in an initial feasibility study. More complex calculations would follow.

In allowing for finance charges on construction costs in the residual valuation, adjustments are made to reflect that funds are borrowed only as they are required, cashflow being critical. Three basic alternative methods are variously employed, all being nothing more than rough estimates. Either half the rate of interest is applied for the full building period, or the full rate is applied for half the building period, or the full rate is applied for the whole period and half the result is taken as the finance charge. All three give different figures, the last quoted producing the highest. In calculating the finance on other components, similar proportions are adopted. For example, the accumulated debt charge on fees is often taken at two-thirds to three-quarters of the interest rate. In fact, a variable percentage, such as 60 per cent or 65 per cent, can be applied to building cost finance to take a rough account of higher charges resulting from such items as costly demolition or site preparation at the beginning of development, or void periods at the end. In practice, the most popular calculation is 50 per cent of total costs for the building period.

Unless special arrangements have been agreed with the vendor, the finance charges on the cost of land and land acquisition are invariably compounded at the full rate of interest over the entire development period and, as stated above, it should be remembered that, if there are any void periods following completion, the total outstanding amount should be rolled-up at the full rate to account for interest on interest, not simply deferred.

The actual rate of interest by which the costs will be rolled-up depends upon the source of finance available to the developer. Conventionally, however, where these are not known or have yet to be agreed, a rate of interest some few percentage points above the base rate (such as London Inter-Bank Overnight Rate, LIBOR) will be employed. Even where a substantially lower rate of borrowing has been negotiated or internal funds are to be employed, it is correct at earlier stages of valuation to adopt a full opportunity cost of finance approach so as to identify other possible bids and a minimum open market value for the land. Again, refinements will follow.

Promotion and marketing

The amount of the budget allowed for promotion and marketing in the development valuation varies considerably and depends largely upon the nature and location of the project concerned. Many schemes are either wholly or substantially pre-let and will require little or no additional funding during the development period. However, it should not be forgotten that an extensive marketing campaign may have been involved prior to construction, and the financing of those costs will have to be carried throughout the gestation period of the scheme.

Because marketing needs will vary so widely between projects, it is unwise to adopt an easy proportion or percentage of some other figure. Rather, a figure related to the probable costs of promoting the individual development must be estimated, and the early advice of agents is desirable.

Likewise, although it is often true that the larger the development the larger the budget, there is no direct relationship with the size of the project, and some of the largest may be relatively easy to let. Nevertheless, it is possible to identify certain fixed costs, and even the very smallest development will rarely require less than £50000 as a promotions budget.

Contingency

There is a certain amount of disagreement within the ranks of development surveyors whether or not a contingency sum should be included within a residual valuation, and if so, how much it should be. It is argued that a contingency should be set aside in the calculation to allow for any unforeseen and financially onerous occurrences that would take place during the development period and affect viability. This might cover such circumstances as the need to provide for unforeseen service requirements, overcome undiscovered physical problems in the land or supply special facilities for a particularly attractive tenant. On the other hand, some would argue that all the other components in the residual should be properly estimated, and that effective project management should ensure that a project or development comes in within total budget. On the whole, however, it is sensible to make provision for a contingency sum. The exact amount will vary, but a commonly accepted margin is around 5 per cent on construction cost or alternatively 3 per cent on gross development value. With schemes of refurbishment it is usual to allow much more. The amount of the contingency item can vary according to the date of the valuation. Prior to the preparation of plans or cost estimates it can be as much as 8 per cent of building cost, after the preparation or sketch plans and cost estimates it is more appropriately put at 5 per cent, and after the award of the building contract it can be reduced to as low as 3 per cent of building cost (Jolly 1979). As an alternative to allowing for a separate item in respect of contingencies, it is common practice to add a further margin to the developer's profit. In Example 1, for instance, a developer's profit of around 17 per cent instead of 15 per cent on gross development value would suffice. In any event, the actual figure should be determined by the degree of detailed research and survey work undertaken both before and during appraisal.

Land acquisition

The very purpose of many residual valuations is to identify the likely price that may be paid or received in respect of an opportunity to develop land. On the other hand, sometimes the cost of land is ignored, sometimes it is known, and sometimes it is assumed. This is either because no change of ownership is contemplated, or because disposition has already occurred at an agreed sum, or because the calculation is being performed against an asking or offer price. In all circumstances, however, it should be remembered that the value of land is a residual, even if it resides from another or previous computation.

As stated above, in the majority of cases the cost of acquiring land is charged at the full rate of discount throughout the entire period of development. However, there may be instances when an arrangement is made between the vendor and the purchaser to phase acquisition or postpone payment. Conversely, an option to buy the land may have been taken out some time prior to purchase and must itself be charged in the calculation. In similar vein, special arrangements regarding the timing or phasing of payment might be agreed between the parties, and adjustments may have to be made to land acquisition costs as a result, depending upon the precise nature of the agreement. Refinements in the purchase agreement leading to delayed, reduced or staged payments should not be ignored, as their effect upon viability can often be quite dramatic.

Theoretically, a formula-based approach incorporating the notional costs and the consequential finance charges should be employed, although in practice some valuers simply apply a discount factor to the sum available for land acquisition at the end of the development period.

Developers' profit

A figure to take account of the reward expected by a developer for taking the risks associated with a scheme of development and applying his management expertise to the project is either included within the residual valuation or is the result of it. Sometimes, indeed, it may be a combination of both, where the calculation is being conducted to ascertain a surplus.

There are two conventional methods by which a developer's profit is included in a residual valuation, the choice depending upon whether or not the cost of land is known. Where land acquisition costs cannot be ascertained and are likely to be the result of the valuation, then a proportion of gross development value is taken, usually 10–20 per cent. Where land costs are known, and can be included as part of total costs, then a proportion of that total cost is adopted, normally 15–25 per cent. Research has shown that a figure of 15–17 per cent is the minimum return on cost accepted by most developers (Marshall & Kennedy 1993).

If the purpose of the valuation is to identify probable levels of developers' profit, then the same proportions of gross development value and total construction cost can be used as measures. In addition, profit may be expressed as a proportion of the yield relationship between anticipated rental income and gross development value. Put another way, a developer will look for a percentage margin above the initial investment yield, normally between 1.5 per cent and 3 per cent, so that if the funding institution requires a 6 per cent return on the project at disposition, the developer will be seeking something between 7.5 and 9 per cent yield in total. Some smaller, more speculative developers might merely look for achieving a simple capital gain and not assess minimum acceptable profit as a percentage of cost or value. In other circumstances, certain development agencies may adopt different attitudes towards development profit. Financial institutions, building firms and major retailers are known at times to operate lower margins of profit, being respectively interested in creating new investment, ensuring continuity of construction work, and obtaining fresh outlets for retailing. In practice, it is also becoming increasingly common to see developers adopting a basic project management fee approach towards their first slice of profit and sharing additional equity in a predetermined manner with a funding institution.

Example 2 shows that the developer's profit on both cost and value can be calculated as being receivable either upon completion or as a discounted sum now. In practice, the former future figure is often used to judge acceptable levels of profit, whereas in theory, the latter discounted figure is more suitable for comparing alternative development schemes having varying periods until completion. In fact, most developers examine profitability from all angles before making a land bid.

The impact of time

In periods of high interest rates, inflation and erratic changes in both costs and rents, the impact of time upon development valuation can be quite startling. In this respect, the residual method is arguably less sensitive to changes through time than the discounted cashflow analysis approach. The most important starting point is to ensure that the appropriate discount rate is employed to defer future income and expenditure. Whereas the initial investment yield is the proper rate to capitalize rental income once the scheme is completed and let, the correct rate at which to discount the residual sum during the development period, whether it represents land value or development profit, is the opportunity cost of capital for internal funding or the cost of borrowed finance for external funding. Any other rate should be based upon explicit policy assumptions made or approved by the client.

In conducting an appraisal it should be appreciated that, whereas rental growth during the development period will have the effect of inflating the value of the completed scheme by the whole amount of the increase, the total costs of construction will only increase by about half the rate of growth. This is because only a proportion of the debt charge is outstanding. This inherent gearing builds in a margin of enhanced profitability and explains why some developers undertake projects that on the face of it appear highly suspect.

Although risk and uncertainty can be incorporated much more easily into residual valuations by courtesy of microcomputers, it must be stressed that more, if not all, appraisals should be subjected to a simple sensitivity analysis by varying the component factors of rent, cost, yield, finance charges and time in order to explore the effects of change and the different attitudes that might be taken by the market. At its very simplest a basic optimistic–realistic–pessimistic set of appraisals should be conducted to establish the range of values.

Taxation and allowances

Allowance for taxation is rarely made in residual valuation. The discounted cashflow technique described below, however, can be used to incorporate the effects of individual tax liabilities, as well as tax relief against interest charges and tax allowances for the installation of plant and machinery, and for construction in assisted areas. In most other circumstances it has been held that the effects of tax on the residual valuation are ignored so that rents, costs and values are calculated on a before-tax basis. So far as the capitalization of rent is concerned, this is a well established principle in any open market valuation where it is likely that potential purchasers will pay tax at the standard rate of corporation or income tax. Tax relief against interest charges and tax allowances for the provision of plant and machinery are again not usually taken into account in an open market valuation, because they are dependent upon the circumstances of the particular developer (Jolly 1979). Likewise, value added tax is usually ignored in residual valuation, but there is evidence that, where appropriate, a majority of developers are allowing for VAT in any cashflow analysis (Marshall & Kennedy 1993).

Criticisms of the residual method

Most notable, and oft quoted, among the critics of the residual method of valuation have been the Lands Tribunal, which has demonstrated a reluctance to accept the technique as a primary method of valuation within the aegis of their jurisdiction. Although it has employed the approach on a few very exceptional occasions, either in whole or in part, the Tribunal has stated that residual valuations are far from being a certain guide to values, because minor adjustments to constituent figures can have a major effect on the resultant valuation. Further, they have argued that "once valuers are let loose upon residual valuations, however honest the valuers and however reasonable their arguments, they can prove almost anything" (*First Garden City Ltd* vs *Letchworth Garden City* 1966). A close examination of some of the cases placed before the Tribunal would seem to support a measure of criticism and, in the notable case quoted above, the continuous revision of figures between disputing parties caused the Tribunal to comment that their process of residual valuation "continued like a seemingly endless game of battledore and shuttlecock, until even such a veteran player as the District Valuer was showing signs of exhaustion". The criticisms made by the Lands Tribunal became even more understandable when one appreciates that the parties before them are not actually intending to use their quoted figures for purposes of disposition for actual development. As the Tribunal itself has stated in another case, the valuations they see are immune from "the purifying fires of open market dealings" and "with captive parties there can be no acid test".

Setting aside the strictures of the Land Tribunal, the residual method was brought into greatest practical disrepute during the worst excesses of the property boom in the early 1970s. A phenomenon aptly described as "130 per cent valuation" was witnessed, whereby negligent, unnerved, and occasionally nefarious valuers sought to establish hyperbolic levels of value in order to secure for clients full funding from banks who would normally advance around two-thirds of the valuation figure. Bullish views of anticipated rents were combined with a bearish attitude towards costs, and compounded by a dismissive approach regarding potential planning problems. Unprofessional practices experienced at that time in the area of development valuation, only some of which have been exposed in the courts, have tended to cast a shadow over the residual method, and while it is true that in many respects it lacks degrees of precision, is often insensitive to changes of cost and value through time and many of the component factors are either crude averages or very approximate guesses, there is another side to the argument. When performed properly with carefully considered assumptions, well researched figures regarding costs and rents, an informed view of the development programme and a justified set of decisions in respect of marketing, management and disposal, it becomes a comparatively overt and reliable means of appraising the viability of, and constructing a valuation for a prospective development scheme relating to, a specific site, a known developer and established conditions for finance, design and building. In any event, it is an appropriate valuation technique where no readily comparable transactions are available or where the scale of the scheme could itself distort the local market.

There are really only two alternative ways to the residual method for valuing development properties: by direct comparable evidence and by discounted cash-flow analysis. Even so, it should be recognized that the first is a derivation of the residual and the second an extension to it.

When employing comparable evidence, it is important to appreciate that the resultant figures are derived from prices achieved in the market and that the sum agreed by an individual vendor and a particular purchaser is likely to be unique, reflecting their personal predilections, tax liabilities and non-property interests. In this way, there is rarely such a thing as a true comparable, and it can be argued that the various adjustments to value or profit that might have to be made to take account of such matters as location, size, date of transaction and proposed use are every bit as contrived and prone to error as the manipulation that takes place in attuning the residual. Furthermore, many of the transactions selected for comparable analysis will, in all probability, have been based upon a residual approach in the first place, and it is surely more credible to construct an explicit and specially prepared residual for the property in question than to rely on the end results of other unknown computations. Markets are notoriously aberrant in both space and time.

Discounted cashflow analysis

The main criticism of the residual method of valuation is that it is not precise enough in the way it reflects the incidence of time and money payments during the period of development. In practice, expenditure upon construction is incurred at regular stages throughout the building contract period, with payments to the contractor usually being made on a monthly basis and assessed on the cumulative value of the work carried out and certified by the quantity surveyor. A typical pattern of payments on a commercial development project has been described as follows:

> During the first few weeks of the building period the valuation will be for relatively small amounts because the contractor is engaged in erecting site offices, taking levels, preparing the site and forming excavations. The rate of expenditure will then start to accelerate as the foundations are put in. If heavy plant, such as a tower crane, is necessary this may be brought in at a fairly early stage and the hire costs will start to be certified by the quantity surveyor after a month or two. Scaffolding costs and structure erection will follow, and the monthly payments will then build up to a fairly consistent level until the first specialist subcontract work begins, such as the installation of lifts and boiler, when there will be a surge in expenditure. After these first large items of equipment have been paid for, there is sometimes a slight fall in the size of the monthly payments until the expensive finishing and fitting out work such as specialist joinery, light fittings, carpeting, panelling and marble work starts. After practical completion, some expenditure may still be outstanding on items such as landscape and planting. There will be an average time lag of approximately five weeks between the date on which the contractor carries out the work on site and the date on which the developer will pay him". (Jolly 1979)

Other items such as professional fees and promotions budget will also display an irregular pattern of expenditure. As a consequence of this variable spending profile, the finance charges will accrue at a similarly fluctuating rate. Furthermore, in many development schemes, particularly those in the residential and industrial sectors, it will be possible to let or sell completed parts of the project as they became available. In this way, rental income or capital sums will be realized during the development period, which can be set-off against expenditure elsewhere.

Because the residual method only "guesstimates" the time value of money, making some heroic assumptions about finance costs, it is at best really a rapid screening device employed in selecting among several alternative projects. What is needed is an approach that examines much more closely the cashflows of expenditure and income throughout the process of development, and apportions them to the appropriate time-periods showing the real cost of finance.

Some advantages have been suggested in using a discounted cashflow analysis (Newell 1989).

- In phased, multi-use developments, the cashflow associated with each phase of the scheme can be spelt out and summed into a monthly or quarterly cash-flow framework.
- The timing of both expenditures (notably building costs, which may be allocated manually or by use of built-in S-curves) and receipts can accurately be allocated to each month or quarter. This will increase the reliability of the interest rate calculation.
- Interest rates may be allowed to vary during the period of the project, allowing greater flexibility and accuracy.
- The developer obtains an accurate picture of potential cash exposure and will be able to identify points of greatest cashflow risk.
- Additional investment criteria including net present value (NPV) and internal rate of return (IRR) may be obtained as a supplement to the traditional "return on cost" measure.

There are different methods by which cashflows during the development period can be valued. These include the:

- phased residual valuation
- residual cashflow valuation
- net present value discounted cashflow analysis
- internal rate of return discounted cashflow analysis

Phased residual valuation

The following example shows how the basic residual method can be modified to take account of phased development projects.

Example 3
Consider the freehold interest in a cleared site that has planning approval for the construction of 90 detached houses. It is thought probable that any prospective purchaser would develop the site in three phases, each of 30 houses. The total development period is estimated at three years, with separate contract periods of

12 months for each of the three phases. The sale price of the houses is set at £150000 each. Construction costs are estimated at £85000 a house and the cost of site works and the provision of services is assessed at an average of £8000 per house plot. Finance is available at 1.5 per cent per month and a developer's profit of 10 per cent on gross development value is considered likely to be sought.

A phased residual valuation can be conducted as in Table 12.3.

It can be seen that the value of each phase is in the order of £386000 if development on all three phases started immediately. However, allowance has been made for the cost to the developer of holding phase 2 for a further 12 months and phase 3 for a further 24 months. Even if the three phases were sold separately to different developers, it is assumed that the local demand for new housing would not hold up sufficiently to permit consecutive development of all 90 houses within the first year. An alternative calculation with adjusted selling prices to reflect increased supply could with advantage be performed.

Table 12.3   Phased residual valuation.

Valuation		
Phase 1		
A. Sale price of house		150000
B. Development cost		
Building costs	85000	
Site works and services	8000	
Professional fees at 10%	9300	
Advertising, say	2000	
Finance on £104300 at 1.5% for 12 months × ½	10201	
Disposal fees at 3% of sale price	4500	
Developer's profit at 10% of sale price	15000	
Total development costs		134001
Balance per plot		15999
C.Site value phase 1		
Number of plots		30
		479970
Amount available in 12 months		
Let site value =	1.000x	
Acquisition costs =	0.040x	
Finance at 1.5% on 1.04x for 1 yr =	0.203x	
	1.243x	
1.243x = 479970		
∴ x = 386138		
Site value of phase 1, say		386000
D. Site value of phase 2		
Site value phase 1	386000	
PV of £1 in 12 months at 1.5%	0.836	
		322696
E. Site value of phase 3		
Site value phase 1	386000	
PV of £1 in 24 months at 1.5%	0.700	
		270200
F. Value of entire site	Say	978896
		£980000

269

Although the method suggested above is an improvement to a global residual, it still gives only a broad indication of value. A detailed discounted cashflow analysis would provide a much better approximation of value.

Residual cashflow valuation

The example below demonstrates that the phased residual valuation can be taken a stage further, so as to produce a residual cashflow valuation.

Example 4

Consider a 10 ha site on a motorway location, which has planning permission for "high technology" B1 industrial development with a site coverage of around 30 per cent. Rents of £120 per m^2 are forecast and a major financial institution has shown interest in buying the scheme once completed if it can show an initial yield of 7 per cent. The total development period will be about three years, but it is considered possible to develop and let the equivalent of 1 ha every three months, starting in month nine. Construction costs are estimated at £500 per m^2 and short-term finance can be arranged at 16 per cent. The site is on offer for £12 million. A residual cashflow valuation, to take account of the effects of expenditure and revenue during the development period and show the likely level of profit, can be performed as follows (Tables 12.4 & 12.5):

Preliminaries
- 10 ha $= 100000 \, m^2$
- Site coverage at 30% $= 30000 \, m^2$ gross.
- Less 5% $= 28500 \, m^2$ net lettable floorspace.
- Building costs of £15000000 averaged at £1250000 a quarter.
- Promotion costs of £300000 spread over the first 2.5 years at an average of £30000 a quarter.
- Professional fees taken at 10% of building costs and paid at an average rate of £125000 a quarter.
- Letting fees taken at 10% of initial annual rents and paid as quarterly rents are received.
- Sale fee of £1466154 being 3% of gross development value payable upon completion and sale.
- Rental income at 10% of the total quarterly rent roll to commence in month 9 and grow by a further 10% each quarter until month 36 when the full quarterly rent roll of £320625 is reached.
- Gross development value of £48871800 calculated by capitalizing rental income of £3420000 a year by 14.29 YP and received in three years' time.
- Annual interest of 16% to be taken at 3.78% a quarter.
- All cashflow figures rounded to the nearest thousand.

Table 12.4   Conventional residual valuation.

		£	£	£
A.	Gross development value			48 872 000
B.	Land and construction costs			
Land		12 480 000		
Building		15 000 000		
Promotion		300 000		
Fees		3 306 000		
Interest		10 490 000		
Total			41 576 000	
Less:				
Revenue during development			4 700 000	
C.	Total development costs			36 876 000
D.	Development profit			
(i)	Development profit in 3 years			11 996 000
(ii)	PV of £1 in 3 years at 16%			0.641
	Development profit now			7 689 436

(iii)   Profit on cost in 3 years =

$$\frac{11996000 \times 100}{36876000} = 32.53\%$$

Profit on cost now

$$\frac{7689436 \times 100}{36876000} = 20.85\%$$

(iv)   Profit on value in 3 years =

$$\frac{1996000 \times 100}{48872000} = 24.55\%$$

Profit on value now

$$\frac{7689436 \times 100}{48872000} = 15.73\%$$

Return on cost

$$\frac{3420000 \times 100}{36876000} = 9.27\%$$

Discounted cashflow analysis (NPV and IRR)

This example compares the conventional residual method of valuation with a discounted cashflow analysis, using both net present value (NPV) and internal rate of return (IRR) approaches, in order to demonstrate the need to be more conscious of the effects of time and the incidence of costs and revenue in the valuation of development of properties.

Table 12.5 Residual cashflow analysis ('000s).

Timescale		Cash outflows				Cash inflows			
Year	Month	Land	Building	Promotion	Fees	Rent	Sale	Cumulative cashflow	Interest at 3.78% pq
0	0	(12480)			(125)			(12510)	(479)
0	3		(1250)	(30)	(125)	85		(13915)	(544)
0	6		(1250)	(30)	(159)	171		(15793)	(618)
0	9		(1250)	(30)	(159)	256		(17691)	(692)
1	0		(1250)	(30)	(159)	342		(19577)	(766)
1	3		(1250)	(30)	(159)	427		(21.452)	(840)
1	6		(1250)	(30)	(159)	513		(23315)	(913)
1	9		(1250)	(30)	(159)	598		(25167)	(986)
2	0		(1250)	(30)	(159)	684		(27006)	(1058)
2	3		(1250)	(30)	(159)	769		(28833)	(1130)
2	6		(1250)		(159)	855		(30616)	(1200)
2	9		(1250)		(159)			(32386)	(1270)
3	0		(1250)		(1466)		48 872	(34140)	
Total		(12480)	(15000)	(300)	(3306)	4700	48 872	11996	(10490)

Example 5

A local property development company have been offered a prime corner site on the high street of a prosperous provincial town for £1.5 million and is anxious to establish the probable viability for development with a view to disposing of it to an institution once fully completed and occupied. The site is currently used as a builder's yard with some vacant and near-derelict shops and has a high street frontage of 120m and a depth of 45m. It lies within an area allocated for shops and offices with an overall plot ratio of 1.5:1 and a general height restriction of three storeys. Preliminary discussions indicate that the usual parking standards of one space to every 200m² of office floorspace and five to every 100m² retail floorspace could be relaxed if 30 spaces are provided on-site and a Section 106 obligation under the TCPA 1990 is entered into, whereby a further 50 spaces are funded by the developer in a nearby local authority carpark to be constructed in one or two years time. A condition limiting a substantial proportion of any office floorspace to local firms will almost certainly be imposed on a planning permission. All ground-floor development must be retail and rear access to shops is considered essential. A small supermarket of approximately 1000m² is thought likely to attract support and, because the local planning authority are concerned that some form of suitable development takes place as soon as possible, negotiations should be relatively straightforward, with permission probably granted in three months.

The quantity surveyor retained by the company has supplied the following information:

- A 6m grid to be used throughout with 5m ceiling heights for retail space and 3m ceiling height for offices.
- Building costs for shops to be taken at £400 per m², excluding fitting out and shop fronts and equally phased over 9 months. Standard shop units to be 6m × 24m.
- Building costs for offices to be taken at £800 per m² for letting, including lifts and central heating and equally phased over 15 months.
- Demolition and site preparation to be allowed for at £20 per m² across the entire site.
- External works, including landscaping, will cost £200000.
- All payments to be made three months in arrears.

The property development company's knowledge of the area indicates rental levels of £150 per m² per annum for supermarket space, an average of £29000 per annum or approximately £200 per m² per annum for a standard shop unit and £100 per m² per annum for offices. Given three months to obtain planning permission and prepare the site and nine months to construct the shops, it is envisaged that a further three months should be time enough to allow for a successful letting campaign and to complete the superstructure of the building, so that the shops could be let at the end of 15 months. In view of the probable local user condition, the letting climate of the offices is slightly more uncertain, and it is considered appropriate to allow a full six months following completion before they are fully

273

let and disposition to an institution can be effected. Professional fees to the architect and quantity surveyor have been negotiated so that £60000 is paid as a lump-sum following planning permission, and the remainder calculated subsequently at 10 per cent of building cost on a three-monthly basis. Short-term finance has been arranged with a merchant bank at 15 per cent (3.56% per quarter).

Table 12.6 Conventional residual valuation.

Preliminaries			m^2
(a)	*Site*		
	Site area = 5400m^2		
	Plot ratio = 1.5:1		
	Therefore, gross permitted commercial		
	floorspace	=	8100
(b)	*Shops*		
	Supermarket 30 × 36m	=	1080
	Standard units 90 × 24m less 2 ground-floor		
	offices entrances 3 × 12m	=	2088
	Total gross retail floorspace	=	3168
(c)	*Offices*		
	(Gross permitted commercial floorspace –		
	gross retail floorspace) 8100–3168m^2	=	4932
	Taking account of 6m grid constraint:		
	2-storey above shops 120 × 18m	=	4320
	Single-storey extension above supermarket		
	18 × 24m	=	432
	Add – 2 ground-floor entrances 3 × 12m	=	72
	Total gross office floorspace	=	4824

(d)	*Gross areas to net*		
	Gross	Deduction	Net m^2
	Supermarket 1080m^2	10%	972
	Standard units 2088m^2	15%	1775
	Offices 4824m^2	20%	3859

(e)	*Income*		£pa
	Supermarket		
	972m^2 at £150 per m^2 pa	=	145800
	Standard units		
	1775m^2 at £200 per m^2 pa	=	355000
	Offices		
	3859m^2 at £100 per m^2 pa	=	385900
			£886700

It is well reported that institutions are interested in schemes of this nature, scale and location, but seek yields of between 7 and 8 per cent. It is therefore necessary to establish whether a yield can be accomplished that provides for this and also allows for the developer's risk.

Notes on Tables 12.6–12.9

- The present value of the profit indicated by the residual is £1575118. This may be compared with an appraisal by discounted cashflow. It is commonly thought that a discounted cashflow analysis produces a more accurate result

Table 12.6 (continued)

Conventional residual		£	£
A.	*Capital value after development*		
(i)	Estimated net rental income	886 700	11 819 711
(ii)	YP in perpetuity at 7 5%	13.33	
(iii)	Gross development value		
B.	*Development costs*		
(i)	Building costs	1 267 200	
	Shops – 3168 m² at £400 per m²	3 859 200	
	Offices – 4824 m² at £800 per m²	108 000	
	Site preparation	200 000	
	External works	5 434 400	
	Total		
(ii)	Professional fees		
	Architect and QS by negotiation	603 440	
(iii)	Contingencies		
	5% on (i)	271 720	
(iv)	Finance on building		
	3.56% pq for 7 quarters × ½ on (i) + (ii) + (iii)	875 297	
(v)	Agents' fees		
	Letting fees 15% on initial rent	133 005	
	Sale fees at 3% on GDV	354 591	
(vi)	Land costs		
	Land	1 500 000	
	Acquisition	60 000	
	Finance at 3.56% for 8 quarters	503 768	
(vii)	Total development costs		9 736 221
C.	*Residual capital value*		
(i)	Capital value in 24 months' time	2 083 490	
(ii)	PV of £1 in 2 yrs at 15%	0.756	
(iii)	Net present value (developer's profit)	£1 575 118	
D.	*Profit*		

(i) Profit on GDV $\dfrac{1575118 \times 100}{11819711} = 13.33\%$

(ii) Profit on cost $\dfrac{1575118 \times 100}{9736221} = 16.18\%$

(iii) Development yield $\dfrac{886700 \times 100}{9736221} = 9.11\%$

(in this case £1572170, virtually the same as the profit produced by the residual method).

- The principal advantage of using cashflows is that there is considerably more flexibility in the timing of payments and receipts. Generally, the same information (costs and values) are used initially in residuals and cashflows such that inaccuracies in these inputs will lead to errors whichever method is adopted. For investment and development appraisal, two discounted cashflow approaches are used commonly.

- The net present value approach involves the discounting of all inflows and outflows. The sum of the discounted inflows and outflows produces the net

275

Table 12.7 Discounted cashflow analysis (NPV).

Item/quarter	0	1	2	3	4	5	6	7	8
Land cost	(1500000)								
Acquisition costs	(60000)								
Site preparation		(108000)							
Building costs:									
shops		(422400)	(422400)	(422400)					
offices		(771840)	(771840)	(771840)	(771840)	(771840)			
other				(25000)	(25000)	(150000)			
Architecture and QS fees		(190224)	(119424)	(121924)	(79684)	(92184)			
Contingency		(65112)	(59712)	(60962)	(39842)	(46092)			
Agency and legal fees						(75120)			(412476)
Shop income						125200	125200	125200	
Sale proceeds									11819711
Cashflow	(1560000)	(1557576)	(1373376)	(1402126)	(916366)	(1010036)	125200	125200	11407235
PV of £1 at 3.56%	1	0.966	0.932	0.900	0.869	0.840	0.811	0.783	0.756
NPV	(1560000)	(1504618)	(1279986)	(1261913)	(796322)	(848430)	101537	98032	8623870
Cumulative NPV	(1560000)	(3064618)	(4344604)	(5606517)	(6402839)	(7251269)	(7149732)	(7051700)	1572170

Table 12.8 Internal rate of return.

Quarter	0	1	2	3	4	5	6	7	8
Cashflow	(1560000)	(1557576)	(1373376)	(1402126)	(916366)	(1010036)	125200	125200	11407235
PV at 6% per qtr	1	0.943	0.890	0.840	0.792	0.747	0.705	0.665	0.627
NPV	(1560000)	(1468794)	(1222305)	(1177786)	(725762)	(754497)	88266	83258	7152336
Total NPV									414716

Quarter	0	1	2	3	4	5	6	7	8
Cashflow	(1560000)	(1557576)	(1373376)	(1402126)	(916366)	(1010036)	125200	125200	11407235
PV at 8% per qtr	1	0.926	0.857	0.794	0.735	0.681	0.630	0.583	0.540
NPV	(1560000)	(1442315)	(1176983)	(1113288)	(673529)	(687835)	78876	72992	6159907
Total NPV									(342175)

Table 12.9 Cashflow analysis. The cashflow is taken from Table 12.7.

Item/quarter	0	1	2	3	4	5	6	7	8
Cashflow	(1 560 000)	(1 557 576)	(1 373 376)	(1 402 126)	(916 366)	(1 010 036)	125 200	125 200	11 407 235
Cumulative costs	(1 560 000)	(3 117 576)	(4 546 488)	(6 061 577)	(7 143 819)	(8 375 552)	(8 512 564)	(8 694 868)	2 398 373
Quarterly interest		(55 536)	(112 963)	(165 876)	(221 697)	(262 212)	(307 504)	(313 994)	(320 715)
Cumulative cost at end each quarter	(1 560 000)	(3 173 112)	(4 659 451)	(6 227 453)	(7 365 516)	(8 637 764)	(8 820 068)	(9 008 862)	2 077 658

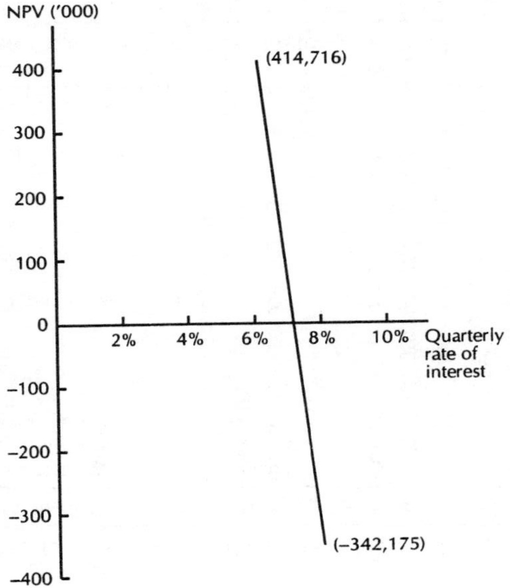

Figure 12.1 Graphical estimation of internal rate of return (see Table 12.8).

Formula calculation of IRR

$$IRR = 6\% + 2\% \ \frac{414716}{414716 + 342175} \quad \text{per quarter}$$

$$= 6\% + 2\% \ \frac{414716}{756891} \quad \text{per quarter}$$

$$= 6\% + 1.096\% \text{ per quarter}$$
$$= 7.096\%, \text{ say } 7.1\% \text{ per quarter}$$
$$\text{Effective annual IRR} = (1.071)^4 - 1$$
$$= 0.316$$

i.e. 31.6% per annum.

present value of the developer's profit. Individual developers have their own "target" discount rates, but for initial appraisals it is logical to use the short-term finance rate. A positive NPV indicates that, potentially, the scheme is profitable, and a negative NPV that a loss is likely.

- Table 12.7 shows how the present value of developer's profit may be calculated. All the costs used are as in the residual, but an attempt has been made to indicate how these costs might be spread throughout the scheme.
- If the finance rate is used for discounting, the difference between the discounted residual profit and the NPV derived from the discounted cashflow results entirely from the treatment of construction finance in the residual and the inclusion of income in the discounted cashflow before the scheme is sold. An alternative discounted cashflow approach enables the calculation of the internal rate of return (IRR) of the scheme. The IRR may be defined as the discount rate that when applied to inflows and outflows, produces a net present value of £0.
- The necessary calculations are shown in Table 12.8, which involve discounting the net cashflows at two trial rates, hopefully producing one negative and one positive NPV.
- The IRR is then found by interpolation, in this case 31.5 per cent pa, confirming that the return exceeds the finance rate of 15 per cent per annum (3.56% per quarter). A full discussion of discounted cashflow theory is beyond the scope of this chapter, but it is felt necessary to repeat that measures of returns produced are not automatically more accurate than those given by the residual.
- Table 12.9 shows a cashflow analysis. With this method an accounting process is undertaken; that is, interest is added to expenditure on a period-by-period basis. The interest in each period is calculated at 3.56 per cent on the cumulative cost in the previous period. This analysis produces a developer's profit of £2077658 comparable approximately with the residual profit of £2083490. (Once again, the difference between these figures is attributable to finance charges and inflows of rent before the development is completed.)
- Cashflows are useful in that they enable a developer (or the provider of finance) to assess the likely financial commitment throughout the scheme (i.e. in quarter 4, total spending amounts to £7365516). This facility is not available with residual or discounted cashflow methods. As a check, the discounted cashflow method should produce the present value of the cashflow profit (subject to rounding).

NPV or IRR?

One of the main advantages of IRR is that it avoids the arbitrary or subjective selection of a discount rate. It is said that the IRR method produces a true yield that obviates the need to anticipate alternative costs of funding. Otherwise, where a net present value approach is adopted, finance charges must be estimated as part of the calculation. Thus, where a project already comprises a mass of complex information regarding cost, rent and time, and the cost of capital is uncertain, it allows the developer to make, accept or reject decisions apart from, or against, the opportunity cost of capital.

On the other hand, it is possible to show that the IRR method is not always reliable in ranking alternative projects in order of their attractiveness. Using a discount rate of 10 per cent to ascertain the net present value of the two projects in Table 12.10, it can be seen that conflicting answers can result.

Table 12.10 Ascertaining net present values using discount rate of 10 per cent.

	Project A (£)	Project B (£)
Outlay	−90000	−90000
Proceeds		
Year 1	+30000	+60000
Year 2	+50000	+40000
Year 3	+60000	+30000
Net present value	+23670	+20140
Internal rate of return	22.5%	24%

Similarly, the method poses problems where projects have unconventional cashflows, such as large negative payments following a series of positive payments. Moreover, it sometimes produces multiple yields; for example, the cashflow series −2000, +5000, −3150 has internal rates of return of 5 and 50 per cent, and some cashflows have no internal rate of return at all. The technique is further affected by the volume of capital expended and the time-period for investment, and is also said to present certain reinvestment problems regarding positive cashflows.

Most of the criticisms levelled at the IRR method, however, apply to cashflows unfamiliar in property development. Comparisons are frequently made between the internal rate of return and the net present value methods of appraisal, and conclusions are drawn as to which approach is best. However, such comparisons are largely invidious, as the two methods can be used to serve quite separate functions.

Currently, the IRR method remains principally a tool of analysis for comparing one project with another or for judging the viability of a project against the opportunity cost of capital where future cashflows are either known or can be anticipated. It is used mainly by development companies, owned by life insurance companies, and by some of the larger and more sophisticated developers. The conventional NPV method is a market-based tool of valuation relying upon a given discount rate, which can be used to determine the capital value of a project as well as explore its feasibility. However, it is fair to say that most appraisals conducted in the development field employ an NPV approach and thereby the market is conditioned by the resultant values and yields.

279

Risk and uncertainty

So far, all the valuations of development properties used as examples have assumed constant factors in terms of such components as rent, yield, cost, finance and time. In practice, of course, all these are a matter of judgement and are subject to change during the development period. Risk is the very business of property development, and uncertainty the prevailing climate within which development takes place. Over the two or three years gestation period that sees many a development project progress from conception to completion, anticipated rental income at the outset may be adjusted several times in response to changing conditions in the demand for and supply of the kind of premises in question; initial yields in the property investment market may fluctuate according to the general state of the economy or the special circumstances of that particular sector; building costs could increase, either as the result of an overall rise of prices across the construction industry, or because of localized difficulties in the provision of labour or materials; the time taken to execute the building works and let or sell the finished development may be longer than originally expected, because of any one of several reasons relating to planning, design, construction or marketing programmes; and finance charges on borrowed money will be affected by any changes in costs or time, and any agreed alterations to the rate of interest that occur during the development period as a result of external forces. In any event, inflation has wreaked havoc upon the best laid of development plans. Therefore, whereas in more stable times the view was taken that any changes in development costs would be roughly set-off by similar changes in development revenues, that sanguine attitude has been shown to be both misleading and dangerous in what has become an increasingly volatile market over recent years.

The traditional method for accommodating the risk of uncertainty in the assessment of the feasibility of projects has been to select a required level of developer's profit that would cover any likely adverse movements in rental income of investment yield, building cost, finance charges or completion time. Typically, high-risk projects would require higher profit levels. Another way of allowing for risk in the construction process is to include an allowance for "contingencies" expressed as a percentage of building cost.

Over recent years a family of techniques drawn largely from the general field of investment analysis have been adopted and adapted for property development appraisal. The main techniques are sensitivity analysis and probability distribution, but there are a variety of related techniques that explore risk and uncertainty and assist in decision-making in development. Moreover, as a result of the increased use of computers and the greater availability of relevant software packages, the use of these techniques is gaining in popularity.

Sensitivity analysis

It is seldom that a development project can be evaluated adequately on the basis of a single set of figures reflecting but a single set of assumptions. For most projects there are degrees of risk and uncertainty surrounding such assumptions as rent, yield, cost and time. Small changes in any one of these prime variables can often exert a disproportionate effect on the residual solution. This uncertainty as to accurate estimation and sensitivity to change is compounded by the fact that the evaluation or feasibility study must take account of likely changes during the development period. A widely used method of dealing with the inherent risk from such uncertainty is sensitivity analysis. The concept is a simple yet effective one, whereby each of the key variables (rent, yield, cost, time) is altered in turn in an informal and realistic way, so that the developer can test how sensitive the profitability of his project or proposed land bid is to possible changes in those variables. The developer is thereby able to identify the critical variables and take suitable action. If it is rent, for example, a pre-let might be sought; if cost, then close attention is paid to the design brief and building contract; if yield, an assiduous search through the investment market is undertaken for a more competitive buy-out arrangement; if time, then a "fast track" programme is devised. In any event, the management capability of the developer is enhanced.

Example 6

This study shows how it is possible to explore the effect of changing levels of performance during the development period among such factors as yield, cost, rent, finance and time. To begin with, a simple sensitivity analysis known as a mini–max evaluation is demonstrated, then the sensitivity of a scheme is tested by the extinguishment of profit method and finally the individual components are measured by the percentage change method.

Consider the position of a developer who has paid £500000 for a plot of land that has planning permission to build a discount cash and carry warehouse of 4000 m^2 gross. Rents of around £85 per m^2 overall have been quoted in the vicinity. Initial yields in the region of 8.5 per cent are reported for similar properties. Construction costs are estimated at £500 per m^2. Finance can be arranged at about 1.2 per cent per month and the development is considered to take approximately 18 months to complete and let.

It can, therefore, be seen that changes to the various components of rent, yield, cost, finance and time can have profound effects upon the profitability of a scheme when acting in concert.

Extinguishment of profit   Another way of testing the sensitivity of individual components is to gauge the degree to which one factor changing independently can extinguish development profit. This is sometimes known as "breakdown analysis'. Given the same circumstances as those above rough calculations show that the various components have to change as follows:

Table 12.11 Minimum–maximum evaluation.

I. Median or realistic valuation			£	£
A.		Gross development value		
	(i)	Rental income at £85 per m² on 4000 m²	340000	
B.	(ii)	YP in perpetuity at 8.5%	11.76	3998400
	(iii)	Gross development value	2000000	3142002
	(i)	Development costs	200000	
	(ii)	Building costs at £500 per m² on 4000 m²	263458	
	(iii)	Professional fees at 10% of (i)	34000	
	(iv)	Finance at 1.2% pm for 18 months × ½	500000	
	(v)	Letting at 10% of rent	20000	
	(vi)	Land	124544	
	(vii)	Acquisition at 4%		
	(viii)	Finance at 1.2% pm for 18 months		
		Total development costs		
C.		Development profit		
	(i)	Sum available in 18 months		856398
	(ii)	PV of £1 in 18 months at 1.2% pm		0.807
		Profit now		691113

(iii)
(iv) Profit on cost $\dfrac{691113 \times 100}{3142002} = 22\%$

Return on cost $\dfrac{340000 \times 100}{3142002} = 10.8\%$

II. Maximum or optimistic valuation

Rents predicted at £100 per m²   £   £
Initial yield taken at 8%
Building costs estimated at £450 per m²
Finance at 1.0% per month
Development period and letting 15 months

A.		Gross development value		
B.	(i)	Rental income at £100 per m²	400000	5000000
	(ii)	YP in perpetuity at 8%	12.5	2783063
	(iii)	Gross development value	1800000	
	(i)	Development costs	180000	
	(ii)	Building costs at £450 per m²	159359	
	(iii)	Professional fees at 10%	40000	
	(iv)	Finance at 1.0% pm for 15 months × ½	500000	
	(v)	Letting at 10% of rent	20000	
	(vi)	Land	83704	
	(vii)	Acquisition		
	(viii)	Finance at 1.0% pm for 15 months		
		Total development costs		
C.		Development profit		
	(i)	Sum available in 18 months		2216937
	(ii)	PV of £1 in 18 months at 1.2% pm		0.861
		Profit		1908783

(iii) Profit on cost $\dfrac{1908783 \times 100}{2783063} = 22\%$
(iv)

Return on cost $\dfrac{400000 \times 100}{2783063} = 14.4\%$

III. Minimum or pessimistic valuation

			£	£
Rents predicted at £70 per m²				
Initial yield taken at 9%				
Building costs estimated at £550 per m²				
Finance at 1.4% per month				
Development period and letting 21 months				
A.		*Gross development value*		
B.	(i)	Rental income at £70 per m²	280000	
	(ii)	YP in perpetuity at 9%	11.11	
	(iii)	Gross development value		3110800
	(i)	*Development costs*		
	(ii)	Building costs at £550 per m²	2200000	
	(iii)	Professional fees at 10%	220000	
	(iv)	Finance at 1.4% pm for 21 months x ½	410251	
	(v)	Letting at 10% of rent	28000	
	(vi)	Land	500000	
	(vii)	Acquisition	20000	
	(viii)	Finance at 1.4% pm for 21 months	176306	
		Total development costs		3554557
C.		*Development profit*		
		A loss of		(443757)

- rent from £85 per m² to £67 per m² = nil profit = 21.2% change
- yield from 8.5% to 10.8% = nil profit = 13.3% change
- building costs from £500 per m² to £615 per m² = nil profit = 18.7%
- finance from 1.2% pm to 2.6% pm = nil profit = 220%

Thus, the scheme can be seen to be relatively sensitive to changes in yield and slightly less so to building cost and rent. However, it is hardly sensitive at all to independent changes in the rate of interest charged on development finance. In reality, of course, these changes would not necessarily take place independently. More likely would be a combination of adjustments, possibly in different directions.

Percentage change   Yet a third approach to testing sensitivity is by subjecting the individual components to a percentage change and assessing the extent to which the level of profit is affected.

- Rent   10% increase = 32.3% profit on cost
                    10% decrease = 11.7% profit on cost
- Yield   10% increase = 12.7% profit on cost
                    10% decrease = 33.5% profit on cost
- Building costs 10% increase = 14.5%
                    10% decrease = 30.7%
- Finance   10% increase = 20.7%
                    10% decrease = 23.3%

(original profit on cost 22%)

Naturally, the same sensitivities emerge, but at the very least a prospective developer is directed towards those aspects of the scheme that merit the closest attention in respect of optimizing profit. Although the way in which these tests are presented here might appear somewhat simplistic, the advent of computer programs permitting detailed and different adjustments to be made to all the various components enables a development analyst to explore a wide range of possible outcomes according to the information available in a comparatively short time and at little additional cost. This has become known as "scenario analysis", which, at its simplest, is shown by the optimistic–realistic–pessimistic approach set out in Figure 12.2.

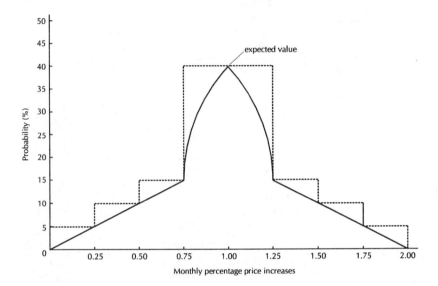

Figure 12.2   Probability distribution.

Probability distribution

Where there are significant uncertainties associated with the result of a development project evaluation, it is sometimes useful to list the range of results thought to be likely and to attach to each result an estimate of its probability of happening. The probability of a result may be expressed in terms of frequency of occurrence, that is, as the proportionate number of times the result would be expected to occur in many trial events. In scientific fields, probabilities are estimated either from the statistical records of past events or by conducting experiments using a sampling procedure. This is scarcely possible in the property development industry. Nevertheless, it is possible to present the estimates as a probability distribution that reflects the subjective views formed by the development analyst, or group of analysts, as a result of their knowledge and experience. If, for example, there is a general expectation in the residential development of a rise in the price of

284

new houses over the next year, but observers are uncertain as to the monthly rate at which they might rise, a survey of informed parties could show the following:

Monthly rate of price rise	Probability of occurrence
0.25%	5%
0.50%	10%
0.75%	15%
1.00%	40%
1.25%	15%
1.50%	10%
1.75%	5%

The example below shows how results from probability analysis can be used in a residual cashflow valuation where probable changes in costs and values are forecast.

Example 7

Consider the conversion of a terrace of eight Victorian houses, which are vacant and somewhat dilapidated, into a block of 24 luxury flats. The houses are situated in a desirable part of north London and similar flats to those planned are selling for around £100000 each, but demand is such that prices are confidently expected to rise by about 1 per cent per month over the next year (12.68% pa). Building costs to effect the conversion are estimated at £25000 a flat but are considered likely to increase by 1.25 per cent per month for the next year (16.08% pa). Building costs are to be evenly spread over a twelve-month development period. It is intended that six flats will be sold in months nine to twelve inclusive. Professional fees are assessed at 10 per cent of building costs, and will be paid by equal instalments of 2.5 per cent a quarter. Agents' and solicitors' fees will be charged at 2 per cent of the sale price of each flat. A development profit of 25 per cent of the sale price is sought and bridging finance is available at 1 per cent a month (12.68% pa).

A prospective developer wishes to know how much he might have to pay for the eight houses now.

Preliminaries

Receipts: six flats sold per month at £100000 each

Month 9: × 1.0937 = £656220

Month 10: × 1.1046 = £662760

Month 11: × 1.1157 = £669420

Month 12: × 1.1268 = £676080

Building costs + fees + profits

Total costs are 24 flats at £25000 = £600000

Average of £50000 a month

Increase by 1.25% per month

£

1. 50625

285

2. 51258
3. 351899 + 10% fees
4. 52548
5. 53205
6. 53870 + 10% fees
7. 54543
8. 55225
9. 55915 + 10% fees + 2% fees + 25% profit
10. 56614 + 2% fees + 25% profit
11. 57322 + 2% fees + 25% profit
12. 58038 + 10% fees + 2% fees + 25% profit

It is assumed that surpluses in the latter few months will be reinvested at the same rate of interest. The resulting residual represents an absolute maximum bid. The developer might offer £1 million for the eight houses

Month	Receipts	Costs	Net cashflow	Capital outstanding	Interest
1		(50625)	(50625)	(50625)	(506)
2	656220	(51258)	(51258)	(102389)	(1024)
3	662760	(67277)	(67277)	(170690)	(1707)
4	669420	(52548)	(52548)	(224945)	(2249)
5	676080	(53205)	(53205)	(280399)	(2804)
6		(69832)	(69832)	(353035)	(3530)
7		(54543)	(54543)	(411108)	(4111)
8		(55225)	(55225)	(470444)	(4704)
9		(249662)	406558	(68509)	(686)
10		(235559)	427201	357925	3579
11		(238065)	431355	792859	7929
12		(257777)	418303	1219091	

Sum available in 12 months = £1219091

$$\text{Let the value of the houses} = 1.0000\,x$$
$$\text{Acquisition costs at 4\%} = 0.0400\,x$$
$$\text{Finance at 12.68\% on } 1.04\,x = 0.1319\,x$$
$$\therefore 1.1719\,x = 1219.091$$
$$\therefore x = 1040269$$

Summary

Although traditional evaluations of development projects have proved effective and simple to use at the initial stages of appraisal, the vagaries of the market and the availability of useful and inexpensive computer software packages have combined to encourage the widespread adoption of cashflow models of one kind or another. It has been found that this wider use of cashflow techniques has prompted greater examination of not only cost but also the likelihood of incurring liabilities on ancillary costs such as planning fees, party-wall awards, rights of light and other elements that might previously have been ignored or included in a general fee or contingency. It is also more generally accepted that property is not an isolated investment, but one that has to be compared constantly and closely with other investments, resulting in cashflow techniques and risk and uncertainty analyses being more commonly used for evaluating alternative investment opportunities, including property. However, developers still regard some of the more theoretical probability and decision theory techniques as being too "academic".

CHAPTER THIRTEEN
Property development finance

It is a truism to state that finance is a critical resource in the process of property development. Nevertheless, when compared to the other resources that combine to produce a development scheme, there often appears to be a disturbing lack of proper understanding about the sources and types of finance for construction and property development, and the arrangements and procedures that accompany them. This is of growing importance, for not only are the margins between revenue and expenditure finer than ever before, but those responsible for providing the bulk of finance to the industry are much more closely concerned, and a great deal better informed, about the management of construction and development projects than they have been in the past. Consequently, they expect and demand development agencies, and those involved in managing their projects for them, to be equally well versed in the evaluation and control of the financial structure and progress of a scheme of development.

A variety of ways exist in which finance for property development can be obtained from a wide array of agencies. The choice normally resting upon the status of the developer and the degree of risk attached to the proposed project. It can almost be stated that every deal dictates its own terms, but for convenience, and to facilitate description, several general areas have been identified below in order to consider the more conventional relationships established between borrowing developers and lending financiers.

In order to explore the increasingly complex subject of property development finance, the chapter is organized as follows:
- sources of development finance
- types of finance
- criteria of funding
- choice of fund
- the financial agreement
- trends and prospects.

Sources of development finance

Most developers will have access to existing sources of finance. Larger companies will usually have multiple funding arrangements with a variety of financial agencies. Nevertheless, the field is becoming so complex and competitive that effective project management is increasingly concerned with the way in which control over a particular scheme will be influenced by the origin and nature of the development finance.

The following selection of possible sources of development finance has no pretensions to be exclusive or exhaustive. However, it does provide an indication of the principal sources that are currently available to the aspiring developer.

Insurance companies and pension funds

Insurance companies and pension funds enjoy a relatively high degree of stability in the availability of funds for investment in development projects, but take a longer-term and more cautious view than most other lenders.

The most popular form of finance provided by the insurance companies and pension funds is the "forward sale", often coupled with short-term bridging finance at preferential rates. Some funds are also prepared to enter into "sale and leaseback" arrangements, mortgage advances or an overall borrowing facility.

The lending policies of those financial institutions are characterized by their "project-based" nature. This means that they tend to exercise extremely tight control over the entire project, including the land acquisition, design, construction and sale or letting programmes. Financial arrangements themselves are almost pre-ordained in terms of yield, interim fixed-rate loans, pre-letting and forward sale. Because of these constraints, a developer might experience problems in maintaining authority, especially once a purchaser or tenant has been found. This situation is further exacerbated where the fund appoints a consultant to monitor development, as happens increasingly.

Another feature is that, because institutions are such big investors in new development, they will usually look for fairly substantial schemes in which to invest. And, not surprisingly, the larger the fund, the larger the average size of scheme financed. But, by far the greatest hurdle a proposed development project must clear before it attracts institutional finance from either an insurance company or a pension fund is that it must be competitive when compared to other forms of investment such as equities, gilts and other forms of property.

Banks

Traditionally, banks are more concerned with the "asset" base of those to whom they lend rather than the project in hand. The emphasis, therefore, will be more upon monitoring the balance sheet and security cover offered by the borrower. For a developer, this provides a more open and flexible climate in which to work, where such factors as time, cost and quality can be traded off against the clients' ability to generate funds or produce additional collateral. Bank finance, therefore, must be carefully tailored to fit the purpose to which it is applied, and a well designed package must be prepared to meet overdraft, term or equity financial requirements. Sometimes the additional flexibility afforded by more expensive arrangements is worthwhile.

Some clearing or retail banks became over-committed to the property development industry during boom years and found themselves slightly embarrassed by the experience. This encouraged them to step aside for a period. Nevertheless, they show a propensity to return quite quickly to the market once a resurgence is evident, and a similar trait to retreat at the first signs of a slump. Although their policies vary widely, not merely between different houses, but within individual banks, they are generally a great deal more flexible and adventurous than the insurance companies and pension funds, being willing to consider, for example, the refurbishment and redevelopment of older buildings and the development of less conventional commercial properties. One principal reason for this is that a clearing bank is as interested in the business as it is in the property, if not more so. This applies whether the business is the intending occupier or a property development company.

Merchant banks have a reputation for having an even more enterprising approach towards development finance. Being concerned primarily with supplying short and medium-term money to the development industry, they have evolved packages for linking their short-term lending with other investors' longer-term aspirations. Most leading merchant banks have established their own specialist property investment departments capable of tailoring bespoke financial arrangements to suit the individual needs of a particular developer. In this way, it is by far the most sophisticated sector of the institutional finance market. The more refined yet venturesome stance of the merchant banks is reflected in the high cost of borrowing from them, and their relative opportunism in respect of equity participation.

One of the more lucrative activities recently undertaken by merchant banks is arranging funding packages or syndications, which are then participated out to other banks. Indeed, it has been reported that in this way some banks can make up to half their income from fees.

Trusts and bonds

Within the category of trusts and bonds can be included real estate investment trusts, investment unit trusts, property unit trusts and property bonds. The structure and purposes of these different media for investment is not explained in detail, because from the standpoint of the developer their policies and practices are much the same and largely resemble those of the insurance companies and pension funds. However, their performance has been extremely variable, and their role in the development field is as yet not great.

Internal finance

Even though it is often alleged that the first rule of the developer is "never use your own money", quite commonly property development agencies either deploy their own surpluses and reserves to support current projects or seek an expansion of their capital base.

Almost by definition, virtually all development undertaken by the major financial institutions, directly or by way of joint venture, can be categorized as internally financed. Similarly, many construction firms acting as developers use their own financial resources to fund projects, as do certain leading business and retail organizations. Funding by prospective owner-occupiers in all sectors of the commercial property market is quite popular. For as long as the capital is available, the risk acceptable and the opportunity cost satisfactory, internal finance has the great attraction of ensuring full recoupment of future rental growth.

A property development company can extend its capital base by increasing its share capital or its loan capital. In simple terms, the holders of the share capital (equity) own the company itself, and the holders of loan capital are creditors of the company. Thus, the holders of share capital are not creditors and have no security, and the holders of loan capital have no rights in the company beyond the receipt of interest and the repayment of the loan in accordance with the terms on which they were issued. The amount a company may borrow by way of loan capital is laid down in the articles of association of the company. There are two principal types of loan capital: debentures and loan stocks. Debentures and debenture stocks are roughly similar to mortgages and are secured either on certain specific assets of the company or as a floating charge over all the company's assets. Secured debts of this kind rank for repayment before unsecured debt in the event of the company being wound up. Unsecured loan stocks, the other form of loan capital, are debts, as their name implies, which are not charged on the company's assets. If the company falls into liquidation, they rank after secured loans along with other general creditors but before the holders of share capital. One kind of unsecured loan stock carries with it the right to convert into share capital on pre-arranged terms and within a limited period: this is known as convertible unsecured loan stock and it comes with a variety of conversion rights. A final form of fixed income company finance is preference shares, which do not form part of the loan capital, and on a winding-up do not rank for repayment until all creditors have been paid in full. Again, there are various types of preference shares, such as "cumulative", where the right to a dividend can be carried forward from one year to another; "non-cumulative", where once a dividend is passed for one year the right to receive it is lost; and "participating" preference shares, where there are rights to share in profits above the fixed dividend.

The share capital held as ordinary shares is usually referred to as the equity. Equity in this sense means that which remains after rights of creditors and mortgagees are cleared and, although different forms of share capital exist, most public property companies do not have very complex share capital structures. The risk-bearing nature of equities is reflected in the "gearing" of a company, that is the ratio of loan or fixed income capital to share or equity capital. In a period of growth and profitability, in a highly geared company, where loan capital is proportionately greater than share capital, holders of ordinary shares gain commensurately. In bad times, the reverse is true, and profits can easily be wiped out.

A detailed examination of how capital can be raised on the stock market is beyond the scope of this text. Suffice it to say that there are two types of new issue by which this can be achieved. First, the bringing to the market of companies that have not previously been quoted. Secondly, the raising of additional capital by companies already quoted. The former will normally be effected by an "offer for sale", whereby an institution such as a merchant bank buys a block of shares from the existing shareholders and offers them to the general public at a fixed price; by a "placing", where an institution may buy the stock or shares and arrange for the placing of the issue with various funds or companies known to be interested; an "introduction" when a company already has many individual shareholdings and Stock Exchange quotation simply provides a public market for shares that previously could only be dealt in privately; or a "tender", which is exactly the same as an offer for sale except that the price of the shares is not fixed in advance. One way in which companies already quoted can raise additional internal funds without increasing their debt charge is the issue of further equity capital. This is normally done by way of a "rights issue", that is, the issue of shares to existing shareholders at a concession.

As with most financial matters, the question of timing is important, not merely in respect of the general climate for borrowing but also the class of capital to be selected. In times of depressed equity prices, a rights issue is normally to be avoided and, if interest rates are at a reasonable level, a prior charge to increase loan capital is usually preferable. Conversely, when equity prices are high, leading property companies might be best advised to make a rights issue rather than increase their loan capital. However, it must be remembered that, although substantial sums can be raised from the market, the costs involved may be considerable, comprising not only the legal and valuation fees but also the costs of underwriting the issue, producing a prospectus, advertising and stockbrokers' charges.

It is in the field of internal or corporate finance that most innovation has been shown by property development companies over recent years. The range of devices, instruments and techniques has appeared endless, with many American mainstream corporate financing practices being adapted and adopted in global financial markets. The amount of "commercial paper' issued by property development companies since the late 1980s has been enormous, largely because of its low cost, high flexibility and simplicity to the borrower, and its competitive yield, liquidity and range of maturities to the lender. However, the inherent dangers of such promissory activity were apparent in a period of worldwide recession during the first half of the 1990s.

The construction industry

Development finance is commonly supplied by the major building firms, either directly from their own cash reserves or through sources with whom they have a funding facility. From a pure funding point of view, this form of finance can be very attractive, because the loan will normally be 100 per cent, to include the cost of land acquisitions, all building costs and fees. Speculative work will also be considered, and the debt rolled up at a small mark-up on the cost of finance to the construction company. From the stance of the developer, however, it is very important to be assured that the right contractor, on the right building contract, is appointed to work to the right price. There is always the danger that the authority of the developer and his project manager is diminished where the contractor is also the funder.

Conversely, this familiarity with the property development industry can often be an advantage and help limit risk. Such collaboration is often the result of a limited loan, say 70 per cent of cost, on the part of a bank, and the need by the developer to fund the shortfall through the good offices of an established construction company. Increasingly, this form of finance takes the form of a joint venture between the two parties. On the other hand, the degree of accountability on the part of the contractor during the construction stage and upon completion is likely to be heightened, and the extent of financial control throughout the building period much tighter than normally experienced. A construction company, however, will normally need to see a clearly identifiable exit in the form of a long-term take-out by a financial institution.

Property companies

A less familiar means of obtaining short-term finance is through one of the larger property investment and development companies. This can be by direct loan or by guarantee, and the principal motive is usually a desire to participate in the equity of the project. Apart from an erosion of profit, another disadvantage is that, as far as the developer is concerned, his funds are coming from a source thoroughly conversant with all aspects of the development process, who is likely to exercise an unusual degree of scrutiny.

293

Government

In a period of continuing worldwide public sector spending constraint, governments find themselves with little enough money for their own national and municipal development projects, let alone to be in a position to fund the private sector. Nevertheless, grants and loans are made available in certain circumstances, and projects are supported in other ways.

Most straightforward is the direct provision of total development finance, which is usually undertaken to promote ventures that would not otherwise attract commercial funds. Government can also provide financial assistance to new or established businesses through loans for land and buildings. A method employed in many industrial development projects has been the "headleasing" arrangement, whereby a government agency takes a lease from the developer to guarantee rental income and then sublets the floorspace to occupiers.

It may be that a government agency acts as a conduit to other funds. Many cities in various countries now offer incentives to encourage firms to invest in designated areas to promote economic and physical regeneration. This includes guaranteeing long-term loans for the conversion, improvement, modification or extension of existing buildings. Some local government authorities have also set up their own enterprise boards to stimulate economic activity. This often includes an extensive programme of property development and refurbishment projects, either independently or more usually in partnership with the private sector.

Another way in which a local government authority can participate in the overall funding of a scheme, without committing actual cash resources, is by providing land already in their ownership. Similarly, although there is a cost to the authority, the supply of certain kinds of directly associated site infrastructure may often be seen as a financial contribution to a development scheme, and treated accordingly in any negotiations surrounding the apportionment of profit.

There is really no limit to the potential sources available to borrow money for property development. Trading companies, financial services firms, charities, churches and wealthy individuals, either alone or in consortia with others, are but a few. Given sufficient time, therefore, a developer could unearth many sources of finance. Indeed, considerable time and effort can often be wasted by directing attention towards inappropriate sources, and it is surprising what an imperfect market the development industry is in respect of a central pool and comprehensive understanding of sources of finance.

Types of finance

Traditionally, the different types of development finance have been examined within the classification of short, medium and long term. Although this remains a perfectly acceptable approach, it tends to oversimplify what has become a more sophisticated and complex market. Indeed, so refined are some funding arrangements that it is increasingly difficult to place them in any particular category, except their own. However, the following description attempts to outline the main methods currently employed in the financing of development.

Development finance

Development finance is also known as building, bridging or construction finance and is used to describe the short-term interest-bearing loans made for periods of anything up to about three to four years, covering all or part of the costs of development. These costs will include land, acquisition, building works, professional fees, marketing, finance itself and any contingencies involved in the development process. Customarily, there have been two main sources for such funds, the commercial banks and the merchant banks, but over recent years other sources have been tapped and other methods of funding employed.

The banks, however, have two basic requirements. First, that the developer must show that they will be able to meet the interest charges, which will usually be "rolled-up" or "warehoused" until the development is completed. Secondly, they must show that they will be able to repay, on time, the principal sum borrowed. This latter requirement implies in most cases the availability of long-term investment funds, out of which the short-term finance may be repaid. The linking of short- and long-term finance must normally be firmly established to the satisfaction of the lender before the development finance is approved. In some circumstances, it is possible that the lending bank might be prepared to assume that long-term financing will be forthcoming before the development is completed, or that the scheme will be sold outright on completion for investment or occupation, and advance the construction finance unencumbered by a forward sale commitment.

As previously intimated, the commercial and merchant banks tend to have slightly different attitudes towards development financing. The former frequently require security over and above that derived from the project in question; they exact a rate of interest 2–4 per cent above base lending rate, depending upon the standing of the borrower; they do not usually demand an equity share; and they provide a procedure that is a relatively simple and standard format, so that the loan is issued quite quickly and with comparative ease. The latter, the merchant banks, in most instances only require the development presented to them as security, but invariably charge a higher rate of interest at about 4–6 per cent above base rate or, more usually, seek to share in the equity of the scheme. In return for the additional cost of the finance, however, the developer will probably find a merchant bank more enterprising than a commercial bank in bearing risk and structuring a loan.

Increasingly, short-term development finance in the institutional market is being provided as part of a complete funding package. A fund will normally acquire a site once planning permission has been obtained and will advance development costs throughout the construction period against architects' certificates and other relevant invoices. Interim finance, as it has become known, is rolled up on the various advances and is payable at an agreed rate that invariably lies mid-way between the prevailing short-term borrowing rate and the ultimate investment yield. Both parties can be seen to gain from such an arrangement. The developer enjoys cheaper finance and the purchaser is afforded more control over the design and progress of development.

Mortgages

For many years up until the early 1960s, the fixed interest mortgage was the predominant form of long-term development finance. Rapid and prolonged inflation then drove lenders away from mortgages towards methods of investment that allowed them some level of inflation proofing through participation in rental growth. From the early 1970s onwards, high interest rates discouraged borrowers from pressing for long-term mortgage advances on fixed rates. The late 1980s and early 1990s witnessed the return of long-term fixed interest mortgage finance to the property development market, with inflation running at relatively low levels, and interest rates showing every prospect of remaining comparatively low for a few years.

The loan term will usually run between 10 and 25 years depending upon the needs of the borrower and the nature of the development project, and the maximum level of advance invariably will be limited to two-thirds of the agreed value of the project acting as security. For other than prime schemes it will often be less, and here lies the biggest drawback in mortgage finance, for a developer will often have to find substantial funds from his own resources if the project in question does not meet certain standard criteria in respect of design and letting.

Unless there are immediate and reliable prospects of an uplift in rents, say within a year of the draw-down of the mortgage facility, then the lending institution will wish to be assured that the initial income produced by the development is sufficient to cover the loan servicing costs. The rate of interest attaching to a loan is usually determined at the date of release of funds by reference to a margin of 1.75–2.25 per cent over the prevailing gross redemption yield on a comparable gilt-edged security on completion. Interest is mostly payable quarterly or half-yearly in arrears.

With most mortgages there will be a choice between interest-only and interest plus capital repayments. Generally, it is only the shorter mortgages of around 10 years that are on an interest-only basis; the longer-term loans of 15–25 years normally require at least 25 or 50 per cent of the capital to be repaid during the term, although they may often begin with a five-year moratorium to allow for rental growth to take place, thereby making the debt easier to service. It is commonly accepted that the annuity-certain method of repaying or reducing a mortgage is probably the fairest and least expensive, both in real terms and as far as

296

cashflow is concerned, as it involves an effective sinking fund under which the benefit of a compound interest rate equal to the mortgage rate is received. Moreover, some companies operate a variable rate system. Although this might seemingly be a more volatile and potentially expensive way to pay off a loan, it will usually be operated on an "even spread" basis, whereby the capital repayments are calculated at a median that, if market interest rates are lower for most of the term, means the loan will be repaid early, and vice versa.

Although mortgages are commonly considered to be medium- to long-term funding arrangements, it is sometimes possible to obtain interim finance against a limited number of architects' certificates as building works progress, in which case adjustments might have to be made to allow for fluctuating interest rates during construction. In any event, this kind of facility would only be countenanced with a pre-let to a good covenant on acceptable terms.

On the question of whether or not a developer should take up long-term fixed interest moneys, one leading specialist in arranging property finance has summarized the situation as follows:

> Our advice to borrowers has always been never to rely on one particular type of finance or one particular lender. A mix of different types of finance is essential to the well-balanced portfolio and a combination of part variable-rate and part fixed-rate mortgage monies will enable the borrower to take advantage of any further fall in interest rates while protecting against an increase. What can be said with reasonable confidence is that the present interest scenario presents an excellent opportunity for borrowers to switch a significant part of their present funding to, or to organize new acquisitions on, a fixed interest rate basis. (Burgess 1982)

As with all other forms of funding, however, mortgage finance has become increasingly sophisticated. For example, repayment patterns can be straight-term, amortized, partially amortized, graduated, renegotiable, shared appreciation or reverse annuity. Interest rate provisions can be straight rate, straight rate with escalator, or variable rate. And the types of security given might relate to what are known as deeds of trust, purchase money mortgages, open-end mortgages, participating mortgages, junior mortgages, and package or blanket mortgages. It has also been reported that financial institutions have started to provide funding in the form of debenture issues as opposed to straight mortgages. A mortgage debenture issue is a method of raising corporate finance whereby the institution makes a loan as a debenture secured against the developer's entire property portfolio. The return from the debenture may be fixed, or yield a "stepped coupon" linked to the rental value of the property. At the end of the loan period the capital is repayable as a lump sum. This type of loan is known in banking circles as a "bullet" loan. A variation upon this theme is the "balloon" mortgage, where the coupon, incorporating both capital and interest repayments, increases and then decreases throughout the duration of the loan.

Two recently popular hybrid varieties of mortgage designed to match the requirements of lenders to the needs of borrowers are the "convertible" mortgage and the "participating" mortgage. These are employed where a borrowing developer is seeking to improve the conditions relating to the loan to value ratio, or the rate of interest, by surrendering a portion of equity or profit. Both the convertible and the participating mortgages are debts secured by way of a full charge over the property concerned and a share in the equity of the scheme at some predetermined point in the future. The convertible mortgage will continue to have an interest in the equity of the development following repayment of the principal and any interest secured under the mortgage. This interest will continue to exist until the agreed profit share is received by the lender at some future time. The participating mortgage is similar, in that the lender has an interest in the equity, but the sharing must be made by a certain point in time. The value of the "equity charge" is usually predetermined, either by amount or by formula, and, whether or not the profits have been realized, the lender's share becomes due. These two instruments are said to be particularly useful in a development scenario where the lender can share in the profits for a higher level of risk (Shayle 1992).

Sale and leaseback

Over the years, the sale and leaseback has been a familiar form of long-term financing in the prime development market. Particularly popular in the 1960s and early 1970s, it returned to favour in the late 1980s and early 1990s. In essence, it involves a developer selling the freehold interest in the completed development to an investor while taking back a long lease at a rent that equates to the initial yield reflected in the selling price. The developer then aims to sublet the property, preferably at a rent in excess of that paid to the investor, thereby creating an immediate profit rent. Sometimes the freehold is owned by a third party, often a local authority, in which case a similar transaction known as a "lease and leaseback" can be conducted, with the investor buying a long lease of, say, 125 years and the developer taking back a sublease of a slightly shorter term.

An alternative approach frequently adopted when the developer is hoping to trade the scheme (that is, to complete let and sell it), is the "leaseback guarantee'. By this arrangement, if the development is not let within, say, six months of practical completion, the developer receives a balancing payment from the fund, representing his profit in return for providing a leaseback guarantee at an agreed base rent. This base rent is usually the same as the rental income estimated at the outset of the scheme, and provision is made for the guarantee to be extinguished once a letting to an occupational tenant has been achieved. If a rent in excess of the base rent is eventually obtained, the agreement will normally provide for that extra rent, often known as "overage", to be capitalized at a more favourable yield to the fund, usually at half the year's purchase applied to the base rent. In this way, the fund is able to share in the growth of rents between commencement and ultimate letting.

Returning to the conventional sale and leaseback, in which the developer is retaining an interest in the project, the most important part of the negotiation between the developer and the fund is the apportionment of rental growth at review. Few funding agreements are now concluded on the basis that the developer receives only an exposed "top slice" income once the fund has taken a guaranteed "bottom slice" return. Most arrangements these days involve some kind of "side-by-side" or "vertical" leaseback, whereby the two parties share the equity in predetermined proportions at, say, three- or five-year review. They also usually include a device in the contract known as a "participation clause", which, like the overage adjustment mentioned above, allows the parties to share in any increase in rental income that is achieved at letting over and above the original estimate of likely rents. The possible permutations by which the returns from property development may be divided between the developer and the fund are many and varied. Different slices of income can be treated in different ways at different times. Inevitably, the eventual contract will be the result of negotiation and compromise, with the outcome depending upon the financial leverage and bargaining powers of the respective parties to the transaction. Who needs whom most is the real key.

One disadvantage of the straightforward sale and leaseback is that the developer is often left with an interest that is difficult to dispose of or refinance except at a value determined by a low capitalization factor. One way of overcoming this disability is to enter into a "reverse leaseback", in which the developer retains a freehold interest at a peppercorn rent and grants a long lease to the fund under which a reviewable ground rent eventually becomes payable on full letting, but one that is subject to a prior charge in favour of the fund in respect of their share. The legal interest held by the developer is thereby made more marketable.

The principal advantage usually claimed for the lessee or vendor is that it frees up capital at a lower cost and for a longer period than would otherwise be available; it can provide 100 per cent financing for a project; the funds released can be used to better advantage or at a higher return; problems of refinancing can be avoided; there can be an appreciation of the leasehold value; it might be possible to pass on certain management responsibilities; retention of use or occupancy can be achieved; and there might be certain tax advantages. In the same way, the main advantages to the lessor or purchaser are said to be that the term of investment is long and thereby early repayment exposure is reduced; it provides an opportunity to invest in large amounts, which reduces management costs; most arrangements, by definition, provide a good covenant; the rate of return after amortization of the principal of the investment is normally relatively high; control over the management of the asset is much higher than with a conventional mortgage; and there may be a substantial remainder of value after the expiry of the lease. There may also be tax advantages to one or both parties.

Forward sale

As mentioned above, most short-term financiers will look for a guarantee that there is an arrangement with a long-term investor or a prospective owner-occupier to "take out" their interest when the project is completed and often occupied. Contractual details regarding the precise sale date, effect of delays in building work, void lettings and rental growth during development will naturally be the subject of negotiation between the various parties. An outright forward sale along these lines takes place, of course, where a developer is trading and not investing. In such circumstances, the main concern of the long-term investor is to secure a guarantee of rent upon completion, and two principal methods are commonly adopted: the "profit erosion" method and the "priority yield" method.

Profit erosion

Also known as the "profit dissipation" method of funding, profit erosion is a form of rental guarantee arrangement whereby the developer wishes to trade-on a scheme. Instead of taking up a leaseback or entering into a leaseback guarantee if the building is not let within, say, six months of practical completion, the developer stakes his profit, no more, against rent and other outgoings. The developer's profit as a balancing payment is placed on a joint deposit account, with interest accruing to the developer, and the fund draws down the base rent and other outgoings at quarterly intervals.

Once this balancing payment has run out, the developer ceases to have an interest and the fund assumes responsibility for letting the scheme. However, if letting takes place at more than the agreed base rent, the overage provision mentioned before generally applies for a limited period as an incentive to the developer.

Profit erosion schemes are held to be particularly useful where a scheme is large and the developer is either of insufficient strength to offer a satisfactory rental guarantee or, more likely, is of sufficient strength but unwilling to enter into a full leaseback agreement. The objectives of both the fund and the developer can be met in this way so long as sufficient rental cover is provided. Two years is generally thought to be an absolute minimum, and in a difficult letting market four might be more appropriate. In any event, given the greater risk borne by the fund, a slightly higher yield of say a 0.25 per cent for prime properties is frequently required.

Priority yield

Priority yield is another variant on the financial sharing theme in trading situations where a fund is looking for a given yield on a development of say 6 per cent and is not prepared to share in anything below that level. If the developer produces a completed development showing an initial return of 7 per cent, then the fund will capitalize this extra point as an additional profit to the developer. Over 7 per cent, and some form of participation would be agreed, usually on an equal share basis.

Priority yield fundings are especially popular when a project of development is difficult to plan in respect of time and cost for one reason or another. It brings the developer and the fund into a close partnership where each party accepts a degree of risk against the potential profit inherent in a speculative development. There is also a considerable incentive for the developer to keep costs down and to complete and let the project as quickly as possible.

Project management fee

Another method of funding relationship becoming increasingly popular is the "project management fee" basis. This is used primarily as a method of funding for major development schemes where the size, impact on the market and time taken to complete and let the premises are such that neither party would wish for anything less than that the funding institution to bear the full risk. In most circumstances the developer would have identified the potential for development and investigated the planning and market conditions. They may even have taken out options on the land and obtained outline planning permission. Upon successful introduction to a fund, a separate fee will usually be agreed. Subsequently, the developer simply receives a fee for project managing the development, which can either be calculated as a fixed percentage of construction cost or geared to the eventual profit of the scheme. Most project management fee arrangements tend to combine both elements, so that a basic minimum fee is agreed as a fixed sum and a proportion of profit over a certain level is offered as a kind of performance incentive.

General funding facility

"General funding facility" refers to an arrangement whereby an overall financial facility is provided to a development company and is not specifically related to any one project. It is secured across the company assets and it enables the developer to carry out a series of projects working within a pre-set lending limit. The loan is normally repayable over a period of up to 40 years, thereby keeping repayments during the early years, when yields may be very low, to a minimum. A comparatively new kind of development finance is the "drop lock loan", which is also a form of general funding facility. In general it allows a developer to have access to predetermined amounts of money over a given period of time. The loans may be for terms of anything between 10 and 35 years, and the period during which a developer may exercise his option to use them between 3 and 7 years. The special feature of a drop lock loan is that, if prevailing interest rates fall below a predetermined base rate during the option period, then the option can be exercised in reverse against the developer who is obliged to take up an agreed tranche or all of the loan at that rate, which is then "locked" for the entire term. If the developer chooses to take up the loan before the predetermined interest rate is reached, he will pay a variable rate linked to that base rate until it falls to

301

the predetermined level, when it is converted into a fixed rate for the rest of the term.

Of increasing popularity in recent years has been the unsecured multiple option financing facility, whereby large loans are made available to property development companies on a broad basis for fixed, but usually extendable, periods of time. One bank will normally act as arranger and facility agent, with anything from between 6 and 30 other institutions supplying or guaranteeing the loan as managers or co-managers. Multi-option financing facilities encompass a variety of alternative financing methods within one package. Short-, medium-and long-term lending can be related in a versatile manner. Syndicated loans, multi-currency arrangements, commercial paper loans and bankers' guaranteed loans can all be selected and mixed, together with choices of swaps, fixed or floating interest rates, bonds with warrants and the like (Pugh 1992). In this way the borrower can choose the best financing package to meet his individual requirements. The loan size is usually large, from around £60 million to £400 million, with £150 million being the average. And maturities normally range from two to ten years, with seven years being most popular (Savills 1990).

Term loans

Term loans provide a development company with the facility to borrow a certain amount from a bank or syndicate of banks, which may be drawn upon immediately or in stated amounts throughout the life of a loan. The loans are always made at rates of interest in line with prevailing market rates during the period of the loan. Such loans will specify the date or dates and manner by which the amount advanced by the banks is to be repaid.

Term loans can also carry the option to convert into a limited recourse loan, where the funds are for a project that will produce income soon after completion. In some cases, the interest rates charged on the loan will fall to a pre-specified level when the property under development has been pre-let. Term loans cannot be called in for repayment before the agreed date, which gives them a distinct advantage over overdrafts. Within the property development sector, most term loans are for amounts of less than £100 million, although loans of up to £350 million are not uncommon. Maturities range from one to seven years, with the two to five-year range being the most popular (Savills 1990).

Overdrafts

In familiar terms, an overdraft occurs when a customer of a bank draws on an account to the extent that he falls into a negative balance. Company overdrafts may be for any size, provided the bank is satisfied by the asset backing and credit standing of the company concerned. Interest on overdrafts is charged at a pre-agreed rate or at the bank's currently published lending rate. Pre-arrangements regarding the interest rate are normally possible only for large corporate customers.

The main disadvantage of overdraft facilities is that repayment may be called for at any time and without notice, and could, therefore, come at a bad time when the company's liquid resources are low. Conversely, the principal advantage of an overdraft facility is that the borrower can repay the whole or part of the debit balance on his account at any time, also without giving notice. This contrasts with a term loan of a fixed amount, where the bank is not obliged to accept repayment before the agreed date, or may charge a penalty for so doing.

In the property development field, overdraft facilities are normally used only as supplementary funds to a principal loan, for exploratory work at the appraisal stage, for financing options to purchase land or for contingency payments.

Standby commitments

Standby commitments arise where a developer needs a temporary loan while seeking a permanent commitment for development finance from another lender. Unlike a take-out commitment in the form of a forward sale, neither the borrower nor lender expects the standby facility to become binding. The developer generally hopes in due course to borrow on more favourable terms elsewhere, but wants to begin development as soon as possible. Often, standby commitments are never concluded and funds never deployed; rather, the facility is used to enhance the confidence of a potential permanent lender in a proposed project. It has been stated, however, that few permanent lenders of development finance are willing to make loans against a standby commitment alone, unless there are very special circumstances (Bruggeman & Stone 1981).

Syndicated loans

The early 1990s witnessed the emergence of the "syndicated" loan, sometimes known as "project" or "consortia" funding. Often arranged by way of tender panels and normally only appropriate for very large schemes, the essential requirement will usually be a blue chip covenant of considerable means, reflected in a substantial asset base, profitability and turnover. This may not be found in the developer client, but with prospective occupiers prepared to lend their covenant to the scheme. The number of parties involved, with their separate interests, can therefore pose problems of authority and control for the developer, as well as time and expense.

Nevertheless, the concept of the syndicated loan has come into prominence because it offers greater flexibility with regard to currencies and interest rates. Other advantages have been said to include flexible maturity, amortization schedules and credit structures, with less rigid documentation requirements than for a securities issue (Savills 1990).

Securitization and unitization

Loan syndication has been supplemented by the securitization of debt, whereby the more conventional loans made by financial institutions are replaced by smaller monetary instruments that can be traded in the investment market. At the time of writing, debate has raged for a few years in the UK about the potential for "unitization", which is very much the same thing as securitization. The idea is to provide a financial vehicle that facilitates the funding of large single development projects, increases liquidity in the market, enables the smaller investor to participate in the market, increases the flow of capital to the property industry, achieves homogeneity of the market by divisibility, permits wider ownership of property, and increases market information and public awareness. Various issues emerge from the debate concerning such matters as valuation, the size and membership of the market, potential conflicts of interest, the management of the property, liquidity, marketability and taxation. Only time will tell how successful will be the notion of unitization.

Non-recourse and limited recourse loans

Non-recourse and limited recourse loans seek to restrict the lending institution to recovering any unpaid debt from the property in question rather than the borrowing developer. From the developer's point of view it obviously limits the risk, minimizing exposure while maximizing profit, and allows him to structure the transaction so that it is "off balance sheet" through a joint venture company. From the lender's viewpoint he can expect higher fees and wider margins. Nevertheless, in reality, no loans are truly non-recourse as such, for the bank will impose conditions relating to the front-end injection of equity finance into the project by the developer as well as seeking guarantees against cost overruns and completion date. These facilities are also only made to property companies with a proven track record in the management of development projects. The average size of non-recourse or limited recourse loans is in the region of £100 million, with a maturity of between two and seven years.

Joint ventures and partnership

Property companies without an adequate financial base to enable them to fund and carry out their own developments often have recourse to joint venture or partnership schemes. Likewise, public and private landowners lacking construction finance and development expertise have frequently entered into similar arrangements.

The advantages of joint ventures are generally obvious and do not need much explanation. However, they can be summarized as follows:

- to spread risk among participating parties
- to enable the development of large projects
- to attract market knowledge and development expertise
- to secure sufficient development finance.

In like manner, the main disadvantages are:

- control over the development project is dissipated
- disposal of a particular interest in a partnership scheme is more difficult
- the value of a part interest is invariably less than the proportionate share in the whole
- there may be double taxation.

Before embarking on a joint venture, the participants will need to identify the most appropriate form of structure to be used. This will normally depend upon the following:

- the number of participants
- the nature of the proposed scheme and the relative risks inherent in development
- the timescale involved, and the policy towards disposal or retention
- how the venture is to be financed, and the desired mix of debt and equity
- responsibility for losses and limitation on liability
- the tax position of the respective parties
- the way in which profits are to be distributed
- any relevant statutory legislation
- the ability and ease of disposing of interests by the parties involved
- any special balance sheet requirements.

There are various legal vehicles by which a joint venture can be effected. These include a trust for sale, a partnership agreement, a limited partnership, a joint venture company and a property unit trust. There are also potential investors looking to collaborate with reputable property development companies. These include local government authorities with land and planning powers but no money; statutory undertakers with surplus land; trading companies and business enterprises looking to participate in the development of property, either for their own occupation or as an investment with shared risk; overseas investors on a learning curve for a particular market or location; life companies and pension funds with money but little expertise; and high net worth individuals. It has been stated that all of the above tend to be looking for the "perfect development property", well let, high yielding and with potential growth. Most of them wish to enter into a 50:50 deal as equal partners, with each party putting up approximately 15 per cent of the equity and the joint venture vehicle borrowing the rest over a five-year term (Bramson 1992).

Venture capital

A phenomenon that has emerged since the mid-1980s is that of "venture capital'. This can mean different things to different people, but is usually employed to describe those sources of finance willing to invest in higher-risk proposals in return for equity participation and a say in project control. The venture capitalist delves much more deeply into a proposition than does a lending banker, and will often seek a close involvement in the management of a project. Venture capital is also expensive, both in arrangement and through profit sharing. The "hands-on" approach can constrain a developer, and it is preferable to try to obtain a "layered" financial package commencing with bank finance, followed by any other loans or grants available and topped off with the venture capital tranche.

Mezzanine finance

With mezzanine finance, a developer seeks the assistance of a second, "mezzanine", financier. Some prime debt lenders may consider providing a limited facility in excess of 70 per cent of value in consideration of a higher interest rate, or a single fee being taken out of the sale proceeds. It is more likely, however, that the top slice of funds will come from a separate specialist lender. These mezzanine financiers have in the past lent up to 100 per cent of the balance of funds required, but now they more usually look for an input from the borrower, in the form of either cash or collateral security. Nonetheless, they are still able to achieve effective gearing of around 85–90 per cent. There are also occasions when the prime debt financier is not prepared to provide as much as 70 per cent of value and the mezzanine financier may again top up the hardcore facility. This form of arrangement is also sometimes known as "wrap-around", "junior" or "subordinate" financing.

Because there are obviously greater risks involved in providing this top slice loan, the mezzanine financier will seek a return that reflects a share in the anticipated profit from the development. Some lenders will insist on taking shares in the development company, whereas others prefer to take a second charge on the project, although the collateral security will rank behind the prime debt financier. The amount of profit share required will naturally depend upon the individual circumstances of the project concerned. The mezzanine financier tends to become more involved with both the developer and the project, often employing a team of property professionals, which can give considerable comfort to the prime debt financier, because in looking after its own interests it will also protect theirs (Berkley 1991).

Commercial mortgage indemnity policies

The use of commercial mortgage indemnity policies (CMIPs) has increased significantly since the late 1980s. Originally used in the residential market, these policies provide a lender with indemnity cover for sums advanced between their normal gearing limits of 70 per cent up to a level of 85 per cent and sometimes even higher. When used properly these policies provide an invaluable tool to lenders, allowing them to bridge the gap between income and interest rates on investments such as development projects, which are not initially self-funding.

It is generally agreed, however, that these CMIPs were greatly abused, and some insurers are now facing considerable claims on development loans. The problem being that these insurers failed to differentiate between the risks involved in indemnifying a comparatively secure investment loan and the risks involved in taking a top slice position on a development proposal. The returns to the insurer were simply pitched too low. Nevertheless, the lessons have been learned and, although CMIPs are more difficult to come by on development schemes, where they are available they are managed in a much more professional and risk-conscious way.

Deep discount and zero coupon bonds

A deep discount bond (DDB) is a debt instrument issued at significantly less than its par value and which is repayable in full on its redemption. It may also carry a low rate of interest, with the lender being compensated by the high capital repayment at the maturity date. A zero coupon bond (ZCB) is similar, but no interest is ever paid during the loan period. The discount is, therefore, like the rolling-up of interest at a full rate until the redemption date. There is also the stepped coupon bond (SCB) whereby the coupon, or interest rate, rises at fixed intervals over the period of the loan by specified amounts. These different versions of the bond may be combined to form variations on the same theme.

The general terms for the issue of such bonds can be summarized as follows:
- maturity between five and ten years
- an interest rate margin of 2–4 per cent over base lending rate for development projects
- fees for arrangement, underwriting and participation totalling around 2 per cent of the loan
- security normally in the range of 70–75 per cent of loan to value, using the full redemption value of the bond
- income cover of at least one times, and preferably one and a half
- a good covenant
- borrower responsible for all associated costs
- early redemption penalties.

Although comparatively rare instruments in the property development finance field, DDBs, ZCBs and SCBs offer attractive rewards in terms of cashflow, running yield and redemption value, as well as certain tax advantages. It has also been suggested that the use of such DDBs and their derivatives could have a role in assisting the development of a securitized property investment market (Shayle 1992).

Hedging techniques

Hedging techniques are used by a borrower to "insure" against adverse interest rate and currency trends. There are a variety of such techniques, the most common of which are:

- "Swaps", where a borrower is allowed to raise capital in one market, and can swap either one interest rate structure for another, or swap the liability for the maturity value and interest from one currency to another. In other words, the simultaneous exchange between two parties of one security or currency for another where there is mutual benefit to both.
- "Caps" and "floors", which are derived from the options and futures market, and guarantee that during the loan period the interest rate paid by the borrower will not rise above (cap) or fall below (floor) a set limit.
- "Collars", where an agreement is reached combining a cap and a floor putting both a maximum and a minimum level on the interest rate paid by the borrower. A premium is normally paid by the borrower for a cap and by the lender for a floor.
- "Droplocks", as already mentioned, this facility enables the borrower to change the loan from a variable to a fixed rate of interest for the remainder of the loan period once long-term interest rates reach a predetermined level.
- "Forward rate agreements", where a borrower can sell the currency in which he has obtained the loan forward by say 12 months in order to lock into a more favourable exchange rate.

Criteria for funding

In most circumstances developers will have well established relationships with the funds from whom they seek development finance. Where it is the first time, a developer approaches a particular source of finance, understandably close scrutiny will be given to the property company as well as the proposal. For new developers setting out to undertake a first project, it is virtually an impossible task to attract financial support from conventional sources, unless on an individual basis they have successfully managed similar schemes for someone else.

In examining the criteria by which development propositions are judged, the following section is based on an established developer making a first approach to a fresh source of funds from a major financial institution.

Past performance

The starting point is bound to be the track record of the developer who is making an application for funding. However subjective the appraisal may be, the financier will probably form a fairly immediate opinion about the developers; in particular, if they were active during the downturn of a previous property cycle, it will reveal quite a lot about their judgement. Increasingly, it is expected that developers should themselves exhibit an expertise in the actual process of development, and the demonstration of true project management skills within the development company is now almost a prerequisite. Moreover, it is not sufficient for those skills merely to exist within the company. It must clearly be shown that they will be fully applied to the scheme in question, for even the most able of project managers can be expected to be responsible for only three or at most four major projects at any one time.

The necessary skills sought are not confined to the physical production of the property. A thoroughgoing competence in all aspects relating to the financial performance of the scheme is of paramount importance, because, when all is said and done, every facet of the development programme has a pecuniary effect. For this reason, it may occasionally be the case that proven financial expertise in another field of business aside from property could be considered as relevant in assessing a request for development funds.

Consideration will also be given to the supporting professional team selected by the developer. Some architects are best suited to particular types of development and certain projects demand the injection of specialist building, engineering, service, surveying and agency skills. The previous record of all the contributing disciplines and their likely corporate chemistry will, therefore, be taken into account.

It should almost go without saying that, even at first blush, the selection of the project by the developer should appear sound and attractive to the fund, for it is well accepted that where a developer sees opportunity a financier sees risk.

Company accounts

The accounts of a property company should tell their own story and will always constitute an essential part of an initial application for development finance. In appraising the assets of the company, the fund will look to see properties of a good physical quality occupied by tenants of repute on beneficial terms with regular upward reviews of rent. They will take note of the portfolio mix of properties owned, with special regard to geographic and sectoral spread. The development programme currently in hand should not appear to be too large for the financial and management resources of the company, and not all the assets of the company should be pledged.

On the other side of the coin, in examining the accounts of the company, an

309

intending financier will be reassured to find a healthy proportion of equity to balance the liabilities. The total term debt borne by the company should ideally have a good balance of fixed rate loans with any variable loans they have taken on. In addition, it is important to ensure that in their financial planning the property company have managed to avoid the bunching of repayments on existing loans and not placed undue reliance on short-term borrowing, both of which could lead to unfortunate pressures to refinance in a manner that might have repercussions upon the security sought by the fund. Where a property company have an overseas position, it is also necessary to establish that their foreign currency liabilities are generally matched by their overseas assets and sources of income.

Overall, therefore, the profit and loss account should demonstrate that the quality and amount of present income should not only be adequate to meet current outgoings, but should also be sufficient to meet any future rises in interest rates and cover any unforeseen exigencies that might occur. In this respect, cashflow is difficult to fudge, but some company accounts are otherwise less than revealing. This is especially true when it comes to the policy adopted towards the revaluation of existing property assets, and most funds pay close attention to how often the property portfolio is revalued, on what basis, and by whom. A careful watch will also be kept for the possibility of any off-balance sheet items, such as guarantees, being in existence and affecting the financial credibility of the company.

The project

From the funds standpoint, the proposed project must not only meet the portfolio objectives of the developer; more importantly, it must meet their own. Broadly speaking, the project should be of a suitable size in terms of value, with no single investment property forming more than about 5–10 per cent total portfolio. It should be in accord with the sectoral balance of the property portfolio, which might be distributed along the lines of 35 per cent to 40 per cent offices, 35 per cent to 40 per cent shops, 10 per cent to 15 per cent industrial and 5 per cent to 10 per cent other forms of land and property investment. Locationally, it should meet the geographical spread adopted by the fund and critically it must be within easy reach of the developer to make certain of proper project management control.

More specifically, the fund will probably wish to assure itself of detailed property considerations, particularly if the developer is not a previous borrower. This might include conducting its own investigations relating to such matters as precise siting, local demand for space, flexibility of use, and market comparables. Design factors and performance standards loom large in meeting the criteria set-up for funding approval by financial institutions, and are dealt with elsewhere according to their special requirements, sector by sector. Furthermore, virtually all funding agreements will reserve to the fund the right to approve tenants for the scheme and, although in practice this condition rarely proves a stumbling block, it is viewed as being a vital power of control over the project and the developer.

Amount to be borrowed

Most financiers will lend only a proportion of the total amount required to fund a development, normally on the strength of a first legal charge over the development, but although with mortgage finance this is usually limited to 70–75 per cent of cost, banks will usually advance anything up to 80–85 per cent for a quality development with a top-class covenant already agreed, and long-term lease-back or forward sale loans from the institutions covering the interim funding during development can often provide 90 per cent or more of total development cost. However, above 70–75 per cent, borrowings will often be considered as equity and deserving of a higher pricing. Almost as a matter of principle, it is felt right that the developer should make a contribution, however small, towards the financing of the project. As a rule of thumb, however, 25–30 per cent is frequently sought.

Sometimes developers will seek a loan geared to the value of the completed development as opposed to the cost. This may be countenanced by the lender, but usually a lower level of advance is made to compensate and ensure security of the loan. Obviously, different lenders in different markets will view funding applications in different lights and adopt differing criteria in relation to acceptable percentages of cost or value accordingly.

Loan periods

Few banks currently wish to consider commitments of longer than five years, but in exceptional circumstances will consider up to 10 years. The insurance companies and pension funds will consider periods of up to 30 years, and often set 10 years as a minimum term.

Interest rates

For straightforward loans, interest rates are pitched at varying points above an agreed base rate. For example, institutional lenders, might look for a margin of 1.5–2.25 per cent over government gilt edged rates. Banks might seek 1.5–2.5 per cent above the prevailing inter-bank lending rate, or even fix the rate for say five years by charging a similar margin over a five-year swap rate.

As already explained, some funding agreements adopt a fixed rate throughout the term, some a floating rate linked to the base rate, and some adopt a mechanism that combines fixed and floating rates. Increasingly, however, the rate of interest applied to a loan is traded against equity participation.

The timing of interest payments is also important, and methods of calculation vary from lender to lender. For example, a few lenders still calculate interest on the balance outstanding at the beginning of each year. If a loan of say £50 million is fully amortized over a period of 20 years at a fixed rate of 12 per cent, it can be shown that this could result in an additional payment of £8 million compared with a calculation on a day-to-day balance.

Yield

The factor by which income, anticipated or actual, derived from a development is capitalized will depend upon the relative degree of risk involved, and the relevant investment yield will be adjusted accordingly.

Where a fund was providing long-term finance for a scheme already completed and let, the appropriate yield might be, say, 5 per cent. If the finance was agreed on a forward commitment only once the scheme was completed and let, with no interim funding, then the yield might be 5.5 per cent. Where a forward commitment also provided interim development finance but a pre-let was concluded on full and acceptable rental guarantees supplied, then the yield could move to 5.75 per cent. If there was no pre-let and rents were only guaranteed for a limited period of, say, two years following practical completion, then a forward commitment with interim funding would require a yield of around 6 per cent. In the highest risk situation, where the fund was working on a priority yield, project management or profit erosion basis, then it would almost certainly look for a yield of about 6.5 per cent.

Rental cover

Very much as a rule of thumb, both fund and developer will be seeking sufficient rental cover in the margin allowed for developer's profit, and held as a balancing payment, to allow the completed building to stand empty for a period of around two and a half to three years. Exactly how long the contingency period should be will rest on the strength of the market at the time. The stronger the market, the less the cover necessary, and vice versa.

Another way in which rental cover is used as a measure of ascertaining the degree of security is the ratio of initial estimated rental income against interest repayments. A ratio of 1. 1 or 1.2 to 1.0 is normally sought.

General funding facility

As already indicated, where a developer has generated a high degree of confidence with a fund, it may often prove beneficial to both parties to agree that a general funding facility should be made available to the property company. These are usually provided by the merchant banking sector. The terms and conditions upon which such loans are made will vary, but they will commonly refer to such matters as the total amount available, the take-up rate, the level and compounding of interest charges, proportion of facility devoted to any individual project, maximum percentage of development cost allowed for any particular scheme, restrictions as to planning consent and land assembly position, right to approve individual projects, obligation to offer certain other development projects over a given period, revaluation rights, buy-out provisions for schemes slow in starting, equity sharing arrangements, institutional long-term take-out requirements upon completion, repayment, and reporting and review procedures. Funding facilities of this kind can either be of a fixed term for, say, five or seven years, or "revolving" subject to review at pre-ordained intervals. Security for the loan may also be attributable to particular assets of the company or arranged as a floating charge across all the company's assets.

More open-ended arrangements

The greater the degree of flexibility and discretion sought by a developer in a funding arrangement, the more a lending institution will look for further security to cover their risk. If the proposed project is anything less than conventional in respect of size, location, design, occupancy or letting terms, then a fund might be persuaded to relax its standard criteria on one or more of the following grounds. The land might already be owned by the developer, the company might be providing a substantial equity injection into the development, cast-iron collateral providing complete cover might be offered from elsewhere within the company's holdings, another financially strong partner such as a major construction firm might put up security alongside the developer, or bank guarantees may be supplied. Although they might not mean much in financial respects, personal guarantees undertaken by principals within the property company are thought to concentrate the mind wonderfully upon the successful outcome of development projects.

Sensitivity

These days it would be unusual for a lending institution not to conduct its own analysis of the sensitivity of a development scheme presented to it to changes in such component parts as rental income, initial yield, construction cost, finance charges and period to complete and let the development. Indeed, they would normally expect to see such an exercise performed for them by the prospective borrower in presenting the development for approval.

313

Tax

Although tax considerations are rarely the most significant issues in determining whether or not a scheme should be funded, they can affect the way in which a financial package is arranged. For example, because in some countries certain financial institutions are either wholly or partially exempt from tax, it is important to structure the funding agreement so that any concessions such as industrial building allowances or capital allowances relating to plant and machinery pass to the developer so that he can write them off against construction costs and improve his net profits position after tax. Further, it is sometimes the case that, whereas capital repayments do not attract tax relief, interest payments do, and in such circumstances borrowers are well advised to ensure that so far as is possible all fees and charges associated with funding the development are expressed in the formal finance agreement, so that they too become eligible for relief.

Costs

Apart from the obvious cost of interest on the loan and any equity share forgone, it should be recognized that the financing of development can be an expensive business. There are arrangement fees of between 0.25 and 1 per cent, payable to the fund or to intermediaries for effecting an introduction and putting a funding package together; commitment fees, which are usually about 1 per cent of the loan amount upon acceptance of a formal offer, and are repayable on completion of the advance but forfeitable if the borrower does not proceed; legal costs, which on the loan can amount to about 1.0 per cent of the advance, although it might be lower if it is a very large loan and higher if the deal is especially complex; valuation fees, which on average can cost up to a further 0.5 per cent of the advance; revaluation fees, during the currency of the loan; penalty fees, if by any chance the developer seeks early repayment of a mortgage advance; tail-end or exit fees; and the costs incurred in making the presentation itself.

Choice of fund

So far, attention has been focused upon the necessary attributes of the developer in the eyes of the fund. However, it is just as important that developers should carefully select their source of borrowing.

General considerations

In the same way that developers' underlying resources would be examined, it is for them to be assured about the financial strength of the fund, although this requirement is not as imperative as it was 25 years ago when there sprung up a crop of suspect secondary banks specializing in property investment. Of greater concern to the developer these days is the speed of response made by funds to a request for finance. Associated with this is the extent to which delegated authority is conferred upon the fund manager or executive director. The very location of the finance house can be a consideration in selecting a likely lender, for some funds can have a special regard for, or relationship with, certain towns or regions. It usually helps if the fund has developed an interest and expertise in property matters, particularly at the development end of the market. If so, it will often pay to make a few inquiries of other borrowers as to their experience of dealing with that fund.

The general attitude of the fund towards an approach for development finance will usually give a fair indication of what kind of business relationship is possible and how it is likely to evolve. As with most transactions, the level of success depends upon mutual trust and confidence, and even within the largest of organizations this often comes down to individual personalities on both sides. In this context, stability of management within both the property development company and the financial institution can only assist in forging close and effective links between the two agencies, but large organizations are notorious for moving people about. With this in mind, therefore, and for several other reasons, it is not always a good idea for a developer to rely too heavily upon a single source of money for funding their development programme. People and policies can change.

Given that most major development schemes in the prime part of the property market are funded either by insurance companies and pension funds in the "institutional" sector, or by clearing, merchant or overseas banks in the "banking" sector, it is worth considering the different characteristics of these alternative sources from the developer's viewpoint.

Institutional lending

By and large, the lending policies of the major insurance companies and pension funds are characterized by their "project"-based nature. This means that they tend to exercise extremely tight control over the entire project, including the design, construction and letting programmes. But although institutions are very risk adverse and maintain strict standards of building design and performance, many will lend up to 100 per cent of development finance to favoured borrowers.

What is required of the developer is a good knowledge of the institutional funding market. This includes an understanding of the locational and sectoral preferences of different funds, their recent transactions, investment objectives, portfolio balance and the amount of money currently available for particular projects. Some will tend to specialize in certain forms of financial arrangement: short-term bridging loan, medium-term mortgage, long-term leaseback or forward sale. Some will not consider a project costing less than £5 million to them, others concentrate on smaller schemes of, say, £1–3 million, and will have a ceiling figure beyond which they cannot lend. Particular funds will also either favour certain types of development – small industrial workshops, provincial shops or city offices, for instance – or be seeking to acquire them in order to balance their portfolios. A shrewd developer will always shop around. Consequently, contact has to be maintained with a range of fund managers and the agents who act on their behalf, so that by knowing who acts for whom, and which funds prefer a direct approach, careful targeting to selected institutions, rather than a shot-gun blast across the market, can be accomplished.

In the same way, the basis of agreement for obtaining finance can vary among funds and between projects. Some funds, for example, are less keen upon sale and leaseback arrangements than others. Similarly, with regard to the desire for a degree of partnership with a developer, some funds prefer the borrower to bear a reasonable proportion of risk, whereas others are less favourably inclined towards side-by-side arrangements, taking the view that too large a share to the developer gives him a disproportionate involvement in overall responsibility. The reverse can also be the case. It may be that the developer in question has no choice and, having to trade on, must opt for a forward sale. The manner in which such matters as bridging finance, rental projection and additional tranches of loans are agreed also varies across the market, and is often a question of careful negotiation.

A critical factor is the need to establish the extent to which potential profits are placed at risk. In this context, some form of equity-sharing leaseback arrangement tends to be less contentious than a straight taking of a capital profit through a forward sale, because both parties share a common interest. Nevertheless, whether the arrangement provides for rental guarantee, profit erosion or priority yield commitments from the developer, he must be aware of the respective consequences from each kind of agreement. In particular, attention should be paid to the length of the agreed letting period, and thus the amount of rental cover provided.

Pre-letting will also frequently be an important consideration. In fact, it will often be a condition of funding. However, despite what might be seen as the security and certainty afforded by a pre-let, for the developer there can be drawbacks that effect time, cost and quality. Not only might the demands of the tenant be in contradiction to the stipulations of the fund, but the added involvement of the tenant and his professional advisers in the construction process and upon completion can cause extra problems. Furthermore, it can affect the overall planning and phasing of the development programme, especially in respect of common parts and facilities. Nevertheless, the securing of a pre-let can attract a premium and avoid contingency payments, void rental periods and heavy marketing costs.

One area of increasing sophistication is that of funding documentation. In the thrill of the moment of approval, or during the cut and thrust of negotiations, certain matters can be overlooked or onerous undertakings entered into too lightly. Thus, the aim of the developer should be for an agreement that is not too tight and not too loose, but, above all, that the offer letter is binding and operable. Care must be taken about conditions relating to every aspect of the project – design, construction, funding and letting – and the result is usually a compromise between strict compliance with institutional criteria and cost minimization to optimize profit. It is more and more common for an institution to appoint their own consultant firm to monitor development, an arrangement that if not properly formulated can be very irksome to the developer and his project manager. Another important aspect of this kind of funding agreement is to ensure that the client's potential liabilities to the fund are matched by those of the contractor to him, and likewise between the developer, the project manager and the other members of the professional team.

Bank lending

Banks are traditionally more concerned with the "asset" base of those to whom they lend rather than upon the particular project in hand. The emphasis, there-fore, will be more upon monitoring and controlling the balance sheet and security cover offered by the borrower. For the developer this can provide a more open and flexible climate in which to work, where such factors as time, cost and quality can be traded off against the client's ability to generate funds or produce addi-tional collateral. However, bank finance is founded on profitable lending rather than by direct investment in a scheme, and, because banks normally neither pro-vide risk capital under conventional arrangements nor seek to participate in equity profits, it is common for only a proportion of development finance (typ-ically around 70%) to be loaned. It is, therefore, imperative for the developer responsible for securing finance to have an understanding of the policies, prac-tices and procedures that determine bank lending. This is of greater moment here, for although institutional negotiations are invariably conducted between survey-ors, bank lending is more usually transacted with a banker. Furthermore, the lending market is far from homogeneous. The banking sector broadly comprises major stock banks, the merchant banks, finance houses and overseas banks. All are different, and all are competitive, so bank finance must be carefully tailored to fit the purpose for which it is applied, and a well designed package prepared to meet overdraft, term or equity financial requirements. And, as interest rates in the market tend to move closely together, so the aim of the developer is to seek the best deal in respect of such matters as quality of service, fees, costs and repayments. Indeed, sometimes the additional flexibility afforded by more expensive arrangements can be worthwhile. For example, the objectives with a smaller project might be for a quick decision, flexibility in execution and an abil-ity to revise arrangements without excessive penalties. With a larger scheme, detailed arrangements regarding the term of the loan, interest rate options and adjustable repayment schedules might be of more concern.

Term loans, which impose a contractual obligation on the bank to provide finance for an agreed period, have become a popular way of funding development projects. Banks are increasingly experienced in tailoring proposals that give flexibility of approach on the one hand but are matched by covenants on the other, which can have considerable effect on the running of the borrowers business in the future. For instance, financial ratios are a valuable tool of control, the breach of which puts the lender in a strong position to call for initial or added security or for changes in the terms of the loan, with such options as accelerating the loan or cancelling any unused part of the facility. There are other alternatives of varying efficacy: the negative pledge, sharing-round clauses and contractual right of set-off. Additionally, where the loan is unsecured, which now is sometimes the case, the bank might also consider various forms of direct involvement in the borrower's company, ranging from the appointment of a nominee director, to a working capital maintenance agreement, with shareholders undertaking to ensure the maintenance of the borrower's capital to satisfy covenanted ratios. Thus, in general, term-lending can afford a flexibility that, depending upon the circumstances, can be preferable to long-term mortgages, sale and leaseback arrangements or debenture borrowing.

A feature of bank lending is that there has been a tendency for the borrower to rely upon the lender to propose the basis and structure of the lending facility. This occurs often through ignorance, and sometimes through a misplaced desire to please. Such a lack of initiative or awareness in negotiations on the part of the developer can all too easily lead to a costly and mismatched facility being accepted.

Customer relationships are a critical factor in bank lending policy. The early training of young bankers dwells on the "cannons of lending" – character, ability, means, purpose, amount, repayment and income (for which the acronym CAMPARI serves as a handy reminder). It is perhaps significant that there is not "S" for security, for banking theory holds that a perfect loan arrangement should be unsecured. Practice, however, dictates otherwise. In many cases the prospective borrower will have developed a relationship with his bank through ordinary business and overdraft lending, and it is a golden rule in the clearing banks that the current account forms the basis of mutual confidence between banker and developer. Where there is no previous relationship, then it will be necessary to establish the financial status of the borrower and the viability of the proposed scheme with great care.

Several other factors warrant attention on the part of the developer when negotiating bank lending. These are:

- The extent to which standby facilities might be required, and the terms that might be attached to them.
- The type of charge secured over the assets of the borrower: making sure that they are neither overcharged, which can reduce the ability to obtain further loans, nor unduly restricted, so that, for example, disposal is limited.

- Ensuring that a proper presentation is made of the man, the market, the margins, the management information systems and the money requirement concerned with a particular project.
- Confirming the "facility letter" from the bank to the borrower setting out the terms on which the loan has been agreed. Apart from specifying the amount, rate of interest, repayment terms and brief details of the security, if any, it will also normally include specific terms and conditions in the form of negative or positive convenants relating to such matters as default, other borrowings, supply of information and provision of warranties.

Whatever detailed arrangements are finally made, the project management objective must be to seek elasticity. Full allowance for the possible effects of inflation, time and cost overruns should be built in. Even the location of the bank and its officials, together with their speed of response, can be of importance. And these days, the very stability of the financial source is equally significant.

Problems in funding

Apart from the basic thesis that lack of knowledge and understanding of the principal sources of finance for property development and their respective policies, practices and procedures presents a major problem for aspiring developers, there are other issues that condition the climate for lending. A few of these are described, in brief, below.

Location
Within and among funding institutions a preferential treatment exists towards certain situations in, around and between selected cities and facilities. Some of this has the smack of hindsight about it, but much has to do with perceptions regarding environment, accessibility and communications. From the point of view of a developer approaching a potential source of funds, therefore, it is helpful to know the attitude and commitment of individual fund managers to particular towns, areas and regions.

Presentation
It is astonishing how little attention is paid to the professional presentation of proposed development schemes. Although not always the declared reason for turning a proposition down, poor presentation probably accounts for many funding refusals. At the very least, the following are required: a detailed appraisal of planning and market conditions, a cashflow analysis and a reasonable set of drawings, together with an explicit statement of the financial position of the intending borrower, contained in a well illustrated, succinct and coherent document.

Personality can also play a part. Character assessment is always a matter of personal judgement, but it is nonetheless important to ensure that any presentation is made in an open, confident, informed and enthusiastic manner.

Speculation

It is almost a cliché to state that one man's profit is another man's risk. Nevertheless, it is probably true to say that developers as a breed are eternally optimistic, whereas bankers, and those of their ilk, are notoriously cautious in their approach towards new developments. Moreover, it is often harder for the small developer to borrow money than for the large established property company, for if one project goes wrong for the former, it will have a more profound effect upon overall security and performance than for the latter.

From the standpoint of the developer or project manager, it is always worth considering the way in which potential profits are placed at risk by the manner whereby funds adjust their yield parameters according to the financial arrangements agreed. For example, as indicated earlier, an office scheme might variously be finely tuned as follows:

> 5%   completed and let
> 5.25%   pre-let, interim finance and forward commitment
> 5.5%   leaseback or lease guarantee
> 5.75%   profit erosion basis
> 6%   priority yield basis.

Collateral

A frequent explanation for funding agencies turning down applications to support proposed development projects is the inadequacy of existing collateral guarantees and proffered future equity participation. In fact, research indicates that this is probably the single most common reason for rejection.

Valuation

Lenders will invariably seek their own valuation of a proposed development project. This may often be at odds with the value perceived by the prospective borrower. In stagnant or recessionary markets, for example, the emphasis by the lender and his valuation advisers will normally be placed upon secure cashflow rather than anticipated capital value allowing for potential growth, which can lead to a wide divergence in estimating current open market value.

Thus, although regard is still paid to the loan to value ratio, the ability of the transaction to service the debt becomes of paramount importance. Pre-letting to a high-quality covenant on beneficial terms is, therefore, a vital factor in obtaining full financing in a falling or static market. In such markets it is always advisable to check that the lender's chosen valuer is prepared to confirm an approximate value, albeit verbal, prior to paying commitment fees, solicitors' costs and, of course, the valuer's full fees for a written report (Berkley 1991). Nevertheless, there are always the twin dangers of initial valuation or appraisal of a proposed development scheme being either too conservative or overoptimistic. Great care must be taken to explore the constituent components of rent, yield, building cost, finance, land cost, profit and time.

Currency

Given the global nature of property development finance, foreign currency loans have become increasingly popular. Interest rates can be lower, capital sums higher and terms easier. Foreign currency markets, however, are prone to constant fluctuations, and, in order to take advantage of such borrowing arrangements, developers should ensure access to any one of a number of different currencies, and be able to switch with ease. There are now versatile "multi-currency" banking facilities available from leading international banks.

Refinancing

In many markets the issue of refinancing is extremely topical. Proper handling of this can often mean the difference between a property company's survival or its insolvency. Refinancing development property presents a particularly formidable challenge in depressed markets, as uncompleted and unlet projects lack the two basic attributes required to reassure a financier: cashflow and marketability.

Developments are most likely to be refinanced as part of an overall corporate refinancing exercise. Alternatively, where the scheme is in an area of strong demand or very prime, a development may be refinanced by the injection of fresh capital by a new equity investor, either as a joint venture partner or as a long-term investor. The unpredictability of development projects is not often compatible with the fine tuning of debt-oriented refinancing packages. A new financier's willingness to provide additional finance will primarily depend upon the quality of the security offered, although the company's past record will also play an important role. An existing financier will look especially at the feasibility of the company's corporate plan in comparison with other realization options, although it has been pointed out that the ultimate decision will invariably turn on the strength of the relationship between the parties involved (Clarke 1991).

Loan workouts

In a period of widespread overbuilding, sluggish leasing activity and other demand-side problems, many development projects are faced with a situation where schemes seem unlikely to service their debt charges upon completion. In these circumstances a lender may agree to what is known as a "loan workout", which provides the developer with sufficient time and support to achieve a turn round in their project.

Essentially, a workout is the debt restructuring for a single project or many projects or properties normally requiring assiduous management, new money and additional collateral.

A developer should seek a workout as soon as a problem is identified and should try to persuade the lender to participate (not always an easy task). At a minimum, a financial workout will allow the developer to make the best of his current position. Ideally, it will enable him to satisfy his obligations while maintaining equity in the property. Thus, a workout provides better odds that the developer will emerge from the crisis with his business intact.

What a developer basically wants from a workout is temporary relief from all or part of the required debt service payment; an extension of a maturing loan without large extra fees; minimal additional encumbrances on the property or further dissipation of equity; personal liability relief; debt reduction, or even forgiveness; minimization of potential tax consequences; and co-operation to sell existing holdings. The incentives to the lender are a belief that with temporary concessions the problem can be solved; minimization of the risk of foreclosure; reduction or elimination of negative media attention; lessening of the impact on the lender's loan portfolio and income recognition; and the avoidance of protracted litigation. It has been stated that the keys to a successful loan workout are the development and implementation of a financial plan that addresses the maximization of return to creditors, and the long-term survival of the debtor as a going concern, together with the smooth interaction of various functions, including legal, accounting, information systems, asset marketing and management, and business operation. A workout can be a very sobering process to even the most sanguine of developers.

From above, it can be appreciated that it is essential to establish the correct financial base for the project, and for the developer to balance their aims with the aspirations of the lending agency, whose risk/reward criteria will determine the scope for negotiation between the parties. It can, therefore, be suggested that three basic elements of funding have to be assessed in any scheme:

- availability – in terms of knowing the range of possible sources of finance, methods of approaching them and their current position
- economy – in respect of interest rates and how they might fluctuate, as well as equity participation, incentives and penalties, and any hidden costs of borrowing
- practicality – with integrates the elements of availability and economy into a feasible arrangement that might otherwise detract from the viability of the project or invalidate it completely.

Financial adaptability on the part of the developer at a time when the investment character of property is changing is now a must.

The financial agreement

Inevitably, perhaps, the aims of the funder and the developer will often conflict. It is increasingly important, therefore, that the respective responsibilities for control during the development period are clearly apportioned and understood, and that the financial agreement is properly documented. Although a developer or project manager will doubtless have recourse to competent legal advice, the cut and thrust of negotiation is often such that certain matters may be misinterpreted or overlooked in the false hope that, once building has begun, the financial agreement will be forgotten or set aside. However, the opposite is more often the case, for it is at those moments of crisis during development that the parties are more likely to spring to the small print and come to realize the true consequences of their earlier bargaining. A better understanding of the objectives and procedures of financial control and documentation on the part of the developer will normally enable him to negotiate with greater confidence and to deploy his professional team more effectively.

Objectives

In structuring the financial arrangement the **funder** will aim to control certain aspects of the proposed scheme, including the:

- criteria by which tenants are selected and leasehold terms agreed
- negotiations conducted and agreements concluded with third parties
- entry by the developer into any special legal agreements with the local government, authority, and the consequent liability if the developer defaults
- nature and level of indemnity policies and collateral warranties held or offered by the developer, his professional team, the contractor and the sub-contractors, so that in the event of failure the developer can be dismissed and the fund can assume full authority for the completion of development
- taxation implications of the project
- the purchase price of the completed project, so that unnecessary premiums and over-rentalization are avoided.

In contrast, the **developer**, whilst wishing to retain long-term goodwill with an interested fund, will seek to ensure that the terms ultimately accepted in the finance agreement provide:

- a smooth flow of funds
- speedy responses by the funder
- minimum interference by the funder's professional consultants
- smooth letting arrangements without undue constraint by the funder.

The "offer" letter

One of the most important stages of the documentation relating to the finance of development arises well before the formal issue of agreements. This is the initial "offer letter" by the funding agency or its professional representatives. In effect, it will set out the basic terms of the deal and outline the intentions and expectations of the funder. Such a letter will have particular significance if the developer has to commit himself to the purchase of land prior to the full finance agreement being formalized. Any condition precedent in the correspondence must, therefore, be carefully appraised as to its implications.

There is no such thing as a standard offer letter, but the following list represents the more usual draft proposed heads of agreement:

- description of the parties concerned
- intention to purchase and basis of acquisition
- type and amount of loan; rate of interest and method of repayment
- identification of site and ownerships
- description of the proposed development
- planning position and local authority interests
- estimate of construction costs
- prospective letting agreements
- initial yield and resultant purchase price
- staged payments of costs and fees
- sharing of surplus rental income
- rental guarantees by developer
- approval building contract
- insurances and warranties.

The contractual agreement

The financial agreement will put into final contractual form the exact degree of control over the scheme of the funder will expect to have. It is important for the developer, therefore, to ensure that the conditions imposed are not so onerous as to prejudice the proper management of the project or jeopardize the profitability through no fault of their own.

Apart from confirming the contents of the original offer letter, renegotiated or otherwise, the financial agreement, which is made under seal, will normally start by defining all the terms, procedures, parties and dates involved in the transaction. Of special concern to the funder will be the terms and conditions relating to any actual or proposed building agreements, or agreements for a lease. If the developer defaults, or if some other specified event takes place, the funder will wish to protect its position in respect of the determination of those agreements. The three main remedies normally incorporated into the financial agreement are:

- the power for the funder to assign the benefits under the agreement to another developer
- the power by the funder to complete the development and sell the created investment without any continuing liability
- an agreement whereby if a third-party freeholder exercises their right to re-enter for any reason under another contract, then the funder receives a payment relating to the improved value of the property achieved by the works to date undertaken by the developer.

Practical problems

It is impossible to cover all the matters that may be included in a financial agreement, and ultimately it is up to the developer whether or not the various terms and conditions are acceptable. Nevertheless, there are issues that recur, and they merit close attention on the part of the developer. In no particular order, these are:

- Design documentation attached to the agreement should clearly set out the objectives of the scheme and, as a general rule, the more details provided by the developer the better, so that subsequently the funder's surveyor cannot alter the initial specification.
- A developer is well advised to attempt to restrict the number of outside consultants the funder may appoint to act on their behalf in relation to the project. A single firm of surveyors should suffice.
- The necessity to obtain written approval for the appointment of subcontractors should be avoided by agreeing a list of nominated subcontractors, although difficulties might arise in the case of a management contract involving many subcontracts, all of which may not initially be known.
- A clear understanding of the definition of the date of practical completion should be established and, wherever possible, the views and visits of the developer's architect and the fund's surveyor should be harmonized.
- The date on which capitalization and transfer of purchase price takes place should be explicit, and not dependent upon the actions of third parties.
- Access to the site by the funder's surveyors and facilities to inspect and test materials and workmanship should be kept within reasonable bounds. Notice of any defects should also be notified at the time of discovery.
- A procedure for arbitration should be agreed.
- It may be necessary for the developer to consider the inclusion of a "walkabout" clause, so that he can approach other sources of finance if a top-up of funds over and above the funder's maximum commitment is required.
- There should be some mitigation in respect of those delays that push the completion date beyond the agreed date, especially where such delays are outside the control of the developer.

Little has been published in the professional press about funding agreements, although a specialist breed of solicitors have grown up who seem to be developing ever more complex documentation, usually for funding-clients. The aspiring developer, therefore, must be increasingly aware of the many pitfalls ahead.

Trends and prospects

This chapter concludes where it started, by stating that finance is a vital dimension of property development, and a principal concern of project management for the real estate industry:

- The globalization of property finance markets will continue.
- Developers and financiers alike will have to become even more aware of occupational demands by property users, and willing to accept greater innovation in the design, construction and management of commercial premises.
- Construction companies are already an attractive source of short-term development finance, not only providing interim funds but also acting as security for a long-term take-out, and entering into a fixed-price contract in return for an equal share of the eventual profit, and it is probable that, with difficulties in the institutional finance market and continuing uncertainty in the construction industry, the number of joint venture schemes between contractors and developers will grow.
- A specialized market in high-risk development schemes will emerge, depending upon more sophisticated market research, superior management skills and the spreading of risk over a well balanced mix of investments and among enterprising investors. Active risk management through various methods of syndication has already had considerable success in America.
- Joint venture and partnership agreements between public and private sector agencies will gain in popularity.
- The consortia approach towards investment in all forms of property development will become increasingly common: small private, as well as public, investors being grouped together to finance relatively small schemes, and large institutional investors collaborating in funding the major development projects.
- Refined funding techniques, which can reduce dependence upon cashflow in the early years after the completion of a development project, will be introduced on a wider scale than hitherto, as will funding schemes that allow for the future consolidation of debt charges into equity interest, such as convertible mortgages, which permit the translation of fixed interest loans into equity shares once an agreed rate of inflation is reached.
- Among new arrangements structured specifically to attract additional funds for property development will be special multi-layered agreements in which each tranche of investment funding is designed to meet the tax needs and positions of the various parties to the deal, so as to take maximum advantage of tax allowances and relief.
- Some experimentation will undoubtedly take place in the property investment market with certain of the new techniques that have been developed in other investment markets, such as indexed mortgages, equity-linked bond issues, shelf registration issues and deep-discounted stock issues.
- A new funding ethic needs to be formulated towards the regeneration of older building stock in inner-city areas.
- Occupiers will be more directly active as developers, since they hold the key to financing.
- Environmental aspects of property development will play a larger part in the appraisal equation.

- Higher standards of professionalism will be demanded at every level.
- Worldwide, there is likely to be a contagious reappraisal of the concept of value.

Whatever happens, structural movements in the international economy have already begun to increase uncertainty in most forms of property investment, and the impact of new technologies is calling into question conventional attitudes about low-risk property development opportunities. Times they are a-changing!

CHAPTER FOURTEEN
Marketing for development

The days of certain markets, easy lettings and malleable tenants have gone, and, for the foreseeable future they are unlikely to return. Property as a product has become more difficult to sell, and those responsible for selling it perforce required to bring a higher degree of professionalism to the market. Users' needs have to be more closely identified and more carefully matched with product design. As with other property services the agency function to date has been performed against a background that has rested heavily upon the historic monopoly enjoyed by established firms and a traditionally constant attitude towards transactions in land and property by owners and occupiers. This is changing.

The chapter is organized as follows:
- the marketing role
- marketing functions
- market segmentation
- selling techniques
- developer's viewpoint

The marketing role

A useful definition of marketing is one provided by the Institute of Marketing, which runs:

> Marketing is the management function which organizes and directs all those business activities involved in assessing and converting customer purchasing power into effective demand for a specific production or service to the final customer or user so as to achieve the profit target or other objective set by the company".

More simply perhaps, marketing is the skill of matching the needs of a buyer with the product of a seller, for a profit. It is probably true to say that development property used to be a soft-sell product. An estate agent would erect a board, place an advertisement and wait. Nowadays, however, those marketing property developments are faced increasingly with a highly competitive and discerning market, and one that demands better information and more active attention to the selling process.

The agency function

The appointment of an estate agent is the usual means by which the commercial sector of the property development industry disposes of completed projects, whereas in the residential sector most major developers perform their own agency functions with or without the help of agents. There has also been a slight tendency on the part of some developers and local authorities to undertake agency on their own behalf. Nevertheless, despite criticism over recent years about the quality of their work, it should nearly always be possible to gain a wider access to the market by retaining an agent. Depending upon the nature of the development and the circumstances prevailing in the market at the time, an agent might be called upon to perform some or all of the following tasks:

- find suitable sites or properties for development, redevelopment or refurbishment on behalf of clients
- receive instructions and liaise with the developer at an early stage in the project to consider the overall concept of the proposed scheme and, in particular, to advise on those features of design and layout that could add to or detract from the marketability of the completed property
- provide general economic advice and investigate rental levels and capital values in respect of the viability of the project
- comment on the planning implications and assist in discussions with local authority officers
- advise on potential occupiers and tenant mix
- advise on the possible need for special building and occupiers' services, as well as considering the general operation of future management services
- advise regularly throughout the period of development on prevailing market conditions
- advise, arrange and implement a marketing strategy
- monitor responses and handle prospective occupiers' inquiries
- conduct negotiations with interested parties and investigate the credentials of potential purchasers or tenants
- advise on and assist with the provision of development finance
- negotiate and conclude the final sales or lettings.

With regard to payment for the various activities described above, it is usual for an agent to negotiate a separate fee for professional services rendered in connection with acquisition, development appraisal, funding, development consultancy, project management, letting and management. An interesting change that has taken place over recent years in respect of offering estate agency services and attracting instructions, is the increasingly liberal attitudes taken by professional institutions towards advertising. Under current regulations and notes for guidance of the RICS, for example, members are actually encouraged to give interviews to the press and media, and the rules are stated to be designed to give the profession "maximum freedom in accordance with current thinking". This has allowed commercial agents quite a broad scope in marketing their own services as well as their clients' property.

There are said to be certain fundamental prerequisites to effective agency, based on the adage "if you have no information, you have no product sell" (Development Systems Corporation 1983). More specifically, the necessary market intelligence can be broken down into the following areas:

- *Knowing the owners*   Thorough market knowledge involves knowing who owns the buildings and the land in the locality. Ideally, a good agent should generate ownership data on every potential development or redevelopment site, for sale or not for sale, within his bailiwick.
- *Knowing the tenants*   An able agent will gather as much information as possible on tenants, large and small, operating within the market area. Particular attention being paid to existing major tenants or high potential tenants. Tenant intelligence should go beyond knowing names to knowing why a tenant is there. Why did a tenant sign a lease on one building and not on another? What is the critical location and site criterion for the tenant? Does the tenant rely heavily on street patterns, demographics, signage, skilled labour?
- *Knowing the deals*   The acute agent will know about all important deals transacted in their territory. Such deals define the economic character of the market, determining the level and pattern of leasing and selling values. The information on current and recent deals is not always easy to uncover, being a matter of confidentiality between the parties involved, but a good relationship is imperative between fellow agents and existing or prospective tenants and purchasers.
- *Knowing the property*   Understanding the physical land and property inventory of an area is the cornerstone of an agent's practice. Knowledge of the types of property in a given area, the amount of each type, the special features of particular properties and the plans for new projects is essential.
- *Knowing the competition*   From the viewpoint of the agent, as well as the client developer, it is important that he is aware of who else is in the market, and what size share of that market they are likely to absorb. Besides market share, it is always wise to know how the competition is operating, its strengths, its weaknesses and its marketing strategies (Development Systems Corporation 1983).

Types of agency

There are four essential bases upon which an estate agent may be instructed to sell a development. These are:

- *Sole agency*   A sole agency arrangement is one in which a single firm is instructed to dispose of a property. Preferred by agents because, if they are successful in selling the development scheme, then they receive the full measure of commission. A normal fee would be 10 per cent of full annual rental value for a letting and between 1.5 and 3 per cent of agreed price for a sale.
- *Joint agency*   Where two agents are instructed by a developer to collaborate in the letting or disposal of a property, a joint agency is established. This arrangement is most commonly used in the sale of provincial property where national and local coverage is required, or in a scheme of mixed development where specialist marketing of particular components is thought desirable. It is also adopted where a property is considered especially difficult to sell and an element of competition is felt advisable, or where one agent has introduced a development to a client on the understanding that they will at least share in the agency, but the developer requires the marketing skills of another firm. Although fees are negotiable, it is probable that the developer will have to pay up to around one and half times the normal fee, divided by the two agents by agreement.
- *Sub-agency*   It is always open for an agent, unless instructed otherwise, to appoint another firm as subagent to assist in the marketing of a particular property. The main difference between sub-agency and joint agency is that the responsibility to the client rests with the principal firm in the former case and commissions tend to be higher in the latter.
- *Multiple agency*   When several agents are individually instructed to dispose of a property and commission is only payable to the agent who achieves the sale, a multiple agency is formed. Resort to such form of agency is not normally taken in the marketing of a development project, because it invariably leads to a confused marketing campaign, abortive costs and a suspicion on the part of potential purchasers that for some reason the property is difficult to sell.

As already mentioned, some development organizations sometimes opt to perform the agency function themselves. In such circumstances, an "in-house" team will assume responsibility for the promotion and disposal of a scheme. However, it should be recognized that established firms of estate agents are bound to be more informed about, and have wider access to, both property and business requirements and opportunities. Only very rarely does it benefit an individual developer to market a project entirely on their own.

The role of the provincial agent has also taken on a greater importance over the past few years in the field of development. Although the major national firms of estate agents based in London can offer unrivalled services in respect of the potential national and international occupancy market, and can also supply certain specialized support services such as research, planning and funding, local firms situated in major regional centres also supply invaluable expertise. The provincial agent tends to have a deeper knowledge of local markets, better information regarding the availability of suitable sites, a heightened awareness of the true state of prevailing planning policy and practice, and a favoured insight into the performance and intentions of local businesses and landowners. Furthermore, they will often have a superior understanding of local values and returns, being privileged with the precise details underlying local sales conducted by private treaty. At the letting stage they will also benefit from the accumulated experience of enquiries received across a whole range of properties over time, giving them a good idea of the vagaries of the market. Their ready availability to react to enquiries and respond informatively to questions regarding local services and conditions is an obvious advantage.

Rules and responsibilities

The year 1991 to 1992 proved something of a watershed for estate agency practice. After a decade or more of threats and promises the profession witnessed the introduction of The Estate Agents (Undesirable Practices) Order 1991, The Estate Agents (Provision of Information) Regulations 1991, both introduced under powers conferred by the Estate Agents Act 1979, and the Property Misdescriptions Act 1991.

The procedures dictated by the former two statutory instruments are wide ranging. But in so far as they touch on agents dealing with clients, they essentially fall into two areas: the course of action to take as soon as a client–agent association begin, and the conduct required as that relationship progresses. The regulations, for example, are explicit about the information that must be furnished to the client and, importantly, the moment at which those details must be provided. A client–agent agreement must be established "before the client is committed to any liability towards the estate agent". An agreement will cover all aspects of agency: the length of instruction, fees and when they become payable, marketing budgets, circumstances in which other payments are due and definitions of "sole agency", "joint sole agency" and the like. Few problems, hopefully, face the experienced developer and worthy agent.

The Property Misdescriptions Act 1991, which became operable from April 1993, presents estate agents, and developers who market their properties directly, with a new form of criminal liability for mis-statements. The kernel of the Act lies in Section 1 (1) which provides:

> Where a false or misleading statement about a prescribed matter is made in the course of an estate agency business or a property development business, otherwise than in providing conveyancing services, the person by whom the business is carried on shall be guilty of an offence under this section.

As one leading authority in the field explains, agents and developers now face a criminal offence of strict liability (i.e. one in which the prosecution need prove neither intent to deceive nor even negligence), subject only to the possibility of avoiding conviction where the defendant can prove that all reasonable steps and due diligence have been taken (Murdoch 1993). Nevertheless, the Act does not require any particular information to be given about property that is being marketed. What it does require is that any information given should be accurate, or at least not false or misleading. The detailed degree of care that must be taken over such marketing tools as photographs, models, artists' impressions or demonstration units is not as yet clear, but considerable caution will have to be exercised with sales aids of this kind, and regular updating undertaken. The measurement of floor areas and rooms, whether relating to commercial or residential properties, requires particular care, and resort will inevitably be made to that ubiquitous caveat "approximately'. With regard to disclaimers, however, the Department of Trade and Industry advises that they must be applied in as bold, precise and compelling a way as the statement to which they relate. Again, developers and agents of good standing will have nothing to fear from the legislation, but the more responsible representatives of the property industry still call for the implementation of Section 22 of the 1979 Estate Agents Act laying down minimum standards of competence and experience, with many preferring a full system of licensing or registration.

Above all else, successful marketing in the property world depends upon confidence and credibility. It is distressing to record the lasting gratitude that both journalists and politicians afford to estate agents for keeping them from occupying the lowest position in repeated professional popularity polls. Nevertheless, in the commercial real estate marketing field, the winning and retaining of trust and confidence by client organizations, whether vendors or purchasers, is critical.

Marketing functions

Current pressures on estate agents to let or sell their clients' buildings is leading to a much higher degree of sophistication in the way development properties are marketed. In addition, as more and more commercial floorspace comes on stream and disposal becomes ever harder to effect, so the realization that getting the product right in the first place grows even stronger. Consequently, however faddish it might seem, the property world must gain a better understanding of the procedures and functions of marketing, and at the same time learn from the array of marketing principles and practices that have been developed in other sales markets. In stating this, however, it should be appreciated that the marketing of planned new developments ahead of construction breaks many basic marketing rules, in that a potential customer cannot test and experience the qualities of a product prior to purchase. The reputation of the developer and the climate of

333

goodwill created between those involved in a potential sale or letting becomes a crucial factor in the marketing campaign.

Marketing tools

A useful classification of the four key tools of the marketing man has been provided as follows:

- *Market research and information* It is suggested that for the purpose of the estates profession these two functions should be distinguished, because the term "research" is used by most major firms of estate agents simply to describe the collection of largely retrospective statistics that show trends and can be used for producing forecasts, whereas market research in the true sense is described as an "action-oriented procedure" aimed at informing the developer of a marketing or advertising plan.
- *Advertising* This is process of spreading information by preparing and placing paid-for material such as space in newspapers and journals or time in the broadcasting media. Advertisements are always identifiable with their sponsor or originator, which is not always the case with other forms of promotion or publicity.
- *Promotion* Covers those marketing activities, other than personal selling, advertising and publicity, that stimulate consumers' purchasing and agents' effectiveness, such as displays, shows, exhibitions, and various non-recurrent selling efforts not in the ordinary routine.
- *Public relations* The role of public relations is to establish and maintain understanding and goodwill for the development organization's product and services, activities and operating policies. In this, it is not only concerned with communicating for marketing purposes, but also for the broader purpose of creating a favourable atmosphere within which the organization may operate successfully.

Marketing research

The whole process of development essentially starts with market research, the goal of which is to project the rate of absorption for a particular property product based on the supply and demand for similar properties in a specified market area. Conducted at the outset of the development process, the developer seeks to identify an unfulfilled market need that might feasibly be met on a specific site. If the signs are promising, a formal market study might be commissioned and a marketing plan of campaign prepared.

The starting point of any marketing plan of campaign is the identification of the target groups of possible purchasers. Research is, therefore, essential, and it is really only in recent years that some of the leading firms of estate agents and a few of the major property development companies have committed themselves to the serious analysis of the markets in which they operate and consideration of the buildings they produce and sell.

It must be said, however, that certain pieces of published research are in fact just so much window dressing. The compilation of crude vacancy rates for particular sectors, for example, says very little about market performance or prospects except at the most superficial level. Broad indications of rental value across wide geographical areas might be useful promotional material for the firms concerned, but cannot be held to contribute greatly to a better understanding of the property market. Effective marketing increasingly will depend upon more rigorous research into the underlying conditions and determinants of demand and supply in the property market.

In practice, marketing research is usually concentrated on a few recurrent problems, often on a continuous basis, which may be grouped as follows:

Up-to-date market knowledge

- The size of the regional and local markets for particular kinds of property, normally measured in floorspace for commercial sectors and dwelling units or habitable rooms for housing.
- Past patterns of demand and underlying economic, social, political, legal and technological factors that are likely to affect future levels of demand, together with an indication of the timescale involved and any cyclical variations.
- Buying or renting habits of consumers, along with an appraisal of the possible changes in attitude and behaviour by both customers and funding institutions that might take place.
- Actual and potential market share commanded by the development organization, and a breakdown of the market shares of major competitors.
- General appreciation of past and possible future trends in broad socio-economic terms covering such matters as population change, national income and expenditure, sales and output, availability of finance, construction industry performance and legislative or political change.

Overall policy and tactics

- An examination of competitive pricing structures and practices, looking at where, how and at what cost competitors promote and advertise their properties.
- A consideration of how marketing costs compare with other costs and with competitive costs, and what effect any change or differential in policy would make.
- An assessment of how sales and lettings differ by dint of location or type of use, and why.
- An evaluation of the probable effects of any radical change in the pricing structure of the developers' or competitors' property.

335

- An appraisal of the effect of promotional activity, looking at the effectiveness of advertising copy and placement and the result of incentive schemes to both agents and purchasers.

The product

- What is the company reputation or image for producing quality buildings and providing a good service to purchasers?
- How are previous developments thought of and used, and what features are found to be most important by occupiers?
- Should any changes be made to current or proposed development projects in respect of design, layout, materials or services?
- What property management, legal or planning restrictions might inhibit the ready sales or letting of a development?
- What are the strengths and weaknesses of previous development schemes constructed by the company and by its competitors?

Primary and secondary data

- The data collection phase of marketing research draws on two main sources of information, which are distinguished as primary and secondary sources, or alternatively desk and field research.
- Secondary sources are those that already exist, but consist of data collected for purposes peripheral to the main line of research inquiry in hand, so care must be taken to ensure that the information is relevant, can be adjusted to the present problem and is reliable.
- There are internal and external secondary sources. Internally, agents and developers will have a mass of marketing information available from their own records, and although it is not always collected systematically or in the most appropriate form, modern computerized data-processing systems are making the access to and extrapolation of suitable information easier and faster. Externally, there is a growing wealth of published information from other agents, consultants, professional bodies, trade associations, research organizations and government departments. Secondary sources should be consulted before primary or original research is undertaken.
- Primary or field research will usually cover the potential market demand, occupiers' preferences, the precise characteristics of the actual or proposed development, the terms of sale or letting, and the methods of advertising. Original data of this sort may be collected by observation, experimentation or survey. Observation depends heavily upon the skill and objectivity of the observer. Experimentation is rarely appropriate to the property market. And survey can be time-consuming and expensive.

Marketing research process

Although research projects in the property development market are not susceptible to a single and inflexible sequence of steps, the following procedure is a useful guide (Giles 1978):

- Definition of the problem, a step of the greatest importance, and one treated in a cursory way too often.

- Specification of the information required.
- Design of the research project, taking into account the means of obtaining the information, the availability and skills of staff, the methods to be used and the time and cost involved.
- Construction and testing of any surveys, questionnaires or interviews.
- Execution of the project, with arrangements for a check on the reliability of data collected.
- Analysis of data.
- Preparation of report and formulation of recommendations.

However, it should be recognized that marketing research neither provides a panacea nor guarantees success, but it does assist in improving the quality and confidence of decision-making.

Marketing strategy

Over the past few years there has been a significant shift towards the devising of more formally structured and deeply considered marketing plans for proposed development projects. The advantages of a more rigorous planning process are that diverse marketing activities can be better co-ordinated, crisis management can either be avoided or reduced to a minimum, measurements of performance are easier to conduct against known standards, corrective measures can be applied in sufficient time when required, and participation by all those involved can be encouraged with improved commitment and motivation (Giles 1978).

It has been stated that a marketing plan for property should be much the same as for any other kind of product, in that it needs to.

. . . strive to create the tangible from the intangible and present a concept that will stimulate the imagination of the potential client . . . This simple need becomes more and more difficult to achieve as the weight of communication channels and the material sent to them increases each year. (Watts 1982)

Accepting that the alliteration is a gross over-simplification, a favourite way of remembering the key variables that form the basis or marketing strategy and mix is known as "the four Ps", namely:

- product
- price
- place
- promotion.

A preferred means of describing the most important steps in preparing a marketing plan to take account of the key variables involved in marketing operations can be more fully stated as follows.

Select the right team

In identifying, anticipating and satisfying customer requirements, profitability – the very nub of marketing – it is essential that all those involved in the entire process of development, from inception to completion and through to management afterwards, are selected with a view of optimizing the collective effort of the professional team. The chemistry between those directly concerned with design and construction and those specifically responsible for the actual marketing campaign must be right. It is not productive, for example, to have an architect who is either oblivious or unsympathetic to the advice of the agent, or to have an agent who is uncomprehending or hostile to those designing and building the project. In the past, the formulation of a marketing strategy has all too often been left to the agent acting alone, and invariably too late in the development process.

Identify the target groups

Properly conducted marketing research as outlined in previous sections should have identified the general categories of occupier that might be interested in the scheme in question, and hopefully the actual manufacturing, trading or business organizations who are either actively looking for new or additional accommodation or who might conceivably be enticed into taking or moving premises. Often the most difficult task is to identify and reach the person within the organization responsible for taking the decision.

Agree the message strategy

This involves deciding on how best to present the special sales characteristics of the building, its situation and wider environs. In the rather "whiz-word" riddled world of marketing, this is known as creating the "unique selling proposition" or "USP", and is concerned with striving to convey a concept that will stimulate the imagination of the potential occupier or purchaser. The overriding aim in designing general and specific "USPs" should be to see the whole strategy in terms of how it might benefit the eventual client. This might seem a trifle obvious, but somehow agency practice in the UK has been extremely slow in breaking away from a fairly standard and somewhat impersonal property-oriented approach towards a more original and individually directed user-based approach.

Write a communication plan

Having established the broad "message" about the property that needs to be conveyed, the next step is to plan how best it is communicated. Any "communications plan" will usually combine a variety of direct and indirect selling techniques, called the "marketing mix", all of which require careful orchestration. Direct methods such as the use of brochure, personalized mail shots, targeted circulation lists, exhibitions and agents' receptions will need to be synchronized with indirect methods involving national and local media, side advertising and contact networks within the property industry. Again, these techniques may seem patent and familiar, but the early and co-ordinated planning is often missing. There is also a positive wealth of face-to-face selling expertise accumulated in other fields of marketing that has lain largely untapped by the property profession, and might with advantage be explored and exploited.

Ensure follow-up activity

There are two distinct aspects to following through on the communications plan. First, there are those endeavours that have to be made to stimulate only very mild expressions of interest. And second, there are those efforts to make in converting strong interest into an actual sale and subsequently keep the purchaser content. With the former, an agent marketing a development should be aware that there are several kinds of barriers that may block their ability to communicate and must be overcome, or at least lowered. These are personal barriers, arising from the fact that individuals differ, and different people have to be approached in different ways: organizational barriers, thrown up by administrative structures and hierarchies, so that finding the right person and presenting the case in a corporately acceptable manner becomes even more vital; and mechanical barriers, which exist because some organizations lack the proper points of contact and channels of communication. With the latter, translating a positive response into a trouble-free transaction, it should simply be a matter of competence and professionalism, keeping the customer informed about progress and handling all inquiries and negotiations promptly, efficiently and pleasantly.

Agree a budget

Ascertaining an accurate figure for the total cost of marketing for development is an extremely difficult task. In the first place, however, there is need for a plan in order to determine a budget. From this plan can be extracted the various marketing activities that are proposed. It has been suggested that the following process be adopted (Miles et al. 1991):

- A plan is formulated to promote the product to the target market by the developers and their agents as early as possible in the development process.
- The plan typically begins with a description of the product and the target market, based on earlier market research including statements about how the product will be attractive to the target market and how those responsible for marketing will reach that market.
- As more detail emerges, an extensive checklist of possible activities within each category of the marketing plan is prepared excluding no reasonable ideas.
- A realistic cost estimate for each marketing activity on the checklist is compiled, sparing no expense at this stage.
- The initial total cost estimate is then scrutinized and pared down by examining closely and squeezing tightly every item. Each activity must justify itself, deleting rigorously those that do not, so that, although the net is cast widely, only the best of what is caught is kept.

- Some of the items in this process might be one-time investments, such as fitting out a show unit, and might last the life of the marketing campaign, whereas others, such as brochures, might have to be replaced periodically. Still others will recur continually, such as media charges, which could keep mounting as the campaign intensifies.
- The grand total is estimated, having predicted how long a presence is required in the market and taking account of likely absorption rates.

Another approach, which can be used as a check on the above, is to pose the question of how many new contacts will have to be made and cultivated in order to generate sufficient positive responses to achieve the predicted absorption rate? The cost of making these contacts can then be gauged. Commercial property marketing relies heavily upon this "prospecting" approach, whereas residential sales rely more upon general advertising (Miles et al. 1991).

Yet a further budgeting procedure has been described, termed the "task method" and based upon a four-stage process:

- Market (what is it? where is it?)
- Message (for that market)
- Media (most effect and most direct)
- Measurement (cost effectiveness and results). (Cleavely 1984)

This task method requires objectives to be set as part of the marketing strategy, which can be monitored and plans adjusted according to the degree of success achieved.

In practice, however, it has to be stated that marketing budgets for property development disposals are generally based upon the experience and judgement of the developer and marketing consultants involved. Moreover, it is important that a high degree of flexibility is afforded to allow for the unexpected in the market.

Methods of selling

An agents' prime objective is to sell or let property for the highest price or rent available in the market, not to pursue his own subjective assessment of value. To achieve this, the property must be freely exposed to the market in an orderly manner. The most appropriate method of selling a particular property largely depends upon the nature of the premises concerned and the prevailing market conditions. Four basic methods of property disposal can be distinguished.

Private treaty

Straightaway, it should be stated that the vast majority of all sales and lettings in the overall property market are normally conducted by private treaty. There have been periods when extreme conditions in the market have encouraged such practices as rental tendering, and formal and informal tenders and public auctions are always popular for certain sectors of the market. It has also been known for various kinds of informal tender to be used in order to resolve difficult and competing negotiations, but such recourse is rare. Private treaty is, therefore, the most prevalent method of selling property across all sectors of the development market. It simply involves the setting of an asking price or rent and negotiating to achieve it. As floorspace in most conventional development schemes, either proposed or completed, is bought and sold between property professionals, the basis of assessing a reasonable level of capital or rental value is likely to be very broadly the same. Therefore, so long as the developer and his agent have set the asking price properly, not so high as to stifle offers and not so low as to cause embarrassment and bad feeling by continued negotiation well above that opening price, all should be well. However, there are two main exceptions in the development world where sale by private treaty is not normally the best means of disposal: first, with the sale of land or buildings possessing development potential, but prior to development taking place, where offers will be determined by many variable and unpredictable factors; and, secondly, where the market is especially uncertain or volatile. One renowned residential development on the riverside in London was quickly taken off the market when, much to everyone's surprise, offers massively exceeded the asking prices.

Public auction

This method should, in theory, ensure an orderly market, for, if the property has been properly advertised, it should attract everyone with a serious interest and force them to reach a decision in a competitive atmosphere and with no opportunity to withdraw. The preparation of particulars is critically important with this method of sale, for they must be detailed and accurate, yet enticing. The overwhelming drawback in selling agreed or completed developments at auction is that the major financial institutions are rarely interested in buying at auction. Moreover, they are normally unwilling to provide a firm commitment to a developer wishing to buy potential development properties at auction, unless perhaps the value of the site or the existing buildings is less than, say, £1 million, and only then if most of the uncertainties about the proposed scheme, particularly in respect of planning permission, have already been resolved.

Formal tender

The formal tender, whereby prospective purchasers are invited to submit sealed bids on or by a particular date, is similar to the auction in that all the bids constitute contractual offers that, if accepted, are binding. As with the auction, it is essential to reduce uncertainties to a minimum, and preferably to obtain planning consent beforehand. This not only takes time, but however assiduous the vendor and his agent, there can be no guarantee that the consent obtained is the most valuable possible, and prospective purchasers will bid for what has been approved and not what they think they get. The great advantage of the formal tender is that the highest possible bid for the property should be attracted, whereas at auction even an especially keen or special purchaser only has to exceed the second highest offer. As has been stated:

Formal tenders are particularly attractive for undeveloped land where the planning situation is quite straightforward. Most housebuilders have adequate finance and are well geared up to acquire residential building land at tender, but bidders for industrial and commercial sites normally require funding from institutions and, quite reasonably, institutions are reluctant to enter into funding commitments until the site is secure. (Armon-Jones 1984)

Informal tenders

The informal tender method involves the selling agent inviting single and highest bids, subject to contract, from prospective purchasers attracted by an initial marketing campaign. Because there is an interval between the acceptance of an offer and exchange of contracts, the method is said to be vulnerable to the successful bidder trying to renegotiate the offer once other tenders have been disappointed and possibly withdrawn. Nevertheless, it is argued that in spite of this weakness the informal tender is often the best form of sale for the disposal of development sites. So long as the procedures are clearly established and abided by, full and consistent information given to all potential purchasers, confidentiality maintained between the parties regarding the various schemes proposed prior to tender, satisfactory financial assurances obtained and a package of relevant legal documents circulated to all serious bidders shortly before the closing date, most of the problems can be reduced or eliminated (Armon-Jones 1984). However, the method does depend upon a high degree of trust and respect on both sides.

Market segmentation

It should almost go without saying that the property market is highly diverse. Not only does this apply to the rich variety of occupational markets it seeks to supply, but also to the varying requirements within those markets, the different sales techniques appropriate to different sectors, the inconsistent attitude of differing client bodies and the divergent approaches taken towards marketing adopted by individual estate agency practices. A brief mention about some of the most notable characteristics of the main sectors of the market, therefore, is appropriate.

Shops

In the context of property development, the marketing of shops normally involves the letting of retail space to tenants and often the sale of the entire scheme to a funding institution. Thus, when an agent is selling shops, he is selling to:
- the investing institutions
- the retail industry
- the shopping public.

Inevitably, any financial institution contemplating the funding of a shopping development will want to be assured about the quality of income and the prospects of rental growth in the future. In large planned shopping centres, it will be necessary to show the actual or probable pre-letting of the major anchor units to one of the leading larger national multiples such as Sainsburys, Boots or W. H. Smith. Smaller schemes would need to be presented to an institution, with commensurate letting agreements involving national multiples and regional superstore chains. A clear indication of the likely overall market penetration for the scheme based upon an assessment of the population catchment area, the accessibility to the development and the existing and possible future competition for trade would have to be shown. And a fund would also be interested in the proposed tenant mix, the leasing structure and the proposals for continuing management services. Pre-letting of a significant proportion of space is often a prerequisite.

In marketing shop premises to retailers, regard should obviously be paid to the general design and layout of the scheme, with special emphasis upon such considerations as access, pedestrian flow, transport and parking facilities, and individual traders' market share. They will also want to know who else might be taking space in the scheme, so that they can evaluate the attraction factor of any anchor tenants and assess the probable degrees of competition and complementarity generated by surrounding units. Naturally, an acceptable level of rent and a lease without excessively onerous conditions will carry most weight in persuading a retailer to take space in a scheme. In addition, they will wish to be convinced by the developers' commitment and ability to promote and market the entire development so as to enhance public awareness of it and to provide reliable and effective management to it.

As far as the public are concerned, a shopping development must show itself to be conveniently accessible, offer a wide range and alternative choice of goods and services, and provide or be close to carparking if possible. With larger planned shopping centres it is also important to create a pleasant atmosphere, make available certain facilities such as restaurants and toilets, and increasingly guarantee a safe, clean and secure environment. It also helps if all or most of the space can be let before opening, and vacant units avoided, or at least attractively maintained.

Offices

In the present competitive climate it is becoming ever more incumbent upon the estate agency profession to possess a thorough-going knowledge and understanding of office users' requirements. Both in terms of crude locational space requirements and the required level of functional performance. An agent seeking to market an office development will, therefore, seek to ascertain if he can identify firms within international, national, regional or local markets who:

- might find advantages from "hiving-off" certain activities or departments

to a new location
- would benefit from consolidating already dispersed operations under a single roof or by bringing them in closer proximity to one another
- could effect substantial savings by moving their entire operation to a new location or new building
- are contemplating expansion
- have already made a decision to search for new or additional premises.

These days, it is essential for an agent marketing an office property to know in a fair amount of detail its relative suitability in respect of different kinds of business operation. Such factors as face-to-face contact within and outside an organization; technological communication, like facilities for satellite, telephone, facsimile, computer link-up and visual display units; internal environment, including temperature range and control, natural light and outside views and type and quality of working space; and corporate image, covering such matters as aspect, setting, entrances, reception area, services and other facilities. A prospective occupier will then primarily be interested in cost. Increasingly, office accommodation is considered by commercial organizations in relation to its "all-in cost'. An agent must, therefore, be prepared to quote figures for rates, service charges, cleaning, security, heating, lighting, insurance and other maintenance and repair obligations, in addition to rent.

Industrial property

In addition to many of the considerations described above in respect of the shop and office sectors relating to questions of rent, lease conditions, design, layout and management, there are a few aspects of industrial property marketing that merit special mention. Generally, a potential occupier of industrial premises is more concerned about the performance factors of a building, such as quality of construction, eaves-heights, floor loadings, column spacing, loading and delivery facilities, and access and egress to and from the site and building.

Location is of course paramount, and an agent must have an intimate knowledge of the special labour, market, materials and component needs in terms of accessibility that are demanded by different trades and industries. In the same way, an understanding of the distributional hinterlands and networks commanded by various commodity markets is essential in the sale or letting of warehouse developments.

As with other forms of commercial property development, flexibility is fast becoming the keynote of successful letting. The particular problem encountered in the industrial sector, however, is that flexibility not only applies to the ease with which it is possible to effect physical or functional changes within a building, but also to the freedom allowed an occupier to change the proportion of space given over to a particular use. This is often a matter of planning consent, and too constrained a permission can inhibit the marketability of a scheme. It must be recognized, in addition, that pre-lets are harder to achieve in the industrial sector.

Two other factors are beginning to characterize successful industrial sales and lettings. First, environmental quality both inside and outside factory premises is becoming more important to prospective occupiers. And, secondly, the availability of certain specialist services, whether on an industrial estate, or in close proximity to a particular development, plays a significant part in the decisions taken by industrial space users.

Residential property

At the outset it should be appreciated that residential development of any scale differs in one major respect from commercial property development in that almost all volume housebuilders tend to employ their own sales teams, and have recourse to estate agents as a second line of support, if at all. Because of this, advertising assumes an even more important role in the marketing of housing estates, for there is no network of agents as with the commercial sector, and not the same degree of high street representation as with the second-hand house market.

Prior to development, whoever is responsible for marketing, having established the basic demand for accommodation in the locality, the suitability of the locality, the amenities of the area and the extent of likely competition, is well advised to study former residential sales records in an attempt to find out why any cancellations took place. Non-buying attitudes are critical in the residential sector. Advertising studies, conversely, can show what features and what kind of presentation is most effective in generating interest in a particular development.

The usual method of marketing employed nowadays by the major housebuilders is to fit out and furnish one of the completed properties in a scheme as a show house. This will then be staffed up to six and half or even seven days a week, remembering that the majority of sales are introduced over the weekend. The advantage to the housebuilder is that the rest of the development can be monitored by their own agent, any damage can be made good immediately, access and response to inquirers is almost instant, all the energies of the sales force can be devoted to the one scheme and, in the case of phased development projects, information on reactions and probable market trends can be fed back to the design team. With show houses, it is always worthwhile laying out the garden to a high standard and making sure that the water and heating systems work efficiently.

In the residential sector, the role of aggressive promotion and marketing is probably most telling at either end of the market. Luxury housing is a volatile and unpredictable product. Well targeted, skilfully presented and extensively placed advertising can reap enormous dividends, for it is really a matter of reaching and attracting individual purchasers to whom marginal amounts of money at or around the asking price are of little consequence once they have decided that they want the house or flat in question. High-quality design and finishes, combined with an elegantly furnished and fitted show unit, are also an essential ingredient in successful luxury developments.

At the other end of the market, competition rages to attract the first-time buyer. A key element of marketing strategy for first-time buyer of housing is the availability of mortgages. Virtually all the major housebuilders have agreements with one or more of the main building societies, giving ready access for potential purchasers to mortgage finance. These block allocations are a particularly valuable marketing tool when high demand causes mortgage queues and lending restrictions make it especially hard for first-time buyers. Other inducements offered as part of a marketing package often include one or more of the following:

- payment by the developer of legal fees, survey fees and stamp duty
- payment of a mortgage protection policy for, say, two to three years to ease the burden of worry; this has been extended by at least one volume housebuilder to the taking out, on behalf of the purchaser, of a personal protection policy against possible redundancy
- provision of items of household furniture and equipment such as cooker, washing machine, refrigerator, fully fitted units and carpets; in some small starter units this can even reach to chairs, tables and beds
- removal expenses
- subsidized mortgage repayments for up to one year
- repurchase at guaranteed levels of value.

All these concessions both help the developers cashflow and give momentum to the sales drive. In a mixed development, moreover, the early sale of the smaller units may prove a useful catalyst in stimulating interest in the remainder of higher-priced units in the scheme.

Selling techniques

It has been stated that there are no new methods of marketing property; all that exists are refinements of long-established techniques (Butler 1982). As with any business venture where management skills count every bit as much as the product, perhaps even more, so with the marketing of property developments, for given similar buildings, in roughly the same location and identical promotion budgets, apart from the unexplained foibles of the markets; it can only be the personal qualities of those managing the marketing campaign that make the difference. Nevertheless, a basic understanding of the techniques brought to bear by estate agents in selling floorspace is an essential part of the overall management of development projects.

Public relations

Public relations is a form of untargeted promotion aimed at the public at large. The best generator of good public relations is ultimately the quality of the development itself. Nevertheless, it is important to recognize that property development is rarely a popular activity to those in proximity of a proposed project. They often view development schemes as being physically intrusive, socially damaging and a threat to property values. Therefore, the sensitivity with which property development proposals are handled can greatly affect the acceptability and hence the feasibility of a project.

The very way in which the developers present themselves, the company and the retained consultants to the political representatives, professional officers, the press, interested parties and the general public can all contribute to fostering a favourable impression. Supplying full information and readily responding to criticism in a sympathetic and constructive manner further assists in creating an open and positive climate of opinion. Some developers establish an information office on the site or near the project, hold exhibitions, make presentations, conduct their own consultation exercises and produce a regular newsletter regarding project progress. In fact, every aspect of the selling process described below should be seen as part of a broad public relations campaign aimed at merchandising the development property.

Brochures and particulars

Naturally, both brochures and more simplified forms of property particulars must describe the intended or completed development and convey all the details that a potential occupier might require. Normally this will include some or all of the following:

- a geographical description of the general area, which identifies the precise location of the site or building
- communications facilities such as road, rail, air and water transport to and around the scheme
- for some kinds of development a brief social and economic profile of the area is advisable, covering such matters as shopping, housing, education and recreational facilities, as well as the presence in the vicinity of leading commercial organizations
- property particulars describing the accommodation, giving areas, heights and specification
- a description of the services supplied to the building, such as gas, water, cabling and electricity
- the nature of the interest being marketed, together with a broad explanation of the lease terms and a declaration about the existence of any restrictions to tenure

- an indication of the price or rent being sought
- who to contact, how and where for more information, assistance or appointment to view
- a saving clause to protect the agent and the developer, which might be along the following lines:

> The agents, for themselves and for the vendors or lessors of this property whose agents they are given notice that plans and drawings are for identification purposes only and do not form part of any contract. Measurements and areas are approximate and although believed to be accurate an intending lessee or purchaser must satisfy himself as to their accuracy. No responsibility is taken for any error, omission or misstatement in this brochure which does not constitute or form any part of an offer or contract. No representation or warranty whatever is made or given in this brochure or during any negotiations consequent thereon.

Vogues and styles in brochures have changed over the years, from the crude letting brochures of the 1960s, through to some of the extravagant productions of the 1970s and 1980s, to the full colour, expertly designed and professionally laid-out publications of today. Even these are being edged out or supplemented by audiovisual cassettes and tapes. Nevertheless, the brochure is likely to remain an important marketing aid, and great care is now given to the presentation of information, so that prospective purchasers or tenants can assimilate the relevant facts quickly. There has also been an increasing emphasis over recent years on the use of good graphic designers, artists' impressions for new development, and specialist photography.

As with direct mailing (discussed below) it is vital that the brochure falls into the right hands. It may be necessary to produce more than one brochure during the course of marketing a development scheme. It also pays to attach a reply-paid card simply requiring interested parties to tick a box if they would like to receive further details.

Press advertising

Press advertising obviously is arranged at reaching the potential occupier or his professional advisers. They will, however, usually have different reading habits. The property professional is fairly predictable, and Saturday's scrutiny of the *Estates Gazette* is something of a time-honoured ritual for the commercial agent. The potential occupier is more difficult to divine, and the agent must attempt to gauge, which professions, businesses or trades might be interested in a particular property or unit. Thus, if the space is clearly located and signed to be attractive to architects, then an advertisement in the RIBA *Journal* or in *Building* might evoke a positive response. Similarly, for computing firms, *Computing* or *Informatics* would be appropriate publications and, for advertising agencies, *Cam-*

paign or *Marketing Week*. National press coverage may also catch the attention of the managing director or decision-taker, and do so in a captive situation or reflective mood, as might more specialist publications such as airline club magazines. Again, agents often prefer to design their press advertising to facilitate a direct response by incorporating a reply form to be filled out and returned.

Commonly, agents have recourse to specialist advertising agencies, although some of the very largest firms have established their own in-house advertising departments. A director of one of the country's leading advertising agencies has commented on the best and worst of the output of property advertising copy where internally or externally prepared (Stewart Hunter 1983). The better advertisements were said to stand out from the crowd and break through the "noise" of competing claims on the readers' attention; be characterized by beautiful photography or illustration; have striking or unexpected headlines; and feature the building attractively or, in advertising language, make the product the "hero" of the advertisement. The worst press advertisements were characterized, almost by definition, by having nothing striking about them, and likely to put off readers by virtue of the clutter, poorly laid out detail and unimaginative headlines and illustrations. Generally, moreover, property advertising was criticized as featuring the identity of the agents too prominently and yet also lacking a consistency in establishing a corporate identity.

It is generally recognized that the market has become increasingly sophisticated and developers far more aware of the power of the advertisement, in particular that potential tenants and targeted agents are different markets requiring different techniques. Some further comments by leading advertising agencies make telling, and sometimes contradictory, points about the advertising culture:

- Good design and clever ideas are not enough to sell a product – you've got to understand what is important to the audience.
- The biggest mistake is to go for too complex an image. It needs to be simple to survive what is a very noisy environment.
- You must not be afraid to be bold. The property press has been flooded with run-of-the-mill building adverts with square footages, agents' logos and piles of shopping bags. Your advert has got to be different.
- Any advertisement should be jazzy to look at, but it should be full of information.
- Humour has proved a particularly rich source of inspiration for corporate communication via advertising.
- A good picture highlights both the building itself and its chief asset, its location.
- Because we are always overestimating the importance of product, accepting that the product can take second place to concept allows to take about something other than the air-conditioning or lighting. (Hall 1993)

One of the frustrations facing the advertising industry, however, is that the relative success of different approaches is difficult to quantify and largely remains a matter of speculation. Alongside press advertising is editorial coverage. It often pays to keep journalists informed of market developments, especially for major or unusual schemes. This is best done in the form of a press release accompanied by a good monochrome photograph with caption and forwarded personally to the appropriate journalist.

Direct mailing

The use of carefully targeted mail shots has become an extremely popular form of marketing communication. The main advantages are that: it enables direct contact to be made with individuals in the target occupational group; it is highly selective and it avoids unnecessary circulation; it does not compete at the same time with other advertising messages; it is flexible in terms of geographical area, frequency and design; and it is relatively quick and cheap to produce and distribute.

Mail shots are normally used to support a wider marketing campaign, and should be released to coincide with other advertising ploys, but they may sometimes be the sole method of promotion. It must be remembered, however, that the bulk of direct mail letters end up in the waste-paper basket. They must, therefore, be simply but compellingly written, preferably well illustrated and addressed to a named managing director or finance director marked "personal" to circumvent over-protective secretaries. It is quite common practice for a local mail shot to precede a more widely directed regional or national mailing using one of the better direct mail houses properly briefed.

Despite a certain scepticism on the part of some developers regarding the effectiveness of using one of the growing breed of direct mail houses, a survey conducted by the *Estates Gazette* showed that more than half of the 300 agents polled believed that direct mail was a very useful or essential mix in the marketing strategy of buildings. Only a fifth found the approach less than useful (*Estates Gazette* 1993). Another piece of research showed that more than 67 per cent of business mailing is not opened by the person to whom addressed and almost 60 per cent of direct mail is binned. Naturally, the response rate of a direct mailing list is governed by the accuracy of its targeting, which in turn determines the cost, and it is scarcely surprising that the service found to be most effect by agents, Executive Information Research, was, at around £3.50 per 1000 mailings, considerably more expensive than others, which ranged from £0.59 to £1.59. Moreover, it should almost go without saying that direct mail is only good if a rapid follow-up is undertaken by a professional person. This is normally done over the telephone, in which context it is worth quoting one agent who states:

> I have almost completely abandoned direct mail. Although the cost of telephone marketing is considerably higher, I have been able to persuade my clients to pay because personal targeting is assured, there is a 100 per cent

contact rate, a known response level and it is easier to interpret levels of interest. (ibid.)

Despite the widespread use of the word-processor and the increased facility to "personalize" letters, however, it is quite possible that the effectiveness of the traditional direct mail shot will diminish. Nevertheless, good clear and precise covering letters accompanying other mailed particulars will always be an important marketing tool.

Siteboards and hoardings

Perhaps the most familiar marketing aid is the agent's board, providing on-the-spot advertising of the availability of property. There is a tendency, however, for development sites during the construction period to be weighed down with a welter of different boards – architects, building contractors, engineers and quantity surveyors, as well as developers and agents. In marketing terms they achieve little or nothing, even when sensibly grouped as a single display, unless considerable thought is given to their function and treatment. Moreover, there is often the lingering suspicion in the mind of the client developer that the board on a completed building does more to promote the image of the agent than it does the identity of the development.

However, the contribution made by sale or letting boards to the overall marketing campaign should not be underrated. On a new development such boards can be used not only to state the details of a proposed building or buildings under construction, but be employed as a linking display describing the programme of work and the progress to date. Casual visitors to the site may well be potential occupiers, and be converted into actual tenants by the continuing advertisement.

Over the past few years it is obvious that much greater care has been expended upon the design and location of siteboards by some leading property development companies. Dignified artists' impressions and stylishly presented wording can only help to enhance both the perceived quality of the building and the corporate image of the developer. Nevertheless, it is important to ensure that boards are regularly inspected and maintained, otherwise the opposite reactions might be engendered.

The development in photographic processing, going by the proprietary name of Scanachrome, offers much more scope for creativity and impact in the use of siteboards, letting boards and posters. Large pictorial boards can be produced as massive enlargements of photographic transparencies or prints at a relatively little cost and can have a physical outdoor life of up to 18 months.

Siteboards and hoardings are now popular vehicles for developers who have become increasingly enterprising in their use of the medium. For about £10000 a first-class hoarding can be commissioned for a fairly large development. A site can be made safer and the incidence of graffiti and vandalism reduced. The local

351

community and emerging young artists can also be involved in the content and design of such hoardings. There is now even an annual competition held by the *Estates Gazette* for the best hoarding of the year.

It should be remembered that if a board is larger than $2-3\,m^2$ it requires advertising consent under town planning controls. Some local authorities apply even stricter controls in what are considered to be sensitive environmental areas. The suggestion has also been made that the creative effort expended in the design and positioning of boards may ultimately be thwarted by the planners, who are increasingly resistant to their use (Wilks & Brown 1980). This notion is reinforced by the activity of a growing number of residents' associations and amenity groups who oppose what they see as a proliferation of estate agent boards, which results in "visual pollution'. Hopefully, however, innovation and imagination in siteboard and hoarding design might temper any overreaction to what remains an effective promotion and selling technique.

Demonstration

The residential sector has long relied upon the tangible demonstration of its wares to sell property. No estate development of any size is complete and properly ready for marketing until a furnished and fitted show house or flat is made available for inspection. Over recent years this approach has spread to the office and industrial sectors. Show suits of offices, fully furnished and equipped, are now a common feature of marketing. Some shrewd consultants have even been able to persuade office furniture and equipment suppliers to fit out such show space at no cost. Reception areas are also invariably completed, decorated and "landscaped" to high standards well before final building works are finished. Good housekeeping is important, with windows washed, rubbish cleared and common parts cleaned.

Many major commercial property developers have adopted the principle set by the volume housebuilders and have put their own people on site so that a constant and knowledgeable marketing presence is maintained. This is the kind of service that prospective tenants are coming to expect in the current letting market.

A modern surrogate for on-site demonstration is, of course, the videotape. In producing these, as well as with actual tours of inspection, it is worth recognizing that there is a best way to show someone over the property. Preferred routes should, therefore, be mapped out in advance, and so arranged as to make the first and last impression of the development the most favourable (Butler 1982).

For major schemes, or ones of an especially sensitive nature, an exhibition might be necessary. Apart from displays put on as part of the process of obtaining a planning consent, the majority of exhibits of development projects are prepared as part of corporate promotions in both the public and private sector. It should be appreciated, however, that the mounting of exhibitions or, for that matter, the participation in exhibitions organized by others, is a costly and time-consuming affair.

Television and radio

The use of commercial television to advertise property is still the exception rather than the rule. The principal reason for this is cost, in terms of both preparation and presentation of material. Despite the expense, television is said to offer wide coverage, to be an intrusive medium that is well suited to demonstrating a building to its best advantage, and to be capable of targeting regional audiences with some precision. View data services such as Prestel, Ceefax and Oracle, however, have not proved as successful as was hoped in the marketing of property.

Local radio is beginning to be used fairly extensively for the advertising of property. Opinions vary as to how effective it is. On the one hand, it is reasonably cheap, offers relatively wide coverage and can lend itself to the creative and striking communication of information. On the other, although it might do wonders for the agent's image, it can be argued that the transitory nature of the message is unlikely to sell property. The right people rarely listen, except at the wrong time.

Incentives

Apart from the traditional agents' lunch, and more recently agents' breakfasts and coffee mornings, more and more incentives seem to be on offer in the market. Luxury cars, holidays abroad and additional cash bonuses are all dangled before those who can introduce a successful letting. At the same time, in a difficult market, there is a continuing pressure to offer ever more attractive inducements to prospective occupiers. Rent-free periods, low starting rentals, fitting-out subsidies, reverse premiums and options to break are all employed at the moment, as incentives during negotiations to secure a letting. They should, however, be introduced with care. For it has been pointed out that if a property has been correctly marketed and stands in rental terms on an equal footing with competition, then to use these factors prematurely can often erode the base for negotiation. In addition, it is argued that very seldom is a businessman lured into the market-place purely by marginal short-term financial inducements. If the property is right, and the terms comparatively competitive, the deal should be struck notwithstanding the trappings. Conversely, because they are known to exist in the market, they become expected. In any event they should be properly costed at the outset of the scheme, as should the reception held on completion to launch the building onto the market, whether it has been pre-let or not. This has now become an important part of the promotion campaign, for the agent and funder as well as the developer, and it deserves careful attention. If, for example, it is a pure letting reception, the individual public relations of those concerned with the development should not be allowed to detract from the essential marketing thrust.

Other approaches

More and more firms of estate agents as well as developers and financial institutions are using the service of public relations advisers. With their consumer-based approach, the range and variety of promotional activities are bound to increase. Marketing plans will be more professionally drawn up and more persistently pursued. Special events and novel programmes will become a more common feature of property promotion and marketing.

The use of display models of a development; special naming of a building or the grant of naming rights; the design of a compelling logo and graphics for a project; ground-breaking, topping-out and opening ceremonies with attendant publicity; the use of holograms in demonstration units; special treatment of entrances and common parts; cold calling of possible purchasers; and the despatch or presentation of novelties are all well tried selling techniques. More recently the possibility of using "interactive" or "virtual reality" techniques has been explored by some property developers to market their buildings, so that at the press of a button you can move around the premises and experience different forms of finish, enclosure and fitting out. However, it is costly.

Again, whatever combination of selling techniques is employed, the importance of effective follow-up activity cannot be stressed enough. Few sales are closed quickly, and patience and perseverance are invariably required. Follow-up should not stop once an agreement has been made or a deal struck. It should continue between signing and moving in, and beyond into occupancy. The good name of the developer and the reputation of the agent are themselves integral aspects of present and future promotion, marketing and sales.

Developers' viewpoint

It should be the overriding objective of all developers operating in the private sector to ensure that the buildings they produce are marketable. They must, therefore, concentrate the minds of all the members of the professional team, whether they be architects, engineers, quantity surveyors, builders or whatever, upon the marketing aspects of the project. Thus, from the developers' viewpoint there are several general factors that should be taken into account in planning the marketing campaign for almost any scheme of development.

The choice of agent

The question of marketing and the selection of those who will be responsible for the choice of agent should be made at the earliest possible stage in the development process. It may well be that a potential development site has been introduced by a particular agent. Alternatively, a firm might have been instructed by the developer, or by a prospective occupier, to find a suitable development site because of their special knowledge of the land market in a given locality. In both circumstances the agent concerned might wish to remain associated with the project and undertake the sale or letting. Indeed, it would be surprising if they did not, and in the case of an introduction to a site it is difficult to arrange otherwise. However, they may not be the best firm for the job. In selecting the right agent several questions can be posed:

- *National or local?* A national firm of estate agents will have a broad coverage of markets and a wide range of business and property contacts, but on smaller or more difficult developments they may not be quite so hungry for success. A local firm might be eager to perform, conveniently available and familiar with the local market, but they may lack the necessary knowledge and network of commercial contacts and be unable to supply certain support services. Often a combination of the two is the best solution.
- *Large or small?* Much the same arguments as above apply to the size of estate agency firm retained. It is remarkable, however, how many major developers are increasingly willing to entrust the marketing of very large schemes to very small practices. Again, the answer is often a joint instruction.
- *Firm or individual?* It is important to select and instruct agents with care to ensure that it is not just the right firm, but also the right person within that firm who is fully responsible for selling the property.
- *Regular or infrequent?* Although there are often compelling reasons for sticking with an agent who has performed well in the past and has become accustomed to the individual ways of a given developer, it can sometimes be beneficial to try out someone different. Even in professional circles, familiarity occasionally can breed contempt, and it is always interesting to compare alternative approaches.
- *Generalist or specialist?* Certain estate agents gain a particular reputation for marketing expertise in special fields, either by sector or by geographical area. Even within such broad categories as shops, offices or industrial premises, performance can vary. With very special types of property, such as leisure or hotel projects, it is a brave developer, or perhaps a foolish one, who does not avail himself of special marketing advice.

To get the best out of an agent it is not only necessary to appoint them at the inception of a project, but equally essential to make sure that they are involved at every stage of the development process. In this way, marketing factors are built into the original design and the agent gains a deeper understanding of the nature of the property. Although this close collaboration throughout the period of development is bound to be to the benefit of all concerned, it is nonetheless imperative that there should be clearly defined terms of reference and established levels of responsibility for marketing. This is especially true where two or more agents are instructed.

The marketing campaign

It is a cardinal priority for both the developer and the agent to satisfy themselves that the marketing campaign is property planned and evenly spaced. As has been contended:

> One of the worst offences is the momentous first push, heavy over-exposure and comparative inactivity thereafter. Plan it so that you have a series of nudges rather than one forgettable blast. (Butler 1982)

Another common failing among development companies is the parsimonious allowance made for marketing at appraisal and project planning stages. It is astonishing that, with the enormous capital sums involved and the difficult market conditions that prevail, how little money is made available for marketing. The developer and agent should, therefore, agree on a reasonable budget for promotion and marketing, remembering that smaller, less prominent, buildings will often require a proportionately higher sum spent on selling them than do their larger, more splendid, counterparts.

As already mentioned, the contribution of the public relations firm to the promotion and marketing of property development schemes has grown over the past decade or so. Although the cost of retaining the services of a good firm of public relations consultants is additional to the usual agency commissions incurred, it is worth the developer of any special kind of development, particularly those dependent upon public custom, considering the use of such expertise. However, experience shows that it is advisable to negotiate a fixed fee rather than work to their preferred quantum merit basis. It is also important to make sure that a good working relationship and clearly defined terms of reference are established between the estate agent and the public relations firm, otherwise an element of suspicion can erode the effectiveness of both.

Naturally, a developer will also wish to approve the proposed selling techniques. Without re-examining the relative merits or otherwise of such methods of selling as brochures, videos, press advertising, direct mailing, siteboards, demonstration units, television or radio, a developer should have a basic understanding of the techniques used by estate agents in selling commercial floorspace. At the very least it is necessary to select the right agent in the first place. At best, it promotes a healthy climate of confidence between the agent and developer.

In any event, it is worth restating that there are really no new methods of marketing property, merely refinements of long-established techniques. But with any business venture where management skills count every bit as much as the product, so with the marketing of property developments. For given similar buildings, in roughly the same location and with identical promotion budgets, apart from the foibles of the market, it can only be the personal qualities of those managing the marketing campaign that make the difference.

With potential occupiers becoming increasingly aware of their space requirements, it is important not to present marketing material in too naïve, or even insulting, a manner. Moreover, if sufficient thought is given early enough in the development programme as to what exactly is involved, and where time and money is best expended, it may transpire that some of the traditional avenues or marketing are not necessary.

Monitoring marketing

Once an agent has been instructed and a marketing campaign agreed, it is essential that the developer retains continuing contact with the agent to monitor progress. Regular meetings, at say, monthly intervals, should be held, preferably on site. Moreover, the client developer should always insist that a written report on the previous month's activity is submitted to him at least two days before the meeting. This would itemize all the inquiries that had been made about the property, the names and positions of those inquiring and whether or not any visit to view had been arranged or taken place, and with what result.

Where appropriate, an explanation of why enquirers had not pursued their interest should be included, together with a reasoned argument examining how lettings have taken place in what are seen as directly competing properties. This discipline is not popular with agents, and there might indeed be occasions when excessive adherence to the routine becomes a contrivance. However, formality is easy to relax, but difficult to reassert. The reporting process must, therefore, be seen as a genuine evaluation of progress and not a mere ritual.

The developer will also normally wish to be consulted regarding the presentation and placement of advertising. Although the agent will be more familiar with the various vehicles for promoting the property to the best advantage, it is as well to check that it is the development that has pride of place in an advert, and not the agent's corporate image. Another avenue worth exploring with the agent is the possibility of trailing editorial comment throughout the course of the campaign. It is hard to assess the true value of editorial exposure, but it is free.

There are several other matters worth mentioning regarding the relationship of the developer and the agent during the marketing process. These can be summarized as follows:

- Resist the natural urge to tinker with such matters as the design and format of the brochure or the structure and content of any covering letter. If dissatisfied, reject them; do not compromise.
- Do not be tempted to cut out the agent if an approach is made direct by a potential purchaser/lessee. Always refer such offers to the agent, for there is little purpose served in retaining an agent and conducting negotiations personally. In this way, a secondary negotiating position is reserved.
- Do not change agents midway through marketing unless there are very good reasons for so doing. Continuity is one of the more important ingredients of a marketing campaign. If the service from the agent is thought to be unsatisfactory, it is often better to give them two months' notice to quit or ask

357

them to re-tender for the instructions against a major competitor. It is remarkable how rejuvenating this particular process can be. If, however, the dissatisfaction is deep-seated, then it is better to cut losses and change agents forthwith.

- Decide the degree to which the property will be finished, and what help might be made available to any incoming tenants for fitting out. There is a growing tendency in the office and industrial development sectors, as there always has been in retailing, to complete buildings only to a shell stage. Tenants are then encouraged to select wall, floor and ceiling materials and finishes, with the developer covering the cost up to a predetermined amount. Some developers are even providing free space-planning advice.

- Consider what kind and level of continuing services could be provided by the client and on what basis. It can be argued that, both to generate initial profitability and maintain income flow, the management of commercial property generally needs to be much more aggressive. To some extent, therefore, development does not end once a building is physically completed, but includes the establishment of a property management system.

- Furthermore, in terms of marketing and management, more flexible leases as well as more flexible buildings are being demanded by tenants, particularly by those in the new technology industries and specialized professional services. Tenants are increasingly looking for shorter leases with one-sided break clauses and a range of supporting business and personal services. Thus, good marketing, which has regard to good management, will play an ever more important part in assuring the success of development projects.

- Pay fees promptly, and once agreed do not attempt to renegotiate. There is almost a paradox in the property world whereby an agent achieving a good quick sale or letting is somehow not felt to have earned their fee, whereas the long and costly campaign is in a strange way thought to have shown value for money.

- Consider within the overall context of marketing the corporate image of the client. In these days of greater accountability and ever-growing public awareness, the image a property development company portrays to the public at large is fast becoming one of its more valuable assets. "Public" in this sense refers to the whole professional and commercial milieu in which the company operates. Thus, it includes clients, competitors, local authorities, the news media, financial institutions, construction firms, professional practitioners and prospective purchasers.

In a business that, rightly or wrongly, is not exactly renowned for its high ethical or aesthetic standards, there is good reason for property development companies to ask themselves a few telling questions regarding their corporate image. It has been suggested that these should include the following:

How do we think we are perceived by the public?
How are we actually viewed by them?

How would we wish to be thought of?

What image is most likely to assist us in achieving our objectives?

(Charlesworth-Jones 1983)

Unless, in the unlikely event of all the answers to these questions coinciding, the next proposition should be, "How do we go about designing and implementing a desirable corporate image?". This may involve a change in attitude by members of the company, an advertising campaign, public relations exercises, or even a change of name. In any event, the very act of self-assessment can be both salutary and rewarding.

Conclusion

Innovation in the process of promotion and marketing is bound to happen. What confronts the agency business is the extent to which property professionals can retain command over the sales team. Already we see leading firms of public relations consultants, with their skilful manipulation of the media and their flair for promotional activities, beginning to make incursions into the agency field. As mentioned earlier, specialist firms of property marketing consultants importing American selling techniques are starting to spring up. Advanced systems of information technology with wider and cheaper accessibility, together with new methods of conducting business, all point to changes in the way we buy and sell development and other properties. Education for marketing, both for existing members in practice and for new entrants to the estates profession, will become ever more essential.

Nevertheless, there are no magic formulae to the art of marketing. It is simply a logical stage-by-stage approach that employs a range of techniques and disciplines, and it is the firm that uses all the appropriate techniques and skills that will create the synergy that sells.

PART FIVE

Real estate
development sectors

CHAPTER FIFTEEN
Retail development

For the 30-odd years following the end of the Second World War, retailing was repeatedly heralded as the most innovative and changeable sector of the property market. New types of shop development emerged one after another: department stores, variety shops, supermarkets, covered shopping precincts, hypermarkets, superstores, district centres and discount warehouses. Preferred locations shifted away from the high street, to adjacent central-area sites, out-of-town to greenfield sites, back to peripheral suburban locations and even "sideways" onto industrial estates. Modern forms of merchandising have altered the shape, size and layout of shops of all kinds, and advances in the methods of distribution have affected the design and position of retail outlets. It can be argued, however, that other commercial sectors are displaying a greater metamorphosis at the present time. Nevertheless, there remains considerable volatility in the shop market and a continuing dynamic in the field of retail development.

This chapter is divided into five sections, as follows:
- the context for retail development
- types of retail development
- planning and retailing
- design and layout
- shopping centre management

The context for retail development

As consumers have become increasingly discerning, affluent and mobile, so retailers have had to respond to changing market conditions and opportunities. In forecasting future trends in shopping and shop development it is worth recording briefly some of the more significant factors that have brought about the process of change in retailing over recent years. These can be summarized as follows:
- Food retailing on any scale has almost disappeared from many traditional town centres as superstore operators have relocated to locations on the edge of or out of town, where they can find sites capable of providing 4645–5574 m^2 (50/60000 ft^2) or more of space with extensive carparking facilities.

- The fashion industry has extended its market to embrace every sector of society, whereas only a generation or so ago it was the preserve of the better-off.
- Likewise, eating-out was something of an occasional treat for most people, but over the past couple of decades a revolution has taken place in the catering industry, with a consequent impact upon all forms of retail property development.
- The majority of the population have more money to spend than at any time in the past. They are also more likely to own a car and gain from greater mobility.
- Retailers have become more inventive and competitive in their promotional, marketing and merchandising policies.
- Low inflation and rising shop rents created a favourable climate for retail development in both in- and out-of-town locations during the late 1980s.
- Government attitude towards new types of retailing became more relaxed during the 1980s than previously.
- For most of the past 20 years, the growth of capital investment in UK retailing has outstripped comparable growth rates in almost all other sectors. Investment in shop development has, therefore, enjoyed continued and expanding support from financial institutions and retail operators alike.
- During the 1970s and early 1980s, retailers and developers increasingly detected a consumer need to provide "one-stop" shopping with a collective grouping of retail outlets offering multiple choice within an easily accessible, traffic-free and preferably enclosed environment.
- Speciality trading has emerged during the 1980s as a powerful force in the retail sector, usually at the expense of the department store.
- As a result of re-targeting and redesigning by retailers, floorspace requirements have constantly been changing. Moreover, unit sizes have been affected by new ways of distributing and storing stock.
- Leisure facilities and catering outlets have increasingly been incorporated into planned shopping centres.

Decentralization of shopping, in its many forms, has, and continues to be, the central issue in the planning and development of retail space. The tide of trade flowing away from the high street can neatly be described as occurring in three waves. The first outward wave was that by the food-based superstores to edge- or out-of-town sites. The second wave, now well established, gained momentum towards the end of the 1970s, included retailers selling bulk items such as DIY, furniture and electrical goods. The third wave is represented by the creation of regional and subregional shopping centres, and also includes the drift out of town of groups of major durable goods traders. There is now a determined attempt to reverse this trend back towards the town centre so as to create a fourth wave.

Forecasting and trends

In the context of retailing it has been said that forecasting is much easier than is generally realized, because what the rich do today creates the appetites of the masses in the future (Schiller 1983, McCollum 1985). Moreover, the USA acts as a kind of window into how people will want to work, live and shop in times ahead. There are, however, a few basic ingredients that help determine the likely future nature and mix of retailing, which are described below:

Population changes

Changes in the size, social and age structure of the population have a considerable influence upon property markets. Birthrate, which has been running at less than replacement level since the early 1970s, seems set to remain at a low level. Life expectancy, on the other hand, has increased by two years over the past decade and is steadily rising. Household size appears likely to reduce even further, so that by the year 2000 almost 60 per cent of all households will consist of only one or two people. This all probably means that, with an ageing population and more households, more people will have more time to spend shopping.

Spatial distribution

Although the overall size of the UK population has changed little over the past 20 years and looks fairly stable, if ageing, for the next 10 or so, the spatial distribution is much more variable. Broadly speaking, the only parts of the country where more than 10 per cent population growth is forecast before the end of the century are 13 counties stretching in a band from Lincolnshire, Cambridgeshire and Suffolk in the east, southwestwards through Northamptonshire, Oxfordshire, Buckinghamshire and Berkshire to Wiltshire, Shropshire, Hampshire, Somerset, Dorset and Cornwall in the south and west. These are the areas where more retail floorspace will be required.

Consumer expenditure

Despite the recession of the early 1990s the shopping public in general is becoming more affluent. Although there will be fluctuations in the short run, the longer-run trend seems to suggest that spending will continue to rise faster than inflation. Some of this growing affluence will naturally go into improved housing, additional leisure and better health and education services, but some will undoubtedly go towards increased retail expenditure.

Mobility and accessibility

Car ownership and its effect upon shopping behaviour is probably even more important than is commonly supposed. The number of cars on British roads is increasing by 2–3 per cent annually. Car ownership doubled between 1960 and 1980, and is likely to double again by the early years of the next century. Among all households with children, 72 per cent have a car.

Work and leisure

The average working week in all industries has fallen from around 42 hours in 1973 to about 40 hours in 1985 and is thought, although conflicting figures are produced, to have decreased to under 37 hours by 1995. In the salaried business sector this is probably lower. Nevertheless, more women will probably work, and "moonlighting" will increase. Not only will people have more time to go shopping, and more money to do it with, but shopping will itself become more of a leisure activity.

Information technology

One of the greatest areas of doubt about the future pattern of retailing surrounds the effect that advanced technology might have upon it. Improved communications could revolutionize the comparison, selection and ordering of goods, and considerable advances have already been made in the stocking, distribution and control of merchandise. However, whether or not any profound change will occur in the immediate future is questionable. It is interesting to note, for example, that mail-order shopping has held at a constant of just under 10 per cent of retail expenditure for some years. The proportion of "distance" shopping may change, but is almost certain that most shoppers in the future will shop at the shops.

Consumer demands

Perhaps above all there has been the realization among retailers and developers that it is the customer that calls the tune. The shopping public constantly have to be wooed. They increasingly demand accessible, convenient, secure and enjoyable shopping environments with adequate parking, a wide and comparative range of goods at reasonable prices and the availability of attractive and useful facilities such as food, child care and leisure.

Basic research procedures

As the retail industry has matured, so shopping centre developers have become more and more aware of the need for reliable market research and analysis. Indeed, such retail studies are of benefit to all concerned. To the developers they confirm the degree of potential opportunity, provide a basis for planning application, set design and site layout constraints, furnish basic data for marketing and funding, and provide information vital to the future sale of the property. To the local community they contribute to the development planning and control processes: identifying existing and future shopping needs, allocating land for retail development, examining and catering for infrastructure consequences, assessing the impact of development proposals upon existing shopping facilities, and determining the outcome of applications for shopping schemes. And to prospective retailers they measure the opportunity for new units, sales potential and floor space, as well as assessing the competitive situation (McCollum 1985).

It should be appreciated that market research is not an exact science, for the analyst is essentially presenting a subjective evaluation of a project's potential based upon available data and drawing upon personal experience and judgement. In fact one leading consultant has gone so far as to state that "traditional catchment analysis is a thing of the past" (Maynard 1990). Nevertheless, the basic procedure for conducting a retail market analysis is typically an economic area analysis, a trade area analysis and an appraisal of optimum size and mix for the proposed project (McCollum 1985).

Economic area analysis

Economic area analysis is conducted to determine whether a particular market can support additional retail development and it includes an investigation of:

- *Employment trends* These are critical as the form and level of employment naturally determine the overall purchasing power of the market area.
- *Population forecasts* Such an analysis would lean heavily upon information compiled and used by the planning authority for the area.
- *Income levels* Extracting per capita and family income levels and estimating likely increases is a vital preliminary step in estimating retail expenditures for the area in question.
- *Retail sales data* This study depicts which retail categories have achieved rapid sales growth, which are declining, and how they relate to population and income growth. They are usually divided into comparison or durable goods sales and convenience goods sales.

The prime objective of the economic area analysis, therefore is to reveal the strength and nature of the employment base, the geographical centres of population and potential for population growth, the strongest retail categories, and the sales potential projected for the area. The analysts will then use these data when delineating a trade area and assessing sales potential for a proposed centre.

Trade area analysis

Assuming the economic base study has shown potential growth for the area, a market analysis of the trade area is undertaken to assess the potential of a given site for a shopping centre development. A trade area is the geographic sector for which the sustaining patronage for steady support of a shopping centre is obtained. Also known as the catchment area or hinterland. The boundaries are determined by various factors, including:

- the size and nature of the site itself, as well as character of the surrounding locality
- present and proposed accessibility to the site
- any physical or artificial barriers limiting the site
- the location of competing facilities
- the limitations of travel time and distance.

The total trade area is normally divided into three or more zones as a means to illustrate and assess variations in the impact of the proposed centre by use of established capture or penetration rates. By reference to population, income and capture estimates, total expenditure can be gauged.

Shopping centre sales potential

The principal aim of the market research is to assess the proposed centre's retail sales potential. This demonstrates ultimate profitability and optimum size and mix. There are two basic approaches to estimating sales potential:

- *Share of the market*   This approach essentially assumes that the shopping centre will gain a certain percentage of the total trade area sales potential. Experience, and the analysis of comparable developments in similar situations elsewhere, will indicate the probable proportion of the population falling within the trade area that will be prepared to travel to the proposed centre. An evaluation of the population employment and income data will show how much they might spend and on what.
- *Residual analysis*   The potential trade for a new centre can also be calculated by employing what is variously described as the "vacuum", "residual", or "remainder" method, whereby the total consumer expenditure going to other centres in the vicinity is assessed at first instance. The procedure briefly includes determining the prospective catchment area, gauging the total population by census district, calculating retail expenditure by goods and socio-economic groups, allocating expenditure to more accessible and convenient centres, allowing for local traders' share and estimating the potential trade remaining, for, where positive, the turnover will be available to the new centre, where negative, the area is already overshopped.

Project size and mix

Once total sales potential has been predicted, the need arises to translate this demand into a physical context, in terms of how much floorspace, in how many shops or what type, to determine the size and mix of the centre. This is achieved by use of conversion factors, which simply express turnover per square metre of gross floorspace. These factors display a variation according to broad region and specific locality. Other changing aspects of shopping also play a part in the steady rise of conversion factors: longer shopping hours, the reduction of non-productive space, and improved merchandising.

In the context of retail market research and analysis, it should be stated that over the years there has been a rapid advance in the development of sophisticated techniques that aim to assist in the assessment of the retail hinterland, the measurement of market penetration, and provide some explanation for retail land-use location. These techniques are grouped together as shopping models. They seek to represent a real world situation in terms simple enough to permit examination of past and present shopping patterns and the prediction of future trends.

These models tend to be employed more by planning authorities and major retail organizations than they do by shopping centre developers. Some members of the property profession remain sceptical about the use of advanced techniques of analysis. But more than ever, given the increasingly complex nature of the retail market, the sector needs to be served by good research, not just in the form of quantitative studies, but in respect of customer behaviour and personnel requirements.

Types of retail development

A useful, but less than traditional, classification of shopping centres has been advanced along the following lines:

- Those centres that are free-standing and suburban in location providing for the general-purpose shopping needs of households. They may be neighbourhood, community or regional in terms of catchment, so that the small strip centre and the large super-regional centre are really subtypes of the same category.
- General-purpose centres located in shopping districts, and are sometimes known as renewal or redevelopment centres. Again there are several subtypes according to size and location, as well as their relationship to the shopping district in which they are positioned.
- Multi-use centres, where shopping is only one of several uses within the overall development. Once more there are several kinds of centre within this category, and they tend to be more common in the USA than they are in the UK. However, this might change.
- Those centres where retailing is ancillary to other commercial activities, and is provided to complement the dominant function of the building complex. The so-called subtypes here would be differentiated according to the dominant activity, whether it be hotel, office or transport interchange.
- The speciality centre that concentrates upon a particular theme or tenant mix, sometimes purpose-built and sometimes housed in a renovated building.
- The focused centre, that concentrates upon a particular theme or tenant mix. Sometimes purpose-built and sometimes housed in a renovated building.

No classification completely satisfies the market, but at least the one outlined above helps distinguish between the different processes of development, methods of funding and styles of operation, as well as forms of retailing. It has also been pointed out that different types of centre will succeed in different ways and must, therefore, be assessed accordingly.

In considering the shopping opportunities that have been taken across the various types of retail operation over the past few years, and exploring those that exist to be exploited in the immediate future, attention is paid primarily to the development side of the market rather than to the investment or business prospects of retailing.

The high street

In the high street it is just about possible to forecast the limited revival of the small shop occupied by a local trader. Some of the leading multiples in certain durable goods markets are also looking more closely at good secondary positions rather than their previous prime pitches, bringing with them a new injection of consumer interest and possible redevelopment potential. Moreover, while there appears to be an inevitable decline in the total number of standard units, it is sometimes surprising to discover the high turnover achieved by individual traders in specialized fields. Locally based development companies are also showing more interest in purchasing, refurbishing and reletting single smaller units. Such developers are inclined to be more sensitive to occupiers' needs. Thus, leases are showing some signs of becoming shorter, review periods more regular and user conditions less onerous. In this way, the rate at which the trading mix of high streets changes is likely to quicken.

Other avenues for possible development in the high street can be summarized as follows:

- The acquisition and exploitation of land to the rear of high street shops to allow for the creation of stores with large floorspace and high street access, but where wide high street frontage for display is not a principal requirement.
- The assembly of several deep standard units, with or without additional rear land, in order to create small malls or precincts branching off the high street.
- The refurbishment of existing units to provide more suitable retail space for the changing needs of multiple traders.
- The incremental upgrading of side streets to the high street to establish a kind of "Latin Quarter" atmosphere, with a grouping of complementary service trades.
- Capitalizing upon the pedestrianization of high streets or adjoining thoroughfares to refurbish or redevelop otherwise redundant or deteriorating premises.
- The renovation and conversion of historic buildings, or buildings of special architectural merit, to produce a type of speciality centre, probably incorporating some form of catering and leisure facility.
- Some braver developers have contemplated the creation of multi-level trading through the conversion of existing high street stores, normally in absolutely prime positions.

Uncertainty engendered by recession heightened the debate on the future of the high street, one element of which is the role that the major retailers play. The increased concentration of ownership and occupation of the high streets in the UK has been said to have brought both benefits and drawbacks (Bernard Thorpe & OIRM 1990). On the plus side, it has seen an immeasurable improvement in the internal and external appearance of shops, the product ranges on offer and the general ambience of shopping. On the minus side, the further decline of independent shops and a wider assortment of multiple retailers has led to a loss of variety and the "higgledy-piggledy" character of older, traditional high streets. It has also been suggested that the 1990s will be the decade of the pan-European retail multiple, and expansion by retailers across national boundaries is already established (Knee 1990). The implications for Britain's high streets is thought to be encouraging, in that a wider variety of multiple trading names will appear, with new standards of shop design and quality of merchandise, provided, that is, that the Europeans accept what are to them unusual leasing and rent review formats.

It cannot be denied, however, that the town centre in general and the high street in particular, face a challenge from accessible, convenient and secure out-of-town centres. Nevertheless, as has been maintained, the disappearance of food retailing from the town centre has been more than compensated for by the opportunity for extra retail floor space for those traders specializing in comparison and durable goods. Moreover, major retailers and investors have enormous capital values and commitments locked into town centres and thereby have a strong vested interest in protecting and preserving their assets for the future. This challenge can be met, but it requires local authorities to address the problems of their town centres on a comprehensive basis. The lessons learned and experience gained from the private sector management of planned shopping centres could be more widely applied to existing traditional town centres.

Speciality centres

Perhaps one of the most exciting areas of retail development facing the property industry over the next decade is the further growth of speciality centres. These centres characteristically are close to prime locations, have no particular anchor tenant, tend to concentrate upon providing a carefully selected mix of retailers, have a high proportion of small units, and place the accent upon high-class merchandise. In addition, great attention is paid to layout, design and finishes in order to give a more friendly and comfortable atmosphere than that experienced in most forms of planned centre.

Most speciality centres aim to attract the better-off shopper willing to spend their income on goods they believe they "want" to buy rather than "need" to buy. Much of floorspace is normally given over to various forms of catering, often around 40 per cent, and the design and environment of the centre usually directed towards a particular theme intended to generate a "shopping experience". The tenant mix tends to favour the small independent retailer, often holding on short-term leases or even inclusive licences. New and expanding traders can, therefore, secure representation in or near town centres away from the competition of the high street and the multiple traders.

Intensive management is essential to the success of a speciality centre. It must be imaginative, flexible and highly involved in the trader's business. One of the problems in this respect is that service charges in speciality centres are inclined to be high, and developers state that they sometimes experience difficulties in demonstrating to tenants the validity of these costs. Such centres also need to be promoted continuously by both advertising campaigns and the staging of live entertainment.

The need for strong and committed management combined with a relative lack of comparable schemes to analyze and appraise has led to a certain degree of institutional caution in terms of investment, and funding is not always easy to obtain. Nevertheless, as standing investments they currently trade at somewhere above more traditional shopping centre yields, although there is evidence that as the market becomes more familiar with them as investment propositions, and witnesses a pattern of good rental growth, these yields are falling. It is probable, therefore, that the speciality centre will play a leading part in helping to retain shopper loyalty to traditional town centres.

One form of speciality shopping that has emerged is "festival" shopping. This has been described as a completely new type of shopping, because people do not go to festival schemes exclusively for shopping, but for the pleasure of visiting. At least 60 per cent of visitors to such projects give the major reason for their trip as "browsing", and only 10–15 per cent go primarily to shop. Familiar in the USA since the beginning of the 1970s, and with Covent Garden an early example in the UK, other schemes such as the Albert Dock, Ocean Village, Cutlers Wharf and Quayside have followed. These schemes are said to accept not only the challenges of a new form of retailing and of a flagship role in urban regeneration, but also of an entirely new approach to retail property development and management (Brown 1990).

Another form of specialized retail development spreading across the USA, and beginning to appear in the UK, is what is known as the "category killer" 1858 to $2787\,m^2$ (20000–30000 ft^2) stores concentrating on such single-product areas as sports, office products and books.

Planned central area schemes

The glamorous end of retail development is unquestionably the planned central area scheme, and it is here that opinions as to future opportunities vary widely. On the one hand, there are those who point to the long and uncertain gestation period, front heavy infrastructure and holding costs, complicated site assembly, political sensitivity and high operating costs attached to such projects. On the other, it has been estimated that about 25 per cent of towns up and down the country remain to be "done'. Moreover, many towns that built centres in the 1960s and early 1970s are now ready to embark upon further phases, and many these centres are already in the course of refurbishment.

What does seem certain is that, where planned shopping centres are developed, they will be smaller, more sensitively handled and afford greater energy efficiency. Many will incorporate elements of renewal and conservation in their basic design, others may concentrate upon the complete redevelopment and upgrading of existing older but outdated planned centres.

A few trends can be discerned. There will be less food shopping, apart from catering, which will increase, and the accent will be placed more upon creating a shopping "experience" with a greater selection and better quality of goods. Centres will depend less and less upon department or variety stores as anchors in the way that they have previously done. More attention will be paid to good management and a satisfactory tenant mix. Turnover rents will become more popular and local traders made more welcome. Leisure and recreation facilities will also figure more prominently.

It has been stated that the early 1990s have already witnessed a tremendous improvement in the general ambience of shopping centres, with vastly better detailed design and good use of natural and artificial lighting. They are friendlier, safer and more security conscious places for the shopper. Great advances have been made in improving the external appearances of the buildings. The difficulty is that the main planned town centre schemes form possibly the largest buildings that will ever be constructed in many towns and are prone to appear monolithic.

In assessing the potential performance of a planned shopping centre, there are factors that have been called the "seven secrets of success" (Ringer 1989). Most of these are dealt with a little later in the chapter, but can usefully be listed here:

- *Location* Shoppers must be able to get in and out of shopping centres with ease, and therefore access for both car and public transport is vital.
- *Planning* This relates to the movement of people around the shopping centre, optimizing the flow of pedestrians and maximizing the total potential of all units.
- *Design* The shopping centre must understand its target audience and then address them through design solutions that create a unique image and communicate the identity of the centre to the public.
- *Amenities* This really includes everything from well lit and safe carparks, through to toilet, crèche, and facilities for disabled persons, so that customers feel good about being within the centre, stay longer and spend more.
- *Mix* The tenant mix should be focused on the target audience, with the developer thinking like a retailer and planning the centre layout as one big department store.
- *Programming* Shopping centre owners, in conjunction with the tenants, should ensure a promotion events programme throughout the year.
- *Management* The centre must be kept clean and safe, with a sense of common purpose shared by the management and the tenants.

The point has been well made that the coming years will undoubtedly reveal increasingly discriminating consumer tastes, which will need to be assessed by research into community needs and implemented by centre management teams ready to run shopping centres as dynamic businesses (Ringer 1989). Developers and landlords who ignore this approach do so at their peril.

District centres

Perhaps the least contentious retail development is the district centre, apparently popular with planners, developers, shoppers, traders and financiers alike. Serving a catchment area of anything between 20000 and 120000 population, but usually around 50000, it normally provides about 9290 to 18580 m^2 (100000 to 200000 ft^2) of retail floorspace comprising anything from 20 to 40 standard units built around a superstore and invariably a few civic facilities such as a library, health centre or sports hall. Occasionally, the term "district centre" is something of a euphemism, being coined by a superstore operator to gain a more favourable response from a planning authority. But despite their seeming acceptance by planning authorities, it could be argued that they pose a greater threat to the traditional high street than do single free-standing superstores.

More constructively, however, the suggestion has been made that the development of district centres in declining inner-city areas could be used as a catalyst to help regenerate the local economy. The idea would be for the land to be made available by the local authority and for a consortia of retail operators to underwrite the scheme with their covenants, with the smaller traders anchored and supported by a major superstore.

Superstores

Once anathema to planners, the superstore or hypermarket has now established itself in the shopping hierarchy. Between 1983 and 1993 the number of superstores operated by the "big four" grew from 178 to 667, as in Table 15.1.

Table 15.1   Superstore size and share.

	1983	1993	Sales area (million ft^2)	Market share, 1993 (%)
Sainsbury	15	186	14.2	14.1
Tesco	79	198	11.4	13.3
Argyll	13	94	8.9	8.7
Asda	71	189	8.2	8.1

Sources: Argyll, Management Horizons and Henderson Crosthwaite.

These four operators have spent £14.4 billion on new stores over the same period and now account for more than half of UK food sales. Various estimations have been made as to the number of locations that could support additional superstores in the UK, but somewhere around 200 to 250 extra developments would seem feasible.

The ideal state-of-the-art superstore has been described as fulfilling the following criteria (Hawking 1992):

- catchment population: minimum of 20000 people
- competition: provision of floorspace and potential trade must be in balance

- location: strategic, preferably stand-alone, positioned on arterial roads
- site acreage: six to eight acres of flat land (maximum slope 1:50)
- carparking: minimum of one space per $9\,m^2$ ($100\,ft^2$) gross
- store size: between $4180-6040\,m^2$ ($45\,000$ to $65\,000\,ft^2$) gross area
- access: "comfortable driving': roundabout or traffic-light junction, clearly signed and visible
- servicing: separate and secure servicing capable of easy access and manoeuvring; able to accommodate three articulated vehicles
- petrol filling station: located on the main exit

The superstore has become more and more accepted as a part of everyday life, and arguably many of the initial fears voiced by planning authorities about the effect of such stores on existing town centres have not really materialized. Indeed, some positive advantages have been experienced in terms of taking the pressure of excessive traffic off many older town centres. Car-borne customers also demand the convenience, quality and service they provide.

Despite the recession of the early 1990s, the pace of expansion of superstores has scarcely slackened, and rental growth and institutional investment interest, where available, has remained buoyant. One reason for this high level of activity is that leading superstore operators frequently act as their own developers, and are not dependent on the vagaries of the financial markets, raising substantial sums through internal cashflow. It has been pointed out, however, that the continuing proliferation of new stores is not just being undertaken for the fun of it. The retailers are not only planning to satisfy what they still see as an expanding market, but there is also an element of "spoiling", whereby they seek to deny rivals access to promising new market areas, to secure sites that are not immediately profitable, and to push up market share by invading territory occupied by competitors (Cole 1993).

Nevertheless, the spread of the discount retail warehouse dealing in food goods, and more recently the advent of the warehouse club, could challenge the pre-eminence of the superstore in the shopping hierarchy.

Retail warehouses

To some extent, superstores have been replaced as the "bête-noir" of planning authorities by retail warehouses. These can best be defined as single-level self-contained retail stores, selling non-food goods, often specializing in a particular trade, with at least $929\,m^2$ ($10\,000\,ft^2$) of floorspace occupying a warehouse or industrial-type building and supported by a carpark. Usually they are around $2322-4645\,m^2$ ($25\,000$ to $50\,000\,ft^2$) in size, and demand a large catchment area of about $100\,000$ population within a 30 minute drive time. Because they concentrate on bulky goods, such as furniture and electrical appliances, out-of-centre locations are required.

The original concept of retail warehousing has seen significant change during its short evolution. Initially, such developments consisted of scattered units, often trading with planning battles unresolved, tucked away on industrial estates, invariably with inadequate parking. They have quickly developed to such an extent that most recent arrivals can be found on new out-of-town retail parks, which provide purpose-built units allowing the warehouse retailers to congregate together. They also permit enough space for retailers to shop-fit the frontage to their own design and fit-out the interiors, which are now used predominantly for retailing as opposed to storage. The whole development is normally surrounded by numbers of carparking spaces undreamed of in the early 1970s. As experience of retail warehouse development grows, so characteristic features emerge in terms of their specification and design. These can be summarized as follows:

- Location is the single most important factor, with an optimum balance between accessibility, hinterland and visibility. A catchment population of 70000 within a minimum drive time of 20 minutes is seen as a minimum.
- Some traders prefer a cluster of complementary retail outlets, and others are perfectly happy with a single free-standing unit.
- Many retailers avoid high-standard specifications and adhere to a "keep-it-simple" approach towards their stores' interiors. However, corporate image is considered important by all.
- As a general rule, pitched roofs tend to be unpopular, because they are difficult to "sign'.
- Direct access and exposure to surface carparking is essential, and an ideal ratio is one space to $19\,m^2$ ($200\,ft^2$), which can be lower in a large retail park where parking facilities can be shared.
- Attention to the internal layout, configuration and subdivision of buildings at design stage is critical. In a park scheme, the design must be flexible enough to allow for a range of unit sizes from, say 464 to $4645\,m^2$ (5000 to $50000\,ft^2$), with a frontage to depth ratio of at least 1:2.
- An increasing number of retailers are incorporating some kind of catering facilities.
- Service vehicles should be separated from customer carparking.
- Pedestrian movement must be facilitated.
- Retail warehouse park layouts have progressed from the initial simple "parade" of units, to a more efficient use of site area by utilizing shared parking between the different units forming two parallel blocks or occasionally an "L" or "U" shaped plan form.
- With regard to tenant mix, an ideal size for a retail warehouse park has been suggested at around $11613\,m^3$ ($125000\,ft^2$) typically comprising (Fletcher King 1989):

DIY and garden centre	$3250\,m^2 +$ ($35000\,ft^2$)
Carpets	$930–2300\,m^2$ ($10–25000\,ft^2$)
Furniture	$2800–3700\,m^2$ ($30–40000\,ft^2$)
Auto	$1400\,m^2$ ($15000\,ft^2$)
Electrical	$650–930\,m^2$ ($7–10000\,ft^2$)

This produces a well balanced park with a variety of users and building size.

- The environment, in terms of landscaping, around retail warehouse parks, is beginning to be improved and some older parks are now being upgraded. As the trend for integrating leisure and retail facilities continues, however, the environmental factor will become increasingly important.
- Building specification has advanced and corporate image has become increasingly significant to retailers who have developed readily identifiable logos, colours and house styles. This is due to both mature traders entering the market and institutional investors setting high standards of building design.
- Pro-active management, earlier neglected in the sector's rapid expansion, is now more and more common.
- Specialist themed retail warehouse parks around a particular use might be the next phase of development.
- The discount food sector seems set to expand, with additional retailers operating simple shop fit, low capital, low storage cost, high-intensity and minimal staff expense outlets.
- The most recent arrival in the discount warehouse sector is the warehouse club, led by Costco, which, although legally not within the strict definition of retailing, are destined to develop as part of the shopping hierarchy.

The 1990s have been christened the "discount decade", and overall the amount of floorspace developed for retail warehousing of one kind another seems destined to grow.

Department stores

The difficulties facing department stores are generally well known and virtually all major operators have experienced serious trading problems since the mid-1980s, mainly as a result of the costly nature of this type of retailing operation. However, these retailing difficulties give rise to some unusual and exciting redevelopment opportunities. The growth in the use of concessions and franchising, promoting the concept of a store within a store, is not a development activity in the true property sense, but a business reorganization along these lines often forms part of a larger redevelopment programme. It also provides more flexibility for achieving an optimum tenant mix within a single large store than within a planned shopping centre comprising many separate shop units. Management services are also easier to co-ordinate.

Many stores came onto the market as a result of the rationalization of the major chains of department store operators. This released development potential, and some interesting schemes have been undertaken. One of the main problems in effecting a redevelopment of department stores is the preponderance of upper floorspace, but a mixed development of offices above retail space on the ground floor is the conventional solution, although the office space so created is often far less than ideal.

In the cyclical way of things, the department store is enjoying something of a revival. The major reasons for this are (Hall 1993):

- A long-standing appeal remains based upon familiarity and confidence.
- Many specialist traders have performed poorly by comparison.
- They did not embark on highly expansionist programmes prior to the recession.
- Many held property on a freehold basis in good locations.
- Their targeted customer base tends to be older and less financially affected by the recession.
- The massive expansion in shopping centre development during the 1980s benefited many stores, with developers eager to lure them into projects at concessionary rates to secure funding and specialist traders.
- Most stores reorganized themselves, often along North American lines, with the removal of certain product lines, including food, once considered fundamental to the traditional department store, and replacing them with a wider range of clothing, footwear, accessories and homeware. Reliance upon concessions was greatly reduced. Thus, many have become large-space speciality retailers appealing to the mass market for mid-price family and home fashions.
- They offer good staffing levels, delivery and after sales service, and also provide such amenities as toilets.

Generally, the changing demographic pattern of an increasingly ageing population is favourable to the future of the revamped department store.

Arcades

Since the mid-1980s the shopping arcade has been resurrected. Built originally on narrow strips of land, usually connecting two main streets, by developers anxious to optimize the use of land or owners seeking to prevent incursion or misuse of their property, they often now occupy prime positions and command high pedestrian flows. Probably the best known of all is the Burlington Arcade connecting Piccadilly with Burlington Gardens, but other notable ones that have been refurbished include the nearby Royal Arcade, the Great Western Shopping Arcade in Birmingham, and the Barton Arcade in Manchester. Units tend to be small, with as little as $11.6 \, m^2$ ($125 \, ft^2$) on the ground floor, and frequently have a basement and two upper floors. However, rents can be high.

Leases are frequently shorter than usual, at around 15 years, and landlords have come to accept that, as they attract specialist traders and not multiples, there can be more problems, and greater understanding must be afforded. Arcades also need very careful and positive management, but where this has been provided there are definite signs of it paying off.

377

Regional shopping centres

In many countries the decentralization of comparison shopping has been accommodated in regional shopping centres. Until the mid-1980s, with the notable exception of Brent Cross in north London, attempts to develop regional shopping centres were thwarted, largely on planning grounds due to their presumed impact upon established town centres. However, the outlook for such centres changed dramatically from about 1985.

New regional shopping centres, strategically located close to the national motorway network and intended to serve an extensive catchment population, became an important feature of retailing in the early 1990s. Such centres comprise $100000\,m^2$ (1 million ft^2 or above) or more of purpose-built retail floor area on a site of 40–60 ha (100 to 150 acres) with a minimum of 5000, and more usually 10000 to 13000 carparking spaces at surface level. It has been argued, moreover, that regional shopping centres must be worthy contenders and an alternative to existing town and city centres. Both Brent Cross and Metro Centre have shown that tradition can eventually be created where none previously existed. The tenant mix, therefore, must be a response to consumer requirements and not just a reflection of the development team's aspirations. It should blend the results of research and experience, from which there has been a welcome and understandable desire to break away from look-alike centres occupied almost exclusively by well known multiples who are controlled by a handful of companies (Hammond 1989).

Leisure has also figured large in the design of regional shopping centres. A good example of this can be seen in the Lakeside scheme at Thurrock in Essex, developed by Capital and Counties. Here, a children's ice rink and landscaped area with a water feature forms the focal emphasis of the central mall. The rink can also be used for promotional events. There is also an Enchanted Forest where smaller children can be left under supervision, a Water World for older children, a multi-screen cinema and a range of theme restaurants and small cafés. Because leisure and catering facilities encourage customers to stay longer, there are as many as 13000 parking spaces. Great care is also taken to locate carparking, model the slope of the land, and design entrances and walkways so as to maximize pedestrian flow equally around the two levels of the centre. The developers recognize that shopping is becoming a leisure activity, and the potential uniformity of shopping malls underlines the need for each of them to be presented as a stylish and individual package.

Although an examination of the potential for regional shopping centre development has suggested that there is capacity for around 35 to 40 full-size schemes in Great Britain, with a third of these in London and the outer Metropolitan area, the number of regional centres opening in the next decade is likely to be severely limited because government planning guidelines towards such out-of-town shopping have become extremely restrictive (Roger Tym 1993).

Planning and retailing

Straightaway, it is tempting to suggest that planners should be more agnostic in their attitudes towards shopping, less afraid of innovation and change, and more prepared to accept the positive part that retail development can play in sustaining the urban economy. Developers, conversely should be more sympathetic to the environmental impact of their projects and sensitive to the needs of the less mobile members of the community. All too often there has been a lack of understanding between local planning authorities and retail developers. The former are seen as prepossessed with protecting and reinforcing the existing shopping hierarchy, whereas the latter are viewed as being narrowly occupied with exploiting a particular trading position for their own gain. There are, of course, merits in both cases, and it is probably fair to say that, of late, much more common ground between the parties has been found.

Development plans

Shopping, as a sector, is prone to sudden and dramatic changes in location, layout, design and operation. Planning authorities, therefore, need to display a fast response towards shifts in retail fashion, facilitating desirable new modes of shopping in line with consumer preference, and controlling the worse excesses of an unfettered competitive market. Some of the major problem areas where planning and development agencies collide can be summarized as follows:
- the development of superstores, retail warehouse parks and regional shopping centres
- the location of retail outlets outside established shopping districts
- the development of large non-food stores
- the loss of local shops and rural shops
- maintenance of a hierarchy of shopping districts
- regeneration of inner-city areas
- urban conservation
- traffic management within established shopping districts
- maintenance of viable shopping districts
- shopping provision on industrial estates.

From the viewpoint of the development industry, those development plans that reflect a traditional shopping hierarchy based upon selective and tightly controlled strategic centres should be re-examined in the face of changing consumer mobility and fluctuations in the economics of shopping development and retail trading. Specialist advice of a kind rarely sought, operational not merely analytical, should be incorporated at plan preparation stage and referred to at regular intervals during implementation. One of the sorrier aspects of retailing in development planning is said to be the conflict that occurs between strategic and local planning authorities. Dissonance of this kind is said not only to produce market uncertainty but

also to discredit the machinery of planning and lower the credibility of the authorities involved. Local government boundary changes may ameliorate this.

From a planning perspective, however, the government has produced guidance reflecting a plan-led approach towards development and reaffirming its
belief that town centres should remain the anchor of the retailing system This
guidance is set down in the revised PPG6 (PPG6) published in July 1993, which
has the main objectives of:

- supporting competition in the retail industry within a clear planning framework
- creating a planning system that was positive about the role of town centres,
  with development plans positive rather than prescriptive
- ensuring that when local authorities judged proposals for retail development,
  these were refused only on grounds of impact if clear evidence exists that
  the development would undermine the vitality and viability of existing town
  centres
- strongly support town centre initiatives, including town centre management
  and strategies for transport and environmental improvements.

The implications of the new PPG6 for the retail development industry are examined in more detail elsewhere, but some of the major issues can be summarized
as follows (Raggett 1993):

- Local authorities will be expected to provide leadership, to facilitate partnership with property owners and to generate civic pride, all within the context of the local plan.
- It is recognized that vitality and viability will be difficult to assess in preparing
  development plans and determining planning applications, but unusually
  assessments of commercial yield and pedestrian flow will be the main criteria.
- Other commercial indicators are also recommended, including retailer representation and mix, levels of and changes in retailer demand, and vacancy
  rates.
- The physical structure of the centre and diversity of uses are seen to be relevant factors.
- Local authorities are expected to provide a choice of retail sites, both in
  and out of town, through their local plan.
- Where plans are up-to-date, and follow the guidance, retail proposals on
  sites allocated for other uses will not normally now be allowed.
- Out-of-town retail development is identified as an option for those centres
  facing congestion, but only if the problem cannot be tackled in any other way.
- Edge of centre superstores or supermarkets are favoured for small towns,
  and the risk of existing stores or district centres closing is regarded as a
  major consideration when assessing out-of-town retail proposals.
- The common use of planning conditions restricting the range of goods sold
  to protect the character of retail developments over time is supported, but
  the use of agreements to keep existing town centre stores open as part of
  an approval is discouraged.

- With regard to out-of-town regional shopping centre development, PPG6 is pessimistic about their prospects unless they are supported by the structure and local plan process. Further, they will be supported only if significant population or expenditure growth is likely; private sector investment in nearby town centres is unlikely to be jeopardized any green belt or other environmental loss can be justified by economic and social benefits; public transport can adequately service a wide population; and there is an acceptable impact on the road network. Environmental, transport and economic assessments will also be required.

Probably the most uncertain and potentially contentious issues relate to the interpretation of the terms "vitality" and "viability" in assessing the impact of large-scale development proposals on existing town centres. This, in turn, has raised the whole question of the use of retail impact assessment techniques. Shopping models, of both the manual and gravity variety, extensively employed in the 1960s and 1970s to forecast the effect of superstores, have been disinterred and employed to predict the consequences of "mega-centre" proposals on existing shopping patterns. A strictly quantitative approach can lead to problems where even small variations in assumptions about trends in turnover, population, expenditure and the efficiency of use of existing floorspace can lead to a wide range of forecasts. Impact assessment has thus been described as an inexact science coloured by the subjectivity of its users, a better practice being to afford greater weight to a qualitative analysis centre-based survey approach that is simple, robust and pragmatic. This is explained elsewhere and involves the construction of an "index of vitality" based upon a comparative study of certain main indicators such as:

a. relative rental levels in centres;
b. vacancy and occupancy rates;
c. relative branch performance of major retailers;
d. level of retailer representation and retail mix;
e. presence of covered malls, speciality centres and new shopping centre proposals;
f. presence of pedestrianization schemes;
g. relative access to the centres for both public and private transport;
h. level of carparking in the centres relative to their net retail floorspace;
i. health of secondary shopping areas;
j. presence of town centre management and promotion schemes;
k. presence of other unique attractions such as tourism, conference venues, cinemas, theatres; and
l. the size of the local town or town centre employment base.

(Norris & Jones 1993, URBED 1994)

This is argued to provide a more detailed insight into the local property market, which should make a significant contribution to the decision-making process at appeal.

Future planning policy for shopping centres

In its objective to preserve town centres and restrict out-of-town retail developments, the DOE received much encouragement from the House of Commons Environment Committee Report on shopping centres published in November 1994. Reinforcing the guidelines set down in PPG6 (DOE 1993a), the report's main recommendations can be summarized as follows:

- Where there is a suitable site either in or on the fringe of the town centre, an out-of-town scheme should not receive planning permission.
- Restrictions should be placed on the type of goods that retail warehouses could sell.
- Local authorities should consider the appointment of a Town Centre Manager at a senior level as a means of mobilizing and co-ordinating activities to improve the shopping environment.
- Adequate finance should be made available for the revitalization of town centres by exploring more fully grant aid, private partnership, tax relief or business rate allocation options.
- Improved arrangements for planning authorities to collaborate over transport planning should be made.
- Better guidance should be given to planning inspectors to improve consistency in policy.
- The problem of the lack of retail expertise and resources possessed by most local authorities in the assessment of development proposals should be addressed.
- Greater control over architectural and merchandising aspects of factory outlet centres should be exercised. However, warehouse club activities should be treated as "normal" retailing operations.
- There should be further clarification of "planning gain" and an endorsement of the principle that no amount of planning gain should render an unacceptable scheme as acceptable.
- In recognition of the reality that certain towns are over-supplied with shops, there is a need to develop policies that "plan for decline".
- Public transport policies should be pursued to reduce reliance on the car.
- Environmental assessments should be provided in the case of retail developments that have a significant effect on the environment.
- There is a need for better quality data and research on retailing.

Few of the Committee's proposals are radical. Mainly, they are an extension of the government's policies relating to town centres and the use of the car. They do, nevertheless, represent a strengthening and growing opinion that out-of-town retailing is acceptable only if it is not detrimental to town centres.

Other planning considerations

An important, although at times forgotten, feature of retail development relates to the level of employment generated by new shopping schemes. Even a small superstore of around $3787\,m^2$ ($40000\,ft^2$) can provide up to 150 full-time equivalent jobs and a hypermarket of $4645\,m^2$ ($50000\,ft^2$) as many as 220. Larger superstores can create work for anything from 300 to 700 people and even most of the new DIY stores employ about 20 to 30 people for every $929\,m^2$ ($10000\,ft^2$). Even more attractive in employment terms is the fact that these jobs are largely aimed at the young, the unskilled and those seeking part-time work. Furthermore, the development of an individual shopping project will usually have multiplier effects in the locality, generating demand for local goods and services and attracting other employers and business to the area. Case studies of two of the earliest hypermarket developments in the UK tend to support this view, although it is pointed out that any losses in employment are often geographically dispersed and therefore not so noticeable.

Not only is the retail sector of the commercial property development market the one in which local planning authorities have become most involved; it is also the one where most opportunity now exists for the extraction of planning gain from individual private development projects or the provision of community benefits in partnership schemes. Leisure and recreation facilities have been a popular addition to many new town centre schemes, and superstore operators have probably shown themselves to be among the most generous and flexible providers of planning gains. Such negotiations need to be carefully prepared and conducted.

Shopping patterns are particularly sensitive to significant changes in road networks and parking provisions. The requirement to refer planning applications for shop developments bordering major roads to highway authorities has often proved to be a rich source of frustrating and expensive delay. Major superstore operators are especially wary about traffic problems when prospecting for sites, and will usually be willing to make the necessary contributions to upgrade a local road network and create a good access. Nevertheless, some local planning authorities tend to over-react to such retail development proposals with regard to traffic generation, for superstore traffic has an uncanny propensity to adjust to peak hour flows.

Most planning authorities operate some form of retail frontage policy for shopping parades. Within primary parades the policy is normally to seek to maintain a level of around 70 per cent of those retail uses falling within Class A1 of the Use Classes Order, but secondary parades are usually treated much more flexibly. Even so, it has been recognized that some strictly non-retail uses can prove an attractive draw and sometimes generate a greater pedestrian flow than conventional retail uses (Unit for Retail Planning Information 1980).

Several other issues are worth mentioning. First, it has been suggested that even the Use Classes Order 1987 remains an ineffective and redundant instrument of development control in terms of retailing and should be scrapped or drastically amended. Secondly, the question of pedestrian flow needs greater comprehension on the part of certain planning authorities, in particular the effects of pedestrian-ization and carparking. Thirdly, a more flexible attitude towards the change of use of accommodation over existing but dated high street shops should be adopted, so as to facilitate redevelopment and refurbishment.

On a more positive note, it is clear that town centres are facing a challenge from out-of-town centres – a challenge of increased accessibility, convenience, environment and security. The argument runs that this challenge can be met pro-vided local authorities look at the problems of their centres on a comprehensive basis. Many planned shopping centres exhibit high-quality management, so there is no reason why local authorities should not examine ways of managing a whole town centre to ensure that it provides the best possible facilities and convenience to the shopping public. This is starting to happen.

Design and layout

It has been said that demographic changes, urban congestion and growing con-cern for the environment will precipitate a radical reappraisal of the purpose of shopping centres, their appeal, how they function and how their returns can be optimized (Walker 1990). An ageing population placing an emphasis on quality, convenience, high standards of service, leisure and life-style will dictate a dif-ferent pattern of consumer behaviour. The design and layout of shopping centres will play an important part in providing a suitable environment to meet these changing expectations.

Whereas inflation fuelled the surge in retailers' sales volumes during the 1970s and 1980s, they are now having to find real sales growth in a highly competitive market, and are turning to design to achieve it. Retailers increasingly see design as more than a mere extension of architecture or shelf engineering, and rather a mainspring of the marketing drive, so that developers in the UK now continually monitor what is happening to the shops and shopping malls in the USA in order to review their approach here. This accent upon good design is underlined by the statement made by one leading retail designer:

At its best shopping is an important experience that triggers off all the senses – visual, tactile, oral, audile and smell.

Planned shopping centres

The practical requirements in shopping are space, servicing, parking and acces-sibility, but increasingly these have to be matched with creative design, visual interest, character and feel. Thus, enormous opportunities exist for both the developer and the architect, and, although there can be no magic formula for success, a few basic principles underlying shopping centre design can be described as follows.

Size and shape

Generally speaking, new centres are becoming smaller and better integrated into the towns they serve. Even within the centres, many major retailers are themselves looking for somewhat smaller premises than they did a few years ago. Elevations are also being designed to a smaller scale. However, there is a recognition that the traditional strict rectangular shape is not essential to successful performance. Knowing retailers' requirements and being flexible enough to accommodate them is the important factor. At the Ashley Centre, Epsom, for example, where Bredero developed a $26016\,m^2$ ($280000\,ft^2$) centre Marks & Spencer increased in size by 25 per cent, Waitrose reduced planned space by 10 per cent and the House of Fraser store was cut by 30 per cent to $4181\,m^2$ ($45000\,ft^2$). With regard to the size of standard units within a centre, the favoured size of the majority of retailers is around $279\,m^2$ ($3000\,ft^2$) with a frontage of $7.3\,m$ ($24\,ft$) and adequate storage and ancillary space either at basement or first-floor level. The choice of size of structural grid is important to efficiency and flexibility, and, although there is no recognized norm, a grid of $11\,m$ ($36\,ft$) allows for a wide variety of unit sizes (Northen 1977).

Enclosure

Opinions vary as to the future of the fully enclosed environmentally controlled shopping centre. Suffice it to say that reports of its imminent demise a few years ago proved to be greatly exaggerated. In fact, many previously open centres have been enclosed. Nevertheless, that fast tempo of centre development during the late 1980s and early 1990s is destined to slacken in future. However, where it takes place one major keynote of enclosure is buildability, because problems of cracking, movement, inadequate drainage and water leaks have been relatively common with older shopping centres. Roofs, for example are frequently a cause for concern, especially with the fashion towards the introduction of atria, and the advice of a specialist roofing contractor early in the design process is imperative.

Cladding

The perimeter of a shopping centre is a massive area, and while light-coloured tiles might be attractive, they can be costly to clean. For this, and for other reasons of taste, there has been a marked return to the use of brick cladding. Whatever material is selected, the important thing is to pay careful attention to the finer detailing, so as to avoid costly difficulties if there is a component failure in the panels of brickwork.

Climate

Where a fully controlled environmental system is provided, the optimum climate is said to be somewhere between an office temperature and the outside tempera-

385

ture. Energy conservation is extremely important, and space heating, lighting and air-conditioning facilities must all be appraised for cost-effectiveness in terms of running costs as well as installation. Nevertheless, architects have become much more skilful at designing centres with a high proportion of natural lighting, but avoiding the excessive heat loss and gain mentioned above.

Environment
Experience drawn from the USA shows that it is crucial for a shopping centre to establish a distinct identity and create a pleasing environment. For too long the temptation has been to mimic successful schemes elsewhere, and, in a sense, one Arndale centre tended to look very much like another. The pressure now is for creativity and innovation, or as one leading American shopping centre developer has described it – "a touch of the ethnic", arguing further that what people want is a return to the feeling of the Middle East bazaar or the market town of the middle ages, not the faceless could-be-anywhere shopping centre that has dominated the scene for so long. Greater use of domestic architecture and materials could be made, and much more tasteful use of colour and texture introduced. Extensive planting along the malls, with more trees, and not just low level shrubs, together with a wider variety of water features such as fountains, waterfalls and streams, should be encouraged, despite cries of high management costs. The use of carpets on stairs and ramps has also proved popular. Generally, therefore, the movement should be more towards the "street scene" approach as opposed to the "grand manner" of so many 1970s centres. As part of this approach, the design of signposting and facades should be sympathetic to the overall theme running through the architecture and landscaping of the centre.

Security
Apart from electrical surveillance equipment and management staff on patrol, the security aspects of a centre should be taken into account during the design stage of the development process. As regards safety, sprinkler systems and fire shutters can sometimes be a headache, and specialist advice is essential. In respect of vandalism and hooliganism, the number and siting of entrances, the clear run of malls, the location of security doors and the existence of blank spots and corners must all be considered.

Mixed use
Large mixed-use development schemes located in central city areas seem to be the order of the day in North America. It has been suggested that the pace of retailing activity fell in shopping centres during the 1970s and 1980s except where such projects were combined with hotels and entertainment facilities. Expert opinions are divided in the UK as to the viability of mixed-use development schemes, but it could well be an area of considerable opportunity, shown the way.

Parking

It is normally uneconomic to provide surface parking for town centre development schemes, but usually essential to provide such a facility in a suburban or edge-of-town location. Carparking, whether it be multi-storey or surface, can be provided specifically for the centre or as part of a wider community facility. Some retail developers, wherever possible, insist upon control over their own parking areas. The ideal provision is about four to six spaces for every 93m^2 (1000ft^2) of retail floorspace, and in town centres this can fall to under three, but the total amount of land for carparking works out to around 32.5m^2 (350ft^2) per space to allow for access and manoeuvring room. In respect of carparking provision there are design issues to be addressed, including:

- the attractiveness of the interface of the carpark and the shopping centre
- visible access and egress points with adequate queuing areas
- the suitability of external screening and the sufficiency of cross-ventilation
- effective control systems and efficient operation
- well placed pick-up points and trolley parks
- good standard finishes and services
- a reasonable standard of lighting.

Servicing

A great deal of space is often wasted in overproviding for servicing, resulting in vast open areas. It is now recognized that only about 25 per cent of lorries using service yards are 15m long (49ft) or more and not every unit in the centre is visited. Most modern town centre schemes now have centralized unloading and servicing bays with localized trolley distribution. Among the questions that arise in the design and layout of service areas are the degree of security afforded; the extent of separation of service and customer traffic; hours of access; level of ground, bays and ramps (not exceeding 1:10); adequate drainage; provision for waste disposal; sufficient turning room; and proper access for fire-fighting vehicles.

Malls

Shopping centre malls are becoming more varied in all respects: length, width, roof height, layout, frontage and decoration. There is really no such thing as an ideal length to a mall; interest and convenience to shoppers are by far the most important factors. Likewise, with mall widths, although there has been a tendency to design narrower double fronted malls of between 5m and 8m (16–26ft) to encourage shoppers to cross over and shop both sides of the mall. Increasingly, moreover, malls are broken up by squares and courts of varying sizes to create an even more attractive environment. With regard to the shopping frontage, popular treatments over recent years have been the cranked line of shop fronts and the repeated bay-window style along a splayed frontage to a court. Apart from visually breaking up a flat surface, cranked or splayed frontages also give tenants two-sided representation. A further refinement is to distinguish separate malls by differing tenant mix. Mall heights are another design consideration. A low ceiling breaks up the perspective of a long mall, reduces building costs and minimizes energy consumption. A high ceiling can allow for unusual architectural treatments, and may be unavoidable in multi-level centres. Some interesting effects can also be achieved by combining a high roof with low eaves heights. Wherever possible, however, the tendency is for lower ceilings, on cost rather than aesthetic grounds. Other considerations to be taken into account in mall design include the sympathetic use of natural light; attractive entrances; rest areas with seating and plants; focal points for displays and promotions; fixed and free standing litter bins; special features, such as water, sculpture or lighting effects; and public information points.

Levels

Traditionally it has been thought daring for a developer in the UK to provide shopping on two levels, let alone more, and always provident to encourage horizontal rather than vertical movement around a centre. However, eight-storey shopping centres in Singapore and Hong Kong manage to break all the rules and succeed. American shopping developments seem to be able to make two-, three- and even four-storey shopping work well. Underground servicing avoids pedestrian and vehicular conflict and permits efficient exploitation of constrained town centre sites. However, it is relatively costly to construct and sometimes it creates difficulties in access.

Amenities

Most successful shopping centres provide, so far as possible, a wide range of amenities to cater for customers' needs. The most common of these are catering, lavatories, crèches, telephones and play sculptures. The provision of catering is a controversial area, and solutions range from somewhere to sit down for a drink and a light meal to a full-blown food court. It has been found that, although food courts generally increase pedestrian flow into shopping centres, they do not necessarily increase retail sales, because well over half of the food court users do not visit other shops. Food courts are also expensive to furnish, maintain and refurbish. However, the food court concept has proved extremely successful in many centres, with location, circulation, visibility, light, height overhead, good service and variety being important factors. Lavatories are now almost essential, sometimes together with a baby-care room, and should be away from major shopping frontages but clearly signed. A crèche tends to be an expensive luxury, but some developers have partially solved the problem of cost by having properly supervised paying playgroups in their centres.

Maintenance

It is important to design for low maintenance costs. Maintenance-free and vandal-proof materials and finishes should be selected wherever possible. Structural components should be designed for ease of cleaning, and services installed to facilitate access for inspection and repair. Circulation areas should be laid out with the need to use cleaning machines on a daily basis in mind.

Pedestrian flow

Shopping centres are all about pedestrian flow: the total amount drawn to the centre and the maximizing of circulation around it. The location of magnet stores, careful siting of entrances, skilful arrangement of malls and subtle manipulation of circulation space to create areas of interest all conventionally contribute to an optimum flow and high trading volume. Some simple guidelines can be laid down from the experience of pedestrian behaviour in various centres developed over the years:

Entrances

The first function of a centre is to attract customers to it. Two basic approaches can be identified to the location and design of shopping centre entrances. First, the strikingly obvious entrance that heralds access to the centre and does not depend overly upon the surrounding area. Featured entrances of this kind are of particular importance to free-standing and wholly enclosed shopping centres as a relief to the otherwise monolithic appearance and as an environmental control barrier; and, secondly, the psychologically more subtle entrance that entices shoppers into the centre. All entrances should be inviting and should not present the shopper with a choice. The use of tenants having interesting displays at the entrance is effective, and striking signing on the exterior of the shopping centre is critical. For out-of-town centres, the customer will already have decided to visit the centre, but helpful signage for parking and shopping must be provided. In major centres it is essential to indicate clearly the various entrances to different sectors.

Magnets and anchors

There are certain tenants and retail uses whose presence in a shopping centre are held to be critical to the success of a scheme of development. Known as the "magnet" or "anchor" tenants, they traditionally comprise department stores, variety stores, superstores and certain other major multiple traders. A magnet not only draws shoppers into a centre, or from one end to another, but as a pre-letting for a new development it is also the bait with which to catch acceptable tenants for the other individual shop units. Variations in layout to generate pedestrian flow by the different siting of magnets have been tried over the years. Sometimes a magnet has been placed at each end of a single mall; sometimes several magnet traders have been placed at extreme ends or at intersections of malls; and, with smaller centres where there is only one obvious major space using anchor, it will normally be placed as far away from the entrance as can be arranged. It is also common practice with stores to try to keep them away from prime frontage posi-

389

tions along the mall, because such kinds of retailer are able to trade from what might be thought inferior pitches because of the immense consumer loyalty they command, whereas the standard unit type of tenant depends upon a high degree of comparison and impulse buying, triggered by prominent window displays. However, times are changing with regard to magnets. Department stores are still opening new outlets, but they are also closing down others, and no longer can a developer rely upon attracting such tenants as John Lewis, Debenhams or Selfridges to a scheme. The superstores are an obvious alternative, and the likes of Waitrose, Tesco and Presto are all prepared to consider town centre locations, but prefer predominantly single-storey space and look for generous parking provision. Supermarkets are only effective as true magnets in conjunction with leading non-food stores in schemes of any significance, and, on their own, they tend to give the centre a convenience-good flavour. More recently, the concept of the food court as an anchor to a planned shopping centre has been adopted from North America.

Vertical circulation

Many planned centres include two, and sometimes more, levels of shopping with varying success. Sloping sites have helped some, such as Brent Cross and the St George's Centre in Preston, where it has been possible to avoid making either level especially dominant. Elsewhere, by skilful design, shoppers must be persuaded to ascend (or preferably to descend, which they are more inclined to do) to secondary floors. This requires the inclusion of strong visual links between floors, usually by means of open balconies, prominent staircases or alluring escalators, assisted by good signposting and seductive advertising. Themed floors are another possibility, for, in one way or another, a prime objective in the design and management of future shopping centres will be to get shoppers to use more than just the ground floor. However, it must be appreciated that multi-level centres create problems of fire control and smoke as well as heavy reliance on artificial lighting and ventilation.

Refurbishment

Most of the major planned shopping centres built a decade or more ago are now obsolescent and in the need of substantial refurbishment. Many of them have problems with open malls or central areas, poor natural light, inadequate services and facilities, and outdated circulation patterns. In addition, many existing centres do not fully comply with stricter fire regulations and they possess certain other inherent design faults. Whereas high streets experience a constant rejuvenation, and leading department stores and superstores under a single ownership have been revitalized in response to economic pressure, shopping centres often have not. With diminishing market share and growing competition, refurbishment is now the name of the game.

Any decision to refurbish on a large scale must obviously be preceded by a careful study to ensure that expenditure is justified. In this, several common problems can be identified:

- The multiplicity of ownership, where there is often a financial institution, a developer, a local authority and sometimes a multiple store holding long-term interests in the property, and it is often necessary to renegotiate the lease structure or buy-in the freehold.
- Retailers are keen to improve their trading prospects, but less willing to pay for the improvements, or suffer the disruption while building works are carried out.
- The formula for viability is extremely difficult to calculate, depending as it does upon renegotiated rents at review related to comparative turnover and profitability.

In the context of the above problems, it has been pointed out that the financial sharing formulae provided in development agreements were often generously loaded in favour of the ground landlord, both in terms of initial rent and sharing provisions. Few imagined that such profound changes at such a high cost would have to be undertaken so soon to sustain the market share and investment worth of centres. The problem is frequently compounded by what is known as "adverse" gearing, which has been described succinctly as follows:

Take a centre which originally cost £10 million to build with the developer achieving a notional return of 7.5 per cent on this amount. The fixed element of the ground rent was, say, £275000 and the original occupational rents amounted to, say £1.3 million with the provision to review the rents to 50 per cent of the occupational rents after allowance for the developers notional return on his investment. If the occupation rents have now increased to say £4.2 million on such a formula, the local authority's share of the income will have increased from 21 per cent of occupational rents at the outset to 42 per cent within a 15 year time-span. The curve is exponential and the situation continuously gets worse at the expense of the management owners.

Thus, the cost versus income equation to the party responsible for necessary comprehensive refurbishment is often a difficult one to balance. With different areas performing differently in different years. A report produced by the British Council of Shopping Centres in 1994 concluded that most refurbishments, stemming from a "defensive" justification, take place at a later point in the economic cycle of the shopping centre than the optimum period, and that by tracking more closely the shopping centre life-cycle investment decisions can be made earlier to reduce time-lag between the deterioration of a centre's performance and the completion of the refurbishment. The report further suggests various evaluation techniques that can be applied to ensure that the timing of refurbishment is undertaken in such a way as to maximize cashflow, taking into account risk, project running costs and the consequence of not refurbishing.

In general, however, if major retail investments are to be protected they must at least hold on to, and preferably increase, their market share. However, the extent to which reconstruction and reorganization takes place will vary according to individual circumstances. But, inevitably, opportunities will be presented to buy-out leases and re-let premises; to create extra letting space in useless voids or by extending the building or narrowing the malls; to enclose open centres; to install new plant and building servicing facilities; to adjust the tenant-mix and add missing traders; and generally upgrade the environment and decor of the centre. If the work is successful, turnover will increase and higher rents will be achieved on review to produce an acceptable return to the investor.

Shopping centre management

Of all the commercial sectors of the property market, shop developments have traditionally depended upon good management, and arguably have much to teach the office, leisure and industrial sectors.

Much also remains constantly to be learned from good practice at home and abroad, especially from North America. Looking towards the year 2000, shopping centre developers and owners are acutely aware of the continuing set of challenges that face them. It is well recognized that the shift to out-of-town locations, the emergence of new retail concepts, a squeeze on retailers' profit margins and low expectation of growth in consumer spending make it even more important to ensure that a centre has the ability to gain market share from its competitors, for the benefit of its retailers, and ultimately the developer and owner. Location, accessibility, local dominance and tenant mix all play a part in this, but it has been stated that of equal importance is the style in which the centre is managed (Saggess 1993).

Tenant mix

The aim of any shopping development should be to attract tenants who will maximize turnover and profitability, so that rental income can also be negotiated to the highest possible level. For a long time, developers in the UK, having conceived a retail scheme, would place the units on the market and allow market forces to determine the ultimate shopping mix.

In some instances this remains true, especially in difficult letting markets where any tenant willing to pay a reasonable rent is likely to be welcome. However, creating and maintaining a productive tenant mix is essential to the economic performance of any centre, although implementation sometimes calls for a steady nerve. In achieving this there are several criteria to be examined:

- cumulative attraction: produced by the clustering of different but related shops, together in a manner that generates the same magnet effect as that

of a major user
- competition and comparison: where several similar shops offering the same kinds of goods are grouped together so that shoppers are attracted to a centre knowing that they will be able to compare and contrast goods and prices
- compatibility: some shops are positively prejudicial to one another in respect of lighting, noise, marketing, smell and crowding, so special care must be taken in both the selection of certain trades and their positioning in a centre.

A useful definition of tenant mix can be provided as follows:

Tenant mix is a continuous policy of maximizing public patronage of a shopping centre by optimizing the number of traders, the size of their premises, their styles and goods sold or services rendered.

In achieving the above, the objective is to secure a range of retailers who will appeal to the largest possible proportion of the catchment population commanded by the centre. The right mix will, therefore, be determined by the size, composition and quality of the catchment area. Large but low-income group hinterlands would justify an emphasis upon a variety rather than a department store and might encourage a developer to include a market in the centre. A smaller, but more affluent local population would suggest a greater concentration upon high fashion and jewellery shops and less accent upon general convenience shopping. The younger the population, the more fashion, children's wear and electrical goods shops, and an extensive and varied catchment area could support a specialist retailer such as a book shop or healthfood shop. Some of the other considerations to be taken into account regarding tenant mix can be summarized as below:
- What proportions of convenience and durable goods shops to include?
- How many, if any, service shops, such as banks, betting shops, gas and electricity showrooms, launderettes and public houses to permit?
- Whether to try to attract small local traders as well as national multiples?
- Is a "themed" floor approach focusing on such topics as "the home" or "women" or "leisure" worth developing?
- What steps must be taken to avoid or overcome the creation of "dead spots'?
- Are fast food outlets to be encouraged and is a gourmet food hall a potential component?
- What is the appropriate ratio between floorspace given over to major "anchors" and to other units (usually about 40:60)?

A survey of retailers showed that tenant mix is the single most important factor in selecting a suitable trading location, and also a major source of occupier dissatisfaction. The same survey also revealed that the role of anchor stores should be re-examined both in terms of the type of store involved and the amount of space allocated (a little less, and more accent on convenience goods); that the independent retail sector should be allocated twice as much space as at present; however, the argument for incorporating considerable leisure facilities within shopping centres has not yet been made (Watt & Valente 1991). It concludes by stressing that a successful tenant mix does not occur naturally, but requires careful consideration of both consumer needs and those of retailers themselves. However, above all it calls for a positive approach to be adopted, that treats the scheme in its entirety and places due emphasis on both primary and secondary space.

Initial research must be coupled with continuous monitoring of the catchment area in order to change the balance of traders as both supply and demand evolve in a particular location. It can still be argued that this pre-supposes a degree of management flexibility, which does not sit entirely comfortably alongside the current landlord–tenant relationship (ibid.).

Leases

For some time there has been considerable debate about the legal relationship between shopping centre owners and retail tenants. The combination of over-supply, recession and national economic policy during the early 1990s has allowed many occupiers to rewrite lease terms, but major issues still persist. These include:

- *Privity of contract* Many retail tenants have found to their cost that if an assignee goes bust, then the responsibility for lease and the payment of rent returns to the original leaseholder. Some landlords refuse a re-let, or accept a lower rent, looking to the head leaseholder for the difference, because of the covenant position. However, the Landlord and Tenant (Covenants) Act 1995 has changed the ground-rules, so that for new tenancies the tenant will cease to be liable on assignment; a tenant may be required to guarantee his immediate successor; a landlord can apply to be released from liability after assignment; the landlord can pre-define terms upon which the tenant will be allowed to assign commercial leases; and all covenants are enforceable by and against assignees. For new and existing leases, a former tenant cannot be liable for variations to the lease and has the right to an overriding lease upon paying the arrears.
- *Length of lease* Pension funds and insurance companies, the major owners of shopping centres in the UK, have traditionally demanded a multiplicity of blue chip tenants contracted on 25-year leases before property investments become acceptable. Turnover rents and short leases, which arguably are needed if a centre is to be run as a business, are treated at valuation as insecure income. There is now a tendency towards shorter leases, prompted by economic circumstance, but also in recognition of the need to concentrate upon quality of income rather than length.
- *Upwards-only rent reviews* Another chief target of retail tenants is the upwards-only rent review, and support for this view is found from those close to government who see such a practice as profoundly inflationary. However, institutional investors funding retail development argue that the whole basis of their equity financing of property requires a relatively low return on the basis that rent will grow. Anything less would represent an unfair balance between return and risk.

Further changes towards a more flexible structure in the leasehold relationship between landlords and tenants in the retail sector seem possible. However, it has to be recorded that it all depends on the state of the economy, and on where you stand, as to the benefits or otherwise of particular terms and conditions at any given time.

Turnover rents

Turnover rents first originated in the USA during the 1930s, and now few units in shopping centres there are ever let on any other terms. However, they remain the exception rather than the norm in the UK. Nevertheless, having been pioneered by Capital and Counties in the early 1970s, the use of turnover rents is now more familiar among shopping centres.

Typically, a turnover rent in the UK comprises two elements. First, a base rent, which is usually expressed as a proportion of agreed open market rental, and commonly set at about 75–80 per cent. Second, a percentage of the annual sales turnover of the tenant, which can be as low as 1.5 per cent and as high as 15 per cent, but normally range from around 7–12 per cent according to trade. The basic formula is subject to any number of refinements. The basic rent may refer to an average of past years' rents; turnover provisions may be delayed until, say, the third year of opening; large stores may claim an exempt first slice of turnover; it may be calculated gross or net of tax; or the percentage figure may change according to different levels of sales. Typically, however, the following provide the example in Table 15.2 (Northen 1987):

The advantages of employing turnover rents are that:
- landlord and tenant share an objective to maximize income
- the landlord has an incentive to promote the centre and provide a high standard of management
- the landlord receives an annual share of rental growth
- rent review problems and negotiations are minimized
- it can be a useful devise in an inflationary period as far as the landlord is concerned
- it can be helpful in circumstances where the trading potential of a new development is uncertain
- more attention is paid by the landlord to establishing the correct tenant mix

On the other hand, there are various difficulties associated with turnover rents. These include:
- some trades, such as television hire, building societies and banks, are not suitable for turnover rents
- new traders might not have a track record and cannot easily be assessed
- the system really works best when traders can quickly and simply be moved around the centre, or poorly performing traders substituted by potential high-turnover ones, as occurs in the USA

Table 15.2 Turnover rent percentages

	Trade	%
1.	Jeweller	10–11
2.	Ladies fashion	8–10
3.	Men's fashion	8–9
4.	Radio and electrical	7
5.	Catering	7
6.	Shoes (fashion)	9–10
7.	Shoes (family)	8–9
8.	Records	9
9.	Sports goods	9
10.	Greengrocer	6
11.	Butcher	4–5
12.	Baker	5

- landlord and tenant legislation in the UK is not designed for turnover rents, for apart from the security of tenure provisions there are some doubts about the status of such arrangements
- problems may arise in controlling assignments, and landlords must take care not to disturb the tenant mix
- some traders are reluctant to disclose turnover figures, and the monitoring of accounts can be difficult and costly, but externally audited certificates are normally provided
- unknown levels of rental income are said to deter financial institutions from funding developments let on a turnover basis, but this criticism is probably exaggerated
- Similarly, it is suggested that valuation is a problematic exercise, but again growing familiarity is showing such fears to be groundless.

In managed centres, overall, the use of turnover rents should forge the relationship between all the parties ever closer and contribute towards mutual success.

Promotion and public relations

A shopping centre will need active promotion before, during and after development. The aim being to increase public interest and awareness and thereby increase pedestrian flow and turnover. To foster or retain goodwill on the part of both shoppers and retailers, there is also a need to ensure a high and constant level of public relations.

The promotion of shopping centres has become almost an industry in itself. Extensive promotional campaigns will normally be mounted at the launch of a new centre, where there are still a substantial number of units vacant or when sales are static, declining or threatened. It is not possible to detail all the techniques of promotion or aspects of public relations that have evolved or emerged over recent years, but some of the most effective policies can be summarized as follows:

- The centre should have a clear identity, reinforced by a memorable name and a striking logo.
- Likewise, a friendly and co-operative stance should be adopted towards local community groupings, such as Chambers of Trade and Commerce, Rotary, Lions Club, Round Table, schools, clubs, women's organizations and the local council.
- Special events of a community nature such as a Christmas carol service, a wine festival or a gymnastics display could be held to draw attention to the centre and make shopping interesting.
- A programme of tenant oriented promotions should be prepared in collaboration with the retailers and might include events such as fashion shows, craft displays or exhibitions.
- Regular press releases should be prepared and carefully placed.
- A survey of shoppers' views about the centre, its competition, travel and parking behaviour, the shopping mix, facilities provided, spending habits and desired changes or additional trades or service should be conducted from time to time.

Most important of all, however, is to ensure that all public relations and promotional activities take place against a deliberate and agreed overall policy, otherwise the image portrayed will be at best commonplace, and at worst counterproductive.

Centre management

The primary functions of a shopping centre management have succinctly been described as (Martin 1982):

- paperwork: the administration of head leases and leases, accounting for rent and service costs and secretarial, insurance and legal services
- people: human relations comprising public relations, publicity, promotion and security.
- premises: maintenance, primarily of common areas in respect of both buildings and plan.

In a shopping centre of any size there will be a shopping centre manager, representing the interests of the developer or owner. Since the late 1980s there has been a tremendous elevation in the status of the shopping centre manager and a consequent rise in the skills and standards of performance expected of them. A good manager can make the difference between a successful centre and mediocre one. Among the many duties falling upon the centre manager will be the following.

Maintenance of common area

Including routine housekeeping, such as cleaning, polishing, rubbish and litter collection, plant watering and changing of light bulbs and air filters; regular maintenance, such as repainting, turning of carpets and overhaul of plant and machinery; repairs, such as cracked floors, chipped walls and broken elements; and occasional replacement of such components as escalators, lights, carpets, toilets, boilers, mall seating and entrance doors.

Security

Depending upon the size and nature of the centre, its location and setting, the kind of traders represented and the availability of regular fire, police and other services, different levels of security will have to be provided. Aspects of security to be considered will include hooliganism, vandalism, shoplifting, lost children, health and safety at work, protection during building work, fire precaution, emergency lighting, illness or accident procedures and employment of suitable staff. Good security has been defined as:

> A state of benevolent vigilance at all times towards the public tenants, staff and contractors by way of well thought out and constantly reassessed routines and resources. (Martin 1982)

Service charge

Being the levy by the landlord upon the tenant for all the operational, maintenance, repair and security charges provided at the centre. Although such charges used to be based upon an agreed sum, the common practice now is for full recovery of all the costs of specified services to take place. Although there are a variety of ways of apportioning charges, in a large enclosed centre this can work out at about £54 per m^2 (£5.00 per ft^2) a year. A proportion of the service charge should also be set aside as a sinking fund for the replacement of major items of plant.

Insurance

The main aspects of insurance with which a shopping centre manager will be concerned are the preservation of income, the reinstatement of property, those liabilities incurred under the terms of the head lease, and any legal liabilities arising out of statute or common law. Rightly, however, it has been stated the insurance is not a substitute for vigilance and good management (Martin 1982).

Traders' associations

There appears to be a notable lack of interest by both landlords and tenants in the formation and running of traders' or merchants' associations in the UK. This is beginning to change as each party recognizes the benefits to be gained. Indeed, most modern leases insist that tenants join an association if one exists. It is really then for the centre manager to ensure that there is an appreciation of the role of the association as being to promote the interests of the centre as a whole.

Town centre management

Many of the principles and practices relating to the effective management of planned shopping centres can equally be applied to town centres themselves. Over recent years the high street has become a fashionable policy focus, which has been formalized with the emergence of Town Centre Management (TCM) initiatives aimed at addressing the issue of enhancing the vitality and viability of town centres. Town centre management has generally been defined by the Association of Town Centre Management as follows:

> Town Centre Management is the effective co-ordination of the private and public sectors, including local authority professionals, to create, in partnership, a successful town centre – building on full consultation.hu bnu b

In particular, TCM is said to provide (Parker 1994):
- a means to co-ordinate the more effective use of public resources
- a new policy/resource priority and focus
- a conduit for establishing private and public sector partnerships
- a lever to secure further private sector investment in the high street
- a co-operative vehicle for community participation and mobilization
- a riposte to out-of-town competitive retail pressures.

Since its inception in 1986, TCM has been adopted by over 80 towns. It has been widely endorsed and actively promoted by government, leading retailers, local community ventures and property-owning institutions, but remains largely a local authority initiative. The origin of TCM lies in the threat posed by out-of-town retail facilities and a growing concern over the health of the high street. It is founded on the property management practices employed by the leading shopping centre owners, but without the legal powers available to them through tenure.

A key element in successful TCM is the appointment of an effective town centre manager whose main functions have been described as follows (Court & Southwell 1994):
- to promote an area rather than a function-based focus to the management of town centres
- to represent the opinions and priorities of all interested public and private sector groups
- to co-ordinate private and public sector roles and policies to achieve a common aim (i.e. the improvement of the town centre)
- to manage effectively town centre initiatives/developments
- to liaise between local authority functions and private sector requirements
- to promote the town-centre and the TCM concept.

Research and experience shows that the application of TCM, to date, varies very substantially in organization, finance, power and purpose. Being primarily local-authority based, it is also largely dependent upon public funding, with notable but limited private sector contributions.

A report produced in 1994 found little to suggest that TCM was not considered to be an effective approach to an urgent and obvious problem. Nevertheless, it suggested that private–public sector co-operation was an integral part of successful TCM, which could be encouraged by:

- real participation
- a town centre manager
- aims beyond the janitorial
- an absence of "political" debate
- effective decision-making
- rational "business" planning projects rather than politically oriented TCMs
- initiatives back by authority.

Conversely, it has been argued that it is important to acknowledge that the high street is a market place and not a homogeneous community of common interests. The application of public resources to one priority over another is also seen as a conflict faced by many elected members, requiring political as opposed to "technical" resolution. In its role as a conduit for public and private sector partnership, moreover, a wider public sector consensus that the high street is worthy of care and that the different cultural approaches to the issues confronted need to be appreciated. Likewise, the argument runs that, for the private sector, whereas the high street is the traditional economic focus of the commercial activities that sustain the urban fabric, it must at the same time be recognized that the high street is also the social and cultural stage for the wider urban community (Parker 1994).

Conclusion

The face of shopping continues to change. Large stores, having gained a place out-of-town, are now to be subject to much more selective planning control. There is an increasing awareness of the vital need to improve and promote traditional town centres, and a conscious attempt by many councils to adopt a management approach towards the issue. Category killers in such areas as electronics, office goods, household linens and sporting goods are arriving, and bound to grow. Likewise with warehouse clubs and factory outlets. Conventional leasehold terms and conditions are already under attack, and will surely change to produce a much more flexible system. Considerable imagination is also being brought to bear upon the retail sector as witnessed by the refurbishment of many old inner-city buildings to form new shopping centres and arcades. Similarly, dated existing planned shopping centres are being revitalized. Nevertheless, in respect of shopping centre management, we still have much to learn from the active and intensive management practices of US centres.

Much has been made about the impending revolution in retailing resulting from the rapid development of a new advanced communications technology. Any major fundamental upheaval in shopping behaviour still seems a long way off,

and the retail industry has shown comparatively little enthusiasm for the introduction of "remote" or "armchair" shopping. It seems more pre-occupied with
the installation of point-of-sale equipment and other in-store technical innovations, and the US experience does not suggest much consumer appetite for home-
based shopping. In any event, the assembly and distribution of goods is an expensive operation, and it is the shopper who bears the hidden costs of this at present.

Shop investors, developers and owners should not, however, be too compla-
cent. The likely over-supply of shopping facilities reminds those involved that
their shop property can no longer be conceived in purely architectural or geographical terms. Successful centres of the future must be consumer-led and innovative to attract and retain their shopping populations.

CHAPTER SIXTEEN
Office development

The world economy is changing, and with it the nature and function of cities, and the way in which work is perceived and performed. One of the most intractable tasks for urban planning and development in the light of such change is the proper provision for all concerned of office and business space. Not only is there a shift of economic growth from the old economies of Europe and North America to the new economies of the Far East and the Pacific Rim, but there is the potentially explosive impact of the full flowering of information technology (IT) and the question as to whether that impact will be evolutionary or revolutionary in character.

In Europe, the advent of modern management systems and the corporate drive for cost effectiveness has been stated to affect the nature of cities in at least four ways:

1 the historic migration of high volume, low value added – so called back office – activity out of the city;
2 the subsequent, and sometimes simultaneous migration of this type of activity to other lower cost countries;
3 the higher value added, lower volume activity remaining within the urban area but now dispersing from the centre;
4 the reverse of these dispersal trends in the new magnetism of the concentration of specialist, relatively low volume, but high value added, activity into the core of the city especially for those activities which require a great deal of co-operation among people. (Chapman 1995)

The continuing search for increased business efficiency, especially by the 40000 or so transnational companies identified in the global economy, has led to the optimization of real estate assets in terms of location, quantity, specification and tenure, as well as the emergence of such corporate restructuring buzzwords as down-sizing, right-sizing, outsourcing, telecommuting, hot-desking and core business concentration. Cities themselves are finding the need to compete as businesses with an awareness of their inherent strengths and weaknesses; an evaluation of the necessary management, skill, resource and marketing abilities required to maintain and enhance the city economy; and the desirability and direction of specialization, excellence and expertise. In this context, it has been argued that effective, properly resourced partnerships of central and local government and the business community, with coherent reliable strategies to underpin the existing economies in order to attract more firms, will be essential for the long-run demand for offices (ibid.).

In the UK the 1980s could fairly be described as having been the era of the office. More was researched and written about modern office needs during that decade than was ever compiled and published over the previous 50 years. This quest continues. However, warnings of the need for change were first signalled during the mid-1970s when, for example, it was stated:

> When planning our buildings we cannot afford to stand still, year by year standards are improving; the office building that was built in the early post-war years began to look a little dated by the 1960s and now in the 1970s that same building will probably require extensive modernization and adaptation to bring it into line with modern requirements. It is reasonable to assume that the rate of change in office standards is accelerating. (CALUS 1974)

Nothing could have been more true. The advent and application of information technology has brought about the need for changing office design and location even more rapidly than most professional observers anticipated. An awareness and understanding of the requirements of information technology can rightly be said to have been the keynotes of successful space management in the 1980s. Office activities and structures need to adjust so quickly and so often in response to new business demands and services that, however much of a cliché it has become, the watchword in office development is flexibility. This is exemplified in the sales literature produced by one leading property development company, which identifies and prioritizes certain advantages to a particular development as follows:

> The first is flexibility. Tenants can make their offices fit the logic of the organization. The floor size gives great freedom of layout. The modular grid places the minimum constraint on partitioning. The raised floor allows cabling to run to any position.[1]

In addition, it has been argued that the workplace has changed for several other reasons (Steelcase Strafor 1990). Information technology has altered the social composition of the office, producing a more equal, demanding and discriminating workforce who expect to enjoy choice at work. There is greater freedom, moreover, in the use of time and the location of the office. And the economics of office space use has changed so that far more money is now spent on relatively short-life interiors and proportionately less on the shell and exterior elements of office buildings.

Many great issues concerning the office are said to be emerging in Europe in the last decade of the twentieth century, which are described by Dr Frank Duffy as:

---

1. Extract from poperty sales brochure produced by Greycoat Estates, 1984.

- harmonization of environmental and product standards throughout the European Community;
- increasing awareness of what can be learned from the best international initiatives North American, Japanese, Scandinavian, German;
- the increasing importance of "green" issues in the workplace; avoiding deleterious products, concerning energy in component manufacturing and building use, sustainability in materials usage;
- rethinking the costs of commuter transportation, given the potential of information technology;
- the increasing power of better educated, more scientific facilities managers;
- the opening up of the design process to end users; and,
- much more inventive use of the increasingly expensive resources of time and space.   (Steelcase Strafor 1990)

It has also been observed that there is an continuing managerial revolution that will eventually change the whole world of work. New managerial ideas, the fruit of the information technology revolution that began in the 1980s are dissolving all the boundaries and constraints that shaped the conventional office of the twentieth century. This, in turn, is breeding a new culture towards work, the main features of which have been described as:

- much greater attention to the fluid and urgent use of time e.g. taking the competitive advantage to be delivered from designing serial processes; taking advantage of the redundancies in space use endemic in conventional office design;
- impatience with conventional organizational boundaries;
- little love of hierarchies;
- a tendency towards smaller more transient organizational units, stripping the organization back to the core, out-stripping redundant and non-central;
- the spatial context and focus for intense, complex open-ended teamwork;
- the obsolescence of clerks and clerical ways;
- total confidence in the intelligent and creative use of information technology;
- a wider range of types of work, settings for work, support for work, places for work.   (Duffy 1994)

It is not difficult to predict that the next five to ten years will witness profound changes in the office function, and require of developers a greater appreciation of not only the tenants' operational needs but also of the staff who are employed in the buildings constructed to house those operations. Nothing can be taken for granted for very long in the office world of work.

In examining trends and prospects for the planning and development of offices, this chapter is divided into the following sections:

- location and provision

- planning and office development
- design and layout
- services and facilities
- business and office parks
- facilities management

Location and provision

Hunch and intuition are no longer sufficient attributes in the analysis of office markets to determine planning policies and development opportunities. Office forecasting has become a more specialized task. For example, trend extrapolation might be a useful starting point in examining market conditions, but as an accurate indicator of future demand it is a poor device. Likewise, vacancy rates give a very broad guide to the imbalance between demand and supply in the market, but conceal the effect of a multitude of determining factors.

What seems clear from a succession of major surveys is that location remains the single most important factor to occupiers out of the four major determinants of location, building design, cost of occupation and lease terms. One report, nevertheless, sums up its findings in these terms:

In spite of the superficial temptation to conclude that the survey supports traditional office locations, we believe that increased car ownership and improved public transport facilities could open up many hitherto shunned office locations. In the future there will be increased emphasis on the quality of accommodation offered, and on physical and leasing solutions that pave the way for painless expansion. (Healey & Baker 1986)

Moreover, the traditional notions of office and business location in respect of towns and cities and town and city centres are being transformed. Advanced tools of communication such as video conferencing, PC video phone, telepresence and remote diagnostics enable business people to be in contact with customers, colleagues, collaborators and support services from almost anywhere to anywhere (Chapman 1995).

In terms of provision, the pre-eminence of London is striking. As an indicator, according to Investment Property Databank, 49 per cent of UK institutional office investments by value were located in Central London at the end of 1993. The rest of London and the South East accounted for a further 29 per cent and the provincial regions only 22 per cent overall. For the purposes of investment decision-making in the development process, an hierarchical classification of UK office markets can be made as follows (Damesick 1994):

1. Central London
2. London suburbs and M25 location
3. metropolitan regional centres such as Birmingham, Bristol, Manchester, Leeds, Edinburgh and Glasgow

4. major second-tier centres such as Leicester, Nottingham, Newcastle, Sheffield and Cardiff

5. minor second-tier centres such as Brighton, Peterborough and Oxford.

Demand

Demand for office accommodation can be said to arise from one of three causes: growth, replacement or relocation. Growth can be the emergence of new businesses or the expansion of existing ones, resulting from general growth within the economy or specific growth within individual sectors. Replacement implies the need for more modern premises and demand for this can often be gauged from a physical analysis of the existing stock. It sometimes leads to the older properties being re-let and the stemming of rental growth. Relocation can be sponsored by reorganization, rationalization, or again by growth.

There are several basic sources from which the demand for office accommodation can stem: central government, local government, quasi-government agencies, private sector service industry and private business firms and corporations. It does not take much inspiration or deep analysis to forecast that the main sources of demand over the remaining years of the 1990s, and probably beyond, will spring from the private sector commercial organizations and, therefore, that the location and design of offices will favour their predilections in respect of dispersal, quality and divisibility. Generally speaking, the total amount of new floorspace requirements emanating from these various sources is likely to rise, but probably at a slower rate than has been experienced over the past 25 years. What will change more radically is the average size, location and type of office accommodation demanded. The demand by major commercial organizations, for instance, is not usually for more space, but for better space. In the same way, the rash of national and multinational takeovers frequently leads to a fall in the overall demand for office accommodation, but can produce a fresh requirement for new space more appropriately designed and positioned. Nevertheless, in such circumstances it is common to find that the headquarters function is significantly reduced and the requirement for decentralized office space enhanced. Although there might be less aggregate demand for accommodation from some of the very largest corporations already established in the UK, there is a constant call for space from other multinational organizations moving into the UK, and a healthy demand from successful small and medium-size companies looking for new offices to accommodate their growth.

Analyzing the market demand for office development is perhaps the most difficult and least accurate of all land uses. Statistics on business use of office space are difficult to come by and are frequently outdated. Wide swings in overbuilding and underbuilding distort market perceptions. The "image" of particular locations or individual buildings or the quality of continuing property management can all conspire to make it hard to forecast market demand. Moreover, office buildings do not have a catchment or trade area in the same way as shopping centres or even housing projects. Nevertheless, there are any number of factors that affect the demand for office space. These can be summarized as follows:

- national, regional and local economic performance
- service sector employment growth
- trends within different categories
- communications
- local planning and amenity
- floorspace to worker ratios
- level of rents and values
- costs of occupation
- lease terms
- building services and facilities
- complementarity of neighbouring occupiers.

In stressing that the modern occupier of office accommodation is becoming much more selective than his predecessor, it is clear that:

- Conventional concepts of location in the office market are rendered redundant by improvements to communications, and although activities such as insurance, shipping and commodities firms are likely to remain grouped in traditional areas, other kinds of business are now much freer in their approach and inclined to be more supply oriented.
- Tenants will be seeking shorter leases with one-sided break options, or a series of renewal options, downward as well as upward rent review clauses, and will tend to rely increasingly on their statutory rights. Although this will cause landlords to look more closely at the flexibility of their buildings, and be happier to accept multi-occupation, it is quite likely that rents eventually will rise in compensation for the diminished certainty of income.
- Facilities managers will play a large part in determining the suitability of premises, and the critical factors will be floor sizes and loading, air conditioning, power supply facilities, self-adjustable working environment, underfloor and vertical communication space, servicing costs, and cost-effective divisibility.
- Security will become a prime consideration, not only in terms of the physical access to and from buildings, but also access to data and external communications systems.

In addition, various research studies have provided strong evidence that "teleworking" is expected to become an important factor in the future of office work. Not just individuals working at home, but corporate, executive and contract teleworkings, using satellite offices, shared access telecentres, telecottages or production centres. It has been suggested, therefore, that the increased use of teleworking, and the need for telecentres, will create a market in suitable commercial properties (Todd 1993).

In assessing the broad measures of demand for offices, it should not be forgotten that, as with other sectors of the property development industry, there is an element of "fashion" to take into account. Certain towns and cities can suddenly be in vogue. In the 1970s around London and the West, for example, Reading, Bristol, Swindon, Watford and Luton were enormously popular. The early 1980s saw the likes of Aylesbury, Chelmsford and Newbury come to the fore and the late 1980s and early 1990s witnessed the re-emergence of regional centres such Birmingham, Glasgow, Manchester and Leeds. It is also now possible to predict that a significant amount of new office development will take place in small growth centres. Moreover, given that 95 per cent of all office-based organizations employ less than 50 people, the creation of smaller office buildings, and the construction of buildings capable of multiple occupation, will be a major area of future development.

Corporate image will even override marginal financial considerations. Many so-called "blue chip" companies either relocating from Central London or moving into the UK from Europe and America are looking for buildings in well landscaped settings in a pleasant locality. The increasingly sophisticated nature of the work undertaken by such companies, and the higher executive status of the staff accommodated there, means that developers can no longer be content with providing standard specification buildings. Special space and performance requirements, coupled with a desire to avoid excessive increases in rent at review, are pushing many potential occupiers towards building their own offices.

The changing nature of work itself will obviously exercise a considerable effect upon the demand for office space. As will be discussed below, the information explosion and the increased need for support services by decision-makers will dictate different space requirements. For a variety of reasons, including more room to accommodate the paraphernalia of information technology and the aspirations of employees to work in a more conducive environment, floorspace to worker ratios will inevitably rise. In this context, the following trends and factors have been recorded:

- Evidence suggests that floorspace to worker ratios have already been increasing since the 1970s. This is explained by the increase in administrative and professional over clerical occupations, the predominance of larger office organizations, which tend to be more generous with space provision, and the scale of office mechanization brought about largely through major advances in information technology.
- Wide variations in individual floorspace to worker ratios can occur, often as a result of different gross to net usable floor area ratios between buildings, but also because of differing sizes and types of office activity between businesses and their stage of commercial development.
- Typical London office workers occupy only about two-thirds of the space occupied by their counterparts in Europe.

Therefore, although it seems possible that worker densities will fall, the extent to which this happens will vary according to the design and age of the building concerned and the business activity, workforce, structure, equipment employed and life-cycle stage. Other factors such as the extension of flexi-time, the introduction of job-sharing, the continuous use of certain office premises, the sharing of space between firms and the movement towards a shorter working week will all combine to influence demand in respect of office location and design decisions.

Supply

It is important to remember that the office sector of the property development industry suffers from a strong counter-cyclical pattern of performance. In other words, responses to increased demand tend to take so long to put into effect that, by the time supply is increased to meet it, the market has changed so that supply greatly exceeds demand. Likewise, as supply is curtailed, so the market recovers and demand picks up again, overtaking declining supply. This counter-cyclical effect in the late 1970s and again in the late 1980s saw a shortage of office property, a rise in rental levels and a fall in investment yields – all of which combined to produce higher capital values in the office market. Not unnaturally, these symptoms encouraged developers to institute new projects. On both occasions, the country moved into severe recession, just as these projects began to come on stream. An extreme example of this phenomenon was seen in the City of London office development market when in the year August 1989/90 more office space was constructed ($47\,806\,m^2$ ($514\,600\,ft^2$) than had been built over the previous decade $47\,639\,m^2$ ($512\,800\,ft^2$).

As with most other sectors of the property market, supply is much easier to assess than demand. The principal factors underlying the supply of office accommodation are:

- government and local authority policy
- existing approvals (as a proportion of stock)
- projects under construction (likewise)
- projects proposed but not yet approved (likewise)
- vacancy rates (likewise)
- rental and yield trends
- availability of utilities and services
- construction cost trends
- availability and terms of finance.

Once data on demand and supply have been assembled, an analysis can take place to assess the relationship between the two, for the developer is not so much concerned with demand and supply as such, but rather the difference between them, which is known as the "absorption rate'. Since it takes two to three years to bring an office building onto the market, the developer is principally concerned with the likely future absorption rate for office space in a given locality, rather than present rate. Simple quantitative market models have been proposed but are rarely employed in practice (Detoy & Rabin 1985).

Decentralization and relocation

Perhaps the most hotly debated issue in respect of office location is that of decentralization and relocation, and, linked with it, the future of the main office centres, especially London. However, conflicting views are advanced regarding the pace, degree and direction of decentralized office development.

During the 1980s one of the most powerful engines of the property boom was the growing number of companies that decided to relocate their business premises. The number of jobs that relocated from Central London, for example, doubled from an annual total of 5675 in 1986 to 11 380 in 1990 (Rawson-Gardiner 1993). With the erosion of the property cost differential between London and the regions, one key incentive for companies to relocate office employment to provincial cities became much more reduced. While rapid rental inflation in Central London in the late 1980s helped trigger a record volume of decentralization in the years 1990–92, this tailed off very sharply in 1993–4. Some increase in out-movement is said to occur in the short term, but longer-distance moves beyond the South East became less popular in currently planned relocations (Damesick 1994).

Research has found the following features in the relocation decisions made by companies (Rawson-Gardiner 1993):

- Relocation will continue, but the forces energizing these moves will be different from those in the late 1980s.
- Relocation decisions made since the recession really took grip were driven more by operational and business factors than by purely property cost considerations.
- The restructuring or reorganization of a company often prompted a move, or conversely, the relocation was used as a catalyst to implement cultural corporate changes.
- A significant proportion of the 500 largest companies in the UK feel that scope remains for further reducing property costs through the rationalization of space requirements.
- Although property costs will continue to play an important role in some relocation decisions over the next few years, relocations will be more likely to take place to achieve savings through the reorganization of the property portfolio and/or a desire to downsize, rather than as a means to escape from exorbitant rents.
- The major problems regarding location related to staff matters, especially with long-distance moves, and the use of relocation consultants specializing in human resources was prevalent.
- Relocation overall is an effective tool for achieving both cost control and corporate change.

Looking at the future of London as a main office centre, it is clear that the process of decentralization has been taking place over a long period of time, and is not a sudden phenomenon. In fact, it is unlikely that the scale and type of decentralization that has happened since the mid-1960s will recur. Nevertheless, it is possible to advance the case that in forthcoming years only those activities that absolutely have to be centred in London will remain. Increasingly, operations that depend upon a high level of close business contact, such as finance, property, advertising and the law, will predominate, together with a concentration of top management in the headquarters offices of major national and international companies. Moreover, the influx of foreign business, especially banks, continues apace, and, initially at least, London is viewed as being the only acceptable location. As a consequence of this constant drift towards the provision or retention of higher-level jobs, the overwhelming demand will be for offices supplying superior space standards.

One very noticeable trend throughout the 1980s and early 1990s had been in London itself. Central area development overspilled into several centres around the City and West End, as well as to various suburban locations, for many national and multinational corporations are willing to make only marginal moves. However, it should be appreciated that this process of intra-city relocation is not confined to London, but is also experienced elsewhere in cities such as Bristol, Birmingham and Manchester.

Notwithstanding that London will always attract a certain kind of commercial activity, there can be little doubt that there will be a sustained flow of business away from the capital. Job losses are also virtually certain, which could lead to a further deterioration in transport and other services, as well as an increase in infrastructure costs. There is already a tendency on the part of large business organizations to situate their corporate headquarters in locations well away from major centres. Even some international banking corporations have opted for decentralized locations and many other traditional central area operations are looking very seriously at the balance of advantages that might lead them to decant a significant part of their business, or to decamp altogether, to more provincial or Home County locations. What could well happen is that office functions and structures might be polarised between very high-order activities occupying top-quality expensive office premises in central-area positions, and all other operations being conducted in low-rise, low-density and relatively inexpensive locations out of town. In this way, it appears almost certain that the South East region outside London is bound to expand. Already, considerable pressure has been placed upon towns along the various motorway corridors; the infrastructure investment in areas such as south Hampshire and Buckinghamshire is proving irresistible; and the completion of the M25 inevitably is exercising a magnetic influence upon commercial property developments.

One of the most recent manifestations arising out of a desire to decentralize is the growth in demand for accommodation sited in office parks. These campus-style developments are characteristically located on the edge of towns and comprise a mix of low-rise low-density buildings with a wide range of business, and sometimes leisure facilities, set in an attractive environment close to good schools and high-grade housing. Frequently, they are not restricted purely to office build-

411

ings but are composed of various business activities, including research and light engineering as well as conventional clerical and administrative functions. (These forms of development are discussed more fully on p. 436.)

Planning and office development

Many of the basic aspects of planning policy and practice affecting office development are beyond the scope of this text. Nevertheless, some comment on specific planning considerations is called for because office development proposals are so frequently singled out for special treatment by local authorities, especially in London and the South East. There has often, in fact, been a heavy bias against office development in certain areas, sometimes politically inspired and sometimes resulting from pressures exerted by vested interest. Somehow, offices attract a degree of vituperation not directed towards other forms of development such as industry and housing. The fact that office-based activities provide a major source of employment is seemingly overlooked by some councils and the lobbies that influence them. Strangely, vacant new industrial estates attract sympathy, whereas vacant recently completed office premises attract opprobrium. A certain underlying rationale can be divined, in that office developers are typically cast in the mould of persons who display a general indifference to the social ramifications of their proposed schemes and have a particular tendency to ignore the public costs of private development. To some extent, recession tempered this reaction, and in any event large-scale town-centre office development is in the doldrums. However, out of town the concept for a new generation of business parks faces probable conflict with local authorities in the light of Department of Environment policies regarding sustainable development.

The general principles that govern the framing of most planning policies as they relate to office development can usefully be summarized as follows:
- to control the scale, standards of design and layout of individual buildings according to established planning objectives.
- to control the location of office development, in accordance with the objectives of land use or spatial planning
- to control the overall level of office development activity with respect to the objectives of economic development policy.

These policies are abstracted from the late Greater London Council's published approach towards office development control and they epitomize the somewhat negative approach often taken towards offices. There has always appeared to be a basic ambivalence by planning authorities at a strategic level regarding a decision as to whether support should be given towards central area development along with better housing and public transport facilities, or whether suburban decentralization with improved road and traffic management schemes should be encouraged. In any event, policies towards offices have proved difficult to formulate, because of what appears to be an inherent inability to examine and interpret true office needs, which is made worse by the lack of a proper database relating to business occupation.

Strategic planning for office development[2]

The London Planning Advisory Committee (LPAC), which has the statutory duty of advising government on the content and extent of strategic planning guidance for London, proposed a new strategic context for office development in late 1994. The advice given to government reflects the dramatic changes that have taken place in the London office market since the boom of the late 1980s when the take-up of new floorspace slumped from a peak of 10.5 million ft^2 to only 2.5 million ft^2, with record vacancy rates and supply far in excess of demand.

As described by Martin Simmons, the Chief Planner for LPAC, the kind of policy framework now proposed is not prescriptive: it does not seek specific levels of office development, nor does it direct development to particular locations against others. It aims to reduce uncertainty by improving the availability of strategic information to planning authorities, and to help the market operate more efficiently by lessening the risks of developers and investors misreading it (Simmonds 1994/5).

This information-oriented planning context is based on identifying London's capacity to sustain future office development. It has the following dimensions:
- the macroeconomic background to future demand
- assessment of the London office market
- the future capacity of the labour market
- the future capacity of the transport network
- environmental factors, including urban quality and residential communities.

Macroeconomic scenarios, with pessimistic and optimistic variations, form the basis for a perspective on office demand. They focus on future performance of the finance and business services sectors, on which London's future as a world city depends, and which are relatively volatile in terms of the employment and the office floorspace demand that they generate.

An optimistic scenario has been adopted and short-, medium- and long-term projections made for the demand and supply of office space, together with an evaluation of the future capacity of the London labour market to sustain growth and the impact upon the existing and planned transport system. The overall analysis has led to the establishment of objectives for a new strategic planning framework as follows:
1. to maintain, taking both existing supply and operational requirements into account, accessible development sites to sustain London's continuing world city success;

---

2. This section is drawn from an article by Martin Simmonds (Chief Planner for the London Advisory Planning Committee) in *Property Review* 4(7), 213–17, 1994.

2. a broad capacity for development that is sustainable in terms of available labour and the transport network;
3. to establish a locational context, regarding extent of concentration in the traditional core of the City and West End, the role of Docklands and East London, the scope for "fringe" locations such as King's Cross, and relationship with other London centres, notably Croydon, taking account of relative costs;
4. to seek improved quality in the urban environment, and a vibrant Central London through more mixed activities and enhanced communities. (LPAC 1994)

The proposed strategic locational framework for office development takes the following factors into account:

- an up-to-date understanding of the relationship between the demand for new space and the pattern of supply, up to 2001 and longer term
- the capacity of the Central Activities Zone and the Isle of Dogs/Canary Wharf, relative to other locations
- the comparative advantage (e.g. labour availability and business contact) accruing from new and enhanced transport infrastructure (under construction or where finance is assured)
- mixed-use areas and vulnerable residential areas
- the part office development can play in economic regeneration
- the capacity of centres in Outer London to sustain development, in terms of labour and transport capacity.

In the rest of the South East, a new strategic context is provided by the government's new Regional Planning Guidance (RPG9, March 1994). This includes a general objective of sustaining the attractions of the region for inward investment and the location of corporate headquarters and facilitating new developments for industry and commerce, but bearing in mind that environmental constraints will limit scope for further growth west and south of London. It acknowledges the extent of vacant space and the very substantial scale of existing planning permissions in all parts of the region. Structure plans provide the existing vehicle for augmenting these regional statements for the main office centres, reflecting local circumstances. However, structure planning, and particularly its function in establishing the basic demand and supply parameters, is under threat from impending local government reorganization and the government's desire to extend unitary government and plan-making for smaller areas.

There is also stated to be clear merit in establishing a similar framework for other regional office centres requiring a city–regional scale of analysis with a strong and coherent planning organization. It is argued that, to deliver this, unitary authorities would need to be brought together in a formal structure. Voluntary arrangements not being likely to command the requisite degree of consensus, nor the resources and expertise (including consultancies) to establish a sound macroeconomic demand scenario and local office market analysis to put with the more traditional planning factors.

Many local authorities traditionally opposed to significant office development proposals are beginning to recognize the importance of the office sector in securing overall employment objectives. In this, the attraction of major corporations moving to the country or relocating from Central London has been seen to play an important role. However, it has been pointed out that at the current time there are probably more towns seeking large single-space users than there are potential occupiers for this type of accommodation. Planners and developers alike, it is argued, would do well to pay attention to the regional and subregional role played by a town, which might in future have a greater effect on the office absorption rate, than continued attempts to entice outsiders from the fast-shrinking pool of large mobile companies. There is also a tendency for many towns to resist office development on the edge of the urban area, and in a few less restrictive towns a dual market has emerged between greenfield and town centre locations.

Planning policy can be highly successful in battening down office development, but it is much less effective in encouraging it. Nevertheless, several principal factors outlined below exercise a considerable effect upon the outcome of office development proposals.

Floorspace

The popular way by which the total amount of planned floorspace for a local authority is calculated is to establish a relationship between predicted population levels, proportion of office employees and consequent office space used. Each of these factors is highly susceptible to error, and this is compounded when they are combined. Employment generation assessed by worker density standards, therefore, is extremely difficult to compute and virtually impossible to enforce. From this it can be argued that floorspace as an indicator or regulator of office development is a very crude instrument. A more discretionary approach is adopted by many planning authorities, although some are peculiarly reluctant to release additional approvals in order to reduce obvious scarcities and deflate excessively high levels of rent, which discourage business activity and employment. A certain amount of discrimination is also required to ensure the sensitive release of sufficient land and planning consents in the right locations, so as to capture internationally footloose companies. One further aspect of floorspace is the means of controlling the intensity of development on individual sites. The nature and operation of plot ratio and floorspace index controls is explained elsewhere, but it is important to recognize that different authorities attach varying degrees of adherence to the precise designation of particular areas and density levels. Some are open to negotiation around an established figure, some are not. In general, however, it is fair to say that most authorities are less rigid and less definitive than previously.

415

Transport and parking

Problems of communication and traffic beset all forms of property development, but despite planning arguments to the contrary, it is possible to put forward the case that in many ways offices cause the least amount of disruption to the transportation system. To a great extent, most office developments are creatures of communications networks, and have a strong capacity to adjust to them. The real question that confronts planning authorities is how, in the aggregate, to preserve a balance between, on the one hand, ensuring that there is a sufficient minimum level of service provision to permit proper access to a proposed development and, on the other, preventing an overload of the existing system. Because of this, sites immediately adjacent to transport termini or interchanges are often favoured. In appraising a potential development, or in making an application for planning permission in respect of offices, there are various factors that should be taken into account. These can be summarized as follows:

- the number of employees who will be working within the building
- the likely number of visitors attracted to the development, and their probable mode of travel
- the amount of delivery and service traffic generated by the prospective users
- the extent to which loading and unloading operations might take place, the noise that could be created, and the times when the building will be used and the various operations occur
- where access is to be provided.

Parking is an important consideration. Standards and regulations vary throughout the country, depending normally upon the proximity to the town or city centre and the degree of congestion enjoyed at the place in question. Some local authorities preclude parking facilities altogether, apart from an absolute bare minimum of spaces. Others insist upon levels as high as one space for every $32.5\,m^2$ ($350\,ft^2$) of floorspace. Outside Central London, however, a commonly sought level of provision for in-town sites separates operational and non-operational requirements, setting standards for the former at around a maximum of one space for every $70\,m^2$ ($750\,ft^2$) of gross floorspace. For out-of-town office parks the standard is around one space to every $23\,m^2$ ($250\,ft^2$), and sometimes as one to every $14\,m^2$ ($150\,ft^2$).

With non-operational parking provision it is not unusual for local planning authorities to try to insist that the carparking spaces should be made available for public use, and also sometimes to look for a commutation of the cost of provision towards the construction of general public carparks. In certain circumstances, where no such commutation takes place, councils will seek to enter into agreements with developers for the transfer of private off-street parks to public use on Saturdays.

The Departments of the Environment and Transport collaborated to produce PPG13 *A guide to better practice* in late 1995, aimed at reducing the need to travel, through land-use and transport planning. The guide provides a practical user's

416

manual for implementing PPG13, which should help local authority planners and councillors in drawing up or revising their development plans and in considering individual planning applications. It should also benefit developers and individuals who wish to see how the concepts in PPG13 can be translated into practice.

Restricted user

As part of a policy of restraint, some local planning authorities attempt to limit or control the use or occupancy of office buildings by means of:

- local user conditions, restricting occupancy to businesses already established and operating in the area
- named user conditions, where specified firms alone are allowed to occupy the premises
- small suite provision, where all or part of the development must be let in small office units of, say, not more than $464\,\text{m}^2$ ($5000\,\text{ft}^2$).

Recent years have seen some relaxation of these policies, and a greater record of success against their imposition at appeal.

A radical change in the restriction of use was introduced by the Town and Country Planning (Use Classes) Order 1987. This lists 16 classes, which are placed in four general use categories:

A shopping area
B other business and industrial
C residential
D social and community uses.

With regard to office development, the Class B1 (Business) brings together offices, so long as they do not provide a service for visiting members of the public, and light industry. For certain projects, therefore, developers might seek a wider range of uses than hitherto had been possible. Nevertheless, local planning authorities still retain their power of development control and can look to restrict the freedom to change uses to a narrower range than the order permits. However, Circular 13/87 makes it plain that the Secretary of State will regard the imposition of such restrictions as unreasonable unless there is clear evidence that the uses excluded would have a serious impact on the environment or on amenity, not susceptible to other control. In practice, the business use class has provided considerable opportunities for the owners of multi-storey industrial buildings to refurbish their properties to meet the demands of a growing studio market.

Planning gain

The subject of extracting community benefits in return for planning consents comes most sharply into focus when considering proposed office developments. Offices are invariably – and often erroneously – taken to be the most profitable form of property development and the essential ingredient in many mixed-use schemes. Local authorities have come to accept, however, that there are often occasions when a certain amount of commercial office space must be included to make some residential or leisure developments viable. It is not uncommon to find phrases along the lines of "office accommodation to be kept to a minimum level required for the successful implementation of the development package" (Kingston Borough[3]) in local plans and planning briefs prepared for areas and sites otherwise deemed undesirable for offices. Given the present state of the market, the assumption that office construction usually produces the most profitable form of development is fallacious. Traditionally, shopping schemes produce high returns, and in many prime locations luxury housing can be the most profitable use. On some sites in Central London, in fact, permission has been sought to change existing planning approvals from office to residential use.

Nevertheless, it is important to establish the prevailing attitude of planning authorities towards the issue of planning gain obligations and agreements at the earliest stage in the process of development.

Urban design

Although beauty is said to lie in the eye of the beholder, it is true to say that over recent years the design and siting of offices has become a very much more critical consideration than hitherto. Many local authorities are willing to extend a greater degree of sympathy towards well designed, sensitively proportioned office buildings, or countenance higher levels of density than would otherwise be the norm if a proposed scheme is attractive and harmonizes with its surroundings. In 1994, for example, the City of London abandoned a strict adherence to the use of plot ratio as an instrument of development control in favour of a more discretionary approach towards building design.

The relative popularity of renovation as opposed to redevelopment is becoming general across all sectors of the commercial property market, but the preference towards refurbishment on the part of planning authorities is particularly marked in the case of office development projects. More than this, there appears to be a growing awareness and understanding of the economics of conservation, so that there is no longer quite the antipathy in some quarters towards the change of use of buildings of architectural or historic interest to offices, where otherwise they might have continued to deteriorate. In most instances, conversion to offices is infinitely preferable to redevelopment or radical refurbishment for shops.

---

3. Extract from the draft town centre plan for Kingston, London Borough of Kingston, 1983.

Regeneration

Although this section on planning and office development opened on a negative note as to how office projects are seen by planning authorities, it ends with a more positive theme: the role that planned office schemes can play in the regeneration of local economies. Increasingly, it is recognized that many older cities with serious problems of social deprivation, high unemployment, environmental degradation and general decline have large sites, which are otherwise well located, that have potential for the development of business parks or office campuses. An excellent example of this is the Newcastle Business Park, which is one of the Tyne & Wear Development Corporation's flagship developments. Here a vacant, derelict and contaminated 24 ha (60 acre) site has been transformed through the expenditure of around £140 million in partnership with the private sector into a major business park, providing around 4000 jobs when fully let. Although such initiatives do not always directly benefit the local population with long-term employment, they do generate short-term job opportunities and act as a general catalyst for economic growth within the urban area.

Design and layout

For almost 30 years following the end of the Second World War, the design of office buildings was uniformly dull and unimaginative. Architects were all too frequently nervous about the mystical design and performance standards laid down by the major financial institutions and their professional advisers, and as a result tended to allow the control of design to pass out of their hands. In matters of new office development it almost appeared as if the accountant had gained ascendancy over the architect, and the approach to commercial development seemed to be the provision of functionally clad and serviced floorspace. The 1980s can be said to have witnessed a constant improvement in the standard of design of office developments. Nevertheless, the trend in low-rise blocks back to brick as a facing material, prompted by demands from property and planning interests alike, gave rise to a certain amount of fresh criticism. This resulted from the rash of three- and four-storey brick-built developments, topped with lead or copper mansard roofs and adorned by dinky dormer windows, some of which were reasonably well done, some decidedly were not.

Above all, however, the 1980s have been generally recognized as a decade that witnessed a quantum leap in the design of office buildings. Until the early 1980s, the process of designing office buildings had been one of steady evolution and refinement, with the product being supply led. But then the more astute developers began to question the conventional wisdom of office design and started to identify and examine some of the changing occupational trends brought about by the increasing impact of information technology, new organizational structures and in London, for a brief period in the late 1980s, the new system of stock market trading.

Broad principles

The main principles by which office design and layout might be judged have been set down as follows:

1. relationship of the building to its surroundings in terms of appearance, height and size, and response to outside factors such as railway lines and noisy streets;

2. pedestrian and traffic access, and the position of entrances and service points;

3. structural grid and facility in meeting subdivision requirements;

4. natural light penetration;

5. floor to floor heights;

6. size and shape of floors in relation to likely tenant demand and flexibility in dividing floors or letting separate floors singly;

7. position and design of service cores;

8. efficiency of building, i.e. relationship between gross area and net lettable accommodation;

9. carparking content and location;

10. extent and suitability of any landscaped or other amenity areas. (Marber 1985)

In terms of the shell, scenery and settings, it has been pointed out that buildings take a long time to build, are difficult to change, and once built are there to last (Worthington & Kenya 1988). Firms, on the other hand, are continuously in a state of flux, as the economy, technology and market changes around them.

Because of this, building design decisions reflect different timescales where:

- building shells have a life-span of around 75 years and may have many owners
- services have a life-span of around 15 years and adjust one shell to specific functions.
- scenery may change every 5–7 years as organizations grow and change
- on a daily, weekly or monthly basis, scenery may be moved to reflect specific activities.

In very general terms, a typical specification for a modern office building has been summarized as providing (Jones Lang Wootton 1990):

Structure
- 4m (13ft) slab to slab height
- 3m (9ft 9in.) clear floor to ceiling height
- 15cm (6in.) accessible raised floor height
- 6m by 9m (19ft 8in by 29ft 6in.) structural grid
- 36kg (80lb) per ft^2 live floor loading + 9kg (20lb) ft^2 for partitions.

420

External fabric
- high-quality curtain walling of aluminium and granite or stone
- double glazing

Building services
- variable air volume air-conditioning
- integral lighting within suspended ceiling – 500 lux lighting level
- small power supply of 3 watts per ft^2
- air-conditioning cooling load of 3 watts per ft^2 (small power)
- additional cooling capacity for specialist areas
- emergency standby generator
- facility for tenant's generator
- building management system
- sprinkler installation
- passenger lift providing a waiting interval of 30 seconds
- separate goods lift and loading bay.

Internal finishes
- Use of high-quality materials (granite, marble, timber, etc.) in entrance halls, lifts, atria and lavatory accommodation.

On the subject of specification, however, the era of speculatively driven development in a landlords' market evidenced in the 1980s has passed to a trend of occupier-driven development in a tenants' market. Many occupiers are now calling for less elaborately specified space that still meets their needs. Huge power and heat-removal capabilities; structural loading provisions twice the British Standard with no credible justification; overestimation of electrical loadings and associated air-conditioning capacity; fitting-out tenant space rather than letting a basic shell; and costly bespoke design of the components – all have led to waste and expense, which with the growing unpopularity of air-conditioning; dropping power consumption needs for information technology; and better building-services control mechanisms, means that the new generation of office buildings could be substantially cheaper than those built during the late 1980s with no loss of effectiveness, and possible gains in occupant wellbeing (Saxon 1993). Stanhope Properties undertook research in this field following its experience with Stockley Park and Broadgate with the results shown in Table 16.1 (Low 1994).

Stanhope also concluded that diversity in a building's occupancy must be addressed in order to design efficiently. Good design will also address how

Table 16.1 Impact on development – building specification.

Feature	Industry norm	Stanhope recommended
Small power	25W per m^2	15W per m^2
Floor loadings	5kN per m^2	2.5kN per m^2
Lighting	500lux per m^2	400lux per m^2
Air conditioning	21–22°C	24°C (max)
Occupation density	1.9m^2	1:14/1:16m^2

upgrading can be achieved economically, for it is more economic in the long term to adapt regular office space than it is to custom-design specialist areas in the base building.

With regard to office building specification, the British Council of Offices has produced a document Specification for Urban Offices that supplies a reference source for those needing, providing or investing in offices (BCO 1994). This document aims to achieve consensus towards the approach to office building specification, reviewed as necessary in the light of new technology. It also aims to standardize, wherever possible, the design approach, the choice of materials and of components as they relate to the issues of specification, so that the practice of "re-inventing the wheel" is eliminated.

Over recent years a recognition has emerged that, in addition to purely economic considerations, there is a need to adopt a more environmentally friendly approach towards office development. To this end, the Building Research Establishment (BRE) has linked with professionals to devise criteria for measuring buildings from an environmental standpoint and has introduced the Building Research Establishment Environmental Assessment Model (BREEAM) together with related certification (Prior 1993).

It is now possible to suggest, therefore, that we stand at something of a threshold in respect of office design, where all concerned with development are being asked to match space utilization to occupiers' requirements, building cost and premises layout. In exploring new dimensions in design it can be stated that four themes increasingly will dominate the creation of good office space:

- attractive external appearance
- low energy cost
- acceptance of new office technology
- adaptability for organization and acceptability to people.

Size and shape

Naturally there will be a continuing demand for new office developments of all sizes from $232\,m^2$ $(2500\,ft^2)$ to $23\,225\,m^2$ $(250\,000\,ft^2)$, all that it is possible to do so is to point to several trends that are likely to be most apparent in the market. Two particular features that will probably typify the sector in respect of the size of offices are worthy of mention. First, it seems almost certain that smaller individual units of office accommodation will be in demand, with the accent being on the provision of buildings in the $929-1858\,m^2$ $(10\,000-20\,000\,ft^2)$ range for single occupancy. Secondly, and related, will be the shift to multiple occupation among business users, and the development of office buildings that have the facility to be divided conveniently into discrete units of anything from $93\,m^2$ $(1000\,ft^2)$ upwards. As a direct corollary of these trends, it would seem reasonable to conclude that the number of large speculative buildings in excess of $9290\,m^2$ $(100\,000\,ft^2)$ will decline significantly.

It is equally difficult to generalize about the likely future shape of office buildings, except again to identify the principal direction in which the market is moving. The probable polarization of the office market between central city area and suburban or greenfield site locations has already been promulgated. Suffice it to say that the former will be inclined to retain a concentration upon multi-storey development, whereas the latter will focus more upon two- and three-storey construction. However, the most significant feature in respect of building shape is the optimum width of offices. The era of the shallow rectangular block is over, and so too for that matter is the very deep-plan office design. Few offices in future will be constructed to a width of much less than 12–14 m (40–45 ft), and much more than 15–17 m (50–55 ft). On large sites and for bigger buildings, therefore, a popular form of development shape will be a roughly square building surrounding a central atrium or courtyard. This trend will be reinforced by the increasing desire on the part of the occupiers to have cellular offices with outside views, which, on average, take up about 60 per cent of usable space. Within sensible limits, however, atria should be designed so that a proportion, if not all, can be infilled at a later date.

The BRE suggests that a plan depth of 15–18 m (50–60 ft) is ideal and permits space planning layout in three zones. Dimensions below 15 m (50 ft) preclude this, but flexible space can still be provided down to 13.5 m (45 ft). Below this, efficient space planning becomes difficult. It is important to remember, however, that some deep space in a building, no more than 25 per cent of net lettable area, is necessary to allow efficient space planning for common areas.

Structural arrangement

It has been argued that the importance of structural design is seldom fully recognized, let alone properly appreciated, for it carries with it the genetic code for a building, comprising (Anderson 1985):

- the method of construction
- the speed of construction
- the cost of the structure and related elements
- the internal planning of the building
- fire resistance
- acoustic performance
- structural stability
- life-span of the building
- elevations of the building
- the articulation of mechanical and electrical services
- the response of the heating and cooling systems
- the ability to change.

All structural design elements are to some extent significant, but several deserve special mention from the developer's standpoint: the structural frame, the service core and the floor arrangements.

423

Structural frame

At the outset of the design process, careful consideration should be given to the position, size and number of columns constituting the vertical dimension of the structural frame, the basic rule being that a building should be as column-free as possible and the main constraint being one of cost. Ideally, columns should form a structural grid more than 8 m apart and preferably situated on a floor edge in order to allow the provision of unobstructed office space. However, structural grids of less than this are quite common. Where columns are placed within the internal area, account must be taken of future division, if desired, and possible corridor construction, if adopted. In the same way, perimeter wall details will need to be able to accept partitioning at many different points. In addition to the structural grid, which dictates the frequency of columns, and both determines, and is determined by, the distance between external walls, there is also the planning grid and the construction grid. The planning grid, of interest to the space planner, is defined by the same items as those of the structural grid, but is further affected by the distances between windows and the frequency of the mullions. The construction, or product grid is the module to which standard building products are made. The successful design is the one in which all these grids are integrated into a harmonious whole (Salata 1990).

The vast majority of modern office buildings have a 1.5 m planning grid and it is considered appropriate to standardize on this dimension. It is ideal for sizing rooms and the provision of corridors. Clearly, the structural or column grids chosen must be a multiple of the planning grid. It is not considered advantageous to try to create column-free space in excess of 9 m width, however, because of the effect on structural depths and therefore building height, and also because buildings are rarely fitted out in a way that column space would gain any visual or space-planning advantage. In choosing the column grid it is necessary to avoid excessive column size, and perimeter and core columns should be integral with or about the perimeter or internal walls. With creative thought, the base can be put to various uses such as circulation, café or exhibition space, but requires additional life safety systems if it is to be used for general office area. In the life of the larger buildings it may well be an advantage to be able to create a large area of deep-plan space on at least one floor.

In terms of the materials to be used for the structural frame, steel or reinforced concrete are equally acceptable. Concrete solutions incorporating pre-stressing, post-tensioning or pre-stressed concrete floors slabs are less flexible and inhibit the user in altering the building to suit varying needs. However, where these design solutions could confer real benefits, they should be considered.

Service core

The service core of an office building consists of lifts, stairs, toilets, service ducts and ancillary accommodation, such as special storage, cleaners' cupboards and machine bays. An optimum placement is a balance between space maximization and construction cost, taking into account such factors as entrances, circulation routes within the building, vertical interdepartmental communications, natural lighting and means of escape. There are advantages and disadvantages to central, peripheral and offset or external core provision, depending upon individual circumstances. The internal finishes to core spaces should generally be simple, hard-wearing, maintenance-free and attractive.

Floor arrangements

It is usually advisable to avoid the use of power-floated *in situ* slabs as a floor finish. If they are employed, it is important to consider the problems that arise in the eventual distribution of electricity and other services to central areas, particularly if no partitions are planned. With regard to live floor loading for the general area, which normally accounts for about 95 per cent of the total space, the British Standard Code of Practice has a minimum threshold of $2.5\,kN$ per m^2 over approximately 5 per cent of the total area. Where there is a dead load, an extra allowance of $1\,kN$ per m^2 should be made for such items as demountable partitions, raised floors, ceilings and building-service equipment.

Another factor that has emerged in the structural design of some modern office developments, principally those located on out-of-town business parks, is that provision should be made for the creation of several potential entrance points, as opposed to a single front door and reception area.

Internal layout

A positive revolution is taking place in the internal layout of office space. The strictly cellular office blocks of the 1940s, 1950s and early 1960s gave over to the deep open-plan offices of the late 1960s and 1970s. Open-plan offices with liberal indoor landscaping, pioneered in Germany as the "burolandschaft", claimed savings of 20 per cent in space and in cost, but overall increases in business efficiency have been seriously contested. In short, what we have arrived at is a combination of space uses comprising a mix of cellular, group and open-plan office space, together with suitable integrated space provision for support services. The physical design and layout of buildings is beginning to respond to the demands of effective business organization and preferred commercial practice. Thus, there has been a breakdown in the rigid compartmentalization of activities throughout commerce and industry, be they industrial, research, distributive, storage, administration, executive, clerical, marketing and the like.

With a modern office building it is likely that up to 50 per cent of space will be given over to what conventionally have always been considered to be ancillary uses, such as meetings, conferences, presentations, training, libraries, relaxation and machine rooms. The advent of advanced technology has obviously quickened the pace of change, but this has been put into proper perspective as follows:

Face to face meetings are likely to remain crucial, with formal technology-based communication channels highlighting rather than detracting from the importance of informal, unofficial and non-routine communication. (DEGW 1983)

An overriding criterion in the layout of offices is an ability to change the physical environment. Divisibility, therefore, is important, both in terms of facilitating different working arrangements within a single organization as well as allowing for simple subletting of parts of the premises. It is also necessary to create convivial space for small teams working within large organizations. As has already been stated, most people desire their individual workspaces to have an external view if at all possible, and, to this end, nearly all ancillary operations can be situated towards the central core of the building.

Less uniformity throughout an office complex along the lines described requires that the keynote must again be flexibility. This used to mean the basic ability to alter internal partitioning. It now means a facility to change the proportion of cellular offices, open-plan offices, support space and service equipment, together with an ability to respond to changing occupancy and methods of work. Much of this flexibility can be achieved by differentiating the building shell from the relocatable elements in the office scenery. Moreover, the use of certain space-defining components, such as fin walls, can give some backbone to office planning and layout, and can even assist in office management.

From the developer's point of view it is essential to optimize the amount of lettable floorspace, and, as has been mentioned elsewhere in the text, a net to gross relationship of about 80 per cent is the normal target in new buildings. It is sometimes possible to accomplish slightly more, and occasionally acceptable to supply a little less, all depending upon the individual circumstances of the scheme. Small suite provision, for example, will normally be lower than single occupancy design. In this context, entrance halls should be as spacious as possible, with a very high standard of finish and separation from certain service functions.

On the subject of space utilization, a note about worker space or occupational density is pertinent. It is commonly accepted at the design stage that an overall figure of one worker to every $9\,m^2$ ($100\,ft^2$) of net floorspace may be assumed as a minimum requirement. The legal minimum is expressed as one worker to every $11\,m^3$ ($388\,ft^3$) on the basis of, say, $5\,m^2$ ($50\,ft^2$) floorspace and $2.44\,m$ ($8\,ft$) ceiling height, but this is extremely low. Open-plan offices are credited with easily achieving a space of $12.5\,m^2$ ($135\,ft^2$) per person as against $14\,m^2$ ($150\,ft^2$), which would be needed in an equivalent conventional corridor and cellular layout. Combination layouts are also very economic because they concentrate upon function rather than a crude average. People do not occupy their workstations continuously, for example, and conference space can achieve high worker to space ratios. This having been stated, it should be appreciated that the nature of many peoples' work is changing. Skills are increasing. There is less clerical activity and more managerial, executive and professional. Consequently, there is a growing demand for a better quality of space, and this usually means more. This is portrayed by the figures for the old Greater London Council area, where in 1961 the ratio of administration to clerical work was 1:2.2, which had fallen to 1:1.7 in 1971 and to about 1:1. 1 by 1986.

Glazing

With regard to the provision and design of windows in new office developments, it is becoming increasingly critical to pay attention to insulation and energy-saving standards. Many of the extensively glazed buildings of the late 1960s and 1970s proved costly to run and uncomfortable to work in. More recent developments, therefore, either employ a much more advanced system of glazing or have reverted to a lower proportion of external fenestration set within opaque cladding, or even more commonly, traditional brickwork. However, unless they are well designed, many buildings with restricted window areas can look extremely austere.

Problems of solar glare can often be overcome by the use of tinted glass or blinds, with or without the complement of air-conditioning. Some of the specially coated glasses can greatly increase the thermal value of the building envelope. With many, if not most, major new office development schemes, the incorporation of an atrium in the basic design enhances the provision of natural lighting.

Although every individual office design must be judged on its merits, it can generally be said that the necessary balance of daylight and energy consumption usually results in a proportion of 25–30 per cent glazing of the external surface. More than one-third of the outside area being given over to single glazing prevents proper thermal insulation. Double glazing only normally being installed to combat particular noise problems, rather than enhance environmental conditions, for thicker plate glass will often suffice in that respect. Turning again to design, it has been found that tall thin windows extending from floor to ceiling give the best daylight penetration. Experience has also shown that a certain proportion of a building's windows should be capable of opening, even by way of a caretaker's key, not merely as a fire precaution but in case the air-conditioning system fails. One problem that has recently arisen, which was not anticipated by developers or their architects, is the nuisance caused to neighbouring buildings by strong solar reflections from extensively glazed buildings.

Office refurbishment

Very crudely, in examining the market for office refurbishment a simple division can be made between the renovation of period buildings and the upgrading of post-war offices.

With period office buildings, the cost of refurbishment can be very difficult to assess, for the main structure can suffer from extensive dry rot to timbers or severe rust to steel frames, which might be uncovered only after work has begun. Planning requirements or aesthetic considerations may dictate or favour the restoration of a period building's existing facade, rather than recladding. And the opportunity to create additional office space by constructing extra mezzanine or gallery floors, or by bringing basement space into more effective use. Local authorities are also now empowered to relax certain statutory regulations where refurbishment would enable an historic building or group of buildings to be given a new lease of life.

Many, if not most, post-war office buildings constructed before the early 1970s are now outdated and are in desperate need of refurbishment. The popular 16.5m width, with a 1.5m wide central corridor, and 6m deep cellular offices leading off it, is normally too inflexible to cater for modern office users' demands. An owner or developer will, therefore, need to ascertain if there are design possibilities of re-arranging the internal layout of such a building to remove the rigidly determined central corridor and utilize the space provided, possibly by introducing a mixture of cellular and open-plan areas. The removal of non-loadbearing walls might also provide opportunities to utilize "dead" areas in the building. Although it will normally prove to be too costly, it can sometimes be worth replacing the central service core with an external core, which creates considerable extra lettable space. In any event, some reduction in the size of the existing core will usually be feasible. A typical refurbishment will also include recladding the building, renewing all the heating and plumbing systems, providing false ceilings and/or raised floors to accommodate new service ducts, as well as upgrading all common parts and renewing windows and window frames.

Services and facilities

The most important change to have taken place in the design and development of offices over recent years concerns building services and facilities. Providing an acceptable level of modern business services within a high-quality working environment has become much more important to the creation of successful office premises than the mere production of a serviced concrete and brick shell it once was. As a consequence, those involved in the process of commercial property development have had to become better acquainted with the range of services available and the level or provision required by occupiers.

In considering the relative importance of different aspects of office design and the provision of services and facilities, a survey of tenants was conducted by Healey & Baker, in which they were asked to rank ten factors in order of importance (Healey & Baker 1989). The results were as follows:
1. internal environmental control and heating system
2. quality of internal finishes
3. external appearance of building
4. carparking

5. provision for cable trunking
6. entrance hall
7. toilet facilities
8. security
9. lift performance reliability
10. arrangement for kitchen catering facilities.

Provision and distribution

To begin with, the modern office building demands an integrated approach towards building fabric and building services. The previous tendency was for services to be planned following the basic design of the building fabric. Unfortunately, with notable exceptions, current designs still attempt to adjust traditional building types to new service demands.

Design should provide for the possible and easy incorporation of additional facilities at a later date. This may involve the trimming of floor slabs in such a way that shafts can readily be added in the future. Some schemes have been drawn up so as to allow extra lift shafts to be inserted if they become necessary. Surplus vertical ducts are also fast being considered as essential in preserving the economic life of a building. One modern office complex, for example, has elevations that include a series of turrets that not only give a pleasing visual effect but also supply internal voids that could accommodate a variety of additional services, if and when required. The space needed for vertical ducting is roughly 2 per cent of the gross floor area and should be distributed among several risers rather than be concentrated at a single core.

The prime difficulties that arise in the provision and distribution of services usually relate to machine rooms, cabling and localized heat concentrations. The first and last are essentially questions of heating and ventilation, dealt with below. With regard to cabling, however, it is not everyone who likes cable drops from a suspended ceiling, and although it is possible to employ wall mounted cabling systems if there is no alternative, the best solution is commonly considered to be the construction of a raised floor, usually of about 150 mm. This is because it is accessible and it lends itself to workstation cabling and local environmental control. Another method is to provide three-channel floor ducts at, say, about 1.5 m centres, but this approach can actually prove to be less flexible and more expensive. In considering the provision of power, it is worth noting that if a standby generator is not installed at the outset then provision should be made for connecting one to the power supply at a suitable point.

As already mentioned, however, the 1980s witnessed something of an over-specification in the provision services of office buildings, largely as a result of the advances in information technology. Flexibility considerations seemed to dictate that it was necessary for every part of a building to be able to carry any load. This notion is now seriously in question.

429

Core and shell

The differing space and facility requirements of different office users has led to a "core and shell" approach on the part of many developers. It was becoming absurd for a tenant to move into a newly completed building only to have to set about changing and removing many of the finishes and fittings so recently installed. Tailoring floorspace areas to the special needs of a particular tenant often involves a great deal of modification in terms of partitioning, lighting and mechanical and electrical distribution.

Core and shell, therefore, aims to provide a development where all common areas are fully finished and the lettable areas are left for tenants to fit out themselves, or for the tenants' particular requirements to be incorporated before fitting-out work is finalized. Cost and time savings accrue to both parties, and the tenant has "customized" accommodation.

Opinions vary as to how much fitting-out work is done by the developer. Generally, all vertical distribution of services would be installed, with the duct work, for instance, blanked off where it enters the shell. Fire protection requirements will apply to the whole building and will usually mean the installation of a full sprinkler system. For finishes to shell areas, some developers do not install any floor, wall or ceiling finishes. Others may install a false floor because it improves the appearance and permits immediate partitioning. The entrance hall, staircases, common parts, toilets and core would be fully finished. The key as far as the developer is concerned is being able to predict, which elements tenants are likely to remove, adapt or change when they take up occupancy and therefore leave them out. Flexibility again enhances lettability. The developer naturally retains the right to approve any deviation from a standard specification, and differences in cost may either be borne by the tenant as a lump sum, or rentalized.

Interestingly, in the Healey & Baker survey of tenants referred to above only 9 per cent of respondents preferred fully fitted offices, and the rest were equally divided between bespoke accommodation and shell and core, although shell and core, with a developer's contribution towards fitting out, was much more popular in the London area than in the provinces.

Internal environmental control

The nature, form and degree of internal environmental control provided within modern office developments depends primarily upon the design, location and use of the buildings, together with the economics of the market and the requirements of the occupier. From the point of view of both developer and occupier, however, the reduction of fuel costs, allied with the maintenance of a comfortable environment, is a principal objective. Broadly speaking, this is best attained by producing a daylight building of energy-efficient design. Put very crudely, a highly glazed day-lit all electric and fully air-conditioned building is roughly twice as expensive as a deep-planned air-conditioned building with gas heating, and three times the cost to run as an energy-efficient daylit and naturally ventilated building.

In looking to adopt a low-energy design for an office building, it has been stated that it is possible to aim for a target of about 150kWh per m^2 gross per annum, which is about half the usual target rate of consumption. This can be done by designing the building fabric to modify the climate, reduce air conditioning, lower the lighting load, recover heat in winter, allow for flexibility in fuel usage and manage energy consumption efficiently (Henney 1983).

Air conditioning is a problematic issue in a country where the climate does not really justify the expense of installing sophisticated systems. Again, to a great extent it all depends upon the location of the proposed office development and the state of the property market whether or not it is necessary to instal artificial air-conditioning equipment. Although it is often seen as a sign of a "prestige" building for marketing purposes, tenants are not always impressed by the existence of the service, and are often concerned at the costs of running and maintaining an air-conditioning system. Sometimes, therefore, it is installed quite unnecessarily. External noise rather than excessive heat being a more popular reason for having such a facility. Nevertheless, where it has not been incorporated initially, provision for future installation should be allowed by ensuring that the basic building design has sufficient floor-to-ceiling heights and that the roof, walls and floors have knock-out panels to permit ready ducting. It has, however, been suggested that, where a developer wishes to include facilities for air conditioning, they should be installed in combination with heating radiators, together with variable volume units, so that the tenant may control the environment in separate parts of the building (Salata 1990). Moreover, it is increasingly advisable to consider the provision of separate floor systems and, even further, to make individual controls available in positions that allow sensible partitioning and maintain the proper balance of the system. Although the installation of an overall system is initially very costly, it is often best to design for the full potential and then add or subtract as required.

Several other factors regarding the provision of heating and ventilation systems are worthy of mention:

- Information technology has posed certain environmental problems, because desk-mounted equipment produces local hot spots and requires the introduction of local cooling facilities in selected 20–30m^2 zones (215–323ft^2).
- Appropriate systems include variable air volume, fan coils, displacement ventilation and chilled ceiling or beams according to circumstances.
- Space should be provided at the busy interconnecting junctions of vertical and horizontal ducts.
- Where the structure is massive, it may not cool down too much overnight, otherwise if economically possible it is normally best to maintain some background heating at all times.
- Most users prefer to have some proportion of natural ventilation, and a minimum of about 15 per cent of windows should be capable of opening.

431

- Packaged ventilating or heating units can often be placed on roofs and terraces to give greater flexibility.
- Water is usually preferred as a heating or cooling transfer medium rather than air, because of its compactness.
- Heat recovery systems are becoming very attractive propositions.
- One very useful and efficient development in the field of heating and ventilation is the heat pump, which is basically a refrigeration machine that generates heat in its cooling.

Lighting

Good lighting is extremely important in modern offices. The 1970s saw a general increase in the levels of lighting, but this was found to be both wasteful and uncomfortable. It was not only the level of illumination that caused discomfort and distraction but also the glare caused by the form of lighting employed; since then the tendency has been to lower internal lighting levels from around 1000 lux to 750 lux and even to 400–500 lux in many instances. Some areas of an office building might be dimmer still, and it is more and more common to install adjustable lighting so that tenants can arrange their own requirements as needs change. With the advent of the new office technology, lighting systems have to be capable of special adjustment in order to cope with different levels of light emission from visual display units. Providing lighting that is suitable for the mix of different office tasks in a modern business organization is a much more demanding design exercise than it has been in the past. The trend is towards the combination of background and "task" lighting, with the developer providing the background fixtures and a sufficiently flexible network of power points for occupiers to install task lighting of their own choosing and at their own expense. Over the past few years there has been greater use of "uplighters" with sodium lamps. These are usually free-standing, which gives a high degree of flexibility and a clean finish to walls and ceilings. They also make the reorganization of partitioned offices much easier, reduce the costs of electricity for lighting by about half, and lower the developers' initial costs of construction. Moreover, soft uplighters are best for users of screen equipment.

Communications

The adoption of ever more sophisticated office machinery and the increasing reliance in business operations of all kinds upon advanced information systems means that modern office building must be designed to house a variety of communications equipment and facilitate flexible usage of it. The need to intercommunicate a range of devices within a building has led to the concept of a local area communications network. Three basic approaches to such networks have been described as follows:

(i) A "stair" that is like a telephone exchange with all devices being wired to an exchange that reroutes data to other devices. The manufacturers of PBX equipment naturally prefer this approach, as they can incorporate it into a digital PBX.

(ii) A "ring" which is like a mains ring with each device attached to a data ring that operates at a very high data rate. Devices put data into the ring addressed to another device and when the data arrives at the recipient device it is read off.

(iii) An "Ethernet" which is like a "bus bar" onto which data is fed from devices, runs up and down it and is picked off by the recipient device.

(Henney 1983)

It is too early to say which are the best systems for what circumstances. Only time and the measure of commercial acceptability will tell.

The most popular form of distribution is by three-compartment trunking, accommodating channels for telephones, telex and VDUs. It is important to ensure that sufficient vertical ducts are made available from corridors and that adequate and correct connections for floor ducts and risers are supplied. Distribution could well be simplified by the increasing development and adoption of fibre optic cables. There is also a growing market in complete workstation systems. Looking at the creation of a total communications system, it is no longer a fanciful notion to suggest that most buildings housing large international organizations will have to have a communications dish on the roof.

Office machinery

Office machinery now includes the possible provision of telephone, word processing, personal computing, facsimile transmission, telex, teletext, electronic mail, information storage and retrieval, Prestel electronic diary, Infac (electronic clipping service) and electronic filing facilities. Although most modern offices will require separate machine rooms, with special control over temperature, humidity, dust, noise and static electricity, the amount and degree of specially prepared and controlled space is likely to decrease as advanced business machines become more mobile and more robust. Increasingly, equipment will be distributed around a building to individual workstations.

One of the consequences of introducing new forms of office machinery is the need to provide more power sources and accommodate heavy-duty cables in the office environment. Another is that the noise of modern word processors is lower than that of traditional typewriters, so that acoustic systems have to be balanced because other sources of noise become more incursive. Humidity levels also have to be regulated, and something within the range of 30–50 per cent is desirable, whereas 20–60 per cent might just be acceptable for most machines.

The creation of workstations is probably the most distinctive feature of the modern office. These combine a degree of personal privacy with varying levels of information technology. There are now a wide range of proprietary packages available on the market. In many, worktops, filing drawers, cupboards and the like are hung from tracks fitted to modular partitions or walls. This permits many variations to be introduced and ensures that there is little waste to floorspace. In this way, workstation systems liberate space, make more efficient use of internal areas, and improve occupancy rates. Increasingly, however, they incorporate sophisticated computing equipment with visual display, and this can give rise to a very high level of heat output, perhaps about 40 W per m^2. For this reason, it may be necessary to install localized but relocatable environmental conditioning and cooling systems, but the development of this area of building service technology is still in this infancy.

Lifts

The planning and development of any substantial office building is inextricably bound up with the matter of lift production. In the past it was a common failure in design to neglect proper consideration of the size, number, type, speed and location of lifts until too late in the process. It is not too much of an exaggeration to state, as has one leading manufacturer, that a successful office scheme of any size and quality has, to a very large extent, to be built around its lifts from the beginning. It is not possible merely to insert them at a later stage in standard-size holes, which have been left in the concrete. The lift manufacturer should, therefore, be brought in at the earliest possible stage of design, preferably in the capacity of a nominated subcontractor.

One of the main considerations in the provision of lifts is the future nature of occupancy that is envisaged. Single tenant or owner-occupation usually calls for a different lift layout and produces a different pattern of lift traffic to multiple occupancy. On the other hand, it is normally advisable to ensure that the flexible letting potential of the building is not circumscribed by an inappropriate lift provision. Lift installation must therefore be capable of satisfying the needs of different users as well as a single occupant. Modern microtechnology now enables lift services to be reprogrammed in accordance with changing occupiers' needs. As a guideline, lift provision of 1 person per 14 m^2 of net lettable area is considered to be good practice.

In order to maximize the amount of lettable floorspace and facilitate the internal organization of business activity, a popular recourse has been to design the lift and stairwell services as a separate external unit adjacent to the office building shell. Alternatively, "wall climber" lifts are beginning to be fashionable for office as well as shopping developments.

With regard to lift lobbies, up to three lifts may conveniently be planned in a row, and a row of four is an absolute limit for efficient use, with two facing two preferred. Where the number of lifts exceeds four, three in a row should be the limit in cul-de-sac lobbies. For very tall buildings, lift provision should be divided into vertical zones of 10–15 storeys to limit the number of floors served and thereby achieve acceptable waiting times (Case 1985).

A local authority may insist that one or more of the lifts in a building is designated for manual operation by visiting firemen, usually at the principal exit floor. Moreover, large office buildings will normally be provided with a goods lift whose main function is the distribution of heavy items of furniture, stationery, equipment, food and other stores. Escalators are still not common in office buildings, but their ability to handle continuous interfloor traffic makes them attractive in owner-occupied buildings (ibid.).

Problems with lifts are frequently the major cause of complaint from tenants and need constant care. Therefore, the treatment of lifts as an important part of the overall design is attracting more attention as developers become increasingly aware of the need to create a more attractive and harmonious environment.

Other services and facilities

Among the other services and facilities that might have to be considered in the design and development of a modern office block are the following:

- *Fire protection system*   With attention paid to hose and reel location, dry and wet risers, alarms, sprinklers, gas suppression systems and external access and areas for fire appliances.
- *Emergency lighting*   Should be installed in staircases, lavatories and other common parts.
- *Escape routes*   Designed in consultation with the fire brigade and with the cost effectiveness of office layout firmly in mind.
- *Lavatories*   For both sexes on each floor, with the potential for additional facilities and finishes and fittings to a high quality as well as good ventilation.
- *Ventilated cleaners' cupboards*   On each floor, with power, water supply and drainage.
- *Drinking water*   Supply on each floor.
- *Tea-making facilities*   On each floor, depending upon the size of building.
- *Waste disposal*   Areas should be provided for the storage of waste material as well as the usual waste disposal facilities.
- *Security*   It is increasingly important to provide a full and integrated manned and electronic intrusion system, which can range all the way from access control through to closed-circuit television and movement monitors detecting body heat.
- *Healthy building control*   More and more attention needs to be paid to designing buildings and providing monitoring systems to counteract the "sick building syndrome".

Serviced offices

There is a growing demand for the provision of serviced offices in the UK, by development, refurbishment and reorganization. Serviced offices have been defined as small office units between $15\,m^2$ ($161\,ft^2$) and $50\,m^2$ ($538\,ft^2$) available to let on short lease or licence terms for periods of one month upwards, but outside the security of the tenure provisions of the 1954 Landlord and Tenant Act. They normally provide a combination of secretarial support, photocopying facilities and post handling, telecommunications facilities, catering and dining room facilities, board room facilities, interview rooms, staffed reception area and electricity, lighting and heating. Payment of rent is on an inclusive basis and covers rents, rates, property insurance, a service charge, and may include the use of many of the facilities described.

It was established that in 1993 there were about 2000 business centres supplying serviced office space with occupiers ranging from starter firms looking for a first base to major foreign corporations (Sands 1993). The size of accommodation and standard of finish and fittings also vary considerably, but the common factor to the success of all serviced office developments is the quality of management.

Business and office parks

The late 1980s witnessed the emergence of the business park as a major new force in the UK property market. Without doubt, the growth in development of business parks was fuelled by the introduction of the B1 Use Class in 1987, but the more perceptive developers had already recognized the need for flexible "office look-alike" space out of town, and had closely researched the American experience (Healey & Nabarro 1988, *Estates Gazette* 1990). However, the early years of the 1990s saw a decline in the fortunes of business parks as dramatic as their earlier rise. Nevertheless, work continued on the size and design of a new generation of "true" business parks and realizing the potential of the best of existing parks (MacRae 1993).

The term business park tends to mean different things to different people, usually according to the particular circumstances pertaining and the position in which they stand. To some, the concept lies somewhere between high-tech and traditional industrial sheds, with elements of both in many schemes. To others the mix is much richer, to include not only business and office users but also retail, leisure and even residential developments. Moreover, the most recent arrival on the scene has been the corporate office park, which is predominantly office-based, with selected support facilities and normally aimed at substantial organizations often within the financial services or marketing sectors of the economy looking for international, national or regional headquarters buildings located in a parkland setting. For the purposes of this section a fairly catholic interpretation is taken towards the general classification of business and office parks, but one that excludes research, science and technology, described as (Holden 1986):

- a good business location, including easy access to road, rail and air transport
- high-quality, low-density development, well landscaped and with good car-parking provision
- an actively managed, well serviced development, including power, security and communications facilities, as well as recreational and business community provision.

Looking more closely at the corporate office or commerce park, the following common characteristics are revealed:

- Most buildings are on two, or possibly three storeys in order to limit the amount of vertical movements.
- Entrances and reception areas should be impressive and spacious, so as to allow tenants to promote a strong corporate image.
- Tenants seem to prefer relatively conventional layout and design specifications, such as an office width of around 14m (45ft), at least 40 per cent of partitionable space to create individual rooms and an occupation density of about one employee to $14m^2$ ($150ft^2$).
- A carparking norm of around one space per $20m^2$ ($215ft^2$) gross being no more than 1 per $25m^2$ and sometimes as low as 1 per $15m^2$ all at ground level, appropriately divided, easy to manoeuvre round, well lit and suitably screened.
- A good image for the park as a whole, as well as for particular buildings, necessitating an attractive approach providing a sense of arrival, clear sign-posting, carefully selected tenant mix and the setting and grouping of individual buildings to create a feeling a dignity and importance.
- A low density of development with a site coverage or "footprint" of around 15 per cent producing about $929-1161m^2$ ($10000-12500ft^2$) of lettable floorspace per acre with a two- to three-storey development.
- High standards of landscape to include such features as streams, sculpture and seating.
- A significant element of brick and tile as opposed to curtain walling seems most popular with tenants, together with tiled sloping roofs on timber trusses and rafters allowing the elimination of internal columns.
- The facility in terms of design for tenants to install their own air-conditioning.
- A raised floor to accommodate complex cabling.
- High quality of management.

Although it is already generally accepted that a true business or office park should stand on at least 40ha (100 acres), the next generation is likely to see larger park developments of 162–202ha (400–500 acres) and more resembling mini new towns. These will be based on a masterplan, which would provide a planned and controlled environment within which companies can retain and express their individual and corporate image, give a clear and functional infrastructure of roads and attractive landscapes, provide a variety of flexible plot sizes that enable occupants to expand and adapt their space to accommodate their own growth, develop a phasing policy to ensure that the development appears complete at each stage while minimizing disruption to existing occupants during construction, and sustain the quality of the original concept through design development guidelines for each plot (Michalik 1990). The attitude of some ambitious developers and their consultants is to create:

> . . . an alternative town centre with a wide range of facilities and amenities provided or close by including shopping, leisure, recreation, childcare and catering with high-quality design building and services standards served by good public as well as private transport facilities so as to recruit and retain key staff. One major obstacle to this is government policy aimed at preserving the status of the town centre and creating a climate of sustainable development. The future of business park development, therefore, has succinctly been stated to be about "the integration of flexible buildings with a quality landscape – within the community". (Auckett, quoted in MacRae 1993)

Facilities management

No examination of office development would be complete without some mention of the emergence of the discipline of facilities management. Until relatively recently the property industry regarded management as very much the unglamorous end of the business – a mixture of rent collection and caretaking. However, property or premises management is changing from being the industry's Cinderella to playing a central role in all sectors of commercial development. Shopping centre management led the way back in the late 1970s and throughout the 1980s. Facilities management for offices is more a creature of the late 1980s and 1990s.

In both private business and public service sectors of society, profound changes are taking place, with a fast-growing emphasis upon the twin related forces of enterprise and quality. Central to this metamorphosis has been the rapid spread of new ideas, technologies and practices resulting from advanced international communications and a much more highly competitive global economy. A major consequence has been the recognition by organizations of all kinds regarding the importance of property – its location, design and use – as a prime asset in the operational effectiveness of commercial and civic undertakings, as well as a principal factor in the equation of capital worth. Simple premises management has, thereby, evolved into the somewhat more complex and sophisticated discipline of facilities management. This is especially true of large corporations and utilities.

It is not surprising, therefore, that facilities management is a sector of property asset appraisal that has evoked increasing interest worldwide from both the design and the real estate professions over the past decade. It is still viewed with uncertainty, however, and remains an ill defined field. Nevertheless, as organizations strive to cope with constantly changing economic conditions, they are obliged to seek ever increasingly efficient and productive work environments.

Information technology

As already intimated, the workplace is swiftly being transformed, largely because of the introduction of an unprecedented scale of new information technologies in organizations. Work processes, physical environments and the social milieu of organizations have been redefined. There is now an emerging body of knowledge and experience enabling design and management problems of high-technology workplaces to be solved in an integrated way. Indeed, it has been argued that the progress of work automation has been so fast over the past decade that the pace has often outstripped the capacity of organizations to absorb new technology and to reap their potential benefits effectively. High-technology, moreover, is seen to be affecting the workplace in two different and complementary ways. Directly, it is being invaded by a whole new range of equipment, with new, and frequently conflicting environmental needs. Indirectly, it must change to adapt to the transformations of work processes and organizations that result from automation (Gourmain 1989).

The advent of the "intelligent building" was a striking feature of the 1980s. Stimulated by the globalization of the financial services industry, with the accompanying cascade of terminals, cables, atria and dealing rooms, it coincided with a radical reassessment of building procurement, construction and management processes (Duffy 1991). Buildings must obviously be capable of accommodating new demands and be developed accordingly. They must also be managed as business assets showing an acceptable return.

The nature, form and effectiveness of the intelligent building has been the subject of much study, definition and debate since the mid-1980s. What seems to be required in the current market is adaptable low-cost space capable of delivering high levels of operationally networked performance providing an integrated environment for those involved. Put another way:

> The intelligent building straddles two vastly different, but essential demands made by the modern firm. Buildings must respond to changing demands effectively and quickly, and must support a high level of inter-working by workers. (Robathan 1993)

The facilities manager

Opinions differ about the nature and scope of facilities management, and thus the role of the facilities manager. From a management perspective, it is suggested that facilities managers may be said to look after five key aspects of an organization:

- Shareholders: by maintaining the asset value – regular checks of fabric, etc.;
- Employees: by creating efficient working environments conducive to high morale and productivity;
- Customers: by maintaining and reinforcing the good image of the organization;
- Community: the impact of the organization on the environment and the local community;
- Suppliers: by ensuring the quality of suppliers and services.

(Powell 1990)

In similar vein, a six-point list of facilities management tasks have been identified as follows:

- Real estate. Purchase of land and building; marketing and management of subleases; lease management;
- Building design and construction. Development of brief; engagement of consultants; project control; field supervision; cost control and financial reporting;
- Building operation. Management of building operating systems; maintenance and repairs; ground maintenance; cleaning, housekeeping and other services; security; emergency systems;
- Office facility planning. Development of facility master plan (short and long term); space standards; furniture and equipment standards; specification and management of shared facilities; maintaining office space inventory; monitoring of quality of workplace environment; project management; management of interior changes; planning and management of moves;
- Interior layout and design. Space planning; layout plans; specification of furniture and fittings; decorative standards; interior design;
- Telecommunications planning and control. Planning individual user needs; co-ordination of installations; maintenance of location plans; cable management. (Akhlaghi, quoted in Powell 1990)

From the above, it can be seen that the responsibilities of the facilities manager are remarkably wide-ranging.

Facilities management and property development

The need to provide premises in the right place, at the right time, with the right services, offering the right level of management and at the right price is paramount. Current user markets have done much to alter the attitude of building owners and developers.

Much lip-service is paid to landlords focusing on the needs of the end user, but because most property is built speculatively, the ultimate occupiers generally have to compromise their requirements or deal with severe restrictions imposed at the design stage. It is suggested that these restrictions fall into two categories: those imposed by the building shell and its plant and equipments; and those dictated by real estate procedures, that frustrate the efficiency of the occupier (Prodgers 1992). Tenants are becoming less and less willing to live with inadequacies in the original design of a building, and more demanding of a flexible and service-oriented approach by the landlord towards tenure than hitherto.

The message is perhaps a simple one: the future management of properties facilities, in the very widest sense, should be incorporated as part of development planning at the very earliest stage of the development process. It has been argued that the management of an organization's facilities, its built environment and its infrastructure must take into account the nature of the activities that take place within the building and which the facilities are serving. Moreover, it must be fitted not only to the formal goals of the organization, but also to the way that the organization is structured: its pattern of work and its pattern of decision-making. Therefore, an approach to facilities management that looks into the late 1990s and beyond should be aware of predicted trends and changes that are already taking place in the productive organization (Baldry & Pitt 1993).

Conclusion

The questions for the future type and pattern of demand for office property are many and complex. They are inextricably linked to questions about the future general role of the city, and in particular the role of the city centre. Moreover, it is argued that developers will have to adopt a different ethos towards office development (Low 1994). They will have to be prepared to manage their developments and buildings they create and provide after-sales care. The real challenge faced by developers is to deliver guaranteed buildings tailored to the company's business plan priorities and reach the level of service attained by other suppliers. Gone are the days of "let and forget" philosophy prevalent for so many years. Developers will have to compete. To do so they will need suitably qualified teams to manage the entire development process, challenge previous accepted norms and preconceptions, transfer experience, knowledge and innovation, enhance the value of advisers and reduce potential conflicts of interest to deliver commercially valuable cost-effective buildings.

441

CHAPTER SEVENTEEN
Industrial development

Rising unemployment, changing industrial processes and new ways of working have all combined to require a reconsideration by both public and private sector agencies involved in the production of industrial and business development properties in respect of what they build, where and for whom. The 1980s witnessed a transformation in both the location and property requirements of modern industries. Changing market conditions and the restructuring of the UK economy resulted not only in a substantial shift from manufacturing to service-led growth, but one that was coupled with the increased use of technology, resulting in new demands being placed upon both industrial and business premises. At the same time this was accompanied by organizational changes within key economic sectors and the emergence of a new wave of companies serving rapidly growing markets, both of which had a fundamental impact on the nature of demand for commercial property as a whole. These trends encouraged the creation of high-technology estates and business parks and are predicted to continue so to do as the economy evolves towards the year 2000 (Debenham Tewson Research 1991). In the context of this chapter, much of the material relates equally to industrial and business property.

The broad shift from manufacturing to a service-based economy is clearly reflected in the composition of both gross domestic product (GDP) and employment structure. Although the contribution made by the manufacturing sector to national GDP remained fairly constant throughout the 1980s, output from the financial and business services sector more than doubled from around 10 per cent in 1980 to well over 20 per cent by 1990. The long-term trend is forecast to continue through the 1990s, with manufacturing output rising by an average of only 2 per cent per annum compared with about 6 per cent per annum for the financial and business services sector.

The restructuring of the country's economy is also reflected in changes to employment structure. Manufacturing employment fell steadily throughout the 20 years between 1970 and 1990, from 8.5 million to 3.1 million employees, a decline of nearly 40 per cent. During the same period, employment in the business and services sector rose from 2.6 million to over 5.6 million, an increase of 120 per cent. This trend is continuing, so that it is predicted that employment in the business and services sector will have increased by a further 20 per cent as opposed to a forecast decline of 6 per cent in the manufacturing sector. It is estimated therefore that, by the year 2000, manufacturing employment will comprise around 16 per cent of total UK employment, and business and services employment will rise to about 25 per cent. In this way, it has been projected that by 2005 the manufacturing workforce will have fallen to 4 million, having halved from 8 million in 1971.

In terms of the broad characteristics of modern industry, research has concluded that:

- The shift in economic activity from manufacturing industry to the information and service sectors has changed the types of sites and buildings required for modern industry.
- These emerging sectors are concerned with mental skills – the applications of specialist knowledge – rather than manual skills. This loosens traditional ties and generates new demands – in particular to provide a "people" rather than machine environment, resulting in a specification more akin to an office than a factory.
- To meet market demands and keep abreast of the latest technology these sectors are also concerned with producing limited product runs of specific customized products. This requires the centralization under one roof of research and design, product assembly and customization, and marketing and consumer services. The building must have flexibility to vary the mix of uses within any part of the building as the organization and its products grow and adapt. (DEGW 1985)

Thus, more than ever, it is essential that the property development industry has a greater understanding of the nature of the changes that are taking place within the economy, the general implications that these changes have for businesses, workers and local authorities, as well as on buildings and the kind of responses that will be needed.

This chapter explores the nature of industrial and business property development by examining the following issues:

- location for industry
- planning policy
- design and layout
- warehousing and distribution
- high-technology development
- estate management.

Location for industry

Conventional industrial location theory has assumed that firms behave in a rational and logical manner and are able to achieve their optimum locations.

Rational behaviour in location decision-making was felt to be determined by the aim of profit maximization. However, it has been pointed out that more recent theories of industrial location have abandoned the pretence of the optimal location and have acknowledged that locational decisions are often surrounded by uncertainty and personal preference. Land may be prevented from passing to the highest possible bidder by factors such as owners' expectations and behaviour, the cost of redevelopment and upheaval, or the existence of planning controls. As with other property sectors, because of substantial imperfections, land markets operate only at partial equilibrium. Supply and demand do not automatically equate, supply being determined primarily through the planning system, whereas demand depends upon private sector actions. This is said to make it extremely difficult to apply competitive market analysis to the industrial land market (Adams et al. 1993).

Basic factors of location

Although it remains broadly true that the combination of correct location and good design sells space everywhere, it has become increasingly clear since the late 1980s that the industrial development market is highly segmented, and different categories of user possess different locational requirements. Likewise, certain parts of the country enjoy strong competitive advantages over others. However, there are several basic factors that exercise a growing influence over the location and demand for industrial and business property. These can be summarized as follows:

- *Communications* The need to have quick and ready access to clients, markets, suppliers, labour, services and complementary parts of the business is an absolute prerequisite to modern industry. Thus, motorway linkage and high carparking standards are crucial.
- *Flexibility* A healthy firm has to be able to adapt quickly to changing requirements in respect of both the amount and the use of available space. Room to expand, and the capacity to reorganize methods of production and alter the nature of activities taking place within a building, are becoming more and more critical. Open flexible space, an easily extendable and convertible structure and low site coverage are, therefore, necessary ingredients.
- *Environment* The image portrayed by the site and building chosen by a firm are increasingly important. So too is the internal working environment, and desired conditions in many industrial premises are fast approaching those demanded in offices. Semi-rural positions on the outskirts of town are proving most popular.
- *Design* From the above it can be seen that modern industrial design must be not only stylish, creating an individual identity through character and quality, but also capable of conversion into offices, research, training and

production space. Moreover, it must create a building that can accept electronic communications systems and be constructed to minimize running costs.

A significant trend since the mid-1980s has been the increasing willingness shown by occupiers to move to off-centre locations. A survey undertaken in 1990 provided evidence that companies in most business sectors would actively contemplate a move away from the town centre, at least for part of their organization (Debenham Tewson Research 1990). The increased attractiveness of off-centre locations is related to the shift in both population and economic activity from major conurbations to smaller urban and rural districts. This urban to rural shift has been evident for some considerable time, but during the 1980s it gained momentum as the population of metropolitan counties fell by over 3 per cent against a rise of 4 per cent in non-metropolitan counties. The evidence of this migration of population and economic activity to smaller centres is also apparent from a study that ranked the economic prosperity of each of the country's 280 local labour market areas. This ranking, according to a basket of socio-economic indicators, shows that recent economic performance is clearly skewed towards smaller, recently industrialized districts, with all of the major urban conurbations placed well down the national hierarchy of economic prosperity.

As with office developments, there is what has been described as a "push-me, pull-you" interplay of factors encouraging companies to locate either in or out of town. The push away from town centres involves increased congestion, rising costs and longer commuting times. Conversely, the out-of-town location may be able to offer cost savings, an attractive working environment, better carparking provision and generally greater accessibility. Against this, however, out-of-town sites often show certain disadvantages, such as inadequate amenities and facilities. The town centre might also have certain advantages in terms of accessibility to the public transport network and benefits from a variety of shopping and recreational activities. A survey of companies showed the relative importance of various locational factors. Proximity to motorways and environmental quality were stressed as of most importance, followed by access to markets, airports, the rest of the company, and staff availability, attraction and skills, all well ahead of the availability of public transport, leisure and housing (Debenham Tewson Research 1990).

Regional trends

The deep structural changes that have been taking place within the economy since the mid-1980s – whereby emerging industries are based upon information and communications more than raw materials and productive processes, with a workforce more dependent upon management and innovation than on handling and manufacturing – has meant that such knowledge-based companies are increasingly mobile. As a result, the concentration of new industrial development upon the South East of England accelerated throughout the 1980s.

445

The much vaunted Golden Triangle, formed within the area marked by Hammersmith, Swindon and Guildford, has grown and changed shape to create a kind of Golden Trapezium bounded by lines joining Bristol to the west and Southampton to the south, as well as those connecting Guildford and Hammersmith. Within this area, demand to occupy industrial floorspace and pressure to release land have become especially focused along the Western Corridor created by the M4 leading again from Hammersmith to Heathrow, Reading, Swindon and Bristol. A premium can be discerned on sites within a 30 minute drive time of Central London and Heathrow, and to a lesser extent along the M1, M3 and, more recently, M40 motorways up to a distance of 75 to 100 miles. Much interest has been stirred by the implementation and proposed widening of the M25 orbital route around London, which has had a dramatic effect upon commercial and industrial location decisions.

Demand for new industrial space in the South East is generated from a variety of sources. There are large multinational and national companies decentralizing from Central London. Then there are major fast-growth companies already located in the South East but in need of new and larger premises. Smaller fast-growth companies, both home grown and from overseas, are also actively seeking and occupying space. Probably the greatest demand for new industrial development since the mid-1980s has, in fact, come from abroad.

Relative economic success within the South East during the 1980s brought with it certain disadvantages that began to impinge upon the ability of existing firms to expand. Problems in the supply of suitably skilled and affordable labour, together with increased congestion and a slowdown in economic growth, resulted in oversupply of exclusively business-use accommodation in certain parts of the South East. This raised questions concerning the nature and location of new development. It encouraged, in part, a shift towards the provision of more traditional industrial premises and, in part, a shift in attention towards other regions within the UK. With regard to the business park type of development, the South West, East Anglia, North West, Yorkshire and Humberside regions all experienced significant increases in floorspace provision in the first few years of the 1990s. Nevertheless, it has been shown that, given the regional distribution of employment the South West, East Anglia and both the East and West Midlands, all continue to be underprovided with business-use accommodation, even though the rate of economic growth in these regions is expected to exceed that of the South East throughout the 1990s. This notwithstanding, the shift in development activity towards other regions should be seen as a long-term trend that is unlikely to challenge the predominance of the South East.

The advent of the Channel Tunnel will inevitably have a growing impact upon industrial and business sector development, especially distribution facilities. Eight of the nine designated Railfreight Distribution Eurofreight terminals were completed by early 1994, but development of associated freight villages is proceeding much more slowly. A declining market, the recession, negative images of British Rail's freight operation, and the uncertainty and lack of confidence caused by rail privatization, are all blamed for creating a climate of caution about the effect of Eurofreight on rail-linked warehouse and distribution space. Nevertheless, the likely scale of planned future investment in rail freight indicates with some confidence that rail can wrest significant market share from road transport, and some of the network of nine new intermodal Eurofreight terminals throughout the UK include proposals for B2 (General Industry) or B8 (Storage and Distribution) freight villages (MacRae 1993). There are also several large leading private sector Euroterminal distribution park development schemes already in the pipeline.

Major transportation infrastructure projects are natural catalysts for industrial and business developments. Another generative factor influencing development growth in the sector is the decision of a single substantial investor or producer to locate in a particular town, city or region. A prime example is in the Tyne & Wear region, where Nissan, the Japanese car manufacturer, has chosen to locate its $140000\,m^2$ plant in Washington, near Sunderland. Known as the "Nissan Effect", the massive investment has brought significant spin-off benefits, not only in terms of the immediate 3500 jobs directly created but also by generating renewed business confidence in the region (Mills 1992).

No examination of regional trends would be complete without some mention of the European dimension. Here it has been found, in a survey from the University of Cambridge, that the quality and size of the labour force is a key factor affecting company location decisions in Europe (Moore et al. 1991). As might be expected, the availability of regional development assistance was identified as being important for production companies and from companies relocating from abroad. However, the level of wage costs was generally less important that the quality and size of the labour supply. It is interesting that the quality of infrastructure did not rate highly, and neither did the level of rents, nor the attractiveness of the environment. On the evidence of the survey, preferred regions are those offering minimal costs, but also good quality and supply of labour and good access to markets. This would suggest the run-down industrial areas of northern France, Belgium, the Netherlands and the Ruhr. In Britain it would point to the Midlands and the North. We have perhaps seen an indication of this with the location of Japanese car firms.

The industrial property market

The industrial sector in the UK has undergone a major process of rationalization and cost cutting to reduce the effects of recession. A combination of difficulties in funding, depleted markets for products, and narrowing profit margins, has led to measures such as staff redundancies and the closure of manufacturing units on a large scale. This, in turn, has resulted in an oversupply of second-hand buildings for which there is only limited demand.

The building boom of the late 1980s in the South East was mainly concentrated on offices and B1 (Business) units with high office content, and the industrial sector was spared the oversupply of buildings currently affecting other property sectors. The existing stock of vacant industrial and warehousing buildings is, therefore, largely made up of second-hand properties.

Problems arise with these buildings where they have been adapted to the use of the operator and are not flexible enough for conversion to other users except at very high cost. Some very attractive tenant incentive packages are being offered on these by occupiers, attempting to cut costs and release themselves from long-term liabilities. Unfortunately, many such buildings may never be let, since they are inflexible, and offer poor access and high maintenance liability.

In the distribution sector there has been a noticeable increase in demand. However, distribution companies operate on the basis that the contracts being awarded to them are short-term and, therefore, often require break clauses in their leases. Choice for the occupier has previously been limited by the unwillingness of owners to bring land forward for this type of use, because of the low value released. As other forms of development are badly hit by oversupply and low demand, land is now more readily released, and speculative schemes are under way in the better locations. Improvements in handling methods with widespread use of computerized stock holding is leading to more intensive use of space and higher eaves height, increasing the efficiency of individual units.

With the concentration of supply in second-hand buildings, the upturn in the market is likely to lead to a shortage of modern well located buildings. At the larger end of the market – $4645\,m^2$ ($50000\,ft^2$) upwards – the demand is likely to be met by purpose-built developments.

At present, there is interest from investors in the industrial market, with funds perceiving a growth in rentals in the future. This interest provides opportunities for sale and leaseback, and funding of expansion space by pre-lettings on new development.

Relatively low building prices and ready availability of land at economic levels suggests the mid-1990s is an ideal time to create purpose-built units, and there is likely to be a trend towards owner-occupation to take advantage of these conditions. When growth in rents and capital values return, the owner-occupier will have the advantage of being able to release asset value by means such as sale and leaseback.

The choice of industrial location for the development of large manufacturing units involves balancing the quality of the local labour force, the availability of strategic sites and of grants, and the quality of infrastructure. The North and the North East in particular have many attractions for the relocating industrialist.

Control over inflation, stable interest rates, the availability of a skilled labour force and greatly improved industrial relations since the mid-1980s make the UK attractive in the context of the Single European Market. As a result, it is likely that major international industrialists will seek to establish themselves in the UK over the next few years, taking advantage of these benefits to serve the European market.

Types of industrial development

It has already been stated that the industrial development sector is highly segmented. An understanding of the different types of industrial development is important, because they invariably involve different user requirements, development agencies, sources of finance, design requirements, and management policies. A useful classification has been devised, which identifies categories of traditional, new growth and innovation industries (Worthington 1982):

Traditional industry
- Community workshop: small workshops aimed at encouraging embryo enterprises by developing skills and providing equipment and administrative support. Located close to residential areas in old buildings.
- Flatted factory: multi-storey industrial buildings, with goods lift and corridor access to some small independent tenancies.
- Industrial estate: mixture of manufacturing and service uses. Industrial character where delivery areas predominate.
- Trading estate: warehouse uses with some office content. May attract retail warehousing and trade outlets.

New growth industries
- Working community: a group of independent small firms co-operating in sharing a building and joint services. The objective is to enjoy a scale of premises and facilities normally available only to larger companies. The group will normally have a policy of selecting compatible or complementary firms.
- Commercial/business park: having a high-quality low-density environment. Aimed at firms requiring prestige or high-calibre workforce. Mixtures of manufacturing, office and sales functions.
- Trade mart: a multiple tenanted building with office showrooms and centrally provided exhibition, conference areas, reception and support services. Normally developed around a theme.
- Research/innovation
- Innovation centre: an individual building, immediately adjacent to a university campus, providing small units $30-150\,m^2$ ($323-1615\,ft^2$) for starter firms growing out of research projects within the university and drawing upon its facilities and support services.
- Research park: sites or advanced units for young or established firms in the field of research or development. Often close to a university and associated with university research laboratories and amenities. Such schemes are often joint ventures.
- Science/technology park: with universities and research institutions within a 30-mile catchment area. Attractive life-style, low-density development aimed at scientific or technology-orientated companies.
- Industrial park: aimed at clean manufacturing organizations with a landscaped setting and leisure amenities for staff.

449

Planning policy

Industrial development is now perceived as a major area of government responsibility in much the same way that public housing was some years ago. At central government level, a report by the Trade and Industry Select Committee in April 1994 told government to shrug off the vestiges of its *laissez faire* approach to industry. The report, in examining competitiveness, urged the government to enshrine the importance of manufacturing in economic policy, reflecting a widespread belief that the decline of Britain's manufacturing industry since the 1960s poses a serious threat to the country's ability to sustain economic growth, and thus employment prospects, post-recession. At local level, many planning authorities are very progressive in their approach towards development proposals and supportive of initiatives, whereas others seem caught in a mesh of plans and policies a decade out of date. The effect of local authority planning can most conveniently be discussed by reference, on the one hand, to the exercise of their negative powers under development control and, on the other, the more positive attitudes that some of them adopt, which are demonstrated through an array of employment generation policies.

The national context

In a report produced in August 1994 by the Employment Policy Institute (EPI) it has been argued that a healthy manufacturing sector is important for the continuing prosperity of the country (EPI 1994). The report points out that rates of productivity growth in manufacturing at an average of around 4 per cent per annum are higher than in services and more than double the productivity growth rate of the economy as a whole. In practice, this means that manufacturing provides more jobs, despite the frequently repeated claim that services are more labour intensive. The EPI report also states that:

- The number of jobs sustained by the sector it not fully reflected by the number of people directly employed there. Some manufacturing and construction processes, for instance, rely on a wide range of outside goods and services.
- Government should consider the issues of new knowledge and product innovations, because industrial advances make an invaluable contribution to technological progress.
- Although manufacturing output only accounts for about 20 per cent of UK GDP it provides in excess of 60 per cent of UK exports, and it is important that this level is maintained.
- The government need to change its approach radically to ensure the right economic environment for manufacturing to prosper.

In respect of the last point, criticisms have been made that the government's view of financial support is too short term; relies heavily on the interplay of market forces, which are not always attuned to the needs of certain businesses; tends to be more concerned about the City of London's financial services sector and large high-profile projects such as Toyota, Nissan and Samsung; and supports insufficient training initiatives to provide an effective skilled labour force. Both France and Germany are cited as examples of government commitment to the support of major industry.

A principle plank in government planning policy is laid down in PPG13, *highways considerations in development control*, which encourages mixed uses in a bid to achieve sustainable development. Factories are envisaged juxtaposed with shops, offices and housing. This move back to mixing development activities is intended to reduce travel to work, cutting down on car use and promoting public transport, cycle routes and walking, with landscaped buffers, public open space and playing fields being used to separate employment and residential areas where appropriate. To accelerate the movement away from private to public transport, the Royal Commission on Environmental Pollution recommended substantial increases in the price of petrol, together with a major shift in public spending away from roads and into public transport. Nevertheless, although society might seem to be heading away from a heavy and growing dependence on cars, which will increase demand for mixed-use development schemes, it has been pointed out that it could be the manufacturers themselves who need the most convincing that it is in their interests to move with the times (Mills 1994).

One problem that has to be faced, given the predicted decline in the manufacturing workforce to around 4 million by 2005, is that of redundant and obsolescent industrial space. With an average floorspace per employee of around $44\,m^2$ ($474\,ft^2$) demand for industrial floorspace in the UK as a whole will be around 175 million m^2 (1884 million ft^2), and it is clear that there will be much less demand for manufacturing floorspace than now. Much existing space will have reached the end of its physical and economic life, and as space is redeveloped it will be the best located, least polluted sites that will be creamed off for redevelopment for alternative uses, leaving a rump of contaminated, derelict land with little or no chance of change.

This, of course, assumes that the planning system allows the situation to develop. Too often the planning system is used to present entrenched opposition to changes in use. The perception is that, by retaining land for industrial development, this will in itself attract industrial employers. However, the planning system simply cannot hold out against the pressures for change caused by a shrinking manufacturing workforce. Pragmatic guidance is urgently required from central government as to the acceptance and control of alternative uses for redundant industrial land (Thomson 1994/5).

Another sector of the industrial property market deserving of government attention and guidance is that of storage and distribution. It can be argued that the planning system has not yet come properly to terms with the explosive nature of the distribution industry. The interests of the national economy might well be served if the DoE were to issue more specific guidance to local planning authorities on the matter, distinguishing the sector from retail activities, otherwise an unproductive disarray might take place, similar to that which took place in the 1980s in respect of major out-of-town shopping centres.

Because of their economic importance, for example, the sanctity of certain strategic gaps and rural sites adjacent to the motorway interchanges should not be squandered unless there are very compelling environmental objections. As has been pointed out, through the years of the B1 (Business) office boom, most such key locations allocated for development have been mopped up for business campus uses, and warehousing has frequently been diverted to low-value sites remote from the communications network. As a result, heavy lorry traffic is often sucked through residential areas, with adverse environmental effects (Vail 1994).

On the question of traffic, a popular sentiment echoes around the property development industry that government lacks a coherent policy towards transport. Despite an amended road-building programme promulgated in *Roads to prosperity* (DOE 1994b), slightly reducing the number of schemes, substantial sums of money continue to be invested in the UK roads network, and PPG13 and other government edicts seek to limit car journeys. The distribution of goods throughout the country depends primarily upon heavy goods vehicles and, although many believe it is lorries that clog up the system, surveys have showed that such carriers typicality account for no more than 15–20 per cent of traffic flows. Persuading passenger traffic to switch to public transport would greatly ease the movement of freight.

Local planning practice

The more detailed application of development control regulations as they apply to industrial property, especially the operation of the Use Classes Order 1987, is dealt with elsewhere (Chs 2 and 3). Suffice it to say that in a post-industrial society, such as that in the UK, distribution between factory-based employment and office-based employment is an artificial and largely unhelpful one. Increasingly this is recognized, but the fact remains that, for whatever reason, many local authorities fear creeping office use in what they ostensibly approved as industrial buildings. The B1 (Business) use class has greatly reduced this problem.

However, another circumstance where difficulties of mixed use emerge is the proposed combination of residential accommodation with workspace. Not only are planning authorities reluctant or unprepared to consider such proposals, but building regulations, in particular those relating to fire, render mixed-use developments of this kind extremely complex and expensive to design and build. Nevertheless, it is an interesting field of possible future invention.

A distinctive feature of local authority policy since the mid-1980s has been the concentration of effort upon the generation of employment, by both the encouragement of existing local industries and the attraction of more mobile ones from elsewhere. Among the initiatives have been taken by councils to support the level of employment in their area and assist the development of industrial property are the following:

- • *Development plans revision* Amendments to structure plans and local plans or unitary development plans releasing additional land for industry or rolling forwards planned future allocations have been made by many authorities. Similarly, site specific planning and development briefs identifying potential industrial estates have become a popular means of attempting to stimulate private sector development.

- *Economic development units* Under a variety of titles many local authorities have established special departments and appointed economic or industrial development officers responsible for employment generation. These offer a wide range of schemes covering both business advice and financial assistance.

- *Serviced sites and development* In order to induce potential firms to come to their area, local authorities have frequently laid out the principal roads and services on selected sites, and sometimes have erected speculative units in advance of demand. Many councils have gone further and acted as developer. The early science parks at Warrington, with the well publicized Genesis Building, and Killingbeck, where Leeds City Council itself funded the first phase of the 12ha (30 acre) estate, were among the most notable initial ventures.

- *Headleasing* Where market uncertainty exists and, because of either doubts about the location of the site or the size and nature of the units, private sector developers are wary about taking all the risks of letting and management entailed in a proposed scheme, it has become quite common for the local authority to take the head-lease of the property and subsequently to sublet the units to occupying firms. A variation to this agreement is typified by the agreement entered into by various councils, whereby they have undertaken to take a head-lease from a developer if the particular project is still unlet after a certain period of unsuccessful marketing.

- *Key worker housing* In an attempt to overcome some of the problems experienced by firms in relocation to new premises, a few local authorities have provided subsidized housing or cheap building land for key workers. The conversion of high-rise flats into hostels for single people or young couples is another way of retaining or attracting desired workers.

- *Other initiatives* It has been suggested, at one time or another, that local authorities might:
  - Introduce special long-term incentives on rates; these remain one of the greatest worries among the business community, which does not always benefit from the services provided.
  - Offer rental guarantees to developers and investors, possibly linked to some form of indexing. In this way, dubious investments let to relatively young companies or firms that are recovering from the recession, will immediately acquire a "blue chip" quality.

453

- Concentrate on improving the physical environment in existing and proposed new business areas through better roads, landscaping (hard and soft), refuse collection, lighting and the like.

Design and layout

Historically, the design of industrial buildings has been poor, often being more the preserve of the engineer than the architect. The adherence to strict zoning regulations tended until recently to constrain any serious consideration of the need for good design. It is really only since the late 1970s that employers and management have become concerned about the working environment of their labour force, realizing that pleasant and effective buildings are synonymous with high productivity and satisfactory returns. Moreover, with the relaxation of rigid industrial zoning policies and a movement away from the separation of industrial processes into large estates, it became obvious that many small industrial developments would have to be sympathetically moulded into existing urban areas, and other large industrial developments would have to be sited in exposed and sensitive rural locations, often close to motorways where they would be most apparent. The general quality of design for industrial development, therefore, has improved enormously, with such leaders in the architectural field as Terry Farrell, Nick Grimshaw and Norman Foster bringing a kind of respectability to what was previously a largely drab utilitarian approach. Nevertheless, a strong conservative influence survives among occupiers, and a degree of tenant reluctance to accept some of the more exciting modern design concepts is exemplified by the initial slow letting of certain notable quality estates.

Changing character

As never before, developers need to market their product largely through excellence of design and specification. Architects, therefore, are having to respond with flair and imagination, for they are being asked to devise new buildings that are economic to construct, suitable for new industries and trades, acceptable to institutions that still have half an eye to long-term flexibility, and are in themselves positive marketing and promotional statements. Not only must the buildings conform to newly established criteria, however, but the settings in which they are placed must generate an attractive and compelling business climate. Developers now demand estates that demonstrate upon entry an excellent working environment with genuine landscaping and full amenities. The main reason for this changing character can be summarized as follows:
- The industrial sector, as such, has given way to a business sector comprising retail, high-technology and office use as well as production and distribution.

- Since the economic recession of the early 1990s, the negotiating balance between landlord and tenant has tilted sharply towards the tenant.
- Businesses are much more mobile than in the past, and tend increasingly to seek a consolidation of their administrative activities with their productive operations.
- Employees are also mobile, with higher levels of car ownership and different perceptions of work opportunities.
- With changing business functions and different forms of productive process, the single-storey rule is disappearing.

Density and layout

Traditionally, an overall site cover of 45–50 per cent was always considered to be an appropriate density for modern industrial estate development. The trend over recent years has been for a lower site coverage, and it is likely that an acceptable average for the foreseeable future will be closer to 30–35 per cent. With certain special developments, such as science parks and office campuses, the average density can fall even lower to between 20–25 per cent and below. However, it must be remembered that a lower site coverage by no means implies a lower density, for many forms of modern industry, it is perfectly acceptable to operate on two or more storeys. In fact, with some processes in both the light electronics and pharmaceutical fields, a "layer cake" concept of factory design is most suitable, whereby the production area is laid out on the ground floor, and one or more levels of service or handling space are built above. Not multi-storey in the true sense, developments of this kind rarely suit a portal frame structure, for it is generally not sufficient to carry the loads involved. Nevertheless, the footprints of buildings across a site so developed can be quite scattered.

With regard to the overall layout of estate roads and parking facilities, changes in both the use of the private car, and in the size and nature of delivery vehicles, have dictated changes in the assessment of siting, road circulation, address and services. Not only is the general level of car ownership much higher these days, but the nature of many new industries creates a greater need for carparking facilities, because of the higher income group of employee, the increased level of office-type activity and the additional amount of visiting traffic from clients and other members of the company. As a guideline, most modern estates require one parking space for every person employed, or alternatively one space for every $23\,m^2$ ($250\,ft^2$). An even higher level of provision is necessary if there is any retail warehouse element within the estate, whereas pure warehousing operations demand very much less. The advent of the juggernaut has meant that all industrial estates now need to cater for $15\,m$ ($49\,ft$) plus lorries. Access and forecourt roads need to be wider, longer and more substantial than hitherto, to allow for manoeuvrability. An incidental gain from this is that it produces large open spaces for landscaping. Forecourt layouts and delivery parking facilities are critical if an

455

estate is to be successful, and certain industrial activities and freight operators will require plenty of parking space for vehicles and trailers. Special trailer parking areas are also sometimes needed. Common open areas of concrete or tarmacadam can be laid out and marked for individual units, or segregated spaces with a physical barrier to prevent encroachment can be provided. Although it is important to supply loading and parking facilities to a high standard, it is also important these days to separate them from the office areas on an estate. The roads themselves can be of either a concrete or a tarmacadam finish. Concrete costs more initially, but tarmacadam is more expensive to maintain, leading to complaints from tenants and high service charges.

Design principles

Although the concept of dual capacity – whereby buildings on industrial estates are designed so that they can be adapted for both warehouse and production uses – in order that institutional investors and developers can cast their letting net as wide as possible, is now regarded as redundant, the keynote of good design remains that of flexibility. The following guidelines represent an attempt to describe good design practice that will retain flexibility of use without sacrificing the individual quality of buildings.

- *Floor slab* This should be designed to ensure that an adequate loading capacity, say 227–340 kg (500–750 lb), can be offered through time to a wide range of uses. Once constructed there is very little that can be done to rectify any deficiency.
- *Eaves height* Reference is often made to the institutional requirement for an 5.5 m (18 ft) eaves height, but in many ways this standard is too high for most modern factory buildings, too low for current warehousing needs and insufficient to allow for horizontal conversion. A clear height of 6.7 m to 7.3 m (21–24 ft) permits the inclusion of a mezzanine floor or the conversion into two-storey offices, and retains the possibility of warehouse use. For purpose-built single-storey light industrial buildings, however, a clear height of 3.7 m to 4.6 m (12–15 ft) is much more popular than the traditional 5.5 m to 6.1 m (18 to 20 ft). Special high-bay warehouses require at least 10 m (33 ft) eaves height for a minimum 10 000 m² (107 639 ft²) floorspace at 45 per cent site cover.
- *Column spacing* As a general rule, columns hinder flexibility. Where the structure, span and loads are such that they have to be provided, it is essential that correct column spacing is planned to allow for the possible need to provide extra support for mezzanine floors, subdivide into self-contained smaller units or facilitate pallet racking.
- *Cladding materials* Once again the aim should be to achieve a reasonable degree of flexibility, not merely in the selection and design of cladding but also in respect of the provision of glazing, doors and bays. In attaining this,

architects have benefited from the development of profiled metal sheeting with factory-bonded insulation. External finishes on profiled metal are virtually maintenance free. Advances have also been made in the use of glass-reinforced concrete and glass-reinforced plastic, which in sheet cladding form are said to offer a whole new range of design possibilities in both aesthetic and practical terms. All these insulated flexible skins can be produced in a variety of modular panel systems incorporating interchangeable door, window and service-bay openings so as to provide a range of sophisticated and highly adaptable facades. However, some doubts have been expressed regarding the extensive and exclusive use of demountable and interchangeable cladding panels. For example, great care is required in their selection, because the testing of new materials is not all it should be. The exclusive use of either glazing or cladding is not always popular with tenants and, although the notion of interchangeability is fine in theory, it is less likely to be adopted in practice, for some developers would say that it is often better to provide for internal flexibility within the building rather than in the structure itself.

- *Roofs*   Until recently it has probably been fair to say that absolutely flat roofs were not acceptable because of performance and maintenance problems, but nearly flat roofs could normally be achieved successfully. Now, however, it is feasible to produce a leak-proof flat roof by using a plastics-based membrane material. The object of obtaining as flat a roof as possible is to optimize the internal volume of the building. Nevertheless, it is commonly accepted that a slightly pitched steel trussed roof, which permits the ready attachment of tenants equipment, is best, so long as the truss is constructed deep enough for the installation and maintenance of services to be easily effected. False ceilings are often installed to facilitate the introduction of additional services, as well as to create a better working environment and reduce energy consumption. In both walls and roofs it should always it should be recognized at the basic design stage that windows and roof lights might have to be added or subtracted at some future date. Likewise, both environmental and process services may have to come through either roofs or walls. Indeed, the very structure should be designed to carry these services, on top of any mechanical handling equipment a tenant may wish to install.

- *Building services*   Although an increasing emphasis is placed upon the provision of adequate internal services, there are a growing number of developers who prefer to construct a simple shell capable of accommodating a wide range of building services, but await an actual letting before the specified services are installed. One of the most effective means of supplying electrical services is by way of a ring main around the perimeter of the building. In respect of distribution across a building, building regulations in the UK insist upon the boxed trunking of electrical transmission, unlike the USA where taped carpet tiles can be employed, giving ultimate flexibility. With

457

regard to lighting, good-quality daylighting factors are often required, and natural lighting to office standards is sometimes sought. Otherwise, artificial lighting to around 500 watts is normally sufficient, often to be found hung from a suspended ceiling. Air-conditioning is fast becoming a sought-after facility in many modern industrial estate developments, and is virtually obligatory in some of the more sophisticated high-technology schemes. In any event, consideration in design should be given to ensure that the basic structure and skin are suitable for power, heat and ventilation systems to be added later if required. Similarly, the fundamental design should aim at high standards of insulation, with a airtight skin, because good insulation can literally halve the heating costs of small units and substantially reduce those of larger ones.

- *Office content* The traditional proportion of ancillary office space, at 10–15 per cent of total floorspace, still adopted as a standard by some local planning authorities, is no longer a reliable guide to real need. In fact, most occupiers of modern industrial premises are rarely satisfied with less than 20 per cent, and with certain high-technology operations as much as 50 per cent or more is required. At planning approval stage, a prospective developer would definitely be well advised to gain consent for around 30–40 per cent office use in any proposed estate development, or alternatively avoid any condition as to a fixed percentage. With regard to design, there is a growing desire on the part of potential occupiers, particularly in the South East of England, to create a headquarters building on an estate alongside their distribution operations. This creates a need for an individual or corporate identity for the firm to be created. At the very least, therefore, it is sensible for a developer to reserve land accordingly, or to make sure that certain buildings could be converted if need be. In the context of office space industrial buildings, it is now a common convention that buildings on industrial estates should not have a rear elevation as such, but rather that there should be a double-sided design, with a separate approach for office staff and visitors, preferably on the south side of the building, on the opposite side to the properly planned loading bays and goods handling facilities. It is also the case that a greater area of glazing to permit views and afford natural light for the workforce, or the ability to create it, is required nowadays.

- *Fire* It is often argued that in the UK the cost of fire prevention and control in the UK is excessive. Nevertheless, such requirements remain an important consideration in all forms of development. Moreover, in the London area, what are known as Section 20 regulations provide that, in order to avoid the need in larger units for complete compartmentalization, they must be served with sprinkler installations. Although some developers still do not supply such facilities, the extra cost and effort on the part of the potential tenant could easily tilt the balance against a letting if two or three possible premises have been short-listed. As a small point, it might be worth noting that the fire-proofing of steel structures has become more economical over recent years with the use of intumescent paints and coatings, which also have the added advantage that they are a more attractive finish than the normal concrete or dry lining.

- *Loading bays* Not only should consideration be given to how many doors there should be, where they might be located and how vehicles will get to and from them, but some thought should be given to the provision of weather-protected tailboard-height bays reached over carefully planned approach areas. For speculative developments it is advisable to provide floodlit unloading areas and adjustable levellers, and to ensure some kind of shelter from the bay to the inside of the building.

- *Office and amenity areas* Provision should normally be made for such facilities as an attractive entrance hall and reception area; well finished and insulated curtain walling systems with double-glazed tinted window units; fully fitted carpets and good quality wallpaper; easy subdivision of open-space office area; suspended ceiling and recessed light fittings; perimeter skirting trunking for power, telephone and VDU installations; double-socket power outlets positioned in the ceiling voids; fully tiled spacious male and female toilets, possibly with shower units and dressing areas; central heating system; and drinking fountain, tea bar and cleaners' cupboards.

- *Energy conservation* Some developers are beginning to give consideration to the incorporation of sophisticated energy-saving systems. One such approach is known as "condition-based maintenance" that uses advanced technologies such as remote temperature sensors, electronic flue gas analyzers and current injection test sets. The savings in running costs and reduction of down-time can be a good selling point in a tight market.

- *Others* Special drainage facilities cannot always be added, particularly in heavy load-bearing floors, and it is often worthwhile providing a flexible facility, either by having a soft floor finish or by incorporating floor trenches at convenient intervals.

  Good toilet facilities are often forgotten by developers, although movable prefabricated toilet modules have been found to be a positive advantage in some industrial estate development schemes. Toxic waste disposal services might be demanded by prospective tenants, not merely those from more traditional noxious industries, but also from some of the newer high-technology firms. Likewise, advanced fume-extraction facilities might have to be incorporated.

Refurbishment of old industrial buildings

It has been estimated that there is well over 16 million m^2 (172 million ft^2) of floorspace left vacant in industrial buildings throughout the country, much of which is no longer needed for its original purpose (Thomson 1994/5). A great deal has been said and written about the need to re-use these old redundant buildings, and since the mid-1980s a growing number of successful refurbishment projects undertaken by a variety of development agencies have been implemented. Many of these fall outside the mainstream of conventional property development; but, equally, many opportunities exist for profitable commercial development to be tackled by entrepreneurs who understand the special factors that underlie the market.

All that is possible in this section is to list some of the more critical factors that determine whether or not a viable refurbishment or conversion can be effected. These can conveniently be summarized as follows:

- *Initial outlay*   This must be kept to a minimum, not merely in respect of the capital sum, carrying a debt charge, expended on the purchase of the building, or the head rent that has to be paid, but also with regard to the cost of works that have to be undertaken before all or part of the building can be let. Wherever possible, it is advisable to try to plan a gradual programme of upgrading, so that some of the costs can be funded from income.
- *Overheads*   In the same vein, most successful conversions of old industrial buildings take place where overheads have been reduced as far as possible. This invariably means that professional fees are minimized or avoided, with developers performing most of the professional tasks themselves. Similarly, contractors' and developers' profits are often absorbed in the same way, so that developer, contractor and project manager, and even agent at times, are all rolled into one, and a single slice of fees and profits is sought by that party.
- *Location*   Experience shows that buildings best suited to conversion are convenient for both staff and customers, say five minutes at most from the nearest public transport, are situated in an area of some existing and potential business demand and have good access off a main road on to a two-way street wide enough for parking.
- *Site coverage*   It is desirable to have 60 per cent or less site coverage and to possess good site access with off-street parking and delivery facilities.
- *Building configuration*   Evidence suggests that deep buildings with poor aspects should be avoided. Under 14–16m (46–52ft) depth is preferable, and in no circumstances should buildings over 18m (59ft) be considered if natural lighting and ventilation are to be exploited. Likewise, a three- or, better still, four-way aspect is best.
- *Structure and condition*   Obviously, a building possessing a superior initial construction, and where there is little need for major structural repair, is most attractive. At least the structure should be fairly sound and the building capable of being made wind-proof and watertight without too much trouble. Ideally, the building should be of fire-proofed frame construction and either brick or concrete. More than three storeys become problematical, and the ground floor should have floor height of 2.5–4m (8–13ft) at most. It is also important that there are wide stairways and the facility for incorporating a goods lift if required.

- *Statutory* It must not be too difficult or costly to have to comply with such statutory requirements as fire or public health, and it often helps if there is no need to apply for planning permission for a change of use. Above all, perhaps, the single common factor that seems to characterize all successful conversions of old industrial buildings is the presence of a strong personality responsible for the development, who is thoroughly committed to the scheme.

As a last word on the subject of the refurbishment of old industrial buildings, where elsewhere so much professional attention is paid to the relatively simple, clean, large estates designed for established national and international organizations, it is worth noting the role that has still to be played by the small business sector of the economy. There is a shortage of very small premises of around 10–$50\,m^2$ (108–538$\,ft^2$) in multiple tenanted accommodation, with shared access on flexible occupancy agreements and offering varying amounts of central support services. Therefore, enormous opportunities exist for the small developer with sufficient initiative and sympathetic funding.

Warehousing and distribution

A key feature of the property scene in the UK since the mid-1980s has been the phenomenal growth of the distribution industry and its consequent land-use and property requirements. Indeed, in a relatively stagnant commercial property market, the distribution industry represents one of the very few sectors of property growth with the demand for increasingly sophisticated warehousing premises.

The traditional concept of the warehouse as a crudely converted simple storage building situated in a run-down industrial area has undergone a fundamental change. There is now a widespread demand among distributors of goods for purpose-built, fully automated storage premises designed to satisfy their operational requirements, located on strategically identified sites within, and adjacent to, urban regions and throughout the country generally (Taylor 1993).

Research undertaken by DTZ Debenham Thorpe pointed to a period of sustained activity in the warehouse property sector throughout the 1990s, as major operators respond to the emergence of new markets. Distribution networks that were once viewed as effective and efficient are becoming less so as a result of the combined effect of lower rates of economic growth, the employment of "just-in-time" methods (JIT) and automation in the warehouse, as well as the effect of existing and proposed legislation. Together, these elements are bringing about a major shift in the location and property requirements of many companies, a shift with implications for both developers and investors.

The distribution sector underpins all economic activity. It provides the link between suppliers, manufacturers and retailers in a complex network that is increasingly taking on a pan-European dimension. The warehouse lies at the heart

461

of the supply chain, providing a buffer between fluctuations in supply and demand. However, throughout the 1990s, warehouses are increasingly viewed not simply as a place to store goods but as an integral element of the logistics network capable of making a positive contribution to corporate wellbeing or, negatively, acting as a major constraint on operational efficiency.

The increasingly widespread use of JIT means that warehouses perform a set of functions different from those undertaken in the past. Much greater emphasis is placed on stock rotation, trans-shipment activities and break-bulk, as well as a range of ancillary activities including repackaging and some light assembly. This range of emerging needs requires a comprehensive reassessment of the location and specification of premises deemed suitable in the late 1990s.

Major issues in warehouse and distribution development

Some major issues affecting the development of warehousing and distribution property over the next decade or so can be identified as described briefly below.

Europe

Manufacturers, retailers and other companies throughout Europe are considering their distribution needs on a pan-European basis, with the increasingly common phenomenon of a single distribution site with a super-warehouse servicing all of Europe. However, several sites are a more popular solution. Although northwest Europe has distribution facilities similar to the UK, including traditional estates and free-standing distribution centres, the region has seen developments rarely witnessed in the UK. They include groups of road-haulage depots on a single site and loose groupings of depots and warehouses offering a range of logistical services at one site, including model interchange. Strong competition, standardization and sophistication are destined to become the themes of European distribution development. Legislation regarding environmental taxes, the exchange-rate mechanism, the Social Chapter and operational constraints, will all have an effect on location.

UK regional distribution centres (RDCs)

An RDC is difficult to define according to size or function, but in very general terms it can be stated that manufacturers tend to be concentrated in the Midlands, whereas retailers are dispersed across the country. Most major retailers prefer no more than 2–2.5 hours between distribution depots. It is predicted that RDCs will grow in size and reduce in number, with significant restructuring of both industrial and distribution activities within the regions, probably favouring the Midlands. In addition, it is thought that road will continue to dominate rail networks for regional distributors, although some companies are now environmentally sensitive enough to prefer rail over roads.

Planning policy

To date, the attitude of planning authorities towards storage and distribution-related development has been relatively low key, with very few specific expressions of interest having been published at either national or local level. There is little to find on the subject in structure plans, local plans or unitary development plans, despite the importance to local as well as regional and national economies. Purely in design terms warehousing is unlikely to present any real issues or major conflicts with local planning authorities, whose prime concern in this respect should be satisfaction that environmental and amenity considerations are met. Despite the fact that the purpose-built warehouse is higher and larger than its single-storey predecessor, there is no reason why warehouses should not be designed to look pleasant. Locational factors are the ones most likely to concern planners. Traditional locations in urban areas are no longer attractive to distributors. They need a great deal of space, which cannot normally be found in built-up areas; rural areas, preferably near to motorway interchanges, are their preferred locations. However, it is at these locations, where planners are anxious not to allow development, that sustainability, environmental and countryside policies take preference. Taking the situation on an ad hoc basis, therefore, it is realistic to assume there would be planning opposition to developments of this nature on these sites, unless sites were identified by planners in advance within the context of a clear policy framework. Such a framework would certainly need to indicate sites for major distribution parks. This property form is seen in some distribution industry quarters as the answer to their property requirements and where planning objections can be overcome through well designed, well landscaped layouts (Taylor 1993).

Classification and specification

In an attempt to understand the various levels of warehouse requirement, a useful classification of operations into simple, medium and sophisticated storage can be made. Simple storage operations are those where the goods in question can be block-stacked to a limited height using ordinary counterbalanced fork lift trucks and need a clear height of up to 5.5–6.0m (18–20ft). Some of the traditional standard units, therefore, are suitable. Medium storage operations take place where goods are stored in racked pallets with wider aisles and handled by the use of reach or turret trucks. Clear heights of up to 8.0–8.5m (26–28ft) are required. Sophisticated storage operations imply the existence of an automated warehouse and thus a high commitment to mechanical handling equipment. Wire guidance systems, automatic stacker cranes and computer-assisted stock control are all features of such operations, and buildings with clear heights of up to 36m (118ft) have been constructed to accommodate demand. In fact there is a burgeoning growth in the development of high-bay warehouses. An early example of such a development was the Associated Biscuit factory at Worton Grange near the M4 Reading junction where stacking to over 12m (40ft occurs, and 40 per cent more storage capacity was created at only 18 per cent more cost than would have been incurred in the construction of a conventional warehouse. The reduced floor area can also mean lower land costs, and the new 6500 m^2 (70000 ft^2) building replaces a traditional multi-storey warehouse of 16700 m^2 (180000 ft^2) floorspace. The basic object of modern warehouse design, therefore, is to maximize the amount of usable storage volume out of the gross volume of a building. Although costs of construction increase with height, the rate of increase falls, and produces what has been described as a lower cost of pallet aperture. Unlike industrial premises, it is important that offices should actually oversee the loading bays. A single-sided approach for cars and trucks is thereby created and consequently back-to-back development is possible. Another difference is that insulation to the skin may or may not be necessary, depending upon what is to be stored.

Distribution parks

The lack of large suitable sites for low-density development, the need for good motorway access and the trend towards 24-hour operations, coupled with the availability of both public transport and ancillary services and facilities are all factors likely to enhance the apparent attractiveness of dedicated distribution parks. Nevertheless, many potential occupiers are strangely suspicious about such developments, preferring stand-alone sites or a location on a more traditional industrial estate. This is probably because of the perceived costs associated with distribution parks and the possible lack of access to an adequate supply of skilled labour, as well as other ancillary facilities such as retail (Debenham Tewson Research 1990).

Europe's largest fully integrated national distribution centre, however, is being developed at Magna Park in Leicestershire. Started in 1988, the entire 715000 m^2 (7696188 ft^2) development will be completed around 1998. Situated in the golden triangle of the country's road network, from this site nearly 92 per cent of the population of Great Britain can be reached with the return journey being undertaken on the same day. The scheme features high-quality designed structures with a distinct architectural style, steel portal-frame warehouses with eaves heights of 10 m or more, leases of 999 years allowing the use of positive covenants to control estate maintenance and management, superior landscaping provision, and a cost-effective, centralized sewerage system. Since its inception, Magna Park has secured an impressive range of tenants and investment deals.

Freight villages

These are massive distribution centres located at strategic points around the country, providing integrated multimodal high-bay facilities based on rail as well as road networks, the rail link being used for long haul and the road service for collection and delivery. The EU has declared war on road freight and the British government is following its lead, with an alternative preference for long-haul, large-load freight movements by trains that carry the equivalent of 50 lorry loads. British Rail proposes nine such freight villages and the private sector more. Nervousness about rail technology, equipment and service, unavailability of information on possible pricing structures, a general lack of confidence in rail management, and a reluctance to be over-dependent upon rail operators – all militate against the ready acceptance of such schemes.

High-technology development

The term "high tech" became the buzz word of the 1980s, but there seemed to be little or no common understanding as to the way it was used in the property world. It would often appear to have had as much to do with industrial marketing and architectural fancy as with the true needs of occupiers. The labelling of estates with colourful claddings, tinted glass and expensive landscaping as being high tech led one leading agent to observe, "It is not entirely unreasonable to regard the high-tech chapter in industrial marketing as something of an elaborate self-deception by a number of architects and agents".

The growth of high-technology estate development has its roots in the USA where, although many early American business parks were actually poorly located, a more risk-conscious and responsive property industry led the way in the design and development of accommodation to suit high-technology based companies. The explosive growth that took place in Santa Clara County ("Silicon Valley") during the 1970s is now familiar. However, there were lessons for the UK to be learned because the rapid establishment of well over a thousand major companies across an area of 70 square miles eventually led to a state of over-development with a fall in environmental and design standards, increasingly inadequate infrastructure services that became seriously overtaxed, and a massive rise in domestic house prices. Nevertheless, the strong trading links between US and UK companies means that high and selective standards of location and design are increasingly sought.

The definition of high-technology development

Perhaps too much time and effort has been expended upon worrying away at what is high tech and what is not. Everyone seems to become very excited about categories and definitions, but it is possible to wonder just how relevant is such sophism. For straightaway, one important distinction to make is that between high-tech buildings and high-tech users. Many high-tech users can happily operate in low-tech accommodation. Many high-tech buildings house very low-tech operations. What has really happened, is that there has been a response to the demand by a variety of industrial and commercial users for adaptable, high quality, comfortable and attractive buildings set in pleasant surroundings, which are well located and available on acceptable terms to potential occupiers. Nevertheless, for the purposes of this text, the term "high-technology property" includes:

465

- buildings in an architectural style of design that has come to be known as "high tech"
- buildings occupied or intended for occupation by high-technology companies
- modern buildings in which mixed and flexible uses of space (including administrative use, laboratory, business, assembly and storage) occur (Fletcher King 1990).

Since the introduction of the 1987 Use Classes Order, the term B1 has been rapidly adopted to imply the multi-use space that was previously described as high-tech, despite the fact that pure office buildings also fall under the B1 heading in planning terms. The high-tech definitions can now be seen as forming two distinct groups. The first is where there is academic involvement or where research and development is an important part of the occupiers' activities; the main group here is science parks, together with research parks, technology parks and innovation centres. The second cluster contains the main group of business parks and also the office parks group, which because of the misuse of the B1 (Business) Class description within the Use Classes Order can be seen almost as a specialized form of business park. These are dealt with elsewhere (Ch. 16).

The high-technology developments identified in the first group above have been defined as follows (Fletcher King 1990).

Science park

A science park is a collection of high-technology companies or research institutes, situated in attractive surroundings developed to a low density, engaged in product research and prototype development, close to a tertiary education establishment with which there are significant opportunities for interaction and cross-fertilization of ideas. The term has suffered from imprecise use, but an attempt has been made to insist on a link with a tertiary education or research establishment in order to constitute a true science park.

Research park

Also known as research science park and discovery park, a research park is a collection of high-technology companies or research institutes situated in attractive surroundings developed to a low density, engaged in product research and prototype development, close to a tertiary education establishment with which there are significant opportunities for interaction and cross-fertilization of ideas, and with conventional production and office activities specifically excluded. A research park is very similar to a science park, but with the specific exclusion of conventional production and office activities.

Technology park

A technology park is a collection of high-technology industrial companies situated in attractive surroundings developed to a low density, engaged in research and manufacturing, probably within a reasonable distance of a tertiary education establishment, but not dependent upon it.

Innovation centre

Also known as science nursery, seed-bed centre and enterprise centre, an innovation centre is a collection of newly formed companies, usually housed in an existing building or buildings, converted to form small units, engaged in developing commercial applications of academic research projects and situated within or alongside a tertiary education establishment.

Upgraded industrial estate

Also known as industrial park, industrial mall and industrial area, an upgraded industrial estate is a development of industrial buildings with certain characteristics of high-technology property, which, although distinguishing it from other more traditional industrial estates, does not change its nature from being an industrial estate. These estates may be designed in a high-tech style or have more extensive landscaping than the previous generation of industrial estates, but despite marketing attempts they do not legitimately fall into any of the previous groups.

Another concept developed in the USA puts occupiers with a common business on one park. Thus, a "medi-park" contains medical research and development tenants with private hospitals, rehabilitation centres and sports clinics. It would seem that a medi-park is a technology park with medicine common to the tenants. Similarly, tenants with other industries as the common denominator would attract a generic title; for example, a park based upon the food industry could constitute a Food Park (Fletcher King 1990).

The features of high-technology development

Although a great deal has been researched and written about high-technology developments, there would seem to be three basic ingredients common to all successful schemes, not always in accord with the definitions given above. These can briefly be described as follows:

Location

Location is critical, and certain locational factors can be categorized as essential, important and relevant. Those deemed essential are proximity to an international airport, a good road network with motorway access, pleasant residential and working environments, and the availability of a specialist skilled workforce. Those considered Important are proximity to markets, proximity to the capital city, good rail links to the capital city, and the availability of support from a university or leading research establishment. Those thought relevant are proximity to suppliers, proximity to a domestic airport, good cultural and recreational amenities, and the existence of selective financial assistance (Williams 1982). Put another way, it has been stated that five factors have a significant influence on the location decisions of high-technology companies (Taylor 1985):

- the market for their product and the proximity of purchasers
- the availability of suitable premises and their cost
- a high-quality environment
- the accessibility of the motorway network
- the residence of directors and key personnel.

Flexibility

With regard to the type of buildings suitable for high-technology users, perhaps the most important factor is flexibility. There are several aspects to this:

- *Flexibility of use within the structure* So that the various functions of research and development, production and offices can mix and match, change emphasis and grow or contract according to the needs of the company, a suitable layout might permit any of the three elements to be changed, with only the removal or fitting of carpets for certain types of space or thermoplastic tiles for others. Some true high-tech tenants are working to state of the art specifications and do not know, almost from one month to another, exactly how they need to organize their space.
- *Flexibility for growth* Many companies active in this sector are expanding at a rapid rate. In one study over 80 per cent of the firms interviewed planned to expand in the forthcoming five years, and about 30 per cent envisaged that their corporate expansion would involve occupying more accommodation. Thus, on the one hand, there is a need to allow for physical flexibility for expansion *in situ* and, on the other, for a flexibility of leasehold terms so that firms can move to alternative accommodation without undue constraint. A 25-year lease is a very long time for a company that can scarcely predict its own market for more than a year or two at a time.
- *Flexibility of covenant strength* Many firms will be relatively new and exploring fresh markets, often without a track record, and sometimes without the necessary three years acceptable sets of accounts.

Design

Some of the emerging interior and exterior designs for high-technology developments rival many prime office headquarters buildings, and probably one of the most powerful motivations behind many moves to new technology parks is the desire for a strong and attractive corporate image. Nevertheless, there is a danger of building to specifications unrelated to consumer demand, as it is often the case that occupiers are perfectly happy to accept traditional exteriors – preferring to spend their money on better interior facilities. The likely truth is that the market comprises a wide range of potential occupiers with varying requirements and perceptions. However, there are a few special points of design worth noting:

- extensive carparking facilities are essential
- adequate underfloor space for cabling must be provided
- roofing must sometimes have to take loads of up to 100lb per m^2
- reinforcement for dish aerials will normally be wanted
- cleanliness is occasionally a problem
- energy-efficient buildings are increasingly sought
- the facility to introduce air-conditioning should be allowed
- very high standards of landscaping must be provided
- a high level of security is often required
- a range of finishes should be on offer rather than the typical tenants' norm
- the preference for two-storey development could well extend to three storeys
- with larger schemes, a village centre with small retail and service outlets could be beneficial.

In the property context of high-technology developments, it should be appreciated that, because of the rapid changes that are taking place in the field and the relatively slow gestation period of development projects, a site being developed in phases over several years can start out in one form and then alter its nature in response to demand. For example, phase I of an upgraded industrial estate may be succeeded by phase II units of multi-use space, more specialist high-technology space or even office or business space, so that taken as a whole the character of the estate may change through time.

Estate management

For many years, a large proportion of industrial estate development in Britain lacked even the most basic level of management services, which accounts for their general unsightly appearance. Apart from the New Town Development Corporations and a few notable private development companies such as Slough Estates and Brixton Estates, the management function was largely eschewed, and the burden or responsibility passed on to tenants. However, over more recent years a realization of the importance of good industrial estate management has dawned upon the property development industry. Most of the fundamental principles relating to the planning and design of estates have already been discussed, but other points are worthy of mention. These are as follows:

- *Image* Not merely for initial marketing, but also for subsequent letting and rent review negotiations, it pays to establish and maintain an appealing corporate image for an industrial estate. The naming of an estate, the creation of a special logo, well designed name boards at access points, the construction of an attractive gateway building, and the publication of professionally presented marketing material all make for a sense of community and a successful letting record.

- *Tenant mix* In the same way that there has been an appreciation of the importance of selecting the right mix of tenants in the management of planned shopping centres over the years, so a similar awareness is beginning to grow in the management of industrial estates. The correct identification of likely occupiers will help in planning estate layout and services, because freight operators, distribution centres, retail warehouses, light industry office and research-based users all dictate different buildings, service and traffic management solutions. Complementarity of use, which generates business between tenants, is also a consideration in small unit estates.

- *Signposting* Although it may not seem to be a major aspect of industrial estate development and management, the careful selection and siting of directional signposts around an estate can greatly enhance the general appearance. The careful incorporation of tenants' logos with a corporate framework, both at the entrances to an estate and on the individual buildings, can also add to the overall impression of the development.

- *Landscaping* What used to be regarded as an unnecessary and expensive luxury, often imposed as a condition of planning approval, is now usually seen as an essential attribute of any successful industrial development by investors, developers and occupiers alike. In fact, it is becoming quite fashionable to retain large striking natural features within an estate plan, or even to create artifacts such as an artificial lake or a folly type of building as a focal point to an estate. However, it should be remembered that even the selection and care of trees and shrubs is a relatively specialist affair. Effective landscaping will also attempt to avoid the fencing-in of industrial plots. As a corollary to this, it has been found that the imposition of positive covenants in the lease upon the tenant is rarely the best way of looking after the common landscaped areas of an estate. It is normally much better for a developer to arrange for the management of the estate as a whole at the outset, and recover the cost by way of a properly accounted service charge.

- *Security* Even on the smallest estates, security is a matter of considerable concern to tenants. Control at gate houses, the entrances to the estate, is often required, and they should be sited for maximum visibility around the estate roads. On larger estates, or where there are special tenants' requirements, it will often be necessary to install cameras around the estate, or even to provide 24-hour security, which can cost around £75000 a year for just a one-man operation. How much security is provided, of what kind and who pays, is obviously a matter of negotiation between landlord and tenant.

- *Power* Some estate developers undertake the bulk purchase of oil and gas, which they make available on a metered supply. Slough Estates is perhaps exceptional in that it generates it owns electricity at a privately operated 90MW power station for its 300 tenants at Slough. It also supplies water and steam to the 700000 m² estate. Central sprinkler installations are another facility commonly provided.

- *Refuse disposal*   Although on most estates this is normally looked upon as a tenant's responsibility, some developers have installed central compactors, where demand for such service is thought likely to be high. Otherwise, one of the main problems encountered in day-to-day industrial estate management is the monitoring and enforcement of conditions relating to the storage of rubbish and the placing of skips.
- *Personal services*   Increasingly, developers are conscious of the need to consider the possible provision of shopping, catering, health, banking, bus services, leisure and recreation facilities.
- *Tenants associations*   Although such organizations are comparatively rare on industrial estates, both landlords and tenants are slowly coming to recognize the mutual benefits that can be gained form the formation of a tenants association.

Conclusion

At the time of writing (1995), the recovery in the industrial property market continues and new industrial development is making a comeback. Spurred initially by investment demand for a prime product missing from the market, the recovery in development is being sustained by the re-emergence of genuine occupier demand. However, in this context the charge has been laid against developers and their advisers that, in the industrial and distribution sectors, specific working knowledge of functions and operations is all too often lacking. In a 1993 study by IBM Consulting Group, for example, only 2 per cent of British factories were deemed to be world class. It would seem that, although methods of manufacturing, storage and distribution have undergone revolutionary changes since the mid-1980s, suppliers of property have been slow to react to changing demand. It can be argued, therefore, that a much greater interest in, and deeper knowledge of, occupiers' requirements is needed. Post-occupancy evaluations should be conducted as standard practice in order to ensure that development practitioners are truly in tune with their clients, and that vital lessons can be learned that can quickly be translated into improved building and services. Thus, it has been opined that:

> He who puts the right product in the right place at the right time will profit. Listening to the needs and concerns of the end-user is the best way of finding out what and where. The firms that will be a force in the next upswing will be those that best understand the businesses of their clients. (*Estates Gazette* 1993)

471

CHAPTER EIGHTEEN
Residential development

> Hampshire says it is full up. In 40 years its population has grown by 60 per cent and its Conservative county council has decided enough is enough. The Council is not proposing to cordon off the county. It envisages 51 000 homes being built in Hampshire between 1991 and 2001. But this is considerably less than the 66 500 homes set for the county in government planning guidance.[1]

Any examination of the many issues surrounding residential development will require knowledge of the detailed nature of design and layout in new-build housing or conversion of existing stock as well as knowledge of the wider debate surrounding the allocation of new housing land. This chapter will consider both issues and will raise contemporary issues relating to both new settlements and urban villages.

The chapter is divided into four sections as follows:
- submitting planning applications for residential development
- housing land availability
- new settlements
- urban villages

The starting point for an examination of residential development issues is to be found in government guidance as set out on PPG3, Housing, which was revised in 1992. This document deals with both design and layout issues and the allocation of housing land.

Paragraph 1 states:

> The planning system must provide an adequate and continuous supply of land for housing, taking account of market demand and of government policies for the encouragement of home ownership and the provision of rented housing. It must also ensure that established environmental policies are maintained and enhanced. These policies, to which the Government is firmly committed, include the continuing protection of the green belts, National Parks and Areas of Outstanding Natural Beauty, the conservation of natural

---

1. "Full of the rows of Spring", *The Guardian*, 9 May 1990

habitats and the protection of the countryside and the best and most versatile agricultural land, and the conservation and enhancement of the urban environment and built heritage.[2]

Government policy is committed to allowing housing development subject to the protection of both the urban and the rural environment. This would in theory restrict the erosion of agricultural and green belt land from development or the "cramming" of new buildings within the urban area. However, with ever-increasing demands for new housing, some new land must be allocated, and although a debate rages about whether greater use should be made of existing derelict or under used land, it is almost inevitable that the objectives of PPG3 paragraph 1 will be compromised in an attempt to meet the housing needs of British society. Town planning represents the arbitrator, seeking to allocate new land for housing and determining planning applications for residential development. Arbitration is required between the housebuilding industry and those promoting the conservation of rural and urban environment whose detailed interests are articulated by lobbying and pressure groups (e.g. Friends of the Earth or the Council for the Protection of Rural England) or by the local politicians who compose the planning committees of local planning authorities.

Submitting planning applications for residential development

It is important to recall that planning consent will be required for:
- operational development, including new buildings and structural alteration, rebuilding, additions to buildings and other operations normally undertaken by a person carrying on business as a builder (such as demolition).[3]
- conversion of one dwelling into two or more dwellings.

Outline or full?

It is common practice for developers to submit an *outline application* when seeking planning permission for major residential development (ten or more dwellings). This establishes whether or not the *principal* of residential development is acceptable. An outline planning permission provides the developer with an element of certainty before drawing up detailed plans and may therefore enhance the valuation of the land prior to its potential sale. The outline application can be made with all "reserved matters"[4] to be considered at a later stage, however, it is usually the practice to submit details of siting of the dwellings and means of access onto

---

2. From PPG3, 1992 Housing
3. Section 55 of the 1990 Act, refer to section beginning on p. 55.
4. Refer to the section beginning on p. 38.

the highway. This allows the local planning authority to consider the safety of the access and relationship of proposed dwellings to adjoining ones at the outline stage. Such issues may be vital in the consideration of whether or not to grant outline consent. Although nothing prevents the developer from submitting a full application, it is most commonly employed in preference to outline/reserved matters, when dealing with minor residential development (less than ten dwellings) or applications within conservation areas. The smaller the site, the greater the potential for concern regarding the impact of the development on adjoining occupiers. For example, by reasons of "loss of light" to habitable rooms in neighbouring properties or by appearing "cramped" and out of character with the surrounding development because the plot is too small. Such smaller plots are mostly found within existing urban areas, where the need for new housing makes the development of small plots economically viable. Such town infilling (i.e. adding built development within the existing urban fabric) has been referred to as "town cramming" by critics who argue that it results in an erosion of character and, despite control exercised by local planning authorities, results in a loss of amenity to adjoining occupiers. During the 1980s the rise in the value of residential property resulted in a dramatic increase of such infilling, especially within the existing London suburbs (Case Study 18.1). Many LPAs felt that the direction of government policy at the time meant they had insufficient grounds to refuse such applications. Some LPAs attempted to bolster their own policies by undertaking environmental appraisals of their residential areas in an attempt to resist such a tide of development.[5] Such infilling proposals could take several forms.

- *Infill* To build one or two dwellings within the gap between existing dwellings and facing onto the same road (Fig. 18.1).
- *Backland* To develop existing large back gardens. Government advice states in PPG3 (para. 26) that "Where development of back garden or back land is allowed, it will require careful planning. This means adequate space between the proposed and existing development, proper means of access and adequate carparking within the site (Fig. 18.2).

CASE STUDY 18.1: Housing layout and backland development

Arcadian Developments acquire a house with a large rear garden located within outer London. They propose to demolish the existing house and run a road into the backland and to build a block of ten flats. The site is large enough to satisfy all local plan policies regarding amenity space, car parking and separation from existing development. The new road width satisfies highway considerations in Design Bulletin 32 and incorporates a sufficient "buffer" width on either side to allow for screen planting, so that the residents on either side are not affected by the movement of vehicles to and from the new development.

---

5. The London Borough of Harrow, an outer suburban local authority, commissioned Wootton Jeffreys (planning consultants) to undertake an environmental assessment of all the borough's residential areas to enhance its chance of winning planning appeals on residential development.

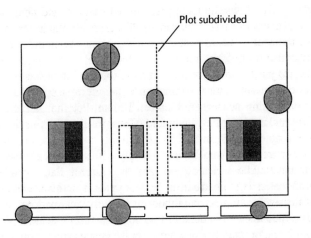

Plot subdivided

Figure 18.1 An example of infill development.

Figure 18.2 An example of backland development.

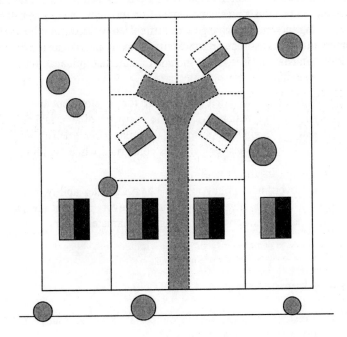

- *Tandem* One house immediately behind another and sharing the same access. This is generally considered to be unacceptable, as the vehicular use of the access would result in a loss of amenity to the occupier of the frontage dwelling (Fig. 18.3).
- *Houses to flats* Since the late 1960s, housebuilding has taken place at higher densities as a direct reflection of the increase cost of land with residential planning permission. Between the late 1960s and late 1980s the price of building land increased sevenfold (Cheshire 1993). Consider the following scenario (Fig. 18.4):

Developers purchase several houses, usually with spacious gardens, and apply to demolish and build a series of two- and three-storey flats (with the second-floor accommodation contained within the roof void). The relative size of the overall plot permits separation from neighbouring property, car parking, sizeable garden/amenity space to satisfy council provision and similar scale of development by maintaining predominantly a two-storey bulk. Permission is granted as the proposal satisfies many of the detailed development control criteria found in local plan policy, as well as meeting the demand for lower-cost one- and two-bedroom residential units. During the next five years many other such applications are submitted and granted. The overall result is that the character of an area has been changed from a low-density residential area to a medium- or high-density one.

This creeping incremental change was difficult to resist during the 1980s and the character of many suburban areas was dramatically altered during this period. When revised in March 1992, PPG3 included additional guidance on this issue, stating:

> Where authorities consider that the pressure for development and redevelopment is such as to threaten seriously the character of an established residential area which ought to be protected, they may include density and other policies in their local plans for the areas concerned while avoiding undue rigidity.

This change in government policy affords LPAs a greater ability to refuse permission for such high-density development. However, it is not always easy to judge the exact point at which such a change in character occurs.

Design and layout

In considering residential design and layout certain specific issues must be considered, as follows (summary as Table 18.1).

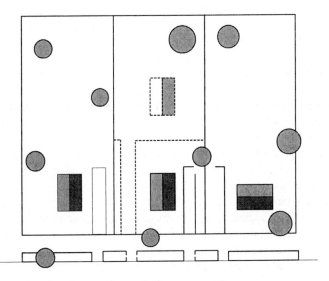

Figure 18.3 An example of tandem development.

Figure 18.4 An example of flatted development on land previously occupied by houses.

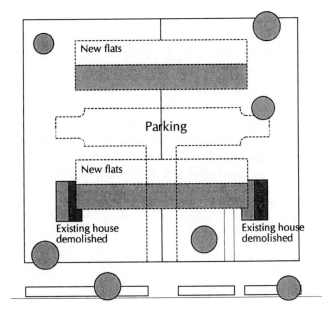

477

Design

Design control as exercised by the LPA is limited. Matters such as the choice of brick colour or mortar detail, the design of a front porch or garage and the proposed fenestration[6] are for the developer to consider and not for the LPA to seek to control. In effect, the ultimate design of a residential development is a reflection of commercial judgement. A reason for refusal based solely on such a design issue would probably constitute unreasonable behaviour for which the LPA could be liable for an award of costs.

Within Conservation Areas, Areas of Outstanding Natural Beauty or in proximity to listed buildings, design control can be exercised more freely. Many Conservation Areas are principally made up of residential buildings and open spaces. Some may comprise fine period-housing layouts such as the Georgian properties in Bath; others may be not so impressive, yet it is important to maintain examples of twentieth century development, for example, "Metroland", 1930s suburban design as found in Harrow, Middlesex (Case Study 18.2).[7] In all these varied cases the role of design control over new development is widely accepted. Many LPAs employ specialist conservation officers to advise on such matters.

Scale, mass and bulk

The following terms are widely used by planning professionals, yet are poorly defined:

- scale refers to the overall size of development.
- bulk refers to the volume of development.
- mass refers to the height and width of elevations.

These concepts should not be confused with that of design. LPAs will seek to ensure that the scale of new development[8] is harmonious with existing development, that the bulk and mass do not result in any demonstrable loss of light or overshadowing of the neighbouring properties. No national planning guidelines exist for dealing with such issues and every site will be considered on its own merits against the judgement of the individual officer. Some guidance on overshadowing is provided by the Building Research Establishment (Littlefair 1991).

---

6. Fenestration refers to the arrangement of windows in a building.
7. Some outer London boroughs have designated certain inter-war suburban roads as conservation areas.
8. PPG3, 1992, *Housing*, states in paragraph 13 that ". . . sites proposed for new housing should be well related in scale and location to existing development".

CASE STUDY 18.2: *Housing development within a Conservation Area*

Arcadia Developments seek outline planning permission to develop a pair of detached dwellings in the Sylvan Park Conservation Area.

The Sylvan Park area was developed between 1890 and 1910 for workers' homes by a local industrialist who was influenced by the writings of Ebenezer Howard. The local planning authority designated the Conservation Area to protect the town planning layout, incorporating deep rear gardens, cul-de-sac road layout and considerable tree planting on both the street frontages and in rear gardens.

The proposal satisfies Council residential standards for existing dwellings and carparking. However, it is considered to result in an erosion of the character of the Conservation Area. The "form" of development is alien to the original layout, and planning permission is refused because:

> The proposal introduced a form of development which is not compatible with the layout of Sylvan Park and therefore harms the character of the Conservation Area.

If the site was **not** within a Conservation Area, the proposal would be considered as an acceptable form of development.

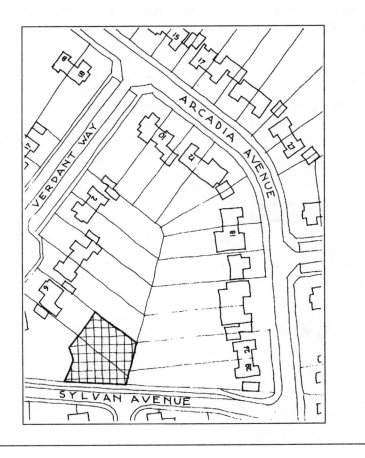

Overlooking

If an LPA were to refuse planning permission on grounds of overlooking, this overlooking would need to be material, that is to say result in a *demonstrable* loss of amenity. This is usually taken to be direct overlooking between habitable rooms. A distance of 21 m window to window is a common standard in many local plan policies, considered sufficient to prevent any serious overlooking.

Highways and carparking

Highway planning criteria have perhaps exercised the greatest impact over residential housing layouts in recent years. The configuration of a road layout effectively dictates the layout of plots and overall urban design of the scheme. The principal source of guidance on this is Design Bulletin 32 (1992), which details standards for road widths, pavement widths and visibility requirements at junctions. For example, the Design Bulletin requires a 5.5 m road width to allow all vehicle types to pass each other, a 4.8 m to allow a car to pass a service vehicle and 4 m for only single file traffic (Fig. 18.5).

Design Bulletin 32 is in itself a technical document prescribing a whole set of criteria dealing with traffic and pedestrian safety. It is widely transposed into practice at the local level by highway engineers, who advise planning officers on highway issues within individual residential applications. This results in little real discretion at the local level, as issues of highway safety predominate, in an attempt to accommodate the motor car within residential layouts. Therefore, the

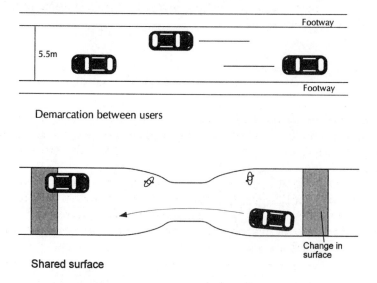

Demarcation between users

Shared surface

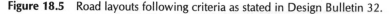

Figure 18.5 Road layouts following criteria as stated in Design Bulletin 32.

480

majority of layouts contain roads of 4–5.5 m width, some with a separate footway and others with no footway (where a shared surface serves both pedestrians and vehicles).

Such road configurations will shape the plot relationships and ultimately the form of the entire scheme. Carparking standards are produced by the LPA usually in the local plan/unitary development plan or in supplementary planning guidance.[9] In most cases these standards distinguish between the various housing types (flats, houses, sheltered accommodation, hostels) and between parking within the curtilage of the property or within a shared parking area.

Dwelling mix/internal standards

Although internal alterations fall outside the definition of development and therefore planning control, the size of individual rooms in new development or resulting from conversion is a material planning consideration. The most complete set of minimum internal space standards were the Parker Morris Standards, which were employed in council housebuilding during the 1960s and 1970s (Parker Morris Committee 1961); for example, a two-storey family dwelling should incorporate 72–92 m^2 (770–990 ft^2) floorspace. Today no such standards exist for public or private sector, although compliance with Parker Morris was always voluntary. As with design issues, the government position is that such matters should be left to the judgement of the developer and not the LPA. The mixture of dwelling types is also of importance and some LPAs, most notably in inner London, will seek to control such dwelling types to meet sectoral needs such as to maintain family housing when faced with increasing pressure to convert existing stock into one- and two-bedroom flats.

Landscaping/amenity space

In similar tone to internal space standards, government guidance on garden sizes is that such matters are best left to the developer. Many LPAs will produce amenity space standards for new residential development or conversion, setting out minimum garden depths or required communal space provision per bedroom or habitable room.

In most major residential proposals the LPA will expect some form of landscaping proposal detailing new tree and shrub planting as well as existing trees/shrubs to be retained. In some schemes the developer may propose a communal play area. The ownership and maintenance may be passed on to the LPA by means of a planning obligation.

9. Supplementary guidance is not a part of development plan policy and will carry weight as a material consideration only if it has been the subject of some public consultation.

Affordable housing

There is no single and widely accepted definition of what constitutes affordable housing. Generally, the term refers to low-cost homes to either rent or buy. Considerable legal attention has also focused upon whether the concept of affordable housing can be considered as a legitimate town planning matter. In the decision of *Mitchell* vs *Secretary of State for the Environment and the Royal Borough of Kensington and Chelsea* (1994), the Court of Appeal reversed a previous decision of the High Court and held that affordable housing does constitute a material planning consideration and local planning authorities may pursue it in local plan policy and in deciding planning application.[10] It will usually be sought in large-scale housing projects and both new settlements and urban villages enjoy potential for a proportion of all dwellings to be low-cost housing. The majority of such housing tends to be provided by housing associations who build and/or manage such property with funding from central and local government or by their own finance, usually raised by market loans. Such provision is necessary in both urban and rural areas.

Table 18.1　Examples of residential town planning standards.

Topic	Standard	Source
Overlooking	21m minimum window to window.	Local plan
Carparking	Varies, but usually one space per dwelling. In flatted developments a percentage for visitors is added.	Local plan
Roads	4.8–5.5m width	Design Bulletin 32
Amenity Space	Flats 10m² per habitable room. Houses 40m² per two bedroom house and 15 for each additional bedroom.	Local plan
Density	Between 70 and 95 habitable rooms per acre.	Local plan
Conversions	To ensure some parking and/or amenity space is provided.	Local plan
Separation of development	Varies between 20 and 30m (taken rear to rear/front elevation).	Local plan
Rear garden depths	Standards discouraged by government yet LPAs do include them at between 10 and 15m depth in new development.	Local plan

10. See Case report in *Journal of Planning and Environment Law,* October 1994, 916–19.

Density

Density is a crude measure of the amount of housing development on a site. However, it is measured in a very exact way as follows:

$$\frac{\text{Habitable room}}{\text{Site area in hectares}} = \text{density, expressed as habitable rooms per hectare.}$$

A habitable room is a bedroom, living room, dining room or kitchen (greater than $13\,m^2$). Site area includes road frontages of the site, which are included to half of the road width.

Housing land availability

The allocation of new housing land has exposed the many political tensions that underlie the British planning system. During the 1980s many LPAs sought to appease strong local opposition to new residential development by refusing permissions and fighting and losing appeals. Planning committees in several London boroughs refused planning permission against officer recommendation that permission be granted. A consortium of major housebuilders sponsored large-scale new settlements to accommodate such demand in major proposals to reduce pressure on existing urban areas. During the 1990s the problem has not gone away, with some Councils seeking to resist further housing growth. The new settlements initiative has enjoyed only limited success and the urban villages have emerged as a new planning innovation. The housing pressures have resulted in the creation of two new acronyms NIMBYISM[11] (not in my back yard) and BANANA (build absolutely nothing anywhere near anyone), reflecting the political impact on the planning system following the local backlash against increasing amounts of residential development. To understand this pressure we must examine the process of housing land allocation and the issues surrounding new settlements and urban villages.

In spite of the lack of a formal system of regional planning within Britain, the allocation of housing targets is the consequence of an "informal" system of consultation between regions and the DOE. Each regional area incorporates its own regional conference, comprising representatives from the constituent Council Councils and district/boroughs. These bodies are invited to submit advice to the Secretary of State for the Environment following their own consultations.[12] The DOE will consider these views, together with a collection of statistical forecasts

11. First used by the late Nicholas Ridley to describe forceful local opposition to the building boom of the late 1980s.
12. Refer to PPG12, *Development plans and regional planning guidance* (1992). Paras 2.1–2.8 provide guidance on the nature of this regional planning guidance.

483

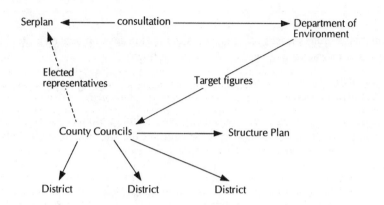

Figure 18.6 Allocation of housing target figures.

dealing with population and housing demand before issuing the housing target figures for the overall region. Such guidance is issued by the Secretary of State for the Environment within Regional Planning Guidance Notes (RPGs). Between 1989 and 1993 seven such RPGs were issued for Tyne & Wear (RPG1), West Yorkshire (RPG2), London (RPG3), Greater Manchester (RPG4), South Yorkshire (RPG5), East Anglia (RPG6) and the northern region of England (RPG7). The individual districts are expected to conform with these *targets* when producing their local plans. The LPA is encouraged to produce allocations on a site-by-site basis, and to set out the policies against which residential applications should be considered. Some allowance should be made for windfall sites up to one hectare in area, where sites are not individually allocated but which may unexpectedly become available and which make an important contribution to housing land supply. LPAs (except London boroughs) are encouraged by government to have a minimum of five-years' supply of housing land. Identified sites must be capable of being developed within this period. In rural areas both PPGs and local policy seek to prevent sporadic housing development in the open countryside and therefore housing land is allocated within or adjacent to existing towns and villages.[13] A good deal of argument is exercised during local plan inquiries on whether or not an adequate supply exists and whether the sites identified by the LPA are economically capable of being implemented and are free from any planning, physical or ownership constraints that would otherwise prevent implementation of a housing scheme. To avoid protracted disputes at Local Plan Inquiry, the LPAs are encouraged to discuss the provision of such sites with representatives of the housebuilding industry. In the absence of a five-year supply the LPA should consider measures to increase provision such as providing an infrastructure to facilitate development or granting more planning permissions for residential development. This process is shown in Figure 18.6.

---

13. Refer to PPG7, *The countryside and rural economy* (1992).

CASE STUDY 18.3: Housing land availability in the South East region

The many political problems surrounding housing allocation within England are most polarized in the South East area. SERPLAN is the regional conference for the 12 South East counties† and 32 London boroughs. Looking at population and household trends (including a significant increase in households due to demographical trends such as more young people leaving home and a greater lifespan) SERPLAN predicted that 730000 additional dwellings would be required between 1991 and 2001. Following consultation the DOE pushed the projection downwards to a figure of 570000 in February 1989. This figure was then divided among the counties, with an allowance made for London. These target agreements came at the end of the building boom of the 1980s with the considerable pressures to build at increased densities on housing land. Local opposition was reflected by district and county councillors and whether or not this was a NIMBY or BANANA reaction, the planners were facing increasing hostility to new housing allocation. The Council for the Protection of Rural England reported that since 1945 the urban area of the South East has grown by almost twice as much as any other region. During this period 188000ha of land have been developed for housing, commerce, industry and roads.‡

Hampshire and Berkshire in particular have sought to confront their housing allocations figures by seeking lower targets. Berkshire proposed 37000 new dwellings against a DOE target of 40000. Berkshire had experienced considerable urbanization since the mid-1960s and the county's strategy was to slow this urbanization by restricting both new housing and industry.

In Hampshire the County proposed 58000 dwellings between 1991 and 2001 against a DOE target of 66500 dwellings. Such battles continued into the structure plan adoption process as developers sought to challenge and oppose such downward trends. Ironically, the outcome in Berkshire was that the structure plan panel, responsible for considering objectives to the new housing policy, recommended a total of 48000 new dwellings over the period 1991–2006, 8000 more than the DOE target figure.

† Hertfordshire, Bedfordshire, Kent, West Sussex, East Sussex, Surrey, Hampshire, Oxfordshire, Berkshire, Buckinghamshire, Essex and the Isle of Wight, represented by the London Planning Advisory Committee.
‡ Sinclair (1992).

The confrontation over housing allocations produced criticisms of the system. Housebuilders criticized some counties for seeking to "cap" housing growth, some lobby groups criticized the planning system for seeking to restrict supply, thereby increasing the price of housing land and restricting access to the housing market by some groups, whereas others such as the CPRE criticized the system for not exercising enough control to prevent the loss of agricultural land.

The current system of land allocation involves an element of consultation but is largely a "top-down" process as the DOE issues target guidelines to counties, and counties allocate to districts (Case Study 18.3). At the local level the districts must allocate sites to provide a five-year supply. Demand for new housing units will continue to grow.[14] Any failure to meet the regional targets will result in increasing pressure on the housing market with consequences for price, density

---

14. Especially so as a result of the increase in the number of households, projected to the end of the century.

and architectural quality. The question now is whether new initiatives to the existing allocation and implementation of housing have to be found. Two important policy initiatives seeking to provide new housing land have emerged from the 1980s and 1990s in the form of new settlements and urban villages.

New settlements

A new settlement is a private sector sponsored new town of between 2000 and 10000 dwellings.

The concept of building new communities away from existing urban areas is not a new phenomenon. The very origins of the British town planning movement and profession can be traced to 1898, when Ebenezer Howard first published his ideas on the "Garden City". Letchworth and Welwyn Garden City were constructed on this model.

The New Towns Act of 1946 introduced a wave of post-war new towns to accommodate overspill housing from Britain's major conurbations. Between 1946 and 1950 a first wave of 14 such new towns were designated in England and Wales, there was one further designation between 1951 and 1961, and then in a second wave an additional 14 between 1961 and 1970. The final designations in the late 1960s included Milton Keynes (1967), Warrington (1968) and Central Lancashire (Leyland) in 1970. The post-war new town Policy was combined with a planned expansion of existing country towns around London during the 1950s and 1960s.

In 1985 a group of major housebuilders[15] formed Consortium Developments Limited (CDL) to submit planning applications for private-sector sponsored new communities or new settlements on several sites. The idea was seen by its promoters as preferable to the town extensions or infilling of existing settlements. This approach permitted a fresh start, with a planned integration of residential, industry–employment, retail and educational uses. New settlements would accommodate housing growth and reduce the pressure for new housing, which had been directed to town cramming within existing urban areas. The concept was in size many ways closer to the Garden City ideas of Ebenezer Howard than the post-war new towns, because it was sponsored by the private and not the public sector. The proposed size of settlement would be much smaller than Howard's population of 30000 in each Garden City or 250000 in the polycentric social city. CDL proposed a population of around 10000 in each new settlement. The idea received favourable, if qualified support, among the planning community, notably the Town and Country Planning Association, an organization founded by Ebenezer Howard.[16] This support expressed a desire that such new settlements

---

15. Barratt, Beazer, Bovis, Ideal, Laing, Lovell, McCarthy and Stone, Tarmac, Wilcon and Wimpey.

must be used to provide a form of balanced development in a good environment, taking pressure away from existing towns and villages and protecting existing countryside. Sites should be carefully chosen to be away from high-grade land while being integrated with existing transport infrastructure (Hall 1989).

It follows that such a new settlement would require careful thought and would be most effectively considered by sponsorship through the development plan process. Ironically, the most significant feature surrounding the early submissions of both CDL and non-CDL sponsored new settlements was that of conflict and not harmony with the planning system.

The three most prominent examples are:

- *Tillingham Hall, Essex*   Proposed 5000 dwellings. Refused planning permission and dismissed on appeal 1988 because of location within Metropolitan Green Belt.
- *Stone Bassett, Oxfordshire (alongside Junction 7 of the M40)*   Proposed 6000 dwellings. Refused planning permission and dismissed on appeal, 1990. The Inspector considered that the siting of a new settlement here would result in an adverse impact on the character of this rural area and create growth and traffic problems. The proposal also conflicted with development plan policies seeking restraint in this part of the county, and no shortage of housing land existed to justify an exception. An application for an award of costs against CDL for unreasonable pursuit of appeal (i.e. no chance of success) was recommended by the Inspector but not accepted by the Secretary of State. This gave a signal to CDL that although such appeals may be dismissed, the government did not consider it unreasonable to pursue the matter to a Public Inquiry.
- *Foxley Wood, Hampshire*   Proposed 4800 dwellings. Refused planning permission and dismissed on appeal in 1989 following a change of Secretary of State for the Environment.

During 1990, two other non-CDL-sponsored new settlement proposals were rejected: at Great Lea near Reading (Speyhawk Developers) and Wymeswold Airfield in Leicestershire (Costain Homes). In all of these cases the planning authorities objected on the grounds of the significant visual impact of the proposals alongside conflict with existing development plan policies.

In both the Foxley Wood and the Stone Bassett decision letters, the government Inspectors acknowledged the harm caused to the character of existing urban areas by past policies of peripheral expansion and infilling. However, these were considered against and outweighed by ecological and environmental harm caused by such large-scale development in these locations. The Foxley Wood Inspector concluded:

---

16. It was suggested by the former Director of the Town and Country Planning Association, David Hall, that about one dozen substantially new towns of 75000–100000 are required in the South East and the southwest Midlands regions of England.

The major cost of the proposed development would be the loss of a significant ecological interest and the urbanization of an attractive rural area of value for its recreational opportunities . . .

As with such major development proposals, both Stone Bassett and Foxley Wood appeals were decided by the Secretary of State for the Environment, with the Inspector's report forming a recommendation. In Stone Bassett the Secretary of State agreed with the Inspector and dismissed the appeal. However, in Foxley Wood the Secretary of State, Nicolas Ridley, although agreeing with the Inspector's identification of the key issues, disagreed with the ultimate *balance* between environmental protection issues and housing need. Ridley considered that Foxley Wood provided an opportunity for much-needed housing provision within northeast Hampshire, about 42 per cent of all new units anticipated being provided within the county between 1991 and 2001.[17] This would relieve housing pressure within the existing urban areas of Hampshire and provide for a "planned" environment with social and physical infrastructure provision built into the proposal. Ridley announced that he was "minded to allow" the appeal, but would await further comments on the matter from all parties. This provoked a mobilization of local opposition to the proposal in what was a solidly Conservative-supporting area of South East England. Such political opposition could not fail to reverberate within a Conservative government. A Cabinet reshuffle during the autumn resulted in Nicolas Ridley being replaced by Christopher Patten. One of Christopher Patten's first decisions at the DoE came in October 1989 when he announced that he was "minded" to accept the Inspector's recommendation and to dismiss the appeal. Following a further round of comments by parties to the appeal, it was dismissed later that year.

In reflecting upon the outcomes of Foxley Wood, Stone Bassett and Tillingham Hall, it is important to distinguish between political and town planning issues:

- *Political issues* The importance of these cannot be underestimated. Foxley Wood and Stone Bassett were sited within areas of strong Conservative support. By allowing both proposals, a Conservative Secretary of State would run the risk of eroding local political support.
- *Town planning issues* None of these proposals were sponsored within the development plan process. They were the subject of speculative planning applications, which were refused by the local planning authority and then considered at appeal. Tillingham Hall was located in green belt and contrary to government and local policy. Foxley Wood adjoined a Site of Special Scientific Interest, that would be affected by the proximity of such a large-scale development. Any new settlement proposal will result in significant impact on the local environment by affecting the highway network and local landscape. The significant outcome from this early wave of proposals was that such major development could be far more acceptably dealt with within

---

17. Northeast Hampshire housing target was adjusted to 11550, Foxley Wood providing 4800.

the town planning system by the promotion within and agreement with the county and district Councils instead of by means of speculative applications and appeals. By 1992 184 new settlements had been proposed, with 60 of them in the South East resulting in a potential for 175 000 new homes if all the schemes had received planning permission.

At the Foxley Wood Inquiry, Hart District Council, the local planning authority for the application site made submissions to the effect that ad hoc appeals do not provide the best process within which to deal with issues of such strategic importance. Government planning policy has supported such a stance:

> The need to respect local preference means that specific proposals for New Settlements should normally only be promoted through the district wide local plan or UDP. . . . local plan policies for New Settlements should address the need for social educational and community facilities and for a wide variety of house types including an element of affordable housing provision. The opportunity to start a New Settlement will be rare and should not be wasted.[18]

Despite such government policy support and the evident desire for such proposals to be the product of liaison between housebuilders and Councils, the subsequent story after 1990 only witnessed a limited improvement in the success of such proposals gaining planning permission.

CASE STUDY 18.4: new settlements and development plan promotion – Cambridgeshire County Council

Cambridgeshire County Council incorporated the allocation of two new settlements within County structure plan policy. Planning professionals felt it was more a case of "where" the new settlement should be located as opposed to "if" a new settlement would be located.[†] A new settlement proposal also received support from the East Anglian Regional Planning Conference. Developers were understandably encouraged by this stance and three schemes were proposed in the corridor of land straddled by the A10 road and a further seven were proposed in the corridor of land straddled by the A45 road. Consideration of these matters was called in by the Secretary of State who appointed an Inspector to hear evidence and report back on the options. The Inspector found that one site on the A45 was acceptable but could not accept any of the A10 corridor. The Secretary of State did not agree with the Inspector's findings on the recommended scheme and rejected the proposal on the grounds that the business park component within the scheme was larger than that envisaged in the appropriate local plan. All proposals were subsequently rejected.

† Nigel Moor, *Housebuilder* (September 1990: 24).

---

18. Refer to PPG3, *Housing* (1992: paras 34 and 35).

New settlement success

In spite of a whole host of setbacks for the promotion of new settlements, both through planning appeals and by working within development plan and review, the concept has enjoyed some success (Table 18.2). Some schemes have received planning permission from the local planning authority and without the use of "call-in" procedure by the Secretary of State.

Table 18.2   New settlements with planning permission.

New settlement success	Details
Chafford Hundred, Grays (Essex)	5000 dwellings and commercial community buildings, 18-hole golf course and built on 234 ha (575 acres) of former chalk quarries
New Ash Green (Kent)	2000 dwellings on 174 ha (430 acres)
Chelmer Village, Chelmsford (Essex)	2500 dwellings and a retail park on 142 ha (350 acres) of land
Church Langley, Chelmsford (Essex)	3500 dwellings on 162 ha (400 acres)
Great Notley Garden Village, Braintree, (Essex)	2000 dwellings, business park, shops, hotel and a country park on a former US Air Force Hospital
Dickens Heath, Solihull (West Midlands)	1100 dwellings on 49 ha (120 acres)
Peterborough Southern Township (Cambridge-shire)	5200 homes, retail centre and business park on 809 ha (2000 acres) of former brick claypits
Kettleby Magna Melton Mowbray (Leicester-shire)	1000 dwellings on former airfield
Martlesham Heath (Suffolk)	1200 dwellings
Bradley Stoke, Bristol	3500 dwellings
Haydonwick Farm, Swindon	3380 dwellings

Government support for the concept of new settlements remained lukewarm during the late 1980s and early 1990s. Despite support for the idea in PPG3 and various ministerial pronouncements on the issue[19] (Case Study 18.4) the identification of such sites is not easy. A new settlement will occupy some 243 ha (600 acres) of land yet must be separated from existing settlements, avoid protected land and be located within an area of housing need, which, like the South East and West Midlands, is already heavily developed (Case Study 18.5). This, combined with local objections and the associated political problems, means that the progress of new settlements as an alternative to town cramming is hampered by a cocktail of political and planning problems that limit the role it will play in satisfying housing provision to the year 2000. Research proposed a major recommendation that larger-scale new settlements (up to 6000 or even 10000 dwellings) will be required in future years to provide one of the most desirable forms of urban development.

19. Such as in a speech by the Housing Minister, George Younger, in December 1993.

CASE STUDY 18.5: new settlements and development plan promotion: Micheldever in Hampshire

This new settlement, Micheldever Station Market Town of 5000 dwellings was as with Cambridgeshire A10 and A45 schemes promoted through the process of structure plan review, but unlike the Cambridge proposals the County Council (Hampshire) opposed the Micheldever proposal set against their own attempts to reduce housing land availability targets from 66 500 (in SERPLAN guidance) to 58 000. Eagle Star Properties, who owned the site, argued that not only is the county's lower figure inadequate to satisfy housing demand, but also that new settlements have distinct advantages over the alternatives of housing provision: relieving pressure on existing communities, minimizing the environmental impact of development, and providing increased access to affordable housing.[†]

† Micheldever Station Market Town. Representations by Eagle Star Properties 1993, to Hampshire County Structure Plan Review.

Summary: new settlements	
Problems/disadvantages	Benefits/advantages
"NIMBYISM" problems of considerable local opposition.	Comprehensive and co-ordinated way of providing for new housing with necessary infrastructure and diverting pressure for "town cramming" away from existing urban areas or land with special value (AONB, SSSI or high-grade agricultural land).
Site assembly – requires some 234 ha (600 acres) of land, which is unlikely to be within one ownership.	Ability to provide for social housing and other forms of planning gain within/adjoining the new settlement.
Difficulty in obtaining planning permission by either speculative planning application (Tillingham Hall, Stone Bassett or Foxley Wood) or by promotion through the structure/local plan review process (A10 and A45 Cambridgeshire). Smaller new settlements (around 2000–3000 dwellings) or on brown land stand the best chances of gaining permission.	The potential to work with the planning system as Councils seek to promote the concept in their planning policy as they realize the benefits of new settlements.
Secretary of State for the Environment faced with problems of local feeling when considering various Inspectors' recommendations, however . . .	Government support for the idea has been published in planning policy advice (PPG3).

Urban villages

An urban village is a mixed-use mixed-ownership urban development based on public–private sector co-operation and covering about 200 acres. (Stubbs)

I am hoping we can encourage the development of urban villages in order to reintroduce human scale, intimacy and a vibrant street life. These factors

491

can help to restore to people their sense of belonging and pride in their own particular surroundings. (HRH The Prince of Wales 1989)

There is already a move away from development monoculture: many developers, architects and planners have been promoting schemes both new-build and refurbishment, which integrate a number of uses into attractive local environments. There is evidence that these can be more stable and attractive and therefore in the longer term a better investment. (Urban Villages Forum 1992)

In 1989 Prince Charles expressed his desire for both investigation and promotion into the concept of planned mixed-use and mixed-tenure developments that would enhance the quality of life for those people who lived and worked in them as well as creating a form of sustainable development. Late in the same year, the Urban Villages Forum was formed to promote the idea. The Forum was an amalgamation of various property-related professions who believed that a new approach was required when building urban areas. This new approach formed a reaction against many forms of post-war urban planning in which planners zoned separate areas for separate uses and developers built mass-volume housing estates on the edge of towns and offices in the centre. The housing lacked any sense of community or urban design and at night the town centres were "dead", devoid of any life or activity. The commuting between the two resulted in a waste of resources. What was needed was a revitalized form of housing and employment land use to bring life back to cities, and new large-scale housing proposals.

The key features of the urban village are:
- Mixed-use buildings and areas comprising housing, small businesses, shops and social amenities. Although one of the key objectives is to provide housing, it is considered important that an urban village maintains a degree of "community" in which people may live and work in the same area.
- Mixed ownership with rented and owner-occupied housing.
- A high standard of urban design to enhance the public spaces and quality of development.
- A total population of between 3000 and 5000 residents.
- A form of development suitable for redevelopment within existing urban areas, but also possible for new-build schemes on greenfield sites. There is some overlap with new settlements because a new settlement could incorporate these urban village features.

A considerable obstacle to this initiative has been that traditionally financial institutions have been reluctant to lend money on buildings that involve a mix of uses on different floors, as this increases the cost of managing the investment and may reduce the future value of the building. For example, a building split into general office and residential results in separate tenants with exclusive tenancy terms and conditions. The letting of the office may be adversely affected by flats above, as occupiers perceive the flats as creating problems of security. This in turn may suppress the value of the offices and therefore the investment potential resulting from the scheme.

How to implement an urban village

The urban villages concept represents a challenge to the land use and development orthodoxy of recent years. This challenge during the 1990s has manifested itself in both seeking to change perceptions of property development and by the implementation of schemes that both foster interest and demonstrate the commercial success of the idea.

Role of the planning system

The implementation of an urban village will be best served through its promotion within the existing development plan and development control system. Local plans should designate areas suitable for such development, detailing the necessary planning obligations or public sector contributions and should also detail the scale of expected development. Such areas should incorporate 40–80ha (100–200 acres) in an area and a combined resident and working population of 3000–5000. Suitable locations would include brown land (vacant inner-city land), suburban or edge-of-town sites or greenfield sites. To engender social and economic integration, the urban village promoter[20] will be encouraged to provide not just a balance of uses but also a variety of housing tenures[21] and commercial freehold and leasehold tenures (Urban Villages Forum 1994, Lichfield 1995).

The urban village concept pushes the planning system towards the greater consideration of creating mixed-use urban neighbourhoods. This will require a rethink of some planning policy standards that prescribe requirements for parking and amenity space. The rigid application of such policies will inhibit the flexibility necessary to create an effective urban village. Further, as planners move away from the "development monoculture" of single-use areas and towards mixed-use areas or buildings, a re-awakening of ideas and training will be required.

Implementation of ideas

Some early examples of urban villages provide an encouraging vision for the further employment of this idea to provide housing and deliver environmental quality.

---

20. Housebuilders, developers and local investors rather than institutions.
21. Owner occupation, rent, equity sharing or retirement.

493

- *Crown Street, Glasgow: the redevelopment of a cleared 16ha (40 acre) site in Glasgow formerly occupied by a 1960s high-rise housing estate* A masterplan was devised, which established layout mix of unit types, including family accommodation and with a split of 75 per cent owner occupation and 25 per cent rented, elevational treatment and creation of a community trust to manage the development. The form of development recreates traditional Scottish tenement living with four storeys incorporating residential accommodation and shops, workshops and studios on the ground floor. Private amenity space would be created within the block. In this case the urban village promoter was a combination of housing developers: City Council, Glasgow Development Agency and a housing association.

- *Poundbury, Dorchester, Dorset: the new development of a 162ha (400 acre) greenfield extension to the west of Dorchester on land owned by the Duchy of Cornwall* The masterplan initially devised by Leon Krier involves an urban form with a medium-density layout with houses (including 20 per cent rented accommodation), offices, shops and industrial space. This mixed-use urban environment has been planned for implementation over many stages, with a development period stretching from 1994 to 2019. Work on the first phase of 61 houses was started in 1994.

- *Hulme, Manchester: the redevelopment of 1km² of 1960s eight-storey deck-accessed concrete housing blocks* Since construction in the early 1970s it had become notorious for its social, economic and health problems, irrespective of the inhuman architecture and planning of the estate.

  Redevelopment work began in 1992, involving the demolition of the housing blocks and the rebuilding of the area employing the principles of mixed-use high-density urban form of redevelopment with a strong element of urban design. The masterplan for redevelopment was a product of public consultation. It emphasizes the fact that merely rebuilding the physical form of an estate such as Hulme is not sufficient; attention is required to create a feeling of community. The Hulme regeneration involves a mix of uses within buildings and areas, as well as a mix of housing tenure and a projected population sufficient to sustain local school, businesses and community facilities into the longer term. The promoter incorporated both City Council, private housebuilder and housing association.

These examples incorporate ideas and concepts drawn from the increasing desire among property professionals to integrate social and economy activity when recreating (as in Hulme) or building afresh (as in Poundbury). The most significant problems facing urban villages as a means of satisfactory new housing targets are that, by the mid-1990s, the total number of units provided is small. The most tangible benefit is the attempt to refocus ideas towards the quality of urban environment.

Summary: urban villages	
Problems/disadvantages	Benefits/advantages
Traditional reluctance by funding institutions to become involved in mixed-use buildings.	Important and significant critique of monoculture of post-war British development, which focuses attention on a change in our approach to urban development and the funding of that development.
Only a few examples implemented during the early 1990s resulting in a small overall contribution to housing land supply.	Creation of a popular "bandwagon" following the successful implementation (financial, social and environmental) of key schemes.
Important mechanism in recreating communities in depressed inner cities.	Few NIMBY problems associated with brownland schemes.
Increased perception of the concept and promotion among the planning community.	

Conclusions

Both new settlements and urban villages should not be viewed as mutually exclusive forms of development. It is conceivable that a new settlement could be developed on the principles of an urban village as promoted by the Urban Villages Forum. Both initiatives have predecessors in planning history, notably the works of Ebenezer Howard and the Garden City movement. The problem of housing demand exceeding supply will remain well into the next century because of the rising number of households. It appears doubtful that the targets for the South East will be satisfied and the planning system will play its part in controlling supply and increasing the value of land with residential permission. However, greater attention than in previous decades is being focused upon the residential quality of new environments. New settlements and urban villages will hopefully improve the quality of life for their inhabitants by utilizing the newly found enthusiasm for the quality design of urban spaces and reacting against the excessive separation of land uses in previous new town developments of the 1950s and 1960s. It is important that both new settlements and urban villages do create the quality of environment that they have set out to achieve and do not become misrepresented as mere marketing catch-phrases to conceal more volume housebuilding for the private sector. Planners and developers have become increasingly aware that new-build housing must form part of a wider mixed-use/mixed-ownership strategy to create a high-quality environment with a social and economic mix that fosters a sense of place or community among its inhabitants.

The initiatives of the Urban Villages Forum are to be welcomed, especially in their attempts to tackle negative perceptions regarding the funding of such projects. Yet, it is important that the idea is widely propagated and, more significantly, that it is widely implemented, otherwise the concept of the urban village will become just another "good idea" in theory, marginalized in practice to a few inner-city redevelopment schemes or novel experiments with famous patronage, such as in Poundbury.

PART SIX

Conclusion

CHAPTER NINETEEN
Trends and prospects

Decisions regarding the nature of urban planning and the performance of the real estate development industry are central to the functioning of society, not the least reason being that by far the largest portion of the nation's wealth is invested in property. The better the quality of planning and development decisions today, the better the quality of the built environment tomorrow. This book concludes where it started, by highlighting some of the major questions that confront those concerned with land, planning and development, and hazarding a view as to how they might be answered. For convenience the various issues to be addressed are grouped as follows:

* urban planning and change
* real estate development and challenge
* sustainability and the built environment

Urban planning and change

The organization of urban planning and the major issues that confront urban planning and development agencies are explored in Parts Two and Three of this book. However, the whole context for urban planning is constantly changing, and communities of all kinds are faced with economic, social and environmental uncertainty. Some of the questions raised or intimated throughout the text are identified and addressed below.

Planning and uncertainty need reconciling

Society seeks certainty, but advances in thought and application lead to the creation of uncertainty as a constant condition. At the same time, however, the whole language of planning implies a high degree of certainty, the very word "plan" implying that some control can be exercised over the future of a given geographical area for which that plan is prepared. Indeed, it has been argued that the fact that we have "statutory" plans and "adopted" plans reinforces the image of planning as a provider of certainty. Further, that the search for certainty within a planning system, managed as it is by democratically elected political bodies, rapidly leads to the general expectation that the planning system exists to maintain the status quo – at least the existing situation is known and to that extent certain. If a community seeks certainty, then the safest course is to stick to what is known and what exists. That message can be accepted readily by local politicians because there are votes in a promise of certainty. Change is inherently uncertain and this has resulted in many local planning officers becoming basically neighbourhood environment protection officers – planners leading the anti-change brigade! (Welbank 1995).

Society's approach to the environment is also changing. It is clear that the world, and the natural world in particular, is not static. It is a dynamic changing scene with every action having a reaction and reactions that cannot be forecast with any certainty at all. Environment has its impact on man and man has an impact on the environment. The interaction is continuous and everyone is part of that process.

The challenge to strategic thinking about the use of land as a resource, therefore, is to be able to offer certainty in planning and environmental progress (ibid.).

Profound changes in the nature of employment will have to be faced

Recognition has at last dawned that the world of work irrevocably has changed. Over the past 30 years or so there have been three distinct employment revolutions: in agriculture, in manufacturing, and more recently in the service sector. Each of these employment sectors has witnessed, or is experiencing, significant shifts in the type and number of jobs it provides. Only about 1 per cent, or 250000, of the working population are now directly employed in agriculture, representing a fall of around 40 per cent over the past 20 years. During the same period the number of employees engaged in all manufacturing and production industries fell from around 8.5 million to 4.5 million, or by almost half, so that less than 22 per cent of the British workforce is now employed in production of one kind or another. The service sector, conversely, has seen employment grow from around 12.25 million to just under 15.3 million over the same years, so that almost three-quarters of the workforce are currently in service sector jobs.

It is in this all-pervasive service sector that revolutionary trends brought about by advances in information technology, privatization, financial liberalization, corporate re-engineering and the general pressure for greater productivity are changing locational preferences, transportation requirements and property needs. On top of this, there is the increasingly familiar "demographic time bomb", with fewer school leavers, more above retirement age and less able to claim unemployment benefit, all contributing to a reduction in the total gainfully employed workforce. With greater global competition, moreover, it means that those in employment will need to be ever more productive, leading to a polarization of work, growing income inequalities and an increasing number of people simply not working.

Certain key factors will determine the level and pattern of work in the service sector. These include: the extent to which producer services, especially financial services, rationalize and reduce employment; how far electronic banking and insurance transfers the location of jobs away from city centres; whether there will be a fundamental shift in core international financial services employment to other European centres such as Frankfurt; whether there may be a similar shift in other headquarters functions to alternative centres such as Brussels, Paris, Madrid, Naples or Strasbourg; and what the knock-on effect would be for associated business services such as law, accountancy, marketing and even real estate consultancy?

Education, health and leisure services are cited as other major clusters of activities carefully to be considered (Hall 1995). Higher education is now one of the largest employers in the country and, as the existing educational institutions and new universities consolidate, expand and restructure the location of their campuses, it becomes a critical catalyst and determinant in employment policy and performance. There are also directly associated development activities such as science parks and student housing to be taken into account. In similar vein, redundant National Health Service hospitals present an opportunity to exploit expensive infrastructure and potentially generative employment openings for private health care operations. London inevitably will become an international medical care centre and selected cities likewise regional centres. Perhaps an even more important source of future employment lies in the complex of leisure, culture, entertainment and sport, all shading into tourism.

Strategic decisions regarding housing provision will have to be made

The stark reality is that, despite a relatively stable population, some 4.4 million extra households will have to be accommodated in the UK over the next 21 years. This "fissioning", as it is known, results from major social changes in the huge growth of independent students, young professionals, childless women, broken families, longevity and the widowed. The traditional nuclear family is no longer the norm.

Because the type, quality and location of housing, together with its availability and "affordability", touches everybody, planning for housing is seen consistently to be one of the most controversial aspects of policy and practice. With current national planning policy constraining the planning system as far as possible to land-use matters, there are recognized limits to that system. Local plan policies, for example, cannot address such issues as that of tenure, and the capture of land values to subsidize new housing is strictly controlled by central government guidance and the law relating to planning gain. Many would wish to see policy pushed into areas beyond the present system, but would be well advised to heed the lessons of the past in respect of public housing provision and betterment taxes.

The future for many must surely be in the creation of planned new settlements. A certain amount of lip service is paid by government to such ventures, and a degree of advocacy advanced by such lobbyists as the TCPA and the Urban Villages Forum. However, there seems to be a fear on the one part and a fragility on the other when it comes to implementation. To think of the worldwide reputation gained by the UK planning system in the development of new towns not that long ago, and the individual achievements of the likes of Unwin and Parker, the LCC and even the great privately developed Victorian villa suburbs before that.

At another level, the new upsurge in non-traditional households should be seen as a tremendous opportunity for revitalizing the inner areas of our towns and cities. It has been argued that many such people are natural city dwellers favouring the urban qualities of proximity, access, gregariousness and conviviality against the conventional calm and space of the suburbs or countryside. However, planning policies do not appear to be positively framed in support of this predilection. Yet many urban problems relating to both housing and the inner city could be tackled together.

However simplistic and grandiose it might sound, therefore, housing policy must confront the concepts of new settlements and renewed centres in a more focused fashion.

British urban planning could look to european counterparts with advantage

There is something that smacks of near xenophobia, or at least self-satisfaction, with the way in which British planning has viewed the work of counterparts abroad, most significantly perhaps in Europe. Apart from the march towards a Single European Market posing questions regarding differing planning systems proving to be a barrier to trade for the development industry in the same way as differential tariffs for commerce, there is also the perceived need to consider if lessons can be learned from other planning systems in Europe. It has been suggested in a planning Compendium of all member-states that, although some are strategically stronger than others and some have a far greater coverage, the systems of planning in the rest of the EU are generally far more protective than in the UK. The plans are seen to be better mechanisms for longer-term public investment planning, the engagement of private sector participation and the demonstration of commitment to the European Commission for funding. Such plans are increasingly at the regional level and are said to express a more integrated approach to social, economic and environmental initiatives. It is also stated that these plans are much clearer on the need to implement sustainable development principles, and environmental assessment is being built into the process of plan development at all stages. In addition, the Compendium document argues that the integrated approach to transport, housing and social welfare creates a sense of purpose and commitment that is not yet apparent in the UK. The difficulties of central government departmentalism in the UK, which have not been solved by the government offices for the regions, are dealt with more coherently in the EU by what are often directly elected politicians. Integration is also the keynote of planning policy at the tier below regional level, and there are proposals from the Committee of the Regions for the incorporation of an "urban competence" again as part of the inter-governmental conference in 1996, which would bring together many of the urban funding schemes and policies already in existence (Morphet 1995).

There is, as always, another side to the story, for whereas the British government stands apart from the rest of Europe, it does so, as with other issues, to preserve a degree of independence and prevent an overly centralized, excessively interventionist and too bureaucratic an approach towards planning within the Union. Nevertheless, British town planning has a poor record of strategic regional planning compared with France, or even Germany, and until there is a much clearer and more certain programme linking guaranteed public expenditure with regional planning aspirations indicating to the private sector where it is best to invest, there is a case for looking at something like the French system again.

Towns and cities should seek their own unique selling proposition (USP)

In the "whizz-word" ridden world of advertising, the successful product is one that occupies and exploits it's own special niche in the market by developing what is known as a unique selling proposition (USP). It is possible to argue that the same could be true for towns and cities. Certainly, it is already the case for individual developments, especially shopping centres, business parks and leisure complexes. Nor is there anything new in the idea. Towns and cities of the nineteenth century gained reputations and prosperity through domination by a particular major industry, activity or employer. In many instances it must be conceded that it was also their downfall, when reinvestment in a new "USP" was eschewed.

Present planning policies tend, consciously or otherwise, towards achieving a common package of activities in the search for the ideal of balanced development. Generative, catalytic or "beehive" effects, call them what may, can be gained from a concentration upon a selected employment base, combined with the enthusiastic attraction and privileged provision of complementary and supportive services. Certain obvious trades, industries and professions quickly suggest themselves in the pharmaceutical, bio-engineering, computing, environmental technology, communications, defence electronics, food, publishing, clothing and leisure fields. Others might be less immediately apparent, and comprise subsectors of the above, but then imagination, innovation and implementation would be the watchwords of such a USP urban policy. There would also be the specialist allied and ancillary activities supporting the core business in terms of highly orientated education, training, research, legal, financial, property, marketing and distribution agencies and services.

Such a notion might seem fanciful, and, unless carefully researched, nurtured and monitored, could admittedly be downright dangerous. But, following the logic that everything is relative, it is the towns and cities that stand above others through fuller employment and higher incomes by developing a USP that will be seen to be successful. The real trick, of course, comes not just in identifying the initial USP, but in recognizing when it has run it's course, and having the foresight, flexibility and will to convert to a new or adapted one. However, time alone will tell whether or not such a concept is meaningful.

Town centre management will come of age

Many town centre problems can be seen as a management rather than a social issue. The economic power of out-of-town retailing lies not only with the efficient layout, controlled environment, plentiful and free parking, but also in its management structure. There is an increasing awareness of the need to manage town centres as businesses.

Research has identified certain key actions for the leading players in town centre management that need to be taken in the coming decade. Retailers need to:

- consider strategies for addressing the static retail spend
- work with local authorities to a common purpose
- ensure that property strategy is reviewed to board level
- utilize their existing property better.

Property developers and investors need to:

- recognize that occupiers are more demanding and improve services to them
- develop a flexible approach to lease structures
- rethink the role of the high street and consider new forms of investment
- overcome fragmented ownership with innovative approaches to partnership
- consider mixed-use developments
- overcome entrenched attitudes to management
- take the lead role in management initiatives.

Local authorities need to:

- decide that their high street is a winner
- exploit the natural resources of the high street
- seek to provide diversity (not just shops)
- not fight the car, but plan for it
- encourage residential and employment opportunities
- promote "civic pride"
- seek flexibility in applying the development regulations.

And town centre managers need to:

- organize appropriate funding
- carry out market and consumer research
- understand the history of the high street concerned
- explore the opportunities
- make better use of what exists

- prepare a realistic business plan
- address access and transport issues through management initiatives
- implement small-scale as well as large-scale projects
- adopt lessons from corporate marketing practice
- compete head on with regional shopping centres (Gerald Eve Research 1995).

The management of high streets should sit alongside the statutory development planning process. Indeed, much of the background information prepared for planning purposes will provide input to the management of the high street. The focus of high street management must be on identifying public and private sector interests, mixing the two together, resolving conflicts and preparing a deliverable action plan.

With approximately 80 per cent of the population living in an urban environment, the role of the high street as the focus of communities is not in question. Despite out-of-town retailing, electronic shopping, and other trends, the high street retains an important role in the lives of most people. The real challenge lies in shaping the future form and environment of the high street. Critical to this is the recognition that different high streets perform different functions for different groups of people. Some high streets will fare better than others and, indeed, some will wither. The planning profession and the property industry must seek to work with retailers and the many others with vested interests to ensure that high streets do not contribute or succumb to some of the more disturbing aspects of social change. In this way, town centre management will come of age.

London will again have a strategic planning authority

Whatever the case for and against the erstwhile Greater London Council (GLC), there are actually very few professionals in either the planning or development spheres who do not accept the need for the re-establishment of some form of strategic planning authority for London, if not the reintroduction of an elected governing body (Simmie 1994). London must be the only capital city in the world without such direction or governance. The return of anything like the GLC is most improbable, but some central agency with actual strategic planning powers, as opposed to mere guidance, seems likely, especially if a Labour government is returned to power.

The London Planning Advisory Committee (LPAC)), composed of all 33 London-based authorities can only be viewed as an inadequate, makeshift and virtually impotent expedient. Apart from being an improvement on its predecessor, the most recent regional planning guidance for London (RPG3) published in March 1995 has satisfied few. The key objectives are outlined in Chapter 16 in the context of office development, but the document has been widely criticized as being full of platitudinous pledges and short on clear and detailed policy measures. One of the strongest themes running through the revised guidance, for example, is the need to make the residents and businesses of London less dependent on the car in order to relieve congestion and meet sustainable development objectives. However, a prerequisite for such a strategy is the provision of efficient and extensive public transport. But positive policies backed by identifiable investment funds seem singularly lacking. Likewise, proposals to provide London with a land bank of sites suitable for all types of industrial and technological use prepared by LPAC officers were excluded from the government's draft.

Cynically, it is possible to suggest that politicians at central government level have grown accustomed to having the ultimate authority to plan the future strategy for the capital, but it is to be hoped that sense and not ascendancy will prevail, and London will once more have a strategic planning authority endowed with the necessary powers to implement policy.

The planning process will have to accommodate the leisure revolution

Despite the recession of the early 1990s, the leisure sector has displayed considerable vitality over recent years. New types of leisure-based activities are emerging, and existing ones are being revived. There are several factors that contribute to what is now recognized as a revolution in leisure activity and a major sector of the economy requiring sympathetic and sensitive planning. These can conveniently be grouped as follows (Watt & Valente 1995):

- *Affluence* Although leisure expenditure is more volatile than consumer expenditure, growth in leisure services has consistently outperformed growth in consumer spending since the early 1980s. Furthermore, the outlook is for growth in leisure expenditure of around 4 per cent per annum compared with annual growth of 1–2 per cent in consumer spending.
- *Demographic shift* Demand for particular leisure facilities will be influenced by the fact that during the 1992–2002 period the number of 15–29 year olds will decline by nearly 1.7 million while the number of 30–59 year olds will rise by 3 million.
- *Consumer expectations* Rising consumer expectations will be as influential in the leisure market as there have been in retailing. The provision of new leisure experiences in attractive and secure environments has been critically important in pulling would-be consumers away from home.
- *Product innovation* The out-of-home leisure market has fought the arrival of VCRs and PCs with a mix of innovation and the introduction of new formats in attractive and accessible off-centre locations. This combination has proved successful in attracting consumers who were believed to have been lost forever to home-based leisure activities. Such supply-led demand has been particularly significant with multiplex cinemas (MPCs) and the new generation of bingo clubs currently being created across the country.
- *Fashion* Changing fashion plays an important role in the leisure market. However, it is doubtful whether this sector can be said to be any more sensitive to the wiles of changing fashion than mainstream retailing, where

505

it is generally seen as a positive influence providing the sector with its underlying dynamism. Cinema-going, bingo-playing and tenpin bowling have all
been around for some considerable time. What has changed is the manner
in which the product is packaged and delivered to an increasingly selective
audience.

Although not afforded a separate chapter in this first edition, the incorporation
of leisure requirements in the statutory planning process will have to be addressed
in a more concerted manner over coming years.

Countryside planning should interlock more with urban planning

The quality of the countryside, in terms of landscape, environmental health, design
of buildings and settlements, access and amenity, matters in varying degrees to
everyone. Modern mobility in all it's manifestations means that the future of the
countryside interlocks with all the major themes of current planning policy – sustainability, transportation, new settlements, employment, housing, energy and
leisure. Although this book is primarily concerned with urban planning and development, some mention, however brief, must be made of changes that are taking
place in the countryside.

To begin with, changes in the political agenda are forcing a rethink in the
approach to the two most extensive land uses in the country: agriculture and forestry. There is likely to be less emphasis on high-intensity farming and more on
non-food crops, the diversification of farm enterprises, the application of agri-
environment measures and the switching of some farmland into forestry, recreation and nature conservation uses (Dower 1995).

With regard to rural communities, the countryside is of course the home and
workplace for many millions of people, and both the economy and the social structure of rural areas have undergone massive changes over recent years with such
trends as a shrinking workforce in farming industries, the loss of village services
and the in-migration of people from the major towns and cities. These trends seem
bound to continue and to provoke the need for policies directly geared to the specific needs of rural areas, such as the provision of affordable housing; the recognition of the dependence of many rural people upon private transport; the
encouragement of small enterprises; and the use of modern telecommunications.

In respect of the leisure revolution mentioned above, the countryside is massively used as a playground for the nation – to the tune of around 1000 million
day-visits a year. These activities include walking, cycling, scenic driving and
sightseeing, which depend on a widespread network of routes through the countryside, plus access to all manner of attractive places; country sports, which put
significant money into the rural economy and help to justify the management of
many countryside features; and other activities of increasing diversity, often
demanding sophisticated equipment and special use of land or water (ibid.).

Given all the growing pressures upon the countryside it is increasingly difficult to segregate the policies, practices and procedures that pertain to urban and rural planning affairs.

The relationship between planning and transport should be brought closer together

There has been a noticeable failure over the years properly to formulate transport policy as an integral part of the planning process. Indeed, this text has not attempted to tackle the topic of transport as a separate issue, but rather incorporate the transport aspects of particular planning and development subjects as and when appropriate. However, several factors combine to make a review of transport policy and its relationship with urban planning at national level timely. These factors are said to include increasing concerns at a local level about pollution and the environmental impacts of traffic and traffic infrastructures; renewed awareness of the impracticability of avoiding worsening traffic congestion by means of road investment; and the inescapable global anxieties about sustainability. Significant shifts in government thinking on transport and the interrelationship between land-use and transport planning are reflected in the UK Sustainable Development Strategy (HMSO 1994a,b,c,d) and more recently in a series of planning policy guidance documents, most especially PPG13 (DoE 1994a) and the subsequent PPG13: *A guide to better practice* (DoE 1995). However, it has been argued that the means of reducing the need to travel, thereby influencing the rate of traffic growth and reducing the environmental impacts of transport, have yet to be worked-out and, more difficult still, "sold" to a populace increasingly accustomed to a life-style designed around the use of the car and dependent upon the mass haulage of goods by road (Parker 1995).

The difficulties of implementing an environmentally sustainable transport strategy formulated in the context of coherent urban, city and regional levels of town and country planning cannot be minimized. Achievement of long-term objectives will continue to be compromised by incremental decisions unless the need for restrictive measures is made clear and the longer-term benefits to society at large, and to future generations, are forcefully spelt-out through expansion of public consultation and involvement. However, it is not realistic simply to look to improved public transport to cater for the diverse pattern of journeys now being made by the private vehicle. Nevertheless, as one leading transport consultant somewhat hopefully avers, in a sustainable future there will have to be less travelling than today; more destinations will be local and reached on foot, by bicycle, by bus and by train; goods movements too will generally have to be shorter, with greater concentration on the marketing of local as against imported goods; private ownership of buses will be widespread, but services and fares will be regulated to contribute to integrated transport and land-use policies; parking, on both public and private land, will be more strictly controlled and priced; vehicle exclusion areas, park-and-ride schemes, bus priority schemes, high-technology information systems and roadside emission checks will be more commonplace; and cycling will be seen as the most efficient, economic and environmentally friendly way, with walking, to get about locally (ibid.). A Utopia indeed, and one requiring not just a closer relationship between transport policy and land-use planning, but unbeknown political courage and determination.

Progress in building energy policies into planning will be slow

There can be little doubt that great strides have been and are being made towards the more efficient use of energy. Equally, there can be no question that considerable scope exists for further advances in this field. The government has accepted that about 20 per cent of the country's expenditure on energy could be avoided if investments in cost-effective energy efficiency measures with pay-back periods of less than two years were made in the domestic, service and industrial services. Others have put the potential for energy savings at around 30 per cent of UK primary energy at or below the cost of supply (Blake 1995).

Realistically, however, a really decisive energy conservation policy, such as exist in Scandinavia, calls for a major shift in the human mind-set and the introduction by government of what would surely be seen as Draconian measures. Such a shift, and such measures, are unlikely to occur in the UK while energy prices are at an historically low level and there is no real prospect of energy shortage in the short to medium term. Moreover, despite the necessary lip-service that has to be paid to "sustainability", energy policy does not occupy a prime position on the political agenda.

The corollary, of course, is that endeavours to build an energy component into planning policies will be weakened. However, planning should keep the efficient use of energy at the forefront of its thinking because, although no energy crisis looms for the time being, planning, by definition, is about the longer-term future, and settlement, design, communications and development decisions made now will affect energy requirements throughout the next century.

It is true that many local authorities now include energy policies in their statutory plans, but invariably they are "exhortatory" in nature, along the lines that energy efficiency will be "encouraged", "promoted", or "taken into consideration". When has a single planning application been refused permission on the grounds that is fails to secure the efficient use of energy?

Exhortation alone is not enough. It has been argued that, if there is serious intent on the part of government to secure energy savings, then sufficient mechanisms should be put in place to ensure that the planning system not merely advocates but actually delivers energy-efficient developments (ibid.). However, the signs for swift action are not that auspicious.

Real estate development and challenge

It has become almost a truism to state that economic growth has broken out across the world, albeit to varying degrees and in differing directions in different regions, but with the common themes of privatization, financial liberalization and corporate restructuring. As part of this international market place, real estate increasingly is developed and traded as a global investment asset. Although Parts Four and Five of this book concentrate upon the workings of the property development industry in the UK, much of what is written relates equally to real estate development in other countries. Similarly, many of the challenges facing the British development industry also confront development agencies worldwide. Some of these challenges are outlined below.

Property will gradually be placed higher on the strategic agenda

Most, if not all, organizations need property to pursue their operations. Over the past few years much research has been directed towards the role and management of corporate property assets and the perception by decision-takers regarding the contribution that property can make to achieving the main objectives of their own organization (Bannock & Partners 1994). The findings from this research highlighted a lack of awareness and understanding by most senior managers of the role of property and the contribution that real estate as a resource could make to the success of their organization (Avis et al. 1989). Although this situation is seen to be improving, with at least some finance directors viewing property as an important strategic resource, there remains a reluctance on the part of many managers to see property in this light.

Since the mid-1980s, the UK has experienced a substantial economic boom succeeded by a sustained period of recession and retrenchment. Inevitably, the property market experienced the same boom and slump, but one augmented by the special characteristics of the real estate market, especially liberality in funding, the development lag and the inflexibility of the building stock.

Much as a consequence, over the same period the balance of power has shifted between the main players in the property industry, from developers and investors to owners and occupiers. The emphasis now being firmly upon cost, efficiency and added value. In fact, the recession has been one of the main driving forces to the raising of the profile of property as a strategic resource.

A survey of major corporations has identified certain key issues critical to success facing organizations over the next decade, the top five being (Gibson 1995a,b):
1. identifying new market opportunities
2. focusing on core business
3. quality improvement
4. investment in new technology

509

5. re-engineering business processes.

In tackling these issues, the effective management and development of corporate property, as a significant organizational resource, will contribute to necessary change and prospective growth. This will include such matters as: the understanding of the property and locational requirements of new markets; synergy with existing space requirements; profitable disposal and exploitation of non-core business property; refurbishment of obsolescent space; and the creation of extra and sometimes more innovative modern technology and new working practices. Nevertheless, the same survey showed, unsurprisingly perhaps, that the vast majority of chief executives of major corporations considered property as a much less important resource than such other factors as information, finance, people and technology. More unexpectedly though, less than a quarter of organizations felt that there was significant change or adaptation required to their property resource over the next decade. Paradoxically, however, almost 40 per cent of those surveyed deemed property a strategic resource central to the main function of their core business (ibid.).

Although major corporations appear to becoming more aware of property as a strategic resource, the pace at which it moves up the management agenda will remain gradual until decision-makers feel that they have a greater degree of control over their organization's real estate resource, and can forecast more accurately the requirements, costs and benefits involved.

The image of the property development industry should be improved

It is sad but true that the widespread image of the property development industry is generally poor. Some of the reasons are relatively easy to identify. As a major agent of change there are tangible and often intrusive physical impacts made by the industry upon local environments. Moreover, they happen quite quickly, unlike most other social and economic changes. The industry is also one where great wealth has accumulated into comparatively few private hands through what is seen to be the exploitation of others. Planners and local pressure groups frequently perceive developers as generally unsympathetic towards the need to protect the environment, to such an extent that they are seen as preoccupied with maximizing floorspace, minimizing cost and optimizing profit, being by nature of a philistine and insensitive disposition towards such issues as the visual quality of the environment, the design and massing of buildings, and the overall amenity of local communities.

This view of the industry does not stand up well to close scrutiny (McKee 1994). The very role it performs is to provide land and buildings for manufacturing industry, commercial businesses, housing, shopping and leisure. Space, therefore, for work and shelter, the two fundamentals of society. By and large it has done it well.

The low esteem in which the property development industry is held needs to be improved. A positive and comprehensive policy should be devised, backed up by a series of initiatives designed to enhance its public standing. Instead of always appearing to be reactive to central and local government proposals, leaders of the industry should seek to be more proactive and try to shape and guide public opinion. Performance standards need to be set, measured and the results published, in much the same way as has been done by local government, the health and education services, and most public utilities. A conscious effort must be made to be more environmentally friendly and subscriptive to the tenets of sustainable development. Studies must be conducted into the operation of the industry, with the findings made readily available. And, most importantly, all those affected by property development decisions, by proximity or by use, should be treated as valued customers.

Both the British Property Federation and RICS have already taken important steps in this direction, but as has been pointed out (ibid.) resources will have to be made available as image has to be paid for as well as earned.

Land and property valuation will be more carefully conducted

Since the mid-1980s there has been something closely akin to a revolution in the valuation profession. Practices and procedures have been criticized, scrutinized and regularised to a degree hitherto unknown. Unfortunately, much of the questioning of professional standards emanated from outside the profession, largely as a result of the traumas experienced in the wake of property market collapses, but also as a continuing consequence of the ravages wreaked by inflation on investments in land and building.

The broad criticisms levelled at the valuation profession can be summarized as follows. Generally, it has adopted an insufficiently questioning approach towards the techniques employed and the basic assumptions on which they are founded. A lack of concern has been displayed regarding the quality of information used in analyzing market transactions and assessing the performance of property investments through time. An unacceptable degree of complacency has led to inadequate attention being paid to the need for rigorous scrutiny of the relevant factors at every stage of the process. Typically there has been a slow response to changing economic conditions within the market and an inability or unwillingness to make informed judgements regarding future trends in value. There has been a wide divergence in the practice of valuation within certain fields of commercial investment and development consultancy, and no consensus as to the terminology employed. Too much reliance has been placed on results achieved in the market, with too little knowledge of what has caused them.

Nevertheless, the valuation profession has come a long way over the past few years in establishing common standards and improving the understanding of techniques. However, it is still possible to suggest a few future directions in which progress can be made. There could, for example, be greater implementation of

511

a code of conduct in respect of valuation standards and procedures and a wider application of disciplinary powers on those who transgress; closer regard to recognized criteria as to "best practice", with a possible move towards the introduction of a practising certificate in order to qualify valuers for specialist purposes; more attention to be paid to the needs of those who might have to use valuations for business and even civic activities; much greater disclosure of information in valuation reports and better access to property records, so that more reliable comparative analysis can be performed; a higher level of consistency and uniformity in the production and presentation of property performance analysis; depreciation to be tackled in a more overt and meaningful way; closer consideration of cost and value factors in appraisal; and improved education and continuing professional training. The "New Red Book", RICS *appraisal and valuation manual* (RICS 1995) should go a long way to improving quality and consistency in valuation performance.

A major debate, however, is bound to rage around how far valuers should be expected to peer into the future, and in what ways adjustments to value or cautions as to changing market conditions should be made. It is disturbing to find so many leading members of the profession implying that a valuation should merely reflect present conditions prevailing in the market. Such an attitude will become less and less acceptable to clients who will be just as concerned with property investment and development worth over time as they are with the likely sale price of a property at a single point in time. Whatever the future holds, better information and higher standards are required in order to improve the professional capacity for assessing how much property is needed, in what form, for whom and where – as well as how much it is worth.

Joint development and partnership ventures will prosper

Although the term "joint development" has no specific legal meaning, it is commonly used to describe a formal arrangement between two or more parties established for the sole purpose of carrying out a specific development, the usual participants being a landowner, a developer and a funder. Such arrangements have a long history, but their use and sophistication grew during the mid- to late 1980s, and tended to be entered into for major complex developments for reasons of spreading risk, obtaining finance, sharing profit, gaining expertise, retaining control, securing planning approval, consolidating landholding, maximizing tax advantages, benefiting from the special powers or position of a particular participant, or as a result of general market conditions. Joint venture arrangements of all kinds are an established and effective method of achieving development project success, but can be a recipe for disaster if not properly constructed and operated. Their use is likely to grow significantly in the immediate future, given the narrow margins that will probably prevail in the development industry in the late 1990s.

One special area of joint development that is worthy of mention is that of

"Partnership". Partnership in the context of planning and development has normally been associated with public and private sector collaboration in implementing inner-city and urban regeneration policy, being seen not only as an essential adjunct to existing policies but as the most important foundation of the government's strategy towards urban areas. It has been stated, indeed, that there is now a broad consensus among the main political parties and practitioners that partnership is now the "only" basis on which successful urban regeneration can be achieved (Bailey et al. 1995).

Whatever the truth of this, it should be stressed that all partnerships are different. However, it is probably correct to state that ultimately all such schemes depend upon a high degree of trust. Unfortunately, suspicion can be a common feature of sharing arrangements, with a public authority nervous of what might appear to be the developer's superior negotiating powers and sceptical of his obsession with the maximization of profits, and the developer harbouring doubts about the strength of the authority's planning and other powers, and apprehensive as to its lack of commercial insight. It is therefore imperative that a bond of goodwill is established in order to surmount the inevitable problems encountered in any major scheme, one aspect of which will be the recognition by each part of the validity and legitimacy of the other's point of view, with the development agency respecting the authority's public accountability and the authority accepting the developer's concern regarding the attainment of a reasonable return. Nevertheless, partnerships in development inevitably will prosper.

Workplace development will continue to evolve

Society is said to be on the threshold of a decade that will change the way in which people work and the workplace environment beyond people's imagination. The challenge for the property industry is to recognize that there is no choice here; these work-style changes will happen and will have an increasingly dramatic effect on users' demand for office space. So, property people need to become more aware of the changing space needs of businesses, how new technologies will influence work-style, the way businesses will utilize space in the future, and the consequential changes in the office market-place (White 1995).

There are various diverse issues that influence the way in which corporations are responding to the increasingly dynamic business environment. These include:

1. *the need to reduce costs* and to use resources, particularly people, just when and where they are needed;
2. *a concentration on the core business* and not on diversionary, peripheral, non-core activities;
3. *the global market-place* in which product life cycles are shortening and new product development costs increasing;
4. *the consequent need to create virtual organizations* – that is the creation of a supply chain from several different sources, to fulfil a particular

513

manufacturing process or service, to deliver particular products;
5. *the shrinking innovation pool* and the niche players who think up new products and services, but who will not fit into corporate structures or locations;
6. *the availability of powerful information technology and communications services* to control and effectively manage distributed and remote businesses irrespective of geography or time." (ibid.)

By the start of the next millennium, the type of office reflecting these pressures will be in regular use, creating an environment in which people are able to work intuitively, and organize information hardware, software, time or space.

The retail development sector has entered a new era

Following the development excesses of the late 1980s and the severity of the recession of the early 1990s, there can be little doubt that the retail market has entered a new era. A new cycle has emerged where the inherent dynamism that typifies so much of retailing has come face to face not only with pedestrian growth in consumer expenditure but also a much more cautious approach on the part of the occupier towards expansion. In parallel, a new range of constraints on development have arisen through the planning process. All this provides a combination that is potent enough to influence every retailer's strategy for growth in the short to medium term. At the centre of such a strategy lies the fight for market share that takes on a new sense of urgency and one that applies equally to occupiers as well as the owners of shopping centres. (DTZ Debenham Thorpe 1995).

Consumer conservatism has replaced the conspicuous consumption of the 1980s, and in the 1990s retailing will be dominated by the need to provide value for money. The nature of retailing is also changing as two distinct types of shopping trip emerge: "purposeful shopping" and "leisure" shopping. Against the current trend of planning policy, purposeful shopping will continue to dictate a move by retailers out of town but, with active management and new forms of partnership, the role of town centres need not be threatened. (Jolly 1995).

Refurbishment will increasingly be placed centre stage. The wave of new supply that reached the market during the late 1980s was of such magnitude that the rate of market growth anticipated over the medium term is insufficient to guarantee the success of each and every new shopping scheme throughout the country. Competition between adjacent schemes will intensify and, against such a background, refurbishment will be embraced by many landlords as a means of simply maintaining as well as enhancing value.

In the longer term, telephone shopping is going to revolutionize consumer habits and emphasize even further the complementary nature of the purposeful and leisure shopping functions. It will be difficult for the telephone and the VDU screen to challenge the social dimension of "leisure" shopping but many "purposeful" shopping trips will become unnecessary leaving capacity in the system for continued innovation and change out of town.

With regard to the current collision between proposed planning policy and commercial realism it has been argued that vested interest and the inherent conservatism of the UK planning system will ensure that viable and attractive town centres do not die in the wake of a mass movement of retailing out of town. There is not going to be a repeat of the relative planning freedom that characterized the 1980s and which resulted in the emergence of dominant out-of-town regional shopping centres such as Thurrock Lakeside, Meadowhall Sheffield, Merryhill Dudley and the Metro Centre at Gateshead. Their value is going to be protected as a result, but, once the few remaining planning consents are taken up, it is most unlikely that there will be any more.

Out-of-town shopping developments will not, in future, be able to achieve the critical mass needed to make them dominant in their region. The threat has passed. Out-of-town retailing is likely to be fragmented and therefore unable to pose a serious challenge to established and well managed town centres. However, town centres, like shopping centres, will have to be well managed and, particularly where there is effective competition from out-of-town retailing, property owners may need to seek a more pro-active partnership with town councils in order to secure the necessary investment in town centre promotion and in access and environmental improvements.

Town centres have a valuable, but changing, role to perform as centres for "leisure" shopping, and sensitive local authorities will therefore both recognize this specialized role and plan for it (Jolly 1995).

Leisure development will flourish

The dynamics of consumer demand regarding growing expectations, long-term demographic shift, increased leisure time and product innovation have already been mentioned in respect of the need to plan more assiduously for the leisure revolution. In terms of the development challenge, the upsurge in the leisure market is, in large part, the result of rationalization among the main operators. This has led to a concentration of market share, the emergence of more standardized trading formats and a willingness on the part of the major players to raise their standards and quality of leisure provision. In turn, this is the result of tougher competition, corporate restructuring and innovation among the leading operators.

Following in the footsteps of food superstores and retail warehousing, there is now the advent of the "Leisure Box", providing a single-point destination able to offer consumers a range of services either within a single envelope or on adjacent sites set in attractive, comfortable and secure environments with adequate parking provision. To provide the necessary degree of flexibility, such leisure boxes require a footprint of at least $4650\,m^2$ ($500000\,ft^2$), eaves height of up to 8m and at least 700–900 parking spaces.

A configuration of this kind can accommodate a range of uses that are emerging as an appropriate tenant mix including a Multiplex cinema of 3250–4200 m² (35–45000 ft²); bingo hall of 2800 m² (30000 ft²); restaurants of 185–325 m² (2000–3500 ft²) and bar of 185–280 m² (2000–3000 ft²). There might also be bowling, night clubs, discovery zones, ice rink, swimming pool, quasar centre or other attraction. The most popular anchor is the Multiplex cinema, where, for example, the number of screens rose from 10 in 1985 to 638 in 1995 and now represent a third of all screens (Watt & Valente 1995).

The leisure market has recently seen an appreciable rise in interest from property investors and, as with any other new and emerging-market, inherent dynamism has to be balanced with caution, it seems certain that the leisure development industry will flourish.

Real estate research must continue to develop

The Orwellian maxim runs that "information is power", and in this the property market is no exception. Naturally, the basic rationale of research in the private sector is to gain a competitive edge by finding ways of reducing risk and maximizing return. Scope for research in the development industry embraces a broad range of factors from demographic trends, general economic performance, social indicators, public policy, consumer demand and expenditure patterns, through to construction costs, finance rates, rental and capital values, property yields, occupational requirements, investment conditions and the like. Increasingly, such data is sought internationally as well as nationally and locally, as the UK property industry strives to retain supremacy in international real estate markets.

In terms of research and analysis, the real estate industry has matured significantly over recent years, and this trend is bound to continue. However, one of the ironies has been that, in the past, money to support the growth of research has been more readily available in boom times, when surpluses obviously exist but decisions on the margin requiring better evidence are rarer, than in periods of recession or recovery when reliable data regarding development opportunities and likely performance are of more aid in decision-taking.

It is generally accepted that the fortunes of the property market are in some way determined by what is going on in the wider economy, but establishing exactly what is that relationship is the difficult task. Previously, there has been a tendency to oversimplify certain cause and effect relationships, but a fuller appreciation is gradually being gained of the complexities of real estate markets, the external influences upon them and the internal mechanisms at play. To some extent it might be said that real estate researchers are in an enviable position, because for generations they have defended their position, and very existence, on the grounds that real estate is a product and a business sufficiently different to require tools of analysis and ways of thinking that go well beyond the static equilibrium models of mainstream finance and economics. To their credit, and no doubt relief, this turns out to be correct. The list of research questions in the general field of property, and the particular discipline of real estate development, grows longer and longer; it now includes international as well as national, regional and local issues, with an historically high level of both public and private sector interest in the answers to questions of what to build, where, for whom and how much.

Sustainability and the built environment

The background to the debate on sustainability and the role of urban planning in helping to limit future environmental degradation is described in Chapter 7, but, at the risk of contributing to any "sustainability fatigue" that might be creeping into the body of planning and development thought, there are a few clear signs for the future.

The goal of sustainable development will endure

At the outset it should be stated that this section makes no pretence to be a theoretical treatise, an economic analysis or social discourse. Nor is it a plea by a dedicated conservationist. Indeed, prior to working overseas this author proselytized an unhampered free-market approach towards most economic activities, especially land-use planning and the property development industry. However, recent experience and current contemplation have produced a conversion of almost Damascene proportions. Put simply, the well accepted basic tenet for future development is that true development must be sustainable development, true growth be sustainable growth. Further, that this "sustainability" is dependent upon a very much greater emphasis being placed by all concerned upon environmental quality as a critical factor in public and private decision-making. Thus, investment and development decisions that satisfy the needs of present producers and consumers should be taken without threatening or compromising those of future ones.

Worldwide there can be few unfamiliar with the range of environmental issues that confront us, either by formal education or by bitter experience. From the threat to the ozone layer, deforestation and the greenhouse effect, through air, water and noise pollution, to soil erosion, energy conservation, nuclear fall-out, traffic congestion, and even "sick" buildings syndrome – everyone is actually or potentially affected.

Almost everywhere there is a mounting criticism of materialism, albeit to different degrees and on different questions. Post-material politics, moreover, have become the order of the day in developed countries, and they now transcend national and international boundaries. A cynical view, but one with more than a kernel of truth, is that increasingly there are votes in it. Politicians are notoriously keen to shifts in public opinion. However, words are cheap and it takes decisive and expensive action to translate political rhetoric into firm government commit-

517

ment.

Environmental economics will flourish as a discipline

To poach and pervert Milton Friedman's popularized catch phrase: there is no such thing as a free environment. Where there is any diminution in the quality of the environment, there is cost – tangible or intangible, measurable or immeasurable. However, ecological losses are not normally allowed for in current accounting practices, although a few industrialized countries are attempting to introduce a system called "resource accounting", and the World Bank is experimenting with a roughly similar approach for use in developing countries.

One set of views that has gained considerable popularity over recent years is that of "environmental economics" or "market environmentalism". This approach argues that environmental resources should be considered in the same way as any other economic good. To achieve this, it would almost certainly be necessary to extend the concept of property rights to environmental resources in the same way as they are applied to land. It would also imply the need for a market in which such resources were bought and sold, which in turn would require a methodology for valuing the various components of the environment in economic terms; of developing prices and incentives to promote environmental improvement; of resolving boundary problems and reciprocal recoupment of payments; and somehow discounting the future, if ever environmental issues are to be given at least parity, if not priority, in the new economic planning that is needed to achieve sustainable development for the future.

A full exploration of this approach is beyond the scope of this text, but a well established theoretical base exists regarding the issues of externalities and public goods, and a growing information base relating to experiments conducted at a range of scales and covering a variety of projects. Let the "polluters" pay is a crescendo call throughout the world. However, in any form of market economy we all pay, depending, somewhat simplistically, upon the relative elasticities of demand and supply prevailing at that time, in that place, for that good.

Environmental protection will gain growing acceptability by development agencies

It is increasingly being recognized in most Western economies that environmental protection is a positive, dynamic and continuous concept that should be integrated with all forms of planning. Inevitably, in balancing economic growth with the conservation of resources and the quality of life, there will be trade-offs. There will also be short-term cost implications that secure long-term growth prospects. However, environmental protection is definitely not anti-development, as many would make out.

518

Looking at North America and much of western Europe, it has been heartening to witness since the mid-1980s that private sector enterprise has noticeably come to equate value with quality. In the property field, environmental quality is now placed at a premium. Clients have become more demanding, better informed, more highly selective and increasingly mobile. Investors have gained greater expertise in financial analysis and portfolio management and, in doing so, started to take a longer and wider perspective in terms of the quality of the city and regional environment, immediate local environs, amenities, services, urban design and the general management of the area. Developers have responded with better design requirements, stricter specification standards, enhanced level of services, better project control and improved property management, in the knowledge that excellence is reflected in rental income and capital value. The various professions concerned with the property development process have, in their turn, generally demonstrated higher levels of expertise, greater initiative, more responsibility and accountability and an increased desire for quality control and building performance. Public opinion is more aware and better organized, with expectations consequently raised. As a result, in most circumstances improved environmental quality has been seen to be not just more acceptable but more profitable.

Awareness of and attitudes towards environmental issues will continue to grow and become more professional

Although many people apparently remain uninformed or uninterested about environmental considerations, there has, as already mentioned, been a marked advance in environmental awareness across communities over the past few years, leading to positive action by governments, the private sector and pressure groups. Many governments have mounted publicity campaigns aimed at the individual, some large international and national companies are displaying a "green" conscience, and a growing number of local environmental groups with general and specific interests have been formed. Moreover, as "green" issues are increasingly taken on board by legislators, lobbyists, administrators and the public at large, environmental policies regarding the land conversion process and the property development industry are likely to become more and more stringent. Buildings will probably become subject to some form of "environmental audit"; clients are already specifying higher environmental quality standards; project managers are having to take account of the environmental dimension in their consideration of the traditional time, cost and performance elements of development; designers and contractors are forced to seek out environmentally "sound" solutions and products; and occupiers demand better environs both inside and around their premises. The movement generally is one from quantitative to qualitative standards, from purely physical to environmental solutions and from a short-term view of capital gain to a longer-term perspective of value and investment worth.

The day is also fast dawning when it is no longer a mere matter of treating

519

each new development separately, since regulations will require a wider view of the impact and desirability of individual schemes. This has already happened in North America and western Europe, and will surely spread in time to the developing world. It is, therefore, propitious for the building and construction industry to adopt a more anticipatory, pro-active and responsible approach towards development, so as to ensure that legislators take into account future development needs as they construct their "green" platforms.

Among professional organizations and disciplines concerned with the development process, there is a fast-growing trend towards a more multidisciplinary approach. This is accompanied by a more comprehensive policy regarding the assessment of projects in order to balance environmental quality against sustainable investment yield. In fact, it is increasingly found that the two go hand in hand. To this end, there will be a greater need for environmental specialists, more awareness of environmental issues among other members of the professional team, and a system of evaluation that will supplant what is traditionally known as quantity surveying in UK-influenced economies. The American term "value engineering" will take on a wider meaning to embrace environmental quality objectives of development schemes. It can be argued that at the moment there is a leadership vacuum in this respect in the industry, and a need for an international forum to discuss the broad issues of environmental quality and sustainable development, the hoped-for result being a cross-industry initiative aimed at establishing a common wide-ranging policy.

A last word

Since the 1960s, the environmental movement has grown apace. "sustainable development" was legitimized as a concept and a goal at the Earth Summit in Rio in 1992 and handed to the world as the destination of the environmental route to a perfect world. It is "sustainable development" that to so many offers a basis for strategic thinking and a new rationale for the relationship between planning and development. Above all, it has a spatial dimension, which is the most distinguishing feature of the planner's medium of activity and is absent from so many general theories on development.

The term "sustainable development" has now slipped into political and professional jargon at all levels and on all occasions. It is endlessly used and misused to justify or attack almost everything around, and is capable of meaning all things to all men as circumstances warrant. The great danger exists that the whole concept could become debased by over-use in policy statements and by indiscriminate application in practical implementation. It is far too important to the future of realistic urban planning and effective real estate development to allow that.

Bibliography

Legal citations
The following citations are referred to in the text when citing sources of relevant case law:
- AC   Appeal cases
- All ER   All England Reports
- EGCS   *Estates Gazette* case summaries
- JPL   *Journal of Planning and Environment Law*
- P & CR   Property Planning and Compensation Reports
- PLR   Planning Law Reports
- WLR   Weekly Law Reports

Adams, C. D., L. Russell, C. S. Taylor-Russell 1993. Development constraints: market processes and the supply of industrial land. *Journal of Property Research* **10**(1), 49–61.

AIREA 1979. *What to look for in an appraisal*. Chicago: American Institute of Real Estate Appraisers.

Anderson, F. 1985. Structural engineering. In *Office development*, P. Marber & P. Marber (eds), 177–203. London: *Estates Gazette*.

Armon-Jones, C. 1984. Revealing the art of estate agency. *Estates Times* (March).

Ashworth, W. 1954. *The genesis of modern British town planning*. London: Routledge.

Association of Metropolitan Authorities 1990. *Costs awards at planning appeals*. London: Association of Metropolitan Authorities.

Atkinson, R. & G. Moon 1994. *Urban policy in Britain*. London: Macmillan.

Audit Commission 1992. *Building in quality: a study of development control*. London: HMSO.

Avis, M., V. Gibson, J. Watts 1989. *Managing operational property assets*. Department of Land Management and Development, University of Reading.

Bailey, N. with Barker, A. and K. MacDonald 1995. *Partnership agencies in British urban policy*. London: UCL Press.

Barnard, L. 1993. The concept of sustainable development and its impact on the planning process. *Property Review* **2**(9), 394–7.

Baldry, C. & D. Pitt 1993. *Building for the new organisation*. In *Facilities management 1993*, K. Alexander (ed.), 78–91. London: Haston Hilton.

Bannock, G. & Partners 1994. *Property in the boardroom – a new perspective*. London: Hillier-Parker.

Barrett, V. & J. Blair 1982. *How to conduct and analyze real estate market and feasibility studies*. New York: Van Nostrand Reinhold.

Bater, J. 1980. *The Soviet city*. London: Edward Arnold.

Baum, A. & D. Mackmin 1989. *The income approach to property valuation*, 3rd edn. London: Routledge.

BCO 1994. *Specification for urban offices*. London: British Council Offices.

Berkley, R. 1991. Raising commercial property finance in a difficult market. *Journal of Property Finance*, **1**(4), 523–9.

— 1992. Funding review. *Journal of Property Finance* **2**(4), 517–19.

Bernard Thorpe & Oxford Institute of Retail Management 1990. *Who runs Britain's high streets?* London: Bernard Thorpe [chartered surveyors].

Blackhall, J. C. 1990. *The award of costs at public inquiries.* Newcastle: Nuffield Foundation and University of Newcastle upon Tyne.

— 1993. *The performance of Simplified Planning Zones.* Working Paper 30, Department of Town & Country Planning, University of Newcastle upon Tyne.

Blake, J. 1995. Energy policies and planning. Paper presented at the Town and Country Planning Association Annual Conference, London, April.

Blowers, A. 1993. *Planning for a sustainable environment: a report by the Town and Country Planning Association.* London: Earthscan.

Bourne, F. 1992. *Enforcement of planning control*, 2nd edn. London: Sweet & Maxwell.

Boys, K. 1983. Bridging the communication gap. *Chartered Surveyor Weekly* (15 September).

Bramson, D. 1992. Joint ventures and partnership funds today: the art and practice of financing property. Paper presented at Henry Stewart Conference, London.

Brindley, T., Y. Rydin, G. Stoker 1989. *Remaking planning.* London: Unwin Hyman.

Brown, C. 1990. Retail property: development in the 1990s. *EstatesGazette* (9004), 20–24.

Brownhill, S. 1990. *Developing London's docklands: another great planning disaster?* London: Paul Chapman.

Bruggeman, W. & L. Stone 1981. *Real estate finance.* Homewood, Illinois: Irwin.

Bruton, M. J. & D. J. Nicholson 1987. *Local planning in practice.* London: Hutchinson.

Bullock, H. 1993. *Commercial viability in planning.* Occasional Paper 21, *Journal of Planning and Environment Law.*

Burgess, K. 1982. Long-term mortgages are back in favour. *Chartered Surveyor Weekly* (9 December).

Butler, J. 1982. Making the most of your marketing. *Estates Times Review* (October).

Byrne, S. 1989. *Planning gain: an overview – a discussion paper.* London: Royal Town Planning Institute.

Cadman, D. & L. Austin Crowe 1983. *Property development*, 2nd edn. London: Spon.

CALUS 1974. The property development process. *The future of the office market.* Derby: The College of Estate Management.

Carnwath Report 1989. *Enforcing planning control.* London: HMSO.

Case, J. 1985. Building services. In *Office development*, P. Marber & P. Marber (eds), 283–315. London: Estates Gazette.

CBI/RICS 1992. *Shaping the nation: report of Planning Task Force.* London: Royal Institution of Chartered Surveyors.

CEC 1990. *Green Paper on the urban environment.* London: HMSO.

CEC Directorate General for Regional Policy 1991. *Europe 2000: outlook for the development of the Community's territory.* Luxembourg: Office for Official Publications of the European Communities.

CEC Directorate General, for Environment, Nuclear Safety and Civil Protection 1992a. *A Community programme of policy and action in relation to the environment and sustainable development*, vol. II: *towards sustainability.* Brussels: Commission.

— 1992b. *The impact of transport on environment – a Community strategy for sustainable mobility.* Brussels: Commission.

Chapman, H. 1995. Tomorrow and beyond: office occupiers. *Property Review* 5(2), 34–6.

Charlesworth-Jones, S. 1983. Promoting the corporate image. *Estates Gazette* 265, 942–4.

CIOB 1992. *The code of practice for project management for construction and development.* Ascot: Chartered Institute of Building.

Cheshire, P. 1993. Why NIMBYISM has gone BANANA's. *Estates Gazette* (9321), 104–105.

Clark, R. 1991. Refinancing. *Journal of Property Finance* 1(3), 435–9.

Cleavely, E. 1984. The marketing of industrial and commercial property. *Estates Gazette* **217**, 1172.

Cole, H. 1993. The irresistible rise of the superstore. *Estates Gazette* (9301), 73.

Coupland, A. 1992. *Docklands: dream or disaster?* In *The crisis of London*, A. Thornley (ed.), 149–62. London: Routledge.

Court, Y. & Z. Southwell 1994. Town centre management: are the initiatives effective? *Estates Gazette* (9436), 138–9.

CPRE 1992. *Where motor car is master*. London: The Council for the Protection of Rural England.

Cullen, G. 1961. *Townscape*. London: Architectural Press.

Damesick, P. 1994. The major provincial office centres: offices opportunities, values and trends. Paper presented at "Offices" (Henry Stewart Conference, London).

Davies, H. W. E & D. Edwards 1989. *Planning control in western Europe*. London: HMSO.

Davies, H. W. E., J. A. Gosling, M. T. Hsia 1993. *The impact of the European Community on land-use planning in the United Kingdom*. London: Royal Town Planning Institute.

Debenham, Tewson & Chinnocks 1988. *Planning gain: community benefit or commercial bribe?* London: Debenham, Tewson & Chinnocks.

Debenham Tewson Research 1990. *Development trends*. London: Debenham, Tewson & Chinnocks.

— 1991. *Business parks*. London: Debenham Tewson.

DEGW 1985. *Meeting the needs of modern industry*. London: DEGW.

DEGW 1983. *ORBIT: office research on buildings and information technology*. London: DEGW.

Derby City Council 1991. *Sir Francis Ley Industrial Park – Simplified Planning Zone: the first three years*. Derby: Derby City Council.

Design Bulletin 32 1992. *Residential roads and footpaths*. London: HMSO.

Detoy, C. & S. Rabin 1985. Office space: calculating the demand. In *Readings in market research for real estate*, J. Vernor (ed.), 243–57. Chicago: American Institute of Real Estate Appraisers.

Development Systems Corporation 1983. *Successful leasing and selling of property*. Chicago: Real Estate Education Company.

DoE 1988. *Town and Country Planning Assessment of environment effects: regulations*. London: HMSO.

— 1990a. *This common inheritance: Britain's environmental strategy* [Cm 1200]. London: HMSO.

— 1990b. *The Urban Programme Management initiative: a consultation on proposal changes*. London: Department of the Environment/HMSO.

— 1991. *Circular 16/91. Planning and Compensation Act 1991. Planning obligations*. London: HMSO.

— 1992a. *The use of planning agreements*. London: Department of the Environment/HMSO.

— 1992b. *Development plans and regional guidance* [PPG12]. London: HMSO.

— 1993a. *Town centres and retail developments* [PPG6]. London: HMSO.

— 1993b. *Alternative development patterns: new settlements*. London: HMSO.

— 1993c. *Reducing emissions through planning*. London: HMSO.

— 1994a. *Transport* [PPG13]. London: HMSO.

— 1994b. *Roads to prosperity*. London: HMSO.

— 1994c. *Sustainable development – the UK strategy*. London: HMSO.

— 1994d. *Planning and pollution control* [PPG23]. London: HMSO.

— 1995. *A guide to better practice* [PPG13]. London: HMSO.

Dobry, G. 1975. *Review of the development control system*. London: HMSO.

Dower, M. 1995. What change for the countryside? Town and Country Planning Association Annual Conference, London, April.

DTZ Debenham Thorpe 1995. *Special report on shopping centre refurbishment* (June).

Duffy, F. 1991. *The changing workplace*. London: Architecture Design and Technology Press.

— 1994. The future of work: renaissance of the city. *Property Review* **4**(1), 7–10.

Dyker, D. A. 1992. *Restructuring the Soviet economy*. London: Routledge.

Eames, R. 1993. *"The enabling council": planning for recovery*. London: Sweet & Maxwell.

Early, J. 1994. Urban regeneration: a developer's perspective. *Property Review* **4**(5), 158–60.

Edwards, M. & J. Martin 1993. Planning notes. *Estates Gazette* (9313), 106–7.

Edwards, R. 1991. *Fit for the future*. Cheltenham: Countryside Commission.

Eldred, G. & R. Zerbst 1985. A critique of real estate market and investment analysis. In *Readings in market research for real estate*, J. Vernor (ed.), 133–42. Chicago: American Institute of Real Estate Appraisers.

Elson, M. 1986. *Green belts: conflict mediation in the urban fringe*. London: Heinemann.

— 1990. *Negotiation the future: planning gain in the 1990s*. Gloucester: ARC Ltd.

Elson, M., S. Walker, R. MacDonald, J. Edge 1993. *The effectiveness of green belts*. London: HMSO.

Elson, M. & A. Ford 1994. Green belts and very special circumstances. *Journal of Planning and Environment Law*, 594–601.

English Heritage 1990. *The conservation areas of England*. London: English Heritage.

— 1992a. *Buildings at risk: a sample survey*. London: English Heritage.

— 1992b. *A change of heart*. London: English Heritage.

EPI 1994. *Why manufacturing still matters*. London: Employment Policy Institute.

Essex County Council 1973. *Design guide for residential areas*. Chelmsford: Essex County Council.

Estates Gazette 1990. Focus on business parks. *Estates Gazette* (9026), 65–157.

Estates Gazette 1993. Focus on marketing: "posting your way to success". *Estates Gazette* (9302), 76–7.

Evans A. W. 1988. *No room! No room! The costs of the British town and country planning system*. London: Institute of Economic Affairs.

Faludi, A. (ed.) 1973b. *A reader in planning theory*. Oxford: Pergamon.

Fletcher King 1989. *Retail warehousing*. London: Fletcher King [chartered surveyors].

— 1990. *Business parks*. London: Fletcher King [chartered surveyors].

Foley, D. 1960. British town planning: one ideology or three?, *British Journal of Sociology* **11**(2), 211–231.

Franks, D. 1957. *Report on the Committee on Administrative Tribunals and Inquiries*. London: HMSO.

French, R. A. & F. E. Hamilton 1979. *The socialist city: spatial structure and urban policy*. Chichester, England: John Wiley.

Fryer, D. 1994. Viewpoint – the European Council of Town Planners. *Town Planning Review* **65**(2), iii–iv.

Gerald Eve Research 1995. *Whither the high street?* London: Gerald Eve.

Gibson, V. 1995a. Is property on the strategic agenda. *Chartered Surveyor Monthly* **4**(3), 34–5.

— 1995b. Is property on the strategic agenda. *Property Review* **5**(1), 104–109.

Giles, G. 1978. *Marketing*, 3rd edn. Plymouth: MacDonald & Evans.

Glasson, J., R. Therivel, A. Chadwick 1994. *An introduction to environmental impact assessment*. London: UCL Press.

Gourmain, P. (ed.) 1989. *High-technology workplaces*. New York: Van Nostrand Reinhold.

Graaskamp, J. 1981. *Fundamentals of real estate development*. Washington DC: Urban Land Institute.

Grant, M. 1989. *Permitted development: the Use Classes Order 1987 and General Development Order 1988*. London: Sweet & Maxwell.

— 1992. Planning law and the British planning system. *Town Planning Review* **63**, 3–12.

— 1993. Planning gain: the legal question. *Housebuilder* **52**(3), 26–7.

— (ed.) 1995a. *Encyclopedia of planning law and practice* [6 vols]. London: Sweet & Maxwell.

— 1995b. Planning obligations: what's going on? *Property Review* **5**(2), 50–52.

Gregory, T. 1989. So we've found another Roman palace. *Estates Gazette* (8922), 20–22, 62–4.

Grime, K. & V. Duke 1993. A Czech on privatisation. *Regional Studies* **27**(8), 751–7.

Hall, D. 1989. The case for new settlements. *Town and Country Planning* **58**(4), 111–14.

Hall, P. 1975. *Urban and regional planning*. London: David & Charles.

Hall, P. 1992. *Urban and regional planning*, 3rd edn. London: Routledge.

— 1993. Forces shaping urban Europe. *Urban Studies* **30**(6), 883–98.

— 1995. Planning strategies for our cities and regions. *Property Review* **5**(10), 302–305.

Hammond, B. 1989. Keys to success. *Estates Gazette* (8945), 95–9.

Harvey, D. 1973. *Social justice and the city*. London: Edward Arnold.

Hawking, H. 1992. Checkout superstores. *Estates Gazette* (9205), 146, 170.

Hawkins, S. 1990. Using your solicitor correctly. *Estates Gazette* (9005), 26, 63.

Hayward, R. & S. McGlynn 1993. *Making better places: urban design now*. Oxford: Butterworth.

Healey, P. 1983. *Local plans in British land-use planning*. Oxford: Pergamon Press.

— 1991. Models of the development process. *Journal of Property Research* **8**(3) 219–38.

Healey, P., P. McNamara, M. Elson, A. Doak 1988. *Land-use planning and the mediation of change*. Cambridge: Cambridge University Press.

Healey, P. & R. Nabarro (eds) 1988. *Applied property research UK 2000: an overview of business parks*. London: Applied Property Research.

Commission for Local Administration in England 1994. *Annual report for the Local Government Ombudsman 1993/94*. London: The Commissioner.

Healey, P., M. Purdue, F. Ennis 1993. *Gains from planning? Dealing with the implementation of planning*. York: Joseph Rowntree Foundation.

Healey, P. & R. Williams 1993. European urban planning systems: diversity and convergence. *Urban Studies* **30**(415), 701–720.

Healey & Baker 1986. *National office design survey*. London: Healey & Baker.

— 1989. *Serviced offices in Central London*. London: Healey & Baker.

Heap, Sir Desmond 1991. *An outline of planning law*, 10th edn. London: Sweet & Maxwell.

Henney, A. 1983. *Tomorrow's office for the 1980s*. London: Town and City Properties.

HMSO 1983. *Streamlining the cities*: government's proposals for reorganising local government in Greater London and metropolitan counties [Cmnd 9063]. London: HMSO.

— 1994a. *Climate change: the UK programme* [Cm 2424]. London: HMSO.

— 1994b. *Sustainable forestry: the UK programme* [Cm 2429]. London: HMSO.

— 1994c. *Biodiversity: the UK action plan* [Cm 2428]. London: HMSO.

— 1994d. *Sustainable development – the UK strategy* [Cm 2426]. London: HMSO.

Holden, R. 1986. Business parks and science parks. *Estates Gazette* **278**, 684–6.

Home, R. 1989. *Planning use classes: a guide to the 1987 Order*, 2nd edn. Oxford: Blackwell Scientific.

Houghton, G. & E. C. Hunter 1994. *Sustainable cities*. London: Regional Studies Association.

Houghton, J., B. Callender, S. Varney (eds) 1992. *Climate change*. Cambridge: Cambridge University Press.

HRH The Prince of Wales 1989. *A vision of Britain*. London: Doubleday.

Jacobs, J. 1961. *The death and life of great American cities*. New York: Random House.

Jennings, R. 1984. *The role of the developer*. London: Henry Stewart.

Jolly, B. 1979. *Development properties and techniques in residual valuation*. Property Valuation Handbook B1, College of Estate Management, Reading.

— 1995. Retailing in the 1990s. *Property Review* **5**(5), 148–50.

Jonas, C. 1994. Property in the European economy. *Property Review* **4**(1), 11–17.

Jones Lang Wootton 1990. *The City office review 1980–89*. London: Jones Lang Wootton.

Joseph, S. 1987. *Urban wasteland now*. London: Civic Trust.

Jowell, J. 1977. Bargaining in development control. *Journal of Planning and Environment Law*, 414–33.

Keeble, L. 1969. *Principles and practice of town and country planning*. London: *Estates Gazette*.

— 1985. *Fighting planning Appeals*. London: Construction Press.

Key, T., T. Key, F. Zarkesh, B. MacGregor, N. Nanthkumaran 1994. Understanding the property cycle. *Property Review* **4**(2), 61–3.

Knee, D. 1990. *Europe's international retailers*. Shopping Centre Horizons No. 18. Reading: College of Estate Management.

Lavers, A. & B. Webster 1990. *Practice guide to town planning Appeals*. London: *Estates Gazette*.

Lawless, P. 1989. *Britain's inner cities*. London: Paul Chapman.

Layfield, F. 1993. *A retrospect: planning inquiries*. Occasional Paper 20, *Journal of Planning and Environment Law*.

Lichfield, N. 1989. From planning gain to community benefit. *Journal of Planning and Environment Law*, 68–81.

— 1995. Economics of urban villages. *Property Review* **5**(2), 42–5.

Littlefair, P. J. 1991. *Site layout planning for daylight and sunlight – a guide to good practice*. Watford: Building Research Establishment.

Low, F. 1994. Development in the 1990s: a developer's perspective. *Property Review* **4**(3), 82–5.

LPAC 1994. *Advice on the revision of RPG3 1989*. London: London Planning Advisory Committee.

MacDonald, R. 1991. *The use of planning agreements by district councils*. Report of research findings, School of Planning, Oxford Polytechnic and Association of District Councils.

MacEwen, A. & M. MacEwen 1987. *Greenprints for the countryside – the story of Britain's National Parks*. London: Allen & Unwin.

MacRae, J. 1993. Rail freight. *Estates Gazette* (9346), 157–8.

Marber, P. 1985. Project managing office development. In *Office development*, P. Marber & P. Marber (eds), 177–201. London: *Estates Gazette*.

Marriott, O. 1989. *The property boom*. London: Abingdon Publishing.

Marshall, P. & C. Kennedy 1993. Development valuation techniques. *Journal of Property Valuation and Investment* **11**(1), 57–64.

Martin, P. 1982. *Shopping centre management*. London: Spon.
— 1993. Review of planning obligations. *Estates Gazette* (9306), 98–100.
Maynard, P. (Jones Lang Wootton) 1990. Contribution during International Council of Shopping Centres, Helsinki 1990.
McCollum, W. 1985. Basic research procedures. In *Readings in market research for real estate*, J. Vernon (ed.), 183–206. Chicago: American Institute of Real Estate Appraisers.
McCoubry, H. 1990. *Effective planning appeals*. Oxford: Blackwell Scientific.
McKee, W. 1994. The image of the property market. *Property Review* 2(11), 466–9.
McLoughlin J. B. 1969. *Urban and regional planning: a systems approach*. London: Faber.
McNamara, P., A. Jackson, S. Mathrant 1985. *Appellants' perceptions of the planning Appeal system: final report to DoE*. Departments of Town Planning and Estate Management, Oxford Polytechnic.
Meadows, H. 1972. *The limits to growth: a report for the Club of Rome's Project on the predicament of mankind*. London: Earth Island.
Michalik, A. 1990. Breathing life into B1. *Estates Gazette* (9026), 110–12.
Miles, M., E. Malizia, M. Weiss, G. Berens, G. Travis 1991. *Real estate development: principles and process*. Washington DC: Urban Land Institute.
Mills, L. 1992. Nissan still drives the market. *Estates Gazette* (9242), 70–71.
— 1994. Planning: a mixed outlook. *Estates Gazette* (9446), 124–5.
Ministry of Transport 1963. *Traffic in towns: a study of the long-term problems of traffic in urban areas* [Reports of the Steering Group and Working Group appointed by the Minister of Transport]. London: HMSO.
Moore, B., P. Tyler, D. Elliot 1991. The influence of regional development incentives and infrastructure on the location of small and medium-sized companies in Europe. *Urban Studies* 28(6), 1001–1026.
Morgan, P. & S. Nott 1988. *Development control: policy into practice*. London: Butterworth.
Morphet, J. 1995. *The planning system: broken or fixed?* Town and Country Planning Association Annual Conference, London (April).
Moss, N. & M. Fellows 1995. A future for town centres. *Estates Gazette* (9506), 141–3.
Murdoch, J. 1993. Property misdescription: staying afloat. *Estates Gazette* (9313), 85–8.

Nairn, I. 1955. *Outrage*. London: Architectural Press.
National Audit Office 1990. *Regenerating the inner cities*. London: HMSO.
Newell, M. 1989. Development appraisals. *Journal of Valuation* 7(2), 123–33.
Norris, S. & P. Jones 1993. Retail impact assessment. *Estates Gazette* (9304), 84–5.
Northen, I. 1977. *Shopping centres: a developer's guide to planning and design*. College of Estate Management, Reading.

Oliver, P., I. Davis, I. Bentley 1981. *Dunroamin: the suburban semi and its enemies*. London: Barrie & Jenkins.

PA Cambridge Economic Consultants 1987. *An evaluation of the enterprise zone experiment DoE Inner Cities Research Programme*. London: HMSO.
Parker Morris Committee 1961. *Homes for today and tomorrow*. London: HMSO.
Parker, A. 1994. Town centre management: a new urban panacea. *Property Review* 4(5), 161–3.
Parker, B. 1995. *Planning and transport – the key relationship*. Town and Country Planning Association Annual Conference, London (April).
Parnell, L. 1991. *A project manager's companion guide*. Paper 3, Project Strategy. RICS Diploma in Project Management, College of Estate Management, Reading.

Pearce, D. 1994. *Blueprint 3: measuring sustainable development*. London: Earthscan.

Pharoah, T. 1992. *Less traffic, better towns*. London: Friends of the Earth.

Planning Inspectorate, The 1993a. *Customer survey: study of the appellants' experience of the Written Representation appeal system*. Epsom, Surrey: W. S. Atkins.

— 1993b. *Customer survey: study of appellants and local authorities experience of the hearings system*. Epsom, Surrey : W. S. Atkins Planning Consultants.

Powell, C. 1990. *Facilities management: nature, causes and consequences*. Ascot: CIOB Technical Information Service.

Prior, J. 1993. *BREEAM: New Offices Version 1/93. Environmental assessment for new office designs, Buildings Research Establishment Report*. Watford: Building Research Establishment.

Prodgers, L. 1992. Facilities management: facing up to responsibilities. *Estates Gazette* 9238.

Property Advisory Group 1980. *Planning gain*. London: HMSO.

Pugh, C. 1992. The globalisation of finance capital and the changing relationships between property and finance – 2. *Journal of Property Finance* 2(3), 369–79.

Punter, J. 1993. *Development design skills for development controllers*. In *Making better places: urban design now*, R. Hayward & S. McGlynn (eds), 10–18. Oxford: Butterworth.

Purdue, M. 1991. *Planning Appeals – a critique*. Buckingham: Open University Press.

Raggett, B. 1993. Implications of the new PPG6. *Estates Gazette* (9330), 78–9.

Rawson-Gardiner, C. 1993. Where next for relocation. *Estates Gazette* (9344), 106–107.

Redcliffe-Maud Report 1969. *Report of the Royal Commission on Local Government in England* [Cmnd 4040]. London: HMSO.

Redman, M. 1991. Planning Gain and Obligations. *Journal of Planning and Environment Law*, 203–18.

— 1993. European Community Planning Law. *Journal of Planning and Environment Law*, 999–1011.

Regional Studies Association 1990. *Beyond green belts – managing urban growth in the 21st century*. London: Regional Studies Association.

RICS & English Heritage 1993. *The investment performance of Listed Buildings*. London: RICS and Investment Property Databank.

Ringer, M. 1989. Is the shopper really king? *Estates Gazette* (8945), 109–112.

Robathan, P. 1993. The intelligent building. In *Facilities management*, K. Alexander (ed.), 50–53. London: Haston Hilton.

Roger Tym and Partners 1984. *Monitoring Enterprise Zones reports*. London: HMSO.

— 1993 *Merry Hill Impact Study* [final report for West Midlands Planning and Transportation Subcommittee, Wyre Forest District Council and DoE]. London: HMSO.

Ross-Goobey, A. 1992. *Bricks and mortals: the dream of the 80s and the nightmare of the 90s, the inside story of the proper world*. London: Century Business.

Royal Commission on Environmental Pollution 1994. *Transport and the environment*. Oxford: Oxford University Press.

Royal Institution of Chartered Surveyors 1995. *RICS appraisal and valuation manual*. London: RICS.

Royal Town Planning Institute 1991. *Planning – is it a service, and how can it be effective?* London: Royal Town Planning Institute.

— 1993. *The character of conservation areas*. London: Royal Town Planning Institute.

Rydin, Y. 1993. *The British planning system: an introduction*. London: Macmillan.

Saggess, J. 1993. *Shopping centre management: the way forward, shopping centre progress 1993–94*. London: British Council of Shopping Centres.

Salata, A. 1990. The starting grid. *Estates Gazette* (9026), 122–3.

Sands, D. 1993. Service with style. *Estates Gazette* (9341), 66.

Savills 1990. *Financing property*. London: Savills.

Saxon, R. 1993. Seeking a consensus. *Estates Gazette* (9318), 70.

Scanlon, K., A. Edge, T. Willmott 1994. *The economics of listed buildings*. MS, Department of Land Economy, University of Cambridge.

Schiller, R. 1983. Shopping trends as they affect the investor. *Estates Gazette* **267**, 420.

Sharp, T. 1942. *Town planning*. London: Penguin.

Shayle, A. 1992. Deep discount bonds, convertible mortgages, participating mortgages: the art and practice of financing property. Paper presented at Henry Stewart Conference, London.

Simmie, J. (ed.) 1994. *Planning London*: London: UCL Press.

Simmonds, M. 1994/5. Planning for office development: a strategic approach. *Property Review* **4**(7), 213–6.

Sinclair, G. 1992. *The lost land: land-use change in England 1945–1990*. London: Council for the Protection of Rural England.

Smith, N. 1994. The end of grants as we know them. *Property Review* **4**(5), 152–5.

Solesbury, W. 1974. *Policy in urban planning*. London: Pergamon Press.

Somers, B. 1984. The role of the contractor. Paper presented at the Property Development Workshop. Henry Stewart Conference, London.

Steelcase Strafor 1990. *The responsive office*. Streatley on Thames: Polymath Publishing.

Stewart Hunter, D. 1983. Property marketing: the impending revolution. *Estates Gazette* **265**, 86.

Stubbs, M. 1994. Planning Appeals by Informal Hearing: an appraisal of the views of consultants. *Journal of Planning and Environment Law*, 710–714.

Stubbs, M. & A. Lavers 1991. Steinberg and after. *Journal of Planning and Environment Law*, 9–19.

Stubbs, M. & J. Cripps 1993. Planning obligations and future prospects. *Property Review* **2**(3), 102–105.

Talbot, J. 1988. Have enterprise zones encouraged enterprise? Some empirical evidence from Tyneside. *Regional Studies* **22**, 507–14.

Taussik, J. 1992. Surveyors and pre-application Inquiries. *Estates Gazette* (9221), 96–100.

Taylor, R. 1985. New high-technology survey. *Estates Gazette* **275**, 20.

Taylor, T. 1993. Shedding light on storage. *The Valuer* **62**(5), 23.

Thame, D. 1992. From the past to the future. *The Valuer* **61**(6), 14–15.

Thomson, R. 1994/5. Manufacturing floorspace demand. *Property Review* **4**(7), 237.

Thorne, J. 1994. Green belts and institutions standing in extensive grounds. *Journal of Planning and Environment Law*, 308–313.

Thornley, A. 1991. *Urban planning under Thatcherism; the challenge of the market*. London: Routledge.

— 1993. *Urban planning under Thatcherism*, 2nd edn. London: Routledge.

Todd, E. 1993. Offices head for home. *Estates Gazette* (9318), 98.

Tugnett, T. & M. Robertson 1987. *Making townscape*. London: Mitchell Publishing.

Unit for Retail Planning Information 1980. *Pedestrian flows at selected retail and service business*. Reading, England: Unit for Retail Planning Information.

Urban Villages Forum 1992. *Urban villages: a concept for creating mixed-use urban development on a sustainable scale*. London: Urban Villages Forum.

— 1994. *Economics of urban villages*. London: Urban Villages Forum.

URBED 1994. *Vital and viable town centres: meeting the challenge*. London: URBED and Comedia Consultants/DoE.

Vail, J. 1994. The ills of over-intensive development. *Estates Gazette* (9414), 118.

Walker, T. 1990. *Design revolution in the 1990s*. London: *Estates Gazette*.

Ward, S. 1994. *Planning and urban change*. London: Paul Chapman.

Watt, D. & J. Valente 1991. Tenant mix – retailers' views. *EstatesGazette* (9143), 82–3.

— 1995. Invest at leisure. *Property Review* 5(7), 220–25.

Watts, R. 1982. Marketing for a pre-let. Paper presented at Henry Stewart Conference, London.

Welbank, M. 1995. Planning and uncertainty. *Property Review* 5(7), 204–207.

White, A. 1995. The future of offices. *Property Review* 5(5), 138–40.

Wilks, D. & H. Brown 1980. Selling techniques have become more vital. *Estates Times Review* (October).

Williams, J. 1982. *A review of science parks and high-technology developments*. London: Drivers Jonas [chartered surveyors].

Wood, C. & G. McDonic 1989. Environmental assessment: challenge and opportunity. *The Planner* 75(11), 12–18.

World Commission on Environment and Development [Brundtland Report] 1987. *Our common future*. Oxford: Oxford University Press.

Worthington, J. 1982. Changing industrial environments. *Architects Journal* 175(16), 80.

Worthington, J. & A. Kenya 1988. *Fitting out the workplace*. London: The Architectural Press.

Index

Notes: 1. References to local planning authorities and England are ubiquitous and have therefore been omitted; 2. References to footnotes have *n* as suffix to page number